G000294650

STREET ATLAS
Suffolk

First published in 2003 by

Philip's, a division of
Octopus Publishing Group Ltd
2-4 Heron Quays, London E14 4JP

First edition 2003
Fourth impression with revisions 2005

ISBN-10   0-540-08334-8 (spiral)
ISBN-13   978-0-540-08334-3 (spiral)

© Philip's 2005

Ordnance Survey®

Printed and bound in Spain
by Cayfosa-Quebecor

Contents

II   **Key to map pages**

IV   **Route planning**

VI   **Administrative and Postcode boundaries**

1   **Key to map symbols**

2   **Street maps** at 1¾ inches to 1 mile

109   **Street maps** at 3½ inches to 1 mile

154   **Street maps of centres of Bury St Edmunds and Ipswich** at 7 inches to 1 mile

156   **Index** of towns and villages

159   **Index** of streets, hospitals, industrial estates, railway stations, schools, shopping centres, universities and places of interest

Digital Data

The exceptionally high-quality mapping found in this atlas is available as digital data in TIFF format, which is easily convertible to other bitmapped (raster) image formats.

The index is also available in digital form as a standard database table. It contains all the details found in the printed index together with the National Grid reference for the map square in which each entry is named.

For further information and to discuss your requirements, please contact Philip's on 020 7644 6932 or james.mann@philips-maps.co.uk

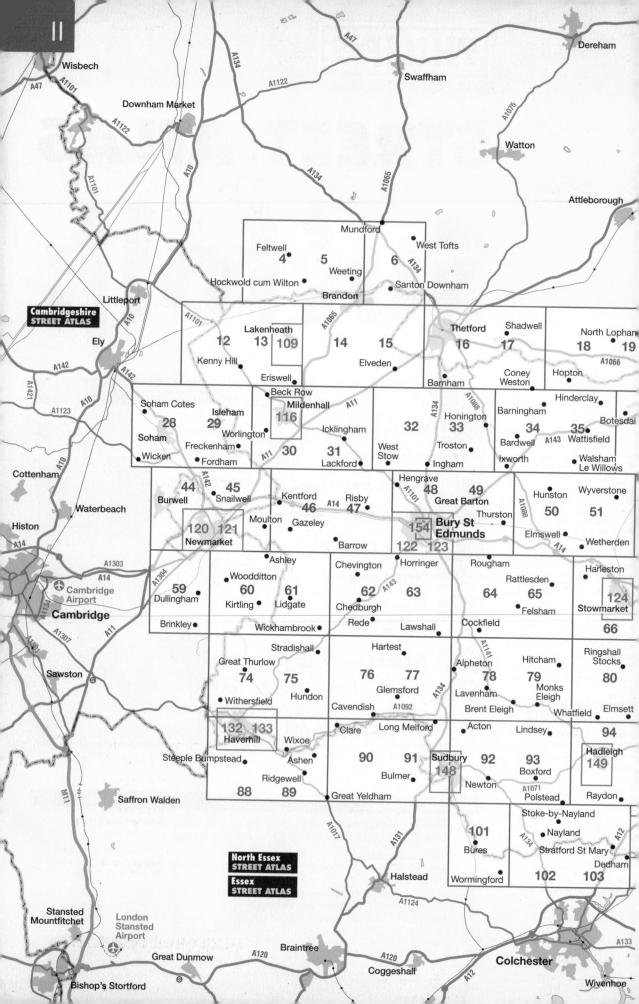

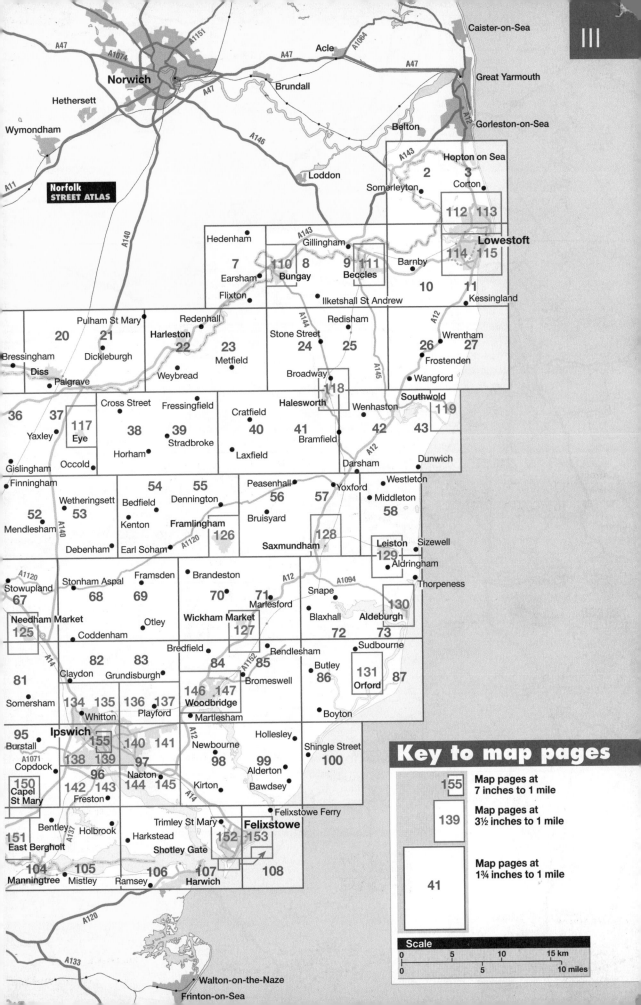

Caister-on-Sea

Great Yarmouth

Gorleston-on-Sea

Norwich

Hethersett

Wymondham

A47

A1151

A1074

A11

A140

A146

A47

A47

Acle

Brundall

Loddon

Belton

A1064

A12

Norfolk STREET ATLAS

A143

Hopton on Sea

2 3 Corton

Somerleyton

112 113

114 115 **Lowestoft**

Hedenham

A143

Gillingham

7 110 8 9 111

Earsham **Bungay** **Beccles**

Flixton

Ilketshall St Andrew

Barnby

10 11 Kessingland

Pulham St Mary

20 21 **Harleston**

Bressingham 22 23

Dickleburgh Metfield

Diss Weybread

Palgrave

Redenhall

A144

Stone Street

24 25

Broadway

Redisham

A145

26 27 Wrentham

Frostenden

Wangford

118

Halesworth

Wenhaston

Southwold

119

36 37 117 38 39 40 41 42 43

Yaxley **Eye** Stradbroke Cratfield **Bramfield**

Gislingham Occold Horham Laxfield Darsham Dunwich

Finningham

Cross Street Fressingfield

Westleton

54 55 Peasenhall Yoxford Middleton

52 53 Bedfield Dennington 56 57 58

Mendlesham Wetheringsett Kenton Bruisyard Sizewell

A140 Debenham Earl Soham **Framlingham** 126 128 **Saxmundham** **Leiston** 129 Aldringham

Thorpeness

A1120

Stowupland

67 68 69 Framsden Brandeston 70 71 Snape 130

Needham Market Marlesford **Aldeburgh**

125 Otley **Wickham Market** Blaxhall 72 73

Coddenham 127 Sudbourne

Bredfield Rendlesham

81 82 83 84 85 Butley 131 87

Claydon Grundisburgh Bromeswell 86 **Orford**

Somersham 146 147 **Woodbridge** Boyton

134 135 136 137 Martlesham

Whitton Playford

95 **Ipswich** 155

Burstall 140 141 Hollesley

A1071 138 139 Newbourne Shingle Street

Copdock 96 97 98 99 100

150 142 143 Nacton Alderton

Capel 144 145 Kirton Bawdsey

St Mary Freston A14

Felixstowe Ferry

151 Bentley Holbrook Trimley St Mary **Felixstowe**

East Bergholt A137 Harkstead 152 153

Shotley Gate 108

104 105 106 107

Manningtree Mistley Ramsey **Harwich**

A120

A133

Walton-on-the-Naze

Frinton-on-Sea

Key to map pages

155	**Map pages at** 7 inches to 1 mile
139	**Map pages at** 3½ inches to 1 mile
41	**Map pages at** 1¾ inches to 1 mile

Scale

0   5   10   15 km

0   5   10 miles

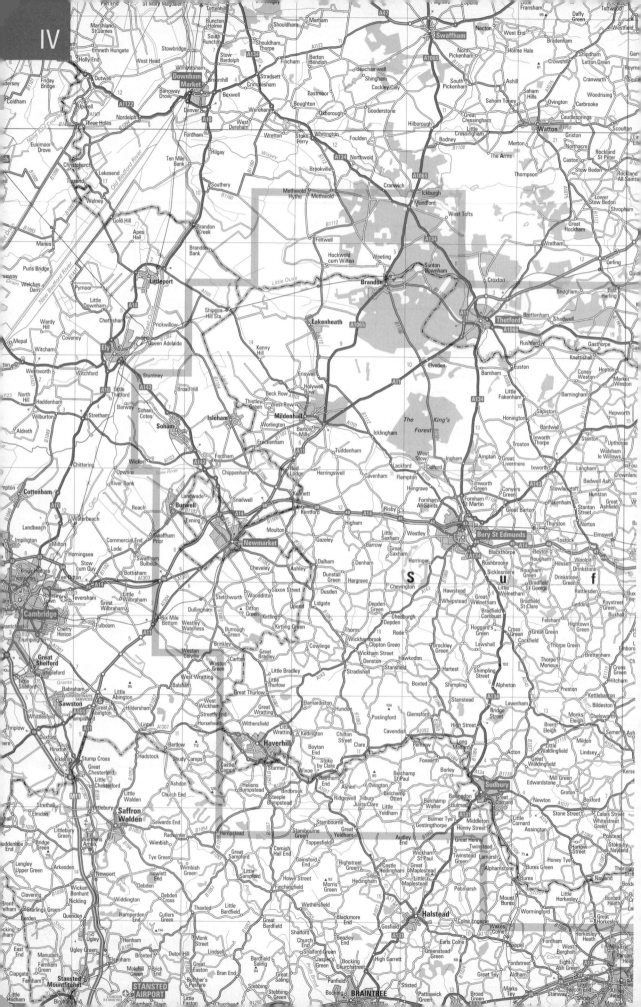

Route planning

Scale

0	5	10	15 km

0	5	10 miles

Administrative and Postcode boundaries

Scale

0	5	10	15	20	25	30km
0	5	10	15	20 miles			

County and unitary
authority boundaries

District boundaries

Postcode boundaries

Area covered by this atlas

22a	**Motorway** with junction number
	Primary route – dual/single carriageway
	A road – dual/single carriageway
	B road – dual/single carriageway
	Minor road – dual/single carriageway
	Other minor road – dual/single carriageway
	Road under construction
	Tunnel, covered road
	Rural track, private road or narrow road in urban area
	Gate or obstruction to traffic (restrictions may not apply at all times or to all vehicles)
	Path, bridleway, byway open to all traffic, road used as a public path
	Pedestrianised area
DY7	**Postcode boundaries**
	County and unitary authority boundaries
	Railway, tunnel, railway under construction
	Tramway, tramway under construction
	Miniature railway
Walsall	**Railway station**
	Private railway station
South Shields	**Metro station**
	Tram stop, tram stop under construction
	Bus, coach station

◆	**Ambulance station**
◆	**Coastguard station**
◆	**Fire station**
◆	**Police station**
✚	**Accident and Emergency entrance to hospital**
H	**Hospital**
+	**Place of worship**
i	**Information Centre** (open all year)
P	**Parking**
P&R	**Park and Ride**
PO	**Post Office**
Δ	**Camping site**
	Caravan site
▶	**Golf course**
✕	**Picnic site**
Prim Sch	**Important buildings, schools, colleges, universities and hospitals**
River Ouse	**Tidal water, water name**
	Non-tidal water – lake, river, canal or stream
	Lock, weir, tunnel
	Woods
	Built up area
Church	**Non-Roman antiquity**
ROMAN FORT	**Roman antiquity**
◀ 87	**Adjoining page indicators and overlap bands**
▼ 228	The colour of the arrow and the band indicates the scale of the adjoining or overlapping page (see scales below)

Acad	**Academy**	Inst	**Institute**	Recn Gd	**Recreation Ground**
Allot Gdns	**Allotments**	Ct	**Law Court**		
Cemy	**Cemetery**	L Ctr	**Leisure Centre**	Resr	**Reservoir**
C Ctr	**Civic Centre**	LC	**Level Crossing**	Ret Pk	**Retail Park**
CH	**Club House**	Liby	**Library**	Sch	**School**
Coll	**College**	Mkt	**Market**	Sh Ctr	**Shopping Centre**
Crem	**Crematorium**	Meml	**Memorial**	TH	**Town Hall/House**
Ent	**Enterprise**	Mon	**Monument**	Trad Est	**Trading Estate**
Ex H	**Exhibition Hall**	Mus	**Museum**	Univ	**University**
Ind Est	**Industrial Estate**	Obsy	**Observatory**	Wks	**Works**
IRB Sta	**Inshore Rescue Boat Station**	Pal	**Royal Palace**	YH	**Youth Hostel**
		PH	**Public House**		

■ The small numbers around the edges of the maps identify the 1 kilometre National Grid lines

■ The dark grey border on the inside edge of some pages indicates that the mapping does not continue onto the adjacent page

The scale of the maps on the pages numbered in blue is 5.52 cm to 1 km • 3½ inches to 1 mile • 1: 18103

0   ¼   ½   ¾   1 mile
0   250m   500m   750m   1 kilometre

The scale of the maps on pages numbered in green is 2.76 cm to 1 km • 1¾ inches to 1 mile • 1: 36206

0   ¼   ½   ¾   1 mile
0   250m   500m   750m   1kilometre

The scale of the maps on pages numbered in red is 11.04 cm to 1 km • 7 inches to 1 mile • 1: 9051.4

0   220 yards   440 yards   660 yards   ½ mile
0   125m   250m   375m   ½ kilometre

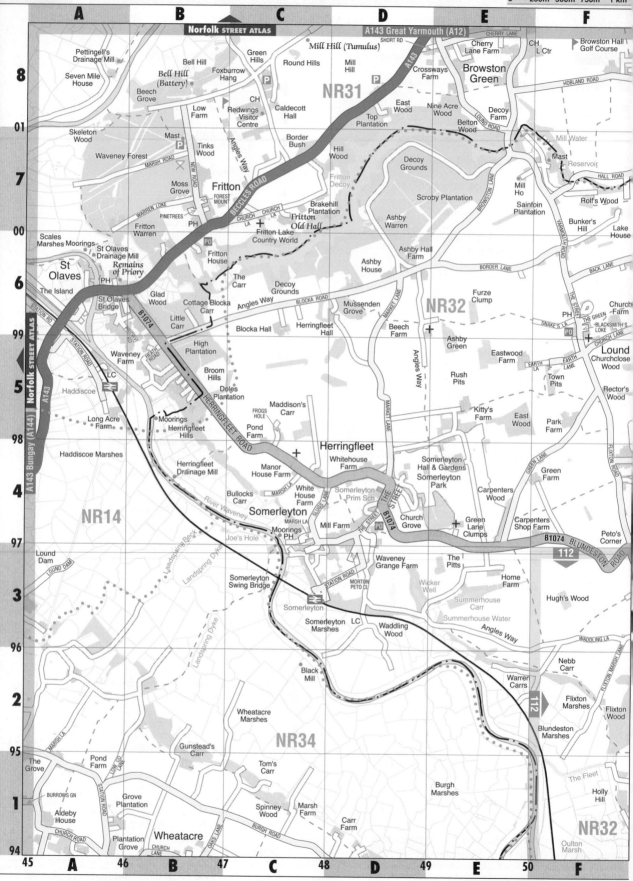

Norfolk STREET ATLAS

A143 Great Yarmouth (A12)

Pettingell's
Drainage Mill
Seven Mile
House
Bell Hill
Skeleton
Wood
Waveney Forest
Scales
Marshes Moorings
St Olaves
Drainage Mill
Remains
of Priory
St
Olaves
The Island
St Olaves
Bridge
Haddiscoe
Long Acre
Farm
Haddiscoe Marshes

NR14

Lound
Dam
The
Grove
Aldeby
House
BURROWS GN
Pond
Farm
Grove
Plantation
Plantation
Grove
Wheatacre

Bell Hill
Foxburrow
Hang
Bell Hill
(Battery)
Beech
Grove
Low
Farm
CH
Redwings
Visitor
Centre
Mast
Tinks
Wood
Moss
Grove
FOREST
MOUNT
Fritton
Fritton
Warren
PINETREES
PH
Glad
Wood
Little
Carr
High
Plantation
Cottage Blocka
Carr
Waveney
Farm
Broom
Hills
Doles
Plantation
Moorings
Herringfleet
Hills
Herringfleet
Drainage Mill
Bullocks
Carr
Gunstead's
Carr
Mill Hill (Tumulus)
Green
Hills
Round Hills
Mill
Hill
Caldecott
Hall
Border
Bush
CHURCH
LA
CHURCH
LA
PO
Fritton
House
The
Carr
Angles Way
Blocka Hall
Blocka
Road
Herringfleet
Hall
Maddison's
Carr
FROGS
HOLE
Pond
Farm
Manor
House Farm
White
House Farm
MARSH LA
Bullocks
Carr
Moorings
PH
Joe's Hole
Somerleyton
Swing Bridge
Somerleyton
Black
Mill
Wheatacre
Marshes
Tom's
Carr
Spinney
Wood
Marsh
Farm
Carr
Farm

NR31
SHORT RD
A143
Mill
Hill
Crossways
Farm
East
Wood
Top
Plantation
Hill
Wood
Fritton
Decoy
Brakehill
Plantation
Fritton
Old Hall
Fritton Lake
Country World
Decoy
Grounds
Mussenden
Grove
Beech
Farm
Herringfleet
Whitehouse
Farm
Somerleyton
Prim Sch
Mill Farm
Waveney
Grange Farm
Station Road
Morton
Peto Cl
Somerleyton
Marshes
Waddling
Wood
Black
Mill
Burgh
Marshes

Cherry
Lane Farm
CH
L Ctr
Browston Hall
Golf Course
**Browston
Green**
CHERRY LANE
Nine Acre
Wood
Decoy
Farm
Belton
Wood
Decoy
Grounds
Scroby Plantation
Ashby
Warren
Ashby Hall
Farm
Ashby
House
Decoy
Grounds
Ashby
Green
Beech
Farm
Rush
Pits
Somerleyton
Hall & Gardens
Somerleyton
Park
Church
Grove
The
Pitts
Wicker
Well
Summerhouse
Carr
Summerhouse Water
HOBLAND ROAD
Mill Water
Mast
Reservoir
Mill
Ho
Sainfoin
Plantation
HALL ROAD
Rolf's Wood
Bunker's
Hill
Lake
House
Back Lane
Furze
Clump
Church
Farm
Blacksmith's
Loke
Lound
Churchclose
Wood
Rector's
Wood
Eastwood
Farm
Town
Pits
Kitty's
Farm
East
Wood
Park
Farm
Carpenters
Wood
Green
Farm
Carpenters
Shop Farm
Peto's
Corner
B1074
Home
Farm
Hugh's
Wood
Nebb
Carr
Warren
Carrs
Flixton
Marshes
Flixton
Wood
Blundeston
Marshes
The Fleet
Holly
Hill
NR32

NR32

NR34

A143 Bungay (A144)

B1074

HERRINGFLEET ROAD

BECCLES ROAD

Angles Way

BLUNDESTON ROAD

112

112

112

10

112

**For full street detail of the
highlighted area see pages
112 and 113.**

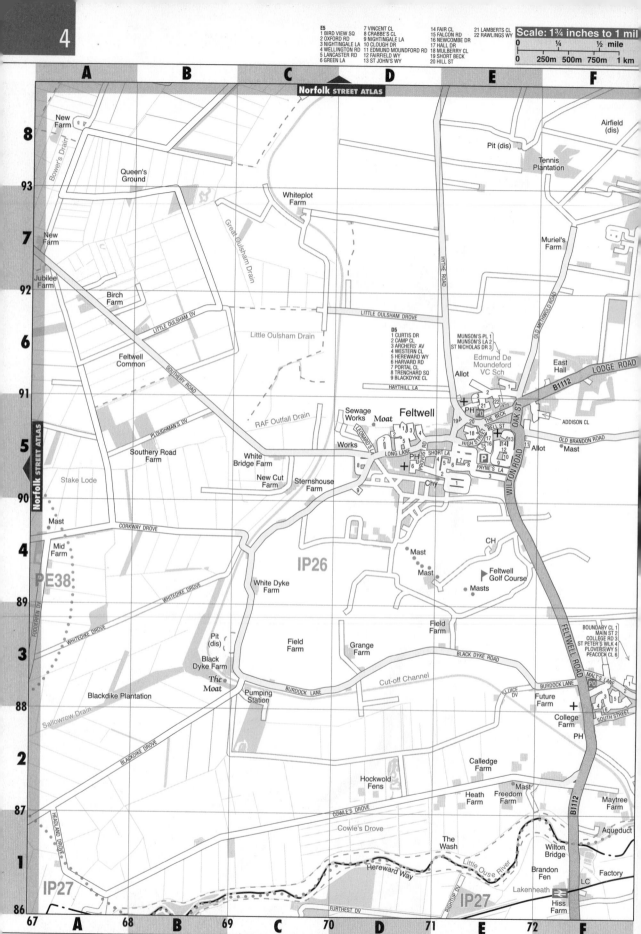

E5
1 BIRD VIEW SQ
2 OXFORD RD
3 NIGHTINGALE LA
4 WELLINGTON RD
5 LANCASTER RD
6 GREEN LA
7 VINCENT CL
8 CRABBE'S CL
9 NIGHTINGALE LA
10 CLOUGH DR
11 EDMUND MOUNDFORD RD
12 FAIRFIELD WY
13 ST JOHN'S WY
14 FAIR CL
15 FALCON RD
16 NEWCOMBE DR
17 HALL DR
18 MULBERRY CL
19 SHORT BECK
20 HILL ST
21 LAMBERTS CL
22 RAWLINGS WY

Scale: 1¾ inches to 1 mil
0   ¼   ½   mile
0 250m 500m 750m 1 km

Norfolk STREET ATLAS

New Farm

New Farm

Queen's Ground

Airfield (dis)

Pit (dis)

Tennis Plantation

Whiteplot Farm

Muriel's Farm

Jubilee Farm

Birch Farm

Little Oulsham Drove

East Hall

B1112

LODGE ROAD

Feltwell Common

Little Oulsham Drain

D5
1 CURTIS DR
2 CAMP CL
3 ARCHERS' AV
4 WESTERN CL
5 HEREWARD WY
6 HARVARD RD
7 PORTAL CL
8 TRENCHARD SQ
9 BLACKDYKE CL

MUNSON'S PL 1
MUNSON'S LA 2
ST NICHOLAS DR 3

Edmund De Moundeford VC Sch

Allot

ADDISON CL

Southery Road Farm

RAF Outfall Drain

HAYTHILL LA

Sewage Works

Moat

Feltwell

PH
PO

Mast

Allot

OLD BRANDON ROAD

Stake Lode

White Bridge Farm

Works

LONG LANE

SHORT LA

PAYNE'S LA

WILTON ROAD

Mast

New Cut Farm

Sternshouse Farm

Chy

Mast

CH

IP26

Feltwell Golf Course

Masts

White Dyke Farm

FELTWELL ROAD

BOUNDARY CL 1
MAIN ST 2
COLLEGE RD 3
ST PETER'S WLK 4
PLOVERS WY 5
PEACOCK CL 6

Field Farm

Field Farm

MALT'S LANE
PO

Pit (dis)

Black Dyke Farm

The Moat

Grange Farm

BLACK DYKE ROAD

BURDOCK LANE

Cut-off Channel

SLUICE DV

Future Farm

BURDOCK LANE

SOUTH STREET

Blackdike Plantation

Pumping Station

College Farm

PH

BLACKDIKE DROVE

Calledge Farm

B1112

Sallowrow Drain

Hockwold Fens

Heath Farm

Freedom Farm

Mast

Maytree Farm

COWLE'S DROVE

Aqueduct

Cowle's Drove

The Wash

Wilton Bridge

HEADLAND DROVE

Hereward Way

Little Ouse River

Brandon Fen

Factory

IP27

FURTHEST DV

RIGHTUP DV

IP27

Lakenheath

LC

Hiss Farm

PE38

FODDERFEN DV

WHITEDIKE DROVE

WHITEDIKE DROVE

CORKWAY DROVE

Mast

Mid Farm

SOUTHERY ROAD

PLOUGHMAN'S DV

LITTLE OULSHAM DV

Great Oulsham Drain

Bower's Drain

HYTHE ROAD

OLD METHWOLD ROAD

OAK ST

BELL ST

HIGH ST

THE BECK

PROVOST LA

LEONARD'S LA

Norfolk STREET ATLAS

5 ◄

Scale: 1¾ inches to 1 mi
0 ¼ ½ mile
0 250m 500m 750m 1 km

A | B | C | D | E | F

A1065 Swaffham

Norfolk STREET ATLAS

SAXON WK 1
CHERRY TREE CL 2
IMPSON WY 3

Mundford Prim Sch

The Grove
Mundford

Water Tower

East Hall Farm

Round Covert Farm

Wellington Plantation

Zigzag Covert

Ash Carr

Iron Carr

West Tofts Covert

Buckenham Tofts Plantation

Glebe Covert

Pumphouse Plantation

Doublebank Covert

Archer's Covert

8

Ickerbuilding Plantation

Attleborough Covert

Marly Covert

Lynford Home Farm

Horseshoe Covert

Moat

Barn Covert

Great Carr

93

Dixon's Covert

DANGER AREA

West Tofts

7

Heath Covert

Big Wood

IP26

Great Covert

Foxtail Farm

Brick Kiln Covert

Sewage Works

Young Salamanca Covert

92

A134

Camp

Watering Carr

West Tofts Mere

Mundford Covert

Water Tower

Foxtail Covert

Gravelpit Plantation

Evergreen Covert

6

Twenty Acre Plantation

Lynford

Oak Covert

DANGER AREA

91

Snake Wood

Oak Farm

Crescent Wood

Tumuli

Flint Mines

DANGER AREA

Youngoak Covert

West Tofts Heath

5

Emily's Wood

Visitor Centre

Grimshoe

Lynford Point

90

Grime's Graves (Flint Mines)

4

Tumuli

MUNDFORD ROAD

Bromehill Cott

A134

IP24

89

A1065

Field Barn Farm

IP27

HARLING DROVE

3

Santon Warren

The Brecks

88

P

LC

Blood Hill

Blood Hill (Tumulus)

Jubilee Wood

MARK LANE

HALL

St Helen's Oratory (site of)

Santon Road Plantation

A134 Thetford

Santon Downham

Water Tower

Sewage Works

Moat

Hereward Way

Santon House

Little Ouse River

Little Lodge Farm

Two Mile Bottom

2

St Edmund Way

Hereward Way

Mayes Plantation

Tumulus

Tumulus

Reed Fen

Thetford Forest

Warren Wood

Chalk Pit

THETFORD ROAD

B1107

BRANDON

80 | B | 81 | C | 82 | D | 83 | E | 84 | F | 85

5 ◄

15 ▼

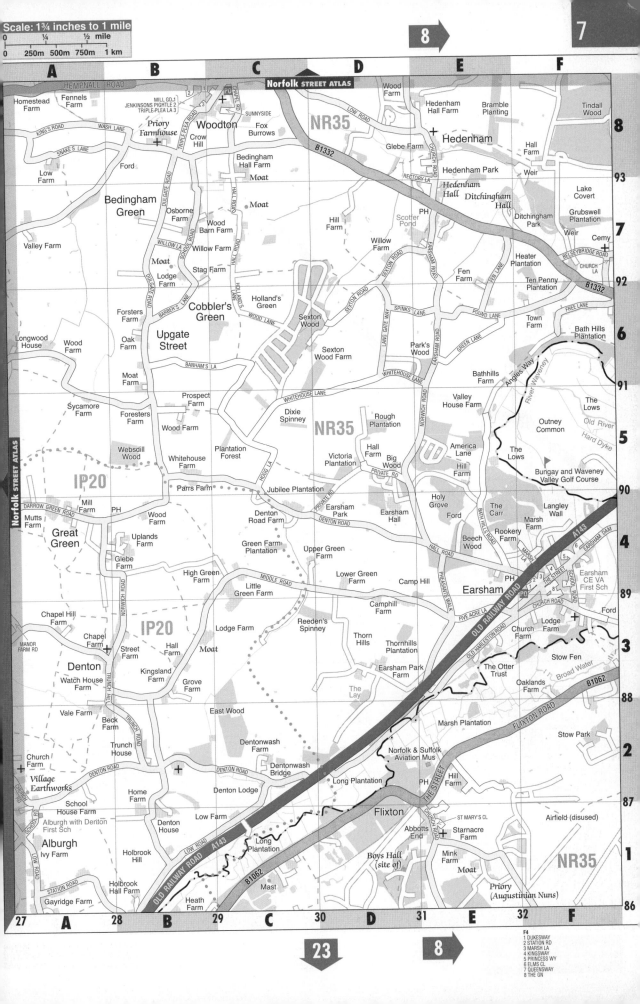

A   B   C   D   E   F

Norfolk STREET ATLAS

Homestead Farm
Fennels Farm
MILL GD 1
JENKINSONS PIGHTLE 2
TRIPLE-PLEA LA 3
Woodton
PO
Chapel Rd
Sunnyside
Fox Burrows
Wood Farm
Hedenham Hall Farm
Bramble Planting
Tindall Wood

NR35
Low Road
Hedenham
Glebe Farm
Hall Farm

8

King's Road
Wash Lane
Priory Farmhouse
Crow Hill
B1332
RECTORY LA
CHURCH ROAD
Hedenham Park
Hall Farm
Weir

Snake's Lane
Low Farm
Ford
Bedingham Hall Farm
Moat
Hedenham Hall
Ditchingham Hall
Lake Covert

93

Bedingham Green
Osborne Farm
Wood Barn Farm
Moat
Hill Farm
Willow Farm
Scotter Pond
PH
Ditchingham Park
Grubswell Plantation
Weir   Cemy

7

Valley Farm
WILLOW LA
Willow Farm
Stag Farm
SCHOOL ROAD
HALL ROAD
OPEN THAI RD
DULGATE ROAD
Moat
Lodge Farm
Willow Farm
SEXTON ROAD
EARSHAM ROAD
Fen Farm
Heater Plantation
Ten Penny Plantation
BELSCYBRIDGE ROAD
CHURCH LA
B1332

92

Forsters Farm
Oak Farm
BARBER'S LANE
Cobbler's Green
HOLLAND'S LANE
Holland's Green
WOOD LANE
Sexton Wood
SEXTON ROAD
LANG GATT WAY
SPINKS LANE
Green Lane
POUND LANE
FREE LANE
Town Farm
Bath Hills Plantation

Longwood House
Wood Farm
Upgate Street
BANHAM'S LA
Sexton Wood Farm
WHITEHOUSE LANE
Park's Wood
EARSHAM ROAD
NORWICH ROAD
Bathhills Farm
Angles Way
River Waveney
The Lows

6

Moat Farm
Sycamore Farm
Foresters Farm
Prospect Farm
Dixie Spinney
WHITEHOUSE LANE
Rough Plantation
Valley House Farm
The Lows
Outney Common
Old River
Hard Dyke

91

NR35
Wood Farm
Whitehouse Farm
Websdill Wood
Plantation Forest
HOGS LA
Victoria Plantation
Hall Farm
Big Wood
America Lane
Hill Farm
Holy Grove
Bungay and Waveney Valley Golf Course

5

IP20
Mill Farm
PH
Wood Farm
Parrs Farm
Jubilee Plantation
PRIVATE RD
Earsham Park
Earsham Hall
PRIVATE RO
BATH HILLS ROAD
The Carr
Langley Wall

90

Mutts Farm
DARROW GREEN ROAD
Great Green
Glebe Farm
Uplands Farm
Denton Road Farm
DENTON ROAD
Green Farm Plantation
Upper Green Farm
Beech Wood
HALL ROAD
Rookery Farm
Marsh Farm
A143
EARSHAM DAM

4

High Green Farm
Little Green Farm
MIDDLE ROAD
Lower Green Farm
Camp Hill
Earsham
PH
Earsham CE VA First Sch
THE STREET
SCHOOL ROAD
Ford

89

Chapel Hill Farm
NORWICH ROAD
Chapel Farm
Street Farm
Hall Farm
Moat
Reeden's Spinney
Camphill Farm
PHEASANT'S WALK
FIVE ACRE LA
Church Farm
Lodge Farm
CHURCH ROAD

3

IP20
Kingsland Farm
Grove Farm
Thorn Hills
Thornhills Plantation
OLD HARLESTON ROAD
OLD RAILWAY ROAD
Stow Fen
Broad Water
B1062

Denton
Watch House Farm
TRUNCH HILL
Earsham Park Farm
The Otter Trust
Oaklands Farm

88

Vale Farm
East Wood
The Lay
Marsh Plantation
FLIXTON ROAD
Stow Park

2

Beck Farm
MANOR FARM RD
TRUNCH ROAD
Trunch House
Dentonwash Farm
Dentonwash Bridge
Norfolk & Suffolk Aviation Mus
Long Plantation
PH
Hill Farm
THE STREET

Church Farm
Village Earthworks
DENTON ROAD
Denton Lodge
Long Plantation
Flixton
Church Road
St MARY'S CL
Airfield (disused)

87

School House Farm
Alburgh with Denton First Sch
Home Farm
Denton House
Low Farm
A143
Abbotts End
Starnacre Farm
Mink Farm
Moat
NR35

Aalburgh
Ivy Farm
Holbrook Hill
LOW ROAD
B1062
Boys Hall (site of)
Priory (Augustinian Nuns)

1

STATION ROAD
Gayridge Farm
Holbrook Hall Farm
Heath Farm
Mast
OLD RAILWAY ROAD

86

27   A   28   B   29   C   30   D   31   E   32   F

F4
1 DUKESWAY
2 STATION RD
3 MARSH LA
4 KINGSWAY
5 PRINCESS WY
6 ELMS CL
7 QUEENSWAY
8 THE GN

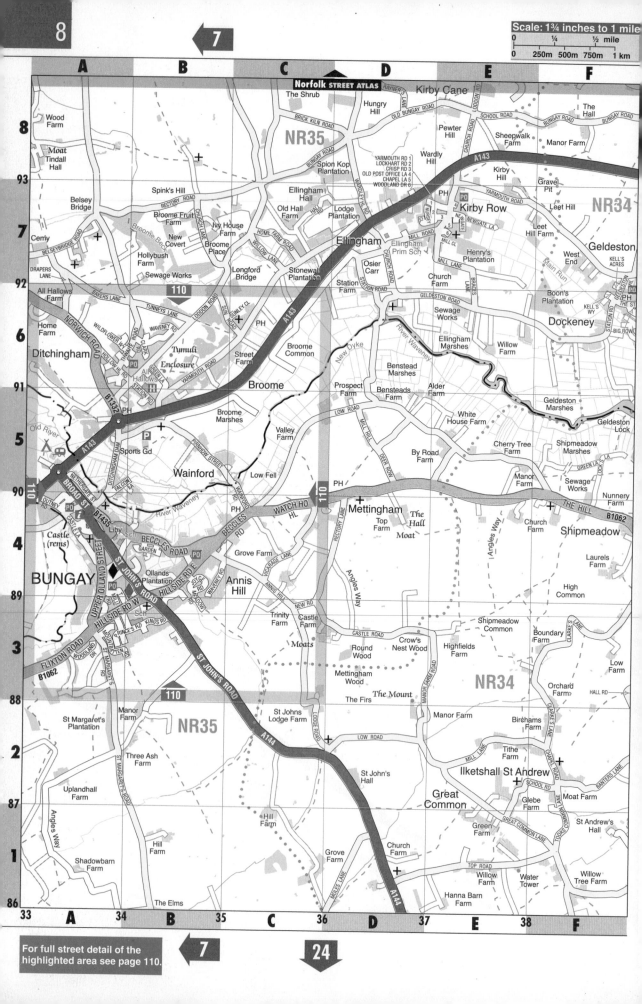

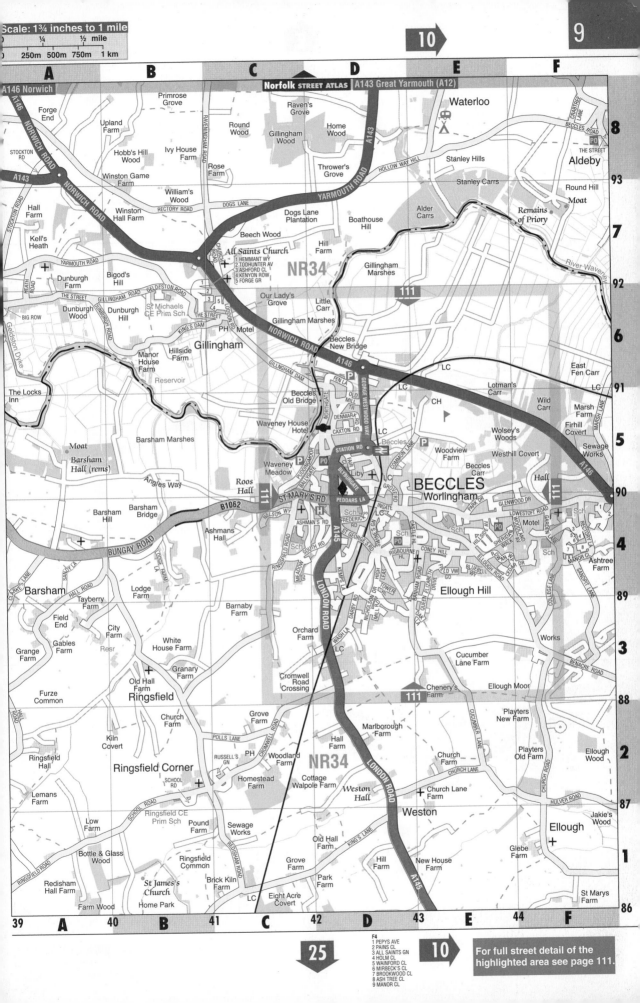

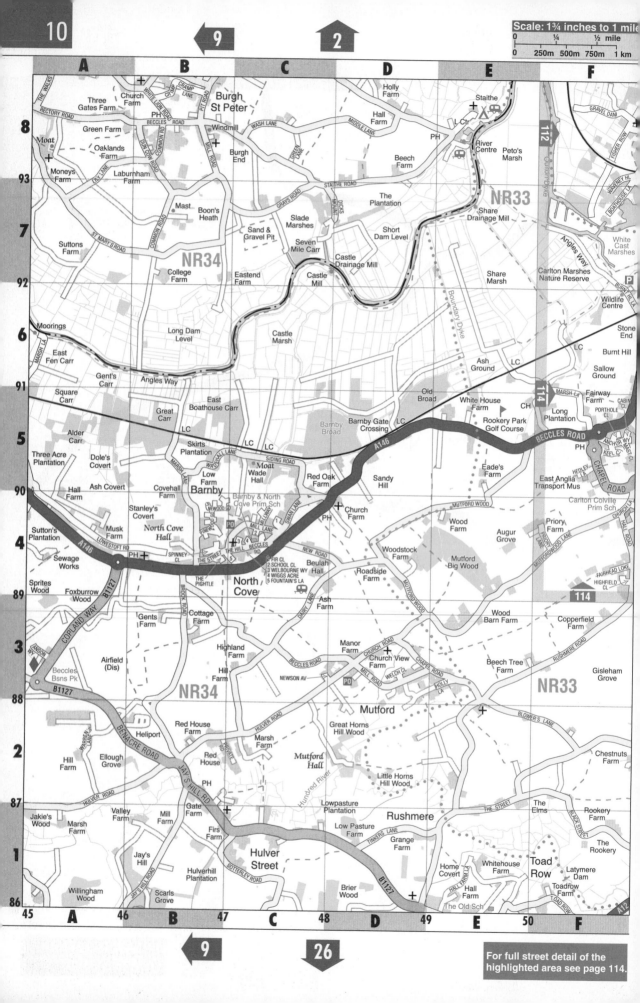

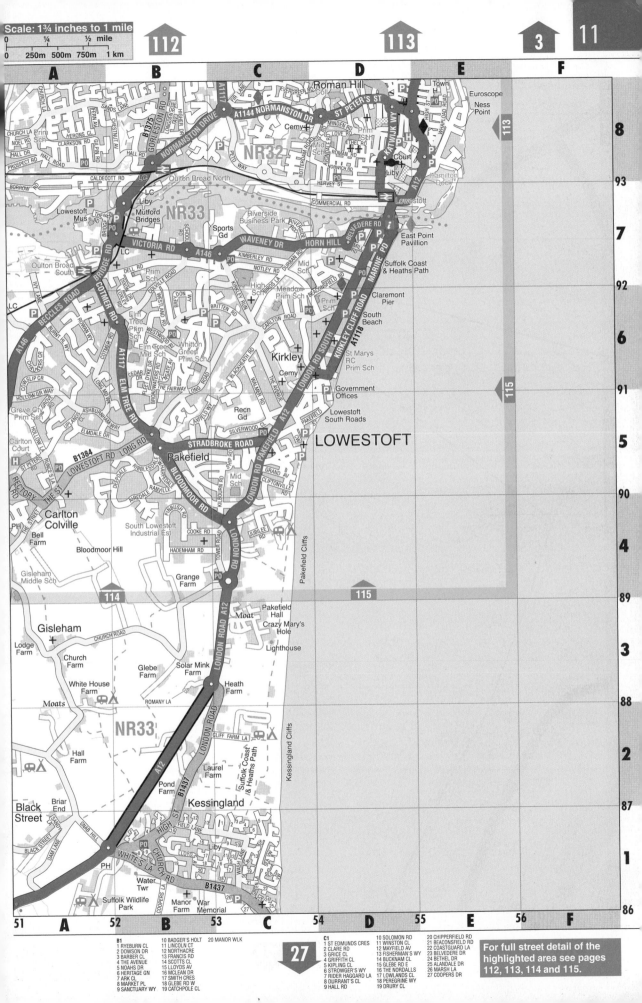

Scale: 1¾ inches to 1 mile

0 ¼ ½ mile

0 250m 500m 750m 1 km

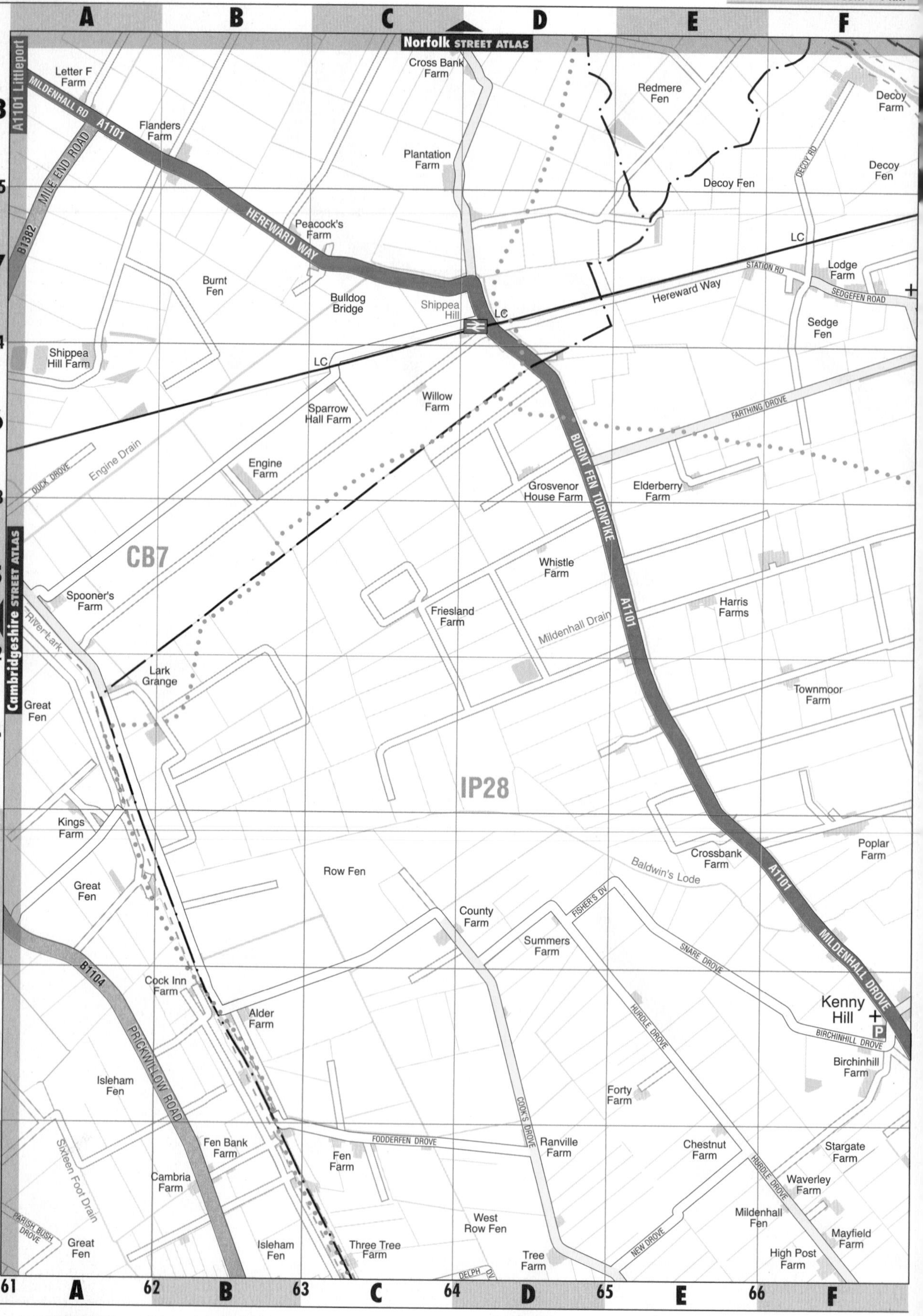

A B C D E F
Norfolk STREET ATLAS
A1101 Littleport
Cambridgeshire STREET ATLAS
8
85
7
84
6
83
5
82
4
81
3
80
2
79
1
78
61 62 63 64 65 66
Letter F Farm
MILDENHALL RD
A1101
MILE END ROAD
B1382
Flanders Farm
Cross Bank Farm
Plantation Farm
Redmere Fen
Decoy Farm
Decoy Fen
Decoy Fen
DECOY RD
HEREWARD WAY
Peacock's Farm
Burnt Fen
Bulldog Bridge
Shippea Hill
LC
Hereward Way
STATION RD
Lodge Farm
SEDGEFEN ROAD
Sedge Fen
Shippea Hill Farm
Sparrow Hall Farm
Willow Farm
FARTHING DROVE
Engine Drain
DUCK DROVE
Engine Farm
Grosvenor House Farm
BURNT FEN TURNPIKE
Elderberry Farm
CB7
Whistle Farm
Spooner's Farm
Friesland Farm
Harris Farms
Mildenhall Drain
River Lark
Lark Grange
Great Fen
Townmoor Farm
IP28
Kings Farm
Crossbank Farm
Poplar Farm
Baldwin's Lode
Row Fen
Great Fen
County Farm
FISHER'S DV
Summers Farm
SNARE DROVE
B1104
Cock Inn Farm
Alder Farm
PRICKWILLOW ROAD
HURDLE DROVE
MILDENHALL DROVE
Kenny Hill
P
BIRCHINHILL DROVE
Birchinhill Farm
Isleham Fen
Forty Farm
COOK'S DROVE
Sixteen Foot Drain
Fen Bank Farm
FODDERFEN DROVE
Ranville Farm
Chestnut Farm
Stargate Farm
Fen Farm
Cambria Farm
Waverley Farm
West Row Fen
Mildenhall Fen
PARISH BUSH DROVE
Great Fen
Isleham Fen
Three Tree Farm
NEW DROVE
Mayfield Farm
High Post Farm
Tree Farm
DELPH DV

28

29

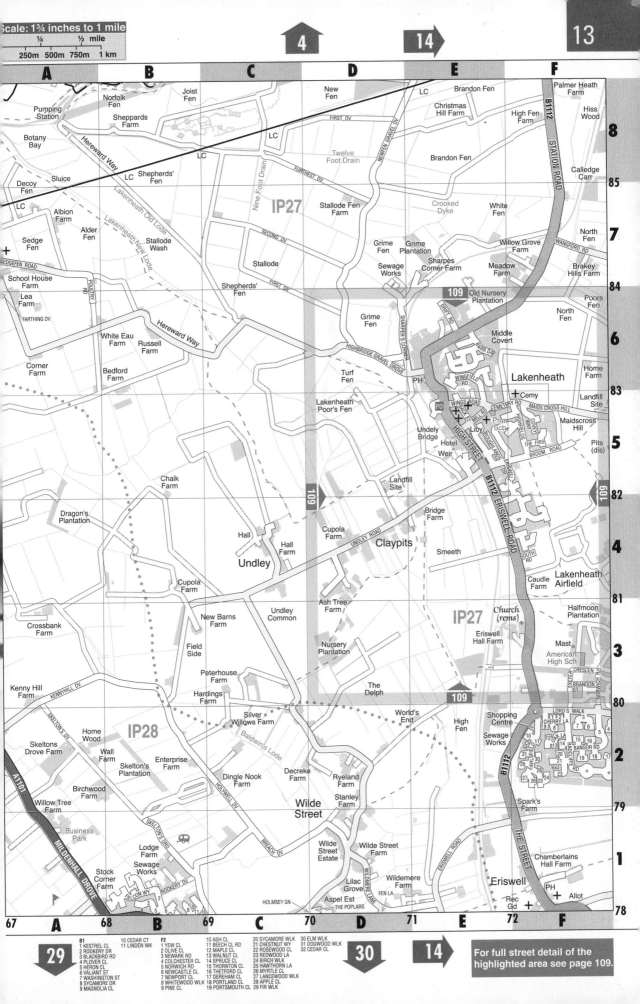

Scale: 1¾ inches to 1 mile

¼ ½ mile

250m 500m 750m 1km

A B C D E F

Pumping Station
Botany Bay
Decoy Fen
LC
Sluice
Albion Farm
Sedge Fen
School House Farm
Lea Farm
FARTHING DV
Corner Farm
White Eau Farm
Russell Farm
Bedford Farm

Norfolk Fen
Sheppards Farm
Joist Fen
New Fen
LC
FIRST DV
Twelve Foot Drain
FURTHEST DV
Stallode Fen Farm
Shepherds' Fen
SECOND DV
Stallode
Stallode Wash
Lakenheath Old Lode
Lakenheath New Lode
Hereward Way
POULTRY RD
Shepherds' Fen
FIRST DV
Hereward Way
NINE FOOT DRAIN

New Fen
LC
Brandon Fen
Christmas Hill Farm
Brandon Fen
Grime Fen
Grime Plantation
Sewage Works
Sharpes Corner Farm
Grime Fen
HIGHBRIDGE GRAVEL DROVE
Turf Fen
Lakenheath Poor's Fen

NEWEN GRAVEL DV
Crooked Dyke
White Fen
Willow Grove Farm
Meadow Farm
109 Old Nursery Plantation
DRIFT RD
Middle Covert
North Fen
SHARPER'S CORNER
PH
WINGFIELD RD
BARR DR
Lakenheath
Cemy
Landfill Site
Maidscross Hill
Pits (dis)

Palmer Heath Farm
Hiss Wood
B1112 STATION ROAD
Calledge Carr
North Fen
WANGFORD RD
Brakey Hills Farm
Poors Fen
Home Farm

8
85
7
84
6
83
5

IP27

Dragon's Plantation
Chalk Farm
Cupola Farm
Crossbank Farm
Kenny Hill Farm
KENNYHILL DV

Hall
Undley
Hall Farm
New Barns Farm
Undley Common
Field Side
Peterhouse Farm
Hardings Farm

UNDLEY ROAD
Cupola Farm
Claypits
Ash Tree Farm
Nursery Plantation

Bridge Farm
Smeeth
The Delph
109

WINGS ROAD
HIGH STREET
Undely Bridge
Hotel
Weir
Landfill Site
POST
Liby
Prim Sch
CEMETERY RD
MAIDS CROSS HILL
HIGHFIELDS
COVERT WAY
THE FIRS
BROOM ROAD
ERISWELL RD
B1112 ERISWELL ROAD
SOUTH RD
Caudle Farm

Maidscross Hill
109
Lakenheath Airfield
IP27
Church (rems)
Eriswell Hall Farm
Mast
American High Sch
CRESCEN
BRANDON ST
EXETER
NORWICH RD
Halfmoon Plantation

82
4
81
3
80

IP28
Home Wood
SKELTON'S DV
Skeltons Drove Farm
Wall Farm
Skelton's Plantation
Birchwood Farm
Willow Tree Farm
A1101
Business Park
MILDENHALL DROVE
Stock Corner Farm
Lodge Farm
Sewage Works
FALCON WY
ROOKERY DV
SKELTON'S DRO
HOLWELL DV
BREACH DV

Silver Willows Farm
Baldwin's Lode
Enterprise Farm
Dingle Nook Farm
Decreke Farm
Wilde Street
Wilde Street Estate
Lilac Grove Est
Aspel Est
HOLMSEY GN
THE POPLARS

World's End
High Fen
Ryeland Farm
Stanley Farm
Wilde Street Farm
Wildemere Farm
WILDEMERE AVE
FEN LA

Shopping Centre
Sewage Works
B1112
Spark's Farm
THE STREET
Chamberlains Hall Farm
Eriswell
PH
Rec Gd
Allot

LORD'S WALK
CHERRY LA
BANGOR RD
RADCLIFFE RD

2
79
1
78

67 A 68 B 69 C 70 D 71 E 72 F

For full street detail of the highlighted area see page 109.

B1
1 KESTREL CL
2 ROOKERY DR
3 BLACKBIRD RD
4 PLOVER CL
5 HERON CL
6 VALIANT ST
7 WASHINGTON ST
8 SYCAMORE DR
9 MAGNOLIA CL

10 CEDAR CT
11 LINDEN WK

F2
1 YEW CL
2 OLIVE CL
3 NEWARK RD
4 COLCHESTER CL
5 NORWICH RD
6 NEWCASTLE CL
7 NEWPORT CL
8 WHITEWOOD WLK
9 PINE CL

10 ASH CL
11 BEECH CL RD
12 MAPLE CL
13 WALNUT CL
14 SPRUCE CL
15 THORNTON CL
16 THETFORD CL
17 DEREHAM CL
18 PORTLAND CL
19 PORTSMOUTH CL

20 SYCAMORE WLK
21 CHESTNUT WY
22 ROSEWOOD CL
23 REDWOOD LA
24 BIRCH WLK
25 HAWTHORN LA
26 MYRTLE CL
27 LANCEWOOD WLK
28 APPLE CL
29 FIR WLK

30 ELM WLK
31 DOGWOOD WLK
32 CEDAR CL

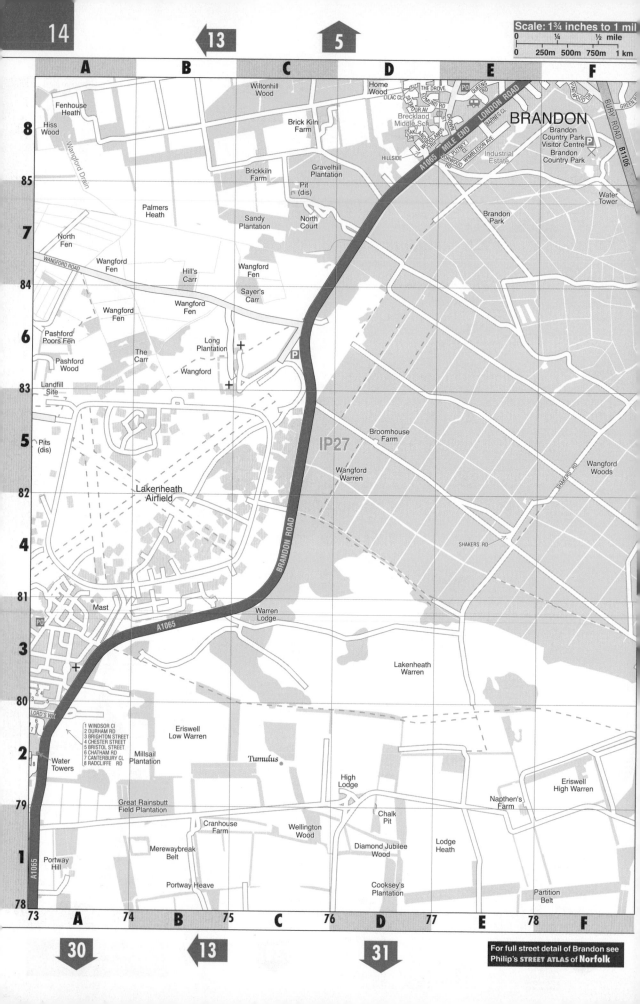

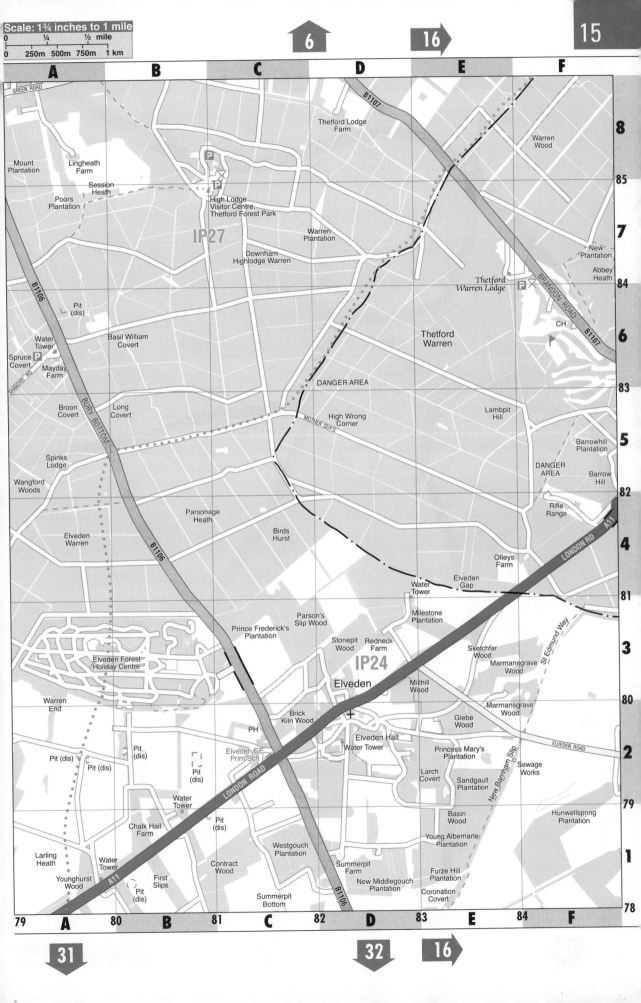

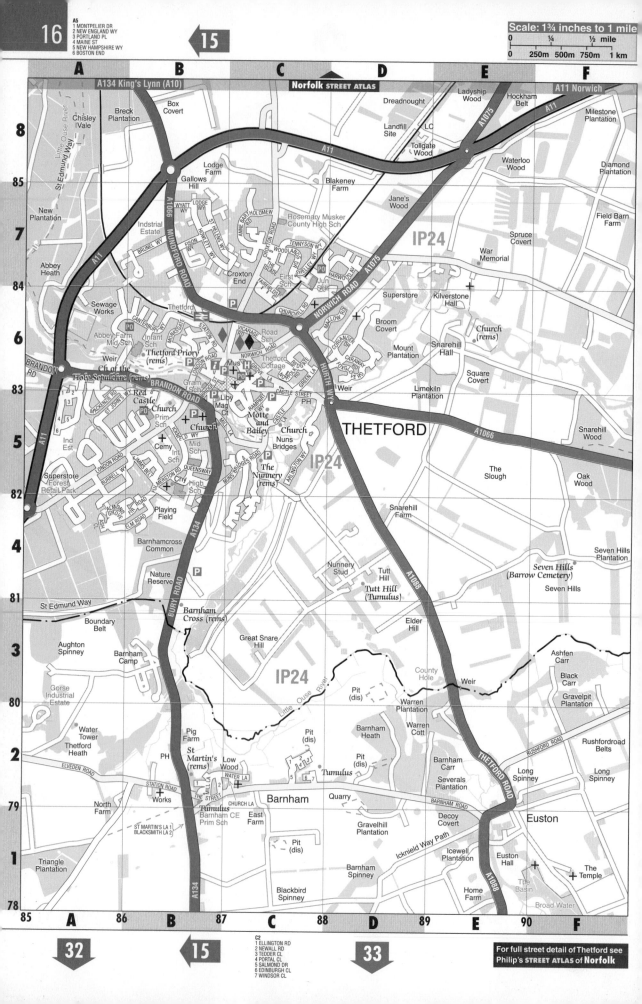

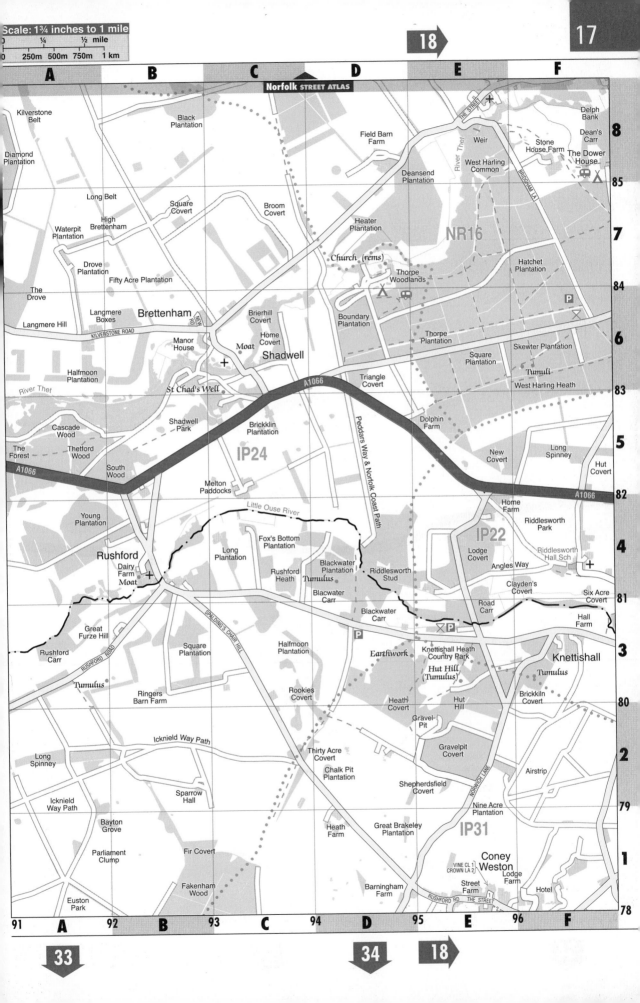

Scale: 1¾ inches to 1 mile

0   ¼   ½ mile
0 250m 500m 750m 1 km

| A | B | C | D | E | F |

Norfolk STREET ATLAS

EAST HARLING ROAD

8

Micklemoor Hill
Settlement
Black Carr
Berdewell Hall Farm

Middle Harling
Mauleys Farm
Middle Harling Farm

WEST HARLING RD

Allot
Cemy
Mauleys Farm
Town Farm

Hill Harling Farm
Hill Harling

Grove Farm

85

WEST Harling

GARBOLDISHAM ROAD

7

Big Wood
Lodge Plantation
Privet Plantation

NR16

LOPHAM ROAD

Flint Hall Farm

Guiltcross Farm

GARBOLDISHAM ROAD

Tumulus

Triangle Covert

84

Ten Acre Plantation

East Harling Heath

HARLING ROAD

Uphall Farm

Dairy Farm

6

Twenty Acre Plantation

Tumulus

Finchams Farm
Dickersons Farm

83

West Harlinghill Plantation

Old Sheep Pen Plantation

Hall Farm

Cranespond Plantation

Garboldisham Manor

Stubbings's Farm

Fir Tree Farm
Whitebreads Farm

Sandy Betty's Plantation

Wilderness Plantation

5

Hut Covert
Fir Covert

Garboldisham Heath

Georgiana Plantation

B1111

Ling Farm

Orchard Farm

Devil's Ditch

The Hall

LYNG LA

82

A1066

Seventeen Acre Plantation

Tumulus

Long Furlong Plantation

BACK ST

WATER LA

Garboldisham

Allotments Farm

Gables Farm

HIGH CO RD

Twelve Acre Plantation
St John's Covert

Hill Plantation

Home Covert

THETFORD ROAD   A1066

CHURCH ST

Garboldisham Rd Prim Sch

DISS RD

ELM GR

DISS ROAD

THETFORD ROAD   A1066

Mill Pond Farm

4

Gasthorpe

St Nichola's Church

LODGE LA

Lodge Farm

Oldoak Plantation

IP22

PO

Church Farm
CHAPEL CL
THOMAS BOLE CL

HOPTON ROAD

SMALLWORTH LA

81

THE STREET

Alder Carr

Angles Way

Fen Farm

Old Fen

HARBOUR LA

Smallworth Farm

Three Wells Farm

3

Six Acre Covert

Wall Covert

Garboldisham Common

FEN LA

Rec Gd

Windmill

Smallworth

Boundary Farm

Willow Farm

White House Farm

Lodge Farm

BLO NORTON RD

All Saints Church

Hopton Fen

Common Farm

MILL LA

Hotel

Fir Covert

Broomscot Common

80

Wall Covert

COMMON ROAD

Hall Farm

Church Farm
MEADOWSIDE

THE STREET

Ash Tree Farm

SELF'S LA

MIDDLE ROAD

2

Dairy Farm

SHICKLE PL 1
LEWIS CL 2
HOLME CL 3
PINE TREE CT 4

Manor Farm

Raydon Common

Angles Way

Moat
Hilldrop Farm

CHURCH LA

Blo' Norton

Manor Farm

Fen Street

NETHERGATE STREET

HIGH STREET

Hopton

PH
PO

Spring Farm

BUGGS HOLE LA

Fen Farm

Willow Farm
The Banks

79

Broom Covert

Robsons Farm

GREYHOUND LA

THELNETHAM ROAD

Thelnetham Windmill

(Nature Reserve)
Thelnetham Fen

FEN ROAD

Little Ouse River

Hinderclay Fen

1

HOLLOW LA

IP31

Weston Fen

Hillside Farm

Hopton CE Prim Sch

WALNUT CL

Church Farm

BURY ROAD

CHURCH ROAD

Kays Farm

Thelnetham

MILL RD

WATER LA

FEN LANE

LOGGERS LA

SCHOOL LA

CHURCH LA

Blo Norton Fen

Holiday Farm

78

Cinque Farm

B1111

Hopton End Farm

Cross Green Farm

HOPTON ROAD

Moat

PH
HINDERCLAY LA

HIGH ST

St Mary's Well (Spring)

FEN STREET

| A | B | C | D | E | F |

97   98   99   00   01   02

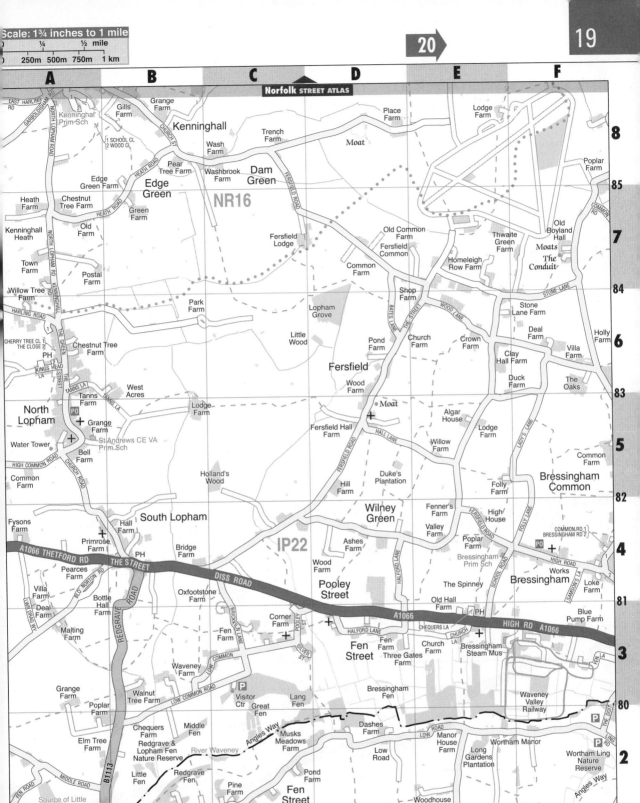

Scale: 1¾ inches to 1 mile

¼   ½ mile
250m 500m 750m 1 km

Norfolk STREET ATLAS

A   B   C   D   E   F

8
85
7
84
6
83
5
82
4
81
3
80
2
79
1
78

EAST HARLING RD

GARBOLDISHAM RD

NORTH LOPHAM ROAD

Kenninghall Prim Sch

Gills Farm

Grange Farm

Kenninghall

Place Farm

Lodge Farm

Poplar Farm

1 SCHOOL CL
2 WOOD CL

Wash Farm

Trench Farm

Moat

CHURCH ST

HEATH ROAD

Pear Tree Farm

Washbrook Farm

Dam Green

FERSFIELD ROAD

COMMON RD

Edge Green Farm

Edge Green

Green Farm

NR16

Old Boyland Hall

HEATH ROAD

Heath Farm

Chestnut Tree Farm

Fersfield Lodge

Old Common Farm

Thwaite Green Farm

Moats

The Conduit

Kenninghall Heath

Old Farm

Fersfield Common

Homeleigh Row Farm

Town Farm

Postal Farm

BATES LANE

THE STREET

WOOD LANE

STONE LANE

Stone Lane Farm

Deal Farm

Holly Farm

Willow Tree Farm

HARLING ROAD

Park Farm

Common Farm

Shop Farm

Church Farm

Crown Farm

Clay Hall Farm

Villa Farm

CHERRY TREE CL 1
THE CLOSE 2

THE GREEN

THE STREET

KENNINGHALL RD

Chestnut Tree Farm

Little Wood

Pond Farm

Fersfield

Wood Farm

Duck Farm

The Oaks

PH

KINGS HEAD LA

West Acres

Lodge Farm

Moat

Algar House

Lodge Farm

LADY'S LANE

Common Farm

North Lopham

TANNS LA

Tanns Farm

Fersfield Hall Farm

HALL LANE

Willow Farm

Bressingham Common

Water Tower

St Andrews CE VA Prim Sch

Grange Farm

Bell Farm

CHURCH ROAD

Lodge Farm

Holland's Wood

Hill Farm

Duke's Plantation

Folly Farm

FERSFIELD ROAD

FOLLY LANE

COMMON RD 1
BRESSINGHAM RD 2

HIGH COMMON ROAD

Common Farm

Wilney Green

Fenner's Farm

High House

Bressingham Common

Fysons Farm

Hall Farm

South Lopham

IP22

Valley Farm

Poplar Farm

SCHOOL LANE

Bressingham Prim Sch

HIGH ROAD

Bressingham

Primrose Farm

Bridge Farm

Ashes Farm

The Spinney

Works

SAMSON'S LA

LOKE LANE

A1066 THETFORD RD

THE STREET

PH

DISS ROAD

Wood Farm

Old Hall Farm

PH

HIGH RD A1066

Blue Pump Farm

Pearces Farm

Pooley Street

HALFORD LANE

A1066

Villa Farm

BLO' NORTON RD

Oxfootstone Farm

Corner Farm

POOLEY ST

Halford Lane

CHEQUERS LA

CHURCH LA

Bressingham Steam Mus

Deal Hall Farm

Bottle Hall Farm

SILVER ST

Fen Street

Fen Farm

Three Gates Farm

Church Farm

FEN LA

Malting Farm

REDGRAVE ROAD

Fen Farm

LOW COMMON

Waveney Fram

Bridge Farm

LANG LA

Bressingham Fen

Waveney Valley Railway

THE DROVE

LONG RD

Grange Farm

Poplar Farm

Walnut Tree Farm

LOW COMMON ROAD

Visitor Ctr

Great Fen

Lang Fen

LON

Manor House Farm

Wortham Manor

Wortham Ling Nature Reserve

Elm Tree Farm

Chequers Farm

Middle Fen

Angles Way

Musks Meadows Farm

Dashes Farm

Low Road

Long Gardens Plantation

FEN ROAD

Redgrave & Lopham Fen Nature Reserve

River Waveney

Little Fen

Redgrave Fen

Pine Farm

Pond Farm

Angles Way

Watch Tower

MIDDLE ROAD

B1113

Source of Little Ouse River

Source of River Waveney

Grove House Farm

Fen Street

Woodhouse Farm

Monument

MAGPIE HILL

Beech Tree Farm

RECTORY RD

Fir Tree Farm

FEN STREET

MILL LA

Fen Street Farm

Moneypot Hill Farm

BIER LA

The Grove

SLADE LA

CHURCH ROAD

WIDWAM HILL

MILLWAY RD

1 WEST HERNE LA
2 SOUTHERN LA

Holly Farm

Magpie Green

Low Farm

Bridge Farm

FEN STREET

HINDERCLAY ROAD

MONEYPOT LA

Moneypot Hill Sewage Works

WASH LANE

Pond Farm

WASH LANE

REDGRAVE ROAD

Sewage Works

THE STREET

Street Farm PH

CHURCHWAY

Crackthorn Corner

03   04   05   06   07   08

A   B   C   D   E   F

Norfolk STREET ATLAS

A **B** **C** **D** **E** **F**

Winfarthing

Holly Farm

Messuage Farm

Marlers Farm

Bridge Farm

Gissing

High London Farm

Church Farm

All Saints CE VA Prim Sch

Hill House Farm

Water Tower

Home Wood

Hotel

Moats

Boyland Common

Moats

Fiddler's Dykes

Mill Farm

Green Dragon Farm

Hamilton House Holly Farm

Top Wood

Old Hall

New Plantation

Elm Tree Farm

Manor Farm

Eaton Farm

Vine Farm

Old Hall Farm Moat

Mill Green

Grove Farm

Wood Cottage Farm

Market Field Plantation

West Hall Farm

Limetree Farm

Street Farm

Shelfanger

Moat

Oak Farm

Laurel Farm

Culpher Farm

Lime Grove

Bridge Green

Osierbed Plantation

Church Farm

Shelfanger Hall

Green Farm

Shelfanger Grove

Home Farm

Far End

Moat

Recn Gd

Manor House Farm

Bridge Green Farm

Hall Farm

Spa Farm

The Heywood

St Martins Farm

Burston

Burston Com Prim Sch

Valley Farm

Moat

Moat

Hazel Farm

Lodge Farm

Dairy Farm

Prospect Farm

Hill Farm

Moat

Market Farm

Audley End

Lark Farm

IP22

Darrow Wood Farm

Farrows Farm

Chestnut Tree Farm

Homeway Farm

The Carr

Misty Wood

Darrow Farm

Wolsey Farm

Westbrook Green

Bow Bridge

Wolsey Bridge Farm

Three Corner Plantation

Bridge Farm

Jubilee Farm

Willow Farm

Stollerie's Farm

Westbrook Green Farm

Walcot Green Farm

Gravel Pit Plantation

Snow Street

Glebe Farm

Boundary Farm

DISS

Walcot Wood

Blackthorn Farm

Coursing Barn Plantation

Gables Farm

Lime Tree Farm

Fir Tree Farm

White House Farm

Algars Farm

Walcot Green

The Grange

Home Farm

Moat

Brewers Green

Cemy

Home Farm

Moat

Grove Farm

Pretoria Plantation

Roydon

High Road

A1066

High Rd

Old High Rd

Roydon Rd

Diss Town FC

Manor Farm

Poplar Farm

Diss Cty High Sch

Alder Carr

Frenze

Scole Common

B1132

Prim Sch

Grove Farm

Allot

Roydon Fen

Cock Street Fen

Stanley Rd

Park Rd

Victoria Rd

Clynt Plantation

Long House

Frenze

IP21

Wortham Ling

Oak Farm

Angles Way

Denmark Bridge

Swimming Pool

Windmill Sewage Works

Frenze Bridge

Angles Way

Waterloo

Pollard Tree Farm

Elm Vale Farm

Flax Farm

Stuston Bridge

River Waveney

Millway Farm

Longs Farm

Cemy

Palgrave VC Prim Sch

Stuston Common

Scole Bridge

Millway Lane

A143

Priory Farm

A143

Stuston

Scole Plantation

The Priory

Palgrave

Orchard End

Willow Farm

Hall Farm

Moat

A3
1 CHURCH CL
2 BLENHEIM WY
3 COPEMAN RD
4 WATERLOO AV
5 TWISS CL
6 OLD RECTORY CL
7 FRERE CR

F1
1 LOW RD
2 IPSWICH RD
3 DISS RD
4 KAREN CL
5 NORWICH RD
6 BRIDGE RD
7 ROBINSON RD
8 CLEMENTS CL

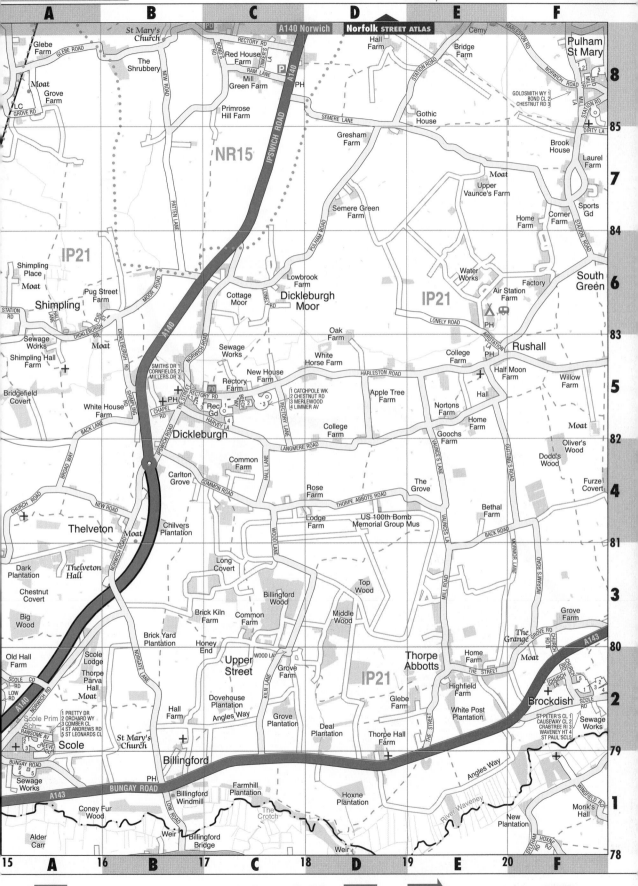

Scale: 1¾ inches to 1 mile

Norfolk STREET ATLAS

A140 Norwich

A B C D E F

St Mary's Church

Glebe Farm
GLEBE ROAD
Moat
Grove Farm
GROVE RD
LC

The Shrubbery

NEW ROAD

RECTORY RD
Red House Farm
TIMBERS LA
BOND'S
RAM LANE
Mill Green Farm
PH
A140
P

Hall Farm

Bridge Farm

STATION ROAD

HARLESTON RD

NORWICH ROAD

Pulham St Mary

MILL DR
STATION RD

GOLDSMITH WY 1
BOND CL 2
CHESTNUT RD 3

8

DIRTY LA

85

Primrose Hill Farm

NR15

SEMERE LANE

Gothic House

Gresham Farm

PULHAM ROAD

Semere Green Farm

Brook House

Moat

Upper Vaunce's Farm

Home Farm

Corner Farm

Laurel Farm

Sports Gd

7

84

IP21

Shimpling Place
Moat
Pug Street Farm
Shimpling
STATION RD
HALL LANE
PUB LANE
DICKLEBURGH RD
Moat
Sewage Works
Shimpling Hall Farm

Lowbrook Farm

Cottage Moor

MOOR ROAD

LONELY RD

Dickleburgh Moor

Water Works

Air Station Farm
PH

Factory

IP21

LONELY ROAD

South Green

Rushall
PH

6

83

Bridgefield Covert

White House Farm

IPSWICH ROAD

CHAPEL RD

A140

THE STREET

SMITHS DR 1
CORNFIELDS 2
MILLERS DR 3
PO
Rectory Farm
RECTORY RD
PH
Rec Gd
BEECH
HARVEY LA

Sewage Works

New House Farm

White Horse Farm

1 CATCHPOLE WK
2 CHESTNUT RD
3 MERLEWOOD
4 LIMMER AV

Oak Farm

HARLESTON ROAD

Apple Tree Farm

College Farm

Half Moon Farm

Hall

Willow Farm

5

BACK LANE

Dickleburgh

Common Farm

RECTORY LANE

HALL LANE

College Farm

LANGMERE ROAD

Nortons Farm

Home Farm

Goochs Farm

Moat

Oliver's Wood

Dodd's Wood

82

BROAD WAY

Carlton Grove

COMMON ROAD

Rose Farm

THORPE ABBOTS ROAD

The Grove

VAUNCE'S LANE

CUTTING'S ROAD

Furze Covert

4

CHURCH ROAD

Thelveton

Moat

Chilvers Plantation

WOOD LANE

Lodge Farm

US 100th Bomb Memorial Group Mus

Bethal Farm

BACK ROAD

81

Dark Plantation

Thelveton Hall

NORWICH ROAD

Long Covert

Billingford Wood

Top Wood

MILL ROAD

MORMOR LANE

INGRAM'S ROAD

Grove Farm

3

Chestnut Covert

Big Wood

Brick Kiln Farm

Common Farm

Middle Wood

The Grange

GROVE RD

CHURCH LA

A143

Old Hall Farm

Brick Yard Plantation

NORGATE LANE

Honey End

WOOD LA

Upper Street

KILN LANE

Grove Farm

Thorpe Abbotts

Home Farm

THE STREET

Moat

Brockdish

80

A140

SCOLE CO RD
LOW RD

Scole Lodge

Thorpe Parva Hall
Moat

1 PRETTY DR
2 ORCHARD WY
3 COMBER CL
4 ST ANDREWS RD
5 ST LEONARDS CL

Hall Farm

Dovehouse Plantation

Angles Way

Grove Plantation

Deal Plantation

IP21

Glebe Farm

Highfield Farm

White Post Plantation

Thorpe Hall Farm

CHURCH LA

SCOLE RD
1
2
3
4
5

ST PETER'S CL 1
CAUSEWAY CL 2
CRABTREE RD 3
WAVENEY HT 4
ST PAUL SCL5

Sewage Works

2

Scole Prim Sch
RANSOME AV
CREEVE CL
Scole
St Mary's Church

79

BUNGAY ROAD
Sewage Works

Billingford
A143
BUNGAY ROAD

PH

LOW ROAD

Billingford Windmill

Billingford Bridge

Farmhill Plantation

The Crotch

Hoxne Plantation

Weir

Angles Way

River Waveney

New Plantation

SYLEHAM HOXNE RD

WINGFIELD RD

Monk's Hall

1

Alder Carr

Coney Fur Wood

Weir

78

A 15 16 B 17 C 18 D 19 E 20 F

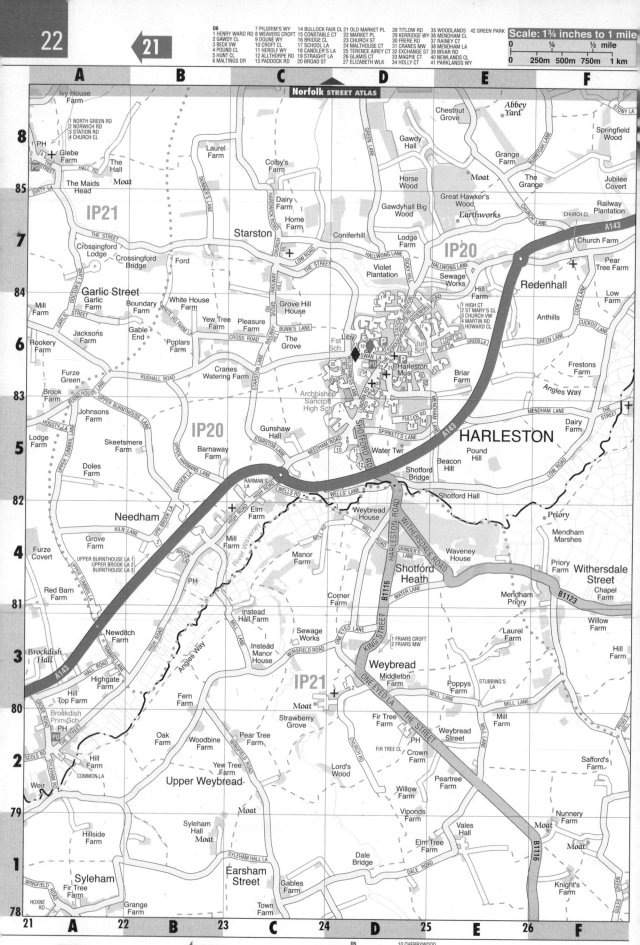

Norfolk STREET ATLAS

D6	7 PILGRIM'S WY	14 BULLOCK FAIR CL	21 OLD MARKET PL	28 TITLOW RD	35 WOODLANDS	42 GREEN PARK
1 HENRY WARD RD	8 WEAVERS CROFT	15 CONSTABLE CT	22 MARKET PL	29 KERRIDGE WY	36 MENDHAM CL	
2 GAWDY CL	9 DOUNE WY	16 BRIDGE CL	23 CHURCH ST	30 FRERE RD	37 RAINEY CT	
3 BECK VW	10 CROFT CL	17 SCHOOL LA	24 MALTHOUSE CT	31 CRANES MW	38 MENDHAM LA	
4 POUND CL	11 HEROLF WY	18 CANDLER'S LA	25 TERENCE AIREY CT	32 EXCHANGE ST	39 BRIAR RD	
5 HUNT CL	12 ALLTHORPE RD	19 STRAIGHT LA	26 GLAMIS CT	33 MAGPIE CT	40 NEWLANDS CL	
6 MALTINGS DR	13 PADDOCK RD	20 BROAD ST	27 ELIZABETH WLK	34 HOLLY CT	41 PARKLANDS WY	

D5		10 CHERRYWOOD
1 THE COMMON		11 NORTHGATE
2 GOTHIC CL		12 SOUTHGATE
3 WILDERNESS CL		13 SPEEDWELL WY
4 PINE CL		14 MAYFLOWER WY
5 WILLOW WLK		
6 PEMBERTON RD		
7 LIME CL		
8 OAK TREE WY		
9 DOVE CL		

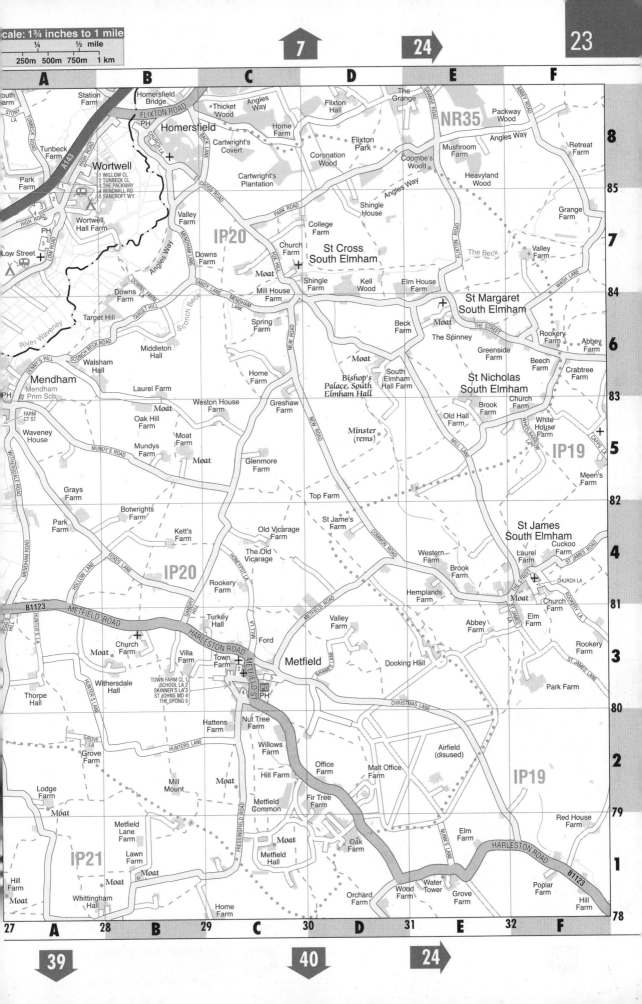

Grid references (top): A B C D E F

Grid references (left): 8 85 7 84 6 83 5 82 4 81 3 80 2 79 1 78

Brewery
St Peter's Hall
Moat
Charity Farm
Elms Farm
School Farm
Ropers Farm
Corner Farm
Church Farm
Highfields Farm
Tithe Farm
Rec Gd
Ilketshall Hall
Moat
Black's Covert
Ant Hill Plantation
Red House Farm
Becks Green Farm

Ilketshall St Margaret
Low Street
Shoe Devil Lane

St Peter South Elmham
Wash Lane
Beckford Farm
Low Farm
Brook House
Moat
Daniels Wood
Old Hall Farm
Tithe Farm
Rosary Farm
Cherry Tree Farm
NR34
Manor Farm
Beck's Green

NR35

Bridge Farm
Mill House Farm
Brook Lane
High Street
High Street
Nest Farm
Common Farm
Green Farm
Mill Farm
Windmill
Little Beck Farm

St Michael South Elmham
Water Tower
Green Farm
Home Farm
Bacons Farm
White House Farm
Highland Farm
Moat Farm
Rookery Farm
Moat Farm
Windmill Farm
Ilketshall St Lawrence

All Saints Common
Croft Farm
Uncle's Lane
Mill Farm
Hulver Farm
Boundary Farm
Rumburgh Lane
Rumburgh Farm
Rookery Farm
Kings Fene Farm
Grub Lane
Hog Lane
School Farm
St Lawrence Prim Sch
School Ww
Stone Street

Church Farm
Moat
The Elms Elms Farm
Monks Farm
All Saints South Elmham
Moat Farm
Moat
Rumburgh Wood
Laurel Farm
Green Lane Farm
Poplar Farm
THE POPLARS
Rose Farm
PH

Ash Farm
Capp's Lane
St James Road
Homestead Farm
Abbey Farm
Rumburgh Priory
Moat
Corner Farm
Gavell Street
Pear Tree Farm
Cutts Farm
Green Lane Farm
Wood Farm
Rookyards

Malt Office Av
Malt Office La
Whyteway
Street Farm
Hattons Farm
Brookhall Farm
Grove House Farm
Spexhall Hall
Moat
White House Farm
Noller's La

Malt Crede Lane
PH
Rumburgh
The Street
Gate Farm
Moat Farm
IP19
Pear Tree Farm
Home Farm
Mill Road
Gray's Lane
Hall Lane
Moat
Spexhall
A144
Stone Street

Bloom's Hall
Red House Farm
Banks' Lane
Scotch Corner Plantation
Pear Tree Farm
High House Farm
Church Lane

Banks Farm
Lodge Farm
White House Farm
Rumburgh Road
Rumburgh Place Farm
Nunn's Hill
Box Farm
Red House
Moat
118
Fairstead Farm

St James La
Hors Farm
Tarleton Farm
Valley Farm
Manor Farm
The Street
St Peters Farm
PH
Bleach Farm
Bonds Farm
Spexhall Manor
Wash Lane
118
Hall Farm
Broadway Farm

Priory Farm
Hill Farm
The Pines
Wissett
Ash Tree Farm
Mill Road

Town Farm
Leggetts Farm
Chediston Road
Lower Grove Farm
Whitehouse Farm
Farm Cl
Wissett Lodge
Grove Farm
Wissett Hall

Grove Farm
The Grove
Manorial Earthworks
Mount Pleasant Farm
Oaklodge Farm
Rosecroft Farm
Ash Farm
Pandi Farm
Wissett Road
Bonners Farm
Grove Farm
Mill Road
Old Station Road
The Av
A144

Cheditson Green
Paradise Farm

33 A 34 B 35 C 36 D 37 E 38 F

40

23

41

118

For full street detail of the highlighted area see page 118.

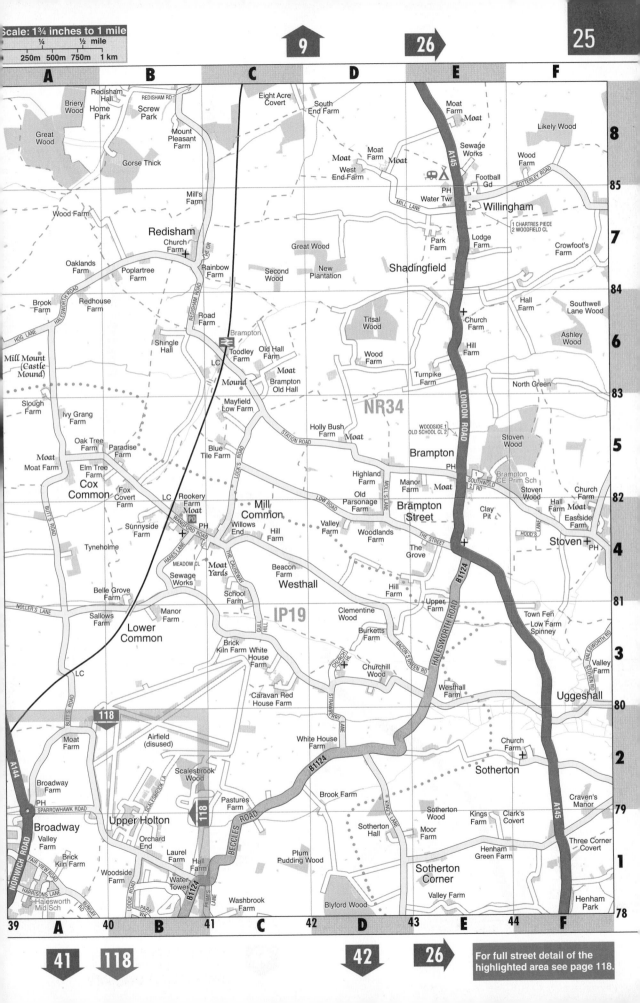

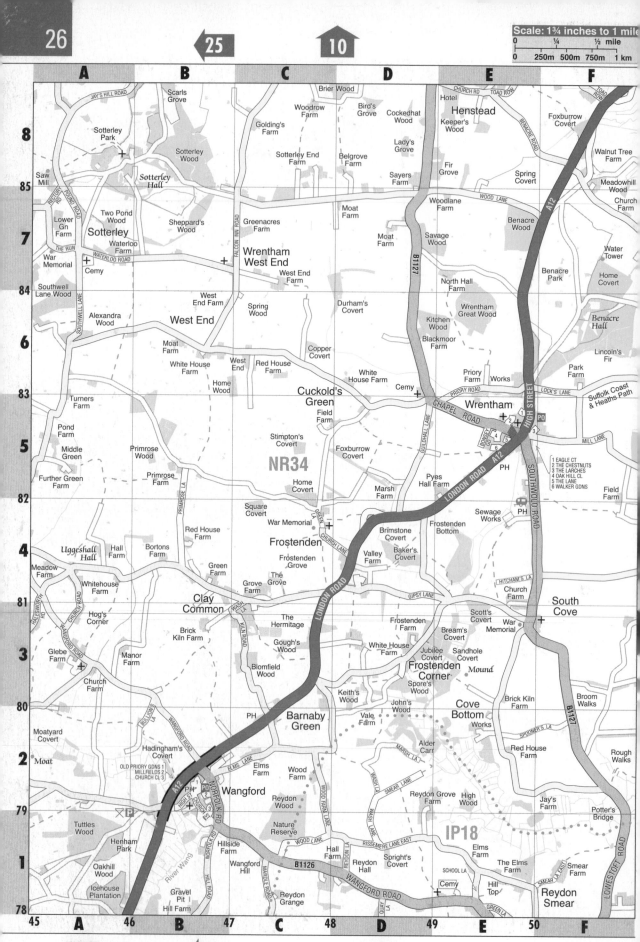

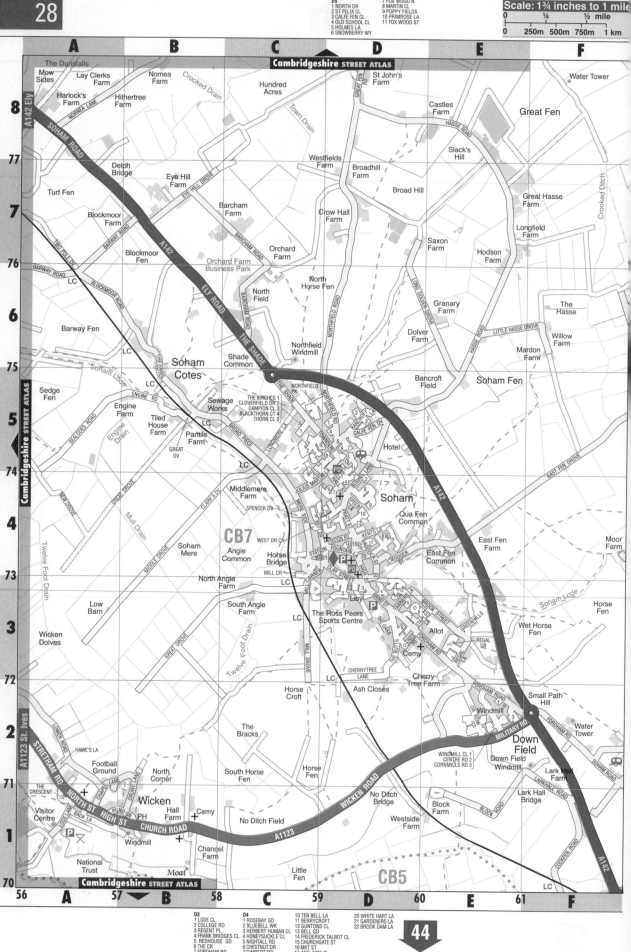

CAMBRIDGESHIRE STREET ATLAS

D5
1 NORTH DR
2 ST FELIX CL
3 CALFE FEN CL
4 OLD SCHOOL CL
5 HOLMES LA
6 SNOWBERRY WY

7 FOX WOOD N
8 MARTIN CL
9 POPPY FIELDS
10 PRIMROSE LA
11 FOX WOOD ST

CAMBRIDGESHIRE STREET ATLAS

44

D3
1 LODE CL
2 COLLEGE RD
3 REGENT PL
4 FRANK BRIDGES CL
5 REDHOUSE GD
6 THE CR
7 FORDHAM RD
8 MEADOW CL
9 MILL CFT

D4
1 ROSEBAY GD
2 BLUEBELL WK
3 HERBERT HUMAN CL
4 HONEYSUCKLE CL
5 NIGHTALL RD
6 CHESTNUT DR
7 GIMBERT RD
8 QUEENSWAY
9 WEATHERALLS CL

10 TEN BELL LA
11 BERRYCROFT
12 GUNTONS CL
13 BELL GD
14 FREDERICK TALBOT CL
15 CHURCHGATE ST
16 MKT ST
17 ADELAIDE CL
18 EASTERN AV
19 BREWHOUSE LA

20 WHITE HART LA
21 GARDENERS LA
22 BROOK DAM LA

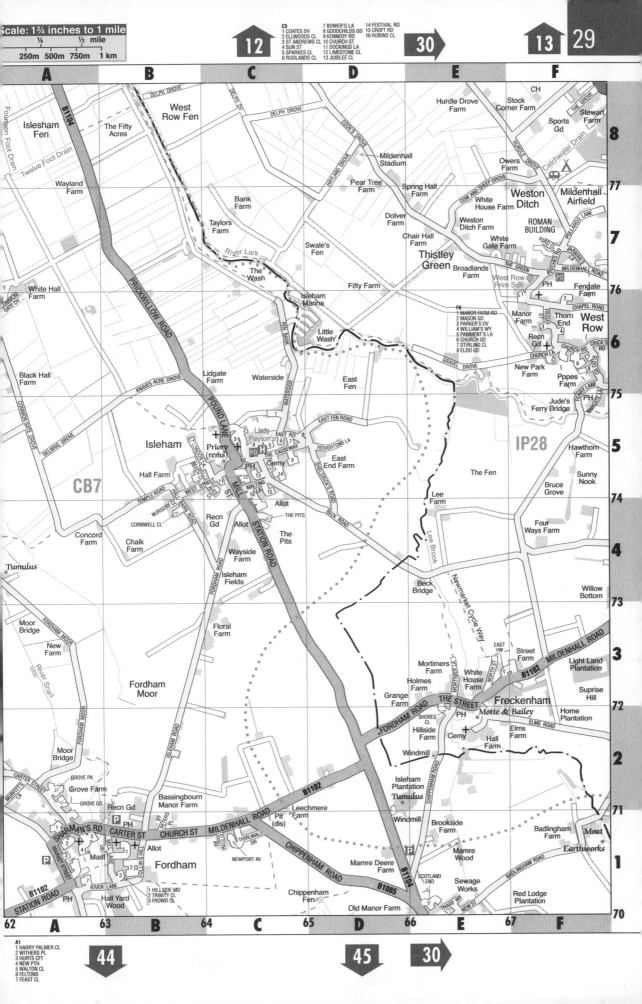

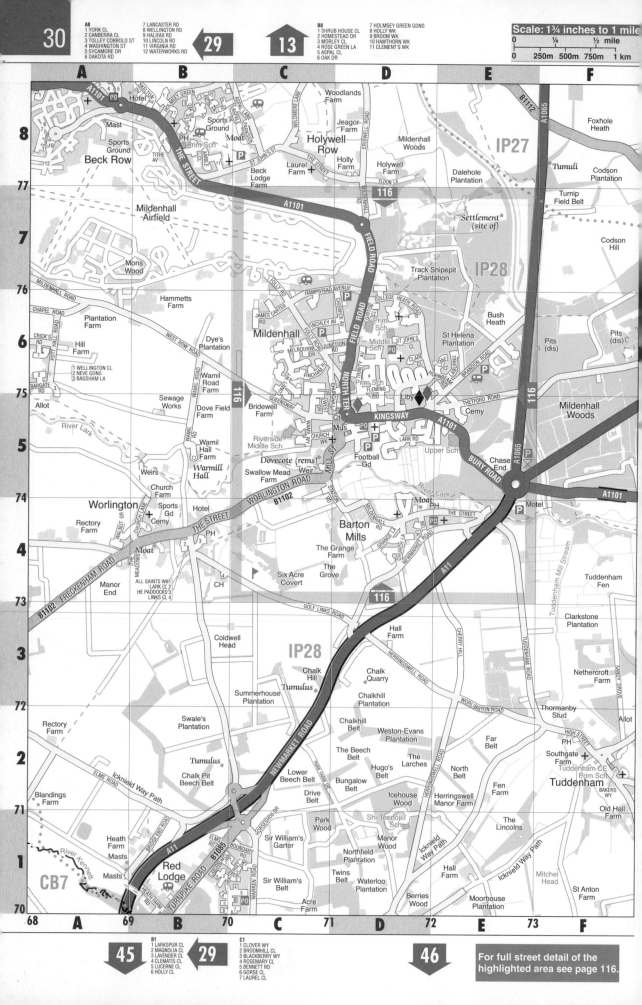

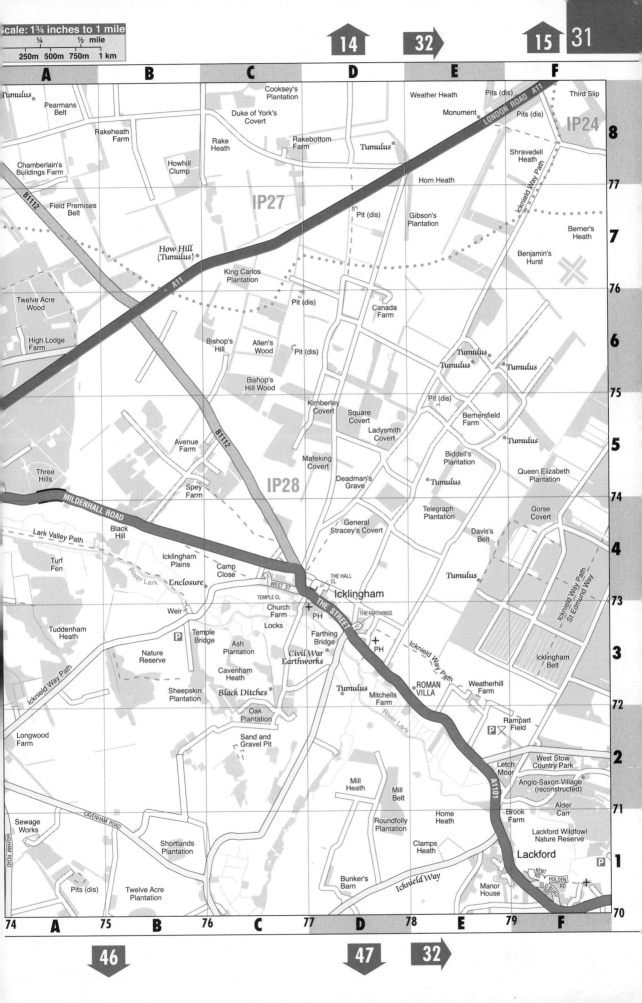

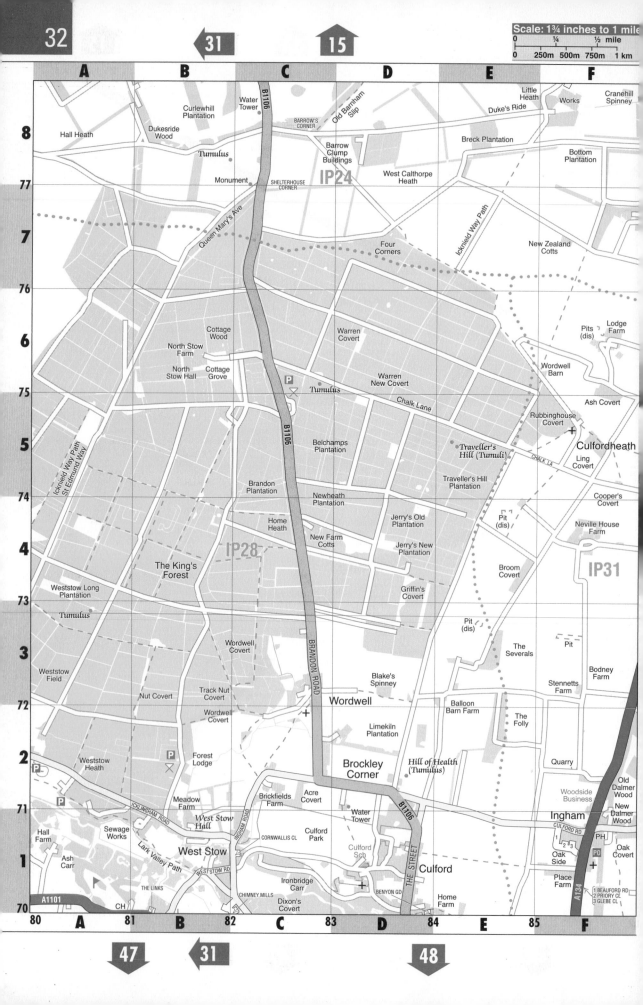

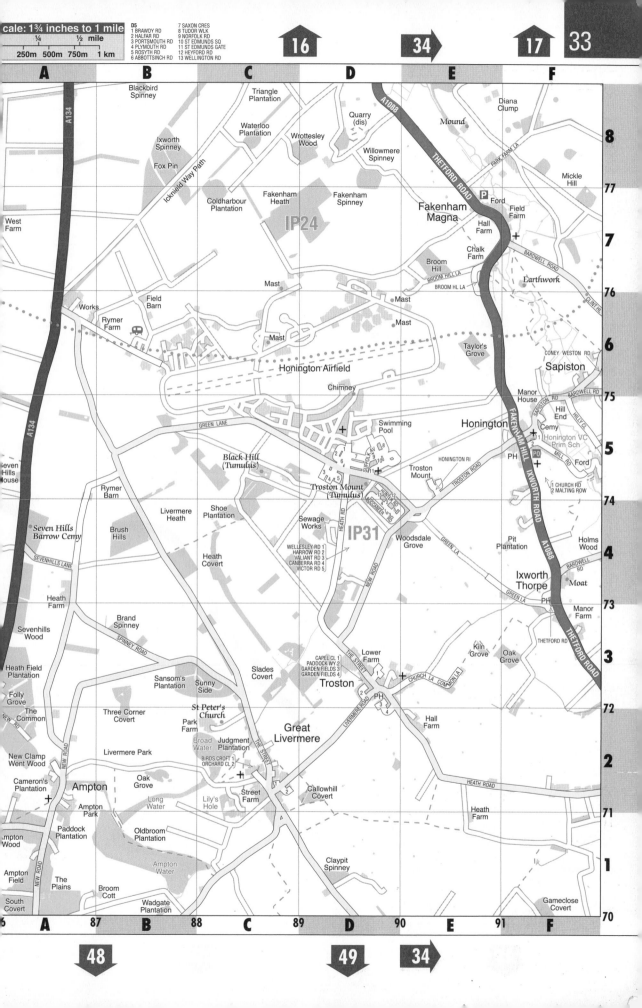

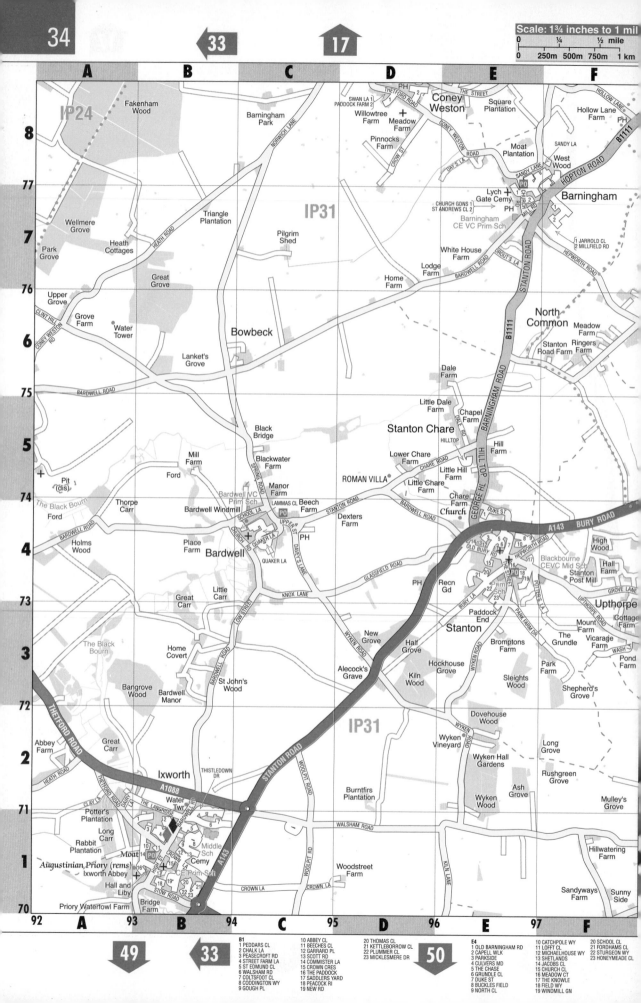

Scale: 1¾ inches to 1 mile

B1
1 PEDDARS CL
2 CHALK LA
3 PEASECROFT RD
4 STREET FARM LA
5 ST EDMUND CL
6 WALSHAM RD
7 COLTSFOOT CL
8 CODDINGTON WY
9 GOUGH PL

10 ABBEY CL
11 BEECHES CL
12 GARRARD PL
13 SCOTT RD
14 COMMISTER LA
15 CROWN CRES
16 THE PADDOCK
17 SADDLERS YARD
18 PEACOCK RI
19 NEW RD

20 THOMAS CL
21 KETTLEBORROW CL
22 PLUMMER CL
23 MICKLESMERE DR

E4
1 OLD BARNINGHAM RD
2 CAPELL WLK
3 PARKSIDE
4 CULVERS MD
5 THE CHASE
6 GRUNDLE CL
7 DUKE ST
8 BUCKLES FIELD
9 NORTH CL

10 CATCHPOLE WY
11 LOFFT CL
12 MICHAELHOUSE WY
13 SHETLANDS
14 JACOBS CL
15 CHURCH CL
16 MEADOW CT
17 THE KNOWLE
18 FIELD WY
19 WINDMILL GN

20 SCHOOL CL
21 FORDHAMS CL
22 STURGEON WY
23 HONEYMEADE CL

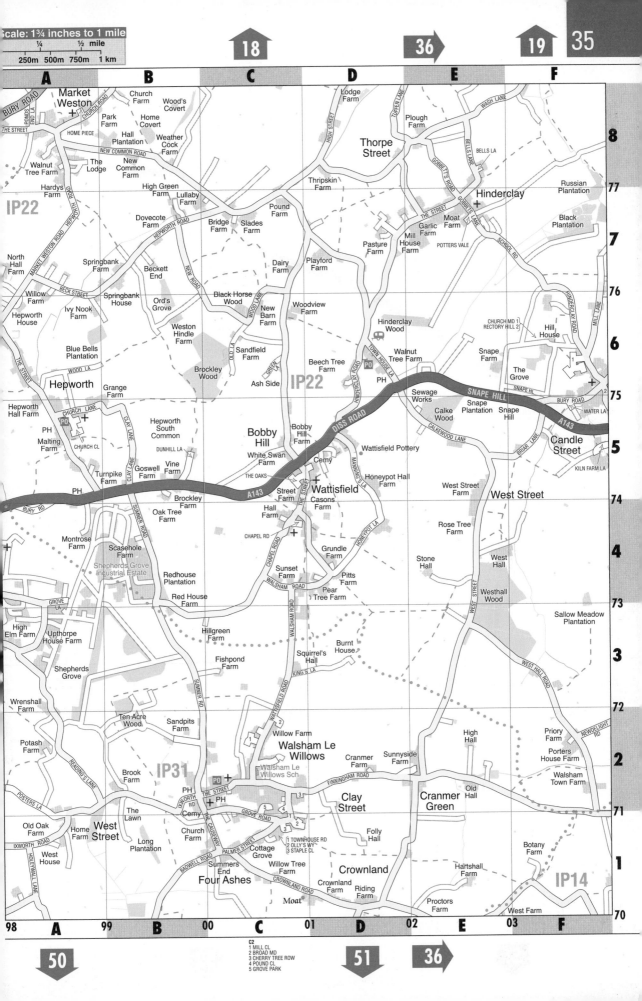

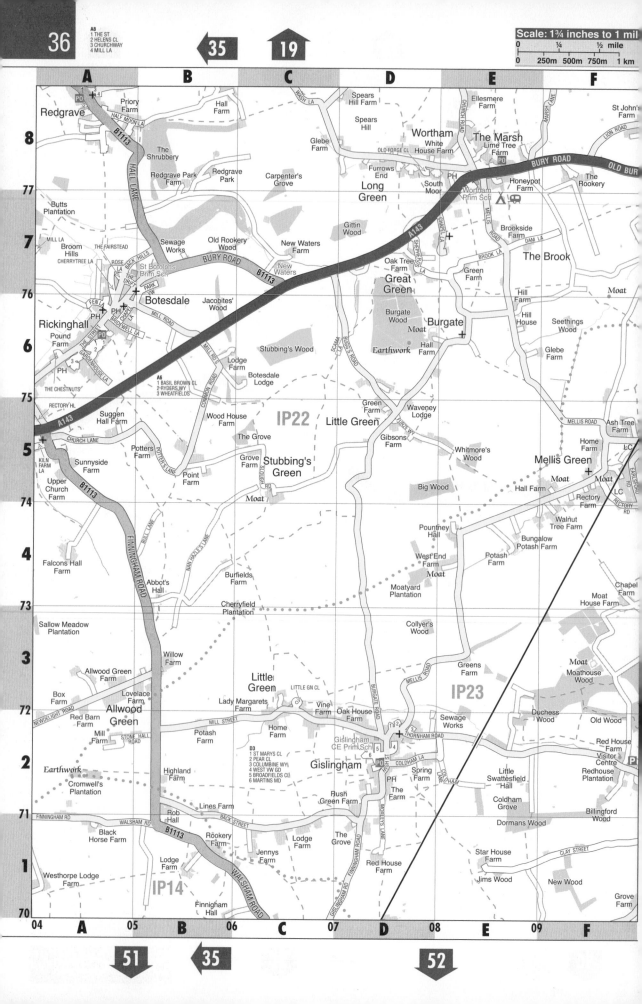

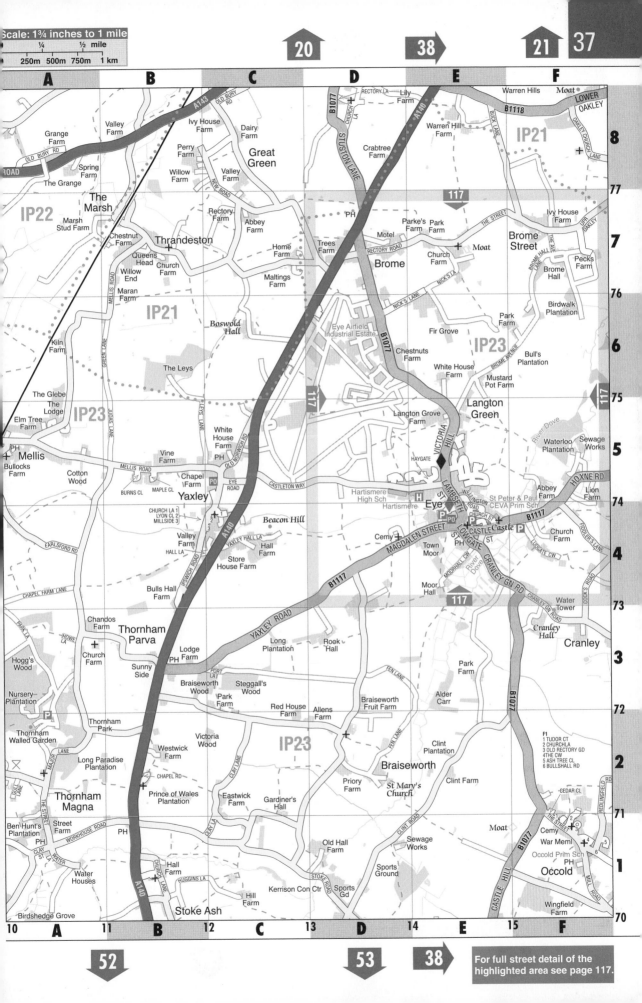

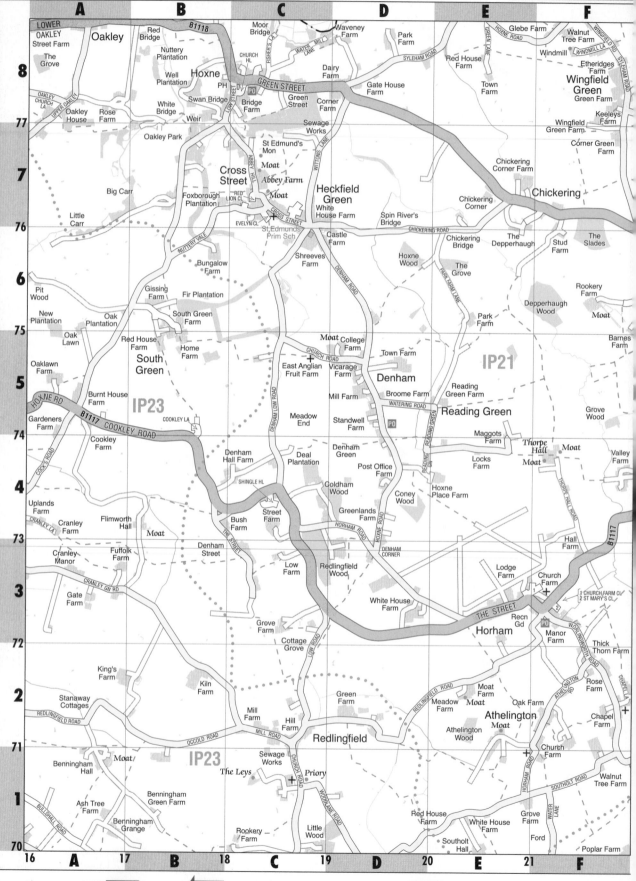

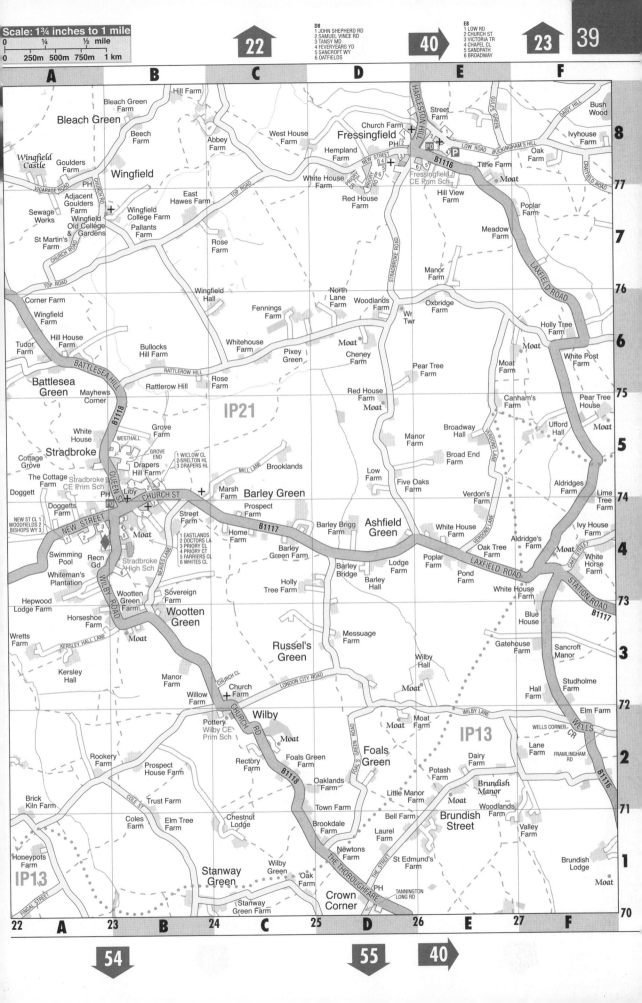

39
23

Scale: 1¾ inches to 1 mile
0 ¼ ½ mile
0 250m 500m 750m 1 km

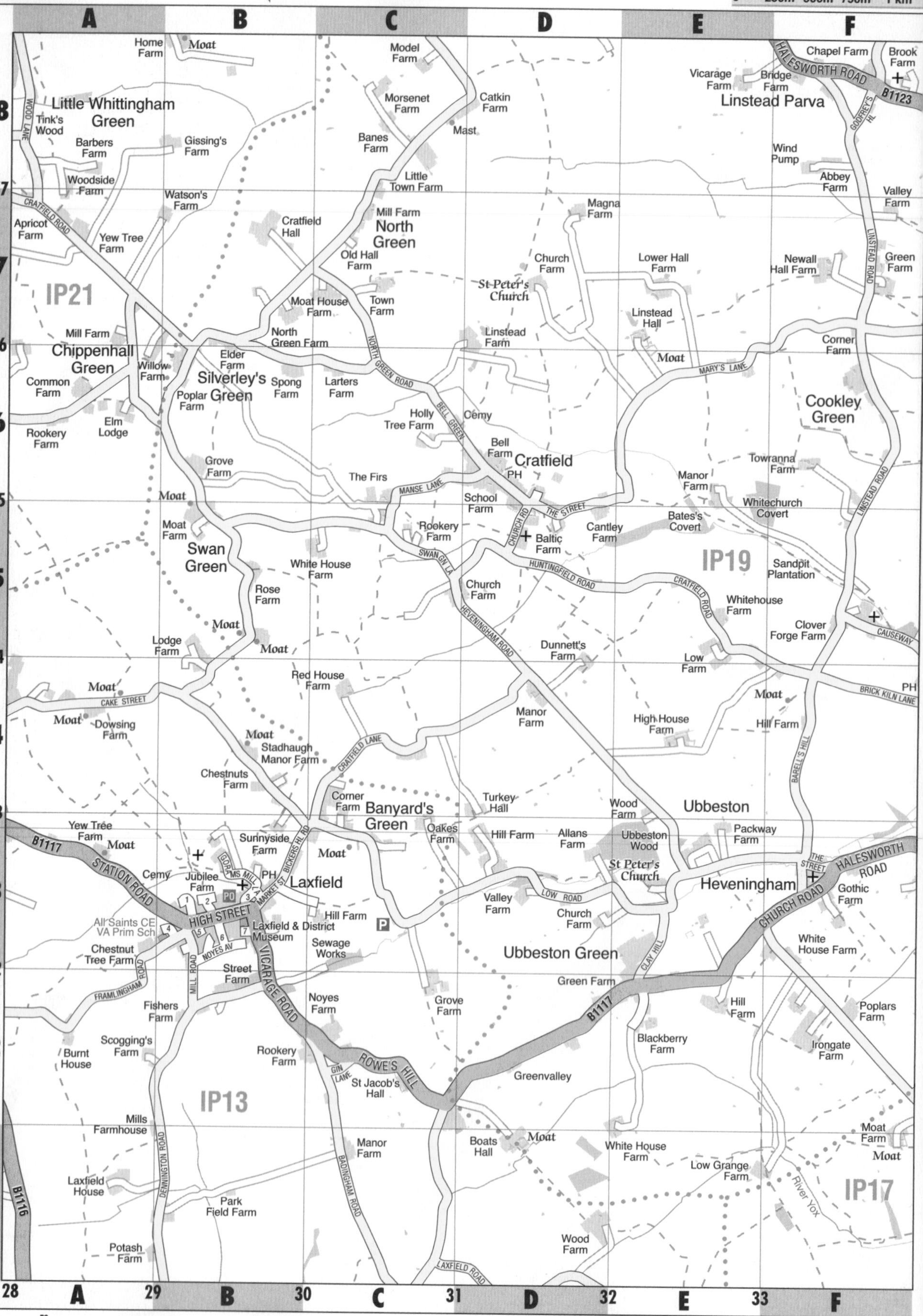
A B C D E F
8 77 7 76 6 75 5 74 4 73 3 72 2 71 1 70
28 29 30 31 32 33
Home Farm
Moat
Model Farm
Little Whittingham Green
Tink's Wood
WOOD LANE
Barbers Farm
Gissing's Farm
Morsenet Farm
Catkin Farm
Mast
Banes Farm
Woodside Farm
Watson's Farm
Little Town Farm
Mill Farm
North Green
CRATFIELD ROAD
Apricot Farm
Yew Tree Farm
Cratfield Hall
Old Hall Farm
IP21
Moat House Farm
Town Farm
Mill Farm
Chippenhall Green
Willow Farm
North Green Farm
Elder Farm
Silverley's Green
Spong Farm
Larters Farm
NORTH GREEN ROAD
Common Farm
Poplar Farm
Rookery Farm
Elm Lodge
Holly Tree Farm
BELL GREEN
Cemy
Bell Farm
Cratfield
PH
Grove Farm
The Firs
MANSE LANE
School Farm
Moat
Moat Farm
Swan Green
Rookery Farm
SWAN GN LA
CHURCH RD
THE STREET
Baltic Farm
White House Farm
Rose Farm
Church Farm
Moat
Moat
Lodge Farm
Red House Farm
HEVENINGHAM ROAD
HUNTINGFIELD ROAD
Dunnett's Farm
Moat
CAKE STREET
Moat
Dowsing Farm
Moat
Stadhaugh Manor Farm
Chestnuts Farm
CRATFIELD LANE
Manor Farm
Corner Farm
Banyard's Green
Turkey Hall
Yew Tree Farm
Moat
B1117
STATION ROAD
Sunnyside Farm
Moat
Oakes Farm
Hill Farm
Cemy
Jubilee Farm
GORAMS MILL LA
PH
MARKET ST
BICKERS HL RD
Laxfield
PO
HIGH STREET
Hill Farm
All Saints CE VA Prim Sch
Laxfield & District Museum
P
Valley Farm
LOW ROAD
Church Farm
NOYES AV
Chestnut Tree Farm
FRAMLINGHAM ROAD
MILL ROAD
Street Farm
VICARAGE ROAD
Sewage Works
Ubbeston Green
Fishers Farm
Noyes Farm
Grove Farm
Burnt House
Scogging's Farm
Rookery Farm
GIN LANE
ROWE'S HILL
St Jacob's Hall
Greenvalley
B1117
IP13
Mills Farmhouse
DENNINGTON ROAD
BADINGHAM ROAD
Manor Farm
Boats Hall
Moat
Laxfield House
B1116
Park Field Farm
Potash Farm
LAXFIELD ROAD
Wood Farm
Magna Farm
Church Farm
St Peter's Church
Linstead Farm
Lower Hall Farm
Linstead Hall
Moat
MARY'S LANE
Vicarage Farm
Bridge Farm
Chapel Farm
Brook Farm
HALESWORTH ROAD
B1123
GODFREY'S HL
Linstead Parva
Wind Pump
Abbey Farm
Valley Farm
LINSTEAD ROAD
Newall Hall Farm
Green Farm
Corner Farm
Cookley Green
Towranna Farm
Manor Farm
Whitechurch Covert
LINSTEAD ROAD
Bates's Covert
Cantley Farm
IP19
Sandpit Plantation
CRATFIELD ROAD
Whitehouse Farm
Clover Forge Farm
CAUSEWAY
Low Farm
PH
BRICK KILN LANE
Moat
High House Farm
Hill Farm
BARELL'S HILL
Wood Farm
Ubbeston
Allans Farm
Ubbeston Wood
Packway Farm
St Peter's Church
Heveningham
THE STREET
HALESWORTH ROAD
CHURCH ROAD
Gothic Farm
White House Farm
CLAY HILL
Green Farm
Hill Farm
Poplars Farm
Blackberry Farm
Irongate Farm
Moat Farm
Moat
White House Farm
Low Grange Farm
River Yox
IP17

55
39
56

B3
1 THE ORCHARDS
2 JUBILEE CL
3 CHURCH WK
4 HOME MD
5 MALT CL
6 THE LINX
7 ELM LODGE RD

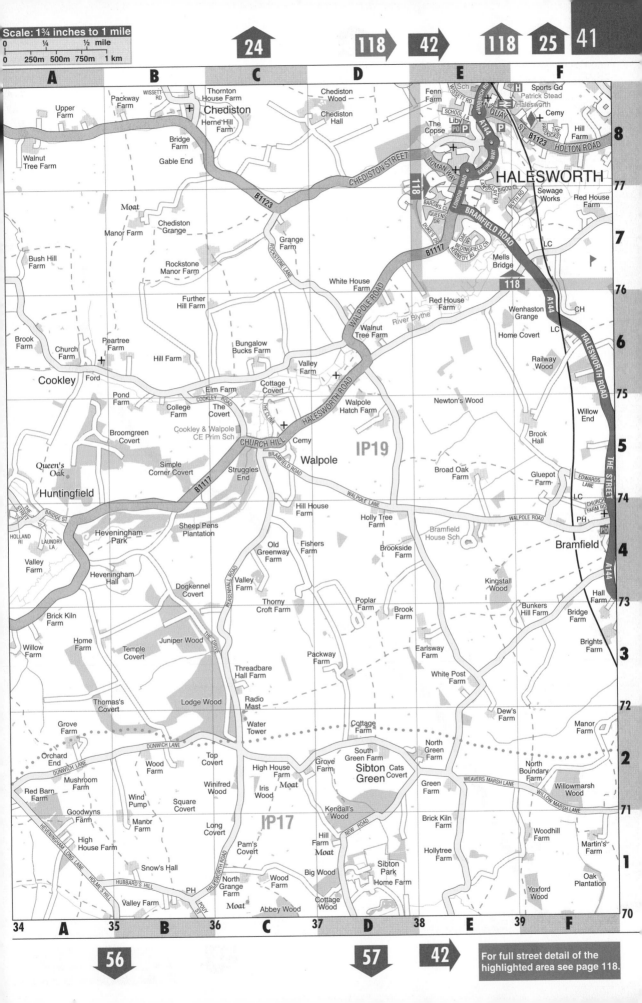

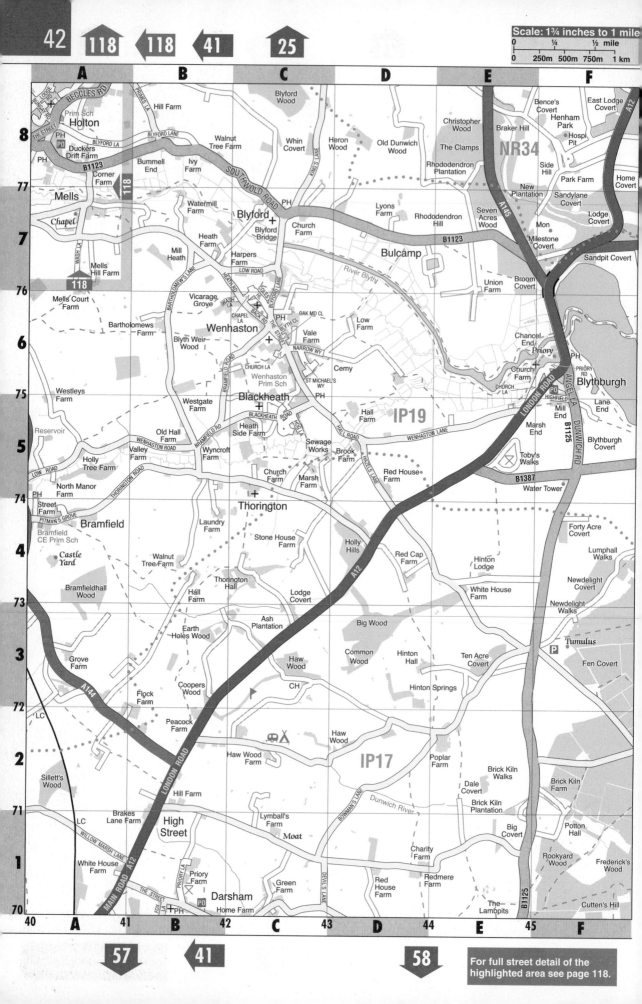

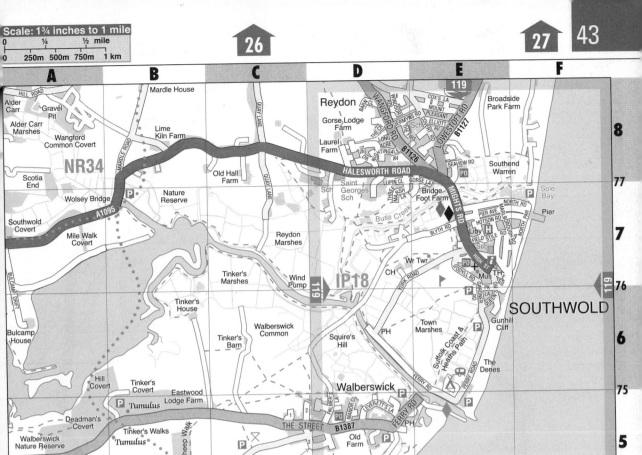

HILL ROAD

Alder Carr

Gravel Pit

Alder Carr Marshes

Wangford Common Covert

NR34

Scotia End

Wolsey Bridge

Mile Walk Covert

Southwold Covert

A1095

MARDLE ROAD

Mardle House

Lime Kiln Farm

Nature Reserve

Old Hall Farm

QUAY LANE

QUAY LANE

Reydon Marshes

Tinker's Marshes

Wind Pump

119

IP18

Tinker's House

Tinker's Barn

Walberswick Common

Squire's Hill

Bulcamp House

BULCAMP DRIFT

Hill Covert

Tinker's Covert

Eastwood Lodge Farm

Deadman's Covert

Tumulus

Tinker's Walks

Tumulus

Walberswick Nature Reserve

EAST SHEEP WALK

LODGE RD

IP19

Sallow Walk Covert

P

P

THE STREET

B1387

1 2

PALMER'S

PO

MANOR CL

LEVERETT'S LA

Old Farm

PH

FERRY RD

Walberswick

3

ADAM'S LA 1
CHURCH LA 2
SHORT LA 3

Hoist Covert

East Hill

Westwood Lodge

Old Covert

Westwood Marshes

Dunwich River

Corporation Marshes

Walberswick Nature Reserve

Dingle Great Hill

Dingle Farm

Fen Hill

Foxburrow Wood

Sandymount Covert

Reedland Marshes

Dingle Marshes

Scheiller's Grove

IP17

Dingle Stone House

Little Dingle

St Helena Farm

Dunwich Forest

Hog's Grove

SUFFOLK COAST & HEATHS PATH

DUNWICH RIVER

P

P

Bridge Farm

BEACH RD

Church Farm

ST JAMES'S ST

Mus

Chapel

Sandy Lane Farm

Dunwich

Broom Hill

The Spinney

MONASTERY HILL

HIGH ST

Mound

Franciscan Friary

Reydon

Gorse Lodge Farm

Laurel Farm

WANGFORD RD

WINDSOR RD

JERMYNS RD

COX'S LA
MOUNT PLEASANT

THE DR

LONG ACRE

THE DR

NIGHTINGALE AV

THREE MARSH LA

Saint Georges Sch

Sch

HALESWORTH ROAD

LUPIN CL

GORSE LA

Bridge Foot Farm

SEAVIEW RD

PO

Buss Creek

Wr Twr

CH

BLYTH RD

YORK ROAD

PH

Town Marshes

FERRY RD

PH

FERRY RD

B1126

119

B1127

Broadside Park Farm

Southend Warren

Sole Bay

P

Pier Ave

NORTH RD

HOTSON RD

Liby
H

FIELD STILE RD

Sch

HIGH ST

PO

MUS

GODYLL RD GARDNER

CH

QUEEN

PK

Gunhill Cliff

The Denes

Suffolk Coast & Heaths Path

119

SOUTHWOLD

Pier

NORTH PAR

MARLBOROUGH RD

TH

119

Suffolk Coast & Heaths Path

119

8

77

7

76

6

75

5

74

4

73

3

72

2

71

1

70

For full street detail of the highlighted area see page 119.

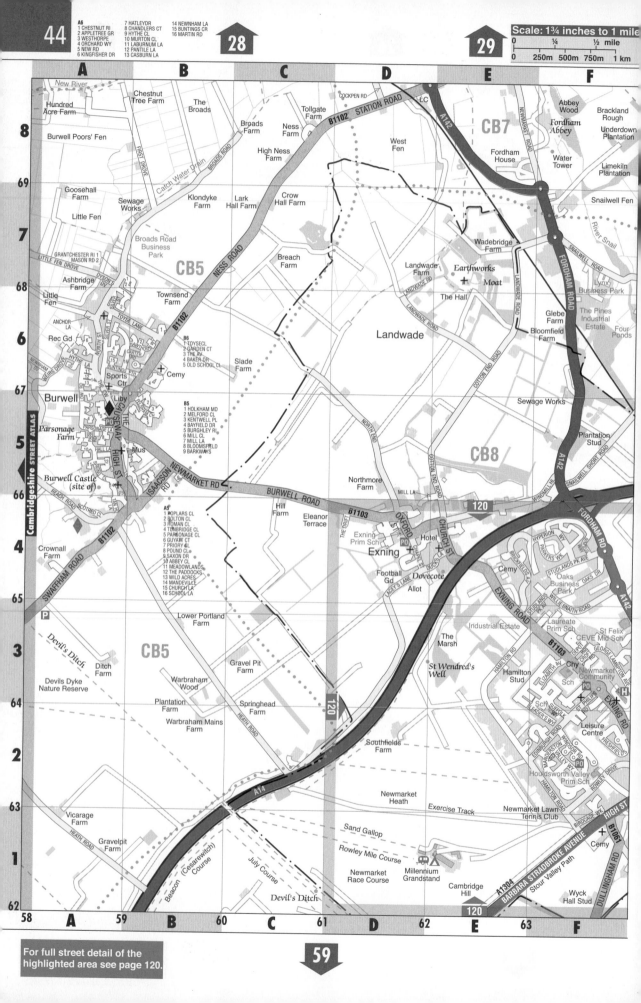

A6
1 CHESTNUT RI
2 APPLETREE GR
3 WESTHORPE
4 ORCHARD WY
5 NEW RD
6 KINGFISHER DR

7 HATLEYOR
8 CHANDLERS CT
9 HYTHE CL
10 MURTON CL
11 LABURNUM LA
12 PANTILE LA
13 CASBURN LA

14 NEWNHAM LA
15 BUNTINGS CR
16 MARTIN RD

Scale: 1¾ inches to 1 mile

0   ¼   ½   mile
0 250m 500m 750m 1 km

Cambridgeshire STREET ATLAS

New River
Hundred Acre Farm
Burwell Poors' Fen
Chestnut Tree Farm
The Broads
Broads Farm
Ness Farm
Tollgate Farm
COCKPEN RD
B1102 STATION ROAD
A142
CB7
Abbey Wood
Brackland Rough
Fordham Abbey
Underwood Plantation
High Ness Farm
Broads Farm
West Fen
Fordham House
Water Tower
Limekiln Plantation
Goosehall Farm
Little Fen
Klondyke Farm
Lark Hall Farm
Crow Hall Farm
Wadebridge Farm
Snailwell Fen
GRANTCHESTER RI 1
MASON RD 2
Ashbridge Farm
Little Fen
CB5
Broads Road Business Park
Breach Farm
Landwade Farm
Earthworks
Moat
Lynx Business Park
The Pines Industrial Estate
Four Ponds
ANCHOR LA
Rec Gd
Townsend Farm
NESS ROAD
B1102
Slade Farm
Landwade
The Hall
Glebe Farm
Bloomfield Farm
Sports Ctr
B6
1 TOYSECL
2 GARDEN CT
3 THE AV
4 BAKER DR
5 OLD SCHOOL CL
Cemy
Sewage Works
Plantation Stud
Burwell
Liby
B5
1 HOLKHAM MD
2 MELFORD CL
3 KENTWELL PL
4 BAYFIELD DR
5 BURGHLEY RI
6 MILL CL
7 MILL LA
8 BLOOMSFIELD
9 BARKWAYS
NORTH END
CB8
A142
Parsonage Farm
Mus
ISAACSON RD
NEWMARKET RD
Northmore Farm
Sewage Works
COTTON END ROAD
MILL LA
Plantation Stud
WINDMILL HL
Burwell Castle (site of)
BURWELL ROAD
120
SNAILWELL SHORT RD
REACH ROAD
SCOTRED CL
A5
1 POPLARS CL
2 BOLTON CL
3 ROMAN CL
4 TUNBRIDGE CL
5 PARSONAGE CL
6 GUYAM CT
7 PRIORY CL
8 POUND CL
9 SAXON DR
10 ABBEY CL
11 MEADOWLANDS
12 THE PADDOCKS
13 WILD ACRES
14 MANDEVILLE
15 CHURCH LA
16 SCHOOL LA
Hill Farm
B1103
Eleanor Terrace
THE THRIFT
Exning Prim Sch
OXFORD ST
CHURCH ST
Hotel
FORDHAM RD
Crownall Farm
SWAFFHAM ROAD
B1102
Exning
PO
Football Gd
Dovecote
Allot
CHAPEL ST
LACEY'S LANE
DUCKS LA
A142
HYPERION WY
PARKERS WK
STUDLANDS PK AVE
Cemy
Oaks Business Park
OAKS DR
WILLIE SNAITH ROAD
Lower Portland Farm
CB5
Gravel Pit Farm
Industrial Estate
The Marsh
EXNING ROAD
BRICKFIELDS A
BELL'S RD
STUDLANDS
LEADER'S WY
Laureate Prim Sch
CEVE Mid Sch
St Felix
Devil's Ditch
Ditch Farm
Warbraham Wood
St Wendred's Well
B1103
HAMILTON RD
Hamilton Stud
ELIZABETH AV
Chy
Newmarket Community
GEORGE LAMBTON AVE
Devils Dyke Nature Reserve
Plantation Farm
Springhead Farm
Sch
ST PHILIP
PO
Warbraham Mains Farm
HEATH ROAD
120
Southfields Farm
HAMILTON RD
EDINBURGH ROAD
MANDERSTON RD
WINDSOR RD
Leisure Centre
FRESKEY RD
Vicarage Farm
Gravelpit Farm
HEATH ROAD
A14
Newmarket Heath
Exercise Track
Houldsworth Valley Prim Sch
HAMILTON DRIVE
ROWLEY DRIVE
Newmarket Lawn Tennis Club
BIRDCAGE WK
HIGH ST
Beacon (Cesarewitch) Course
July Course
Sand Gallop
Rowley Mile Course
Newmarket Race Course
Millennium Grandstand
Cambridge Hill
B1061
Cemy
A1304 BARBARA STRADBROKE AVENUE
Stour Valley Path
Devil's Ditch
120
Wyck Hall Stud
DULLINGHAM RD

For full street detail of the highlighted area see page 120.

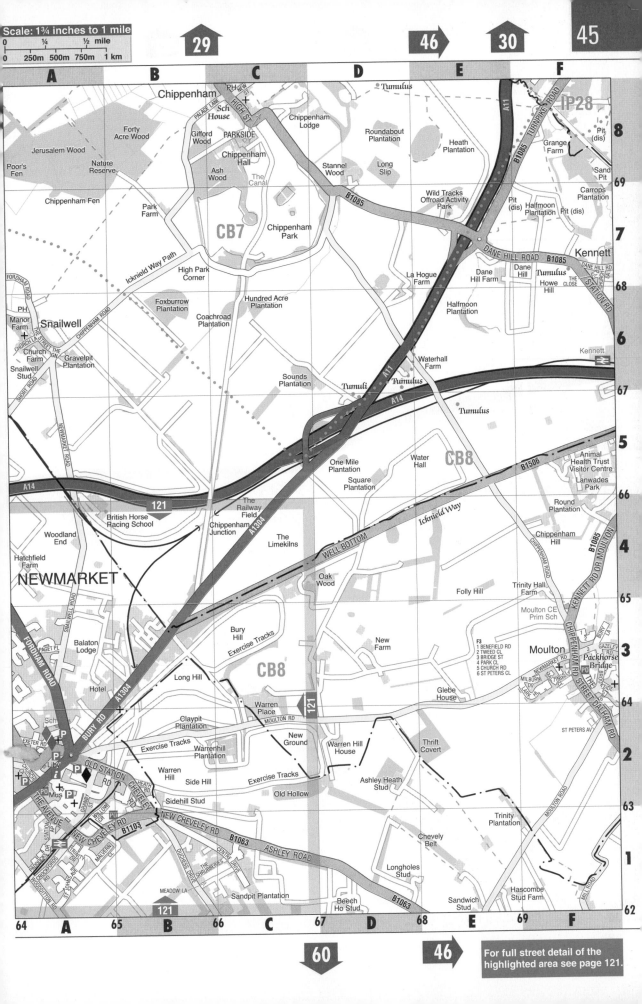

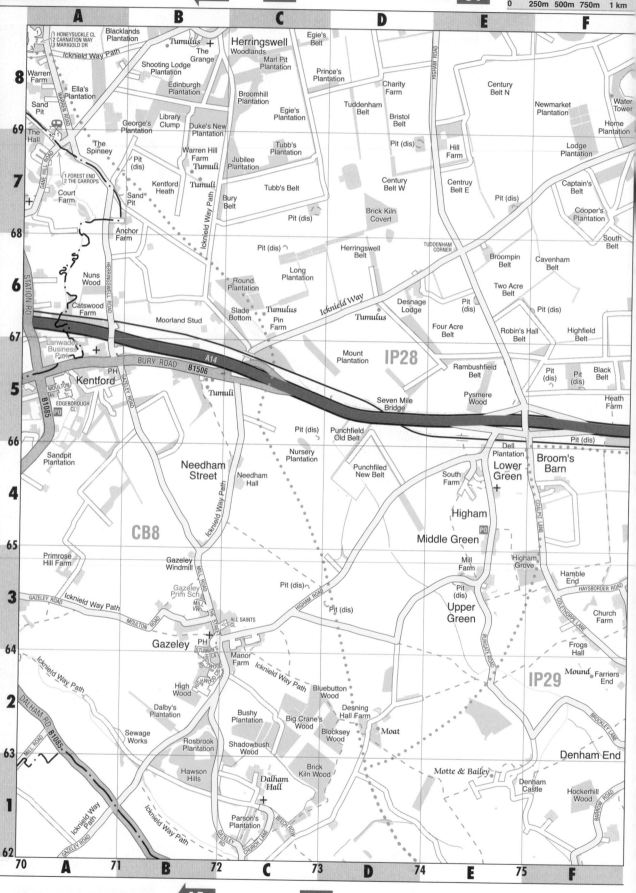

A B C D E F

8

1 HONEYSUCKLE CL
2 CARNATION WAY
3 MARIGOLD DR

Blacklands
Plantation

Tumulus
The Grange

Herringswell
Woodlands

Egie's
Belt

Warren
Farm

Ella's
Plantation

Shooting Lodge
Plantation

Marl Pit
Plantation

Prince's
Plantation

Charity
Farm

Century
Belt N

Newmarket
Plantation

Water
Tower

Sand
Pit

Edinburgh
Plantation

Broomhill
Plantation

Egie's
Plantation

Tuddenham
Belt

Bristol
Belt

Home
Plantation

69

The Hall

George's
Plantation

Library
Clump

Duke's New
Plantation

Tubb's
Plantation

Pit (dis)

Hill
Farm

Lodge
Plantation

7

The Spinney

1 FOREST END
2 THE CARROPS

The
Spinney

Warren Hill
Farm

Jubilee
Plantation

Tumuli

Tumuli

Tubb's Belt

Century
Belt W

Centruy
Belt E

Pit (dis)

Captain's
Belt

Court
Farm

Kentford
Heath

Pit
(dis)

Sand
Pit

Bury
Belt

Cooper's
Plantation

68

Anchor
Farm

Pit (dis)

Herringswell
Belt

TUDDENHAM
CORNER

Broompin
Belt

Cavenham
Belt

South
Belt

Nuns
Wood

Long
Plantation

Round
Plantation

Two Acre
Belt

6

Catswood
Farm

Slade
Bottom

Tumulus

Icknield Way

Desnage
Lodge

Pit
(dis)

Pit (dis)

Highfield
Belt

Moorland Stud

Pin
Farm

Tumulus

Four Acre
Belt

Robin's Hall
Belt

67

Lanwades
Business
Park

A14

BURY ROAD B1506

Mount
Plantation

IP28

Rambushfield
Belt

Pit
(dis)

Pit
(dis)

Black
Belt

5

MOULTON AV

Kentford

GAZELEY ROAD

Tumuli

Seven Mile
Bridge

Pysmere
Wood

Heath
Farm

B1085

EDGEBOROUGH
CL

PO

66

Sandpit
Plantation

Pit (dis)

Punchfield
Old Belt

Nursery
Plantation

Punchfiled
New Belt

Dell
Plantation

Lower
Green

Broom's
Barn

Pit (dis)

4

Needham
Street

Icknield Way Path

Needham
Hall

South
Farm

Higham

CB8

Mill
Farm

Higham
Grove

Hamble
End

65

Primrose
Hill Farm

Gazeley
Windmill

Middle Green

HAYSBORDER ROAD

3

GAZELEY ROAD

Icknield Way Path

MOULTON ROAD

Gazeley
Prim Sch

MILL ROAD

THE STREET

Pit (dis)

HIGHAM ROAD

Pit (dis)

Pit
(dis)

Upper
Green

COLTHORPE LANE

BURGATE ROAD

Church
Farm

MILL
VW

ALL SAINTS
CL

64

Gazeley

PH

STUBBIN'S

Manor
Farm

Icknield Way Path

IP29

Mound

Frogs
Hall

Farriers
End

HIGHWOOD
RD

2

DALHAM RD B1085

High
Wood

HIGHWOOD CR

Bluebutton
Wood

Desning
Hall Farm

BROCKLEY LANE

Dalby's
Plantation

Bushy
Plantation

Big Crane's
Wood

Moat

63

MILL RD B1085

Sewage
Works

Rosbrook
Plantation

Shadowbush
Wood

Blocksey
Wood

Denham End

Motte & Bailey

Denham
Castle

Hockerhill
Wood

Hawson
Hills

Brick
Kiln Wood

1

Icknield Way Path

Dalham
Hall

BARROW ROAD

Parson's
Plantation

BEECH ROW

62

Icknield Way Path

Icknield Way Path

GAZELEY RD

CHURCH LANE

70 A 71 B 72 C 73 D 74 E 75 F

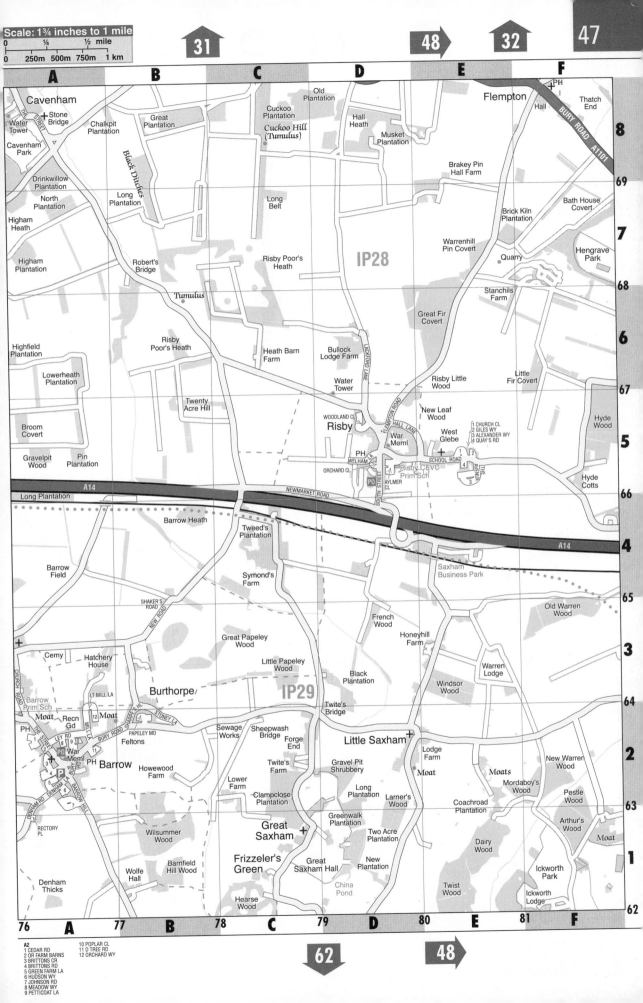

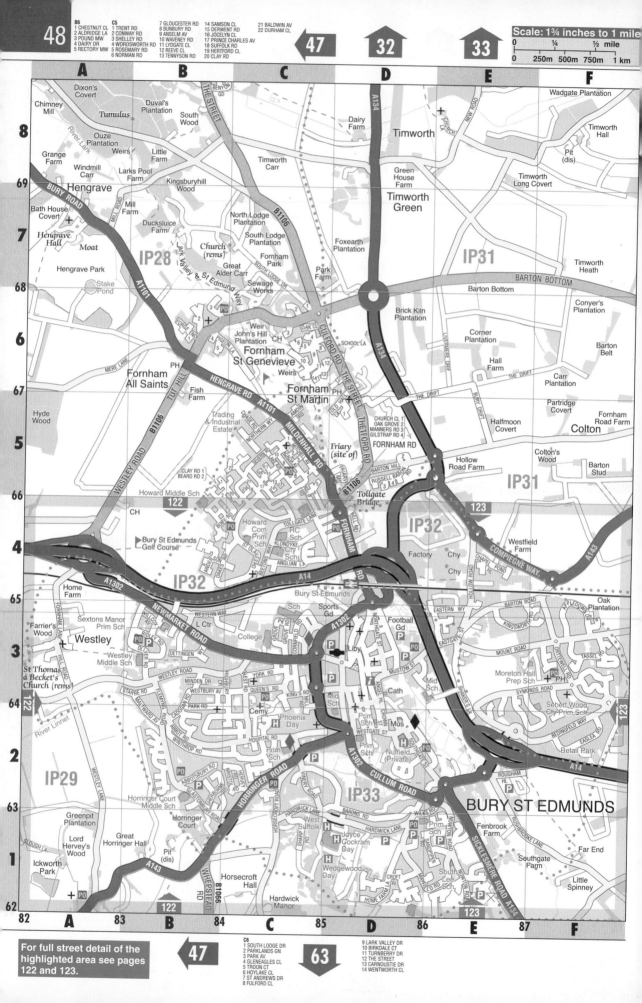

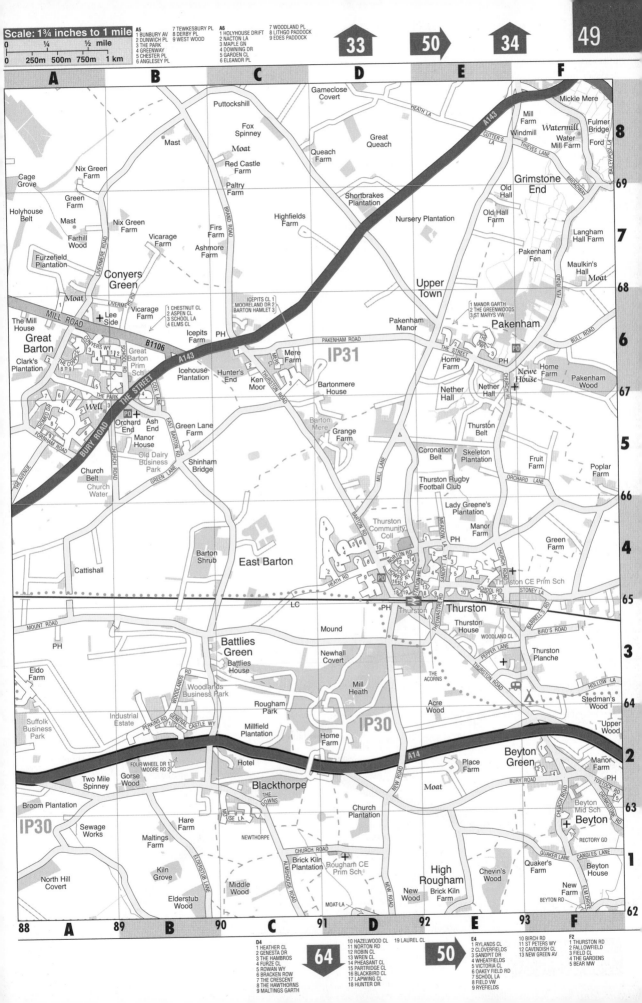

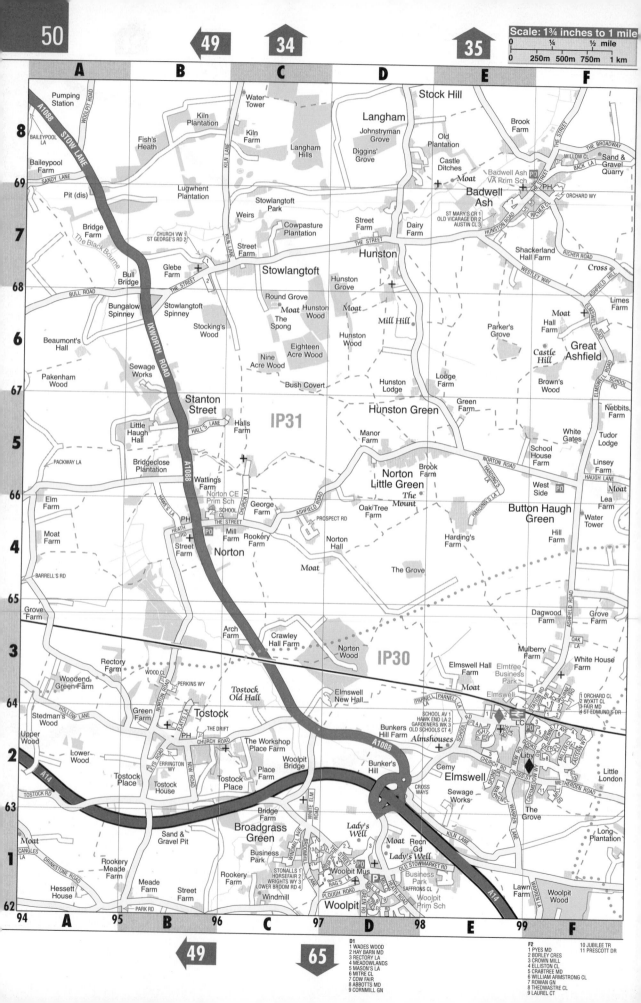

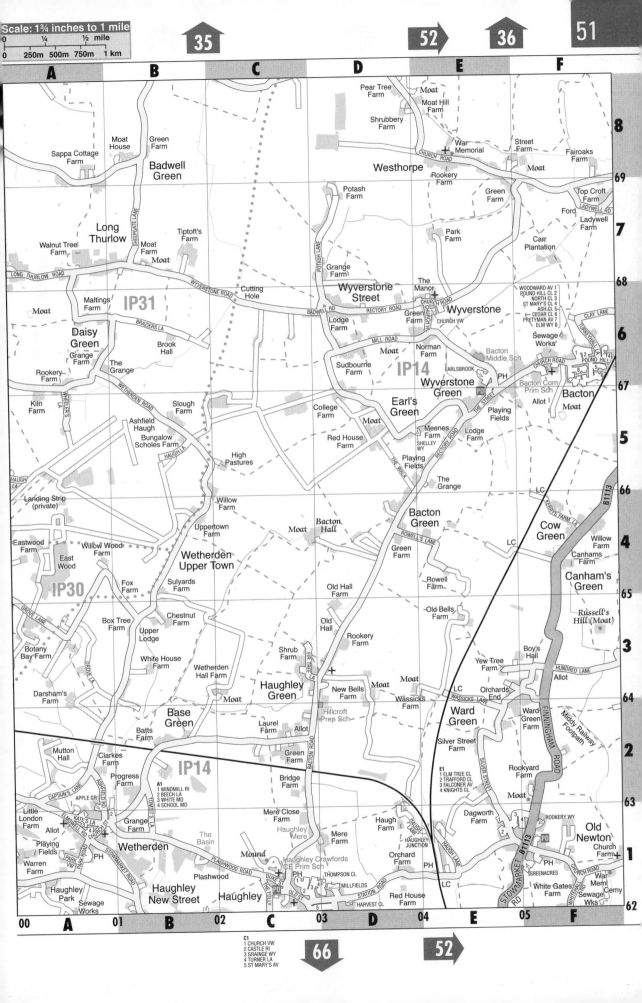

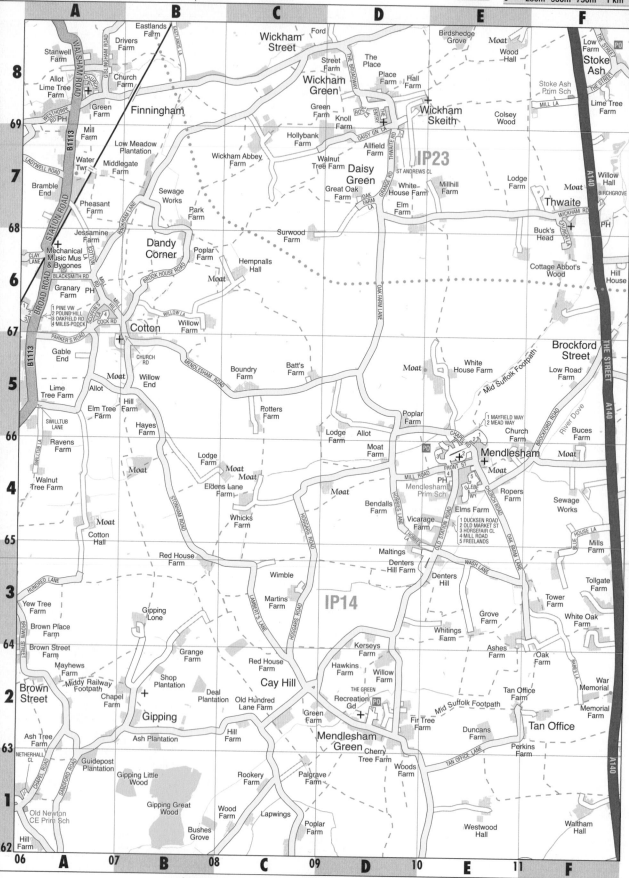

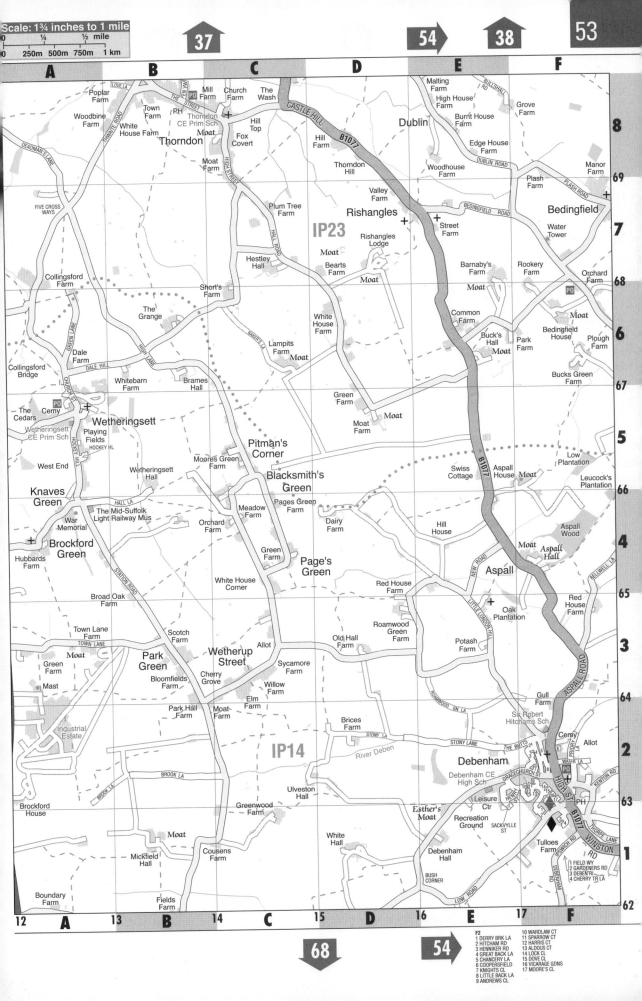

A · **B** · **C** · **D** · **E** · **F**

Poplar Farm
Woodbine Farm
LOVE LA
THE STREET
FEN VW
PO
Mill Farm
Church Farm
The Wash
CASTLE HILL
Malting Farm
High House Farm
Burnt House Farm
Grove Farm
8

Town Farm
White House Farm
RH
Thorndon CE Prim Sch
Moat
Hill Top
Fox Covert
Dublin
Woodhouse Farm
Edge House Farm
DUBLIN ROAD
Plash Farm
Manor Farm
69

Thorndon
THWAITE ROAD
DEADMAN'S LANE
Moat Farm
HIGH STREET
Hill Farm
B1077
Thorndon Hill
Valley Farm
Street Farm
BEDINGFIELD ROAD
PLASH ROAD
Bedingfield
7

Five Cross Ways
HALL ROAD
Plum Tree Farm
IP23
Rishangles
Rishangles Lodge
Barnaby's Farm
Rookery Farm
Water Tower
Orchard Farm
PO
Water Tower

Collingsford Farm
GREEN LANE
HIGH LANE
Short's Farm
Hestley Hall
Moat
Bearts Farm
Moat
Moat
Common Farm
Moat
Bedingfield House
Moat
Plough Farm
68

The Grange
Dale Farm
DALE HILL
Whitebarn Farm
BAKERS LA
Lampits Farm
Moat
White House Farm
Buck's Hall
Moat
Park Farm
Bucks Green Farm
6

Collingsford Bridge
CHURCH ST
PO
Cemy
Wetheringsett
HOCKEY HILL
Brames Hall
Green Farm
Moat Farm
Moat
67

The Cedars
Wetheringsett CE Prim Sch
Playing Fields
HOCKEY HL
Moores Green Farm
Pitman's Corner
Swiss Cottage
Aspall House
Moat
Low Plantation
Leucock's Plantation
5

West End
Wetheringsett Hall
Blacksmith's Green
Pages Green Farm
Hill House
Aspall Wood
66

Knaves Green
HALL LA
The Mid-Suffolk Light Railway Mus
Meadow Farm
Orchard Farm
Green Farm
White House Corner
Page's Green
Dairy Farm
Moat
Aspall Hall
4

War Memorial
Brockford Green
STATION ROAD
Red House Farm
Aspall
Red House Farm
Oak Plantation
NEW ROAD
BELLWELL LA
65

Hubbards Farm
Broad Oak Farm
Roamwood Green Farm
LITTLE LONDON HILL
Potash Farm
Gull Corner
ASPALL ROAD
3

Town Lane Farm
TOWN LANE
Scotch Farm
Wetherup Street
Allot
Old Hall Farm
ROAMWOOD GN LA
Sir Robert Hitchams Sch
Cemy
Allot
2

Moat
Green Farm
Park Green
Bloomfields Farm
Cherry Grove
Sycamore Farm
Willow Farm
Brices Farm
STONY LA
Debenham
Debenham CE High Sch
GRACECHURCH ST
HIGH ST
PO
PRIORY
KENTON LA
PH

Mast
Park Hall Farm
Moat Farm
Elm Farm
River Deben
STONY LANE
THE BUTTS
Leisure Ctr
HENLEY
B1077
WINSTON RD
THORPE LANE

Industrial Estate
IP14
BROOK LA
Ulveston Hall
Greenwood Farm
Esther's Moat
Recreation Ground
SACKVYLLE ST
Tulloes Farm
IPSWICH RD
DEBENHAM RD
1

Brockford House
BROOK LA
Moat
White Hall
Debenham Hall
BUSH CORNER
LOW ROAD
F1
1 FIELD WY
2 GARDENERS RD
3 DEBEN RI
4 CHERRY TR LA
62

Boundary Farm
Mickfield Hall
Fields Farm
Cousens Farm

F2
1 DERRY BRK LA
2 HITCHAM RD
3 HENNIKER RD
4 GREAT BACK LA
5 CHANCERY LA
6 COOPERSFIELD
7 KNIGHTS CL
8 LITTLE BACK LA
9 ANDREWS CL
10 WARDLAW CT
11 SPARROW CT
12 HARRIS CT
13 ALDOUS CT
14 LOCK CL
15 DOVE CL
16 VICARAGE GDNS
17 MOORE'S CL

Scale: 1¾ inches to 1 mile

0   ¼   ½ mile
0   250m   500m   750m   1 km

A | **B** | **C** | **D** | **E** | **F**

The Rookery

Oaklands Farm

IP21

Poplar Farm

Potash Farm

Lodge Farm

8

Carters Farm

Yew Tree Farm

Redhouse Farm

Valley Farm

WATER LANE

FRIGAL STREET

69

Bedingfield

Park Farm

PARK ROAD

WOODLANE ROAD

Town Farm

White Hall Farm

Oak Tree Farm

Pond Farm

Home Farm

Newtown

Worlingworth

THE STREET

Moat

Willow Farm

Southolt

Sycamore Farm

Mill Farm

SHOP STREET

Paradise Farm

Red House

1 PIPERS MD
2 OLD STORES CL
3 WILLOW GN
4 LABURNUM CL
5 CHURCH RD

Sewage Works

CHURCH STREET

Oak Farm

NEW ROAD

7

IP23

Patrick Lane Farm

MILL ROAD

MAISIE'S MD

Worlingworth CE Prim Sch

Beecrofts Farm

CHURCH ROAD

68

Moat

Fleming's Hall

HALL ROAD

Moat

Bedingfield Hall

Charity Farm

Bond's Farm

CHARITY LA

Grove Farm

Willow Farm

Grange Farm

Chandos Farm

SWAN ROAD

6

Spring Farm

Fleming's Hall Farm

Bedingfield Plantation

Sewage Works

Poplar Farm

Moss Farm

Boxbush Farm

Lodge Farm

SOUTHOLT ROAD

Wood Farm

Low Farm

67

Low Farm

Broadway Farm

Bull's Hall

Trust Farm

Oak Farm

Kenton Plantation

Green Farm

Bulls Hall Farm

IP13

Ivy House Farm

5

Green Farm

Potash Farm

The Firs

Moat

Bedfield

Bedfield Hall

Moat

CHURCH ROAD

Low Farm

Sycamore Farm

Messuage Farm

Monk Soham Green

Cottage Glebe

Boltons Farm

White House Farm

Mill Farm

Crown Farm

CHURCH LA

66

Moat

Moat

White House Farm

Kenton

PO

Oakwood Farm

Grants Farm

Bedfield CE Prim Sch

Leucock's Plantation

BELLWELL LANE

CHURCH LANE

Suddon Hall

Moat

Hill Farm

Abbey House

Glebe Farm

Hungers Green

Primrose Farm

The Grove

Tavern Farm

4

Bellwell Plantation

Kenton Corner

Mole End

School Road

Home Farm

White House Farm

Bedfield Little Green

Green Farm

Red-House Farm

65

Moat

Kenton Hall

Cottage Glebe

Kenton Lodge

Earl Farm

Church Farm

Grove Farm

Red House

HOLLOW LA

3

Blood Hall

Oak Tree Farm

LOW ROAD

Soham Town Corner

BEDFIELD ROAD

Pages Farm

Woodcroft Hall

Driver's Farm

White House Farm

64

WADDLEGOOSE LANE

Hill Farm

WADDLEGOOSE LA

WADDLEGOOSE LA

Windwhistle Farm

Moat

Cemy

2

IP14

Grove Farm

Page's Wood

Ashfield Lodge

Clowes's Corner

LOW ROAD

Earl Soham

THE CAUSEWAY

GLEBE MS

Camp Green Farm

KENTON RD

GROVE LANE

Crowborough Farm

Timber Top Farm

Peartree Farm

Earl Soham Prim Sch

Earl Soham Lodge

PO

63

Great Wood

Heater Plantation

Ashfield

THE STREET

Rookery Farm

Church Farm

Crows Hall

Moat

THE ASHES

Hill Farm

MILL HILL

Street Farm

BRANDESTON ROAD

1

Fen Street

Nuttery Belt

Ashfield Cum Thorpe

Warners End

Stone House Farm

Sewage Works

VICARAGE ROAD

B1077

Winston Grange

THORPE LANE

Thorpe Hall

High Row Farm

THE STREET

Cretingham Lodge

Boundry Farm

King's Hill

62

WHITEPOST CORNER

A1120

SWAN LANE

18 | **A** | **19** | **B** | **20** | **C** | **21** | **D** | **22** | **E** | **23** | **F**

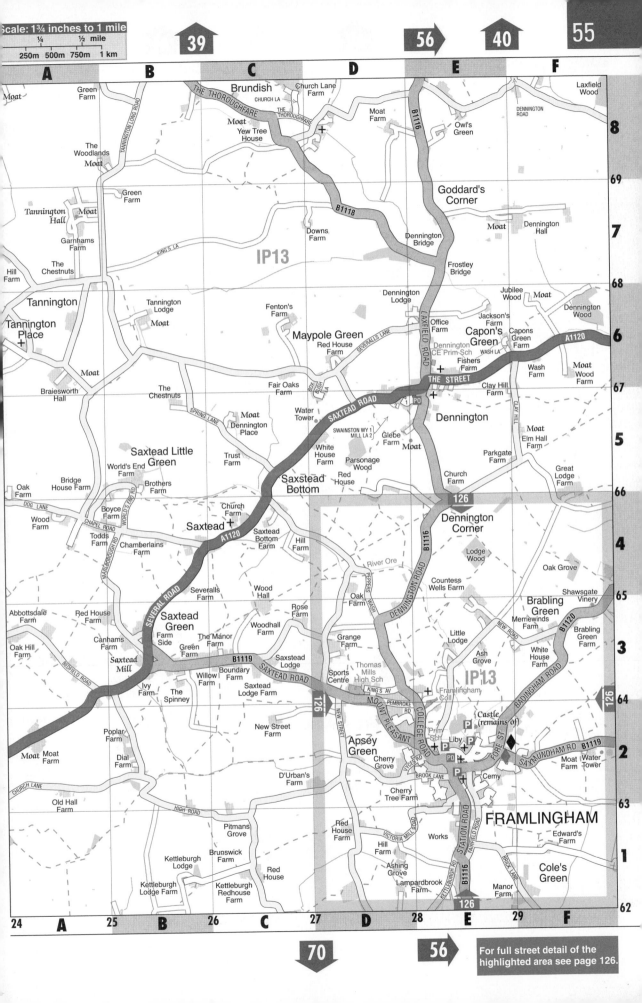

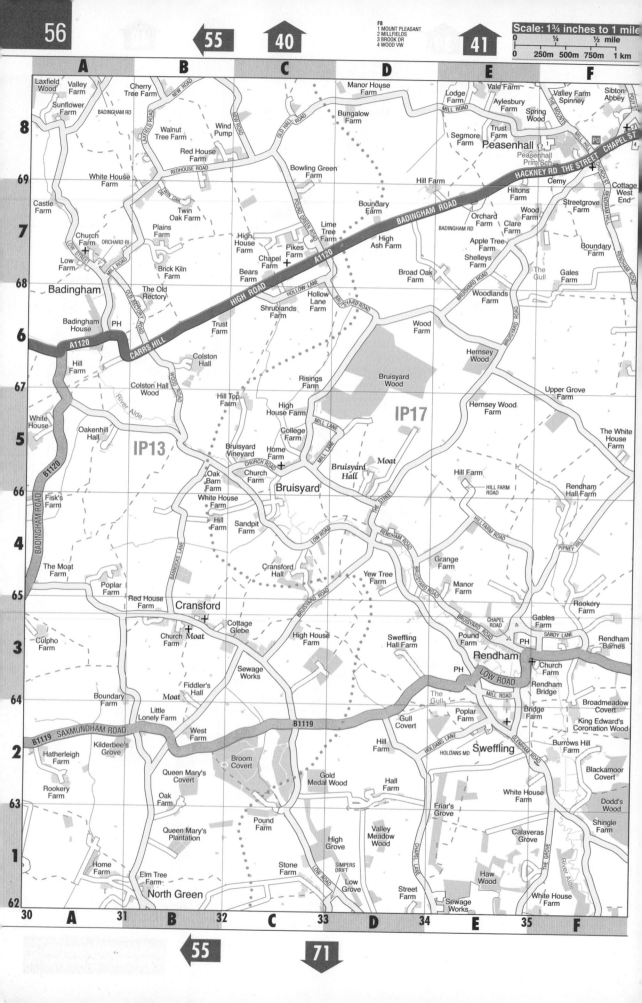

42 A 43 B 44 C 45 D 46 E 47 F 48

57 129 73

For full street detail of the highlighted area see page 129.

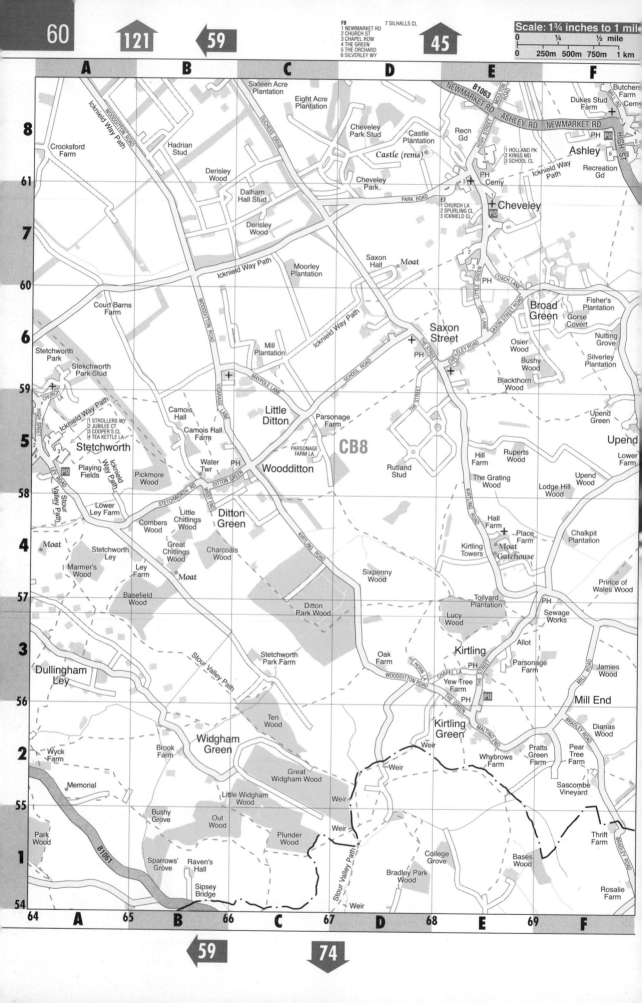

F8
1 NEWMARKET RD
2 CHURCH ST
3 CHAPEL ROW
4 THE GREEN
5 THE ORCHARD
6 SILVERLEY WY
7 SILHALLS CL

Scale: 1¾ inches to 1 mile

| 0 | ¼ | ½ | mile |
| 0 | 250m | 500m | 750m | 1 km |

Butchers
Cemy
Dukes Stud
Farm
Crocksford
Farm
NEWMARKET RD
B1063
MILL RD
ASHLEY RD
NEWMARKET RD
HIGH ST
Hadrian
Stud
Sixteen Acre
Plantation
Eight Acre
Plantation
Cheveley
Park Stud
Castle
Plantation
Recn
Gd
PH
PO
Ashley
Derisley
Wood
Castle (rems)
1 HOLLAND PK
2 KINGS MD
3 SCHOOL CL
Recreation
Gd
Dalham
Hall Stud
Cheveley
Park
PH
Cemy
Icknield Way
Path
Derisley
Wood
PARK ROAD
Park Road
E7
1 CHURCH LA
2 SPURLING CL
3 ICKNIELD CL
PO
Cheveley
Icknield Way Path
Moorley
Plantation
Saxon
Hall
Moat
PH
COACH LANE
Broad
Green
Fisher's
Plantation
Court Barns
Farm
Icknield Way Path
Saxon
Street
Gorse
Covert
Nutting
Grove
Stetchworth
Park
Mill
Plantation
PH
Osier
Wood
Silverley
Plantation
Stekchworth
Park Stud
MAYPOLE LANE
SCHOOL ROAD
Bushy
Wood
Blackthorn
Wood
CHURCH LA
VICARAGE LANE
Camois
Hall
Little
Ditton
Parsonage
Farm
Upend
Green
HIGH STREET
1 STROLLERS WY
2 JUBILEE CT
3 COOPER'S CL
4 TEA KETTLE LA
Icknield Way Path
Camois Hall
Farm
THE STREET
Hill
Farm
Ruperts
Wood
Upend
Lower
Farm
Stetchworth
Playing
Fields
Icknield
Way
Path
Water
Twr
PH
PARSONAGE
FARM LA
Wooddition
Rutland
Stud
The Grating
Wood
Upend
Wood
Lodge Hill
Wood
PO
Pickmore
Wood
STETCHWORTH RD
DITTON GREEN
WEST END
Ditton
Green
Hall
Farm
Place
Farm
Chalkpit
Plantation
Moat
LEY ROAD
Lower
Ley Farm
Combers
Wood
Little
Chitlings
Wood
Kirtling
Towers
Moat
Gatehouse
Stour Valley Path
Marmer's
Wood
Stetchworth
Ley
Great
Chitlings
Wood
Charcoals
Wood
KIRTLING ROAD
Sixpenny
Wood
Toilyard
Plantation
PH
Prince of
Wales Wood
Ley
Farm
Moat
Lucy
Wood
Sewage
Works
Basefield
Wood
Ditton
Park Wood
Kirtling
Allot
Stour Valley Path
Dullingham
Ley
Stetchworth
Park Farm
Oak
Farm
THORN LA
CHAPEL LA
PH
Parsonage
Farm
Jamies
Wood
WOODDITTON ROAD
Yew Tree
Farm
THE GREEN
PO
Mill End
Wyck
Farm
Ten
Wood
Kirtling
Green
MALTING END
Whybrows
Farm
Pratts
Green
Farm
Pear
Tree
Farm
Dianas
Wood
MILL ROAD
BRADLEY ROAD
Memorial
Widgham
Green
Brook
Farm
Weir
Sascombe
Vineyard
Great
Widgham Wood
Weir
Bushy
Grove
Out
Wood
Little Widgham
Wood
Weir
College
Grove
Bases
Wood
Thrift
Farm
Park
Wood
B1061
Sparrows'
Grove
Raven's
Hall
Plunder
Wood
Stour Valley Path
Weir
Bradley Park
Wood
Rosalie
Farm
Sipsey
Bridge
Weir

CB8

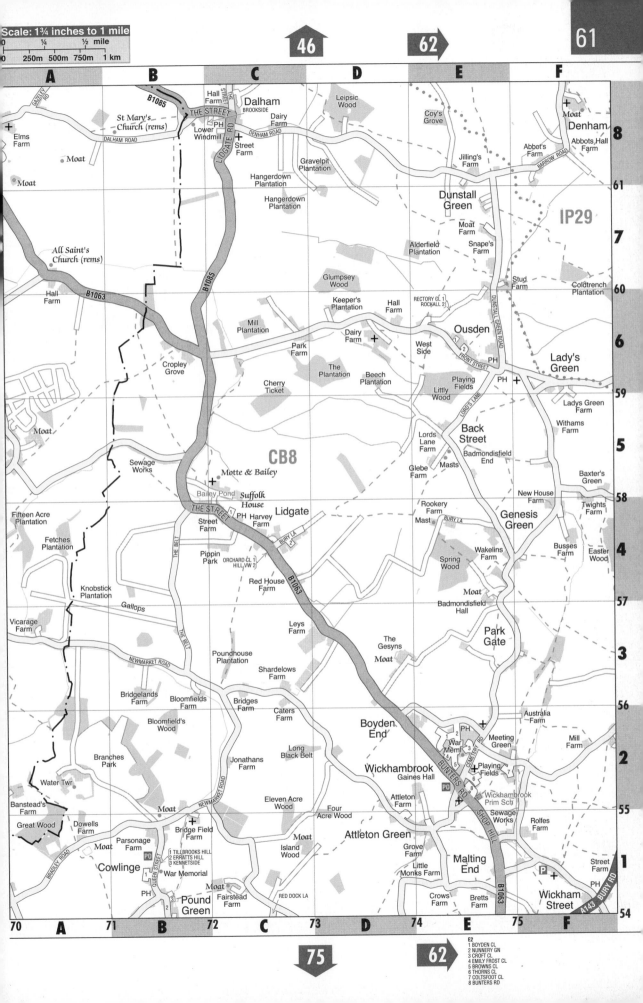

0   ¼   ½ mile
0   250m   500m   750m   1 km

A   B   C   D   E   F

GAZELEY RD

+ Elms Farm

Moat

B1085

St Mary's Church (rems)

THE STREET

Hall Farm

Dalham
BROOKSIDE

Leipsic Wood

Coy's Grove

+ Moat

Denham

DALHAM ROAD

Moat

Lower Windmill

PH

LIDGATE RD

Street Farm

+ DENHAM ROAD

Dairy Farm

Abbot's Farm

Abbots Hall Farm

BARROW ROAD

8

Hangerdown Plantation

Gravelpit Plantation

Jilling's Farm

61

All Saint's Church (rems)

B1063

Hall Farm

B1085

Hangerdown Plantation

Dunstall Green

IP29

7

Mill Plantation

Alderfield Plantation

Snape's Farm

Moat Farm

Stud Farm

Coldtrench Plantation

60

Cropley Grove

Park Farm

Glumpsey Wood

Keeper's Plantation

Hall Farm

Dairy Farm

+

RECTORY CL 1
ROCKALL 2

Ousden

West Side

PH

DUNSTALL GREEN ROAD

FRONT STREET

Lady's Green

6

Moat

Sewage Works

Cherry Ticket

The Plantation

Beech Plantation

Littly Wood

Playing Fields

PH +

Ladys Green Farm

Withams Farm

59

CB8

Fifteen Acre Plantation

Fetches Plantation

+ Motte & Bailey

Bailey Pond

Suffolk House

PH Harvey Farm

Lidgate

Street Farm

LORD'S LANE

Lords Lane Farm

Back Street

Badmondisfield End

Masts

Glebe Farm

Baxter's Green

New House Farm

Genesis Green

5

58

Knobstick Plantation

THE BELT

Pippin Park

ORCHARD CL 1
HILL VW 2

Red House Farm

BURY LA

Rookery Farm

Mast

BURY LA

Wakelins Farm

Spring Wood

Busses Farm

Twights Farm

Easter Wood

4

Gallops

Vicarage Farm

Leys Farm

The Gesyns

Moat

Badmondisfield Hall

Moat

Park Gate

57

NEWMARKET ROAD

Poundhouse Plantation

Shardelows Farm

3

Bridgelands Farm

Bloomfields Farm

Bridges Farm

Caters Farm

Boyden End

Australia Farm

56

Bloomfield's Wood

Branches Park

Jonathans Farm

Long Black Belt

Wickhambrook
Gaines Hall

PH
War Meml

Meeting Green

Playing Fields

Mill Farm

2

Water Twr

Banstead's Farm

Great Wood

Dowells Farm

Moat

NEWMARKET ROAD

Eleven Acre Wood

Four Acre Wood

Attleton Farm

BUNTERS RD

PO

Wickhambrook Prim Sch

Sewage Works

Rolfes Farm

55

Parsonage Farm

PO

Bridge Field Farm

QUEEN STREET

1 TILLBROOKS HILL
2 ERRATTS HILL
3 KENNETSIDE

Moat

Island Wood

Moat

Attleton Green

Grove Farm

Little Monks Farm

Malting End

SHOP HILL

Street Farm

P +

Wickham Street

PH

BURY RD

1

Cowlinge

PH

War Memorial

Pound Green

Fairstead Farm

RED DOCK LA

Crows Farm

Bretts Farm

B1063

A4143

54

70   A   71   B   72   C   73   D   74   E   75   F

E2
1 BOYDEN CL
2 NUNNERY GN
3 CROFT CL
4 EMILY FROST CL
5 BROWNS CL
6 THORNS CL
7 COLTSFOOT CL
8 BUNTERS RD

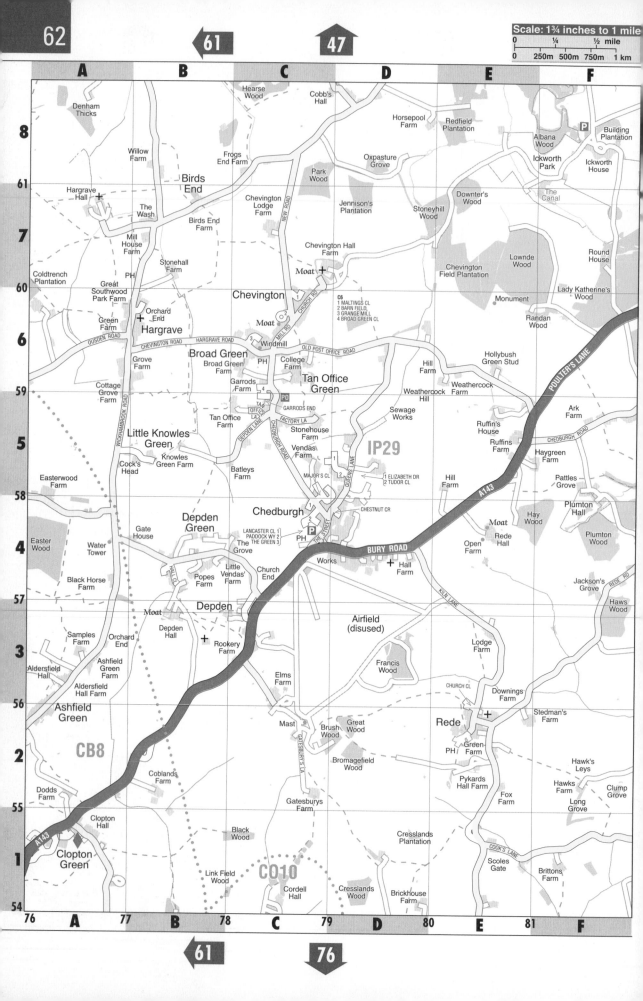

Scale: 1¾ inches to 1 mile

0   ¼   ½ mile
0 250m 500m 750m 1 km

8
61
7
60
6
59
5
58
4
57
3
56
2
55
1
54

A   B   C   D   E   F

Denham
Thicks

Willow
Farm

Hearse
Wood

Cobb's
Hall

Horsepool
Farm

Redfield
Plantation

P
Albana
Wood

Building
Plantation

Ickworth
Park

Ickworth
House

Hargrave
Hall

Birds
End

The Wash

Frogs
End Farm

Chevington
Lodge
Farm

New Road

Park
Wood

Oxpasture
Grove

Downter's
Wood

The
Canal

Birds End
Farm

Jennison's
Plantation

Stoneyhill
Wood

Mill
House
Farm

Chevington Hall
Farm

Chevington
Field Plantation

Lownde
Wood

Round
House

Coldtrench
Plantation

PH

Stonehall
Farm

Moat

Church Rd

Lady Katherine's
Wood

Great
Southwood
Park Farm

Chevington

Moat

Monument

Randan
Wood

Green
Farm

Orchard
End

Hargrave

Windmill

Mill La

C6
1 MALTINGS CL
2 BARN FIELD
3 GRANGE MILL
4 BROAD GREEN CL

Ousden Road

Chevington Road

Hargrave Road

Broad Green

Old Post Office Road

Hollybush
Green Stud

Poulter's Lane

Grove
Farm

Broad Green
Farm

PH

College
Farm

Tan Office
Green

Hill
Farm

Weathercock
Farm

Weathercock

Cottage
Grove
Farm

Garrods
Farm

PO

Weathercock
Hill

Ark
Farm

Little Knowles
Green

Tan Office
Farm

Depden Lane

TAN
OFFICE
LA

Garrods End

Factory La

Sewage
Works

Ruffin's
House

Chedburgh Road

Wickhambrook Road

Stonehouse
Farm

IP29

Ruffins
Farm

Haygreen
Farm

Easterwood
Farm

Cock's
Head

Knowles
Green Farm

Batleys
Farm

Vendas
Farm

Queens Lane

1

1 ELIZABETH DR
2 TUDOR CL

Hill
Farm

A143

Pattles
Grove

Plumton
Hall

MAJOR'S CL

Chestnut Cr

Moat

Hay
Wood

Plumton
Wood

Easter
Wood

Water
Tower

Gate
House

Depden
Green

Chedburgh

The
Street

P

Open
Farm

Rede
Hall

Black Horse
Farm

Hall Cl

LANCASTER CL 1
PADDOCK WY 2
THE GREEN 3

PH

The
Grove

Popes
Farm

Little
Vendas'
Farm

Church
End

Works

Bury Road

Hall
Farm

Kiln Lane

Jackson's
Grove

Rede Rd

Haws
Wood

Samples
Farm

Orchard
End

Moat

Depden

Airfield
(disused)

Lodge
Farm

Aldersfield
Hall

Ashfield
Green
Farm

Depden
Hall

Rookery
Farm

Francis
Wood

Church Cl

Downings
Farm

Stedman's
Farm

Aldersfield
Hall Farm

Elms
Farm

Rede

Ashfield
Green

CB8

Mast

Brush
Wood

Great
Wood

PH

Green
Farm

Hawk's
Leys

Dodds
Farm

Coblands
Farm

Gatesbury's La

Bromagefield
Wood

Pykards
Hall Farm

Hawks
Farm

Clump
Grove

Clopton
Hall

Gatesburys
Farm

Fox
Farm

Long
Grove

A143

Clopton
Green

Black
Wood

Cresslands
Plantation

Cook's Lane

Scoles
Gate

Brittons
Farm

CO10

Link Field
Wood

Cordell
Hall

Cresslands
Wood

Brickhouse
Farm

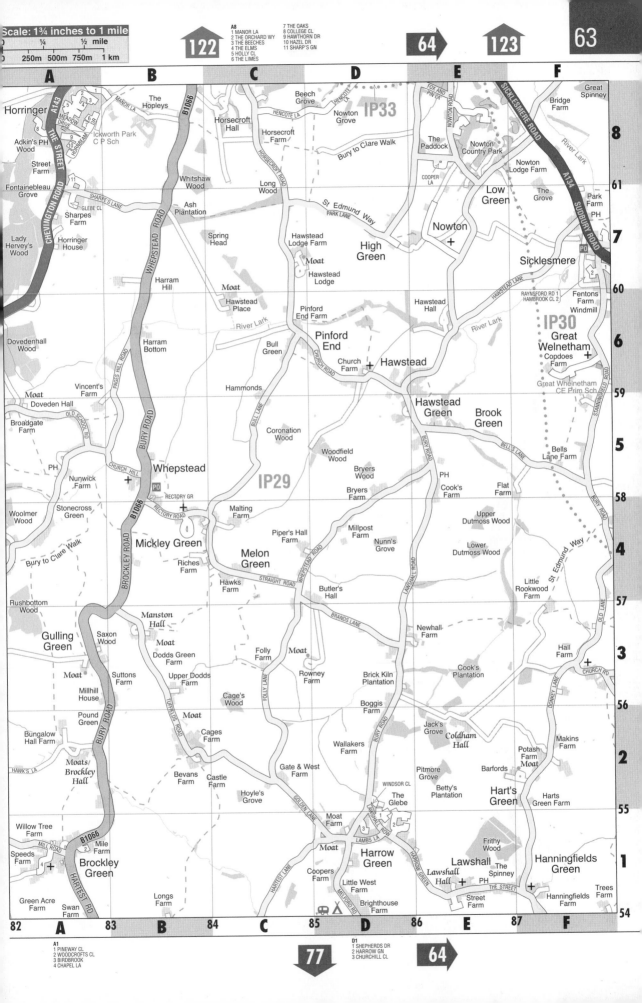

Scale: 1¾ inches to 1 mile

¼ ½ mile
250m 500m 750m 1 km

A8
1 MANOR LA
2 THE ORCHARD WY
3 THE BEECHES
4 THE ELMS
5 HOLLY CL
6 THE LIMES
7 THE OAKS
8 COLLEGE CL
9 HAWTHORN DR
10 HAZEL DR
11 SHARP'S GN

122   64   123   63

A   B   C   D   E   F

Horringer
A143
THE STREET
CHEVINGTON ROAD
Adkin's PH Wood
Street Farm
Fontainebleau Grove
Sharpes Farm
Lady Hervey's Wood
Horringer House

The Hopleys
MANOR LA
MEADOW DRIVE
HARBUROUGH
Ickworth Park C P Sch
GLEBE CL

Whitshaw Wood
Ash Plantation
B1066
WHEPSTEAD ROAD
SHARPE'S LANE

Horsecroft Hall
Horsecroft Farm

Beech Grove
HENCOTE LA

IP33
Nowton Grove
Bury to Clare Walk

FOX AND PIN LA
The Paddock
NOWTON ROAD
Nowton Country Park
COOPER LA

SICKLESMERE ROAD
River Lark
Bridge Farm
Great Spinney

A34
SUDBURY ROAD

8

Long Wood

St Edmund Way
PARK LANE

Low Green
Nowton
The Grove
Park Farm
PH

61

7

Spring Head
Harram Hill
Moat

Hawstead Lodge Farm
Moat
Hawstead Lodge
Pinford End Farm

High Green

Hawstead Hall
River Lark

Sicklesmere
PO
RAYNSFORD RD 1
HAMBROOK CL 2
Fentons Farm
Windmill

IP30
Great Welnetham

60

PAGES HILL ROAD

Moat

Harram Bottom

River Lark
Bull Green
Pinford End

CHURCH ROAD
Church Farm
Hawstead

Copdoes Farm

6

Dovedenhall Wood

Vincent's Farm

Hammonds

BULL LANE

Hawstead Green

Brook Green

Great Welnetham CE Prim Sch

59

Moat
Doveden Hall
OLD SCHOOL RD
Broadgate Farm

BURY ROAD
CHURCH HILL

Coronation Wood
Woodfield Wood
Bryers Wood

BELL'S LANE
Bells Lane Farm

STANNINGFIELD ROAD
BURY ROAD

5

PH
Nunwick Farm
Whepstead
PO
RECTORY GR

IP29
Bryers Farm

PH
Cook's Farm
Flat Farm

58

Woolmer Wood
Stonecross Green
BROCKLEY ROAD
RECTORY ROAD
Malting Farm
Piper's Hall Farm
Millpost Farm
Nunn's Grove

Upper Dutmoss Wood

St Edmund Way

4

Rushbottom Wood
Mickley Green
B1066
Riches Farm
Melon Green
STRAIGHT ROAD
Hawks Farm
Butler's Hall

WHEPSTEAD ROAD
LAWSHALL ROAD
Lower Dutmoss Wood
Little Rookwood Farm

OLD LANE

57

Bury to Clare Walk
Manston Hall
Saxon Wood
Moat
Dodds Green Farm
Upper Dodds Farm
Folly Farm
Moat
Rowney Farm
Brick Kiln Plantation

BRANDS LANE
Newhall Farm
Cook's Plantation
Hall Farm
CHURCH RD

DONKEY LANE

3

Gulling Green
Suttons Farm
Moat
Millhill House
TUFFIELDS ROAD
Cage's Wood
FOLLY LANE
Boggis Farm
BURY ROAD

56

Bungalow Hall Farm
Pound Green
Cages Farm
Jack's Grove
Coldham Hall
Potash Farm Moat
Makins Farm

2

HAWK'S LA
Moats/ Brockley Hall
Bevans Farm
Castle Farm
Hoyle's Grove
Wallakers Farm
Pitmore Grove
Betty's Plantation
Barfords
Hart's Green
Harts Green Farm

GOLDEN LANE

WINDSOR CL
The Glebe
LAMBS LA
LAWSHALL ROW

55

Willow Tree Farm
B1066
MILL ROAD
Mile Farm
Longs Farm
HARTEST'S LANE
Moat Farm
Moat
Coopers Farm
Little West Farm
Harrow Green

Frithy Wood
Lawshall
The Spinney
Hanningfields Green
Trees Farm

1

Speeds Farm
Green Acre Farm
Swan Farm
HARTEST RD
Brockley Green

MELFORD RD
HARROW ROAD
Brighthouse Farm
LAWSHALL ROW
Lawshall Hall
PH
Street Farm
THE STREET
Hanningfields Farm

54

82   A   83   B   84   C   85   D   86   E   87   F   54

A1
1 PINEWAY CL
2 WOODCROFTS CL
3 BIRDBROOK
4 CHAPEL LA

D1
1 SHEPHERDS DR
2 HARROW GN
3 CHURCHILL CL

77   64

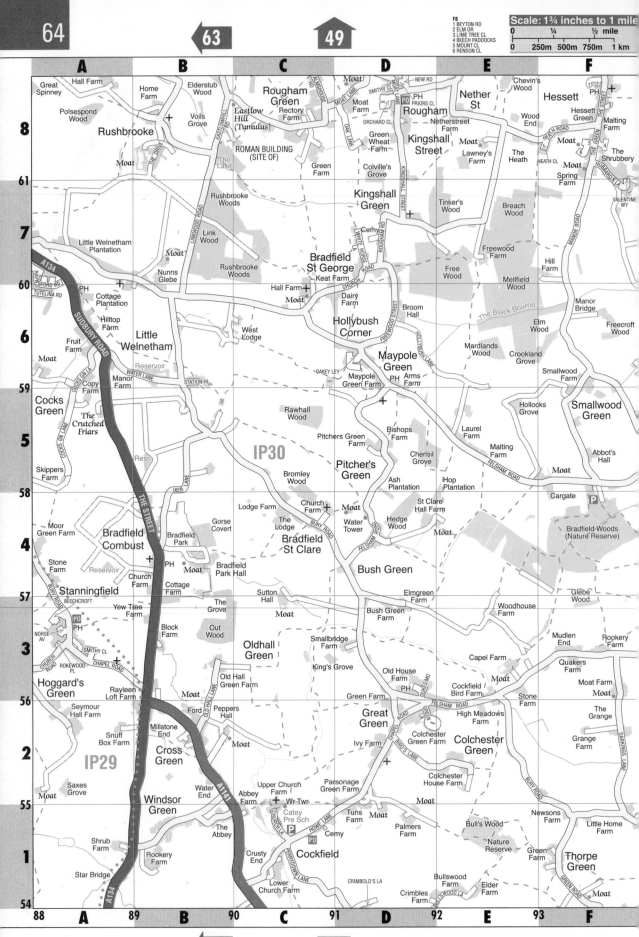

F8
1 BEYTON RD
2 ELM DR
3 LIME TREE CL
4 BEECH PADDOCKS
5 MOUNT CL
6 RENSON CL

Scale: 1¾ inches to 1 mile

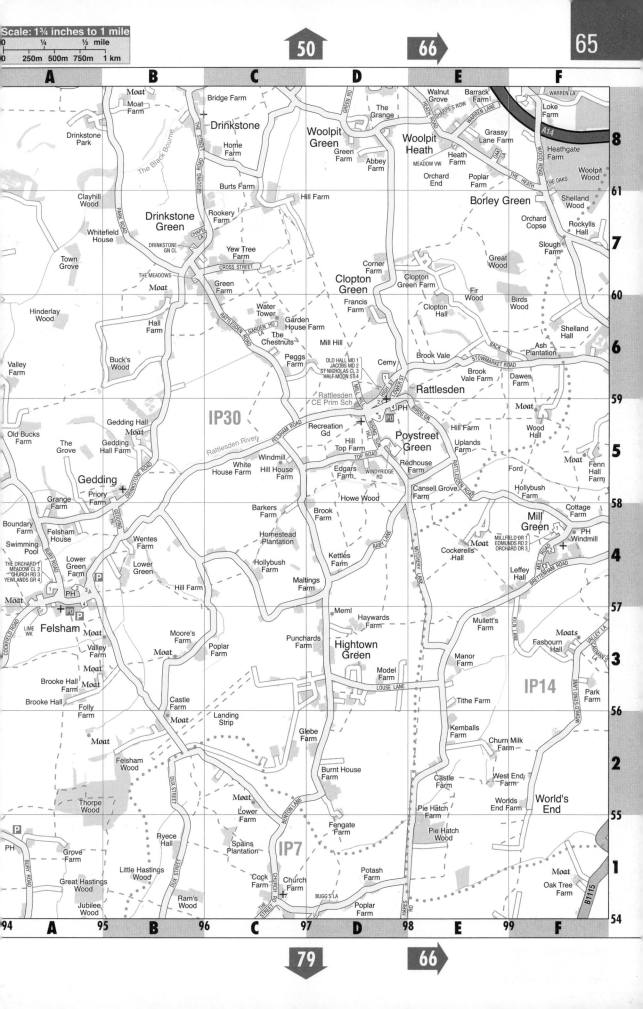

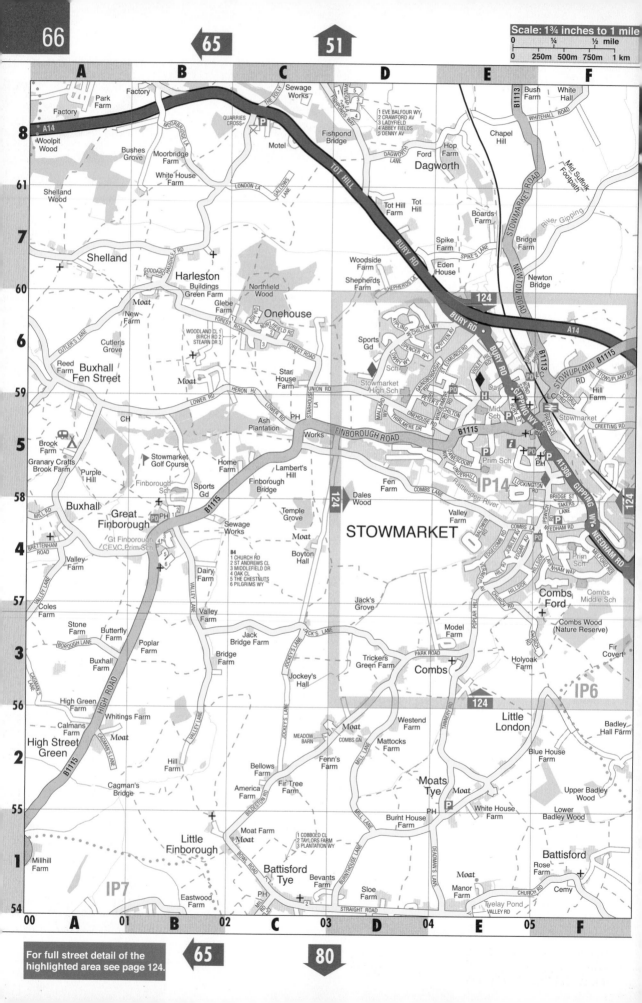

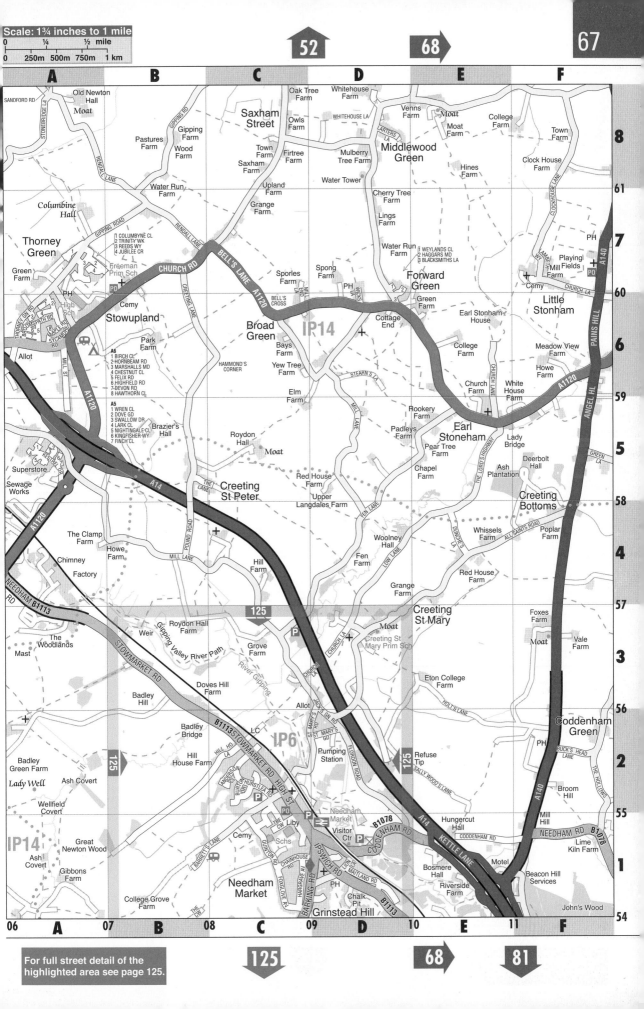

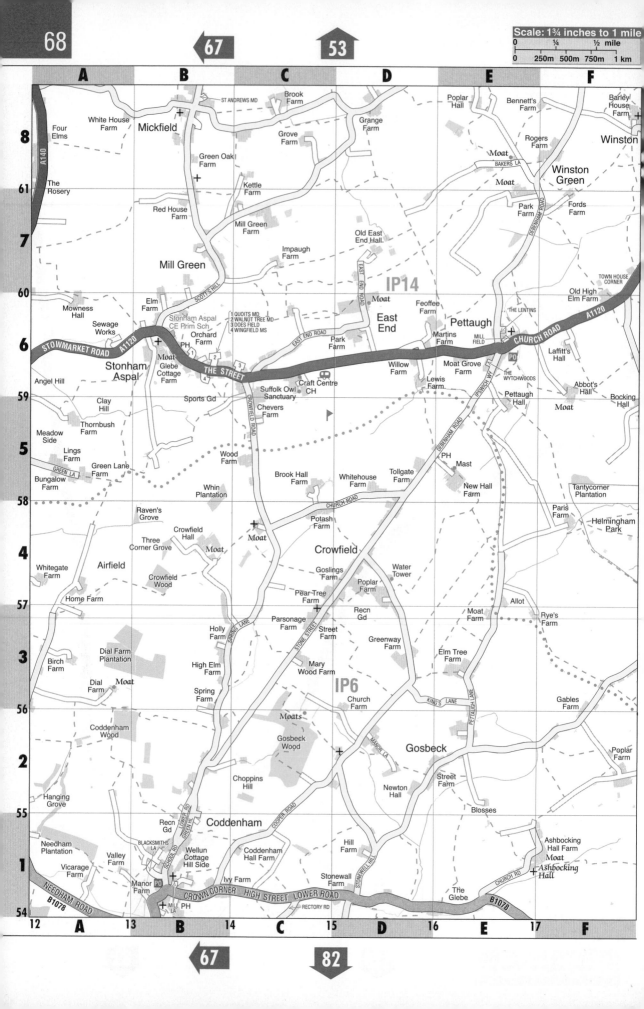

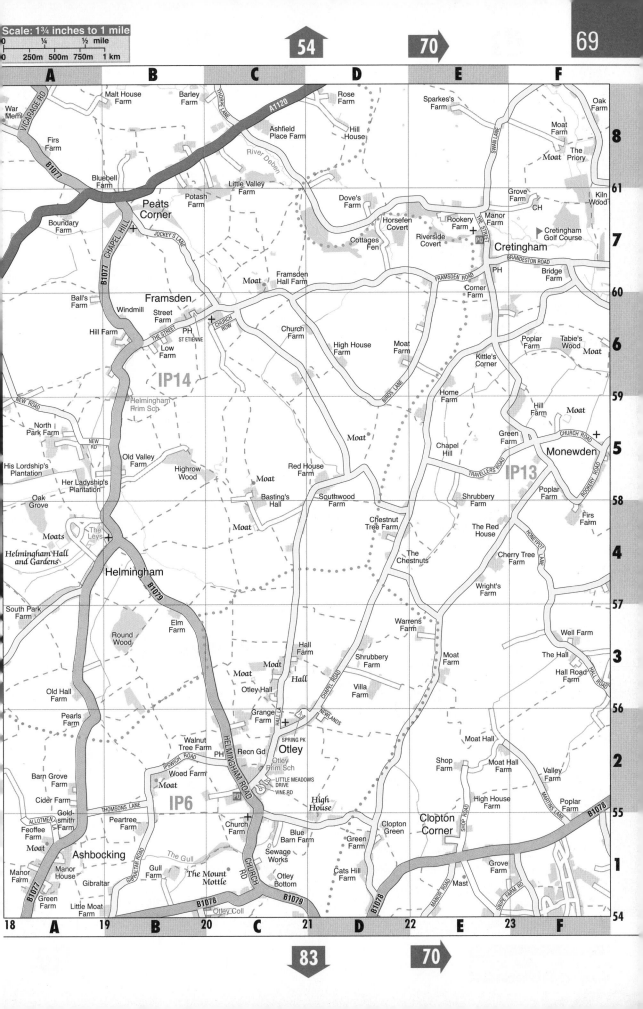

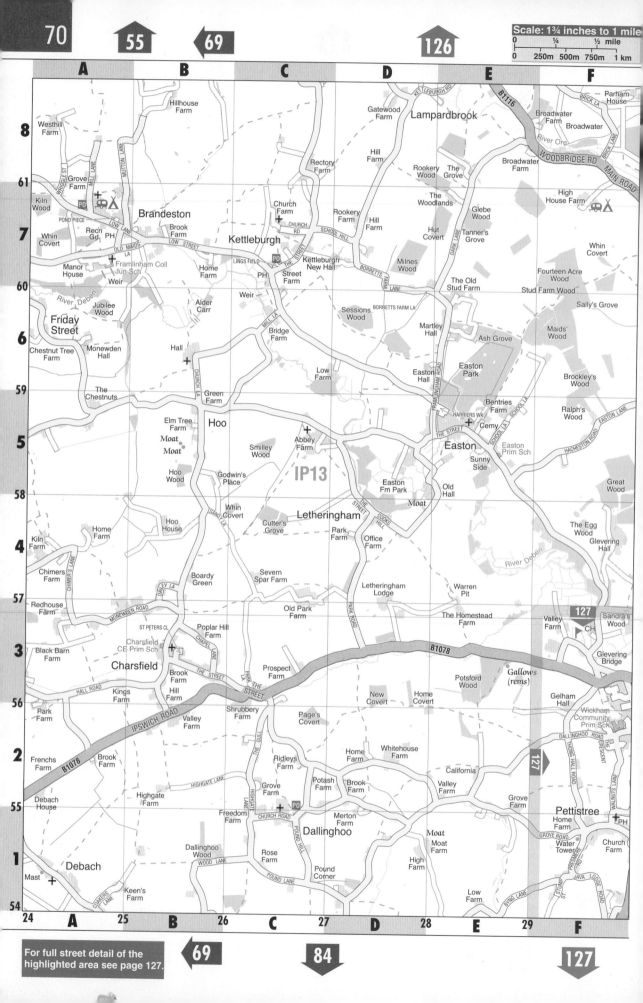

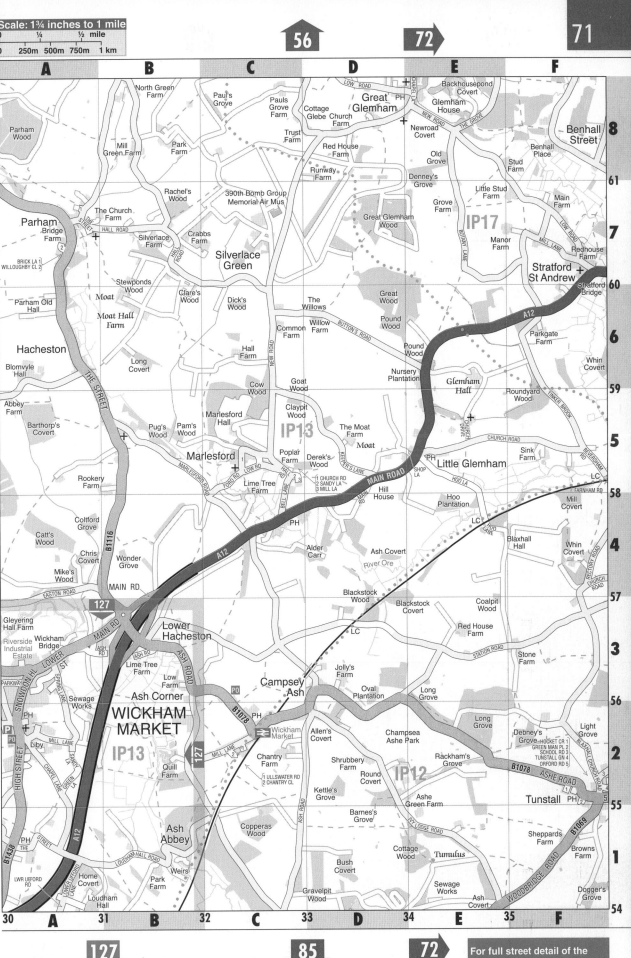

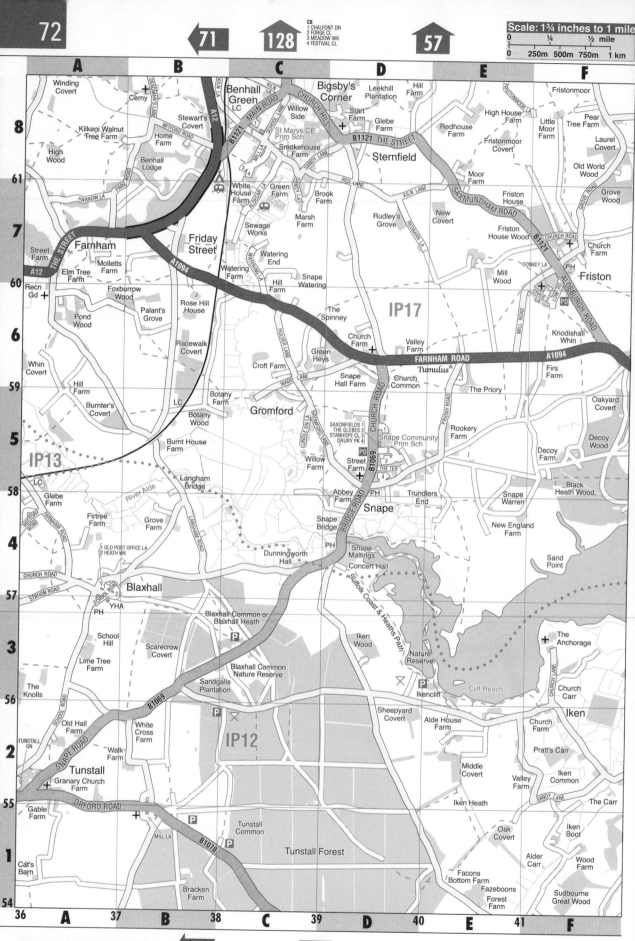

60

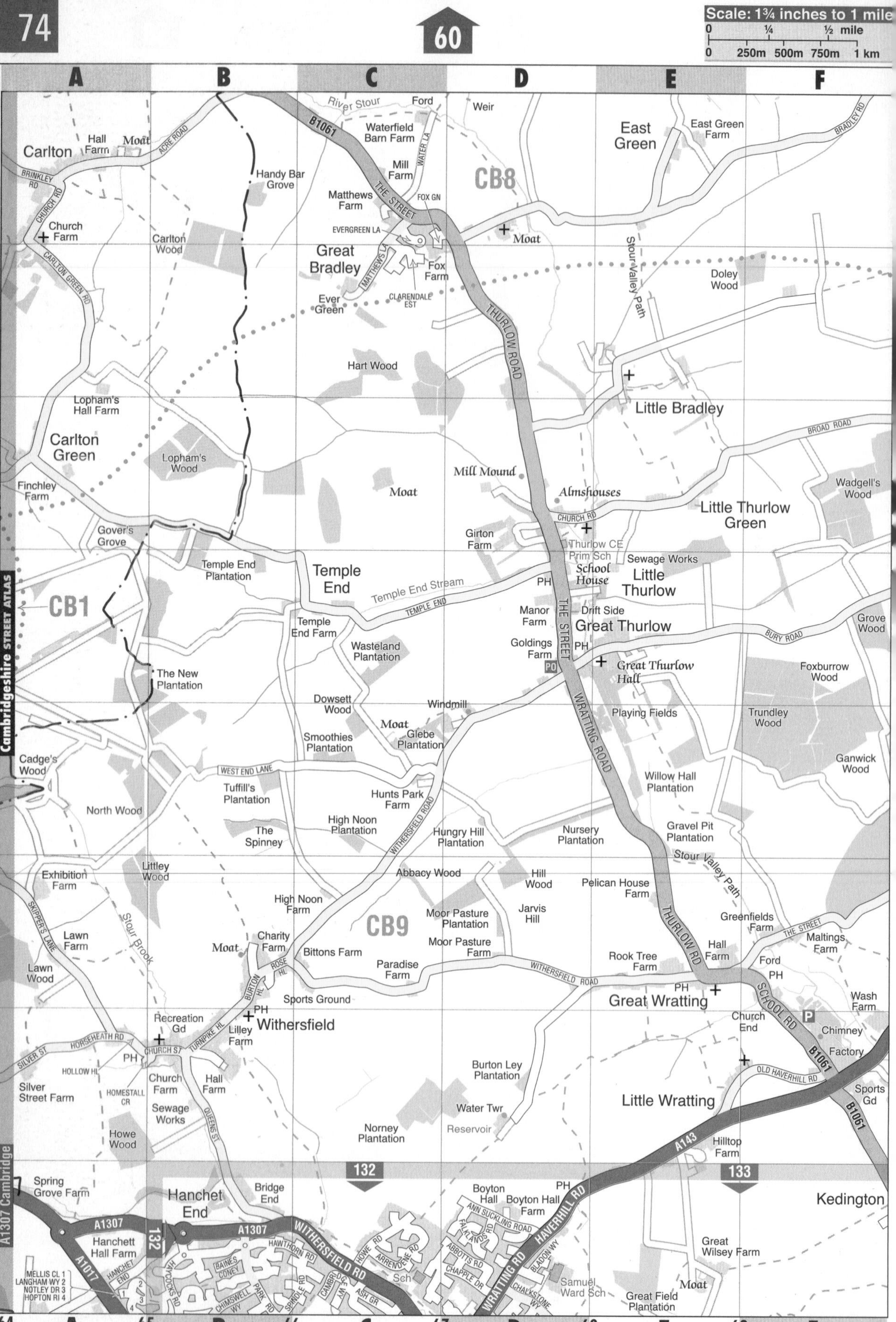
Scale: 1¾ inches to 1 mile
0 ¼ ½ mile
0 250m 500m 750m 1 km
A B C D E F
Carlton
Hall Farm
Moat
ACRE ROAD
River Stour
Ford
Weir
B1061
Waterfield Barn Farm
East Green
East Green Farm
BRADLEY RD
Handy Bar Grove
Mill Farm
WATER LA
CB8
Matthews Farm
THE STREET
FOX GN
BRINKLEY RD
CHURCH RD
Church Farm
Carlton Wood
EVERGREEN LA
Moat
Great Bradley
MATTHEWS LA
Fox Farm
Stour Valley Path
Doley Wood
CARLTON GREEN RD
Ever Green
CLARENDALE EST
THURLOW ROAD
Hart Wood
Lopham's Hall Farm
Little Bradley
BROAD ROAD
Carlton Green
Lopham's Wood
Mill Mound
Moat
Wadgell's Wood
Finchley Farm
Almshouses
CHURCH RD
Little Thurlow Green
Gover's Grove
Girton Farm
Thurlow CE Prim Sch
Temple End Plantation
Temple End
School House
Sewage Works
Little Thurlow
PH
CB1
Temple End Stream
TEMPLE END
Manor Farm
Drift Side
Temple End Farm
Great Thurlow
BURY ROAD
Grove Wood
Wasteland Plantation
Goldings Farm
PH
PO
THE STREET
Great Thurlow Hall
Foxburrow Wood
The New Plantation
Dowsett Wood
Windmill
Playing Fields
Trundley Wood
Moat
Glebe Plantation
WRATTING ROAD
Smoothies Plantation
Cambridgeshire STREET ATLAS
Cadge's Wood
WEST END LANE
Willow Hall Plantation
Ganwick Wood
Tuffill's Plantation
Hunts Park Farm
North Wood
WITHERSFIELD ROAD
High Noon Plantation
Hungry Hill Plantation
Nursery Plantation
Gravel Pit Plantation
The Spinney
Stour Valley Path
Littley Wood
Abbacy Wood
Hill Wood
Exhibition Farm
Pelican House Farm
High Noon Farm
SKIPPER'S LANE
Stour Brook
Jarvis Hill
Moor Pasture Plantation
THURLOW RD
Greenfields Farm
THE STREET
CB9
Lawn Farm
Charity Farm
Moat
Moor Pasture Farm
Maltings Farm
Bittons Farm
Hall Farm
Lawn Wood
Rook Tree Farm
Ford
ROSE HL
Paradise Farm
WITHERSFIELD ROAD
PH
BURTON HL
PH
SCHOOL RD
Wash Farm
Sports Ground
Great Wratting
PH
Recreation Gd
Withersfield
Church End
P
Lilley Farm
Chimney
HORSEHEATH RD
TURNPIKE HL
Factory
SILVER ST
CHURCH ST
PH
B1061
HOLLOW HL
Burton Ley Plantation
OLD HAVERHILL RD
Church Farm
Hall Farm
Sports Gd
Silver Street Farm
HOMESTALL CR
Sewage Works
Little Wratting
Water Twr
QUEENS ST
Reservoir
B1061
Howe Wood
Norney Plantation
A143
Hilltop Farm
132
133
A1307 Cambridge
Spring Grove Farm
Bridge End
Boyton Hall
PH
Boyton Hall Farm
HAVERHILL RD
Kedington
Hanchet End
A1307
ANN SUCKLING ROAD
A1307
FALKLANDS RD
WITHERSFIELD RD
Hanchett Hall Farm
HAWTHORN RD
HOWE RD
ARRENDENE RD
ABBOTTS RD
Great Wilsey Farm
A1017
HANCHET END
HAYCOCKS RD
BAINES CONEY
CHAPPLE DR
BLADON WY
Sch
WRATTING RD
Moat
MELLIS CL 1
LANGHAM WY 2
NOTLEY DR 3
HOPTON RI 4
CHIMSWELL WY
PARK RD
SPINDLE RD
CAMBRIDGE WY
ASH GR
CHALKSTONE WY
Samuel Ward Sch
Great Field Plantation
64 65 66 67 68 69
8 53 7 52 6 51 5 50 4 49 3 48 2 47 1 46

88
For full street detail of the highlighted area see pages 132 and 133.
132
133

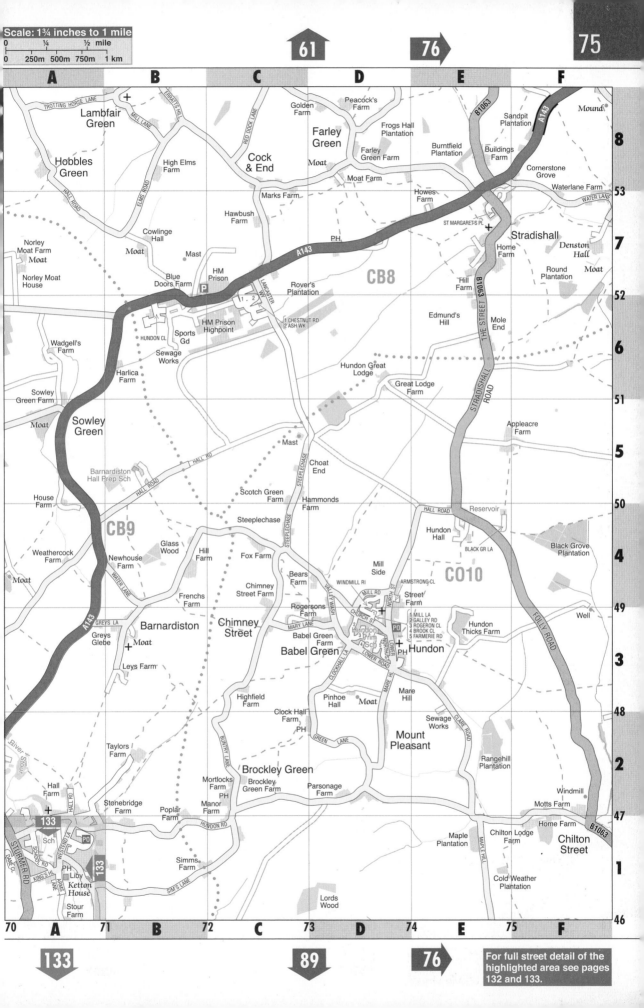

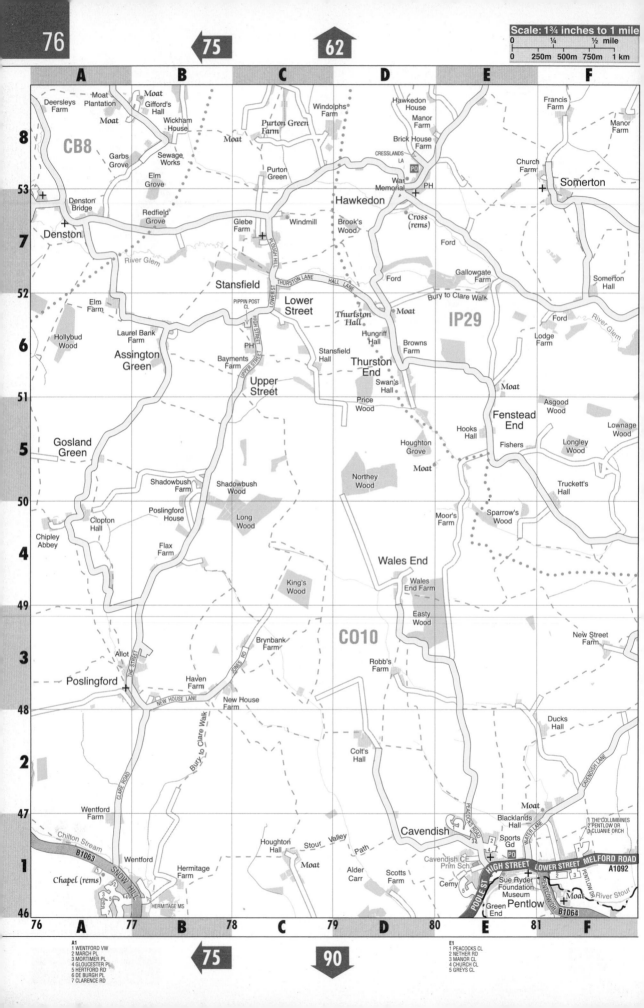

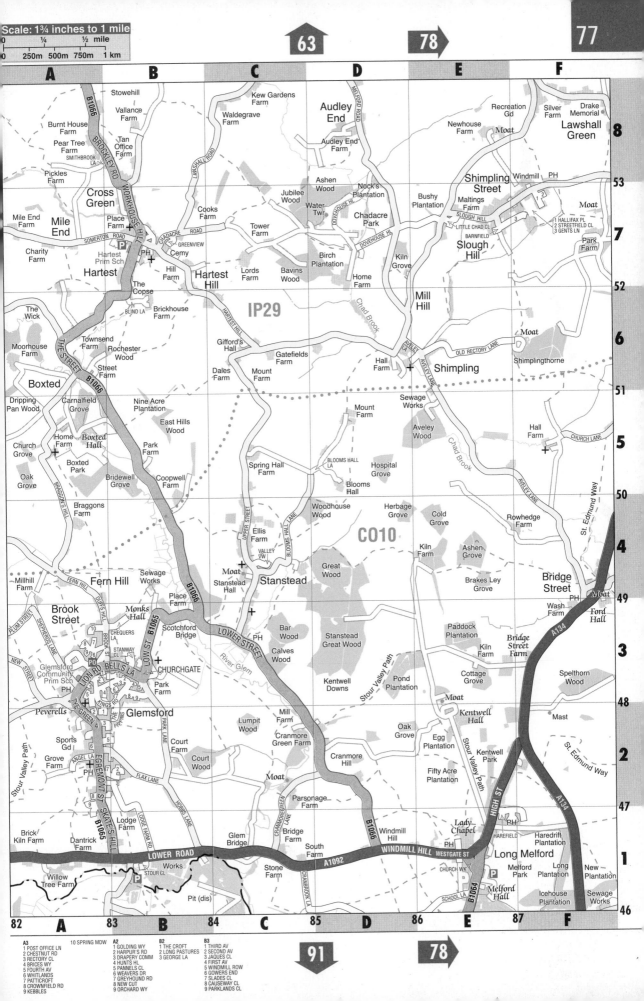

A3
1 POST OFFICE LN
2 CHESTNUT RD
3 RECTORY CL
4 BRICES WY
5 FOURTH AV
6 WHITLANDS
7 PATTICROFT
8 CROWNFIELD RD
9 KEBBLES

10 SPRING MDW

A2
1 GOLDING WY
2 HARPUR'S RD
3 DRAPERY COMM
4 HUNTS HL
5 PANNELS CL
6 WEAVERS DR
7 GREYHOUND RD
8 NEW CUT
9 ORCHARD WY

B2
1 THE CROFT
2 LONG PASTURES
3 GEORGE LA

B3
1 THIRD AV
2 SECOND AV
3 JAQUES AV
4 FIRST AV
5 WINDMILL ROW
6 GOWERS END
7 SLADES CL
8 CAUSEWAY CL
9 PARKLANDS CL

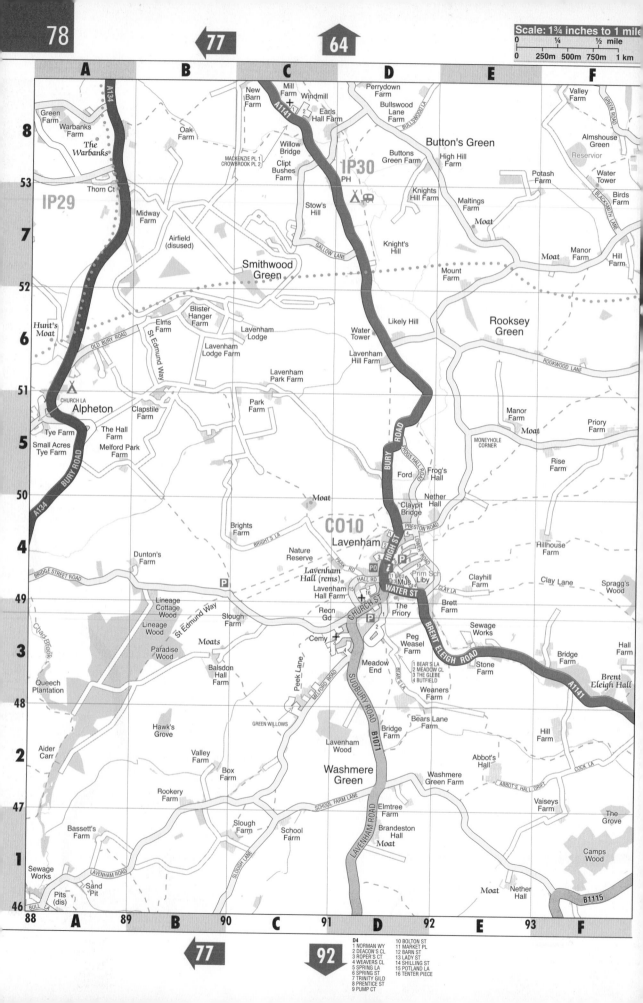

A   B   C   D   E   F

8
Green Farm
Warbanks Farm
The Warbanks
New Barn Farm
Mill Farm
Windmill
Earls Hall Farm
Perrydown Farm
Bullswood Lane Farm
Button's Green
Buttons Green Farm
High Hill Farm
Valley Farm
Almshouse Green
Reservoir
BULLSWOOD LA
GREEN ROAD

53
Thorn Ct
A1134
MACKENZIE PL 1
CROWBROOK PL 2
Willow Bridge
Clipt Bushes Farm
IP30
PH
Stow's Hill
Knights Hill Farm
Maltings Farm
Moat
Potash Farm
Water Tower
Birds Farm
BLACKSMITH LANE

IP29
7
Midway Farm
Oak Farm
Airfield (disused)
Smithwood Green
GALLOW LANE
Knight's Hill
Mount Farm
Moat
Manor Farm
Hill Farm
A1141

52
Hunt's Moat
Elms Farm
Blister Hanger Farm
Lavenham Lodge
Lavenham Lodge Farm
Water Tower
Likely Hill
Rooksey Green
Moat

6
OLD BURY ROAD
ST EDMUND WAY
Lavenham Park Farm
Lavenham Hill Farm
ROOKWOOD LANE

51
CHURCH LA
Alpheton
Clapstile Farm
Park Farm
Manor Farm
Moat
Priory Farm

5
Tye Farm
Small Acres Tye Farm
The Hall Farm
Melford Park Farm
MONEYHOLE CORNER
Rise Farm
BURY ROAD
Frogs Hall Road
Ford
Frog's Hall

A1134
4
Dunton's Farm
Brights Farm
Moat
Nature Reserve
Lavenham Hall (rems)
CO10
Lavenham
Claypit Bridge
Nether Hall
PRESTON ROAD
Hillhouse Farm
Clay Lane
Spragg's Wood
BRIDGE STREET ROAD
BRIGHT'S LA
PARK RD
HALL RD
HIGH ST
PO
P
Prim Sch
Liby
Mus
Clayhill Farm

49
Lineage Cottage Wood
Lineage Wood
Slough Farm
ST EDMUND WAY
The Priory
WATER ST
CHURCH ST
Brett Farm
CLAY LA

3
Queech Plantation
Paradise Wood
Moats
Balsdon Hall Farm
Recn Gd
Cemy
Peg Weasel Farm
Sewage Works
Stone Farm
Bridge Farm
Hall Farm
Brent Eleigh Hall
PEEK LANE
MELFORD ROAD
Meadow End
1 BEAR'S LA
2 MEADOW CL
3 THE GLEBE
4 BUTFIELD
BEAR'S LA
BRENT ELEIGH ROAD
A1141

2
Aider Carr
Hawk's Grove
Valley Farm
Box Farm
Green Willows
Lavenham Wood
Weaners Farm
Bears Lane Farm
Abbot's Hall
Hill Farm
Vaiseys Farm
SUDBURY ROAD
B1071
Washmere Green Farm
ABBOT'S HALL DRIFT
COCK LA

47
Rookery Farm
Washmere Green
The Grove

1
Sewage Works
Bassett's Farm
Slough Farm
School Farm
Elmtree Farm
Brandeston Hall
Moat
Camps Wood
LAVENHAM ROAD
SCHOOL FARM LANE
SLOUGH LANE
LAVENHAM ROAD
Moat
Nether Hall

46
Sand Pit
Pits (dis)
BULL
LAVENHAM ROAD
B1115

88   A   89   B   90   C   91   D   92   E   93   F

D4
1 NORMAN WY
2 DEACON'S CL
3 ROPER'S CT
4 WEAVERS CL
5 SPRING LA
6 SPRING ST
7 TRINITY GILD
8 PRENTICE ST
9 PUMP CT
10 BOLTON ST
11 MARKET PL
12 BARN ST
13 LADY ST
14 SHILLING ST
15 POTLAND LA
16 TENTER PIECE

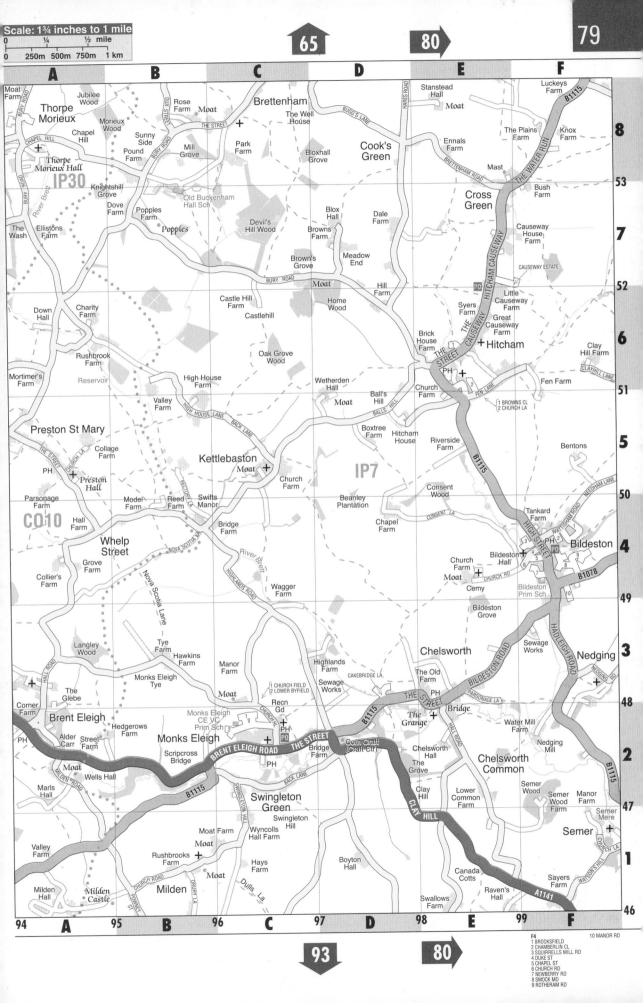

A **B** **C** **D** **E** **F**

8

Moat Farm

Thorpe Morieux

Jubilee Wood

Rose Farm

Moat

Brettenham

The Well House

Stanstead Hall

Moat

Luckeys Farm

B1115

Knox Farm

Morieux Wood

Chapel Hill

Sunny Side

Mill Grove

BURG'S LANE

Cook's Green

Ennals Farm

The Plains Farm

Bush Farm

53

Chapel Hill

Thorpe Morieux Hall

IP30

Pound Farm

Park Farm

Bloxhall Grove

Mast

BRETTENHAM ROAD

Cross Green

Knightshill Grove

Old Buckenham Hall Sch

Devil's Hill Wood

Blox Hall

Dale Farm

Causeway House Farm

7

The Wash

Ellistons Farm

Dove Farm

Popples Farm

Popples

Browns Green

Meadow End

CAUSEWAY ESTATE

HITCHAM CAUSEWAY

52

Brown's Grove

Moat

Hill Farm

Little Causeway Farm

Great Causeway Farm

Down Hall

Charity Farm

Castle Hill Farm

Home Wood

Syers Farm

Brick House Farm

Hitcham

THE CAUSEWAY

Clay Hill Farm

6

Rushbrook Farm

Castlehill

THE STREET

PH

CLAYHILL LANE

Mortimer's Farm

Reservoir

Oak Grove Wood

Wetherden Hall

Church Farm

Fen Farm

51

High House Farm

Moat

Ball's Hill

1 BROWNS CL
2 CHURCH LA

FEN LANE

Preston St Mary

Valley Farm

HIGH HOUSE LANE

BACK LANE

BALL'S HILL

Boxtree Farm

Hitcham House

Riverside Farm

Bentons

5

Collage Farm

Kettlebaston

Church Farm

IP7

NEEDHAM LANE

THE STREET

CHURCH LA

Moat

Beanley Plantation

Consent Wood

Tankard Farm

50

Preston Hall

Parsonage Farm

CO10

Model Farm

Reed Farm

Swifts Manor

Chapel Farm

CONSENT LA

Bildeston

HIGH STREET

WATTISHAM ROAD

Bildeston

PH

Hall Farm

Bridge Farm

Church Farm

4

Whelp Street

Grove Farm

NOVA SCOTIA LA

River Brett

Wagger Farm

Church Farm

Moat

Cemy

B1078

Bildeston Prim Sch

Collier's Farm

HIGHLANDS ROAD

Bildeston Grove

49

Langley Wood

Tye Farm

Hawkins Farm

Manor Farm

Highlands Farm

Chelsworth

BILDESTON ROAD

Sewage Works

Nedging

3

Nova Scotia Lane

CAKEBRIDGE LA

The Old Farm

HADLEIGH ROAD

NEDGING RD

Monks Eleigh Tye

Moat

Sewage Works

1 CHURCH FIELD
2 LOWER BYFIELD

Recn Gd

PH

The Street

PH

Bridge

Water Mill Farm

48

Corner Farm

Brent Eleigh

Hedgerows Farm

Monks Eleigh CE VC Prim Sch

PO

The Grange

Chelsworth Hall

Nedging Mill

PH

Alder Carr

Street Farm

Monks Eleigh

Scripcross Bridge

BRENT ELEIGH ROAD

THE STREET

Bridge Farm

Corn Craft (Craft Ctr)

The Grove

Chelsworth Common

2

The Glebe

BACK LANE

PH

Clay Hill

Lower Common Farm

Semer Wood

Manor Farm

Marls Hall

Moat

Wells Hall

SWINGLETON HILL

Swingleton Green

B1115

CLAY HILL

Semer Wood Farm

Semer Mere

47

Valley Farm

MILDEN ROAD

Moat

Rushbrooks Farm

Swingleton Hill

Wyncolls Hall Farm

Hays Farm

Boyton Hall

Canada Cotts

Raven's Hall

Semer

B1115

CHURCH HILL

1

Milden Hall

Milden Castle

POVINEY

Milden

DRURY LA

Moat

DULLS LA

Swallows Farm

A1141

Sayers Farm

WATSON'S HILL

46

94   **A**   95   **B**   96   **C**   97   **D**   98   **E**   99   **F**

F4
1 BROOKSFIELD
2 CHAMBERLIN CL
3 SQUIRRELLS MILL RD
4 DUKE ST
5 CHAPEL ST
6 CHURCH RD
7 NEWBERRY RD
8 SMOCK MD
9 ROTHERAM RD

10 MANOR RD

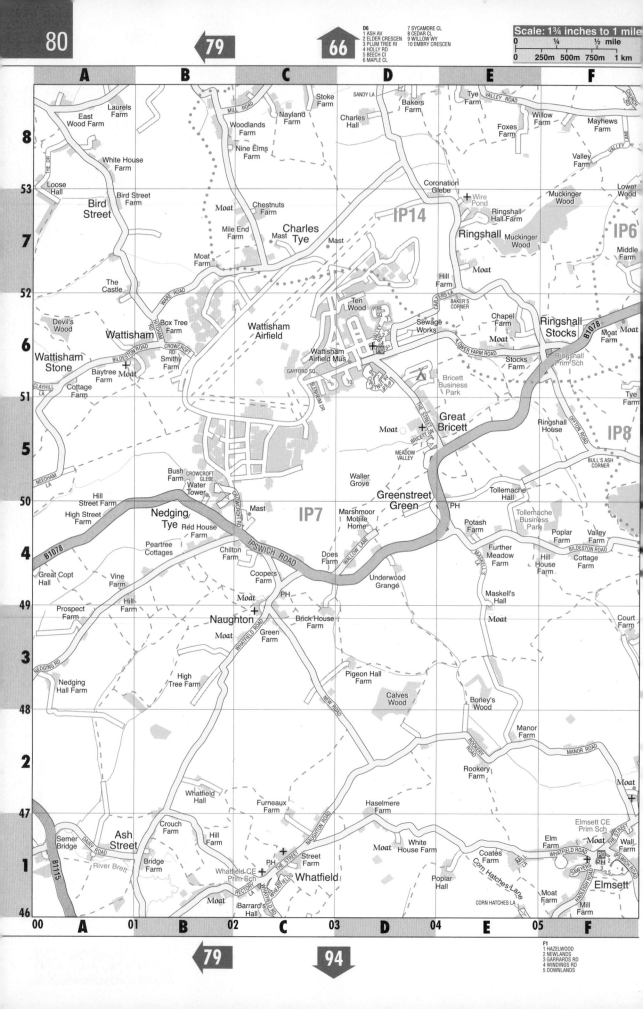

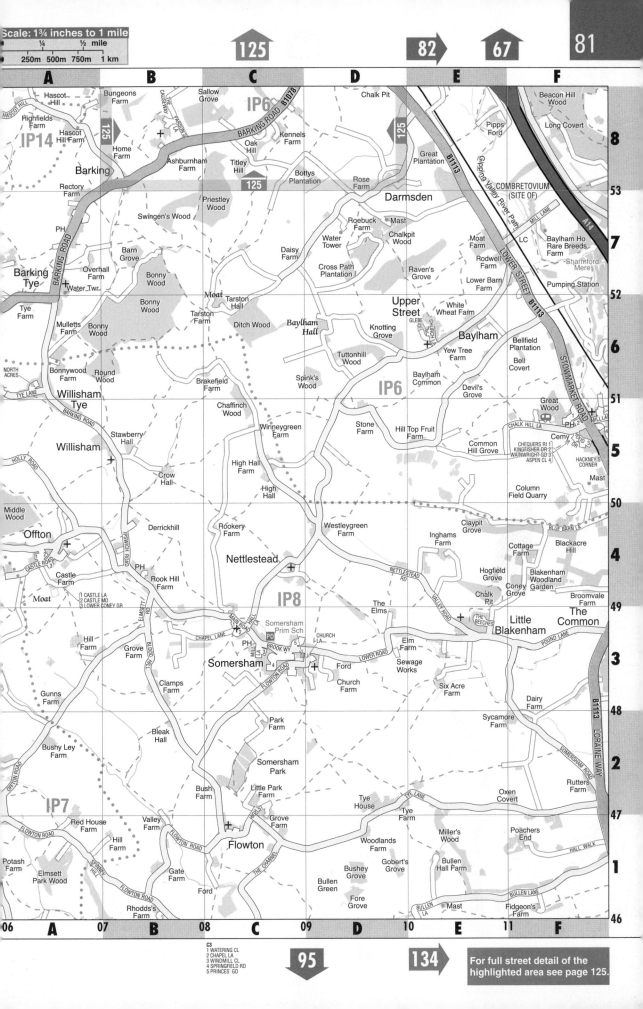

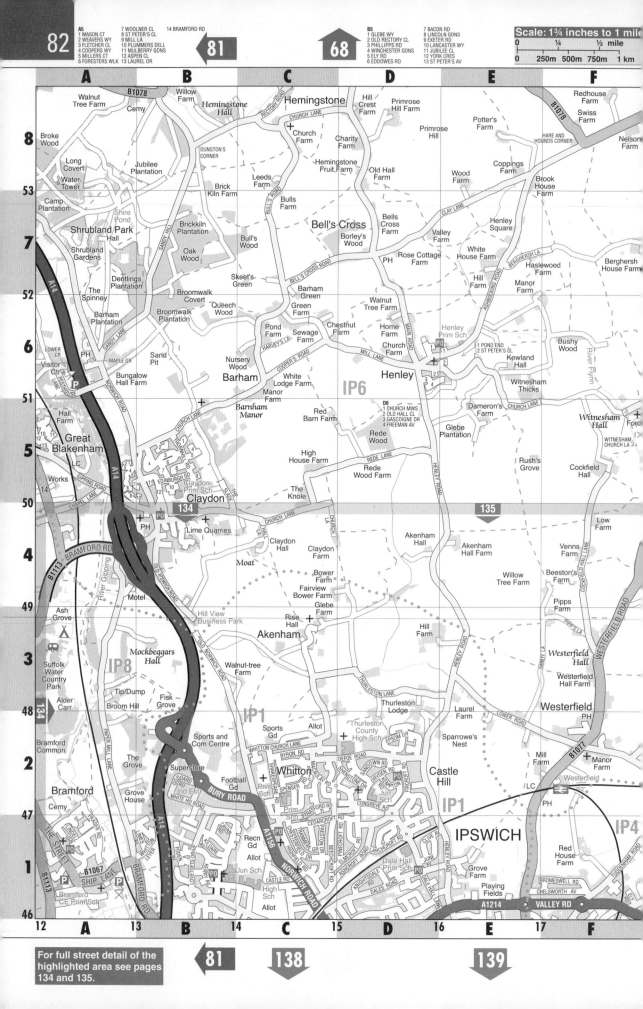

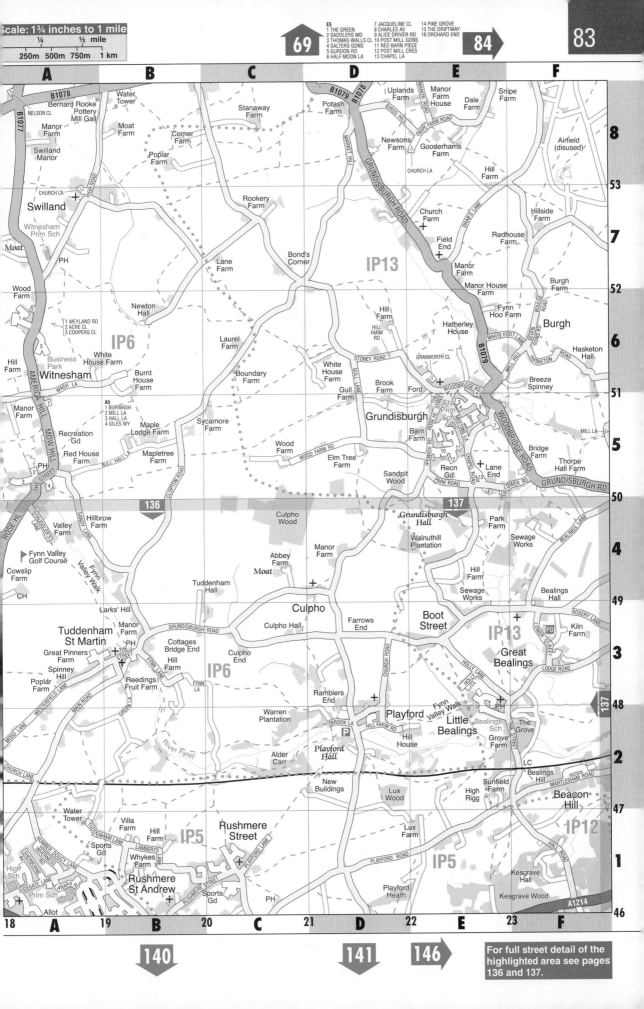

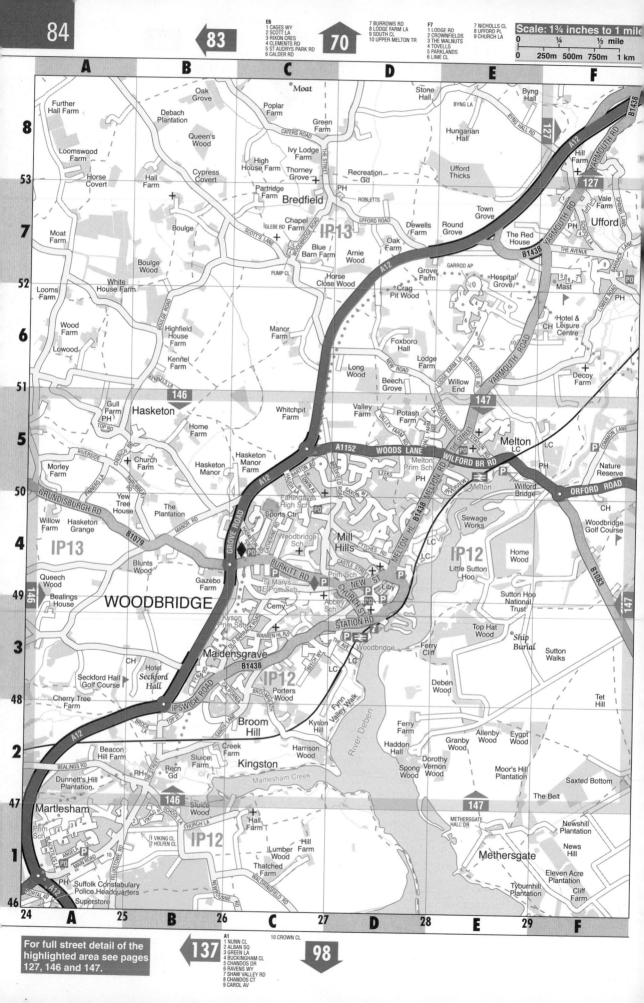

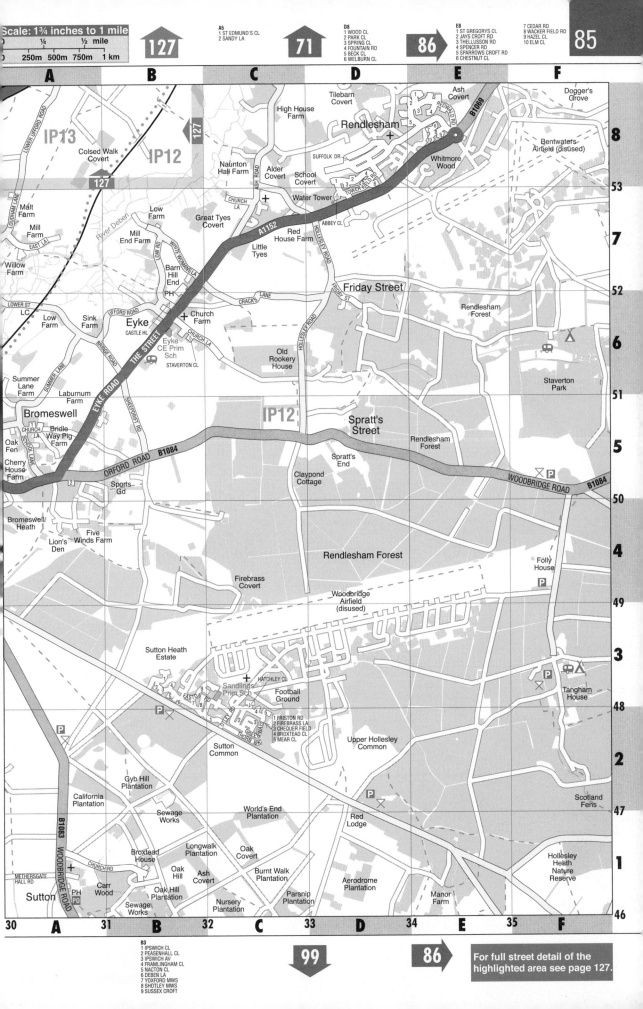

Scale: 1¾ inches to 1 mile

¼	½	mile	

250m 500m 750m 1 km

127

A5
1 ST EDMUND'S CL
2 SANDY LA

71

D8
1 WOOD CL
2 PARK CL
3 SPRING CL
4 FOUNTAIN RD
5 BECK CL
6 WELBURN CL

86

E8
1 ST GREGORYS CL
2 JAYS CROFT RD
3 THELLUSSON RD
4 SPENCER RD
5 SPARROWS CROFT RD
6 CHESTNUT CL

7 CEDAR RD
8 WACKER FIELD RD
9 HAZEL CL
10 ELM CL

85

A **B** **C** **D** **E** **F**

IP13

Colsed Walk Covert

IP12

127

127

Malt Farm

LOUDHAM LANE

EAST LA

Mill Farm

Willow Farm

River Deben

Low Farm

Mill End Farm

LOW RD

WHITE WOMANS LA

Barn Hill End

PH

Naunton Hall Farm

Alder Covert

School Covert

CHURCH LA

ASH ROAD

A1152

Great Tyes Covert

Little Tyes

Red House Farm

High House Farm

Tilebarn Covert

Rendlesham

SUFFOLK DR

Water Tower

ABBEY CL

TOWER FIELD RD

Ash Covert

Dogger's Grove

Bentwaters Airfield (disused)

REDWALD RD

B1069

Whitmore Wood

8

53

7

LOWER ST
LC

Low Farm

Sink Farm

UFFORD ROAD

Eyke

CASTLE HL

THE STREET

Eyke CE Prim Sch

STAVERTON CL

CHURCH LA

Church Farm

CRACKS LANE

Old Rookery House

HOLLESLEY ROAD

FRIDAY ST

Friday Street

Rendlesham Forest

52

6

51

Summer Lane Farm

SUMMER LANE

Laburnum Farm

BRIDGE ROAD

EYKE ROAD

SHEEPDIRT RD

Bromeswell

CHURCH LA

Oak Fen

Bridle Way Pig Farm

SCHOOL LANE

Cherry House Farm

ORFORD ROAD

B1084

Sports Gd

IP12

Spratt's Street

Spratt's End

Claypond Cottage

Rendlesham Forest

WOODBRIDGE ROAD

B1084

Staverton Park

5

50

Bromeswell Heath

Lion's Den

Five Winds Farm

Firebrass Covert

Rendlesham Forest

Woodbridge Airfield (disused)

Folly House

P

4

49

Sutton Heath Estate

EASTON RD

TOTLEY RD

HATCHLEY CL

Sandlings Prim Sch

Football Ground

GREENWAY

THORN WS

1 FRISTON RD
2 FIREBRASS LA
3 CHEQUER FIELD
4 BROXTEAD CL
5 MEAR CL

Upper Hollesley Common

Tangham House

P

3

48

B1083

WOODBRIDGE ROAD

P

Sutton Common

Gyb Hill Plantation

California Plantation

Sewage Works

World's End Plantation

Red Lodge

P

Scotland Fens

2

47

METHERSGATE HALL RD

Sutton

PH
PO

CHURCH RD

Carr Wood

Broxtead House

Oak Hill

Oak Hill Plantation

Sewage Works

Longwalk Plantation

Ash Covert

Nursery Plantation

Oak Covert

Burnt Walk Plantation

Parsnip Plantation

Aerodrome Plantation

Manor Farm

Hollesley Heath Nature Reserve

1

46

30 **A** 31 **B** 32 **C** 33 **D** 34 **E** 35 **F**

B3
1 IPSWICH CL
2 PEASENHALL CL
3 IPSWICH AV
4 FRAMLINGHAM CL
5 NACTON CL
6 DEBEN LA
7 YOXFORD MWS
8 SHOTLEY MWS
9 SUSSEX CROFT

99

86

For full street detail of the highlighted area see page 127.

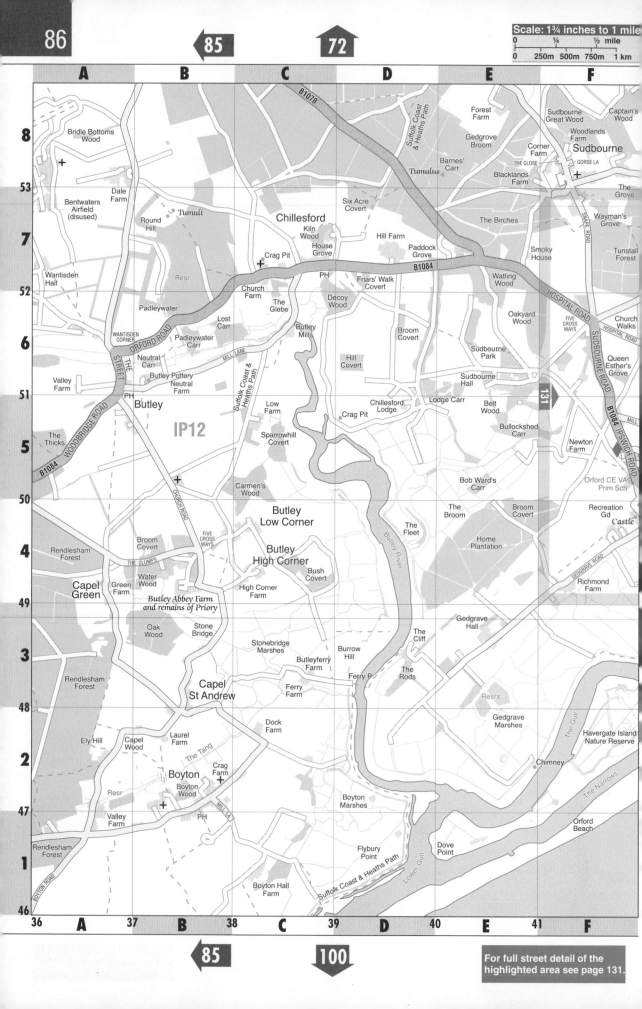

A B C D E F

Firs Farm
Longdrift Carr
Sudbourne Marshes
Aldeburgh Bay
The Firs
The White House
SCHOOL ROAD
131
Valley Farm
River Alde
Sudbourne Beach
8
53
High House Farm
HIGH HOUSE FARM ROAD
Elm Covert
Crag Farm
Crag Pit
FERRY ROAD
CRAG FARM ROAD
Chaplin's Carr
Blackstakes Reach
7
52
Church Farm
Moss' Carr
Ox Carr
Lantern Marshes (NT)
Masts
Prettyman's Whin
Masts
6
IP12
Lodge Farm
131
51
Cobbins Farm
FERRY ROAD
Bullockshed Grove
Ash Carr
Wireless Station
BROADWAY
BULLOCKSHED LA
Raydon Hall
Pig Pail Bridge
5
RAYDON LANE
Town Marshes
Orford
RECTORY RD
PH
FRONT ST
HIGH ST
DAPHNE
BROAD ST
King's Marshes
50
Mus
PH
QUAY ST
Town Hall
P P
IP12
P
Chantry Farm
River Ore
4
Sewage Works
Orfordness National Trust
Orford Ness
49
131
Chantry Point
Orford Ness National Nature Reserve
Orfordness Lighthouse
Stony Ditch
3
Stonyditch Point
Cuckold's Point
48
Orford Beach
2
47
1
46

42 A 43 B 44 C 45 D 46 E 47 F

For full street detail of the highlighted area see page 131.

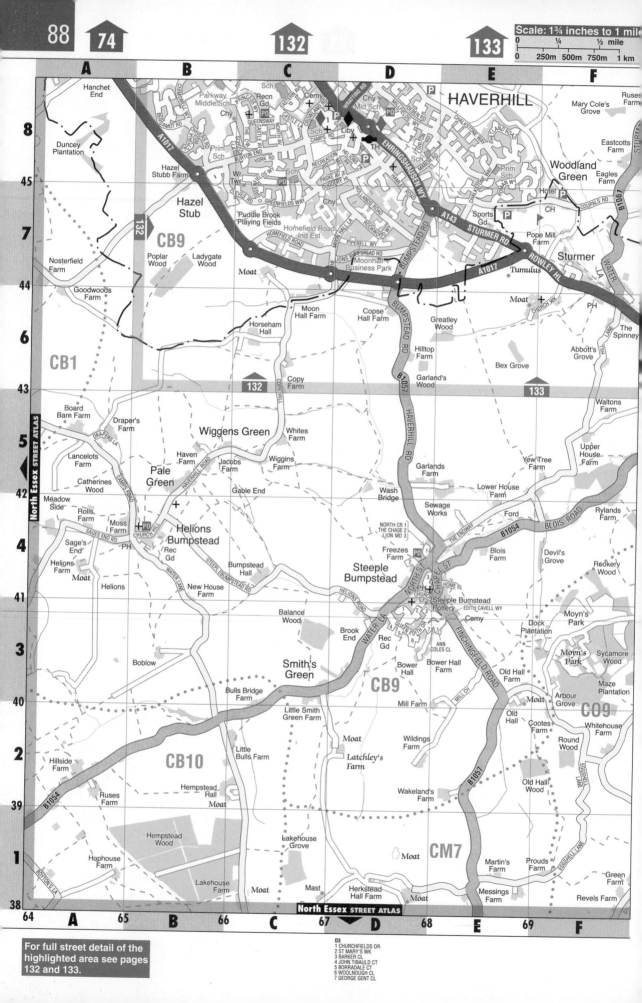

A   B   C   D   E   F

8   Hanchet End

Duncey
Plantation

45

Parkway
Middle Sch
Recn
Gd
Cemy
Chy
Mid Sch
PO

HAVERHILL
Mary Cole's
Grove
Ruses
Farm

Sch
Queensway
Prim
Sch
Liby
TH
Eastcotts
Farm

Woodland
Green
Eagles
Farm

Hazel
Stubb Farm
Wr
Twr
PO
CH
Hotel
P

Coupals Rd

7   Hazel
Stub

CB9

Poplar
Wood

Ladygate
Wood

Homefield Road
Ind Est

Homefield Road

Chy

Bumpstead Rd

Moonhall
Business Park

Sports
Gd
P

Pope Mill
Farm

Sturmer

44

Nosterfield
Farm

Goodwoods
Farm

Moat

Horseham
Hall

Moon
Hall Farm

Copse
Hall Farm

Greatley
Wood

Tumulus

Moat
Church Wk
PH

The
Spinney

6   CB1

Copy
Farm

Hilltop
Farm

Bex Grove

Abbott's
Grove

43   132   Copy Hill

133

Garland's
Wood

Waltons
Farm

5   Board
Barn Farm
Draper's
Farm

Wiggens Green

Whites
Farm

Garlands
Farm

Yew Tree
Farm

Upper
House
Farm

42

Lancelots
Farm
Haven
Farm
Jacobs
Farm
Wiggins
Farm

Lower House
Farm

Rylands
Farm

Meadow
Side
Catherines
Wood
Pale
Green
Gable End

Wash
Bridge

Ford

Sewage
Works

4   Rolls
Farm
Moss
Farm
PO
PH
Church Hill

Helions
Bumpstead

Rec
Gd

Bumpstead
Hall

Sage's
End
Helions
Farm
Moat

Steeple Ebumpstead Rd

NORTH CR 1
THE CHASE 2
LION MD 3

Freezes
Farm
PO
Steeple
Bumpstead

Blois
Farm

Devil's
Grove

Rookery
Wood

41   Helions

New House
Farm

Balance
Wood

Helions Road
North St
Chapel St
PH
Steeple Bumstead
Pottery

Home Cl

Edith Cavell Wy

Cemy

Moyn's
Park

3   Boblow

Smith's
Green

Brook
End
Rec
Gd
Water La

Finchingfield Road

ANN
COLES CL

Moyn's
Park

Sycamore
Wood

CB9

Bower
Hall
Bower Hall
Farm

Dock
Plantation

Maze
Plantation

CO9

40   Bulls Bridge
Farm

Little Smith
Green Farm

Mill Farm
Mill Ch

Old Hall
Farm
Old
Hall
Moat

Arbour
Grove

Whitehouse
Farm

2   Hillside
Farm

CB10

Little
Bulls Farm

Moat

Latchley's
Farm

Wildings
Farm

Old Hall
Wood

Cootes
Farm
Round
Wood

39   Ruses
Farm
Hempstead
Hall
Moat

Wakeland's
Farm

B1057

Eggshell Lane

1   Hophouse
Farm

Hempstead
Wood

Lakehouse
Grove

Moat

CM7

Martin's
Farm
Prouds
Farm

Green
Farm

38   Lakehouse
Farm
Moat
Mast
Herkstead
Hall Farm
Moat
Messings
Farm
Revels Farm

64   A   65   B   66   C   67   D   68   E   69   F

For full street detail of the
highlighted area see pages
132 and 133.

D3
1 CHURCHFIELDS DR
2 ST MARY'S WK
3 BARKER CL
4 JOHN TIBAULD CT
5 BORRADALE CT
6 WOOLNOUGH CL
7 GEORGE GENT CL

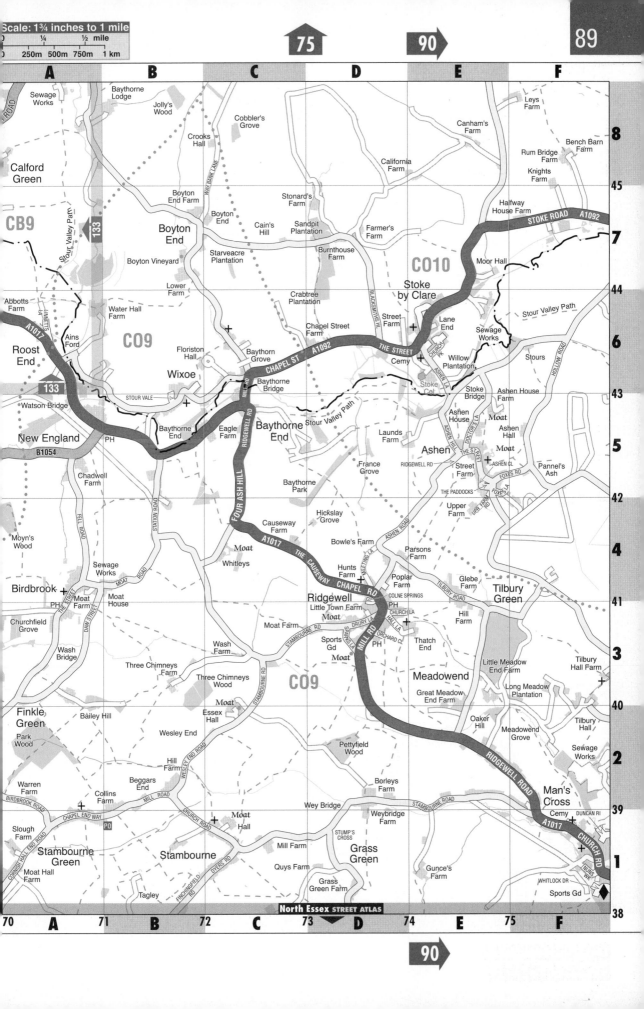

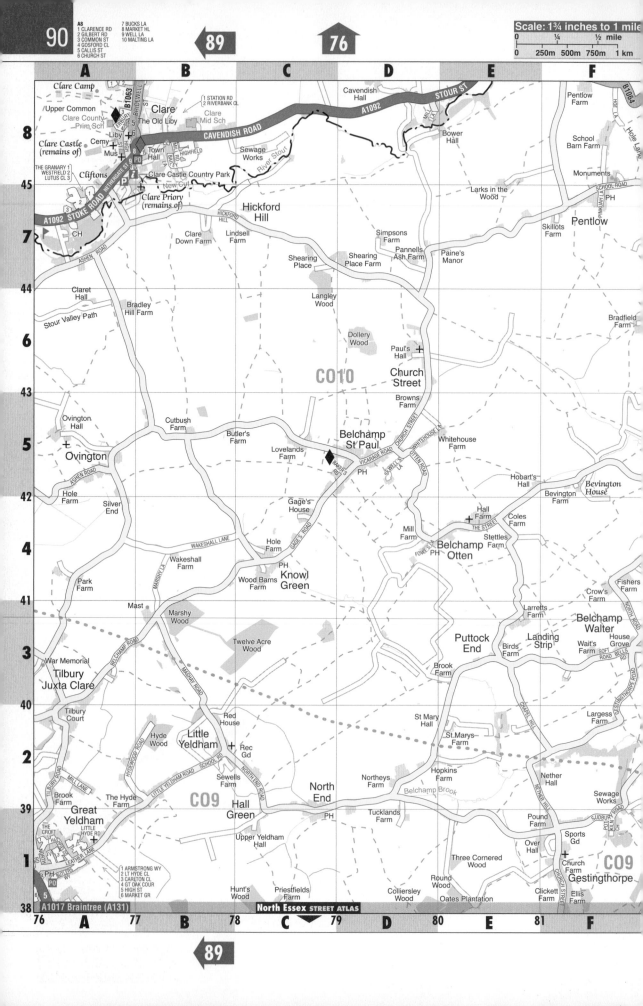

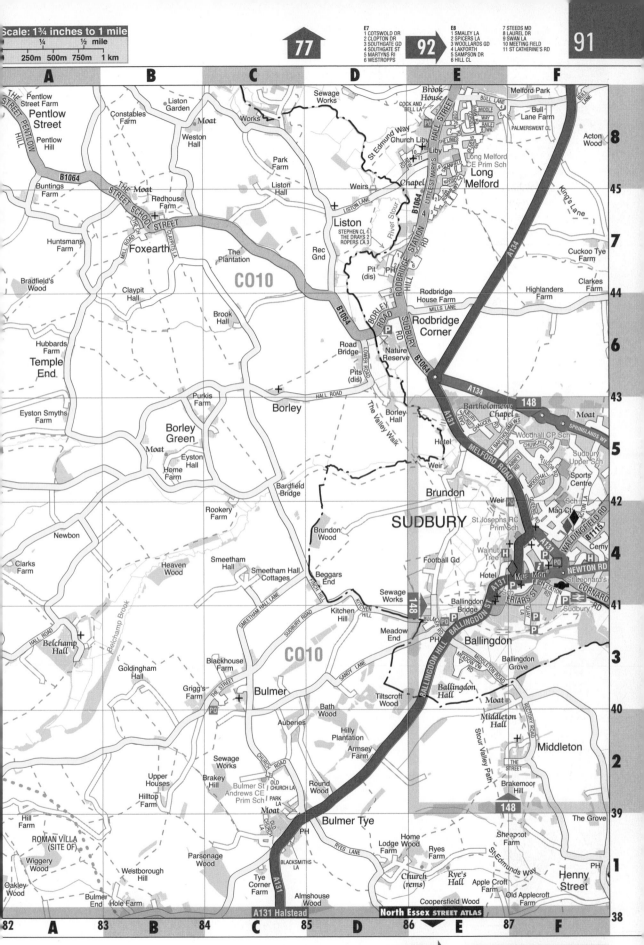

E7
1 COTSWOLD DR
2 CLOPTON DR
3 SOUTHGATE ST
4 MARTYNS RI
5 WESTROPPS

E8
1 SMALEY LA
2 SPICERS LA
3 WOOLLARDS GD
4 LAKFORTH
5 SAMPSON DR
6 HILL CL

7 STEEDS MD
8 LAUREL DR
9 SWAN LA
10 MEETING FIELD
11 ST CATHERINE'S RD

A B C D E F

8
45
7
44
6
43
5
42
4
41
3
40
2
39
1
38

The Street
Pentlow Street Farm
Pentlow Street
Pentlow Hill
PENTLOW HILL
B1064
Buntings Farm
Huntsmans Farm
Bradfield's Wood
Temple End
Eyston Smyths Farm

Constables Farm
Liston Garden
Moat
Weston Hall
Park Farm

Works
Liston Hall

Sewage Works

Redhouse Farm
The Moat
STREET SCHOOL
Foxearth
MILL ROAD
CLAYPITS LA
The Plantation
CO10

Claypit Hall
Brook Hall

Purkis Farm

Liston
Liston Lane
Rec Gnd
Pit (dis)

STEPHEN CL 4
THE DRAYS 2
ROPERS LA 3

Weirs
Chapel
PH

St Edmund Way
Church Liby
Liby

Brook House
COCK AND BELL LA
BULL LANE
MIDDLE WAY
RAILE BWX
PALMERSWENT CL

Melford Park

Bull Lane Farm
Long Melford
Long Melford CE Prim Sch
THE LIMES

Acton Wood

King's Lane
Cuckoo Tye Farm

45
7
Clarkes Farm

River Stour

B1064
RODBRIDGE STATION RD
Rodbridge House Farm
MILLS LANE
Rodbridge Corner

Highlanders Farm

44

BORLEY ROAD
Road Bridge
P
Nature Reserve
Pits (dis)
LOWER ROAD
HALL ROAD
Borley

The Valley Walk
Borley Hall

A134
A131

Bartholomews Chapel
148
Moat
SPRINGLANDS WY

43

Borley Green
Moat
Eyston Hall
Home Farm
Bardfield Bridge

Hotel
Weir

Woodhall CP Sch
MELFORD ROAD
Woodhall
CHURCHILL RD
TUDOR RD

Sudbury Upper Sch
Sports Centre
Sch

5
42

Newbon
Clarks Farm

Rookery Farm

Smeetham Hall
Smeetham Hall Cottages

Brundon Wood
Beggars End

Weir
Brundon

SUDBURY
St Josephs RC Prim Sch

QUEENS RD
Mag Ct
B1115
WALDINGFIELD RD
Cemy

4
41

Belchamp Brook
Belchamp Hall
HALL ROAD

Heaven Wood
SMEETHAM HALL LANE
FINCH HILL
SUDBURY ROAD

Kitchen Hill
KITCHEN HILL

Sewage Works

148
BULMER RD

Football Gd
Walnut Tree
Hotel
H
Mus
A131
FRIARS ST
Mon
Liby
STATION
Sudbury
NEWTON RD
CORNARD RD
St Leonard's

Goldingham Hall
Grigg's Farm
THE STREET
PO
Blackhouse Farm
Bulmer
CO10

SANDY LANE
Kitchen Hill

Meadow End
PH

Ballingdon Bridge
BALLINGDON HILL
BALLINGDON ST
PO
Ballingdon

MEADOW VW
MIDDLETON RD
Ballingdon Grove
Ballingdon Hall
Moat

3

Hall Road
Hill Farm
ROMAN VILLA (SITE OF)
Wiggery Wood
Oakley Wood

Bath Wood
Auberies

CHURCH ROAD
Brakey Hill
Sewage Works
Bulmer St Andrews CE Prim Sch
OLD CHURCH LA
PARK LA
Moat

Hilly Plantation
Armsey Farm

Round Wood

Tiltscroft Wood

Middleton Hall

Middleton
THE STREET
Brakemoor Hill

RECTORY ROAD

40
2

Upper Houses
Hilltop Farm

OLD CHURCH LA
PH
Westborough Hill

Bulmer Tye
RYES LANE
Blacksmiths LA
A131

Home Lodge Wood Farm
Ryes Farm
Ryes Hall

Stour Valley Path

Sheepcot Farm
The Grove
ST EDMUNDS WAY

39
1
Henny Street
PH

Parsonage Wood
Bulmer End
Hole Farm
Tye Corner Farm
Almshouse Wood

Church (rems)

Apple Croft Farm
Coopersfield Wood
Old Applecroft Farm

For full street detail of the highlighted area see page 148.

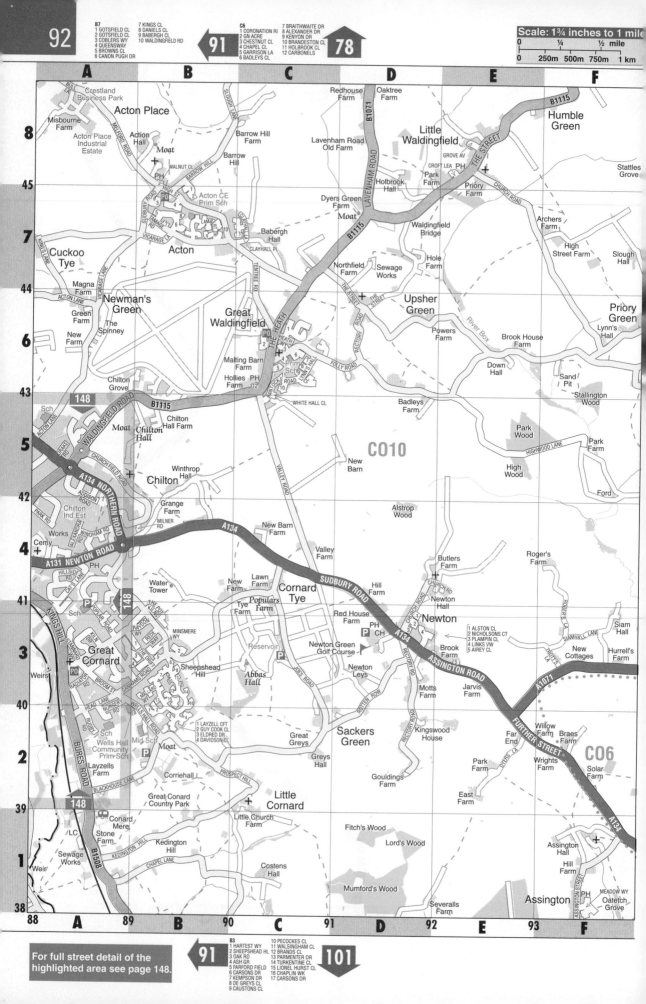

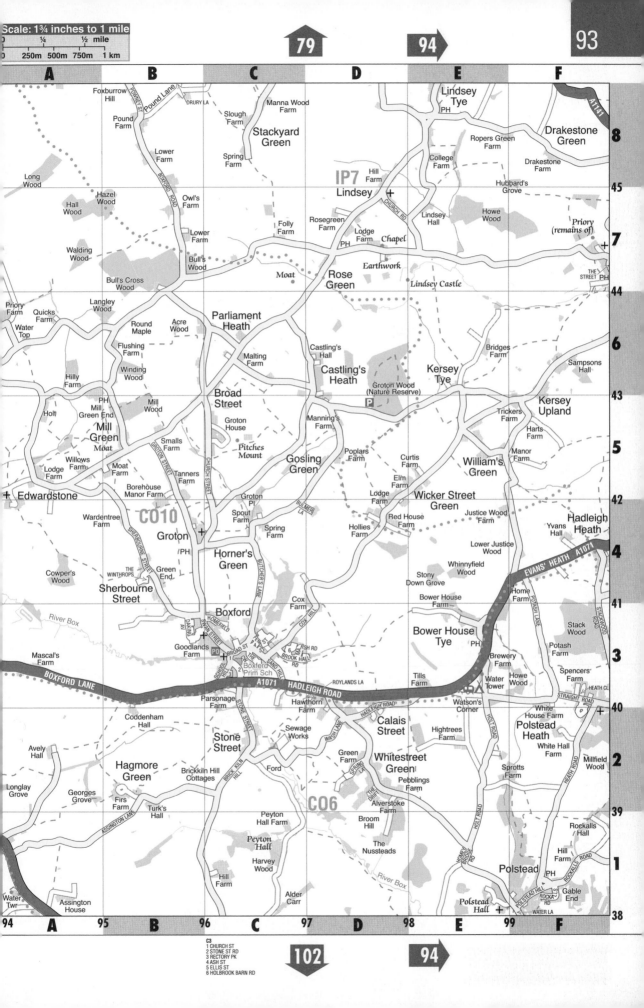

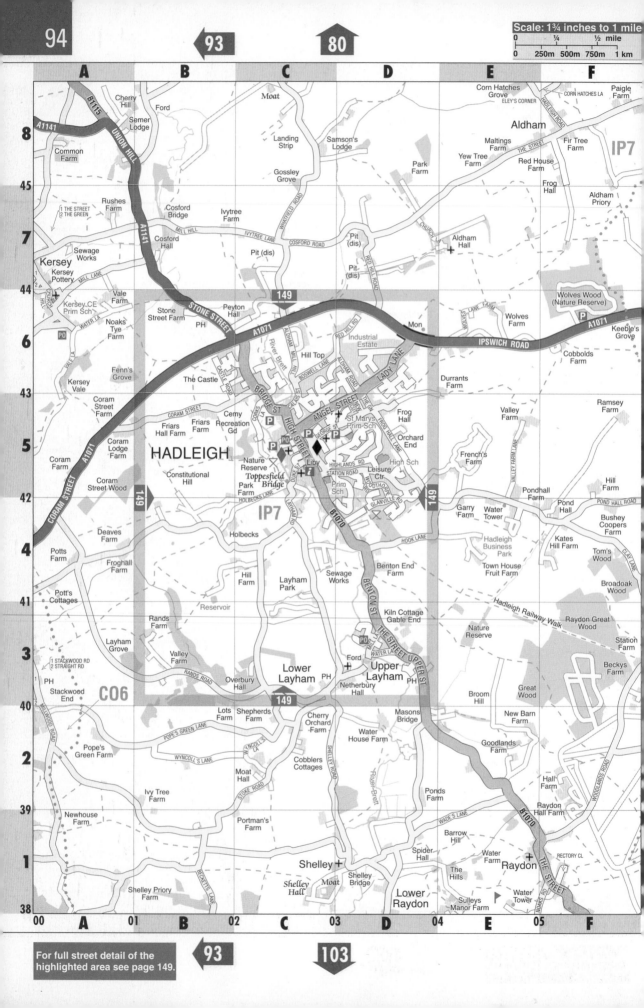

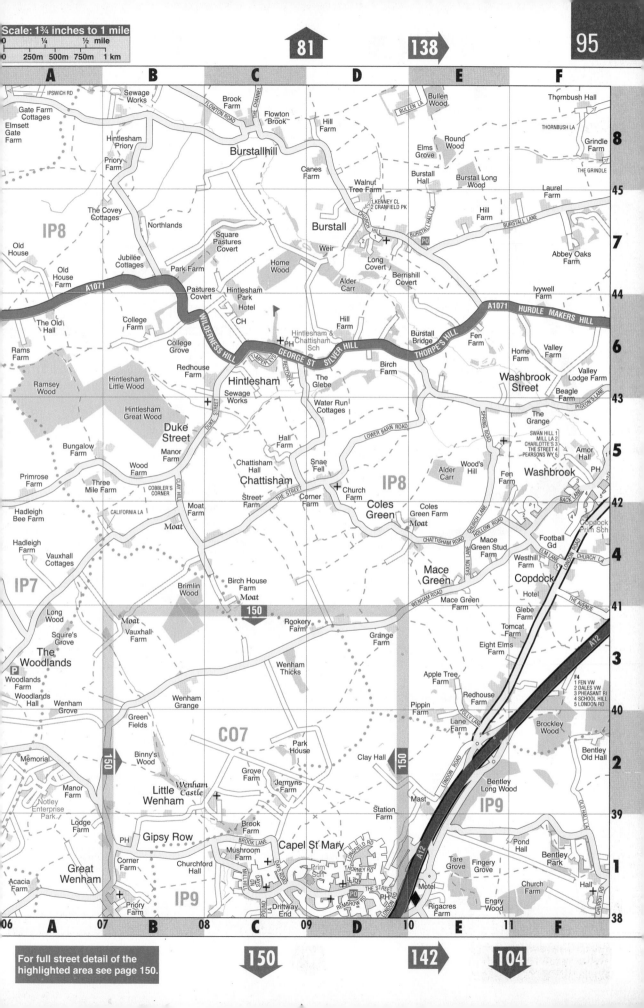

Scale: 1¾ inches to 1 mile

134 ◀ 95 135

For full street detail of the highlighted area see pages 138, 139, 142 and 143.

◀ 95   105

IPSWICH

Sproughton · Westbourne · Chantry · Stoke · Maidenhall · Stoke Park · Greenwich · Gainsborough · Belstead · Wherstead · Freston · Tattingstone White Horse

IP8 · IP1 · IP2 · IP3 · IP4 · IP9

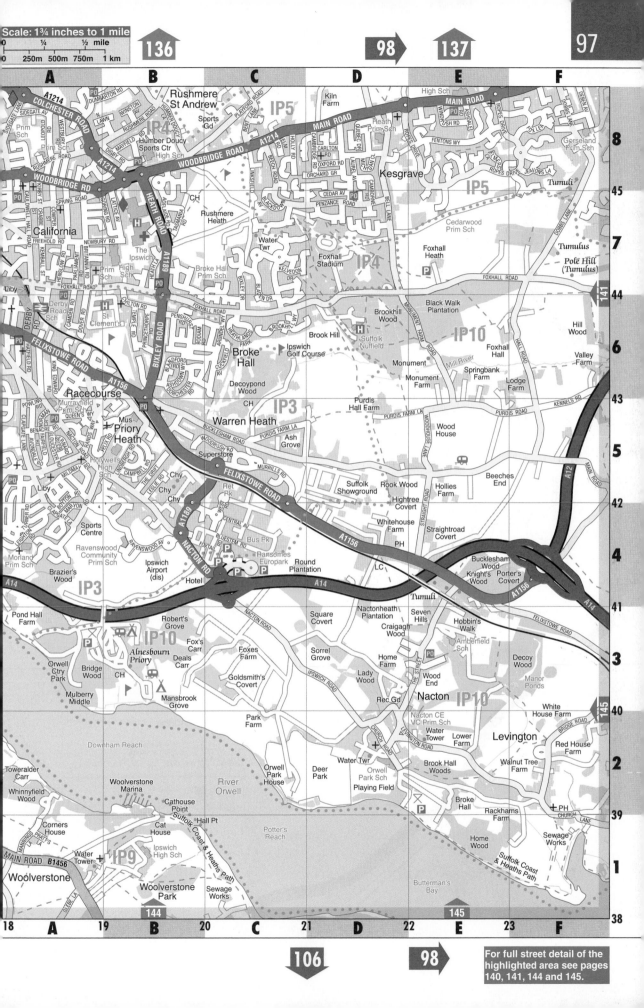

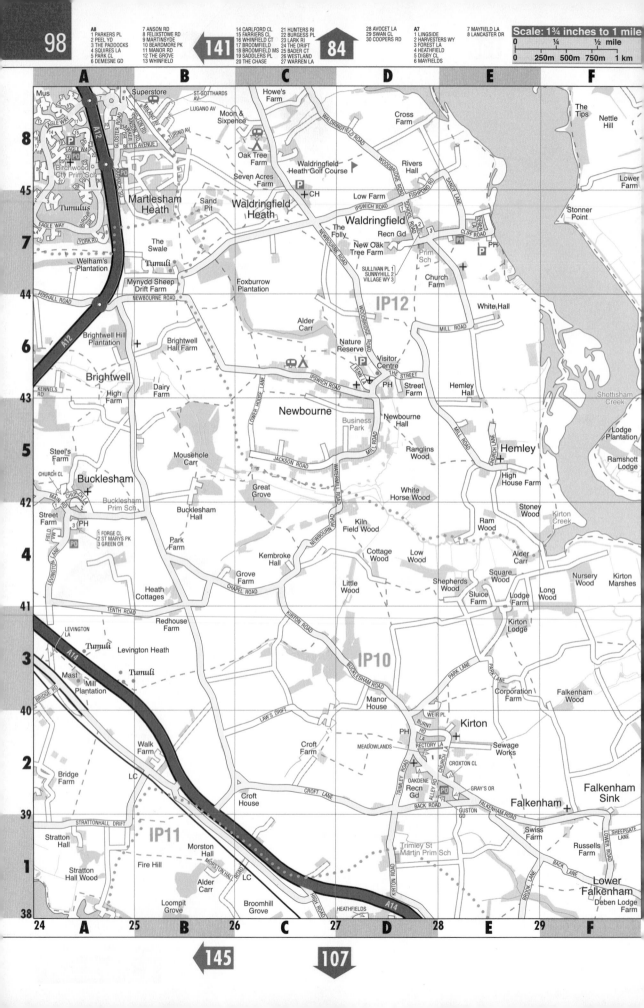

A8
1 PARKERS PL
2 PEEL YD
3 THE PADDOCKS
4 SQUIRES LA
5 PARK CL
6 DEMESNE GD

7 ANSON RD
8 FELIXSTOWE RD
9 MARTINSYDE
10 BEARDMORE PK
11 MANOR RD
12 THE GROVE
13 WHINFIELD

14 CARLFORD CL
15 FARRIERS CL
16 WHINFIELD CT
17 BROOMFIELD
18 BROOMFIELD MS
19 SADDLERS PL
20 THE CHASE

21 HUNTERS RI
22 BURGESS PL
23 LARK RI
24 THE DRIFT
25 BADER CT
26 WESTLAND
27 WARREN LA

28 AVOCET LA
29 SWAN CL
30 COOPERS RD

A7
1 LINGSIDE
2 HARVESTERS WY
3 FOREST LA
4 HEATHFIELD
5 DIGBY CL
6 MAYFIELDS

7 MAYFIELD LA
8 LANCASTER DR

Scale: 1¾ inches to 1 mile

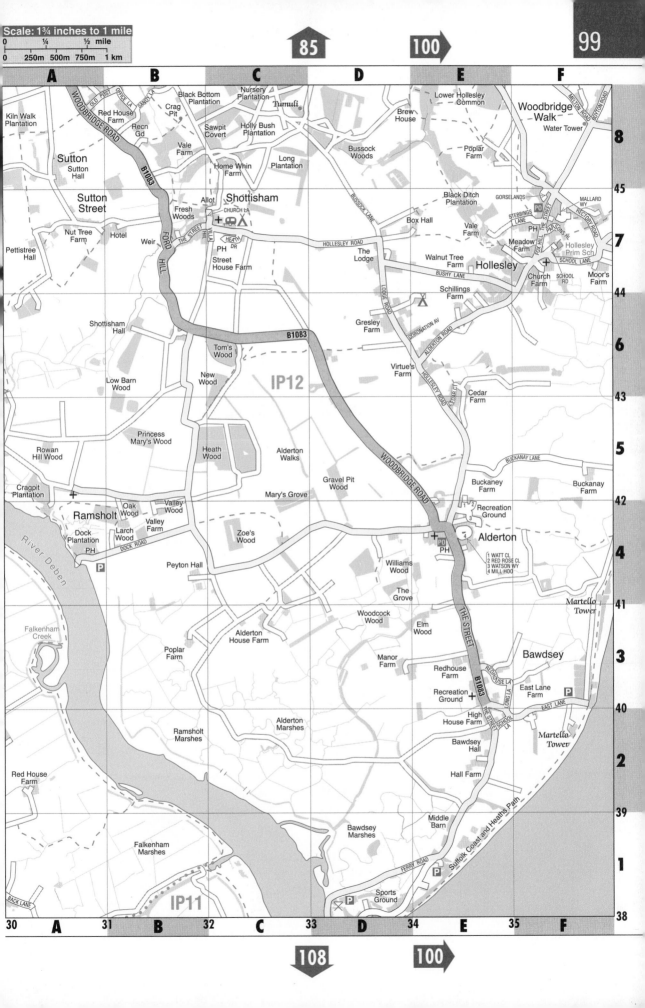

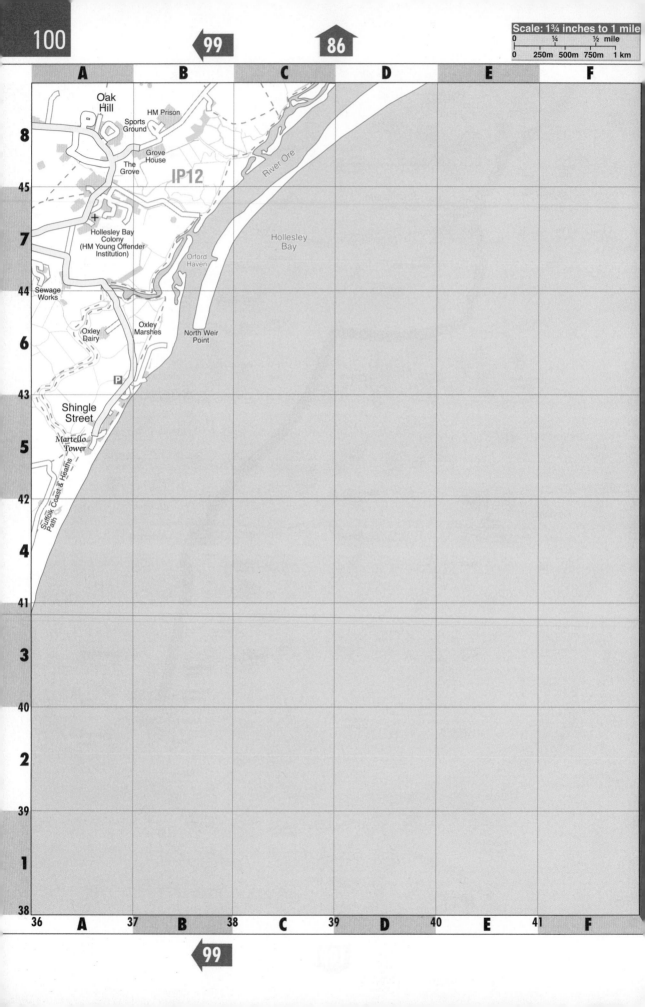

A   B   C   D   E   F

Oak Hill

HM Prison

Sports Ground

Grove House

The Grove

IP12

River Ore

45

Hollesley Bay

7

Hollesley Bay Colony
(HM Young Offender Institution)

Orford Haven

44

Sewage Works

Oxley Dairy

Oxley Marshes

North Weir Point

6

P

43

Shingle Street

Martello Tower

5

Suffolk Coast & Heaths Path

42

4

41

3

40

2

39

1

38

36   A   37   B   38   C   39   D   40   E   41   F

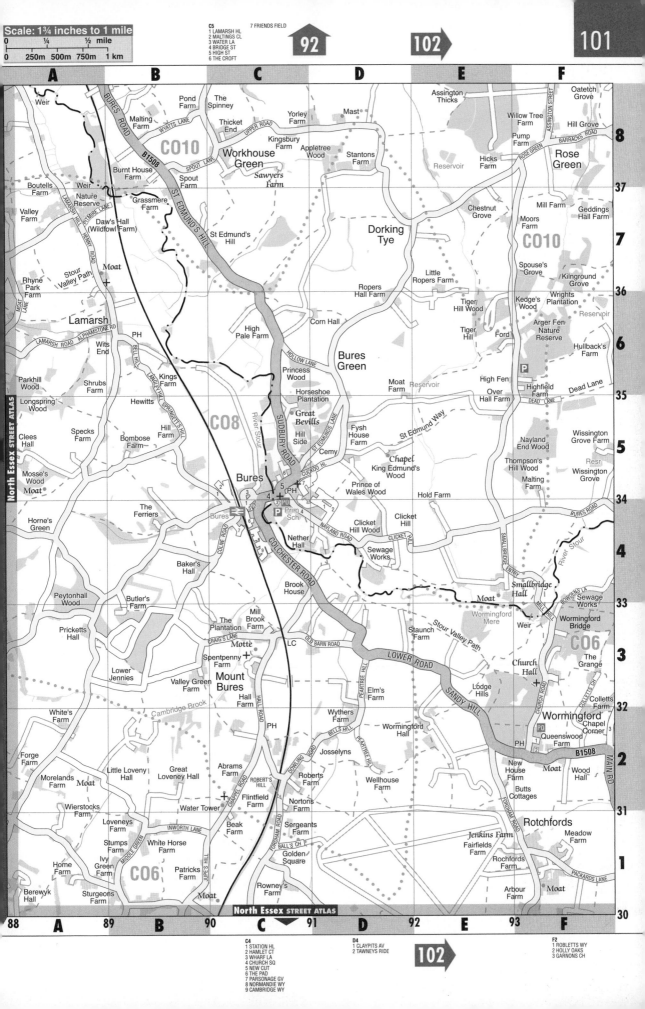

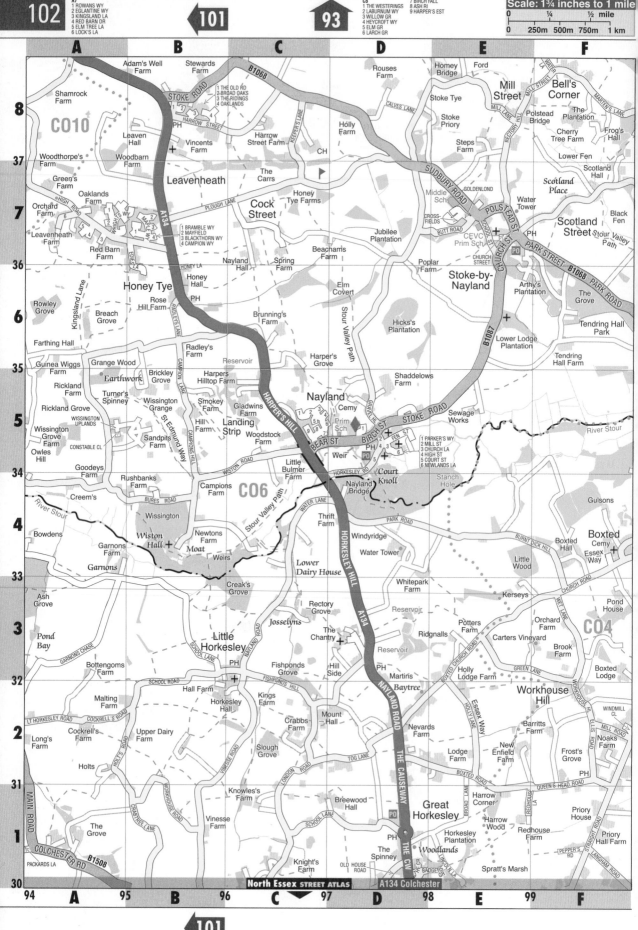

A7
1 ROWANS WY
2 EGLANTINE WY
3 KINGSLAND LA
4 RED BARN DR
5 ELM TREE LA
6 LOCK'S LA

101

93

C5
1 THE WESTERINGS
2 LABURNUM WY
3 WILLOW GR
4 HEYCROFT WY
5 ELM GR
6 LARCH GR

7 BIRCH FALL
8 ASH RI
9 HARPER'S EST

Scale: 1¾ inches to 1 mile

0   ¼   ½   mile
0   250m 500m 750m 1 km

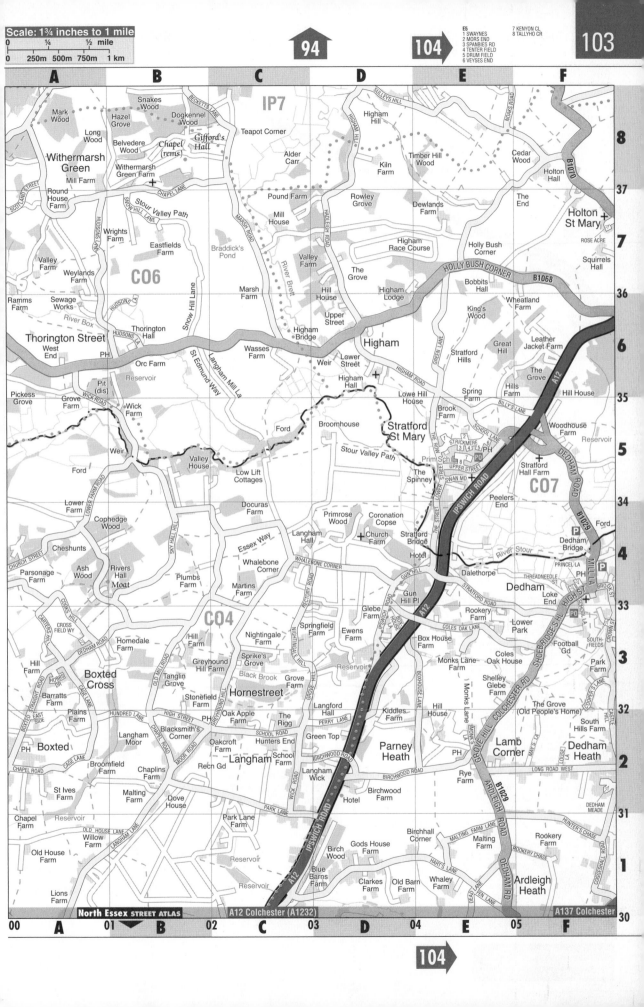

103 | 150 | 95

E4
1 PINE CL
2 GROVE RD
3 ASH GROUND CL
4 PATTERN BUSH CL
5 MERRIAM CL
6 WESTERN'S END

7 ROWLEY CL
8 HARDY CL
9 GRIMWADE CL
10 BROWNING RD
11 TEMPLE PATTLE
12 CATTAWADE ST

E5
1 BROOM KNOLL
2 THE DRIFT
3 THE POPLARS
4 VALLEY CL
5 SCHOOL LA
6 ELM CL

7 CEDAR CL
8 BIRCH DR
9 QUINCE CL
10 BLENHEIM CL

Scale bars: 0 ¼ ½ mile · 0 250m 500m 750m 1 km

Map labels

IP7 · Wenham Place · Sewage Works · Springhill · Capelgrove · Capelgrove Farm · RED LANE · A12 · White Horse Farm · Grove Farm · Potash · POTASH LAN · Church Road · Falslaff Manor

Wenham Hill · Lattinford Bridge · Boydland · Old London Road · Great Gilberts Farm · BLUEGATE LANE · Boynton Hall · Windy Farm · Berry Farm · Potash Farm · Bentley · Bentley CEVC Prim Sch · CASE LA

Oaks Farm · Lattinford Hill · Manor House · Hill Farm · Chaplain's Farm · IP9 · Tawneys Farm · Holly Wood · STATION ROAD · PH · PO · LC

Four Sisters Farm · WENHAM LANE · A12 · WOODGATES ROAD · CUTLERS LANE · Hustlers Grove · Great Martin's Hill Wood · Martins Hill Farm · Willow End · Bentley Grove · THE LINK 1 / LINK LA 2 · 1 HIGHFIELDS 2 SILVER LEYS 3 CHURCH RD 4 EAST MILL GN 5 SOUTH VIEW GN 6 WEST MILL GN

Four Sisters · Woodgates Farm · Sports Centre · Rookery Farm · Ford · Martins Glen · Dodnash Wood · Coppey Farm · Dodnash Coppey Farm

Hughes Corner · Road Covert · East Bergholt · HEATH RD · PITTICKS LANE · Meadow Farm · Ford · The Grange · Augustinian Priory · Dodnash Priory Farm · Little Charles New Plantation

Lodge Plantation · Allen's Farm · East Bergholt CE Prim Sch · GASTON END · MILL ROAD · Elm Farm · MISSION LA · Laurel Grove · East End · Church Barn Farm · Keeble's Grove · Willow Spinney

Ackworth House · Swimming Pool · CO7 · Whistler's Wood · Willowtree Farm · Highlands · Home Farm · EAST END ROAD · Woodlands Farm · GRAVEL PIT LANE · Mower's Spinney

Vale Farm · Cemy · PH · PO · Sports Gd · Smart's Wood · Park House · Park Farm · PARK ROAD · SLOUGH ROAD · Church Farm · CHURCH LANE · IPSWICH ROAD · THE CRESCENT

Fishpond Wood · Old Hall · PH · WHITE HORSE ROAD · RECTORY HILL · ORVIS LANE · Gardens · Warren Wood · Touchey's Lane · Braham Wood · Brookland Farm · Brantham · Brantham Glebe

St Edmund Way · Clapper Farm · FENBRIDGE LA · FLATFORD ROAD · Baker's End · Orvis Farm · Spooner's Wood · Braham Hall · Orchard End · BRANTHAM HILL · Brooklands · Sewage Works

Fen Bridge · Gossnalls Farm · Sewage Works · DAZELEY'S LANE · B1070 · BERGHOLT RD · Decoy Pond

Rare Breeds Farm · National Trust · Mus · Flatford Lock Mill · Valley Farm · Stour Valley Path · Braham Hall · PH · FACTORY LANE · Cattawade · Wks · F

Pound Farm · MANNINGTREE ROAD · Weirs · White Bridge · A137 · CAUSEWAY END 1 / NASH CL 2 / MUNNINGS WY 3 · Nature Reserve · F2 1 KILN LA 2 THE GREEN 3 THE LANE 4 SCHOOL LA

East House · Lower Barn Farm · St Edmund Way · Manningtree · LC · Hopping Bridge · Mistley Towers Craft Centre

Castle House · Dedham Heavy Horse Centre · Stour House · Tumulus · Lawford Hall · CO11 · B1352 · STATION RD · High St · PO · P · Superstore · THE WALLS · Mistley Place Park · HIGH STREET

PH · LIPES HILL · Hill Farm · Jupes Hill Farm · Mill Hill · DEDHAM ROAD · Lawford Hall · Bromley Corner · High Sch · Sports Ctr · Dale Hall · COLCHESTER RD · Liby · Mus · MILL HL · Mistley · Lawford · Chy · Recreation Ground · School Wood · 1 ANCHOR LA 2 THE CHASE 3 THE HEATH 4 COGGESHALL RD

LONG RD WEST · LONG RD EAST · Essex Way · Birchetts Wood · WIGNALL ST · CHURCH HILL · COX'S HILL · LONG RD · B1352 · Mistley Wood · Long Plantation · Laundry Wood · Mistley Hall · Furze Hill · Manningtree

Keepers End · BARGATE LANE · Heath Farm · Bargate Farm · FOXWOOD CL · HARWICH ROAD · Recreation Ground · 1 SCHOOL LA 2 CLAUDE OLIVER CL 3 MILTON RD · NEW RD · Dairy Wood · B1035

Great Hickle Farm · TILE BARN LANE · KINGSDOWN LANE · Lower Farm · Glanfields · GRANGE ROAD · BROMLEY ROAD · Lawford House · DEAD LANE · Aldhams Farm · CHEQUERS ROAD · Mistley Hall · CLACTON ROAD · Beech Plantation

Cherry Tree Farm · A137 · Foxash Estate · Grange Farm · Lawfordhouse Farm · Aldhams · Stacies Farm · Ford Farm · Brickkiln Grove

For full street detail of the highlighted area see pages 150 and 151.

103

D2
1 TURNER AV
2 KEATING CL
3 CONSTABLE CL
4 FITZGERALD CL
5 BURROWS CL
6 BARKER CL
7 BLAKE CL
8 COTMAN AV
9 STUBBS CL

10 STANTON HUGHES WY
11 DIXON CL
12 SITWELL CL
13 CORNFORD WY
14 LODGATE CL
15 EDGEFIELD AV
16 SPRINGBANK AV
17 MERIVALE RD
18 SEATON CL
19 HUNTER DR

20 LINDEN CL
21 CAVENDISH DR
22 MEADWAY
23 WALDEGRAVE CL
24 NICHOLS CL
25 CORNWALL CL
26 PARRINGTON WY
27 STOURDALE CL

E2
1 KINGS CL
2 VICTORIA CR
3 QUEENSWAY
4 THE ROOKERY
5 LUSHINGTON RD
6 KNIGHTS CL
7 HARVEY CL
8 TAYLOR CL
9 SKELTON CL

10 COLCHESTER RD
11 NORTH ST
12 SOUTH ST
13 QUAY ST
14 ERSKINE RD
15 HILTON CL
16 ST MICHAELS CT
17 STOUR ST
18 MILL LA
19 RAILWAY ST

20 REGENT ST
21 FALKLANDS CL
22 MALTHOUSE RD
23 NORMAN RD
24 PARSONS YD
25 OXFORD RD
26 BARNFIELD
27 THE CHASE
28 TRINITY CL
29 ELMDALE DR

30 CEDAR CR
31 THE BEECHES

E3
1 SOUTH STRAND
2 GREENSMILL
3 COMMERCE WY
4 RIVERSIDE AVENUE W
5 JUBILEE END
6 RIVERSIDE AVENUE E

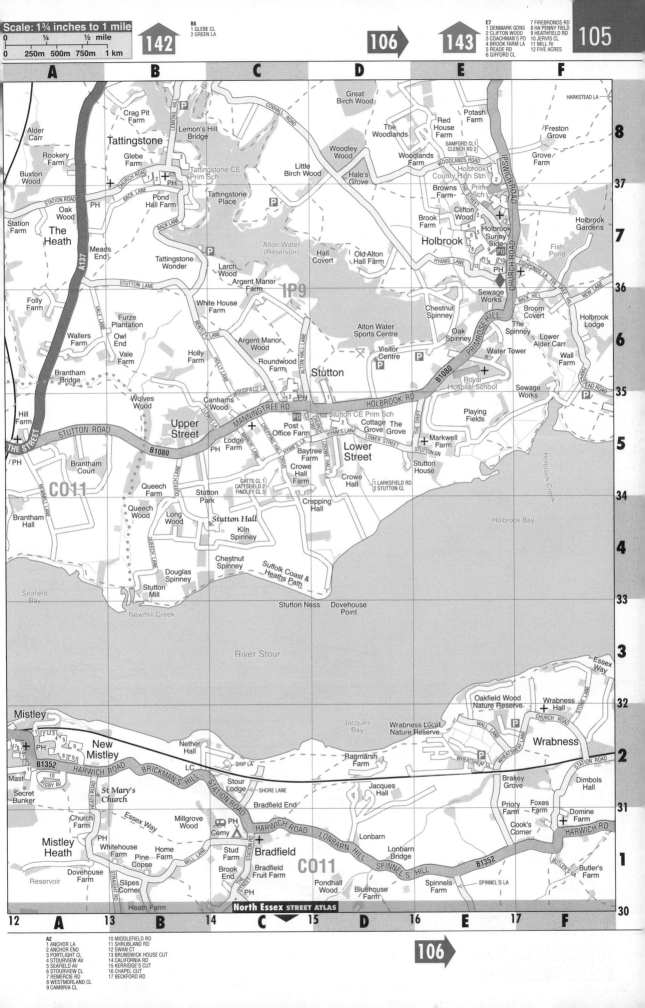

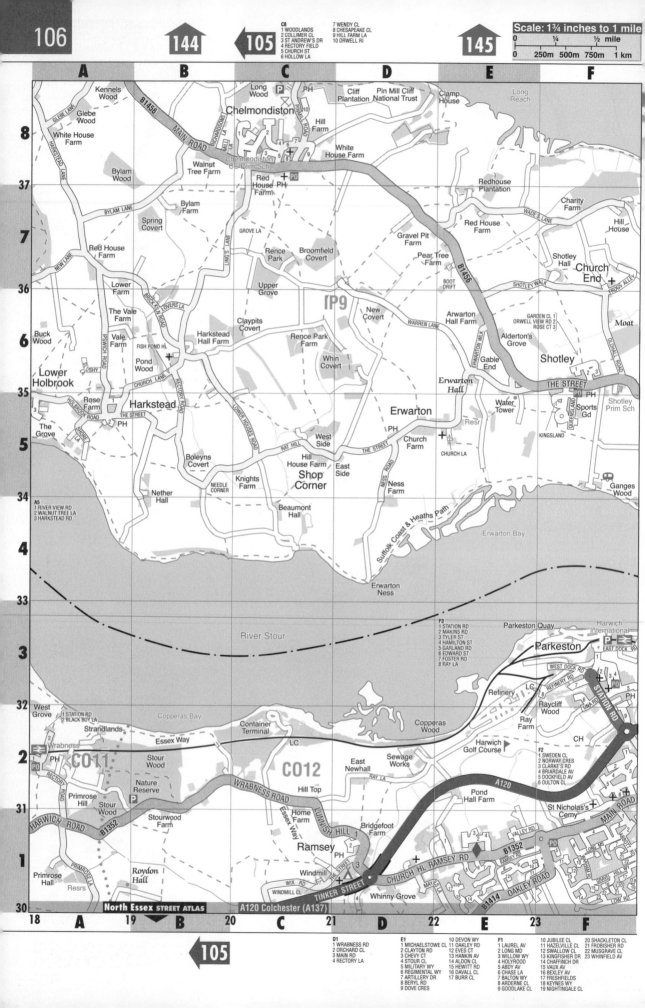

Scale: 1¾ inches to 1 mile

| 0 | ¼ | ½ mile |
| 0 | 250m | 500m | 750m | 1 km |

A5
1 CHILDERS CL
2 GATE FARM RD
3 TUDOR CL
4 BLAKE AV
5 KITCHENER WY
6 HERVEY CL

7 LINK RD

D8
1 MILL CL
2 HIGH HALL CL
3 RED HOUSE CL
4 CAPEL CL
5 SANDY CL
6 CROWSWELL CT

7 CRAIG CL
8 MEADOW CL
9 JASMINE CL
10 ASH GROUND CL
11 JUBILEE CL
12 HEATH CT
13 BLUE BARN CL

14 ST MARTINS GN
15 BRICK KILN CL

98   108

For full street detail of the
highlighted area see page 152.

107

Marina
Little Grove
Loompit Grove
Loompit Lake

Jill's Hole
Collimer Pt
Suffolk Coast & Heaths Path
Twelve Acre Covert
Crane's Hill
Lower Reach

Broomhill Grove
Little Grove
LC
Thorpe Common
Goslings Farm
Florys Farm
Trimley Lower Street
Grimston Hall
THORPE LANE
GRIMSTON LANE
Sports Gd
Trimley St Martin
PO
CHURCH LA
Trimley St Mary
Prim Sch
LC
IP10
Capel Hall Lane
CAPEL HALL LA
Capel Hall
BROOK LA
KIRTON RD
CAPEL HALL LANE
A14
Egypt Wood
Candlet Farm
Hill House Farm
Gulpher Business Park
152

River Orwell

Cuttings Grove
Kiln Grove
Painter's Wood
Trimley Marshes
Salter's Wood
Searson's Farm
Garden Wood
Searsons Farm
Trimley
Chapman's Grove
Clickett Hill
IP11
152
CANDLET RD
GULPHER RD
Walton
Sch
Sch
Cemy
Deben High Sch
FELIXSTOWE
Superstore
Sch
152
35

Shotley Marshes
Fagbury Point
Shotley Point
Marina
IP9
Sports Gd
Over Hall
Martello Tower
HMS Ganges Mus
Martello Tower
Container Park
PARKER AV
TRINITY AV
A154
PORT OF FELIXSTOWE
Container Park
FERRY LANE
WALTON AV
A154
WALTON AV
Leisure Centre
LANGER RD
Suffolk Coast & Heaths Path
GARRISON LA
34

Shotley Gate
A4
1 GANGES RD
2 BAKER RD
3 LLOYD RD
4 LOWER HARLINGS
5 ESTUARY CRES
6 BROADWATER GDNS
7 ESTUARY RD
8 CALEDONIA RD
9 SCHOOL RD
10 BATTERY LA
PH
BRISTOL HILL
KING EDWARD VII DR
Harwich Harbour
Ferry P
Ferry P

B3
1 THE QUAY
2 GEORGE ST
3 CHURCH LA
4 GEORGE ST
5 GOLDEN LION LA
6 ALBEMARLE ST
7 MARIA ST
8 ALEXANDRA ST
9 FERNLEA RD

Ha'penny Pier Visitor Centre
WEST ST
Harwich Town
Bath Side
Tower Hill
High Lighthouse Wireless Museum
Low Lighthouse Maritime Mus

C3
1 ST AUSTIN'S LA
2 KING'S HEAD ST
3 MARKET ST
4 ANGELGATE ESPLANADE
5 CHURCH ST
6 WELLINGTON RD
7 HARBOUR CRES
8 MAYFLOWER AV

Ship Ferry (Vehicular) Terminal
Freightliner Terminal
CARR RD
MANOR RD
MANOR TR
Landguard Common
IP11
E3
1 CARR RD
2 ADASTRAL CL
3 DOCK RD
33

HARWICH
Dovercourt
A120
Cemy
CO12
Superstore
B1352
HIGH ST
MARINE PD
Liby
1 BEACON HILL AV
2 BARRACK LA
Landguard Fort
Felixstowe Museum
Landguard Nature Reserve
Landguard Fort
32

Dovercourt
FRONK'S ROAD
B1414
Lower Marine Parade
B1
1 BEACH RD
2 ST GEORGE'S AV
3 FRONK'S AV
4 ST MICHAEL'S RD
Landguard Point
31

Dovercourt Swimming Pool
Promenade
North Essex STREET ATLAS
108
30

A1
1 DEANE'S CL
2 WILLIAM GROOM AV
3 ALLFIELDS
4 QUEEN'S RD
5 GORDON RD
6 SEAFIELD RD
7 KRESWELL GV
8 RICHMOND CRES
9 REBOW RD
10 HUDSON CL
11 ST DENIS CL
12 ST EDMUNDS CL
13 LOUVAIN RD
14 BRUGES CL
15 BRUSSELS CL
16 WEST END LA

A2
1 HARCOURT AV
2 THE VINEWAY
3 KING GEORGE'S AV
4 SHAFTESBURY AV
5 LARKSFIELD CRES
6 DEEPDALE RD
7 FRYATT AV
8 POUND FARM DR
9 THE CLOSE
10 THE RIDGEWAY
11 DOUGLAS RD
12 PRINCES RD
13 OLD VICARAGE RD
14 MANOR LA
15 ELIZABETH RD
16 GRANGE RD
17 NEWTON RD

B2
1 INGESTRE ST
2 GRAFTON RD
3 PARK RD
4 GWYNNE RD
5 WADDESDON RD
6 EAST ST
7 VICTORIA ST
8 STATION RD
9 KINGSWAY
10 ORWELL RD
11 AY RD
12 MARINE PARADE
13 STATION LA
14 BROOKLYN RD
15 OAKLAND RD
16 PORTLAND AV
17 ELMHURST RD

108

For full street detail of Harwich see Philip's
STREET ATLAS of North Essex

107
99

Scale: 1¾ inches to 1 mile

0	¼	½ mile
0	250m 500m 750m	1 km

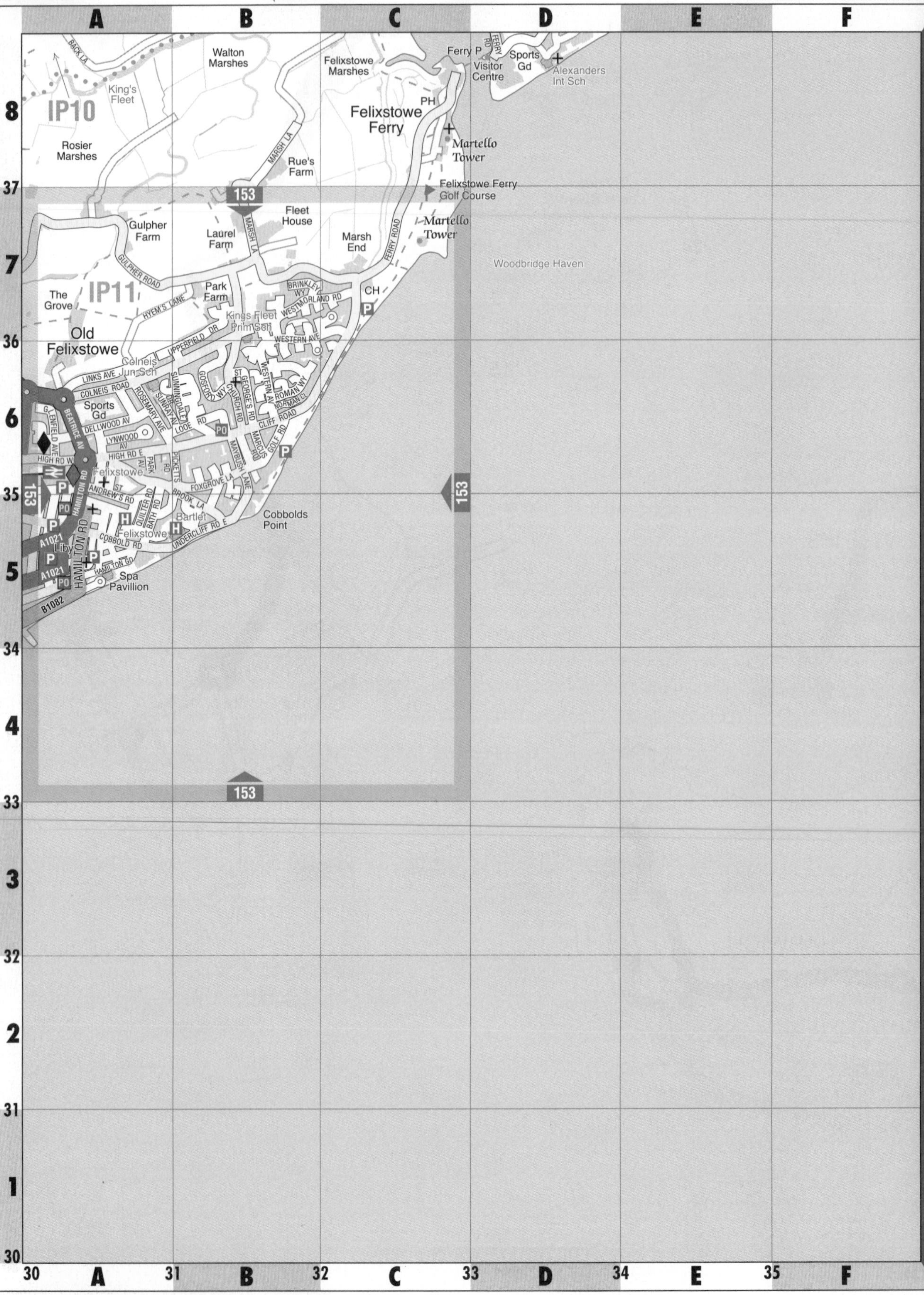

A   **B**   **C**   **D**   **E**   **F**

BACK LA

Walton Marshes

Felixstowe Marshes

Ferry P

Sports Gd

8

King's Fleet

MARSH LA

Felixstowe Ferry Visitor Centre

PH

Alexanders Int Sch

IP10

Rosier Marshes

Rue's Farm

Felixstowe Ferry

Martello Tower

37

153

Fleet House

Felixstowe Ferry Golf Course

Gulpher Farm

Laurel Farm

Marsh End

Martello Tower

7

GULPHER ROAD

IP11

Park Farm

FERRY ROAD

Woodbridge Haven

The Grove

HYEM'S LANE

BRINKLEY WY

WESTMORLAND RD

CH P

Kings Fleet Prim Sch

36

Old Felixstowe

UPPERFIELD DR

WESTERN AVE

Colneis Jun Sch

LINKS AVE

COLNEIS ROAD

SUNNINGDALE WY

GOSFORD WY

CHURCH RD

GEORGE'S RD

ROMAN EL

Sports Gd

ROSEMARY AVE

SUNRAY AV

LOOE RD

CLIFF ROAD

6

DELLWOOD AV

LYNWOOD AV

HIGH RD E

PARK RD

MARCUS RD

GOLF RD

P

GLENFIELD AVE

BEATRICE AV

PICKETTS

MARSH LANE

FOXGROVE LA

HIGH RD W

Felixstowe

ST ANDREW'S RD

QUILTER RD

BROOK LA

Cobbolds Point

35

153

HAMILTON RD

BATH RD

HAMILTON GD

H

H

Bartlet

UNDERCLIFF RD E

153

A1021

Libv

COBBOLD RD

P

5

A1021

P

Spa Pavillion

B1082

34

4

33

153

3

32

2

31

1

30

30		31		32		33		34		35	
	A		**B**		**C**		**D**		**E**		**F**

107

For full street detail of the highlighted area see page 153.

A B C D E F

8

First Drove
Grime Fen
Old Nursery Plantation
Plantation Farm
North Fen
Poors Fen

Newren Gravel Dro
Sharper's Corner
Station Road
Drift Road
B1112

Highbridge Gravel Drove
Middle Covert
Home Farm

Millmarsh Dv
Sharpes Cr
Meadow Dr
Woodlands
Birch Cr
Barr Dr
Cornfield Cl
Larch Cl

7

Mutford Gn
Elm Cl
Quayside Ct
Hall-Fields
Arrowhead
Delph Rd
Woodcutters Wy
Woodcut
Wingfield Av
Breckland

PH
Halfmoon La
Palmer Dr
Mayfields
Wingfield Rd
Lakenheath
Sharper's Cr
Dumpling Bridge La

83

Cemy
Football Gd
Wings Road
Cross La Cl
Cemetery Road
Maids Cross Hill
Landfill Site
Maids Cross Wy

Turf Fen
Anchor La
PO
P
Lakenheath Prim. Sch.
Highfields Dr
Covey Wy
Covey Dr
Maidscross Hill

6

Brewers Cl
Liby
Mill Road
Lilac Dr
Sandgalls Rd
Pashford Cl
Highfields
Covey Wy

Lakenheath's Poor's Fen
Springfield Dr
Roughlands
Back St
The Firs
Pits (dis)

Undely Bridge
Weir
Hotel
High Street
Warren Cl
Broom Rd Cl
The Elders
Broom Road

The Mallands
Eriswell Drive

5

IP27
Curlew Cl
B1112
Eriswell Dr
Lime Cl
Eriswell Dr

Turf Fen
82

Roebuck Dr
Gorse Cl
Caudle Av
Caudle

Compass Cl
North Rd

4

Undely Road
Bridge Farm
Claypits
Eriswell Road
Ave Rd
Albert Rolph Dr

Cupola Farm
South Road

Caudle Farm
Lakenheath Airfield
3

Ash Tree Farm
81

Church (rems)
Halfmoon Plantation
2

Eriswell Hall Farm
Mast
Lakenheath American High Sch

Nursery Plantation
Exeter Crescent
Brandon Street
Ipswich St
Norwich Rd
Windsor

1

The Delph
High Fen
B1112
Halifax St
Hull St
Dudley
Windsor

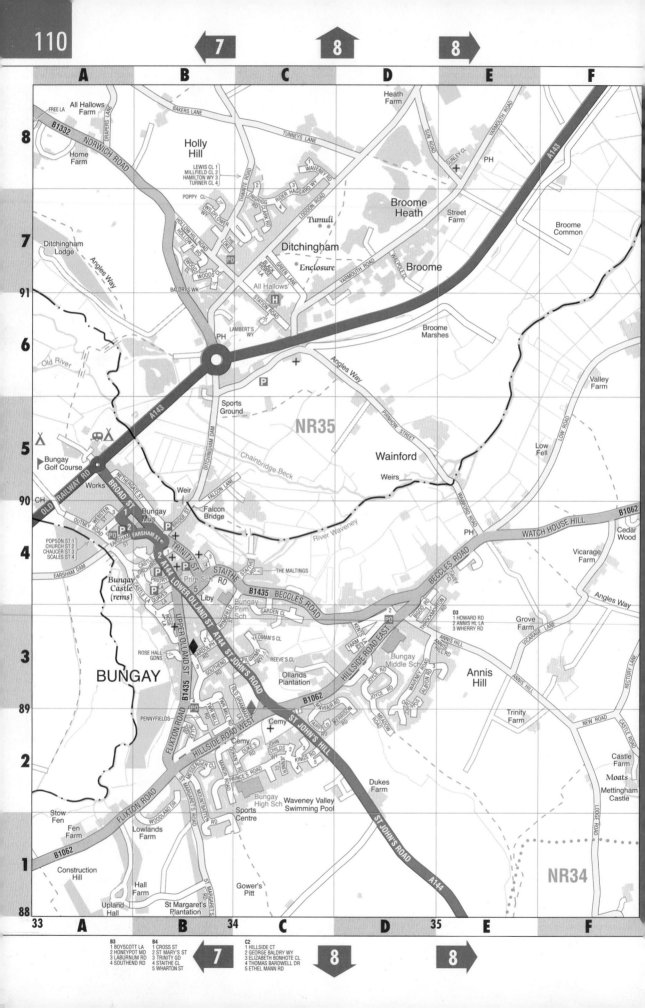

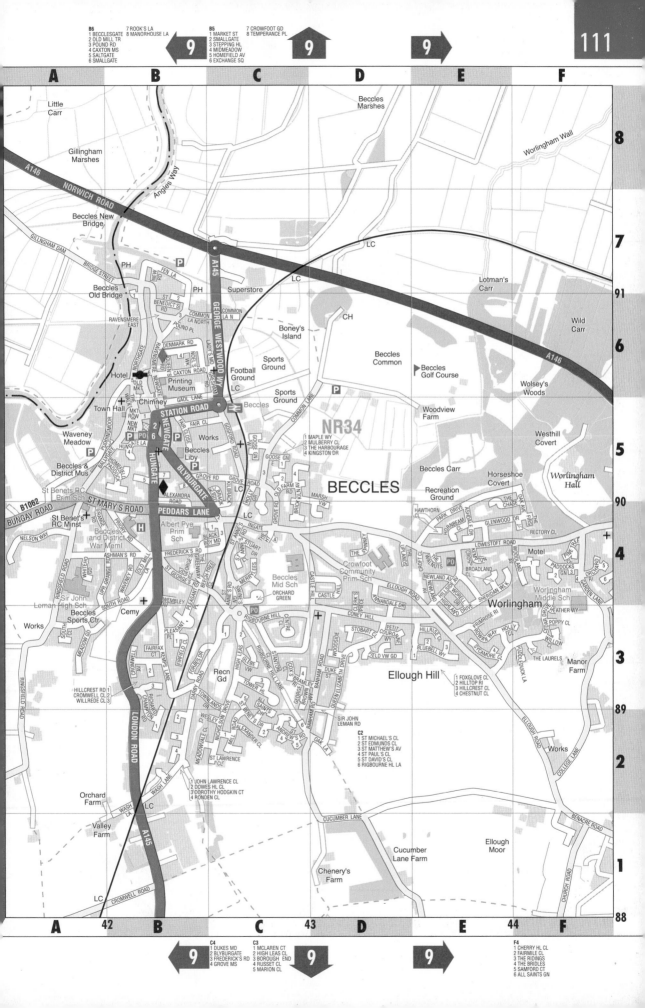

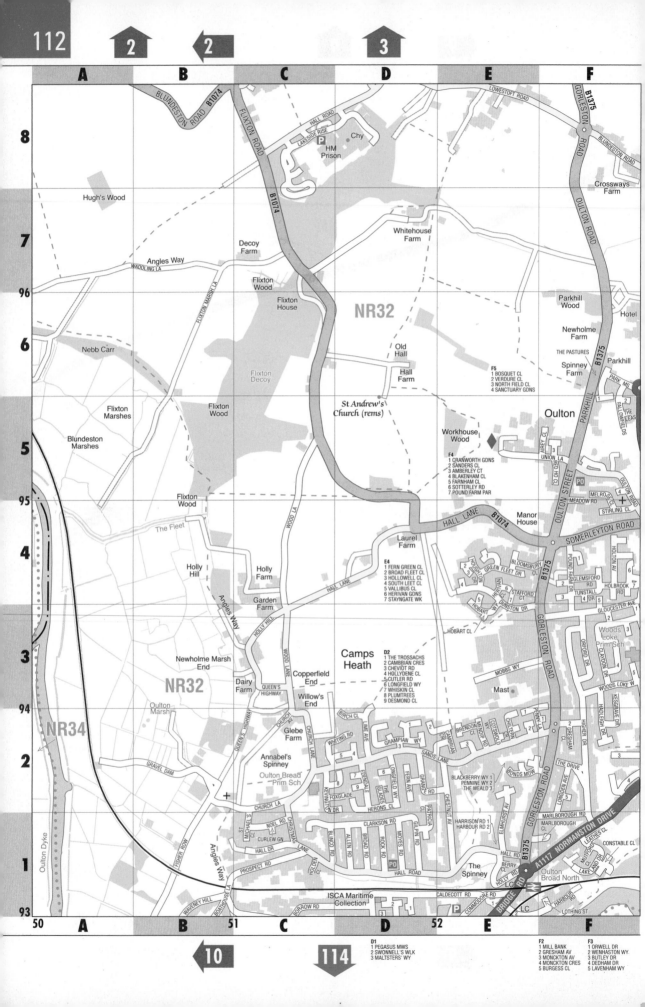

A **B** **C** **D** **E** **F**

8
7
96
6
5
95
4
4
3
94
2
1
93

BLUNDESTON ROAD B1074
FLIXTON ROAD
LOWESTOFT ROAD
GORLESTON ROAD B1375
BLUNDESTON ROAD
Crossways Farm

HALL ROAD
LAKESIDE RISE
P
HM Prison
Chy

B1074

Hugh's Wood

Decoy Farm
Angles Way
WADDLING LA

Whitehouse Farm

NR32

Parkhill Wood

Hotel

Flixton Wood

Flixton House

Newholme Farm
THE PASTURES

Nebb Carr

Old Hall

Spinney Farm Parkhill

Flixton Decoy

Hall Farm

F5
1 BOSQUET CL
2 VERDURE CL
3 NORTH FIELD CL
4 SANCTUARY GDNS

B1375
PARK MS
THE PLEAS
FALLOWFIELDS

Flixton Marshes

Flixton Wood

St Andrew's Church (rems)

Oulton

Blundeston Marshes

Workhouse Wood

F4
1 CRANWORTH GDNS
2 SANDERS CL
3 AMBERLEY CT
4 BLAKENHAM CL
5 FARNHAM CL
6 SOTTERLEY RD
7 POUND FARM PAR

AIREY CL
UNION LA
PO
MELRO
MEADOW RD
STIRLING CL

Flixton Wood

The Fleet

WOOD LA

Laurel Farm

HALL LANE B1074

Manor House

SOMERLEYTON ROAD

Holly Hill

Holly Farm

HALL LANE

E4
1 FERN GREEN CL
2 BROAD FLEET CL
3 HOLLOWELL CL
4 SOUTH LEET CL
5 VALLIBUS CL
6 HERIVAN GDNS
7 STAYNGATE WK

HOLTON DR
GREEN FLEET DR
BLOOMSBURY
STAFFORD CT
HOBART
DUNSTON DR

HOLTON AV
GLEMSFORD RD
HOLBROOK RD
TUNSTALL
GLOUCESTER AVE

Angles Way

Garden Farm

HOBART CL

B1375

Woods Loke Prim Sch

Newholme Marsh End

NR32

Dairy Farm

QUEEN'S HIGHWAY

Copperfield End

Camps Heath

D2
1 THE TROSSACHS
2 CAMBRIAN CRES
3 CHEVIOT RD
4 HOLLYDENE CL
5 CUTLER RD
6 LONGFIELD WY
7 WHISKIN CL
8 PLUMTREES
9 DESMOND CL

MOBBS WY

Mast

ORFORD RD
CLAYTON RD
WOODS LOKE W

NR34

Oulton Marsh

Willow's End

WOOD LANE

GORLESTON ROAD
PENLA
KESGRAVE DR
HADLEIGH DR

Oulton Dyke

GRAVEL DAM

Glebe Farm

CHURCH LANE

Annabel's Spinney

Oulton Broad Prim Sch

BIRCH CL
LIME AVE
GRAMPIAN WY
SANDS LANE
CAMBRIAN
BRENDON
MENDIP RD
COTSWOL
CHILTERN

Blackberry Wy 1
Pennine Wy 2
The Weald 3

PONDS MDW

THE DRIVE

MARLBOROUGH RD
Marlborough CL
CONSTABLE CL

WHITING RD
EVERDALE
THE GLADES
FERN AVE
GRANGE RD
PATRICIA

LONGDEN AVE
GRESHAM
ELMHURST AV

FOXGLADE
HERONS CL
KEVINGTON DR

Harrison Rd 1
Harbour Rd 2

FISHER ROW

Angles Way

ST MICHAEL'S
NOEL RD
CHRISTMAS LANE

CLARKSON RD
BLINCO RD
ALLEN RD
BROAD RD
ROCK RD
MOYES RD
GILPIN RD
CHESTNUT RD

HALL RD
BERRY
HOLLY RD
LC RD

CURLEW GN
HALL DR
PROSPECT RD
HOLDEN RD
HALL ROAD
PO

The Spinney

A1117 NORMANSTON DRIVE
B1375
Oulton Broad North
LAKE
MUTFORD
LAND DR
CONSTABLE CL

WAVENEY HILL
BROADHOUSE LA
BORROW RD

ISCA Maritime Collection

CALDECOTT RD
COMMODORE RD
P
BRIDGE RD
LC
LOTHING ST
HARBOUR

50 51 52

A **B** **C** **D** **E** **F**

B5
1 MONET SQ
2 RENOIR PL
3 KNIGHTSWOOD
4 VILLAGE WY
5 PLEASUREWOOD CL
6 ASTBURY RD

A6
1 GREENWOOD WY
2 LEONARD DR
3 STIMPSON CL
4 WAINWRIGHT CL
5 QUINNELL WY

B6
1 DEGAS GDNS
2 HOLBEIN WY
3 COTMAN CL
4 CANALETTO CL
5 VERMEER CL
6 ROMNEY PL
7 BURWOOD PL
8 HOGARTH WLK
9 VAN DYCK CL

C6
1 MURILLO DR
2 HUBBARD'S AV
3 REMBRANDT CL
4 TURNER CL

E3
1 CART SCORE
2 LIGHTHOUSE SCORE
3 ST MARGARET'S RD
4 OSBORNE ST
5 CAMDEN ST

E2
1 ALBANY RD
2 MARINERS ST
3 COMPASS ST
4 WHITE HORSE ST
5 CROWN ST EAST
6 DUKES HEAD ST
7 HIGH ST
8 OLD MARKET PLAIN
9 TRIANGLE YARD
10 ST PETER'S ST
11 ARTILLERY WY
12 SPURGEON SCORE
13 CUMBERLAND PLACE

E1
1 CHRIST CHURCH SQ
2 HERRING FISHERY SCORE
3 ARNOLD ST
4 OLD NELSON ST
5 BATTERY GREEN RD
6 MARINA
7 BATTERY GN

C1
1 THE CROFT
2 UNION RD
3 STANFORD ST
4 TRAFALGAR ST

A3
1 PEMBROOKE WY
2 COLLEGE MWS
3 MAGDALEN CL
4 FASTOLF CL
5 CHATSWORTH CL
6 RINGSFIELD RD
7 CAVENDISH CL
8 WALBERSWICK WY

A4
1 CULZEAN GDNS
2 ASHNESS CL
3 PATTERDALE GDNS
4 KIRKSTONE WY
5 DERWENT GDNS
6 SNAPE DR
7 WORLINGHAM PK
8 LULWORTH PK
9 PENTLAND WLK

B2
1 GREENACRE CRES
2 BROOM RD
3 MAGNOLIA CT
4 MARHAM RD
5 NORMANSTON DR
6 MYRTLE CL
7 NORMANSTON DR
8 SOUTH VIEW CL

B4
1 FROSTENDEN CRES
2 SPASHETT RD
3 CRISP CL
4 HOPELYN CL
5 CASTLETON CL
6 GODETIA CT

C2
1 NEWSON'S MW
2 NICHOLSON SQ
3 CROWN MEADOW WLK
4 LATTENS SQ

D1
1 ETHEL RD
2 RAGLAN RD
3 CLAPHAM RD CENTRAL
4 LEISTON RD
5 POLICE STATION RD
6 SURREY ST
7 RISHTON RD
8 SUMMER RD
9 CAMP RD

D2
1 CLARENCE RD
2 THE HEMPLANDS
3 THURSTON RD
4 ST PETER'S ST
5 ARNOLD ST
6 ADRIAN RD
7 JACOBS ST
8 CATHCART ST

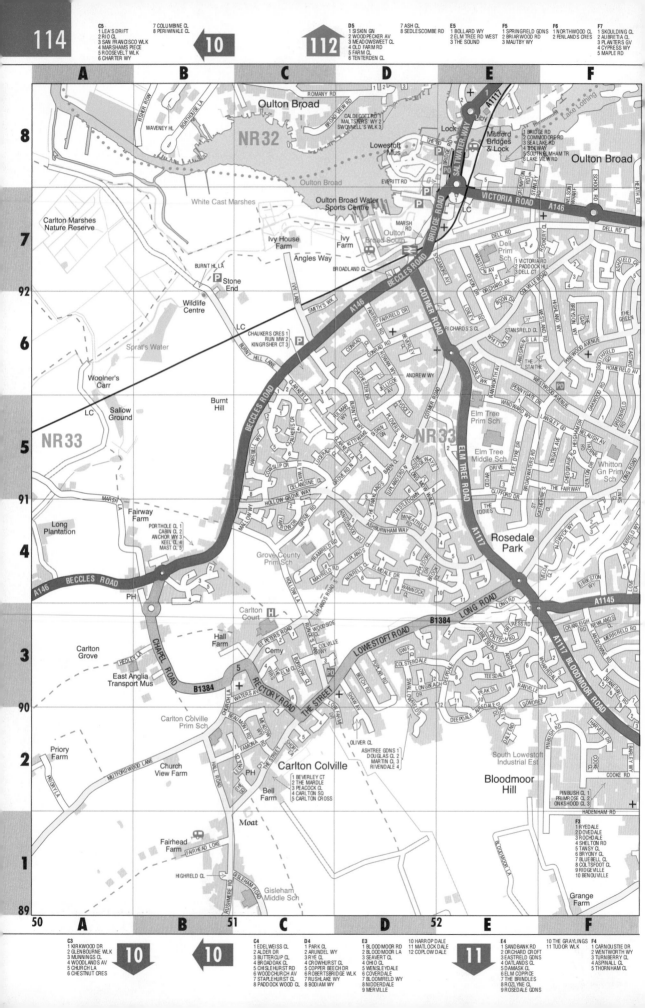

10

112

10

Oulton Broad
NR32
Carlton Marshes Nature Reserve
White Cast Marshes
Oulton Broad Water Sports Centre
Ivy House Farm
Ivy Farm
Oulton Broad South
Angles Way
Stone End
Wildlife Centre
Sprat's Water
Woolner's Carr
Sallow Ground
Burnt Hill
NR33
Long Plantation
Fairway Farm
Grove County Prim Sch
Carlton Court
Hall Farm
Carlton Grove
East Anglia Transport Mus
Carlton Colville Prim Sch
Priory Farm
Church View Farm
Bell Farm
Carlton Colville
Moat
Fairhead Farm
Gisleham Middle Sch
Elm Tree Prim Sch
Elm Tree Middle Sch
Whitton Gn Prim Sch
Rosedale Park
South Lowestoft Industrial Est
Bloodmoor Hill
Grange Farm
Lowestoft Mus
Mutford Bridges & Lock
Oulton Broad

10

10

11

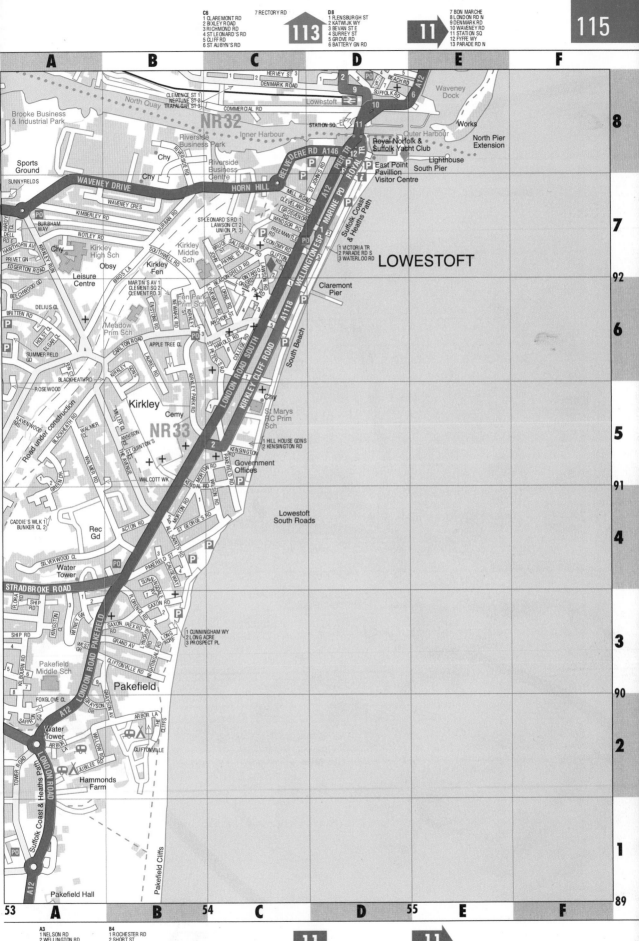

C6
1 CLAREMONT RD
2 BIXLEY ROAD
3 RICHMOND RD
4 ST LEONARD'S RD
5 CLIFF RD
6 ST AUBYN'S RD

7 RECTORY RD

113

D8
1 FLENSBURGH ST
2 KATWIJK WY
3 BEVAN ST E
4 SURREY ST
5 GROVE RD
6 BATTERY GN RD

11

7 BON MARCHE
8 LONDON RD N
9 DENMARK RD
10 WAVENEY RD
11 STATION SQ
12 FYFFE WY
13 PARADE RD N

A3
1 NELSON RD
2 WELLINGTON RD
3 WITNEY RD
4 CRANFIELD CL
5 MARSDEN CL
6 KILBOURN RD
7 SPEEDWELL CL
8 HONEYSUCKLE CL

B4
1 ROCHESTER RD
2 SHORT ST
3 DOLPHIN CL
4 KIRKDALE CT

 11

 11

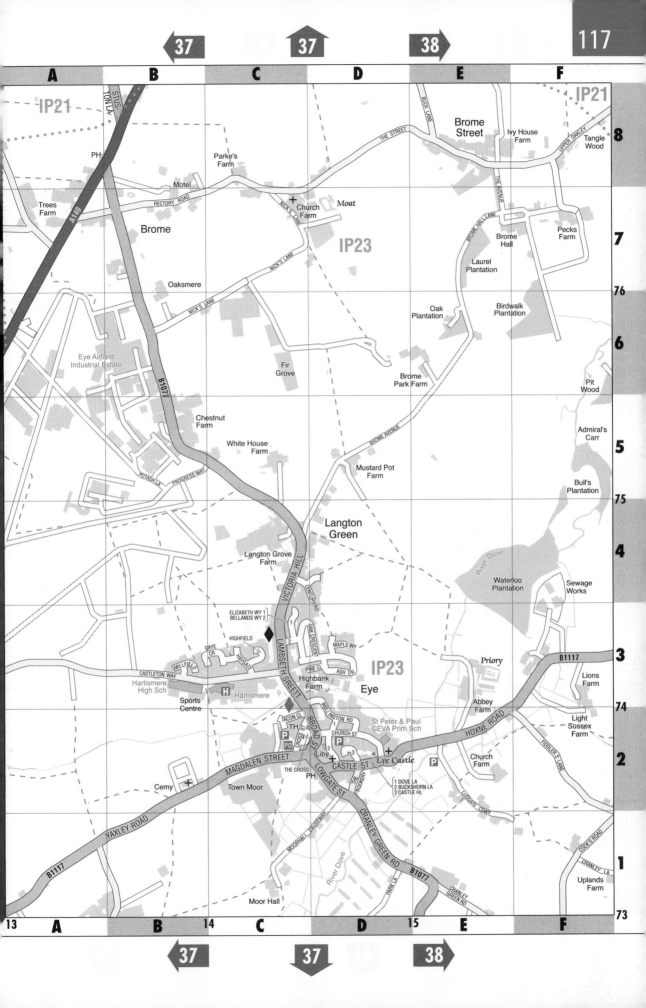

IP21
IP21

8

Brome Street

The Street

Buck Lane

Ivy House Farm

Upper Oakley

Tangle Wood

PH

Trees Farm

A140

Motel

Parke's Farm

RECTORY ROAD

Moat

Church Farm

NICK'S LANE

THE AVENUE

7

Brome

IP23

Brome Hall

Pecks Farm

BROME HALL LANE

Laurel Plantation

Oaksmere

NICK'S LANE

NICK'S LANE

76

Oak Plantation

Birdwalk Plantation

6

Eye Airfield Industrial Estate

B1077

Fir Grove

Brome Park Farm

Pit Wood

Chestnut Farm

BROME AVENUE

Admiral's Carr

5

White House Farm

Mustard Pot Farm

Bull's Plantation

POTASH LA

PROGRESS WAY

75

Langton Green

River Dove

4

Waterloo Plantation

Sewage Works

Langton Grove Farm

VICTORIA HILL

CENTURY RD

Elizabeth Wy 1
Bellands Wy 2

HIGHFIELD

OAK CRESCENT

MAPLE WY

Priory

B1117

3

Lions Farm

GAYE CR

HAYGATE

MILLFIELD

LAMBSETH STREET

PINE CL

ASH DR

IP23

Eye

Light Sussex Farm

CASTLETON WAY

Highbank Farm

Abbey Farm

HOXNE ROAD

74

Hartismere High Sch

H Hartismere

Sports Centre

WELLINGTON RD

St Peter & Paul CEVA Prim Sch

FIDDLER'S LANE

P TH
P PO

TACON CL

CROSS ST

BROAD ST

CHURCH ST

P

Liby

Church Farm

2

Cemy

Town Moor

MAGDALEN STREET

THE CROSS

PH

LOWGATE ST

CASTLE ST

Eye Castle

THE ROOKERY

P

1 DOVE LA
2 BUCKSHORN LA
3 CASTLE HL.

LUDGATE CSWY

COCK'S ROAD

YAXLEY ROAD

MOORHALL CAUSEWAY

CRANLEY GREEN RD

PARK LA

B1077

CRANLEY GREEN RD

CRANLEY LA

1

B1117

River Dove

Moor Hall

Uplands Farm

73

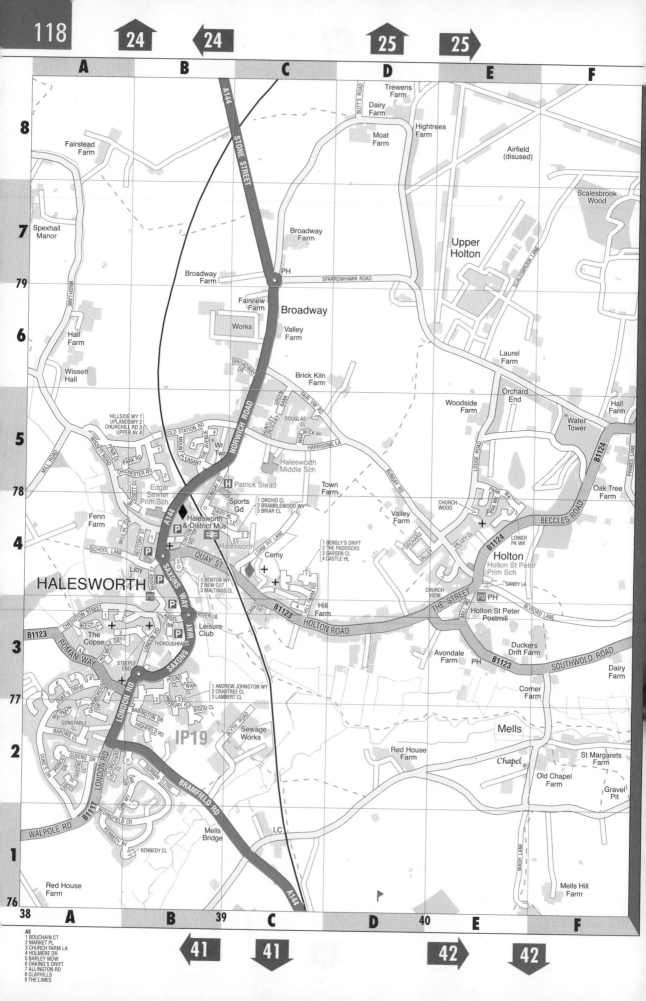

A B C D E F

8

7

79

6

5

78

4

3

77

2

1

76

Fairstead Farm

Spexhall Manor

Hall Farm

Wissett Hall

Fenn Farm

HALESWORTH

The Copse

ROMAN WAY

B1123

Red House Farm

WALPOLE RD

B1117

LONDON RD

BRAMFIELD RD

Mells Bridge

LC

A144

STONE STREET

NORWICH ROAD

BROADWAY DR

SAXONS WAY

SAXONS WAY

QUAY ST

Halesworth

Broadway Farm

Broadway Farm

Fairview Farm

Works

Valley Farm

Brick Kiln Farm

Broadway

PH

SPARROWHAWK ROAD

Butts Road

Dairy Farm

Moat Farm

Trewens Farm

Hightrees Farm

Upper Holton

Airfield (disused)

Scalesbrook Wood

SCALESBROOK LANE

Laurel Farm

Orchard End

Woodside Farm

Water Tower

Hall Farm

B1124

Oak Tree Farm

BECCLES ROAD

PRIMES LANE

Halesworth Middle Sch

Patrick Stead

H

Sports Gd

Town Farm

Valley Farm

CHURCH WOOD

PARK WK

LOWER PK WK

B1124

Holton

Holton St Peter Prim Sch

Edgar Sewter Prim Sch

Halesworth & District Mus

P

Liby

Leisure Club

River La

ANGEL INK

Cerny

Cemy

1 BENSLY'S DRIFT
2 THE PADDOCKS
3 SARSEN CL
4 CASTLE HL

1 ORCHID CL
2 BRAMBLEWOOD WY
3 BRIAR CL

1 BENTON WY
2 NEW CUT
3 MALTINGS CL

Hill Farm

B1123

HOLTON ROAD

THE STREET

ORCHARD

VALLEY CL

CHURCH VIEW

SANDY LA

PO PH

Holton St Peter Postmill

BLYFORD LANE

Avondale Farm

PH

B1123

SOUTHWOLD ROAD

Duckers Drift Farm

Corner Farm

Dairy Farm

Mells

Chapel

St Margarets Farm

Old Chapel Farm

Gravel Pit

1 ANDREW JOHNSTON WY
2 CRABTREE CL
3 LAMBERT CL

IP19

Sewage Works

Red House Farm

WASH LANE

Mells Hill Farm

MILL ROAD

WASH LANE

Spexhall Manor

HILLSIDE WY 1
UPLANDS WY 2
CHURCHILL RD 3
UPPER AV 4

Old Station Rd

THE AVENUE

MOUNT PLEASANT

PARK RD

CHICHESTER RD

WISSETT ROAD

FENN CL

MILL HL DR

SCHOOL LANE

RECTORY ST

DAIRY HL

BUNGAY RD

FAIR VW RD

HUNTLEY GREEN BANK

DOUGLAS CL

WAR WICK AV

HARRISONS LA

WR TWR

HALESWORTH

Fenn Farm

CHEDISTON STREET

BEECH CL

HOLMERE DR

LONDON RD

THOROUGHFARE

STEEPLE END

POUND CL

SWAN CL

GAINSBOROUGH

DUKE'S DRIVE

CONSTABLE CL

BARONS CL

QUEENS DR

DUKE'S DR

PRINCES CL

EARL CL

QUEENS CL

ORCHARD GW

DURBAN CLOSE

BABINGTON DR

KINGSBURY RD

BIGOD CL

HIGHFIELD RD

BLYTH ROAD

KENNEDY AV

KENNEDY CL

BEDINGFIELD CR

OAK WY

STATION RD

LOAM PIT LANE

CLARKS PIT

HILL FARM RD

BUNGAY RD

LODGE ROAD

PARK WK

MILL RD

VALLEY

A3
1 BOUCHAIN CT
2 MARKET PL
3 CHURCH FARM LA
4 HOLMERE DR
5 BARLEY MDW
6 DAKING'S DRIFT
7 ALLINGTON RD
8 CLAYHILLS
9 THE LIMES

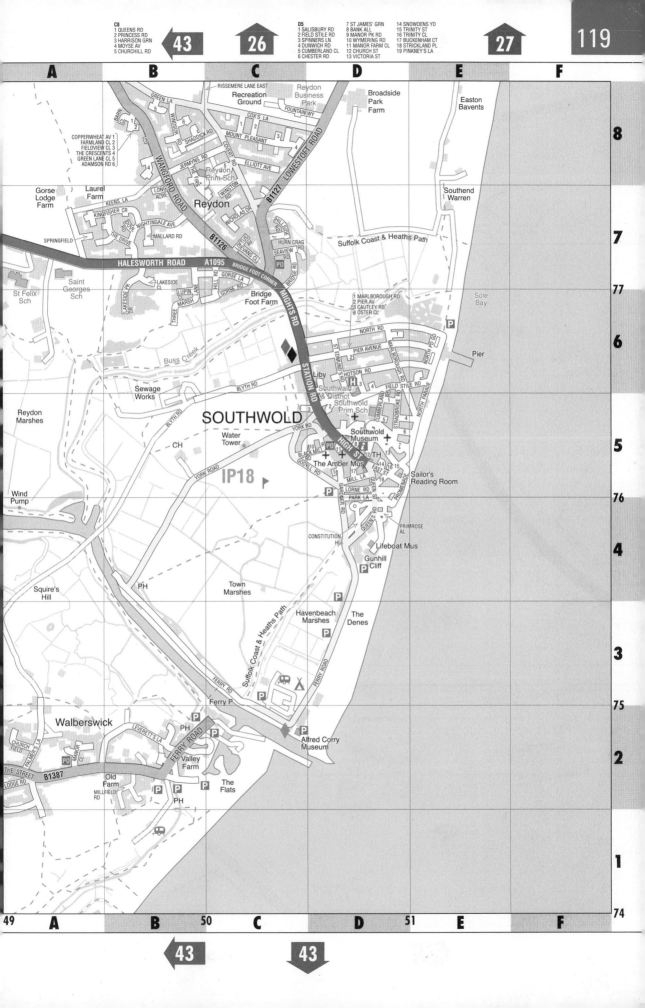

C8
1 QUEENS RD
2 PRINCESS RD
3 HARRISON GRN
4 MOYSE AV
5 CHURCHILL RD

43

26

D5
1 SALISBURY RD
2 FIELD STILE RD
3 SPINNERS LN
4 DUNWICH RD
5 CUMBERLAND CL
6 CHESTER RD

7 ST JAMES' GRN
8 BANK ALL
9 MANOR PK RD
10 WYMERING RD
11 MANOR FARM CL
12 CHURCH ST
13 VICTORIA ST

14 SNOWDENS YD
15 TRINITY ST
16 TRINITY CL
17 BUCKENHAM CT
18 STRICKLAND PL
19 PINKNEY'S LA

27

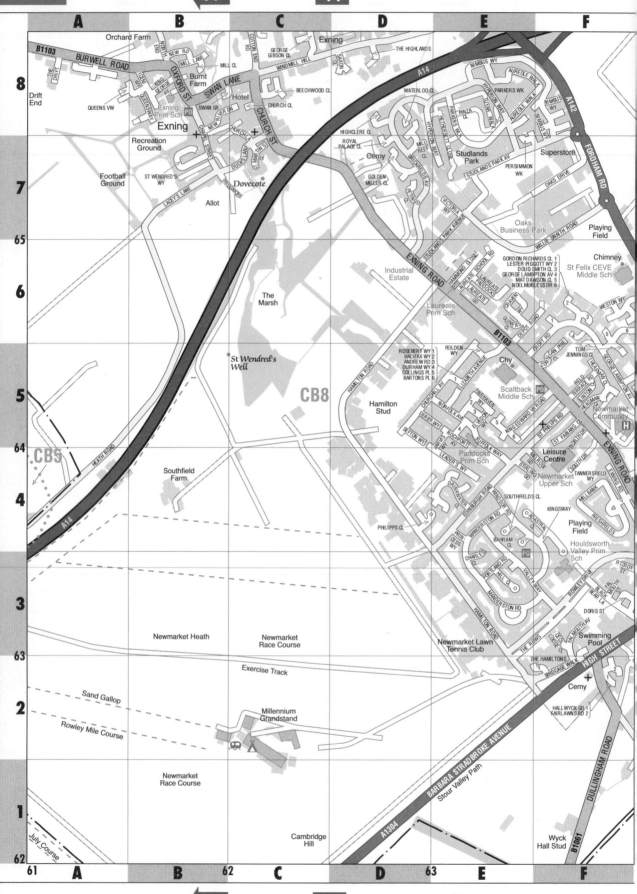

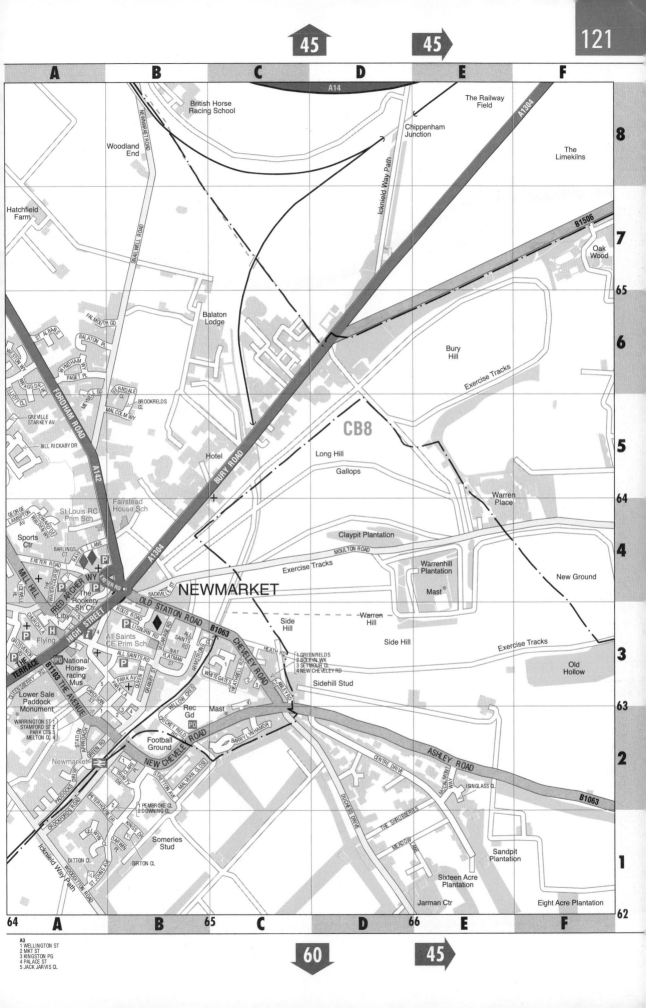

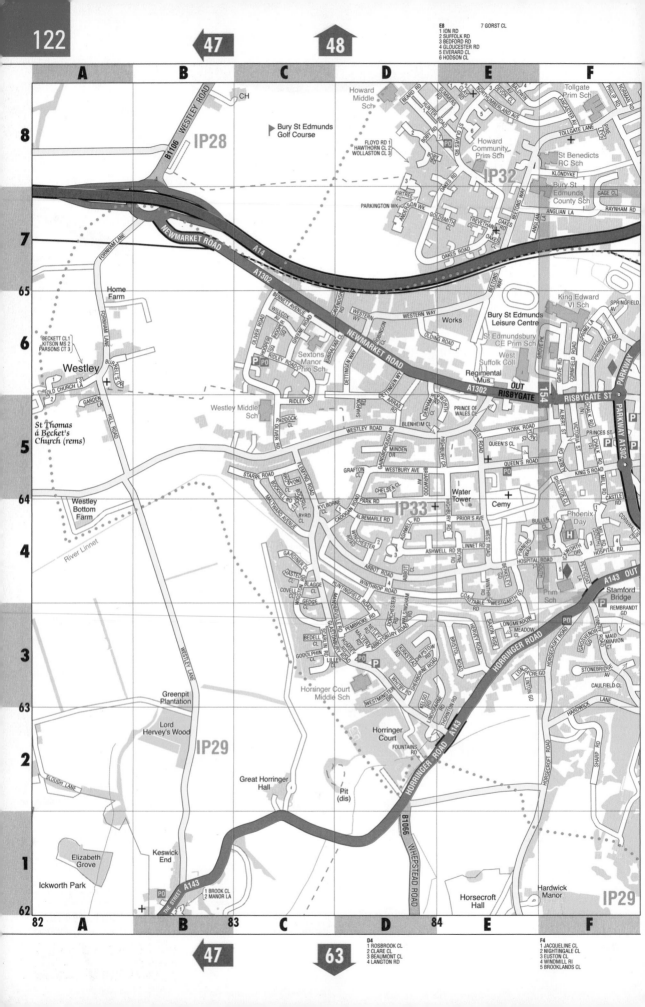

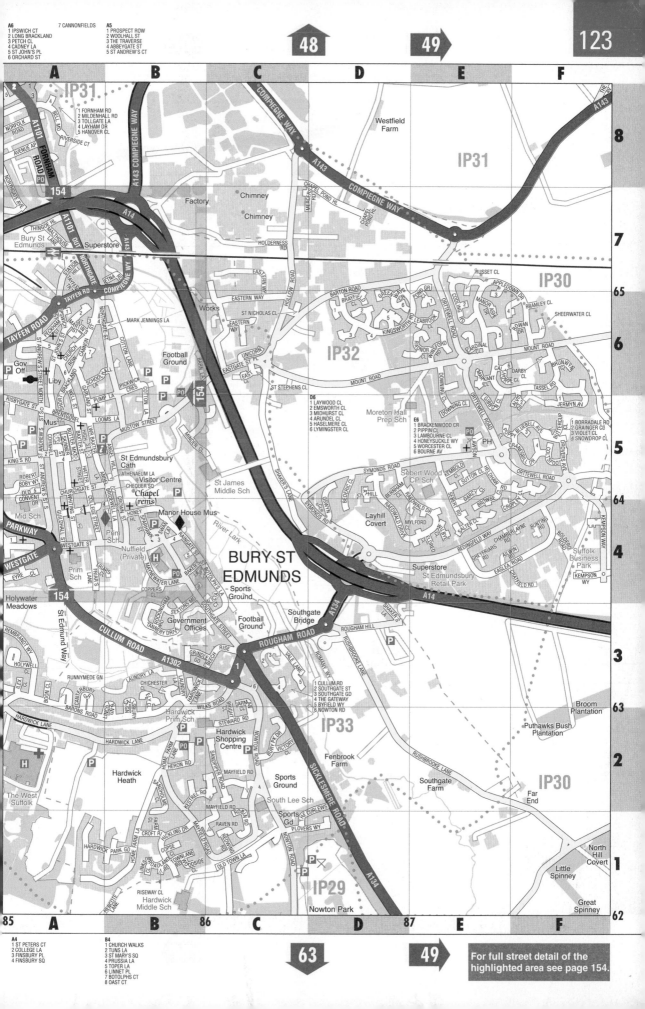

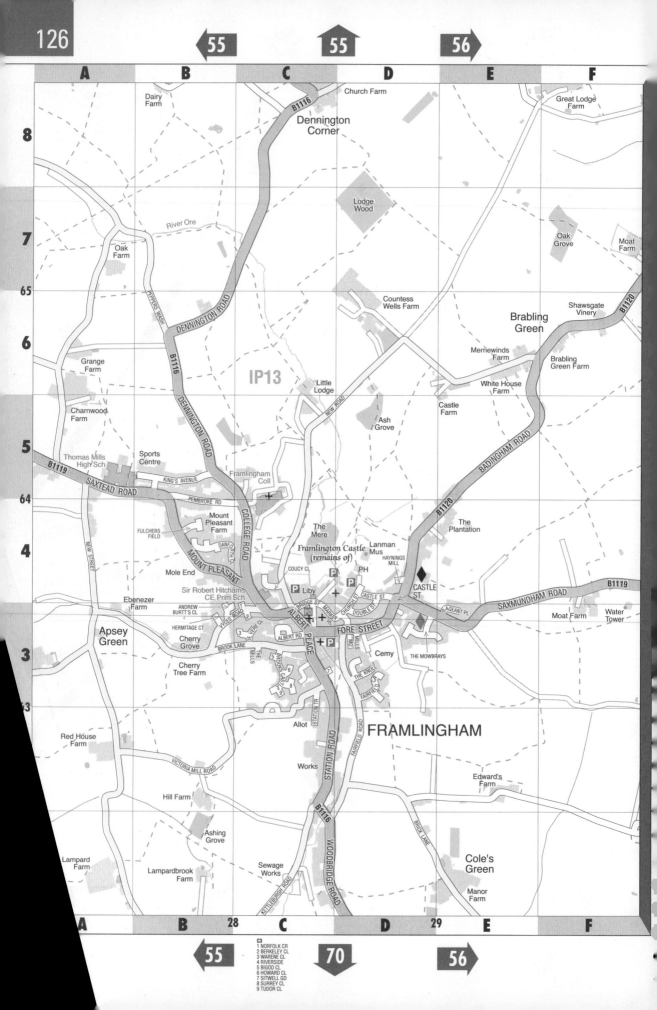

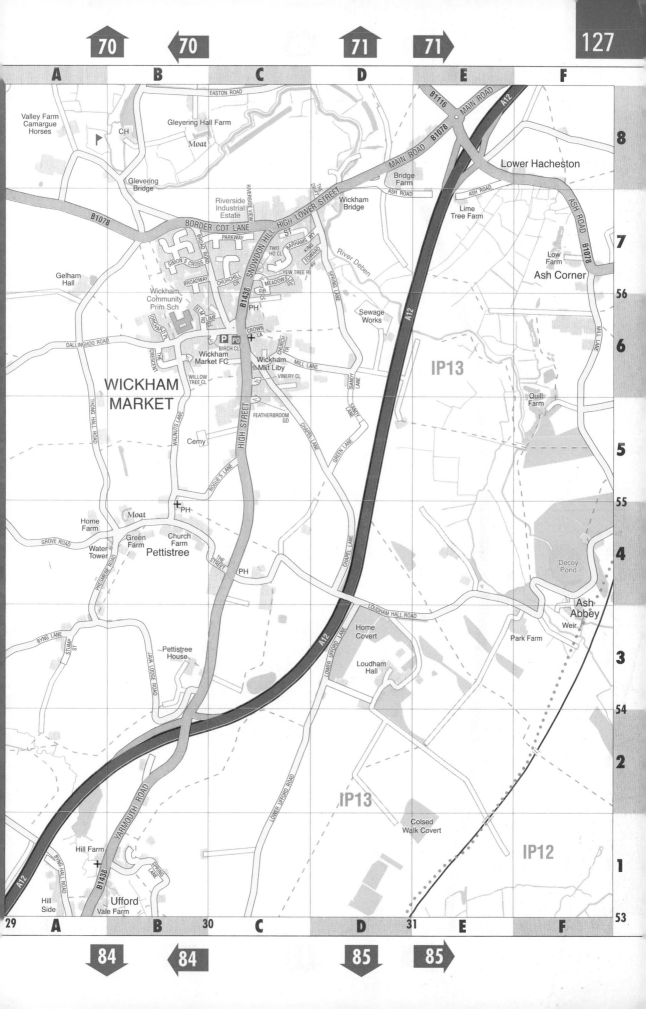

A B C D E F

8

Valley Farm Camargue Horses

CH

Gleyering Hall Farm

Moat

EASTON ROAD

Lower Hacheston

Glevering Bridge

B1116

MAIN ROAD

A12

MAIN ROAD

B1078

Bridge Farm

ASH ROAD

Lime Tree Farm

ASH ROAD

B1078

Gelham Hall

B1078

Riverside Industrial Estate

RIVERSIDE VIEW

BORDER COT LANE

PARKWAY

BROAD ROAD

SIMON'S CROSS

CHURCHILL CR

BROADWAY

SNOWDON HILL

HIGH LOWER STREET

ST

TWO HO CL

BARHAMS WY

KING EDWARD AV

YEW TREE RI

Wickham Bridge

River Deben

Low Farm

Ash Corner

7

56

Wickham Community Prim Sch

ELM RD

ORCHARD PL

LIME

FIR CL

B1438

MEADOWSIDE

PH

SPRING LANE

Sewage Works

MILL LANE

IP13

Dallinghoo Road

DALLINGHOO ROAD

THE CRESCENT

BIRCH CL

P PO

CROWN LA

CHURCH LA

CHURCH TR

Quill Farm

6

WICKHAM MARKET

Wickham Market FC

WILLOW TREE CL

Wickham Mkt Liby

VINERY CL

MILL LANE

SANDY LANE

55

THONG HALL ROAD

WALNUTS LANE

HIGH STREET

FEATHERBROOM GD

CHAPEL LANE

SANDY LANE

GREEN LANE

Cemy

ROGUE'S LANE

5

Home Farm

Moat

Green Farm

PH

Church Farm

Pettistree

THE STREET

PH

CHAPEL LANE

Decoy Pond

4

GROVE ROAD

Water Tower

PRESMERE ROAD

LOUDHAM HALL ROAD

Park Farm

Ash Abbey

Weir

55

54

BYNG LANE

STUMP ST

JAVA LODGE ROAD

Pettistree House

A12

LOWER UFFORD LANE

Home Covert

Loudham Hall

3

YARMOUTH ROAD

LOWER UFFORD ROAD

IP13

IP12

54

2

Hill Farm

SPRING LANE

Colsed Walk Covert

1

A12

BYNG HALL ROAD

B1438

Hill Side

Ufford

Vale Farm

53

29 A B 30 C D 31 E F 53

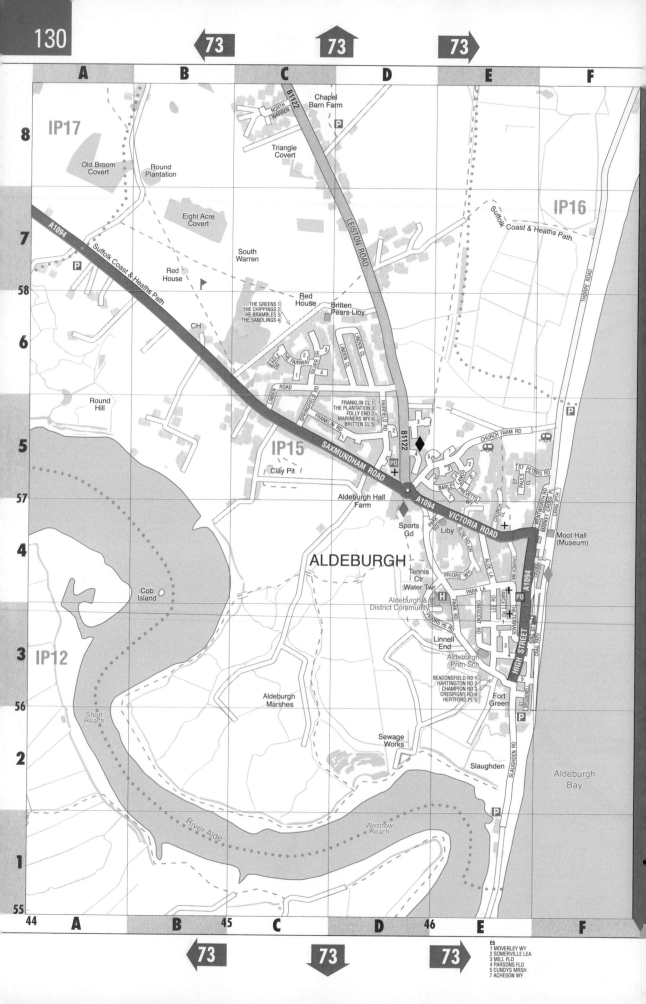

73   73   73

A **B** **C** **D** **E** **F**

8 IP17

Old Broom
Covert

Round
Plantation

Triangle
Covert

Chapel
Barn Farm

7 A1094

Eight Acre
Covert

South
Warren

Suffolk Coast & Heaths Path

IP16

Suffolk Coast & Heaths Path

58

Red
House

Red
House

LEISTON ROAD

6 CH

THE GREENS 1
THE CHIPPINGS 2
HE BRAMBLES 3
THE SANDLINGS 4

Britten
Pears Liby

LINDEN CL

LINDEN CL

SILVER DR

THE FAIRWAY

EAGLE DR

LINDEN ROAD

SPRINGFIELD RD

FRANKLIN RD

FAIRFIELD RD

FRANKLIN CL 1
THE PLANTATION 3
FOLLY END 2
MARINERS WY 4
BRITTEN CL 5

CHURCH FARM RD

5 IP15

SAXUNDHAM ROAD

B1122

PO

ST PETERS RD

ST PAULS CL

Clay Pit

Round
Hill

Aldeburgh Hall
Farm

BARLEY
LANDS

THELVETTS WY

WENTWORTH RD

MARKET CROSS PL

CRAG PTH

57

A1094

VICTORIA ROAD

CHURCH CL

Moot Hall
(Museum)

4 Cob
Island

ALDEBURGH

Sports
Gd

Liby

PARK RD

PRIORS WY

ALDE MDW

ALDE LA

CRESCENT RD

CHURCH WY

A1094

CRAG PATH

Tennis
Ctr
Water Twr

Aldeburgh &
District Community

H

PARK LA

FAWCETT RD

LEE RD

PO

THE TERRACE

KING ST

3 IP12

Linnell
End

Aldeburgh
Prim Sch

PRIORS HL RD

HIGH STREET

BEACONSFIELD RD 1
HARTINGTON RD 2
CHAMPION RD 3
CRESPIGNY RD 4
HERTFORD PL 5

Fort
Green

ST DUNSTAN

56

Short
Reach

Aldeburgh
Marshes

Sewage
Works

SLAUGHDEN RD

2

Slaughden

Aldeburgh
Bay

1 River Alde

Westrow
Reach

55

44 **A** **B** 45 **C** **D** 46 **E** **F**

73   73   73

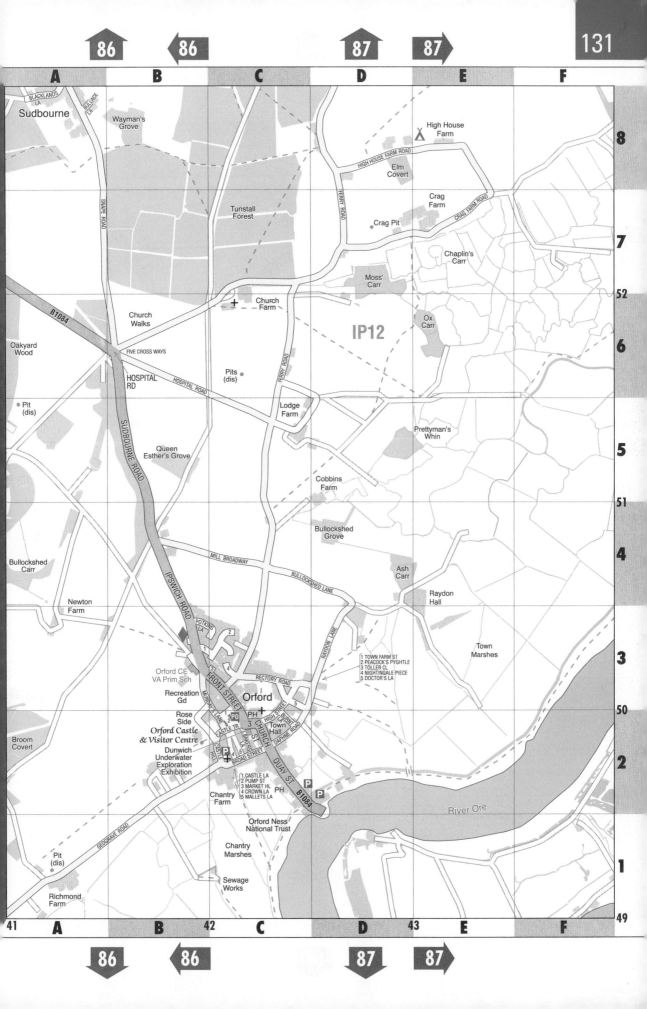

A B C D E F

8

7

52

6

51

5

4

3

50

2

1

49

BLACKLANDS LA
Sudbourne
BULLACE LA
Wayman's Grove
SNAPE ROAD
Tunstall Forest
High House Farm
HIGH HOUSE FARM ROAD
FERRY ROAD
Elm Covert
Crag Farm
CRAG FARM ROAD
Crag Pit
Chaplin's Carr
Church Farm
Moss' Carr
IP12
Ox Carr
B1084
Church Walks
Oakyard Wood
FIVE CROSS WAYS
HOSPITAL RD
HOSPITAL ROAD
Pits (dis)
FERRY ROAD
Pit (dis)
Lodge Farm
SUDBOURNE ROAD
Queen Esther's Grove
Prettyman's Whin
Cobbins Farm
Bullockshed Grove
51
Bullockshed Carr
MILL BROADWAY
BULLOCKSHED LANE
Ash Carr
Raydon Hall
Newton Farm
IPSWICH ROAD
POTKINS LA
1 TOWN FARM ST
2 PEACOCK'S PYGHTLE
3 TOLLER CL
4 NIGHTINGALE PIECE
5 DOCTOR'S LA
Town Marshes
PAYTON LANE
RECTORY ROAD
Orford CE VA Prim Sch
FRONT STREET
Orford
MUNDAY'S LANE
Recreation Gd
Rose Side
PH
PO
CHURCH ST
Town Hall
HIGH STREET
QUAY ST
DAPHNE ROAD
Orford Castle & Visitor Centre
CASTLE TR
CASTLE HILL
BAKER'S
BROAD STREET
Dunwich Underwater Exploration Exhibition
1 CASTLE LA
2 PUMP ST
3 MARKET HL
4 CROWN LA
5 MALLETS LA
PH
B1084
P
Broom Covert
GEDGRAVE ROAD
Chantry Farm
Orford Ness National Trust
Chantry Marshes
River Ore
Pit (dis)
Sewage Works
Richmond Farm

41 A 42 B C 43 D E F 49

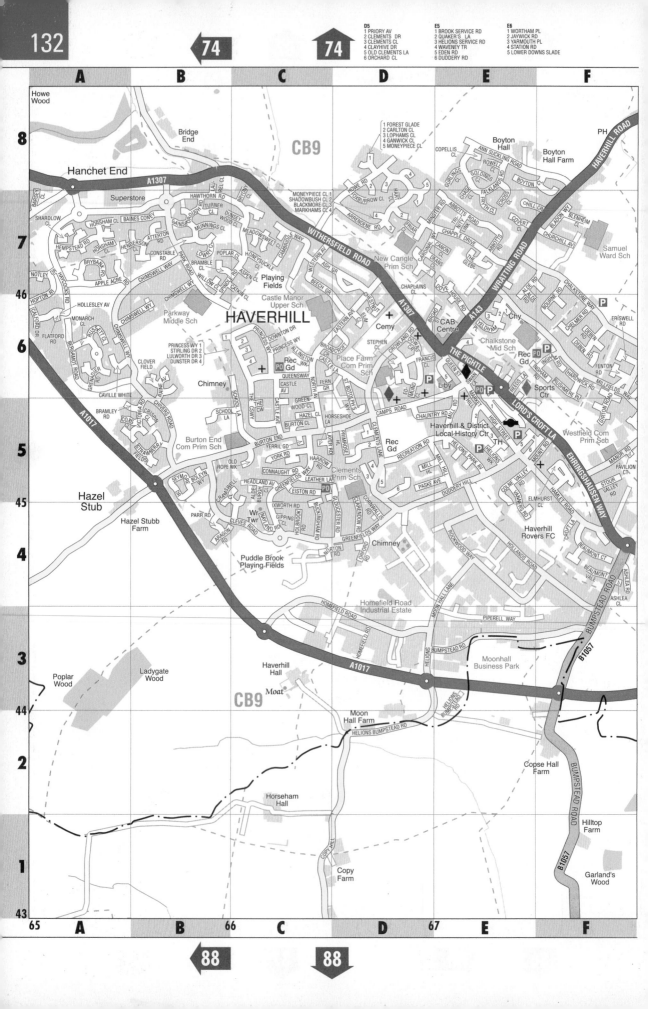

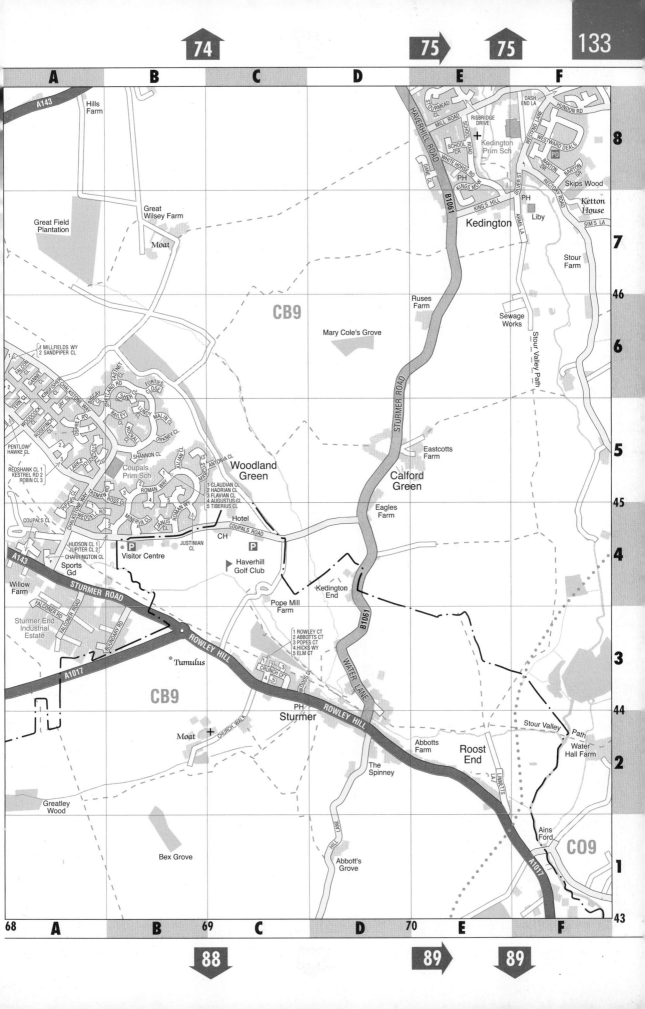

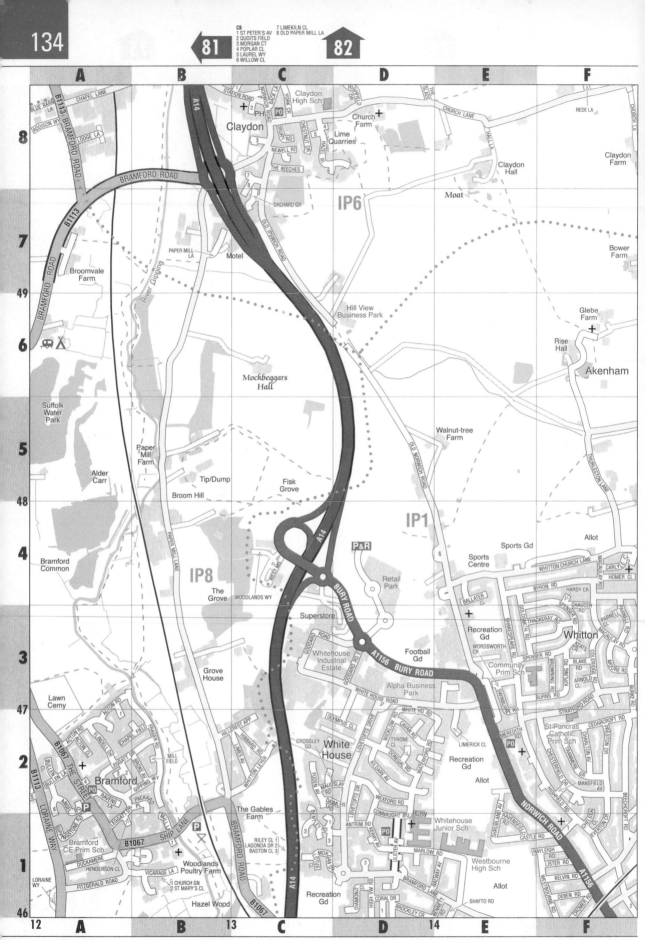

81
82

C8
1 ST PETER'S AV
2 QUOITS FIELD
3 MORGAN CT
4 POPLAR CL
5 LAUREL WY
6 WILLOW CL
7 LIMEKILN CL
8 OLD PAPER MILL LA

A2
1 ACTON GDNS
2 LACON RD
3 BUSHMAN GDNS
4 WALNUT TREE CL
5 BULLEN LA
6 ORCHARD RD

D1
1 OPAL AV
2 AGATE CL
3 BRAMFORD LA

F1
1 HIGHFIELD APPROACH
2 MORNINGTON AV

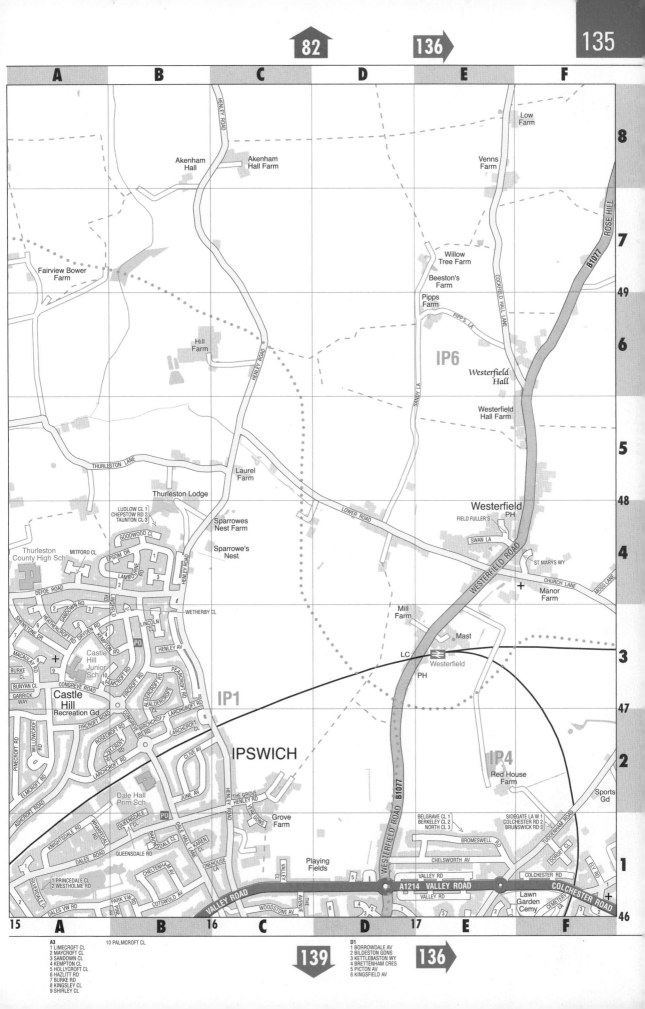

A B C D E F

8
7
49
6
5
48
4
3
47
2
1
46

Low Farm
Venns Farm
Akenham Hall
Akenham Hall Farm
Fairview Bower Farm
Willow Tree Farm
Beeston's Farm
Pipps Farm
Hill Farm
IP6
Westerfield Hall
Westerfield Hall Farm
Thurleston Lane
Laurel Farm
Thurleston Lodge
Westerfield PH
Field Fuller's
SWAN LA
St Marys Wy
LUDLOW CL 1
CHEPSTOW RD 2
TAUNTON CL 3
Sparrowes Nest Farm
Sparrowe's Nest
LOWER ROAD
WESTERFIELD ROAD
CHURCH LANE
Manor Farm
MOSS LANE
Thurleston County High Sch
MITFORD CL
GOODWOOD CL
EPSOM DR
LAMBOURNE RD
HENLEY ROAD
WETHERBY CL
Mill Farm
Mast
DEFOE ROAD
SANDOWN RD
INGFIELD
KEMPTON RD
DRYDEN RD
LINCOLN CL
HENLEY AV
LC
Westerfield
PH
SHENSTONE DR
HEATHERCROFT RD
PO
MACAULAY RD
BURKE CL
BUNYAN CL
GARRICK WAY
Castle Hill Junior Sch
CONGREVE RD
PALMCROFT RD
ALDERCROFT RD
PEASCROFT RD
FIRCROFT RD
LARCHCROFT RD
Castle Hill
IP1
Castle Hill Recreation Gd
PINECROFT RD
WILLOWCROFT RD
ELMCROFT RD
ASHCROFT ROAD
FIRCROFT ROAD
ROSECROFT RD
CONGREVE RD
BIRCHCROFT
LARCHCROFT RD
CLIVE AV
IPSWICH
IP4
Red House Farm
Sports Gd
KNIGHTSDALE RD
WHARFEDALE RD
QUEENSDALE CL
BARNSDALE CL
DALE HALL LANE
KAREN CL
JUNE AV
THE GROVE
HENLEY RD
GROVE GDNS
Grove Farm
WESTERFIELD ROAD
B1077
BELGRAVE CL 1
BERKELEY CL 2
NORTH CL 3
BROMESWELL RD
SIDEGATE LA W 1
COLCHESTER RD 2
BRUNSWICK RD 3
THORNHAM ROAD
DORSET CL
Dale Hall Prim Sch
QUEENSDALE RD
DALES ROAD
CHELTENHAM AV
ONEHOUSE LA
VALLEY CL
Playing Fields
CHELSWORTH AV
VALLEY RD
COLCHESTER RD
ELY CL
1 PRINCEDALE CL
2 WESTHOLME RD
SILVERDALE CL
DALES VW RD
PARK VW RD
PINE VW
COTSWOLD AV
WOODSTONE AV
THE AVENUE
VALLEY ROAD
A1214 VALLEY ROAD
VALLEY RD
Lawn Garden Cemy
COLCHESTER ROAD
CEMETERY LA

HENLEY ROAD
ROSE HILL
B1077
COCKFIELD HALL LANE
PIPP'S LA
SANDY LA

15 A B 16 C D 17 E F 46

A3
1 LIMECROFT CL
2 MAYCROFT CL
3 SANDOWN CL
4 KEMPTON CL
5 HOLLYCROFT CL
6 HAZLITT RD
7 BURKE RD
8 KINGSLEY CL
9 SHIRLEY CL

10 PALMCROFT CL

D1
1 BORROWDALE AV
2 BILDESTON GDNS
3 KETTLEBASTON WY
4 BRETTENHAM CRES
5 PICTON AV
6 KINGSFIELD AV

	A	B	C	D	E	F

8

Wells Farm
PO
THE STREET
B1077 ROSE HILL
STRUGGLER'S LANE
Valley Farm
Hillbrow Farm
SANDY LANE
Culpho Wood

7

Fynn Valley Walk
Fynn Valley Golf Course
CH
Cowslip Farm
WITNESHAM LANE
CLOPTON ROAD
Abbey Farm
Moat
Tuddenham Hall

49

Larks' Hill
IP6

6

Manor Farm
GRUNDISBURGH ROAD
Culpho Hall
PH
THE GRANARIES
Culpho End

Great Pinners Farm
KEIGHTLEY WY
THE PADDOCKS
HIGH STREET
THE STREET
MAIN RD
FYNN RD
Spinney Hill
Poplar Farm
+ +
Tuddenham St Martin
Hill Farm

5

WESTERFIELD LANE
Reedings Fruit Farm
GREEN LA
Oak End
FYNN LA

48

MOSS LANE
MAIN ROAD

4

Warren Plantation

River Fynn
Alder Carr

CHURCH LANE

3

TUDDENHAM ROAD
Laceys Farm
Westerfield House Farm

47

Water Tower
Villa Farm
Hill Farm
IP5

2

Sports Gd
TUDDENHAM LANE
Sports Gd
SEVEN COTTS LANE
LAMBERTS LANE
Rushmere Street
HOLLY LA
PLAYFORD LANE

Northgate Sports Ctr
HUMBER DOUCY LANE
SHERBORNE AV
INVERNESS RD
Ipswich Rugby Union FC
Whykes Farm
THE LIMES
BIRCHWOOD DR
RUSHMERE STREET
CHESTNUT RD

IP4
Northgate County High Sch
WINSTON CL
SIDEGATE LANE
LANARK RD
ANGUS CL
KINROSS RD
ROXBURGH RD
LABURNUM GD

1

Suffolk Fire Service Headquarters
SHERBORNE AV
MOFFAT AV
ROSS RD
RENFREW RD
FIFE RD
GLENCOE RD
HUMBER DOUCY LANE
ST ANDREW'S CHURCH CL
Rushmere St Andrew
PH

Allot
SIDEGATE LA
+
Rushmere Hall Prim Sch
Allot
ABERDEEN WY
SELKIRK RD
+
Sports Gd

46

	A	B	C	D	E	F

18   19   20

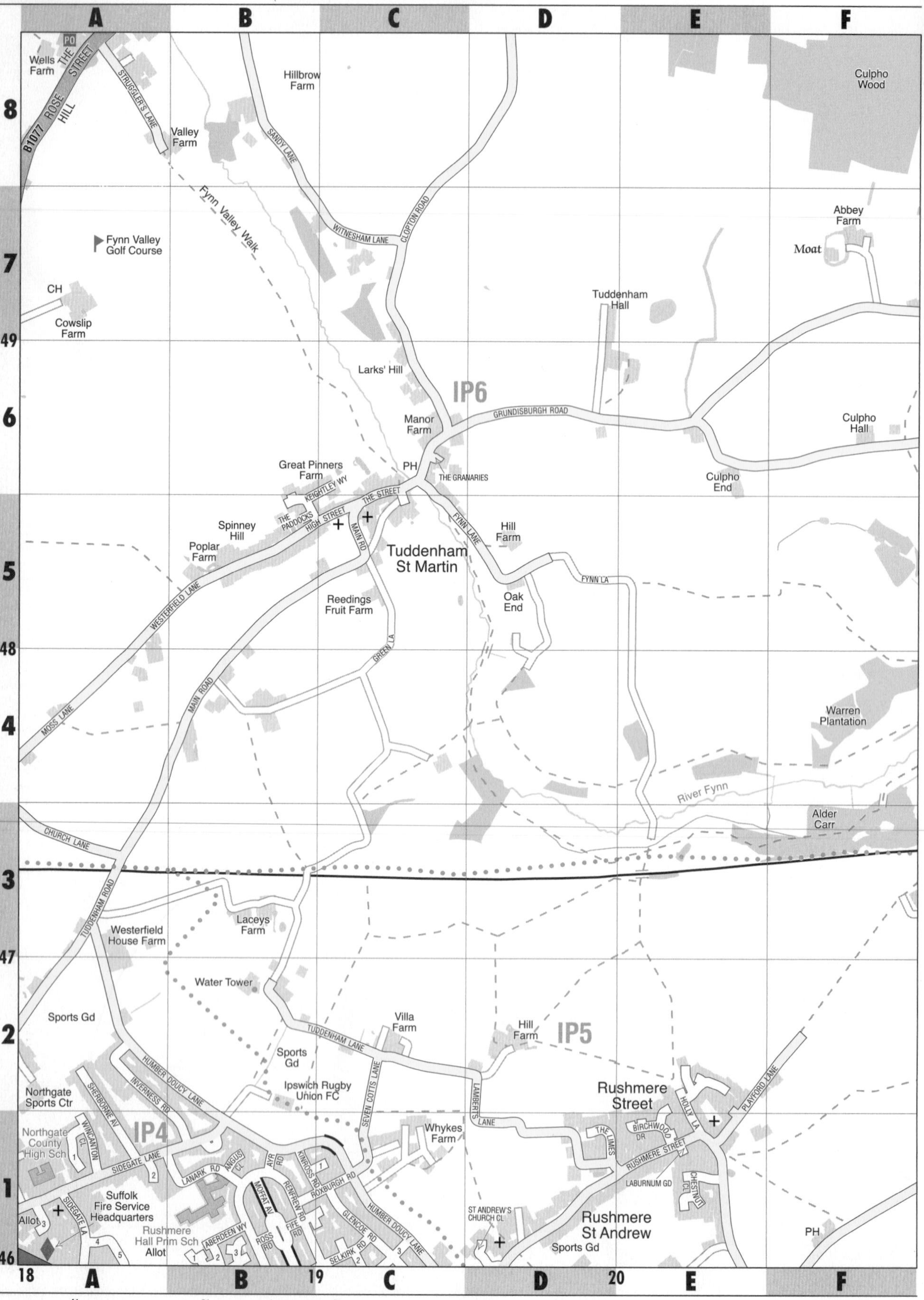

A1
1 CRANBORNE CHASE
2 FAIRLIGHT CL
3 ALMA CL
4 ORKNEY RD
5 SHETLAND CL

B1
1 GRETNA GDNS
2 FORFAR CL
3 TROON GDNS

C1
1 ABERFOYLE CL
2 DUMFRIES RD
3 DUMBARTON RD

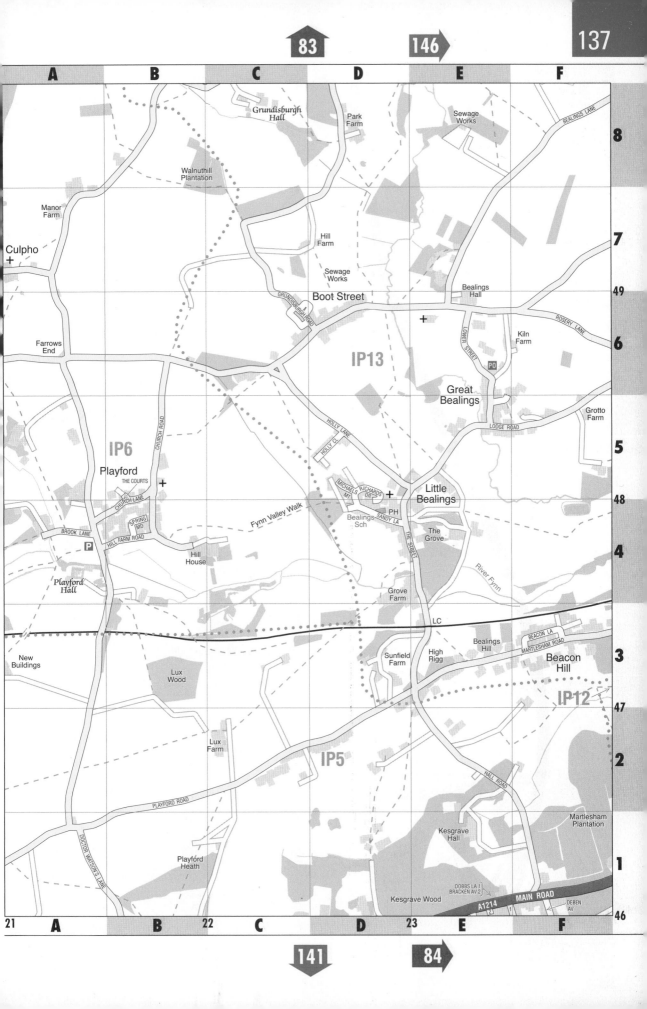

95
134

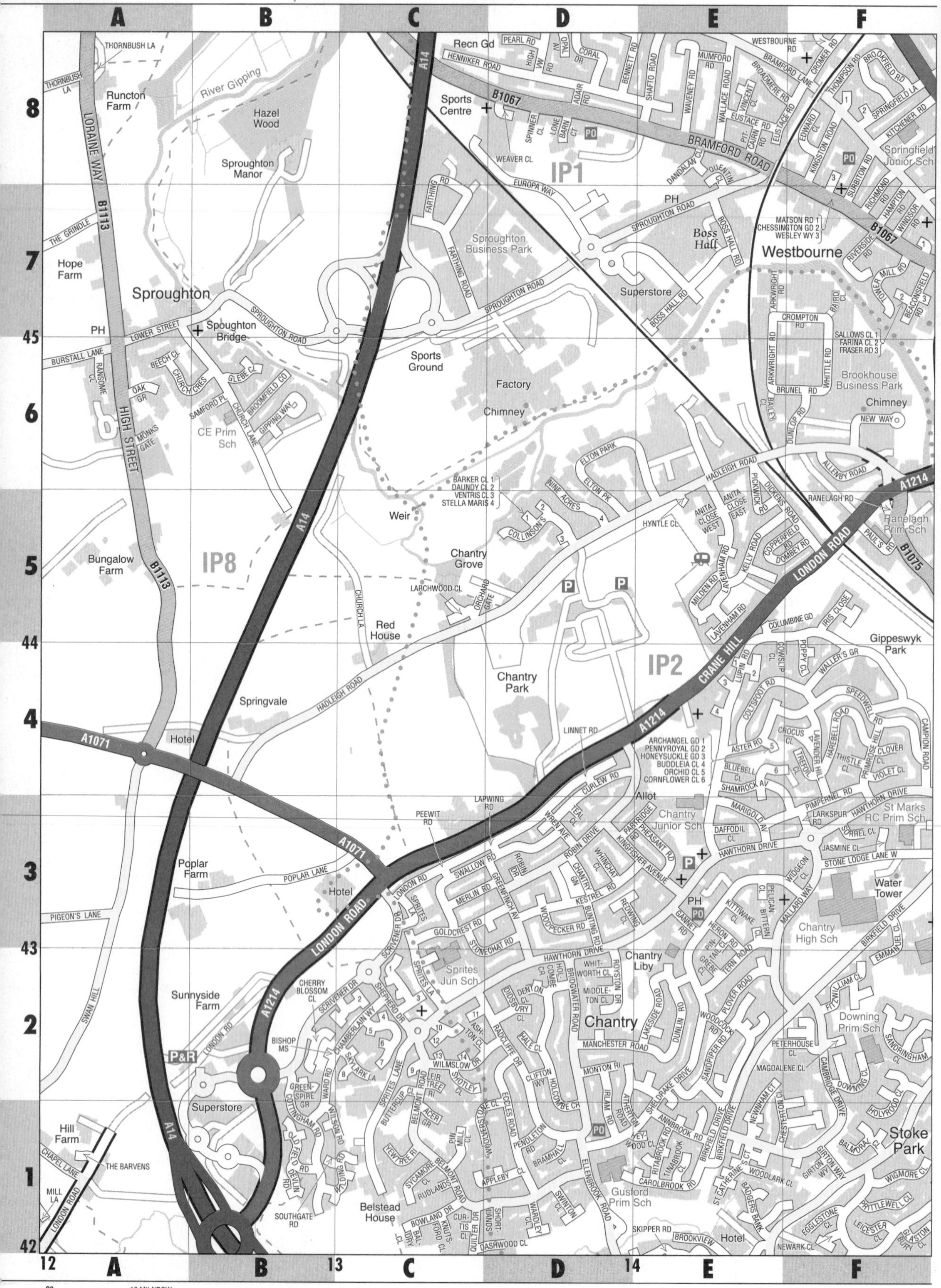

C2
1 BRAMBLEWOOD
2 BROAD MD
3 LABURNUM CL
4 INNES END
5 PEACOCK CL
6 HALFORD CT
7 WENTWORTH DR
8 MAGPIE CL
9 ACORN CL
10 MILNROW
11 THE CHESTNUTS
12 MERRION CL
13 MATLOCK CL
14 MOTTRAM CL

95
142

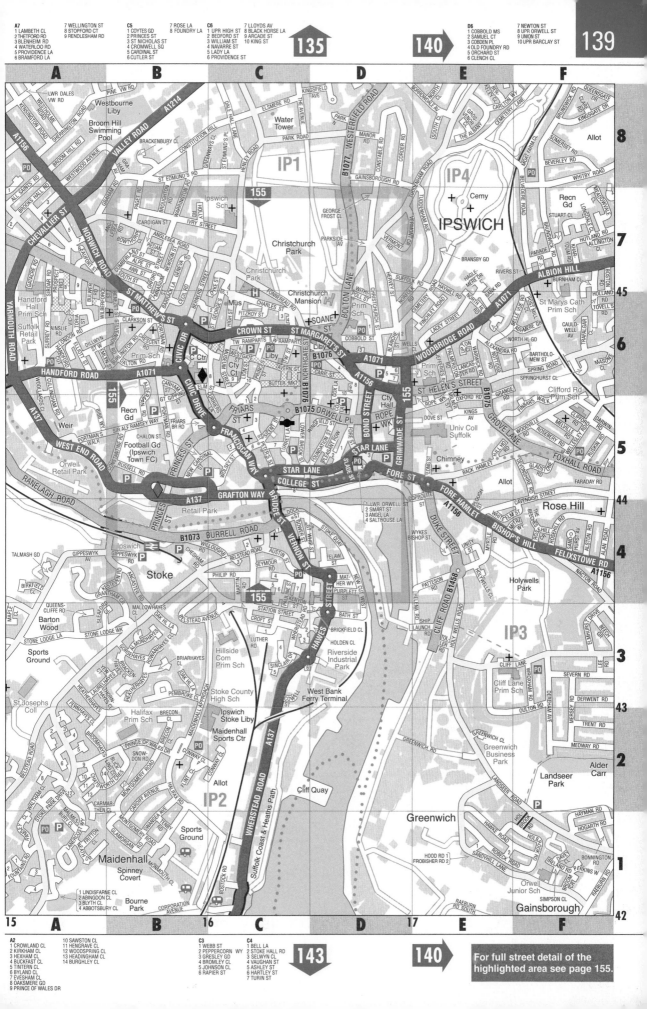

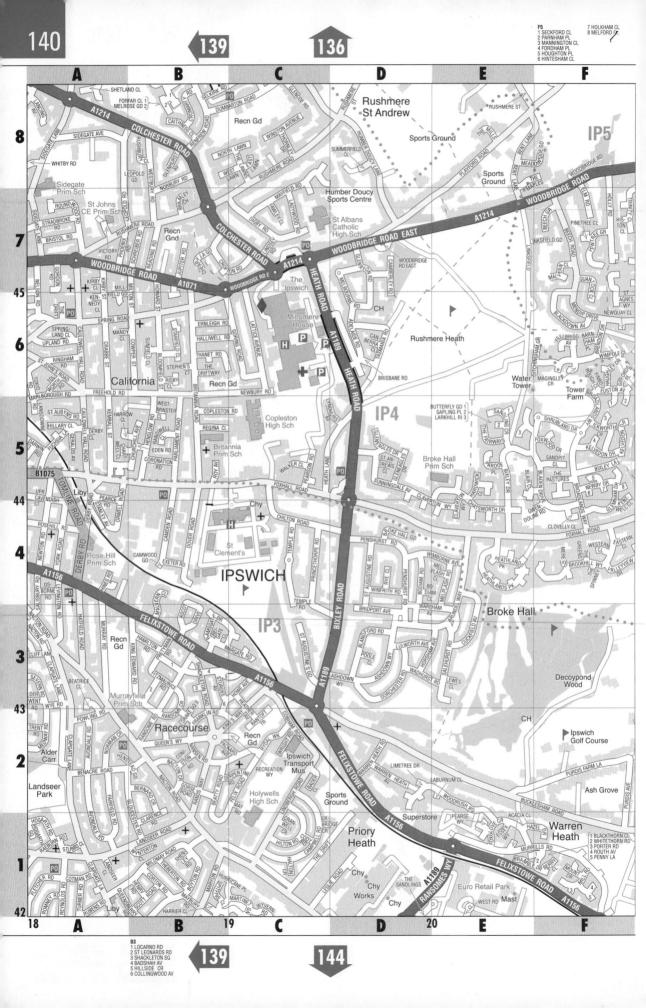

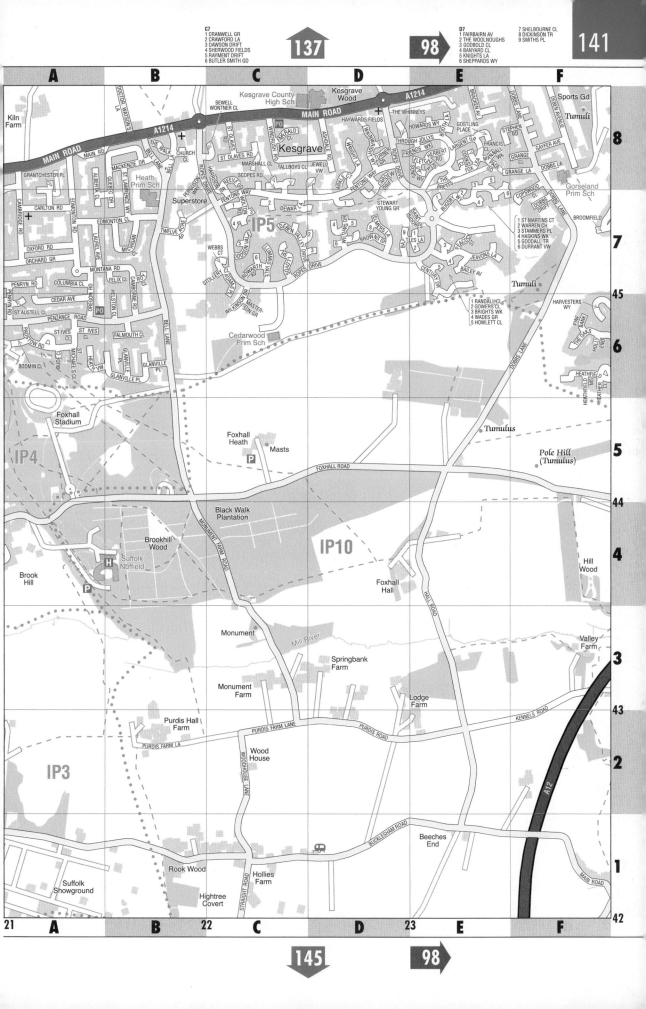

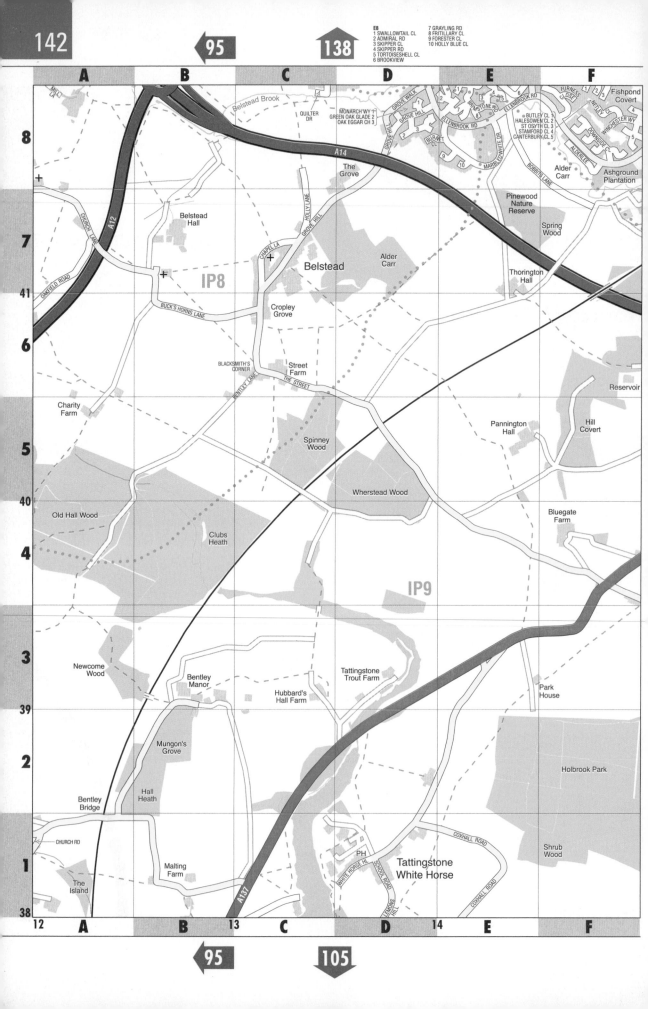

95

138

E8
1 SWALLOWTAIL CL
2 ADMIRAL RD
3 SKIPPER CL
4 SKIPPER RD
5 TORTOISESHELL CL
6 BROOKVIEW

7 GRAYLING RD
8 FRITILLARY CL
9 FORESTER CL
10 HOLLY BLUE CL

A B C D E F

MILL

Belstead Brook

QUILTER DR

MONARCH WY 1
GREEN OAK GLADE 2
OAK EGGAR CH 3

GROVE WALK

GROVE HILL

BUTLEY CL 1
HALESOWEN CL 2
ST OSYTH CL 3
STAMFORD CL 4
CANTERBURY CL 5

FURNESS
CLOSE

NETLEY CL

WINCHESTER WY

Fishpond
Covert

8

CHURCH LANE

A12

A14

OAKFIELD ROAD

The
Grove

ELLENBROOK RD

BRANSTONE RD

ELLENBROOK RD

MARBLE DWHITE DR

BOBBITS LANE

DOWNSIDE CL

ALDERLEE

Alder
Carr

Ashground
Plantation

Belstead
Hall

CHAPEL LA

Belstead

GROVE HILL

HOLLY LANE

Alder
Carr

Pinewood
Nature
Reserve

Spring
Wood

Thorington
Hall

7

41

IP8

BUCK'S HORNS LANE

Cropley
Grove

Reservoir

BLACKSMITH'S
CORNER

BENTLEY LANE

Street
Farm

THE STREET

6

Charity
Farm

Spinney
Wood

Pannington
Hall

Hill
Covert

5

40

Old Hall Wood

Clubs
Heath

Wherstead Wood

Bluegate
Farm

4

IP9

Newcome
Wood

Bentley
Manor

Hubbard's
Hall Farm

Tattingstone
Trout Farm

Park
House

3

39

Mungon's
Grove

Holbrook Park

2

Bentley
Bridge

Hall
Heath

CHURCH RD

COXHALL ROAD

Shrub
Wood

1

The
Island

Malting
Farm

A137

WHITE HORSE HL

SCHOOL ROAD

PH

Tattingstone
White Horse

COXHALL ROAD

LEMONS HILL

38

12 A B 13 C 14 D E F

95

105

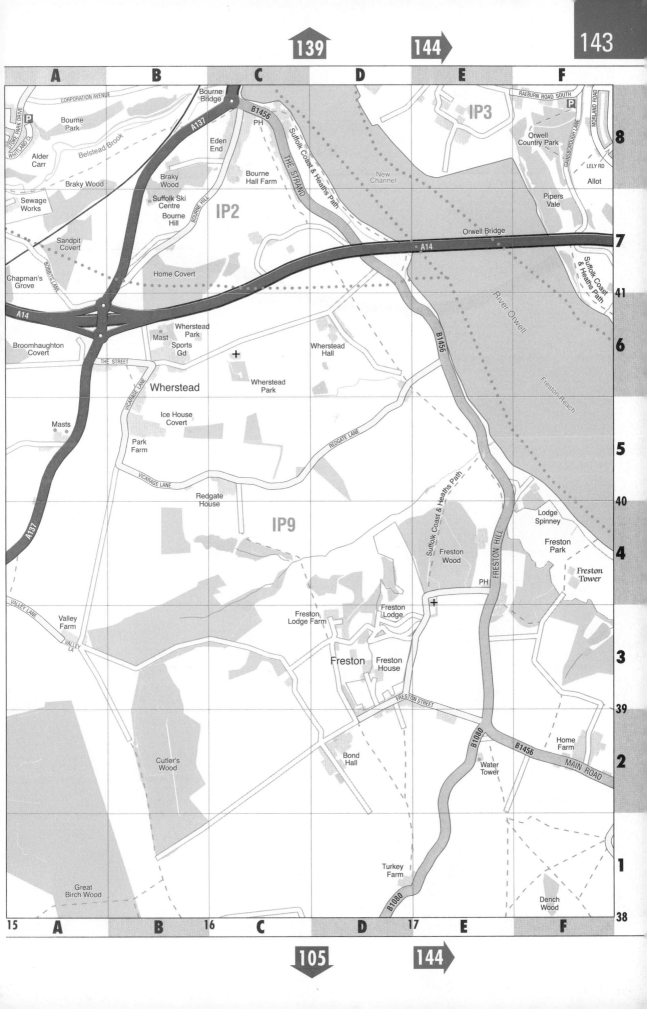

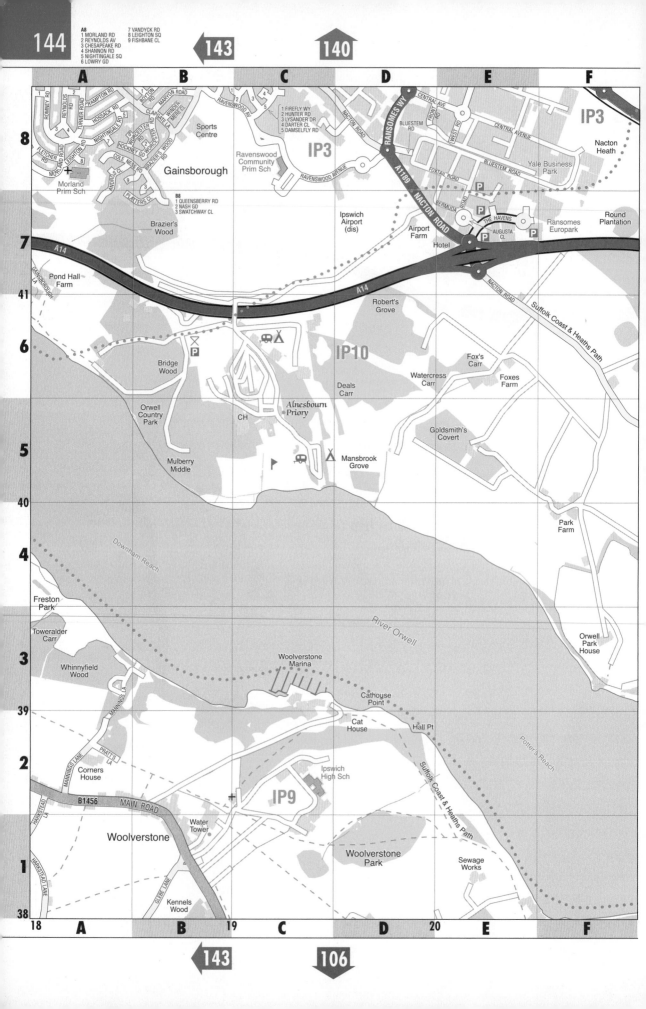

144

A8
1 MORLAND RD
2 REYNOLDS AV
3 CHESAPEAKE RD
4 SHANNON RD
5 NIGHTINGALE SQ
6 LOWRY GD
7 VANDYCK RD
8 LEIGHTON SQ
9 FISHBANE CL

143

140

IP3

Nacton
Heath

Gainsborough

1 FIREFLY WY
2 HUNTER RD
3 LYSANDER DR
4 DARTER CL
5 DAMSELFLY RD

IP3

Sports
Centre

Ravenswood
Community
Prim Sch

RANSOMES WY

CENTRAL AVE

Bluestem
RD

WEST RD

CENTRAL AVENUE

Yale Business
Park

A1189

FOXTAIL ROAD

BLUESTEM ROAD

Morland
Prim Sch

Brazier's
Wood

B8
1 QUEENSBERRY RD
2 NASH GD
3 SWATHWAY CL

Ipswich
Airport
(dis)

NACTON ROAD

Airport
Farm

Hotel

BERMUDA

THE HAVENS
AUGUSTA
CL

Ransomes
Europark

Round
Plantation

A14

Pond Hall
Farm

A14

NACTON ROAD

Suffolk Coast & Heaths Path

Robert's
Grove

IP10

Fox's
Carr

Foxes
Farm

Bridge
Wood

Watercress
Carr

Orwell
Country
Park

Deals
Carr

CH

Alnesbourn
Priory

Goldsmith's
Covert

Park
Farm

Mulberry
Middle

Mansbrook
Grove

Downham Reach

Freston
Park

River Orwell

Orwell
Park
House

Toweralder
Carr

Whinnyfield
Wood

Woolverstone
Marina

Cathouse
Point

Potter's Reach

Corners
House

PRATTS LA

MANNINGS LA

Cat
House

Hall Pt

Ipswich
High Sch

Suffolk Coast & Heaths Path

B1456

MAIN ROAD

IP9

HARKSTEAD LA

Woolverstone

Water
Tower

Woolverstone
Park

Sewage
Works

HARKSTEAD LANE

GLEBE LANE

Kennels
Wood

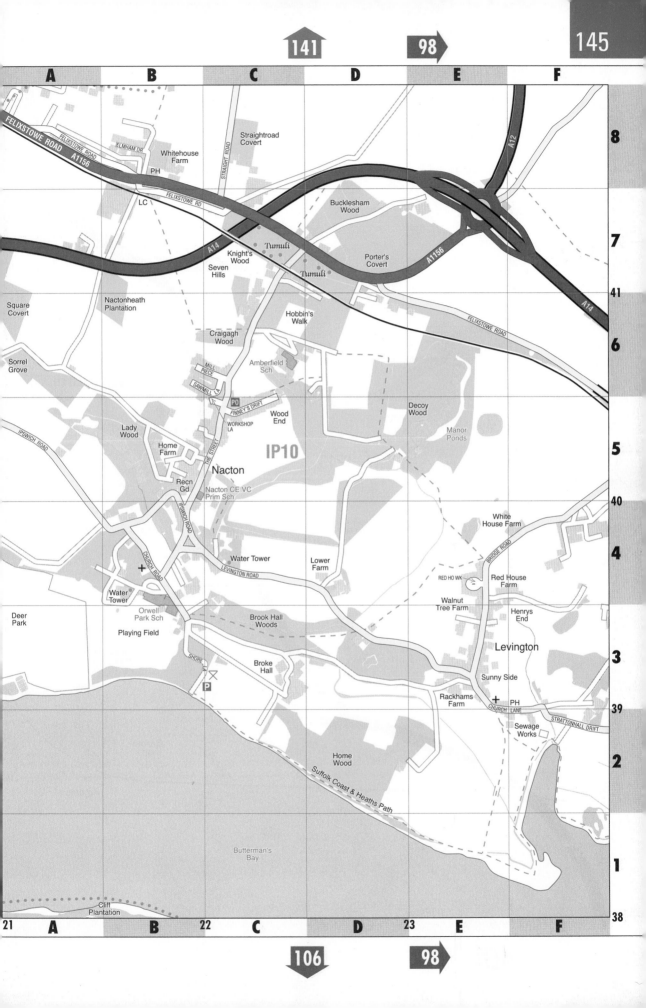

A B C D E F

8

KENNELS LA

Gull Farm

Home Farm

Whitchpit Farm

MILL LA
WATER LANE
PH
LOW RD
TOP RD
Hasketon
BULGE ROAD
TYMMES PL
TYMMES PL

7

FARLINGAYES 1
COLLINGWOOD RD 2
RODNEY CT 3
NELSON WY 4

Morley Farm

MILL LANE
RIVERSIDE
CHURCH RD
Church Farm
SHRUBBERY ROAD
PINNERS LANE

Hasketon Manor
Moat

Hasketon Manor Farm

BARTON RD
COLNE RD
HAUGH LA
BERESFORD DR
EDWIN AVENUE

50

B1079
GRUNDISBURGH ROAD

BEALINGS LA

HASKETON RD

Sports Centre

Farlingaye County High Sch

OSBOLD
MISTLEY WAY
HAUGHGATE CLOSE
WARWICK AVE
PO

6

Willow Farm

Hasketon Grange

Grange Farm

Yew Tree House

Shrubbery Farm

The Plantation

MANOR ROAD

PRENTICES LA
GROVE ROAD
TENNYSON CV
HASKETON RD
RANSOM RD
CATHERINE ROAD
UPR

MOORFIELD RD
WOOLNOUGH RD

WOODBRIDGE

Woodbridge Sch

BREDFIELD ST
NORTH HL

5

IP13

Blunt's Wood

Gazebo Farm

GRUNDISBURGH ROAD
B1079
GRUNDISBURGH RD

OLNEY RD
GROVE ROAD
NAUNTON RD
MILL VW CL
COLLETT'S WLK
WILMSLOW AV
CONNACH RD
MOOR'S WY
PO
Buttrum's Mill
St Marys CE Prim Sch
BURKITT ROAD
THEATRE ST
SECKFORD ST
PO

49

Queech Wood

Bealings House

Wood Farm Cottages

BULLARD'S LA
PEMBROKE AV
DIR BRIDGE HL
BRIDGEWOOD RD
Woodbridge Cemy
CEMETERY LA
PORTLAND CR
Queen's Head La
MARKET HILL

4

ROSERY LA
LODGE RD
Rosery Farm

LADY MARGARET GD 1
GREYFRIARS 2
ST PETER'S CL 3

A12

PETERHOUSE CR
NEWNHAM AV
CLARE AVENUE
GIRTON CL
Kyson Prim Sch
OLD BARRACK ROAD
WARREN HILL RD
HILLY FIELDS
WESTHOLME CL
MORLEY AV
CHERRY TREE RD
BIRCH CL
BEECH WAY

3

CH

Hotel Seckford Hall

Seckford Hall Golf Course

ST ANNES CL 1
TRINITY CL 2
CHRISTCHURCH DR 3
BORRETT PLACE 4
TURNER GD 5
CLAYTON CT 6

OXFORD DR
MAGDALEN DR
SECKFORD HALL RD
PYNN RD
CRANC CL
THROUGH DUNCANS
DUNCANS
The Lancers
IPSWICH ROAD
PINEWOOD
BRIARWOOD RD
Maidensgrave
Porters Wood

IP12

48

Cherry Tree Farm

Football Ground

High Grove

DUKE'S MD
DUKE'S PK
CALIFORNIA

Broom Hill

Kyson Hill National Trust

2

River Fynn

A12

BROCK LANE
TOP STREET
SANDY LANE

BROOMHEATH

Kingston

Harrison Wood

Martlesham Creek

1

MARTLESHAM RD
BEALINGS ROAD

Beacon Hill Farm

Gorse Fell

PH
THE STREET
Recreation Ground

MAIN ROAD
SCHOOL LA
TOP ST
PIGHTLE LANE

Creek Farm

Sluice Farm

Sewage Works

Dunnett's Hill Plantation

REDWALD CL

Sluice Wood

47

24 A B 25 C D 26 E F

E-4
1 GONVILLE CL
2 DOWNING CL
3 ST EDMUNDS CL
4 PORTLAND CR
5 QUEENS AV
6 FITZWILLIAM CL
7 CHURCHILL CL
8 ANDERSON'S WY

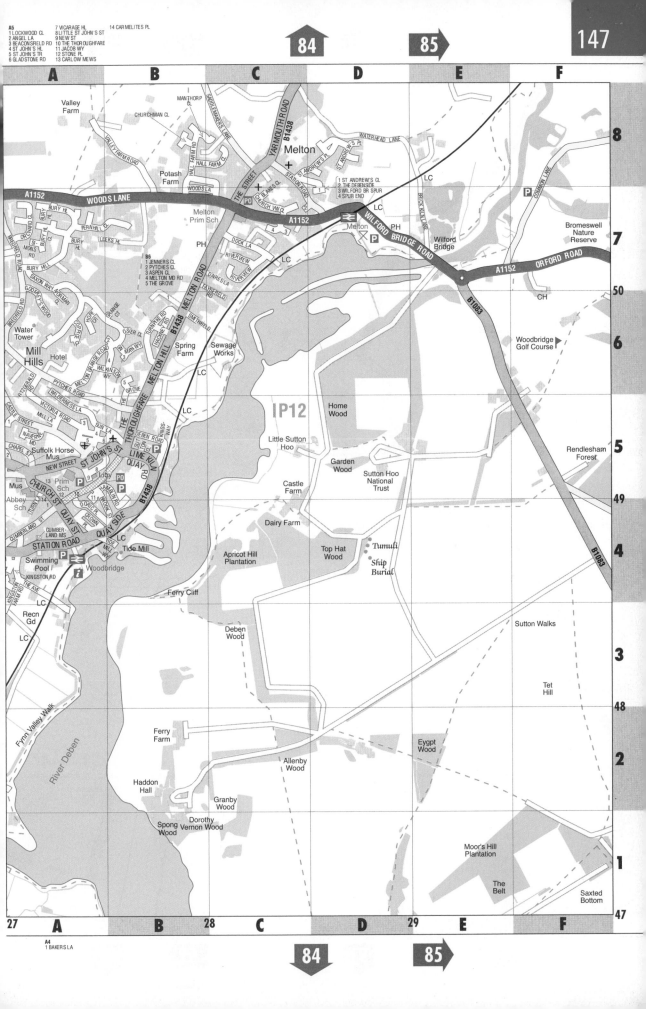

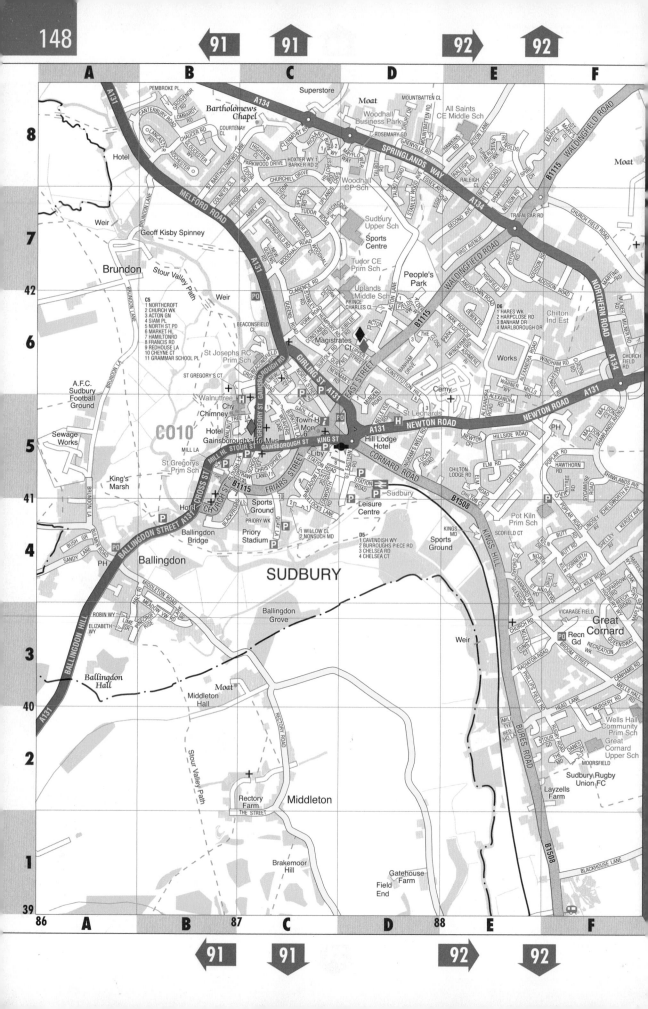

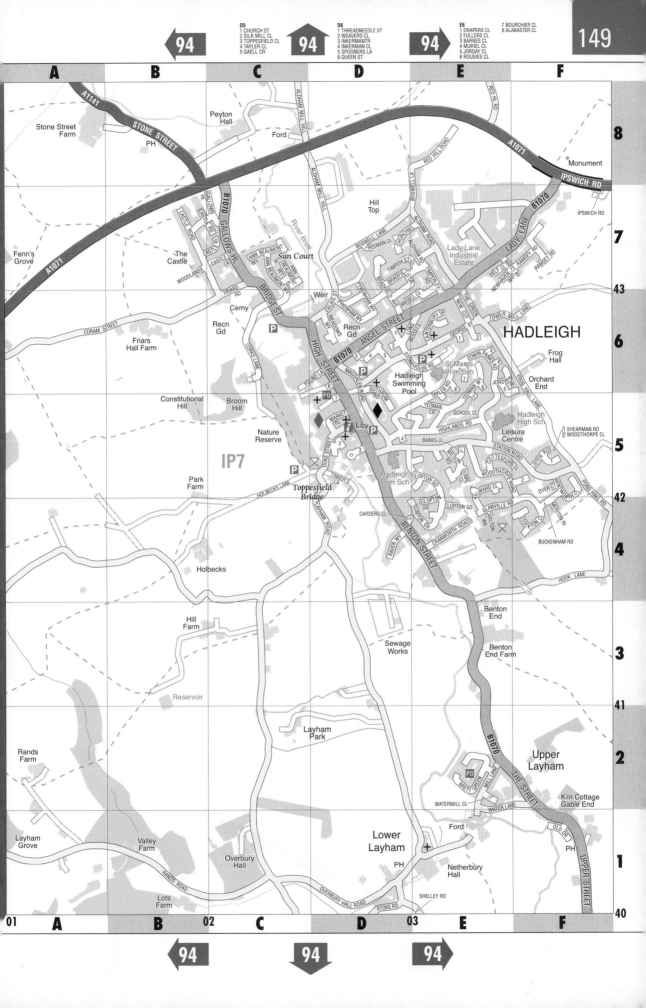

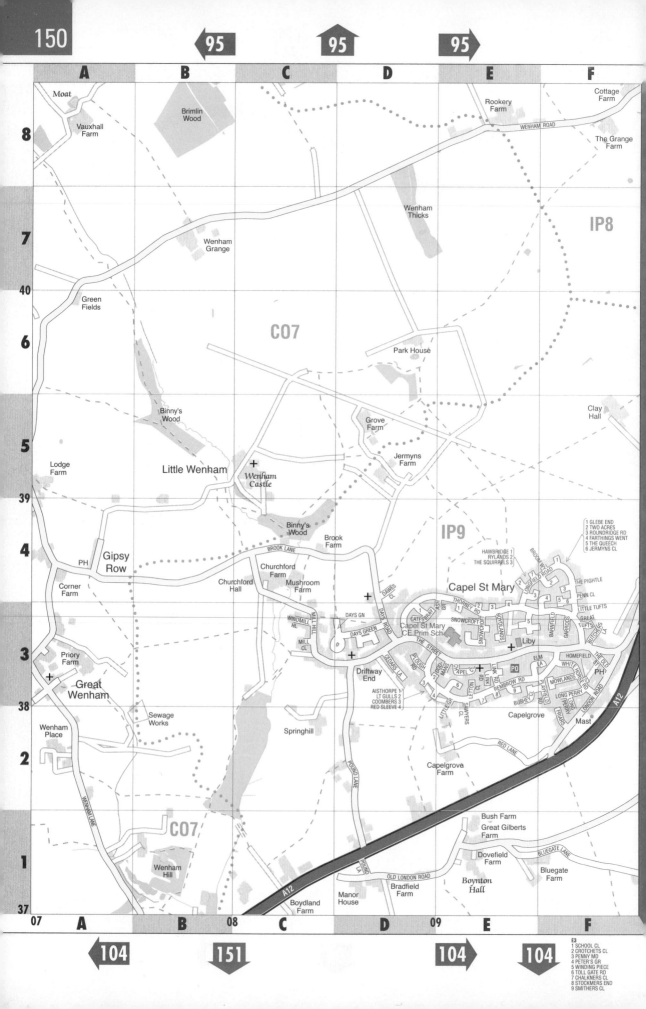

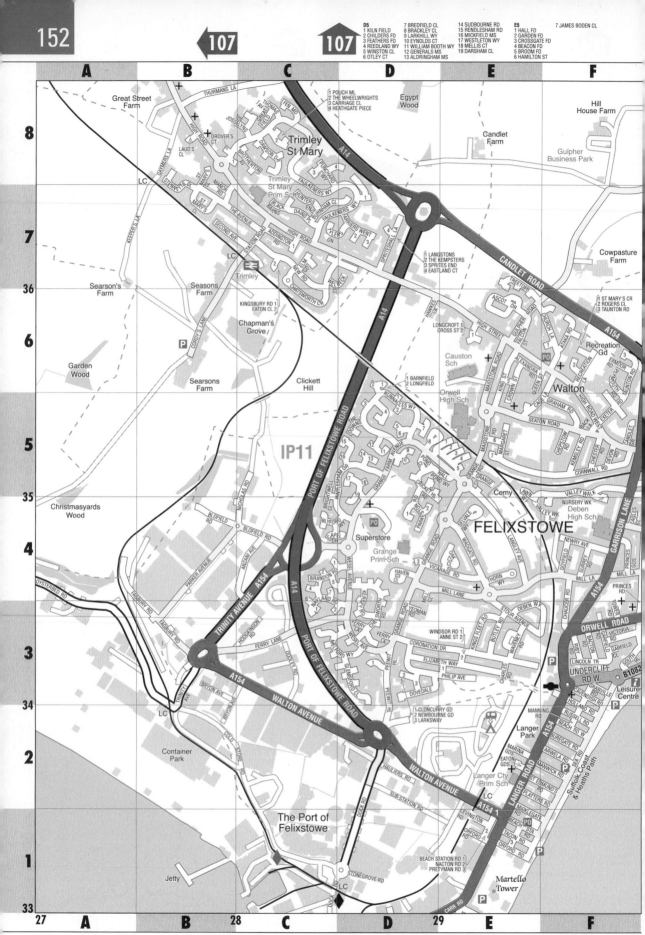

D5
1 KILN FIELD
2 CHILDERS FD
3 FEATHERS FD
4 REEDLAND WY
5 WINSTON CL
6 OTLEY CT

1 POUCH ML
2 THE WHEELWRIGHTS
3 CARRIAGE CL
4 HEATHGATE PIECE

7 BREDFIELD CL
8 BRACKLEY CL
9 LARKHILL WY
10 EYNOLDS CT
11 WILLIAM BOOTH WY
12 GENERALS MS
13 ALDRINGHAM MS

14 SUDBOURNE RD
15 RENDLESHAM RD
16 MICKFIELD MS
17 WESTLETON WY
18 MELLIS CT
19 DARSHAM CL

E5
1 HALL FD
2 GARDEN FD
3 CROSSGATE FD
4 BEACON FD
5 BROOM FD
6 HAMILTON ST

7 JAMES BODEN CL

C3
1 NAYLAND RD
2 ICKWORTH CT

C4
1 LIDGATE CT
2 WICKHAMBROOK CT
3 SUDBURY RD
4 EUSTON CT
5 KENTFORD RD
6 THURSTON CT
7 BOXFORD CT

D3
1 SHOTLEY CL
2 HOLBROOK CR
3 PARSONAGE CL

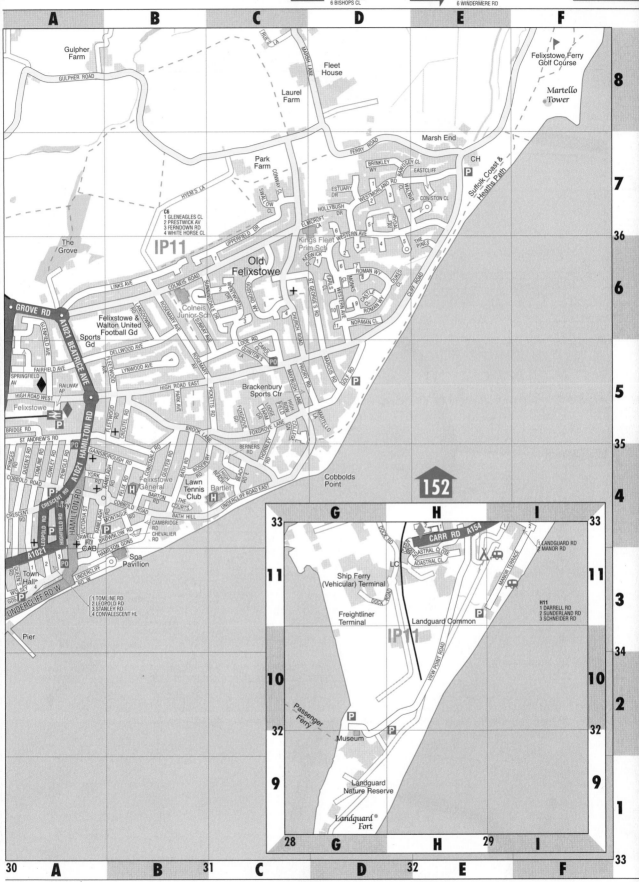

D6
1 TARN HOWS CL
2 ENNERDALE CL
3 LANGDALE CL
4 CUMBERLAND CL
5 GRASMERE AV
6 BISHOPS CL

7 FRIARS CL
8 DEACON CT
9 BARONS CL
10 KNIGHTS CL
11 SAXON CL

D7
1 RUSHMEADOW WY
2 WRENS PK
3 WHINYARD WY
4 ULLSWATER AV
5 STUARTCL
6 WINDERMERE RD

Gulpher
Farm

GULPHER ROAD

Fleet
House

Laurel
Farm

FERRY ROAD

Marsh End

Felixstowe Ferry
Golf Course

Martello
Tower

Park
Farm

CONWAY CL

HYEM'S LA

SWALLOW CL

BRINKLEY WY

BAWDSEY CL

EASTCLIFF

CH

Suffolk Coast &
Heaths Path

C6
1 GLENEAGLES CL
2 PRESTWICK AV
3 FERNDOWN RD
4 WHITE HORSE CL

ESTUARY DR

WESTMORLAND RD

WALNUT

CONISTON CL

RYDAL

HOLLYBUSH DR

ELMCROFT LA

WESTERN AVE

THE PINES

IP11

The
Grove

UPPERFIELD DR

Old
Felixstowe

Kings Fleet
Prim Sch

KESWICK

EARLS

ROMAN WY

MOINS

CASTLE

DUKES CL

CLIFF ROAD

GROVE RD

A1021 BEATRICE AVE

LINKS AVE

COLNEIS ROAD

SHANNINGDALE DR

Colneis
Junior Sch

WESTWORTH

GOSFORD WY

+

CHURCH ROAD

CARLS

WESTERN AVE

ROMAN WY

NORMAN CL

GLENFIELD AVE

Felixstowe &
Walton United
Football Gd

Sports
Gd

LANGDOWNE

ROSEMARY AVE

DELLWOOD AVE

LYNWOOD AVE

HIGH ROAD EAST

PARK AVE

LOOE RD

CAROL

QUINTON'S PO

PRIORY RD

MARCUS RD

GOLF RD

P

FAIRFIELD AVE

FLEETWOOD

FELD RD

FOXGROVE

LODGE LA

MARTELLO

Springfield
Av

Railway
AP

HIGH ROAD WEST

Felixstowe

GAINSBOROUGH RD

FLEETWOOD RD

CROUTEL RD

BROOK LANE

FOXGROVE GD

HIGH FIELD

FARM

COLLEGE GN

Brackenbury
Sports Ctr

BRIDGE RD

ST ANDREW'S RD

CONSTABLE RD

QUILTER RD

PICKETTS RD

ROSEBERY

HIGH BEACH

BEACH RD

BERNERS RD

RODNEY RD

UNDERCLIFF ROAD EAST

Cobbolds
Point

PRINCES RD

QUEEN'S RD

COWLEY RD

PENFOLD RD

A1021 HAMILTON RD

YORK

RANELAGH RD

FELIX RD

MONTAGUE RD

BARTON RD

Felixstowe
General

Lawn Tennis
Club

H

Bartlet

H

COBBOLD ROAD

CRESCENT RD

HIGHFIELD RD

P

Liby

VICTORIA ST

BROWNLOW RD

THE COURTS

BATH HILL

CAMBRIDGE RD

CHEVALIER RD

CRESCENT RD

P

A1021

CAB

HAMILTON GDNS

Spa
Pavillion

1 TOMLINE RD
2 LEOPOLD RD
3 STANLEY RD
4 CONVALESCENT HL

QUEEN'S RD

WOLSEY RD

GDS

UNDERCLIFF RD W

UNDERCLIFF RD W

Town
Hall

PO

Pier

Inset map

33

G   **H**   **I**

CARR RD   A154

33

DOCK RD

ADASTRAL CLOSE

ADASTRAL CL

LC

Ship Ferry
(Vehicular) Terminal

MANOR TERRACE

1 LANDGUARD RD
2 MANOR RD

11

11

Freightliner
Terminal

DOCK ROAD

Landguard Common

P

H11
1 DARRELL RD
2 SUNDERLAND RD
3 SCHNEIDER RD

IP11

VIEW POINT ROAD

10

10

Passenger
Ferry

P

32

Museum

P

32

9

Landguard
Nature Reserve

9

Landguard
Fort

28   **G**   **H**   **29**   **I**

33

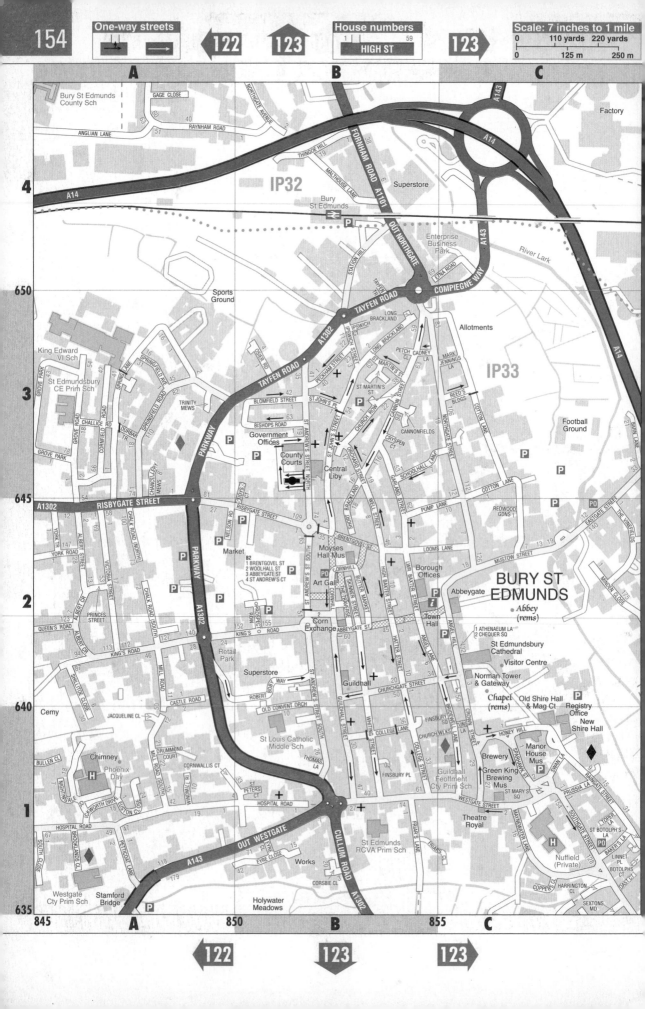

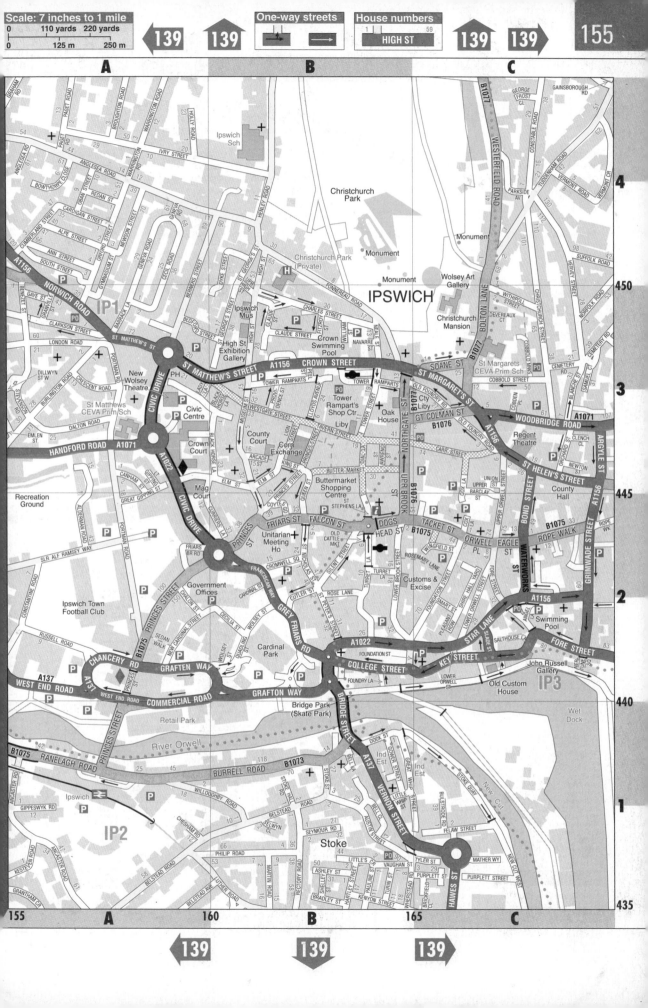

Index

Church Rd **6** Beckenham BR2..........**53** C6

Place name	Location number	Locality, town or village	Postcode district	Page and grid square
May be abbreviated on the map	Present when a number indicates the place's position in a crowded area of mapping	Shown when more than one place has the same name	District for the indexed place	Page number and grid reference for the standard mapping

Public and commercial buildings are highlighted in magenta   **Places of interest** are highlighted in blue with a star★

Abbreviations used in the index

Acad	Academy	Comm	Common	Gd	Ground	L	Leisure	Prom	Prom
App	Approach	Cott	Cottage	Gdn	Garden	La	Lane	Rd	Road
Arc	Arcade	Cres	Crescent	Gn	Green	Liby	Library	Recn	Recreation
Ave	Avenue	Cswy	Causeway	Gr	Grove	Mdw	Meadow	Ret	Retail
Bglw	Bungalow	Ct	Court	H	Hall	Meml	Memorial	Sh	Shopping
Bldg	Building	Ctr	Centre	Ho	House	Mkt	Market	Sq	Square
Bsns, Bus	Business	Ctry	Country	Hospl	Hospital	Mus	Museum	St	Street
Bvd	Boulevard	Cty	County	HQ	Headquarters	Orch	Orchard	Sta	Station
Cath	Cathedral	Dr	Drive	Hts	Heights	Pal	Palace	Terr	Terrace
Cir	Circus	Dro	Drove	Ind	Industrial	Par	Parade	TH	Town Hall
Cl	Close	Ed	Education	Inst	Institute	Pas	Passage	Univ	University
Cnr	Corner	Emb	Embankment	Int	International	Pk	Park	Wk, Wlk	Walk
Coll	College	Est	Estate	Intc	Interchange	Pl	Place	Wr	Water
Com	Community	Ex	Exhibition	Junc	Junction	Prec	Precinct	Yd	Yard

Index of localities, towns and villages

A

Acton 92 B7
Acton Place 92 B8
Akenham 134 F6
Alburgh 7 A1
Aldeburgh 130 D4
Aldeby 9 F8
Alderton 99 E4
Aldham 94 E8
Aldringham 129 D3
All Saints
  South Elmham 24 B5
Allwood Green 36 A2
Alpheton 78 A5
Ampton 33 A2
Annis Hill 110 E3
Apsey Green 126 A3
Ardleigh Heath 103 F1
Ash Abbey 127 F3
Ashbocking 69 A1
Ash Corner 127 F7
Ashen 89 E5
Ashfield 54 D2
Ashfield Cum Thorpe ..54 C1
Ashfield Green
  Stradbroke 39 D4
Ashfield Green
  Wickhambrook 62 A2
Ashley 60 F8
Ash Street 80 A1
Aspall 53 E4
Assington 92 F1
Assington Green 76 B6
Athelington 38 E2
Attleton Green 61 D1
Audley End
  Burston and Shimpling ..20 E5
Audley End Lawshall 77 D8

B

Babel Green 75 D3
Back Street 61 E5
Bacton 51 F5
Bacton Green 51 E4
Badingham 56 A6
Badwell Ash 50 E7
Badwell Green 51 B8
Ballingdon 148 B4
Banyard's Green 40 C4

Bardwell 34 C4
Barham 82 C6
Barking 125 A1
Barking Tye 81 A7
Barley Green 39 C5
Barnaby Green 26 C2
Barnardiston 75 B3
Barnby 10 B5
Barnham 16 C2
Barningham 34 F7
Barrow 47 A2
Barsham 9 A4
Barton Mills 116 D2
Base Green 51 B2
Bath Side 107 B3
Battisford 66 F1
Battisford Tye 66 C1
Battlesea Green 39 A6
Battlies Green 49 C3
Bawdsey 99 F3
Baylham 81 E6
Baythorne End 89 C5
Beacon Hill 137 F3
Beccles 111 D5
Beck Row 30 A8
Bedfield 54 E5
Bedingfield 53 F7
Bedingham Green 7 B7
Belchamp Otten 90 E4
Belchamp St Paul 90 D5
Belchamp Walter 90 F3
Bell's Corner 102 F8
Bell's Cross 82 D7
Belstead 142 C7
Benacre 27 A7
Benhall Green 72 C8
Benhall Street 71 F8
Bentley 104 F8
Beyton 49 F1
Beyton Green 49 F2
Bigsby's Corner 72 D8
Bildeston 79 F4
Billingford 21 B1
Birdbrook 89 A4
Birds End 62 B7
Bird Street 80 A7
Blackheath 42 C5
Blacksmith's Green ...53 C5
Black Street 11 A2
Blackthorpe 49 C2
Blaxhall 72 B4
Bleach Green 39 A8
Blo' Norton 18 E2
Bloodman's Corner 3 A6

Bloodmoor Hill 114 E2
Blundeston 3 A4
Blyford 42 C7
Blythburgh 42 F6
Bobby Hill 35 C5
Boot Street 137 D6
Borley 91 C5
Borley Green Borley ...91 B5
Borley Green Woolpit ..65 E7
Botesdale 36 B6
Bowbeck 34 C6
Bower House Tye 93 E3
Boxford 93 C3
Boxted 102 F4
Boxted 77 A6
Boxted Cross 103 A3
Boyden End 61 D2
Boyland Common 20 A7
Boyton 86 B2
Boyton End 89 B7
Brabling Green 126 E6
Bradfield 105 C1
Bradfield Combust 64 A4
Bradfield St Clare 64 C4
Bradfield St George ..64 D7
Braiseworth 37 D2
Bramfield 41 F4
Bramford 134 A2
Brampton 25 E5
Brampton Street 25 E4
Brandeston 70 B7
Brandon 6 A1
Brantham 104 F4
Bredfield 84 C7
Brent Eleigh 79 A2
Bressingham 19 F4
Bressingham Common ..19 F5
Brettenham 17 B6
Brettenham 79 C8
Brewers Green 20 B3
Bridge Green 20 F6
Bridge Street 77 F4
Brightwell 98 A6
Brinkley 59 E2
Broadgrass Green 50 C1
Broad Green Cheveley ..60 F6
Broad Green Chevington ..62 B6
Broad Green Creeting St Peter or
  West Creeting 67 C6
Broad Street 93 C5
Broadway 118 C6
Brockdish 21 F2
Brockford Green 53 A4
Brockford Street 52 F5

Brockley Corner 32 D2
Brockley Green Hartest ..63 A1
Brockley Green Hundon ..75 C2
Broke Hall 140 E3
Brome 117 B7
Brome Street 117 E8
Bromeswell 85 A5
Brook Green 63 E5
Brook Street 77 A3
Broome 110 D7
Broome Heath 110 D7
Broom Hill 146 E2
Broom's Barn 46 F4
Brown Street 52 A2
Browston Green 2 E8
Bruisyard 56 C5
Brundish 55 C8
Brundish Street 39 E1
Brundon 148 A7
Bucklesham 98 A5
Bulcamp 42 D7
Bulmer 91 C3
Bulmer Tye 91 D1
Bungay 110 B3
Bures 101 C5
Bures Green 101 D6
Burgate 36 E6
Burgh 83 F6
Burgh St Peter 10 B8
Burrough End 59 E2
Burrough Green 59 F2
Burstall 95 D7
Burstallhill 95 C8
Burston 20 E6
Burthorpe 47 B3
Burwell 44 A5
Bury St Edmunds 154 C2
Bush Green 64 D4
Butley 86 B5
Butley High Corner ...86 C4
Butley Low Corner 86 C4
Button Haugh Green ..50 F4
Button's Green 78 E8
Buxhall 66 A4
Buxhall Fen Street 66 A6

C

Calais Street 93 D2
Calford Green 133 D5
California 140 B6
Camps Heath 112 D3

Candle Street 35 F5
Canham's Green 51 F4
Capel Green 86 A4
Capel St Andrew 86 B3
Capel St Mary 150 E4
Capon's Green 55 E6
Carlton 74 A8
Carlton
  Kelsale cum Carlton ..128 C6
Carlton Colville 114 C2
Carlton Green 74 A6
Castle Hill 135 A3
Castling's Heath 93 D6
Cattawade 104 E4
Cavendish 76 D1
Cavenham 47 A8
Cay Hill 52 C2
Chantry 138 D2
Charles Tye 80 C7
Charsfield 70 B3
Chattisham 95 C5
Chedburgh 62 C4
Chediston 41 C8
Chediston Green 24 C1
Chelmondiston 106 C8
Chelsworth 79 E3
Chelsworth Common ..79 E2
Cheveley 60 E7
Chevington 62 C6
Chickering 38 F7
Chillesford 86 C7
Chilton 92 B5
Chilton Street 75 F1
Chimney Street 75 C3
Chippenhall Green 40 A6
Chippenham 45 C8
Church End 106 F7
Church Street 90 D6
Clare 90 B8
Clay Common 26 B4
Claydon 134 C8
Claypits 109 B4
Clay Street 35 D2
Clopton Corner 69 E1
Clopton Green
  Wickhambrook 62 A1
Clopton Green Woolpit ..65 D7
Cobbler's Green 7 C6
Cock & End 75 C8
Cockfield 64 C1
Cocks Green 64 A5
Cock Street 102 C2
Coddenham 68 C1
Coddenham Green 67 D2

Colchester Green 64 E2
Coldfair Green 129 B2
Coles Green 95 D4
Cole's Green 126 E1
Colton 48 F5
Combs 124 C1
Combs Ford 124 D4
Coney Weston 17 E1
Conyers Green 49 B7
Cookley 41 A6
Cookley Green 40 F6
Cook's Green 79 D8
Copdock 95 F4
Cornard Tye 92 C4
Corton 3 C4
Cotton 52 B6
Cove Bottom 26 E3
Covehithe 27 B4
Cow Green 51 F4
Cowlinge 61 B1
Cox Common 25 A5
Crackthorn Corner 19 A1
Cranley 37 F3
Cranmer Green 35 E2
Cransford 56 B3
Cratfield 40 D6
Creeting Bottoms 67 F5
Creeting St Mary 125 F8
Creeting St Peter 67 C5
Cretingham 69 F7
Cross Green Cockfield 64 B2
Cross Green Hartest 77 A7
Cross Green Hitcham 79 E7
Cross Street 38 C7
Crowfield 68 D4
Crown Corner 39 D1
Crownland 35 D1
Cuckold's Green 26 C6
Cuckoo Green 3 A6
Cuckoo Tye 92 A7
Culford 32 D1
Culfordheath 32 F5
Culpho 137 A7
Curlew Green 128 C7

D

Dagworth 66 E8
Daisy Green Great Ashfield 51 A6
Daisy Green
  Wickham Skeith 52 D7
Dalham 61 C8
Dallinghoo 70 D1
Dam Green 19 C8
Dandy Corner 52 B6
Darmsden 125 F1
Darsham 42 C1
Debach 70 A1
Debenham 53 E2
Dedham 103 F4
Dedham Heath 103 F2
Denham 61 F8
Denham Hoxne 38 D5
Denham End 46 F2
Dennington 55 E5
Dennington Corner 126 C8
Denston 76 A7
Denton 7 A3
Depden 62 B3
Depden Green 62 B4
Dickleburgh 21 B5
Dickleburgh Moor 21 D6
Diss 20 C4
Ditchingham 110 C7
Ditton Green 60 B4
Dockeney 8 F6
Dorking Tye 101 D7
Dorley's Corner 128 D8
Dovercourt 107 B2
Down Field 28 F2
Drakestone Green 93 F8
Drinkstone 65 C8
Drinkstone Green 65 B7
Dublin 53 E8
Duke Street 95 B5
Dullingham 59 F5
Dullingham Ley 60 A3
Dunstall Green 61 E7
Dunwich 43 B1

E

Earl's Green 51 D5
Earl Soham 54 E2
Earl Stoneham 67 E5
Earsham 7 E4
Earsham Street 22 C1
East Barton 49 C4
East Bergholt 151 C4
Eastbridge 58 D4
East End East Bergholt 104 E6
East End Stonham Aspal 68 D6
East Green
  Kelsale cum Carlton 57 E4
Easton 70 E5
Edge Green 19 B8
Edwardstone 93 A5
Ellingham 8 D7
Ellough 9 F1
Ellough Hill 111 D3
Elmsett 80 F1
Elmswell 50 E2
Elveden 15 D3

Eriswell 13 F1
Erwarton 106 D5
Euston 16 F1
Exning 120 B8
Eye 117 D3
Eyke 85 B6

F

Fakenham Magna 33 E7
Falkenham 98 E2
Falkenham Sink 98 F2
Farley Green 75 D8
Farnham 72 A7
Felixstowe 152 E4
Felixstowe Ferry 108 C8
Felsham 65 A3
Feltwell 4 D5
Fenstead End 76 E5
Fen Street Hopton 18 B2
Fen Street Redgrave 19 C2
Fern Hill 77 B4
Fersfield 19 D6
Finkle Green 89 A2
Finningham 52 B8
Flempton 47 F8
Flixton 7 D1
Flowton 81 C1
Foals Green 39 D2
Fordham 29 B1
Fornham All Saints 48 B6
Fornham St Genevieve 48 C6
Fornham St Martin 48 C6
Forward Green 67 E7
Four Ashes 35 C1
Foxash Estate 104 B1
Foxearth 91 B7
Framlingham 126 D2
Framsden 69 B6
Freckenham 29 F3
Frenze 20 F3
Fressingfield 39 D8
Freston 143 D3
Friday Street Benhall 72 B7
Friday Street Brandeston 70 A6
Friday Street Rendlesham 85 D7
Friston 72 F7
Fritton 2 B7
Frizzeler's Green 47 C1
Frostenden 26 C4
Frostenden Corner 26 D3

G

Gainsborough Ipswich 139 F1
Gainsborough Ipswich 144 B8
Garboldisham 18 D4
Garlic Street 22 A6
Gasthorpe 18 A4
Gazeley 46 B3
Gedding 65 A5
Geldeston 8 F7
Genesis Green 61 F4
Gestingthorpe 90 F1
Gillingham 9 C6
Gipping 52 B2
Gipsy Row 150 A4
Gisleham 11 A3
Gislingham 36 D2
Gissing 20 D3
Glemsford 77 B2
Goddard's Corner 55 E7
Gosbeck 68 D2
Gosland Green 76 A5
Gosling Green 93 C5
Grass Green 89 D1
Great Ashfield 50 F6
Great Barton 49 A6
Great Bealings 137 E6
Great Blakenham 82 A5
Great Bradley 74 C7
Great Bricett 80 E5
Great Common 8 E2
Great Cornard 148 C2
Great Finborough 66 B4
Great Glemham 71 D8
Great Green Burgate 36 D7
Great Green Cockfield 64 D2
Great Green Denton 7 A4
Great Green Thrandeston 37 C8
Great Horkesley 102 E1
Great Livermere 33 C2
Great Saxham 47 C1
Great Thurlow 74 E5
Great Waldingfield 92 C6
Great Welnetham 63 F6
Great Wenham 150 A3
Great Wratting 74 C3
Great Yeldham 90 A1
Greenstreet Green 80 D5
Greenwich 139 E1
Grimstone End 49 F8
Grinstead Hill 125 E3
Gromford 72 C5
Groton 93 B4
Grundisburgh 83 D5
Gulling Green 63 A5
Gunton 113 C6

H

Hacheston 71 A6

Hadleigh 149 F6
Hadleigh Heath 93 F4
Hagmore Green 93 B2
Halesworth 118 A4
Hall Green 90 C2
Hanchet End 132 A8
Hanningfields Green 63 F1
Hargrave 62 B6
Harkstead 106 B5
Harleston 66 B7
Harleston
  Redenhall with Harleston 22 E5
Harrow Green 63 D1
Hartest 77 A7
Hartest Hill 77 C7
Hart's Green 63 E2
Harwich 107 A3
Hasketon 146 E5
Haughley 51 C1
Haughley Green 51 C3
Haughley New Street 51 B1
Haverhill 132 C6
Hawkedon 76 D7
Hawstead 63 D6
Hawstead Green 63 E5
Hazel Stub 132 A5
Heckfield Green 38 D7
Hedenham 7 E8
Helions Bumpstead 88 B4
Helmingham 69 B4
Hemingstone 82 C8
Hemley 98 E5
Hemp Green 57 C8
Hengrave 48 A7
Henley 82 D6
Henny Street 91 F1
Henstead 26 E8
Hepworth 35 A6
Herringfleet 2 D4
Herringswell 46 C8
Hessett 64 F8
Heveningham 40 F3
Hickford Hill 90 C7
Higham 103 D6
Higham 46 E4
High Green 63 D7
High Rougham 49 E1
High Street Darsham 42 E1
High Street Iken 73 B2
High Street
  'St Margaret, Ilketsall' 24 D7
High Street Green 66 A2
Hightown Green 65 D3
Hinderclay 35 E7
Hintlesham 95 C6
Hitcham 79 E6
Hobbles Green 75 A8
Hockwold cum Wilton 5 A3
Hoggard's Green 64 A3
Holbrook 105 E7
Hollesley 99 E7
Hollybush Corner 64 D6
Holly Hill 110 B8
Holton 118 E4
Holton St Mary 103 F7
Holton St Mary 151 A8
Holywell Row 30 C8
Homersfield 23 B8
Honey Tye 102 B6
Honington 33 E5
Hoo 70 B5
Hopton 18 C2
Hopton on Sea 3 C7
Horham 38 E3
Horner's Green 93 C4
Hornestreet 103 C3
Horringer 63 A8
Hoxne 38 B8
Hulver Street 10 C1
Humble Green 92 F8
Hundon 75 E3
Hunston 50 D7
Hunston Green 50 D5
Huntingfield 41 A5

I

Icklingham 31 D4
Iken 72 F2
Ilketshall St Andrew 8 E2
Ilketshall St Lawrence 24 F6
Ilketshall St Margaret 24 E8
Ingham 32 F1
Ipswich 155 B3
Isleham 29 B5
Ixworth 34 B2
Ixworth Thorpe 33 F4

K

Kedington 133 E7
Kelsale 128 C7
Kennett 45 F7
Kenninghall 19 B8
Kenny Hill 12 F2
Kentford 46 A5
Kenton 54 B5
Kenton Corner 54 C4
Kersey 94 A7
Kersey Tye 93 E6
Kersey Upland 93 F5
Kesgrave 141 C8
Kessingland 11 C2
Kessingland Beach 27 C8

Kettlebaston 79 C5
Kettleburgh 70 C7
Kingshall Green 64 D7
Kingshall Street 64 D8
Kingston 146 F2
Kirby Cane 8 E8
Kirby Row 8 E7
Kirkley 115 B5
Kirtling 60 E3
Kirtling Green 60 E2
Kirton 98 E2
Knaves Green 53 A5
Knettishall 17 F3
Knodishall 73 A8
Knodishall Common 129 A2
Knowl Green 90 C4

L

Lackford 31 F1
Lady's Green 61 F6
Lakenheath 109 E7
Lamarsh 101 A6
Lamb Corner 103 E2
Lambfair Green 75 A8
Lampardbrook 70 E8
Landwade 44 D6
Langham 103 C2
Langham 50 D8
Langton Green 117 D4
Lattinford Hill 151 D8
Lavenham 78 D4
Lawford 104 E2
Lawshall 63 E1
Lawshall Green 77 F8
Laxfield 40 C3
Leavenheath 102 B7
Leiston 129 B5
Letheringham 70 C4
Levington 145 E3
Lidgate 61 C4
Lindsey 93 D7
Lindsey Tye 93 E8
Linstead Parva 40 E8
Liston 91 D7
Little Bealings 137 E5
Little Blakenham 81 F3
Little Bradley 74 E6
Little Cornard 92 C2
Little Ditton 60 C5
Little Finborough 66 B1
Little Glemham 71 E5
Little Green Burgate 36 D5
Little Green Gislingham 36 C3
Little Horkesley 102 B3
Little Knowles Green 62 B5
Little London 66 E2
Little Saxham 47 D2
Little Stonham 67 F6
Little Thurlow 74 E5
Little Thurlow Green 74 E6
Little Waldingfield 92 B8
Little Welnetham 64 B6
Little Wenham 150 B5
Little Whittingham
  Green 40 A8
Little Wratting 74 E4
Little Yeldham 90 E6
Long Green 36 D8
Long Melford 77 F1
Long Melford 91 E8
Long Thurlow 51 B7
Lound 2 F5
Lower Common 25 B3
Lower Falkenham 98 F1
Lower Green 46 E4
Lower Hacheston 127 F8
Lower Holbrook 106 A6
Lower Layham 149 D1
Lower Raydon 94 D1
Lower Street Stansfield 76 C6
Lower Street Stutton 105 D5
Lowestoft 113 F1
Low Green 63 E7
Lynford 6 C5

M

Mace Green 95 E4
Magpie Green 19 E1
Maidenhall 139 B1
Maidensgrave 146 E3
Malting End 61 E1
Manningtree 104 F2
Man's Cross 89 F2
Market Weston 35 A8
Marlesford 71 C5
Martlesham 84 A1
Martlesham Heath 98 B7
Maypole Green
  Bradfield St George 64 D6
Maypole Green
  Dennington 55 D6
Meadowend 89 E3
Mellis 37 A5
Mellis Green 36 F5
Mells 118 E2
Melon Green 63 C4
Melton 147 C8
Mendham 23 A6
Mendlesham 52 E4
Mendlesham Green 52 D2
Metfield 23 C3
Methersgate 84 E1

Mettingham 8 D4
Mickfield 68 B8
Mickley Green 63 B4
Middle Green 46 E4
Middle Harling 18 B8
Middleton 148 C2
Middleton 58 B6
Middleton Moor 58 A6
Middlewood Green 67 D8
Milden 79 B1
Mildenhall 116 D6
Mile End 77 A7
Mill Common 25 C4
Mill End 60 F3
Mill Green
  Burston and Shimpling 20 E7
Mill Green Buxhall 65 F4
Mill Green Edwardstone 93 B5
Mill Green Stonham Aspal 68 B7
Mill Hill 77 E6
Mill Hills 147 A6
Mill Street 102 E8
Mistley 105 A2
Mistley Heath 105 A1
Moats Tye 66 E2
Monewden 69 F5
Monks Eleigh 79 B2
Monk Soham 54 D4
Moulton 45 F3
Mount Bures 101 C3
Mount Pleasant 75 D2
Mundford 6 B8
Mutford 10 D2

N

Nacton 145 C5
Naughton 80 C3
Nayland 102 C5
Nedging 79 F3
Nedging Tye 80 B4
Needham 22 B4
Needham Market 125 E5
Needham Street 46 B4
Nether St 64 E8
Nettlestead 81 C4
Newbourne 98 C5
New England 89 A5
Newman's Green 92 A6
Newmarket 121 B4
New Mistley 105 A2
Newton 92 D3
Newtown 54 D7
Normanston 113 B3
North Common 34 F6
North Cove 10 C4
North End 90 C2
North Green Cratfield 40 C7
North Green
  Kelsale cum Carlton 57 D5
North Green Parham 56 B1
North Lopham 19 A5
Norton 50 B4
Norton Little Green 50 D5
Nowton 63 E7

O

Oak Hill 100 A8
Oakley 38 A8
Occold 37 F1
Offton 81 A4
Old Felixstowe 153 C6
Oldhall Green 64 C3
Old Newton 51 F1
Onehouse 66 C6
Orford 131 C3
Otley 69 C2
Oulton 112 F5
Oulton Broad 114 C8
Ousden 61 E6
Ovington 90 A5

P

Page's Green 53 C4
Pakefield 115 C3
Pakenham 49 E6
Pale Green 88 B5
Palgrave 20 C1
Parham 71 A7
Parkeston 106 F3
Park Gate 61 E3
Park Green 53 B3
Parliament Heath 93 C6
Parney Heath 103 D2
Peasenhall 56 E8
Peats Corner 69 B7
Pentlow 76 E1
Pentlow 90 F7
Pentlow Street 91 A8
Pettaugh 68 E6
Pettistree 127 B4
Pinford End 63 D6
Pitcher's Green 64 D5
Pitman's Corner 53 C5
Playford 137 B5
Polstead 93 F1
Polstead Heath 93 F2
Pooley Street 19 D4
Poslingford 76 A3
Potash 104 F8

Pound Green 61 B1
Poystreet Green 65 E5
Preston St Mary 79 A5
Priory Green 92 F6
Priory Heath 140 D1
Pulham St Mary 21 F8
Puttock End 90 E3

R

Racecourse 140 B2
Ramsey 106 C1
Ramsholt 99 A4
Rattlesden 65 E6
Raydon 94 E1
Reading Green 38 E5
Rede 62 E2
Redenhall 22 E7
Redgrave 36 A8
Redisham 25 B7
Redlingfield 38 D2
Red Lodge 30 B1
Rendham 56 E3
Rendlesham 85 D8
Reydon 119 C7
Reydon Smear 26 F1
Rickinghall 36 A6
Ridgewell 89 D4
Ringsfield 9 B3
Ringsfield Corner 9 B2
Ringshall 80 E7
Ringshall Stocks 80 F6
Risby 47 D5
Rishangles 53 D7
Rodbridge Corner 91 E6
Roman Hill 113 C1
Rooksey Green 78 E6
Roost End 133 E2
Rosedale Park 114 E4
Rose Green Assington ...101 F8
Rose Green Lindsey ...93 D7
Rose Hill 139 F4
Rotchfords 101 F1
Rougham 64 D8
Rougham Green 64 C8
Roydon 20 A3
Rumburgh 24 B4
Rushall 21 F5
Rushbrooke 64 B8
Rushford 17 B4
Rushmere 10 D1
Rushmere St Andrew ..136 E1
Rushmere Street 136 E2
Russel's Green 39 C3

S

Sackers Green 92 D2
St Cross
  South Elmham 23 D7
St James
  South Elmham 23 F4
St Margaret
  South Elmham 23 E6
St Michael
  South Elmham 24 A6
St Nicholas
  South Elmham 23 E6
St Olaves 2 A6
St Peter South Elmham .24 A7
Santon Downham 6 C2
Sapiston 33 F6
Saxham Street 67 C8

Saxmundham 128 D3
Saxon Street 60 D6
Saxstead Bottom 55 C5
Saxtead 55 C4
Saxtead Green 55 B3
Saxtead Little Green ..55 B5
Scole 21 A2
Scole Common 20 F3
Scotland Street 102 F7
Semer 79 F1
Shadingfield 25 E7
Shadwell 17 C6
Shelfanger 20 C6
Shelland 66 A7
Shelley 94 C1
Sherbourne Street ...93 B4
Shimpling
  Burston and Shimpling .21 A6
Shimpling 77 E6
Shimpling Street 77 E8
Shingle Street 100 A5
Shipmeadow 8 F4
Shop Corner 106 C5
Shotford Heath 22 D4
Shotley 106 F6
Shotley Gate 107 A4
Shottisham 99 C7
Sibton 57 A8
Sibton Green 41 D2
Sicklesmere 63 F7
Silverlace Green 71 C7
Silverley's Green 40 B6
Sizewell 58 F1
Slough Hill 77 E7
Smallwood Green 64 F5
Smallworth 18 D3
Smith's Green 88 C3
Smithwood Green 78 C7
Snailwell 45 A6
Snape 72 D4
Snow Street 20 A4
Soham 28 D4
Soham Cotes 28 B6
Somersham 81 C3
Somerton 76 F8
Sotherton 25 E2
Sotherton Corner 25 E1
Sotterley 26 A7
South Cove 26 F4
South Green Hoxne ...38 B5
South Green
  Pulham St Mary 21 F6
South Lopham 19 B4
Southolt 54 B7
Southwold 119 C5
Sowley Green 75 A5
Spexhall 24 F3
Spratt's Street 85 D5
Sproughton 138 A7
Stackyard Green 93 C8
Stambourne 89 B1
Stambourne Green ...89 A1
Stanningfield 64 A4
Stansfield 76 C7
Stanstead 77 C4
Stanton 34 E3
Stanton Chare 34 D5
Stanton Street 50 B5
Stanway Green 39 C1
Starston 22 C7
Steeple Bumpstead ..88 D4
Sternfield 72 D8
Stetchworth 60 A5
Stock Hill 50 E8
Stoke 155 B1
Stoke Ash 37 B1
Stoke by Clare 89 E6

Stoke-by-Nayland ...102 E6
Stoke Park 138 F1
Stone Street Boxford ..93 C2
Stone Street Spexhall ..24 F5
Stonham Aspal 68 A6
Stoven 25 F4
Stowlangtoft 50 C7
Stowmarket 124 E6
Stowupland 67 B6
Stradbroke 39 A5
Stradishall 75 F7
Stratford St Andrew ..71 F7
Stratford St Mary ...103 D5
Stubbing's Green 36 C5
Sturmer 133 C2
Stuston 20 E1
Stutton 105 D6
Sudbourne 86 F8
Sudbury 148 C4
Sutton 85 A1
Sutton Street 99 A7
Swan Green 40 B5
Sweffling 56 E2
Swilland 83 A7
Swingleton Green 79 C2
Syleham 22 A1

T

Tannington 55 A6
Tannington Place 55 A6
Tan Office 52 F2
Tan Office Green 62 C6
Tattingstone 105 B8
Tattingstone
  White Horse 142 D1
Temple End Foxearth .91 A6
Temple End Little Thurlow .74 C5
Theberton 58 B4
The Brook 36 E7
The Common 81 F3
The Heath 105 A7
Thelnetham 18 D1
Thelveton 21 A4
The Marsh 25 E8
The Port of Felixstowe .152 C1
Thetford 16 D5
The Woodlands 95 A3
Thistley Green 29 E7
Thorington 42 C4
Thorington Street ...103 A6
Thorndon 53 B8
Thorney Green 67 A7
Thornham Magna ...37 A2
Thornham Parva 37 B3
Thorpe Abbotts 21 E2
Thorpe Common ...107 C5
Thorpe Green 64 F1
Thorpe Morieux 79 A8
Thorpeness 73 E6
Thorpe Street 35 D8
Thrandeston 37 B7
Thurston 49 E3
Thurston End 76 D6
Thwaite 52 F7
Tilbury Green 89 E4
Tilbury Juxta Clare ..90 A3
Timworth 48 D8
Timworth Green 48 D7
Toad Row 10 F1
Tostock 50 B2
Tower Hill 107 C3
Trimley Lower Street .107 C7
Trimley St Martin ...107 D8
Trimley St Mary 152 C8

Troston 33 D3
Tuddenham 30 F2
Tuddenham St Martin .136 C5
Tunstall 71 F2

U

Ubbeston 40 E4
Ubbeston Green 40 D3
Ufford 127 B1
Ufford 84 F7
Uggeshall 25 F3
Undley 13 C4
Upend 60 F5
Upgate Street 7 B6
Upper Green 46 E3
Upper Holton 118 F2
Upper Layham 149 F2
Upper Street Baylham ..81 E6
Upper Street
  Dickleburgh and Rushall ..21 C2
Upper Street Stansfield ..76 C6
Upper Street Stutton .105 B5
Upper Town 49 E2
Upper Weybread 22 B2
Upsher Green 92 D6
Upthorpe 34 F3

W

Wainford 110 D5
Walberswick 119 A2
Walcot Green 20 D4
Waldringfield 98 D7
Waldringfield Heath ..98 C7
Wales End 76 D4
Walpole 41 C5
Walsham Le Willows ..35 C2
Walton 152 F6
Wangford 26 B2
Ward Green 51 E2
Warren Heath 140 F1
Washbrook 95 F5
Washbrook Street ...95 F6
Washmere Green 78 D2
Waterloo Aldeby 9 E8
Waterloo
  Dickleburgh and Rushall ..20 F2
Wattisfield 35 D5
Wattisham 80 B6
Wattisham Stone 80 A6
Weeting 5 E3
Wenhaston 42 C6
Westbourne 138 F7
Westbrook Green 20 C4
West End 26 B6
Westerfield 135 E4
Westhall 25 C4
West Harling 18 A8
Westhorpe 51 D8
Westleton 58 B7
Westley 122 A6
Westley Waterless ...59 E3
Weston 9 D1
Weston Ditch 29 F7
West Row 29 F6
West Stow 32 B1
West Street
  Rickinghall Inferior ..35 E5
West Street
  Walsham-le-willows ..35 A1
West Tofts 6 E7
Wetherden 51 B1

Wetherden Upper Town ..51 B4
Wetheringsett 53 A5
Wetherup Street 53 C3
Weybread 22 D3
Whatfield 80 C1
Wheatacre 2 B1
Whelp Street 79 B5
Whepstead 63 B5
Wherstead 143 B6
Whitestreet Green ...93 D2
Whitton 134 F3
Wicken 28 B1
Wicker Street Green ..93 E5
Wickhambrook 61 E2
Wickham Green 52 C8
Wickham Market ...127 B6
Wickham Skeith 52 E8
Wickham Street
  Wickhambrook 61 F1
Wickham Street
  Wickham Skeith 52 C8
Widgham Green 60 B2
Wiggens Green 88 C5
Wilby 39 C2
Wilde Street 13 D2
William's Green 93 E5
Willingham 25 E7
Willisham 81 A5
Willisham Tye 81 A6
Wilney Green 19 D4
Windsor Green 64 B2
Winfarthing 20 B8
Wingfield 39 B8
Wingfield Green 38 F8
Winston 68 F8
Wissett 24 D2
Withermarsh Green ..103 A8
Withersdale Street ...22 F4
Withersfield 74 B2
Witnesham 83 A6
Wixoe 89 B6
Woodbridge 146 F6
Woodbridge Walk ...99 F8
Woodditton 60 C5
Woodland Green ...133 C5
Woodton 7 C8
Woolpit 50 D1
Woolpit Green 65 D8
Woolpit Heath 65 E8
Woolverstone 144 B1
Wootten Green 39 B8
Wordwell 32 D3
Workhouse Green ..101 C8
Workhouse Hill 102 F2
World's End 65 F2
Worlingham 111 F3
Worlington 30 A4
Worlingworth 54 F8
Wormingford 101 F2
Wortham 36 D8
Wortwell 23 B8
Wrabness 105 F2
Wrentham 26 E5
Wrentham West End ..26 C7
Wyverstone 51 E6
Wyverstone Green ...51 E6
Wyverstone Street ..51 D6

Y

Yaxley 37 B5
Yoxford 57 D7

390th Bomb Group Meml Air
Mus★ IP13 ....71 C7

A

Abbey Cl 10 Burwell CB5 ..44 A5
10 Ixworth IP31 ....34 B1
Rendlesham IP12 ......85 D7
Abbey Farm Mid Sch
IP24 ....16 B6
Abbey Fields IP14 ....66 D8
Abbey Hill IP21 ......38 C7
Abbey La IP16 .....129 C7
Leiston IP16 ....129 C7
Sudbury CO10 ....148 C7
Abbey Rd Flixton NR35 ...23 F8
Abbey Sch IP12 .....147 A4
Abbeygate St 3 IP33 ..154 B2
Abbot Cl IP33 ....122 D4
Abbot Rd IP33 ....122 D4
Abbot's Hall Drift CO10 .78 E2
Abbots Hall Prim Sch
IP14 ....124 D5
Abbot's Hall Rd IP14 ..124 D5
Abbotsbury Cl IP2 ...139 A1
Abbotsbury Rd IP33 ..122 D3
Abbott Rd CO12 ......106 F1
Abbotts Ct CB9 ......133 C1
Abbotts Mdw 8 IP30 ..50 D1
Abbotts Rd CB9 ......132 E7
Abdy Ave 5 CO12 ....106 F1
Aberdeen Way IP4 ...136 B1
Aberfoyle Cl 1 IP4 ..136 C1
Abingdon Cl IP2 ....139 A1
Acacia Ave IP32 .....48 C5
Acacia Cl IP3 ....140 E1
Acer Gr IP8 ....138 C1
Acheson Way 7 IP15 .130 E5
Acorn Cl 9 IP8 .....138 C2
Acorns The IP30 .....49 E3
Acre Cl IP6 ....83 A6
Acre Rd CB8 ....74 B8
Acton CE Prim Sch
CO10 ....92 B7
Acton Cl Bramford IP8 ..134 A2
Sudbury CO10 ....148 D6
Acton Gdns 1 IP8 ...134 A2
Acton Gn 3 CO10 ....148 C5
Acton La Acton CO10 ..92 A6
Sudbury CO10 ....148 D6
Acton Pl Ind Est CO10 ..92 A8
Acton Rd Bramford IP8 ..134 A2
Lowestoft NR33 ......115 B4
Adair Rd IP1 ....138 D8
Adam's La IP18 ....43 C5
Adams Pl IP5 ....141 C7
Adamson Rd IP18 ....119 B8
Adastral Cl
Felixstowe IP11 .....153 H11
Newmarket CB8 ......120 E4
Addington Rd IP11 ..152 C7
Addison Cl IP26 ......4 F5
Addison Rd CO10 ....148 E7
Addison Way IP8 ....134 A8
Adeane Mdw IP26 ....6 A8
Adelaide Cl 17 CB7 ..28 D4
Adelaide Rd IP4 ....140 D6
Admiral Rd IP8 .....142 E8
Admirals Jun Sch IP24 ..16 C7
Adrian Rd 6 NR32 ...113 D2
Ailwin Rd IP32 .....123 E4
Ainslie Rd IP1 .....139 A6
Airedale NR33 ......114 E2
Airey Cl Lowestoft NR32 ..112 F5
Newton CO10 ....92 E3
Airstation La IP21 ...21 E6
Aisthorpe IP9 ......150 D3
Akethorpe Way NR32 .113 A3
Alabaster Cl 8 IP7 ..149 E6
Alandale Dr 25 NR23 ..11 C1
Alan Rd IP3 ....139 F4
Albany Rd 1 NR32 ...113 E2
Albany The IP4 .....139 E8
Albemarle Rd IP33 ..122 D4
Albemarle St 6 CO12 ..107 B3
Albert Cres IP33 ....154 A2
Albert Pl IP13 .....126 C3
Albert Pye Prim Sch
NR34 ....111 B4
Albert Rd IP13 .....126 C3
Albert Rolph Dr IP27 .109 E4
Albert St IP33 ......154 A2
Alberta Cl IP5 .....141 A8
Albion Hill IP4 ....139 F7
Albion Rd NR35 .....110 D3
Albion St IP7 ....154 A2
Alburgh with Denton Fst Sch
IP20 ....7 A1
Alde House Dr IP15 ..130 E4
Alde La IP15 ....130 E4
Alde Rd CB9 ....132 E7
Aldeburgh Cl CB9 ...132 C5
Aldeburgh Com Hospl
IP15 ....130 D4
Aldeburgh Prim Sch
IP15 ....130 E3
Aldeburgh Rd
Friston IP17 ....72 F7
Leiston IP16 ....129 D4
Aldecar La IP17 .....72 C7
Alder Dr 2 NR33 ....114 C4

Alder Way CO10 .....148 D6
Aldercroft Cl IP1 ...135 B3
Aldercroft Rd IP1 ..135 B3
Alderlee IP2 ....142 F8
Alderman Rd IP1 ....155 A2
Alderton Rd IP12 .....99 E6
Aldham Gdns IP14 ..124 E4
Aldham Mill Hill IP7 .149 C8
Aldham Rd IP7 .....149 E7
Aldis Ave IP14 .....124 D4
Aldon Cl 14 CO12 ...106 E1
Aldridge La 2 IP28 ..48 B6
Aldringham Mews 13
IP11 ....152 D5
Aldringham Pk IP16 .129 D3
Aldringham Rd IP17 .129 B3
Aldwyck Way NR33 ..114 F4
Alexander Cl IP11 ..152 F6
Alexander Dr
8 Great Waldingfield CO10 ..92 C6
Needham Market IP6 ..125 C3
Alexander Way IP28 ..47 C5
Alexanders Int Sch
IP12 ....108 D8
Alexandra Rd
Beccles NR34 ....111 B5
Felixstowe IP11 .....152 E6
Ipswich IP4 ....139 E6
Lowestoft NR32 .....113 D1
Sudbury CO10 ....148 C5
Alexandra St 8 CO12 ..107 B3
Alfred Corry Mus★
IP18 ....119 C2
Algar Dr CB8 ....59 F4
Alice Driver Rd 9 IP13 ..83 C3
Alicia Ct IP33 ......123 C3
All Hallows' Hospl
NR35 ....110 C7
All Saints IP14 ......5 E3
All Saints CE Mid Sch
CO10 ....148 E8
All Saints CE Prim Sch
CB8 ....121 A3
All Saints CE VA Prim Sch
Laxfield IP13 ....40 A3
Winfarthing IP22 .....20 B8
All Saints Cl CB8 ....46 C3
All Saints Dr NR34 ..111 C3
All Saints Gn
3 Beccles NR34 ....9 F4
6 Beccles NR34 ....111 F4
All Saints Rd IP6 ..125 B4
All Saints' Rd
Ipswich IP1 ....139 A7
Lowestoft NR33 .....115 B4
All Saints Wlk IP28 ..30 B4
Allen Rd NR32 .....112 D1
Allenby Rd IP2 .....138 F6
Alley Rd IP10 ....98 D2
Allfields 3 CO12 ...107 A1
Allington Cl IP4 ...139 F7
Allington Rd 7 IP19 .118 A3
Allington Wlk CB9 ..132 C6
Allotment La IP6 .....69 A1
Allthorpe Rd 12 IP20 ..22 D6
Alma Cl 3 IP4 ......136 A1
Alma Pl IP17 ....128 D3
Alma Rd NR32 ......113 C1
Almond Gr IP24 .....16 A4
Almondhayes IP2 ...139 B3
Almshouse Rd IP30 ..49 C1
Alpe St IP1 ....155 A4
Alpha Bsns Pk IP1 ..134 D3
Alphamstone Rd CO8 ..101 A6
Alston Cl CO10 ......92 D3
Alston Rd IP3 ......139 F4
Alton Hall La IP9 ..105 C6
Alton Wr Sports Ctr
IP9 ....105 D6
Alton Wr Visitor Ctr★
IP9 ....105 D6
Alvis Cl IP32 ....123 F5
Amber Mus The★
IP18 ....119 D5
Amberfield Sch IP10 .145 C6
Amberley Ct 3 NR32 .112 F4
America Hill IP6 .....83 A6
Amy Johnson Ct 6
IP28 ....116 B5
Ancaster Rd IP2 ....155 A1
Anchor End 2 CO11 ..105 A2
Anchor La Burwell CB5 ..44 A4
Dedham CO7 ....104 A2
Lakenheath IP27 ....109 C6
1 Mistley CO11 ....105 A2
Anchor St NR33 .....115 C6
Anchor Way NR33 ..114 B4
Ancient House Mus★
CO10 ....90 A8
Anderson Cl IP6 ...125 C5
Anderson Wlk IP32 .122 D7
Anderson's Way 8 IP12 ..146 E4
Andrew Burtt's Cl
IP13 ....126 B3
Andrew Cl 7 IP16 ..129 D5
Andrew Johnston Way
IP19 ....118 B3
Andrew Rd CB8 .....120 E6
Andrew Way NR33 ..114 D6
Andrews Cl 9 IP14 ..53 F2
Andros Cl IP3 ......144 A7
Angel Hill
Bury St Edmunds IP33 ..154 C2
Stonham Earl IP14 ...67 F5
Angel La Blythburgh IP19 ..42 F6

Angel La continued
Bury St Edmunds IP33 ..154 B2
Glemsford CO10 ......77 A2
Ipswich IP4 ....155 C2
2 Woodbridge IP12 ..147 A5
Angel Link IP19 ....118 B3
Angel Rd IP8 ....134 A2
Angel St IP7 ....149 D6
Angela Cl IP12 ......84 A1
Angelgate Espl 4 CO12 ..107 C3
Angerstein Cl IP27 ....5 C3
Anglesea Rd IP1 ....155 A4
Anglian La IP32 ....154 A4
Anglian Way NR31 ...3 B7
Angus Cl IP4 ....136 B1
Animal Health Trust Visitor
Ctr★ CB8 ....45 F5
Anita Cl E IP2 .....138 E5
Anita Cl W IP2 ....138 E5
Ann Beaumont Way
IP7 ....149 C7
Ann Coles Cl CB9 ...88 E3
Ann St IP1 ....155 A4
Ann Suckling Rd CB9 .132 E8
Annandale Dr NR34 ..111 D4
Annbrook Rd IP2 ...138 E1
Anne Bartholomew Rd
IP24 ....16 C7
Anne St IP11 ....152 E3
Annesons Cnr IP17 ..58 B6
Annis Hill NR35 ....110 D3
Annis Hill La 2 NR35 ..110 D3
Annis Hill Rd NR35 ..110 D2
Annison Cl NR33 ...115 B5
Ansell Cl IP7 ......149 D6
Anselm Ave 9 IP32 ..48 C5
Anson Rd 7 IP5 ....98 A8
Anson Way NR34 ....10 A3
Antonia Cl CB9 ....133 C5
Antrim Rd IP1 .....134 D1
Anzani Ave IP11 ...152 C4
Apple Acre Rd CB9 ..132 A7
Apple Cl 28 IP27 ....13 F2
Apple Gr IP14 ....51 A2
Apple Tree Cl IP15 ..115 B6
Appleby Cl IP8 .....138 C1
Appledore Dr NR33 ..114 D4
Appledown Dr IP30 ..123 F7
Appletree Gr 2 CB5 ..44 A6
Appletree La IP22 ...20 C3
Aragon Rd CB9 .....132 B4
Arbor La NR33 .....115 A2
Arcade St IP1 ......155 B3
Archbishop Sancroft High
Sch IP20 ....22 C6
Archers' Ave 3 IP26 ..4 D5
Arderne Cl 8 CO12 ..106 F1
Ardleigh Rd CO7 ...103 E2
Argyle St IP4 ......155 C3
Ark Cl 7 NR33 ......11 B1
Arkle Ct IP5 ....141 D7
Arkwright Rd IP2 ..138 E6
Arlington Way IP24 ..16 C5
Arms La IP25 ......133 F7
Armstrong Cl
Hundon CO10 ....75 D4
Newmarket CB8 .....121 B3
Armstrong Way CO9 ..90 A1
Arnhem Cl NR32 ...113 C4
Arnhem Rd IP16 ...129 D5
Arnold Cl IP1 ......134 F3
Arnold St
5 Lowestoft NR32 ..113 D2
6 Lowestoft NR32 ..113 E1
Arras Rd IP33 .....122 D5
Arrendene Rd CB9 ..132 D7
Arrowhead Dr IP27 .109 C7
Artillery Dr 7 CO12 .106 E1
Artillery Way 11 NR32 ..113 E2
Arundel Cl 4 IP32 ..123 D6
Arundel Way
Ipswich IP3 ....140 E3
2 Lowestoft NR33 ..114 D4
Arwela Rd IP11 ....152 F2
Ascot Dr
Felixstowe IP11 ....152 E6
Ipswich IP3 ....140 B3
Ash Ave 1 IP7 ......80 D6
Ash Cl Bacton IP14 ..51 F6
10 Lakenheath IP27 ..13 F2
7 Lowestoft NR33 ..114 D5
Thetford IP24 ....16 A4
Woodbridge IP12 ...146 F4
Ash Dr IP23 ....117 D3
Ash Gd Cl
3 Brantham CO11 ..104 E4
10 Felixstowe IP11 ..107 D8
Ash Gr
Capel St. Mary IP9 ..150 E3
Haverhill CB9 ......132 C7
4 Sudbury CO10 ....92 B3
Ash Rd
Campsey Ash IP12 ...71 C1
Hacheston IP13 .....127 F7
Onehouse IP14 ......66 C6
Rendlesham IP12 ....85 C7
Ash Rise 8 CO6 ....102 C5
Ash St 4 CO10 .....93 C3
Ash Tree Cl
8 Beccles NR34 .....9 F4
9 Occold IP23 ....37 F1
Ash Wlk CB8 ....75 C6
Ashbocking Rd IP6 ..82 E6
Ashburnham Rd IP6 .125 C4
Ashburnham Way
NR33 ....114 D4

Ashby Rd NR32 .....113 C1
Ashcroft Rd IP1 ...135 A1
Ashdale NR34 ......111 E4
Ashdale Rd IP5 ....141 D8
Ashdown Way IP3 ..140 D3
Ashe Rd IP12 ....71 F2
Ashen Cl CO10 ......89 E5
Ashen Hill CO10 ....89 E5
Ashen La CO10 .....89 E6
Ashen Rd Ashen CO10 ..90 A7
Ridgewell CO9 ......89 D4
Ashes The IP14 .....54 D1
Ashfield Cres NR33 ..114 F7
Ashfield Dr IP16 ...129 C5
Ashfield Hill IP31 ...50 F6
Ashfield Rd
Elmswell IP30 ....50 F3
Norton IP31 ....50 C4
Wetherden IP14 ....51 A2
Ashford Cl NR34 .....9 B6
Ashlea Cl CB9 .....132 F4
Ashlea Rd CB9 .....132 F4
Ashley Downs NR32 .113 C3
Ashley Rd Cheveley CB8 ..60 E8
Harwich CO12 ......107 A4
Newmarket CB8 ....121 E2
Ashley St IP2 ......155 B1
Ashman's Rd NR34 ..111 A4
Ashmere Gr IP4 ...139 F6
Ashmere Rise CO10 .148 E6
Ashness Cl 2 NR32 ..113 A4
Ashton Cl 2 IP2 ...138 C2
Ashtree Gdns NR33 .114 D3
Ashwell Rd IP33 ...122 D4
Askins Rd CO7 .....151 C5
Aspal Cl 5 IP28 .....30 B8
Aspal Hall Rd IP28 ..30 C8
Aspal La IP28 ....30 C8
Aspal Pk IP28 ......30 B8
Aspall Rd IP14 .....53 F3
Aspel Est IP28 .....13 D1
Aspen Cl Claydon IP6 ..81 F5
Great Barton IP31 ...49 B6
Haverhill CB9 ......132 C5
3 Woodbridge IP12 .147 B6
Aspinall Cl 4 NR33 .114 F4
Assington La CO6 ...93 A1
Assington Rd CO10 ..92 D3
Assington St CO10 ..92 F1
Astbury Rd 6 NR32 .113 B5
Aster Cl IP2 ....138 E4
Aston Cl IP1 ....134 C1
Ataka Rd IP11 .....152 F6
Athelington Rd IP21 .38 F2
Athenaeum La IP33 ..154 C2
Atherton Rd IP2 ...138 D2
Atterton Rd CB9 ...132 B7
Aubretia Cl 2 NR33 .114 F7
Audley End IP21 ....20 F5
Augusta Cl IP10 ...144 E7
Augustus Cl CB9 ..133 B5
Aureole Wlk CB8 ..120 E8
Austin Cl IP31 .....50 E7
Austin St 7 IP2 ...155 B1
Aveley La CO10 ....77 D6
Avenue App IP23 ...123 A8
Avenue Rd IP27 ...109 E4
Avenue The
Brome & Oakley IP23 ..117 E8
Copdock & Washbrook
IP8 ....95 F4
Felixstowe IP11 ....152 B7
Great Barton IP31 ..123 F8
Halesworth IP19 ...118 B5
Ipswich IP1 ....135 C1
4 Kessingland NR33 ..11 B1
Lowestoft NR33 ....115 B5
Newmarket CB8 ....121 A3
Risby IP28 ....47 E5
Ufford IP13 ....84 F7
Woodbridge IP12 ...147 A4
Aves Cl CB7 ....29 C5
Avocet Cl NR33 ....114 D5
Avocet La 28 IP5 ...98 A8
Avondale Rd
Ipswich IP3 ....140 A2
Lowestoft NR32 ....113 C1
Aylmer Cl IP28 .....47 D5
Aylward Cl IP7 ....149 E4
Ayr Rd IP4 ....136 B1

B

Babb's La IP14 .....52 F2
Babergh Cl 9 CO10 ..92 B7
Babington Dr IP19 ..118 B2
Baby La IP30 ....65 D4
Back Hamlet IP3 ...139 E5
Back Hill IP9 ......105 F6
Back Hills IP22 .....36 A7
Back La
Badwell Ash IP31 ....50 F8
Burrough Green CB8 ..59 F2
Claydon IP6 ....134 C8
Copdock & Washbrook
IP8 ....95 F5
Diss IP22 ....20 D7
Falkenham IP10 ....98 F1
Felixstowe IP11 ....152 F5
Kettlebaston IP7 ....79 C5
Lound NR32 ....3 D4
Monks Eleigh IP7 ...79 C2
St Mary, South Elmham
Otherwise Homersfield
IP20 ....23 C8
Scole IP21 ....21 A5

Back La continued
Tattingstone IP9 ....105 B7
Wicken CB7 ....28 A1
Back Rd Brockdish IP21 ..21 E4
Middleton IP17 ......58 B6
Rattlesden IP30 .....65 E6
Trimley St Martin IP10 ..98 D2
Wenhaston With Mells Hamlet
IP19 ....42 C6
Back St
Garboldisham IP22 ..18 D5
Gislingham IP23 ....36 B1
Lakenheath IP27 ...109 D6
Bacon Rd 7 IP6 .....82 B5
Bacon's Gn Rd IP19 ..25 D3
Bacton Com Prim Sch
IP14 ....51 F6
Bacton Mid Sch IP14 ..51 E6
Bacton Rd
Felixstowe IP11 ....152 F3
Haughley IP14 ....51 C2
Bader Cl IP3 ....140 C2
Bader Ct 25 IP5 .....98 A8
Badgers Bank IP2 ..138 E1
Badgers Gr CO6 ...102 D1
Badger's Holt 10 NR33 ..11 B1
Badingham
Badingham IP13 .....56 A4
Framlingham IP13 ..126 E5
Laxfield IP13 ....40 C1
Peasenhall IP17 .....56 D7
Peasenhall IP17 .....56 E7
Badley Hill IP6 ....125 B7
Badley Wlk IP6 ....125 A7
Badleys Cl 6 CO10 ..92 C6
Badlingham Rd CB7 ..29 E1
Badshah Ave 4 IP3 .140 B3
Badwell Ash VA Prim Sch
IP31 ....50 E8
Badwell Rd
Walsham-le-willows IP31 ..35 B1
Wyverstone IP14 ....51 C6
Bagsham La IP28 ...30 A6
Bahram Cl CB8 .....120 E4
Bailey Ave IP5 .....141 E7
Bailey La Haverhill CB9 ..133 B5
Ipswich IP2 ....138 E6
Baileypool La IP31 ..49 F8
Baines Coney CB9 ..132 A7
Baird Cl IP3 ....138 F7
Bakehouse Hill CB8 .59 F4
Baker Dr 4 CB5 ....44 B6
Baker Rd 2 IP9 ....107 A4
Baker St Bury St Edmunds IP32 ..48 C5
Bury St Edmunds IP32 ..122 E8
Baldwin Rd IP14 ...124 C4
Ballater Cl IP1 ....134 E4
Ballingdon Hall★
CO10 ....148 A3
Ballingdon Hill CO10 ..148 A4
Ballingdon St CO10 .148 A4
Ball's Chace CO6 ..101 C1
Balls Hill IP7 ....79 D5
Balmoral Cl IP2 ...138 F1
Balton Way 7 CO12 .106 F1
Bancroft La CB7 ....28 C5
Bangor Rd IP27 .....13 F2
Banham Dr 3 CO10 ..148 D6
Banham Rd NR34 ...111 C2
Banham's La NR35 ...7 B6
Bank Alley 8 IP18 ..119 D5
Bank Rd IP4 ....139 E6
Banks Cl IP7 ......149 E5
Banks' La IP19 .....24 C3
Bannocks La IP13 ...56 B4
Banters La NR34 .....8 F2
Bantocks Rd CO10 ..92 C5
Bantoft Terr IP3 ...140 C2
Banyard Cl 4 IP5 ..141 D7
Barbara Stradbroke Ave
Newmarket CB8 ....120 D1
Stetchworth CB8 ....59 D8
Barber Cl 3 NR33 ...11 B1
Barber's La NR35 ....7 B6
Barcham Rd CB7 ....28 C7
Bardolph Rd NR35 ..110 B3
Bardwell Rd IP31 ...33 C5
Bardwell VC Prim Sch
IP31 ....34 C5
Barell's Hill IP19 ...40 F4
Bargate La
Beck Row, Holywell Row
& Kenny Hill IP28 ...29 F5
Dedham CO7 ....104 A2
Bargate Rd IP28 ....30 A6

Barham Picnic Site Visitor Ctr★ IP6 ... 82 A6
Barhams Way IP13 ... 127 C7
Barker Cl Ipswich IP2 ... 138 D5
6 Manningtree CO11 ... 104 D2
3 Steeple Bumpstead CB9 ... 88 D3
Barker Rd CO10 ... 148 C8
Barking Rd
Barking IP6 ... 125 A1
Willisham IP8 ... 81 A5
Barkis Mdw NR32 ... 3 A4
Barkways 9 CB5 ... 44 B5
Barley Lands IP15 ... 130 E5
Barley Mdw 5 IP19 ... 118 A3
Barley Way NR33 ... 114 F2
Barlings Ct CB8 ... 121 A4
Barn Cl
2 Hopton on Sea NR31 ... 3 C7
Lowestoft NR33 ... 114 D5
Southwold IP18 ... 119 B8
Barn Field 2 IP29 ... 62 C6
Barn La IP33 ... 154 C3
Barn St 12 CO10 ... 78 D4
Barnardiston Hall Prep Sch CB9 ... 75 B5
Barnards Way NR32 ... 113 B1
Barnby & N Cove Prim Sch NR34 ... 10 C4
Barnes Cl Brandon IP27 ... 14 E8
3 Hadleigh IP7 ... 149 E6
Barnfield
Capel St. Mary IP9 ... 150 F3
Felixstowe IP11 ... 152 D6
26 Manningtree CO11 ... 104 E2
Barnham CE Prim Sch IP24 ... 16 B1
Barnham Pl IP5 ... 140 F6
Barnham Rd IP24 ... 16 E2
Barningham CE VC Prim Sch IP31 ... 34 E7
Barningham Rd IP31 ... 34 E5
Barons Cl
9 Felixstowe IP11 ... 153 D6
Halesworth IP19 ... 118 A2
Barons Rd IP33 ... 123 A2
Baronsdale Cl IP1 ... 135 B1
Barr Dr IP27 ... 109 D7
Barrack La
Harwich CO12 ... 107 C2
Ipswich IP1 ... 155 A3
Ufford IP13 ... 84 F7
Barrack Sq IP5 ... 98 A8
Barracks Rd CO10 ... 101 F8
Barrell's Rd IP31 ... 49 F3
Barrett's La IP6 ... 125 C4
Barrow Hill Acton CO10 ... 92 B8
Barrow IP29 ... 47 A2
Barrow Prim Sch IP29 ... 47 A3
Barrow Rd IP29 ... 46 F1
Barrow's Cnr IP24 ... 32 C8
Barry Lynham Dr CB8 ... 121 C2
Barsey Cl CB9 ... 132 A7
Bartholomew St IP4 ... 139 F6
Bartholomew's La IP19 ... 42 B6
Bartlet Hospl IP11 ... 153 C4
Barton Bottom IP31 ... 48 E7
Barton Dr CB9 ... 133 F8
Barton Gr CB9 ... 133 F8
Barton Hamlet IP31 ... 49 C6
Barton Hill IP31 ... 48 D5
Barton Rd
Bury St Edmunds IP32 ... 123 D6
Felixstowe IP11 ... 153 B4
Thurston IP31 ... 49 D4
Woodbridge IP12 ... 146 F7
Bartons Pl CB8 ... 120 E5
Barvens The IP8 ... 138 A1
Barway Rd CB7 ... 28 A6
Basil Brown Cl 1 IP22 ... 36 A6
Bates La IP22 ... 19 D6
Bath Hill IP11 ... 153 B4
Bath Hills Rd NR35 ... 7 E4
Bath Rd IP11 ... 153 B4
Bath St IP2 ... 139 D3
Battery Gn 7 NR32 ... 113 E1
Battery Gn Rd
5 Lowestoft NR32 ... 113 E1
6 Lowestoft NR32 ... 115 E8
Battery La 10 IP9 ... 107 A4
Battles La IP5 ... 141 D7
Battlesea Hill IP21 ... 39 A6
Bawdsey Cl IP11 ... 153 D7
Bay Rd 11 CO12 ... 107 B2
Bayfield Dr 4 CB5 ... 44 B5
Baylham House Rare Breeds Farm★ IP6 ... 81 F7
Baynard's La IP22 ... 20 A3
Bays The 4 IP16 ... 73 F6
Beach Rd Dunwich IP17 ... 43 B1
1 Harwich CO12 ... 107 B1
Hopton on Sea NR31 ... 3 C6
Kessingland NR33 ... 27 C8
Lowestoft NR32 ... 115 D8
Beach Rd E IP11 ... 153 C4
Beach Rd W IP11 ... 152 F2
Beach Sta Rd
Felixstowe IP11 ... 152 E1
Felixstowe IP11 ... 152 E1
Beacon Field 4 IP11 ... 152 E5
Beacon Hill Ave CO12 ... 107 C2
Beacon Hill La IP16 ... 73 F7
Beacon La IP13 ... 137 F3
Beaconsfield Cl CO10 ... 148 C6
Beaconsfield Rd
Aldeburgh IP15 ... 130 E3
Beaconsfield Rd *continued*
Ipswich IP1 ... 138 F7
21 Kessingland NR33 ... 11 C1
Lowestoft NR33 ... 115 C6
Sudbury CO10 ... 148 C6
3 Woodbridge IP12 ... 147 A5
Bealings La IP13 ... 137 F8
Bealings Rd IP12 ... 146 A1
Bealings Sch IP13 ... 137 D4
Bear Mdw 5 IP30 ... 49 F2
Bear St CO6 ... 102 C5
Beard Rd IP32 ... 122 D8
Beardmore Pk 10 IP5 ... 98 A8
Bear's La CO10 ... 78 D3
Beatrice Ave IP11 ... 153 A5
Beatrice Cl IP3 ... 140 A3
Beatty Rd Ipswich IP3 ... 140 B2
Sudbury CO10 ... 148 E7
Beauford Rd IP31 ... 32 F1
Beaufort St IP1 ... 139 A7
Beaumont Cl 3 IP33 ... 122 D4
Beaumont Ct CB9 ... 132 F4
Beaumont Rd NR33 ... 114 B2
Beaumont Vale CB9 ... 132 F4
Beaumont Way IP14 ... 124 B5
Beccles & District Mus★ NR34 ... 111 A5
Beccles & District War Meml Hospl NR34 ... 111 B4
Beccles Bsns Pk NR34 ... 10 A3
Beccles Mid Sch NR34 ... 111 C4
Beccles Rd Aldeby NR34 ... 9 F8
Aldeby/Wheatacre/Burgh St Peter NR34 ... 10 B8
Blyford IP19 ... 25 C1
Bungay NR35 ... 110 C4
Bungay NR35 ... 110 D4
Carlton Colville NR33 ... 114 A4
Fritton & St Olaves NR31 ... 2 C7
Holton IP19 ... 118 F4
Lowestoft NR33 ... 114 D7
Mutford NR34 ... 10 C3
Beccles Sports Ctr NR34 ... 111 A3
Beccles Sta NR34 ... 111 C5
Becclesgate 1 NR34 ... 111 B6
Beck Cl 5 IP12 ... 85 D8
Beck Rd CB7 ... 29 D4
Beck Row Prim Sch IP28 ... 30 B8
Beck St IP22 ... 35 A7
Beck The IP26 ... 4 E5
Beck View 3 IP20 ... 22 D6
Beckett Cl IP33 ... 122 A6
Becketts La IP7 ... 94 B1
Beckford Rd 17 CO11 ... 105 A2
Beckham Rd NR32 ... 113 C1
Becks Gn La NR34 ... 24 F8
Bedell Cl IP33 ... 122 C3
Bederic Cl IP32 ... 123 D4
Bedfield CE Prim Sch IP13 ... 54 E5
Bedfield Rd IP13 ... 55 A3
Bedford Rd 3 IP32 ... 122 E8
Bedford St IP1 ... 155 A3
Bedingfeld Way IP32 ... 123 E4
Bedingfield Cres IP19 ... 118 A1
Bedingfield Rd IP23 ... 53 E7
Beech Cir 5 IP7 ... 80 D6
Beech Cl
Halesworth IP19 ... 118 A3
Isleham CB7 ... 29 B5
11 Lakenheath IP27 ... 13 F2
Sproughton IP8 ... 138 A6
Beech Croft CB8 ... 59 E1
Beech Gr Haverhill CB9 ... 132 C7
Ipswich IP3 ... 139 F3
Ipswich IP5 ... 140 F7
Beech La 2 IP14 ... 51 A1
Beech Paddocks 4 IP30 ... 64 F8
Beech Rd Ipswich IP5 ... 140 F7
Lowestoft NR33 ... 114 D3
Sudbury CO10 ... 148 F4
Beech Rise IP33 ... 123 C3
Beech Row CB8 ... 46 C1
Beech Terr IP14 ... 124 D7
Beech Tree Cl NR34 ... 111 B4
Beech Way
Dickleburgh IP21 ... 21 C5
Woodbridge IP12 ... 146 F3
Beech Wlk IP16 ... 129 C5
Beechcroft IP29 ... 64 A3
Beechcroft Rd IP1 ... 134 F2
Beeches Cl 11 IP31 ... 34 B1
Beeches Rd IP28 ... 29 F7
Beeches The
Claydon IP6 ... 134 C8
Horringer IP29 ... 63 A8
Ipswich IP3 ... 139 F4
31 Lawford CO11 ... 104 E2
Little Blakenham IP8 ... 81 E3
Beeching Dr NR32 ... 113 D4
Beechwood Cl CB8 ... 120 C8
Beechwood Gdns NR33 ... 115 A6
Beetons Way IP32 ... 122 F7
Belaugh Ave NR33 ... 114 F5
Belchamp Hall★ CO10 ... 91 A3
Belchamp Rd CO9 ... 90 A3
Belgrave Cl IP4 ... 135 E1
Bell Cl IP2 ... 155 B1
Bell Gdns 13 CB7 ... 28 D4
Bell Gn IP19 ... 40 C6
Bell Hill CO8 ... 101 B6
Bell La
Barton Mills IP28 ... 116 D2
Ipswich IP2 ... 155 B1
Bell La *continued*
Marlesford IP13 ... 71 C4
Bell Mdw IP32 ... 123 A8
Bell St IP26 ... 4 E5
Bellands Way IP23 ... 117 C3
Belle Vue Rd
Ipswich IP4 ... 139 F6
Sudbury CO10 ... 148 D5
Bell's Cross IP14 ... 67 C6
Bell's Cross Rd IP6 ... 82 C7
Bells Hill CO8 ... 101 D2
Bell's La Hawstead IP29 ... 63 E5
Stowupland IP14 ... 67 C7
Bells La Glemsford CO10 ... 77 A3
Hinderclay IP22 ... 35 E8
Bells Rd CO10 ... 90 F3
Bellwell La
Debenham IP14 ... 53 F4
Kenton IP14 ... 54 A4
Belmont Gdns NR32 ... 113 B3
Belmont Rd IP8 ... 138 C1
Belseybridge Rd NR35 ... 7 F7
Belstead Ave IP2 ... 155 A1
Belstead Rd IP2 ... 155 A1
Belt The CB8 ... 61 B4
Belvedere Dr 23 NR33 ... 11 C1
Belvedere Rd
Ipswich IP4 ... 139 F8
Lowestoft NR33 ... 115 C7
Benacre Rd
Ellough NR34 ... 111 F1
Henstead with Hulver Street NR34 ... 26 E8
Ipswich IP3 ... 140 A2
Benefield Rd 1 CB8 ... 45 F3
Benezet St IP1 ... 155 A3
Benjamin Britten High Sch NR32 ... 113 A5
Bennett Ave
Bury St Edmunds IP33 ... 122 C6
Elmswell IP30 ... 50 F2
Bennett Rd
Ipswich IP1 ... 134 E1
5 Red Lodge IP28 ... 30 C1
Benouville 10 NR33 ... 114 F3
Bensly's Drift IP19 ... 118 C4
Bent La IP4 ... 140 E8
Bentley CE VC Prim Sch IP9 ... 104 F8
Bentley Dr NR32 ... 113 A6
Bentley La
Belstead IP8 ... 142 C5
Stutton IP9 ... 105 B6
Bentley Rd IP1 ... 134 C2
Benton La IP7 ... 65 C1
Benton St IP7 ... 149 D4
Benton Way IP19 ... 118 B4
Benyon Gdns IP28 ... 32 D1
Beresford Dr IP12 ... 146 F7
Beresford Rd NR32 ... 113 D2
Bergamot Rd CB9 ... 132 A6
Berghersh La IP6 ... 82 E7
Bergholt Rd CO11 ... 104 D4
Berkeley Cl
2 Framlingham IP13 ... 126 C3
Ipswich IP4 ... 135 E1
Berkeley Gdns
Bury St Edmunds IP33 ... 122 E4
Lowestoft NR32 ... 113 A4
Bermuda Rd IP10 ... 144 D7
Bernard Cres IP3 ... 140 B2
Bernard Rooke Pottery Mill Gall★ IP6 ... 83 A8
Berners Rd IP11 ... 153 C4
Berners St IP1 ... 155 A3
Bernham Cl IP32 ... 123 D5
Berry Cl Ipswich IP3 ... 140 F1
Lowestoft NR32 ... 112 E1
Berrycroft 11 CB7 ... 28 D4
Beryl Rd 8 CO12 ... 106 E1
Bethel Dr 24 NR33 ... 11 C1
Betts Ave IP5 ... 98 A8
Bevan St E 3 NR32 ... 115 D8
Bevan St W NR32 ... 113 C1
Beverley Cl NR33 ... 114 D6
Beverley Ct NR33 ... 114 C2
Beverley Rd IP4 ... 139 F8
Beversham Rd IP13 ... 71 F5
Bexley Ave 16 CO12 ... 106 F1
Beyton Mid Sch IP30 ... 49 F2
Beyton Rd IP30 ... 49 F1
Bibb Way IP1 ... 139 A5
Bickers Hill Rd IP13 ... 40 B3
Bier La IP22 ... 19 C1
Big Row NR34 ... 8 F6
Bigod Cl
5 Framlingham IP13 ... 126 C3
Halesworth IP19 ... 118 B2
Bigod Rd NR35 ... 110 D3
Bildeston Gdns 2 IP1 ... 135 D1
Bildeston Prim Sch IP7 ... 79 F4
Bildeston Rd
Chelsworth IP7 ... 79 E3
Combs IP14 ... 124 A1
Offton IP7 ... 80 F4
Wattisham IP7 ... 80 A6
Bill Rickaby Dr CB8 ... 121 A5
Billy's La CO7 ... 103 E5
Bilney Rd IP12 ... 146 E5
Birch Ave CO12 ... 107 A2
Birch Cl
Lowestoft NR32 ... 112 D2
1 Stowupland IP14 ... 67 A6
Wickham Market IP13 ... 127 C6
Woodbridge IP12 ... 146 F3
Birch Cres IP27 ... 109 D7
Birch Dr 8 CO11 ... 104 E5
Birch Fall 7 CO6 ... 102 C5
Birch Gr IP5 ... 98 A7
Birch Rd Onehouse IP14 ... 66 C6
10 Thurstow IP31 ... 49 E4
Birch St CO6 ... 102 D5
Birch Wlk 24 IP27 ... 13 F2
Birchcroft Rd IP1 ... 135 B2
Birches The CB7 ... 28 C5
Birchgrove IP23 ... 52 F7
Birchinhill Dro IP28 ... 12 F2
Birchwood Cty Prim Sch IP5 ... 98 A8
Birchwood Dr IP5 ... 136 E1
Birchwood Rd CO7 ... 103 D2
Bird View Sq 1 IP26 ... 4 E5
Birdbrook 3 IP29 ... 63 A1
Birdbrook Rd CO9 ... 89 A2
Birdcage Wlk CB8 ... 120 F2
Birds Croft IP31 ... 33 C2
Birds Gn IP30 ... 65 E5
Birds Hill IP13 ... 83 D8
Bird's La IP30 ... 64 D2
Birds La Framsden IP14 ... 69 D5
Lowestoft NR33 ... 115 B6
Bird's Rd IP31 ... 49 F3
Birkdale Ave IP28 ... 116 B5
Birkdale Ct 10 IP28 ... 48 C6
Birkfield Cl IP2 ... 139 A4
Birkfield Dr IP2 ... 138 E1
Biscay Cl CB9 ... 133 A5
Bishop Mews IP8 ... 138 B2
Bishops Cl 6 IP11 ... 153 D6
Bishop's Hill IP3 ... 139 E4
Bishop's Palace S Elham Hall★ IP20 ... 23 D6
Bishops Rd IP33 ... 154 B3
Bishops Way IP21 ... 39 A4
Bishops Wlk
10 Hopton on Sea NR31 ... 3 B7
Lowestoft NR32 ... 113 D5
Bittern Cl IP2 ... 138 E3
Bittern Rd IP17 ... 128 B3
Bixley Dr IP4 ... 140 E5
Bixley La IP4 ... 140 F5
Bixley Rd Ipswich IP3 ... 140 D3
2 Lowestoft NR33 ... 115 C6
Black Barns IP11 ... 152 C7
Black Bear La CB8 ... 120 F3
Black Boy La CO11 ... 106 A2
Black Boy Mdw NR34 ... 111 B4
Black Dyke Rd IP26 ... 4 E3
Black Gr La CO10 ... 75 E4
Black Hill (Tumulus)★ IP31 ... 33 C5
Black Horse La
Ditchingham NR35 ... 110 C7
Ipswich IP1 ... 155 A3
Black Mill Rd IP18 ... 119 C5
Black Slough IP17 ... 58 B7
Black St NR33 ... 10 F1
Blackberry Way
Lowestoft NR32 ... 112 E2
3 Red Lodge IP28 ... 30 C1
Blackbird Ave IP27 ... 6 A1
Blackbird Cl 16 IP31 ... 49 D4
Blackbird Rd 3 IP28 ... 13 B1
Blackbourne CE VC Mid Sch IP31 ... 34 F4
Blackbourne Rd IP30 ... 50 F3
Blackdike Dro IP26 ... 4 A2
Blackdown Ave IP5 ... 140 F6
Blackdyke Cl 9 IP26 ... 4 D5
Blackfriars CO10 ... 148 B4
Blackheath Rd
Lowestoft NR33 ... 115 A5
Wenhaston With Mells Hamlet IP19 ... 42 C5
Blackhouse La CO10 ... 148 F1
Blacklands La IP12 ... 131 A8
Blackmore Cl CB9 ... 132 D7
Blacksmith La
Barnham IP24 ... 16 B2
Thorpe Morieux IP30 ... 78 F7
Blacksmith Rd IP14 ... 52 A6
Blacksmith's Cnr IP8 ... 142 C6
Blacksmiths Hill CO10 ... 89 D6
Blacksmiths La
Bulmer CO10 ... 91 C1
Coddenham IP6 ... 68 B1
Stonham Earl IP14 ... 67 D6
Blacksmith's Loke NR32 ... 2 F6
Blackthorn Cl IP3 ... 140 F1
Blackthorn Ct CB7 ... 28 C5
Blackthorn Way CO6 ... 102 B7
Blacktiles La IP12 ... 84 A1
Bladen Dr IP4 ... 140 F5
Bladon Way CB9 ... 132 F7
Blagge Cl IP33 ... 122 C4
Blair Cl IP4 ... 140 E5
Blake Ave 4 IP9 ... 107 A5
Blake Cl 7 CO11 ... 104 D2
Blake Rd Ipswich IP1 ... 134 F3
Stowmarket IP14 ... 124 B7
Blakenham Cl 4 NR32 ... 112 F4
Blakes Cl IP12 ... 147 C7
Blanche St IP4 ... 155 C3
Blandford Rd IP3 ... 140 D3
Blaxhall Church Rd IP12 ... 71 F2
Blaxhall Comm Nature Reserve★ IP12 ... 72 C3
Blenheim Cl
10 Brantham CO11 ... 104 E5
Bury St Edmunds IP33 ... 122 D5
Haverhill CB9 ... 132 F7
Blenheim Dr IP7 ... 80 C6
Blenheim Rd 3 IP1 ... 139 A7
Blenheim Way 2 IP22 ... 20 A3
Blickling Cl IP2 ... 139 B2
Blinco Rd NR32 ... 112 C1
Blind La IP29 ... 77 B6
Blo' Norton Rd
Blo' Norton IP22 ... 18 F3
South Lopham IP22 ... 19 A4
Block Rd CB7 ... 28 E1
Blocka Rd NR32 ... 2 C6
Blockmoor Rd CB7 ... 28 A6
Blofield Rd IP11 ... 152 B4
Blois Rd CB9 ... 88 F4
Blomfield St IP33 ... 154 B3
Blood Hill IP8 ... 81 B3
Bloodmoor La 2 NR33 ... 114 E3
Bloodmoor Rd
1 Lowestoft NR33 ... 114 E3
Lowestoft NR33 ... 114 F3
Bloomfield St IP4 ... 140 B6
Bloomfield Way 7 NR33 ... 114 E3
Blooms Hall La CO10 ... 77 D5
Bloomsbury Cl NR32 ... 112 E4
Bloomsfield 8 CB5 ... 44 B5
Blower's La NR33 ... 10 E2
Blue Barn Cl 13 IP11 ... 107 D8
Blue Barn La IP8 ... 134 A8
Blue House La IP14 ... 52 F3
Bluebell Ave IP32 ... 123 F5
Bluebell Cl Ipswich IP2 ... 138 E4
7 Lowestoft NR33 ... 114 F3
Bluebell Gr IP6 ... 125 D3
Bluebell Way NR34 ... 111 E3
Bluebell Wlk 2 CB7 ... 28 D4
Bluegate La IP9 ... 150 F1
Bluestem Rd IP3 ... 144 D8
Blundeston CE Prim Sch NR32 ... 3 A4
Blundeston Rd
Corton NR32 ... 112 F8
Somerleyton, Ashby & Herringfleet NR32 ... 112 B8
Blyburgate
Beccles NR34 ... 111 B5
2 Beccles NR34 ... 111 C4
Blyford La Blyford IP19 ... 42 B8
Holton IP19 ... 118 E3
Wenhaston With Mells Hamlet IP19 ... 42 C6
Blyford Rd NR32 ... 113 A5
Blyford Way IP11 ... 152 C4
Blyth Cl Ipswich IP2 ... 139 A1
Wenhaston IP19 ... 42 C6
Blyth Rd
Halesworth IP19 ... 118 C2
Southwold IP18 ... 119 B5
Blythburgh Rd IP17 ... 58 C8
Boathouse La
Carlton Colville NR32 ... 114 B8
Lowestoft NR32 ... 112 B1
Bobbits La
Pinewood IP9 ... 142 E8
Wherstead IP9 ... 143 A7
Boby Rd IP32 ... 122 D8
Bockhill Rd IP33 ... 122 C5
Bodiam Cl IP3 ... 140 D4
Bodiam Rd IP3 ... 140 D4
Bodiam Way 8 NR33 ... 114 D4
Bodmin Cl IP5 ... 141 A6
Boeing Way IP28 ... 116 B5
Boldero Rd IP32 ... 123 F4
Boleyn Way CB9 ... 132 B5
Boleyn Wlk CB8 ... 121 C3
Bollard Way NR33 ... 114 E5
Bolton Cl 2 CB5 ... 44 A5
Bolton La IP1 ... 155 C3
Bolton St 10 CO10 ... 78 D4
Bon Marche 7 NR32 ... 115 D8
Bond Cl IP21 ... 21 F8
Bond St Ipswich IP4 ... 155 C2
Stowmarket IP14 ... 124 D7
Bonds Mdw NR32 ... 112 E2
Bond's Rd NR15 ... 21 C8
Bonnington Rd IP3 ... 139 F1
Bonsey Gdns NR34 ... 26 E5
Boon Cl IP33 ... 123 A3
Boon Dr NR33 ... 114 E6
Boot Drift IP9 ... 106 E7
Booth La IP5 ... 141 E8
Border Cot La IP13 ... 127 B7
Border La NR32 ... 2 E6
Borley Cres 2 IP30 ... 50 F2
Borley Rd CO10 ... 91 D6
Borough End 3 NR34 ... 111 C3
Borough La IP14 ... 66 A3
Borradale Ct 5 CB9 ... 88 D3
Borradale Rd IP32 ... 123 F5
Borrett Pl IP12 ... 146 D3
Borretts Farm La IP13 ... 70 D6
Borrow Cl NR33 ... 114 C3
Borrow Rd NR32 ... 112 C1
Borrowdale Ave
1 Ipswich IP4 ... 135 D1
Ipswich IP4 ... 139 D8
Bosmere Prim Sch IP6 ... 125 D4
Bosquet Cl 1 NR32 ... 112 F5
Boss Hall Rd IP1 ... 138 E7
Bostock Rd IP2 ... 139 C1
Boston End 6 IP24 ... 16 A5
Boston Rd Ipswich IP4 ... 139 F7
Lowestoft NR32 ... 113 D2
Boswell La IP7 ... 149 D7
Botany La IP17 ... 71 E7
Botolphs Ct IP33 ... 154 C1
Bouchain Ct 1 IP19 ... 118 A3
Boulevard The NR32 ... 114 D8
Boulge Rd Burgh IP13 ... 83 F6
Hasketon IP13 ... 146 B8
Boulters Cl IP14 ... 124 B6

Boulters Way IP14 . . . . .124 B6
Boundary Cl IP26 . . . . . . .4 F3
Boundary Rd
  Haverhill CB9 . . . . .133 B3
  [1] Hockwold cum Wilton
  IP26 . . . . .5 A3
  Red Lodge IP28 . . . . .30 C1
Bourchier Cl [1] IP7 . . .149 E6
Bourne Ave [6] IP32 . . .123 E6
Bourne Hill IP2 . . . . . .143 B7
Bourne Rd
  Haverhill CB9 . . . . .132 F6
  Lowestoft NR32 . . . . . . .113 B3
Bowdens La CO6 . . . . .101 F3
Bower's La [7] CB7 . . . .29 C5
Bowl Rd IP14 . . . . .66 C3
Bowland Dr IP8 . . . . . .138 C1
Bowman's La IP17 . . . . .42 D1
Bowthorpe Cl IP1 . . . .155 A4
Box Bush La IP13 . . . . . .55 D5
Boxford Cl [2] IP14 . . .124 E3
Boxford Ct [7] IP11 . . .152 C4
Boxford La CO10 . . . . .93 A3
Boxford Prim Sch
  CO10 . . . . .93 C3
Boxford Rd IP7 . . . . . . .93 B8
Boxhouse La CO7 . . . .103 D3
Boxted Church Rd
  CO6 . . . . .102 E2
Boxted Rd CO6 . . . . . .102 E2
Boxted Straight Rd
  CO4 . . . . .103 A2
Boyden Cl [1] CB8 . . . . .61 E2
Boydlands IP9 . . . . . . .150 E3
Boyne Rd IP33 . . . . . . .122 E4
Boyscott La [1] NR35 . .110 B3
Boyton Cl CB9 . . . . . . .132 E8
Boyton Rd
  Hollesley IP12 . . . . .86 A1
  Ipswich IP3 . . . . .140 B1
Boyton Vineyard★ CO9 .89 B7
Boyton's La CB10 . . . . .88 A1
Braces La NR35 . . . . . . .8 E7
Bracken Ave IP5 . . . . .137 E4
Bracken Rise IP6 . . . . . .6 A8
Bracken Row [6] IP31 . .49 D4
Brackenbury Cl IP7 . . .139 B8
Brackenbury Sports Ctr
  IP11 . . . . .153 C5
Brackenhayes Cl IP2 . .139 B3
Brackenwood Cres [1]
  IP32 . . . . .123 E6
Bradfield Ave IP7 . . . .149 D7
Bradfield Cres IP7 . . . .149 D7
Bradley Rd Cowlinge CB8 .60 F1
  Great Bradley CB8 . . . . . .74 F8
  Kirtling CB8 . . . . .60 F2
Bradley St IP7 . . . . . . .155 B1
Braggon's Hill IP29 . . . .77 A5
Braithwaite Dr [7] CO10 .92 C6
Bramble Cl CB9 . . . . . .132 B7
Bramble Dr IP3 . . . . . .140 E1
Bramble Way CO6 . . . .102 B7
Brambles The IP15 . . . .130 C6
Bramblewood [1] IP8 . .138 C2
Bramblewood Way
  IP19 . . . . .118 C4
Brames La IP20 . . . . . . .23 D3
Bramfield CE Prim Sch
  IP19 . . . . .42 A4
Bramfield House Sch
  IP19 . . . . .41 E4
Bramfield Rd
  Halesworth IP19 . . . . . . .118 B2
  Lowestoft NR32 . . . . . . .113 A3
  Walpole IP19 . . . . .41 C5
  Wenhaston With Mells Hamlet
  IP19 . . . . .42 B5
Bramford CE Prim Sch
  IP8 . . . . .134 A1
Bramford La
  [3] Ipswich IP1 . . . . . . .134 D1
  [6] Ipswich IP1 . . . . . . .139 A7
Bramford Rd
  Bramford IP8 . . . . .134 B1
  Claydon IP6 . . . . .134 A8
  [14] Great Blakenham IP6 .82 A5
  Great Blakenham IP6 . . .134 A8
  Ipswich IP1 . . . . .138 E8
Bramhall Cl IP2 . . . . . .138 D1
Bramley Chase IP4 . . . .140 B7
Bramley Cl IP32 . . . . . .123 F6
Bramley Rd Diss IP22 . . .20 B3
  Haverhill CB9 . . . . .132 A5
Bramley Rise NR34 . . . .111 C4
Brampton CE Prim Sch
  NR34 . . . . .25 C5
Brampton Sta NR34 . . . .25 C6
Brand Rd IP31 . . . . .49 C7
Brandeston Cl [10] CO10 .92 C6
Brandeston Rd
  Cretingham IP13 . . . . . . .69 E7
  Earl Soham IP13 . . . . . . .54 F1
Brandon Ctry Pk Visitor Ctr★
  IP27 . . . . .14 F8
Brandon Her Ctr★ IP27 .5 F1
Brandon Rd
  Felixstowe IP11 . . . . . . .152 C4
  Lakenheath IP27 . . . . . . .14 C4
  Methwold IP26 . . . . .5 B8
  Mildenhall IP28 . . . . . . .116 C5
  Thetford IP24 . . . . .15 F6
  Weeting IP27 . . . . .5 F3
  Wordwell IP28 . . . . .32 C3
Brandon St IP27 . . . . . .109 F1
Brandon Sta IP27 . . . . . .5 F2
Brands Cl [12] CO10 . . .92 B3

Brands La IP29 . . . . . . .63 D3
Bransby Gdns IP4 . . . .139 E7
Brantham Hill CO11 . . .104 E4
Brawdy Rd [1] IP31 . . . .33 D5
Brayfield Cl IP32 . . . . .123 D6
Braziers La IP31 . . . . . .51 B6
Brazier's Wood Rd
  IP3 . . . . .144 B8
Breach Dro IP28 . . . . . .13 C1
Breckland Ave IP7 . . . .109 D7
Breckland Mid Sch
  IP27 . . . . .14 D8
Breckland Way
  Lowestoft NR32 . . . . . . .113 A3
  Mildenhall IP28 . . . . . . .116 C5
Brecklands [5] IP26 . . . .6 B8
Brecon Cl IP2 . . . . . . .139 B2
Bredfield Cl [7] IP11 . . .152 D5
Bredfield Rd IP12 . . . . .147 A7
Bredfield St IP12 . . . . .146 F5
Brendon Cl NR32 . . . . .112 C8
Brendon Dr IP5 . . . . . .140 F6
Brent Cl IP28 . . . . .116 D4
Brent Eleigh Rd
  Lavenham CO10 . . . . . . .78 D3
  Monks Eleigh IP7 . . . . . .79 B2
Brentgovel St
  [1] Bury St Edmunds IP33 .154 B2
  Bury St Edmunds IP33 . .154 B2
Bressingham Prim Sch
  IP22 . . . . .19 E4
Bressingham Rd IP22 . .19 F4
Bressingham Steam Mus★
  IP22 . . . . .19 E3
Brett Ave IP7 . . . . .149 E7
Brett Gn IP7 . . . . .149 E2
Brettenham Cres [4]
  IP1 . . . . .135 D1
Brettenham Rd
  Buxhall IP14 . . . . .65 F4
  Hitcham IP7 . . . . .79 E8
Bretts The IP5 . . . . . . .141 E8
Brewers Cl IP27 . . . . . .109 C6
Brewers Gn La IP22 . . . .20 B3
Brewhouse La [19] CB7 . .28 D4
Breydon Way NR33 . . . .114 F6
Briar
  Halesworth IP19 . . . . . . .118 C4
  Lowestoft NR32 . . . . . . .113 B5
Briar Hill IP30 . . . . .50 D1
Briar La IP22 . . . . .35 F5
Briar Rd [89] IP20 . . . . .22 D6
Briardale Ave [4] CO12 .106 F2
Briarhayes Cl IP2 . . . . .139 B3
Briarwood Ave IP33 . . .122 D5
Briarwood Rd
  Lowestoft NR33 . . . . . . .114 F5
  Woodbridge IP12 . . . . . .146 E3
Brices Way [4] CO10 . . .77 A3
Bricett Bsns Pk IP7 . . . .80 E6
Bricett Gn IP7 . . . . .80 D5
Brick Kiln Ave NR34 . . .111 C4
Brick Kiln Cl [15] IP11 . .107 D8
Brick Kiln Hill CO6 . . . .93 C2
Brick Kiln La
  Huntingfield IP19 . . . . . . .40 F4
  Melton IP12 . . . . .147 E2
Brick Kiln Rd
  Ellingham NR35 . . . . .8 C8
  Harkstead IP9 . . . . .106 B6
  Mildenhall IP28 . . . . . . .116 D5
Brick La
  Framlingham IP13 . . . . . .126 D1
  Parham IP13 . . . . .71 A7
Brickfield Ct IP2 . . . . . .155 C1
Brickfields Ave CB8 . . .120 D7
Brickfields The IP14 . . .124 C6
Brickkiln La IP22 . . . . . .19 C3
Brickman's Hill CO11 . .105 B2
Bridewell Ct IP28 . . . . .116 B4
Bridewell La
  Botesdale IP22 . . . . .36 A6
  Bury St Edmunds IP33 . .154 A2
Bridewell St CO10 . . . . .90 B8
Bridge Cl [16] IP20 . . . .22 D6
Bridge Cottage (National
  Trust)★ CO7 . . . . .151 D1
Bridge End Rd IP28 . . . .30 B1
Bridge Foot Corner
  IP18 . . . . .119 C7
Bridge Pk (Skate Park)★
  IP1 . . . . .155 B1
Bridge Rd
  Bromeswell IP12 . . . . . . .85 A6
  Burston & Shimpling IP22 . .20 E7
  Felixstowe IP11 . . . . . . .153 A5
  Levington IP10 . . . . .145 E4
  Lowestoft NR32 . . . . . . .112 E1
  Reydon IP18 . . . . .119 C7
  [6] Scole IP21 . . . . .20 F1
  Snape IP17 . . . . .72 D4
Bridge St Beccles NR34 .111 A7
  Brandon IP27 . . . . .5 F1
  Bungay NR35 . . . . .110 B4
  [4] Bures Hamlet CO8 . . .101 C5
  Carlton CO17 . . . . .128 D6
  Framlingham IP13 . . . . . .126 C3
  Hadleigh IP7 . . . . .149 C7
  Halesworth IP19 . . . . . . .118 B4
  Huntingfield IP19 . . . . . . .41 A4
  Ipswich IP1 . . . . .155 B3
  Moulton CB8 . . . . .45 F3
  Needham Market IP6 . . . .125 D5
  Stowmarket IP14 . . . . . .124 F5
  Thetford IP24 . . . . .16 B5
Bridge St Rd CO10 . . . .78 A3
Bridgewood Rd IP12 . . .146 E5
Bridgham La NR16 . . . . .17 F8

Bridgwater Rd IP2 . . . .138 D2
Bridles The [4] NR34 . .111 F4
Bridport Rd IP3 . . . . . .140 D3
Bright Cl IP33 . . . . .123 C3
Brighton St [3] IP27 . . . .14 A3
Bright's La CO10 . . . . . .78 C4
Brights Wlk IP5 . . . . . .141 E7
Brightwell Cl IP11 . . . . .152 C4
Brimstone Rd IP8 . . . . .142 E8
Brindles The [7] NR33 . .114 E4
Brinkley Rd Brinkley CB8 .59 E1
  Carlton CB8 . . . . .74 A8
  Dullingham CB8 . . . . .59 F4
Brinkley Way IP11 . . . .153 D7
Brisbane Rd IP4 . . . . . .140 D6
Bristol Hill IP9 . . . . . . .107 A4
Bristol Rd
  Bury St Edmunds IP33 . .122 C4
  Ipswich IP4 . . . . .140 A7
Bristol St [5] IP27 . . . . .14 A2
Britannia Prim Sch
  IP4 . . . . .140 B5
Britannia Rd IP4 . . . . . .140 B6
Britten Ave IP14 . . . . . .124 C7
Britten Cl IP15 . . . . . . .130 D5
Britten Rd NR33 . . . . . .115 A6
Brittons Cres [3] IP29 . . .47 A2
Brittons Rd [4] IP29 . . . .47 A2
Broad Fleet Cl [2] NR32 .112 E4
Broad Gn Cl [4] IP29 . . .62 C6
Broad La CO6 . . . . .102 E1
Broad Mdw
  [2] Ipswich IP8 . . . . . . .138 C2
  [2] Walsham-le-willows
  IP31 . . . . .35 C2
Broad Oaks CO6 . . . . . .102 B8
Broad Piece CB7 . . . . . .28 C5
Broad Rd Cotton IP14 . . .52 A6
  Little Thurlow CB9 . . . . . .74 F6
  Lowestoft NR32 . . . . . . .112 D1
  Wickham Market IP13 . . .127 E7
  Orford IP12 . . . . .131 C2
Broad View Rd NR32 . . .114 C8
Broad Way IP21 . . . . . . .21 A4
Broadcroft Cres IP8 . . .132 C6
Broadfields Rd [5] IP23 . .36 D2
Broadland Cl
  Beccles NR34 . . . . .111 E4
  Lowestoft NR34 . . . . . . .114 C7
Broadland Rd IP33 . . . .123 B1
Broadlands Way IP4 . . .140 F5
Broadmere Rd IP1 . . . .138 E8
Broadoak Cl [4] NR33 . .114 C4
Broads Rd CB5 . . . . . . .44 B8
Broads Rd Bsns Pk CB5 .44 B7
Broadwater Gdns [6]
  IP9 . . . . .107 A4
Broadwaters Rd NR33 . .114 E5
Broadway
  [6] Fressingfield IP21 . . . .39 E8
  Pakenham IP31 . . . . .49 F8
  Wickham Market IP13 . . .127 B7
Broadway Dr IP19 . . . . .118 C6
Broadway The
  Badwell Ash IP31 . . . . . . .50 F8
  Wickham Skeith IP23 . . . .52 D8
Brock La IP13 . . . . .146 C2
Brockdish Prim Sch
  IP21 . . . . .22 A2
Brockford Rd IP14 . . . . .52 F4
Brockley Cres IP1 . . . . .134 D1
Brockley La IP29 . . . . . .46 F2
Brockley Rd
  Hartest IP29 . . . . .77 A8
  Whepstead IP29 . . . . .63 B4
Broke Ave IP8 . . . . .134 B2
Broke Hall Gdns IP8 . . .140 D4
Broke Hall Prim Sch
  IP4 . . . . .140 E5
Brome Ave IP23 . . . . . .117 D5
Brome Hall La IP23 . . . .117 E7
Bromeswell Gn Nature
  Reserve★ IP12 . . . . . . .147 F7
Bromeswell Rd IP4 . . . .135 E1
Bromley Cl [4] IP2 . . . .139 C3
Bromley Rd CO11 . . . . .104 D1
Bronyon Cl IP33 . . . . . .122 C5
Brook Cl
  Horringer IP29 . . . . .63 B8
  Hundon CO10 . . . . .75 D3
  Lowestoft NR33 . . . . . . .114 A4
  Stowmarket IP14 . . . . . .124 B7
Brook Dam La [22] CB7 . .28 D4
Brook Dr [3] IP7 . . . . . . .56 F8
Brook Farm La [4] IP9 . .105 E7
Brook Farm Rd IP17 . . .128 B4
Brook Hall Rd CO10 . . . .93 C3
Brook House Rd IP14 . . .52 B6
Brook La Burgate IP22 . . .36 E7
  Capel St Mary IP9 . . . . . .150 C4
  Felixstowe IP11 . . . . . . .153 B5
  Framlingham IP13 . . . . . .126 B3
  Mickfield IP14 . . . . .53 A2
  Needham IP20 . . . . .22 B4
  Playford IP6 . . . . .137 A4
  St Margaret, Ilketshall
  NR35 . . . . .24 C7
  Trimley St Martin IP10 . . .98 E1
Brook Rd NR34 . . . . . . .10 B4
Brook Service Rd [1]
  CB9 . . . . .132 E5
Brook St Dedham CO7 . .103 F4
  Glemsford CO10 . . . . . . .77 A3

Brook St continued
  Soham CB7 . . . . .28 D3
  Woodbridge IP12 . . . . . .147 A5
  Yoxford IP17 . . . . .57 D7
Brook Way IP8 . . . . .81 C3
Brooke Bsns & Ind Pk
  NR33 . . . . .115 A8
Brookfield Rd IP1 . . . . .138 F8
Brookfields Cl CB8 . . . .121 B5
Brookhouse Bsns Pk
  IP2 . . . . .138 F6
Brooklands Cl IP33 . . . .154 A1
Brooklands Rd CO11 . . .104 E4
Brooklands Rise CO11 . .104 E4
Brooklyn Rd [14] CO12 . .107 B2
Brooks Castle IP33 . . . .126 C3
Brooks Hall Rd IP1 . . . .139 A7
Brookside [1] IP7 . . . . . .79 F4
  Moulton CB8 . . . . .45 F3
  Dalham CB8 . . . . .61 C8
Brookview Ipswich IP3 . .142 E8
  Pinewood IP2 . . . . .138 E1
Brookwood Cl [7] NR34 . .9 F4
Broom Cres IP3 . . . . . .139 F1
Broom Field [5] IP11 . . .152 E5
Broom Hill La IP24 . . . . .33 E7
Broom Hill Rd IP1 . . . . .139 A8
Broom Hill Swimming Pool
  IP1 . . . . .139 A8
Broom Knoll [1] CO11 . .104 E5
Broom Rd
  Lakenheath IP27 . . . . . .109 E5
  [2] Lowestoft NR32 . . . .113 B2
Broom Rd Cl IP27 . . . . .109 E5
Broom St CO10 . . . . . . .148 F3
Broom Way IP9 . . . . . .150 E4
Broom Wlk [9] IP28 . . . .30 B8
Broomfield
  Martlesham IP5 . . . . .141 F7
  [17] Martlesham Heath IP5 .98 A8
Broomfield Comm
  IP8 . . . . .138 B6
Broomfield Mews [18] IP5 .98 A8
Broomhayes IP2 . . . . . .139 A2
Broomheath IP12 . . . . .146 F2
Broomhill Cl [2] IP28 . . .30 C1
Broomhill La IP30 . . . . . .50 C1
Broomspath Rd IP14 . . . .67 A6
Brotherton Ave IP11 . . .152 B8
Broughton Rd IP1 . . . . .155 A4
Brown St IP14 . . . . .52 A3
Browning Rd
  [10] Brantham CO11 . . .104 E4
  Ipswich IP1 . . . . .134 F3
Brownlow Rd IP11 . . . . .153 A4
Browns Cl [5] Acton CO10 .92 B7
  Hitcham IP7 . . . . .79 E6
  [5] Wickhambrook CB8 . . .61 E2
Browns Gr IP5 . . . . . . .141 D7
Browse Cl IP32 . . . . . . .123 E4
Browston La NR32 . . . . . .2 E7
Broxtead Cl IP12 . . . . . .85 C2
Bruce St IP15 . . . . .115 C7
Brudenell St IP15 . . . . .130 E3
Bruges Cl [14] CO12 . . .107 A1
Bruisyard Rd IP13 . . . . .56 C3
Bruisyard Vineyard★
  IP17 . . . . .56 C5
Brundon La CO10 . . . . .148 A5
Brunel Rd IP2 . . . . .138 E6
Brunel Way IP24 . . . . . .16 B7
Brunswick House Cut [18]
  CO11 . . . . .105 A2
Brunswick Rd IP4 . . . . .135 F1
Brunwyn Cl NR32 . . . . .123 F6
Brussels Cl [15] CO12 . .107 A1
Brybank Rd CB9 . . . . . .132 A7
Bryon Ave IP11 . . . . . . .152 B2
Bryony Cl Haverhill CB9 .132 C7
  [6] Lowestoft NR33 . . . . .114 F3
Buccaneer Rd IP31 . . . . .33 D5
Buck La IP23 . . . . .117 E8
Buckanay La IP12 . . . . . .99 E5
Buckenham Ct [17] IP5 . .119 D5
Buckenham Rd IP7 . . . .149 F4
Buckfast Cl [4] IP2 . . . .139 A2
Buckingham Cl [4] IP12 . .84 A1
Buckingham Rd CB9 . . .132 C4
Buckingham's Hill IP21 . .39 E8
Buckles Field [8] IP31 . . .34 C7
Bucklesham Prim Sch
  IP10 . . . . .98 A4
Bucklesham Rd
  Ipswich IP3 . . . . .140 E2
  Kirton IP10 . . . . .99 B6
Buckleswood Rd IP16 . .129 A7
Bucknam Cl [14] NR33 . .11 C1
Buck's Head La IP6 . . . . .24 F7
Buck's Horns La IP8 . . .142 B6
Bucks La [2] CO10 . . . . .90 A8
Buckshorn La IP23 . . . .117 D2
Buddleia Cl IP2 . . . . . .138 E4
Bude Cl IP5 . . . . .141 A6
Buggs Hole La IP22 . . . .18 D2
Bugg's La
  Brettenham IP7 . . . . .65 D1
  Hitcham IP7 . . . . .79 D8
Bugg's Rd IP22 . . . . . . .36 D6
Bugsby Way IP5 . . . . . .141 E7
Bulcamp Drift IP19 . . . . .43 A7
Bull Hall La IP6 . . . . . . .83 A5
Bull La Acton CO10 . . . .78 A1
  Hawstead IP29 . . . . .63 C5
  Long Melford CO10 . . . . .91 B8
  Rickinghall Superior IP22 . .36 B4
Bullace La IP31 . . . . . . .131 A8

Bullard's La IP12 . . . . .146 E5
Bullen Cl Bramford IP8 . .134 A2
  Bury St Edmunds IP33 . .154 A1
Bullen La [5] IP8 . . . . . .134 A2
Buller Rd IP16 . . . . .129 C6
Bullion's La NR34 . . . . . .26 B2
Bullock Fair Cl [14] IP20 . .22 D6
Bullocks La CO10 . . . . .148 C5
Bullockshed La IP12 . . .131 C4
Bull's Ash Cnr IP7 . . . . .80 F5
Bull's Rd IP6 . . . . .82 C7
Bullshall Rd
  [6] Occold IP23 . . . . .37 F1
  Occold IP23 . . . . .53 E8
Bullswood La IP30 . . . . .64 D1
Bulmer La CO10 . . . . . . .93 C4
Bulmer Rd CO10 . . . . . .148 A4
Bulmer St Andrews CE Prim
  Sch CO10 . . . . .91 C2
Bulstrode Rd IP2 . . . . .155 C1
Bulwer Rd IP1 . . . . . . .139 A6
Bumpstead Rd CB9 . . . .132 F3
Bunbury Ave
  [1] Great Barton IP31 . . . .49 A5
  Mildenhall IP28 . . . . . . .116 C5
Bunbury Rd [8] IP32 . . . .48 C5
Bungay Castle (rems)★
  NR35 . . . . .110 A4
Bungay High Sch
  NR35 . . . . .110 C2
Bungay Mid Sch NR35 . .110 D3
Bungay Mus★ NR35 . . .110 B4
Bungay Rd Barsham NR34 . .9 F4
  Beccles NR34 . . . . .111 A4
  Dickleburgh & Rushall
  IP21 . . . . .21 B1
  Ellingham NR35 . . . . .8 C8
  Halesworth IP19 . . . . . . .118 B4
  Scole IP21 . . . . .21 A1
  Stockton NR34 . . . . .8 F8
Bunker Cl NR33 . . . . . .115 A5
Bunn's La IP20 . . . . .22 C6
Bunters Rd
  [8] Wickhambrook CB8 . . .61 E2
  Wickhambrook CB8 . . . . .61 E2
Bunting Rd
  Bury St Edmunds IP32 . .123 F4
  Ipswich IP2 . . . . .138 D3
Buntings Cres [15] CB5 . .44 A6
Buntings Path CB5 . . . . .44 A6
Buntry La CO10 . . . . . . .75 C2
Bunyan Cl IP1 . . . . .135 A3
Burch's Cl IP17 . . . . . . .129 C3
Burdock La IP26 . . . . . . .4 C3
Buregate Rd IP11 . . . . .152 F2
Bures Cl IP14 . . . . .124 E4
Bures Prim Sch CO8 . . .101 C4
Bures Rd
  Little Cornard CO10 . . . .101 A8
  Nayland-with-wissington
  CO6 . . . . .101 F4
  Sudbury CO10 . . . . .148 E2
Bures Sta CO8 . . . . . . .101 C4
Burgate Rd
  Gislingham IP23 . . . . .36 D3
  Higham IP28 . . . . .46 E3
Burgess Cl [5] NR32 . . .112 F2
Burgess Pl [22] IP5 . . . .98 A8
Burgh Rd NR34 . . . . .2 C1
Burghley Cl IP12 . . . . . .139 A2
Burghley Rise [5] CB5 . . .44 B5
Burke Cl IP1 . . . . .135 A3
Burke Rd [7] IP1 . . . . . .135 A3
Burkitts La CO10 . . . . . .148 C5
Burlington Rd IP1 . . . . .155 A3
Burnet Cl IP8 . . . . .142 D8
Burnham Cl
  Felixstowe IP11 . . . . . . .152 C7
  Ipswich IP4 . . . . .139 F7
Burnham Way NR33 . . . .115 A7
Burns Cl IP23 . . . . .37 B5
Burns Rd IP1 . . . . .134 E3
Burnt Dick Hill CO4 . . . .102 E4
Burnt Fen Turnpike
  IP28 . . . . .12 D6
Burnt Hill La NR33 . . . .114 D4
Burnt Hill Way NR33 . . .114 D5
Burnt House La IP10 . . . .98 D2
Burnt La IP12 . . . . .131 C2
Burnthouse La
  Battisford IP14 . . . . .66 D1
  Needham IP20 . . . . .22 B4
Burntoak La IP20 . . . . . .22 E8
Burr Cl [17] CO12 . . . . .106 E1
Burrell Cres IP28 . . . . . .116 D2
Burrell Rd IP2 . . . . .155 B1
Burrell Way IP24 . . . . . .16 A5
Burrell's Orch IP33 . . . .122 A6
Burroughs Piece Rd [2]
  CO10 . . . . .148 D5
Burrows Cl [5] CO11 . . .104 D2
Burrows Gn NR34 . . . . . .2 A1
Burrows Rd [7] IP12 . . . .84 E6
Burstall Hall La IP8 . . . . .95 E7
Burstall La IP8 . . . . .95 E7
Burston Com Prim Sch
  IP22 . . . . .20 F6
Burston Rd
  Dickleburgh & Rushall
  IP21 . . . . .20 F4
  Diss IP22 . . . . .20 D4
  Gissing IP22 . . . . .20 F5
Burton Cl CB9 . . . . .132 C5
Burton Dr IP6 . . . . .125 C5

Burton End CB9 ....**132** C5
Burton End Com Prim Sch
CB9 ....**132** B5
Burton Hill CB9 ...**74** B3
Burton St NR32 .....**113** D2
Burwash ◻ IP6 ......**83** A5
Burwell Mus★ **44** B5
Burwell Rd CB8 .....**120** A8
Burwood Pl ◻ NR32 ..**113** B6
Bury Bottom IP27 ....**15** A5
Bury Drift IP31 ......**48** E6
Bury Hill IP12 ......**147** A7
Bury Hill Cl IP12 ...**147** A7
Bury La Lidgate CB8 ...**61** C4
Moulton CB8 ....**45** F3
Stanton IP31 ......**34** E3
Wickhambrook CB8 ...**61** E4
Bury Pk Dr IP33 ....**123** C2
Bury Rd Alpheton CO10 ...**78** A5
Barrow IP29 ....**47** A2
Beyton IP30 ....**49** E2
Botesdale IP22 .....**36** B7
Bradfield St Clare IP30 ...**64** C4
Brandon IP27 ......**14** F8
Brettenham IP7 ....**79** C7
Brockley IP29 ......**63** A2
Chedburgh IP29 ....**62** D4
Felsham IP30 ......**65** A4
Flempton IP28 .....**47** F8
Great Barton IP31 ...**49** A5
Great Thurlow CB9 ...**74** F5
Great Whelnetham IP30 ...**63** F4
Haughley IP14 .....**66** D7
Hengrave IP28 .....**48** A7
Hepworth IP22 .....**35** A4
Ipswich IP1 ....**134** D4
Kentford CB8 ......**46** B5
Lavenham CO10 ....**78** D5
Lawshall IP29 ......**63** D2
Market Weston IP22 ...**18** B1
Mildenhall IP28 ....**116** E4
Newmarket CB8 ....**121** C5
Rickinghall Inferior IP22 ...**35** F5
Stanton IP31 ......**34** F4
Stowmarket IP14 ...**124** C8
Stowmarket IP14 ...**124** C8
Thetford IP24 ......**16** B3
Thorpe Morieux IP30 ...**64** E2
Wickhambrook CB8 ...**61** F1
Wortham IP22 .....**36** E8
Bury St ◻ IP14 .....**124** D6
Bury St Edmunds Art Gall★
IP33 ....**154** B2
Bury St Edmunds Cty Sch
IP32 ....**154** A4
Bury St Edmunds Leisure Ctr
IP33 ....**122** E6
Bury St Edmunds Sta
IP32 ....**154** B4
Bush Cnr IP14 ......**53** E1
Bush Gr CO10 ......**148** A4
Bushel La CB7 ......**28** D4
Bushey Cl IP9 ......**150** E3
Bushman Gdns ◻ IP8 ..**134** A2
Bushy La IP12 ......**99** E2
Bussock La IP12 ....**99** D7
Butchers La IP9 .....**150** F3
Butcher's La CO10 ...**93** C4
Butcher's Rd IP17 ...**128** E7
Butfield CO10 ......**78** D3
Butler Smith Gdns ◻
IP5 ....**141** C7
Butlers La CO11 ....**105** F1
Butlers Way CO9 ....**90** A1
Butley Cl IP2 ......**142** E8
Butley Dr ◻ NR32 ...**112** F3
Butley Pottery★ IP12 ...**86** B6
Butley Rd IP11 .....**152** E3
Butt Rd
Stoke-by-nayland CO6 ...**102** E7
Sudbury CO10 .....**148** F4
Butter Mkt
Bury St Edmunds IP33 ...**154** B2
Ipswich IP1 ....**155** B3
Buttercup Cl
Bury St Edmunds IP32 ...**123** F5
Ipswich IP8 ....**138** C1
◻ Lowestoft NR33 ..**114** C4
Butterfly Gdns IP4 ..**140** E5
Button's Rd IP13 ....**71** D6
Buttrum's Mill★ IP12 ..**146** E5
Butt's Rd Holton IP19 ...**118** D8
Spexhall IP19 ......**25** A4
Butts The
Debenham IP14 .....**53** E2
Soham CB7 ....**28** D3
Buxlow Cl IP17 .....**129** B2
Byfield Way IP33 ....**123** C3
Bylam La IP9 ......**106** A4
Byland Cl ◻ IP2 ....**139** A2
Byng Hall Rd
Pettistree IP13 .....**84** E8
Ufford IP13 ....**127** A1
Byng La IP13 ......**127** A3
Byrd Cl IP33 ......**122** C4
Byron Rd IP1 ......**134** E4

C

Cabin Cl NR33 ......**114** B4
Caddie's Wlk NR33 ...**115** A5
Cadiz Way ◻ NR31 ..**3** C6
Cadney La IP33 .....**154** B3

Cadogan Rd IP33 ....**122** D4
Cage La Boxted CO4 ...**103** A3
Felixstowe IP11 ....**152** E5
Cages Way ◻ IP12 ...**84** E6
Cagman's La IP14 ...**65** F3
Caithness Cl IP4 ....**140** B8
Cake St IP13 ......**39** F4
Cakebridge La IP7 ...**79** D3
Calais St IP7 ......**149** D6
Caldecott Rd NR32 ...**112** D1
Calder Rd ◻ IP12 ...**84** E6
Caledonia St ◻ IP7 ..**107** A4
Calfe Fen Cl ◻ CB7 ..**28** D5
Calfe Fen Dro CB7 ...**28** D5
Calford Dr CB9 .....**132** A6
California IP12 .....**146** D3
California La IP8 ....**95** B4
California Rd ◻ CO11 ...**105** A2
Calkewood La IP22 ...**35** E5
Callis St ◻ CO10 ...**90** A8
Calthorpe Cl IP32 ...**123** E6
Calves La CO6 .....**102** D8
Camberley Rd IP4 ...**140** D7
Camborne Rd IP5 ...**141** B7
Cambria Cl ◻ CO11 ..**105** A2
Cambrian Cres ◻ NR32 ...**112** D2
Cambridge Rd
Felixstowe IP11 ....**153** B4
Ipswich IP5 ....**141** A4
Lowestoft NR32 ....**113** D3
Cambridge Way
◻ Bures CO8 ......**101** C4
Haverhill CB9 ......**132** C7
Camden Rd IP3 ....**140** B4
Camden St ◻ NR32 ..**113** E3
Camp Cl ◻ IP26 ....**4** D1
Camp Rd NR32 .....**113** D1
Campbell Cl ◻ IP28 ..**116** B5
Campbell Rd IP3 ....**140** C1
Campion Cl CB7 ....**28** C5
Campion Cres IP14 ..**124** C4
Campion La CO6 ....**102** B6
Campion Rd IP2 ....**138** F4
Campion Way CO6 ...**102** B7
Campions Hill CO6 ..**102** B5
Camps Rd
Haverhill CB9 ......**132** D5
Helions Bumpstead CB9 ...**88** A5
Camwood Gdns IP3 ..**140** B4
Canaletto Cl ◻ NR32 ..**113** B6
Canberra Cl
Ipswich IP4 ....**140** D6
◻ Mildenhall IP28 ...**30** A8
Canberra Rd IP31 ...**33** D4
Candler's La ◻ IP20 ..**22** D6
Candlet Gr IP11 ....**152** F5
Candlet Rd IP11 ....**152** F5
Cangles La IP30 ....**49** F1
Canham St IP1 .....**155** A4
Canhams Rd CO10 ...**148** F3
Cannon St IP33 ....**154** B3
Cannonfields IP33 ...**154** B3
Canon Cl CB9 .....**132** D7
Canon Pickering VC Jun Sch
IP20 ....**22** D6
Canon Pugh Dr ◻ CO10 ...**92** B7
Canterbury Cl
Ipswich IP2 ....**142** F8
◻ Lakenheath IP27 ..**14** A2
Canterbury Gdns IP7 ...**149** E6
Canterbury Gn IP33 ..**123** A3
Canterbury Inf Sch
IP24 ....**16** B6
Canterbury Rd CO10 ...**148** B8
Canterbury Way IP24 ...**16** B6
Capel Cl
◻ Felixstowe IP11 ..**107** D8
Troston IP31 ......**33** D3
Capel Dr IP11 .....**152** C4
Capel Hall La IP11 ...**107** E8
Capel St Mary CE Prim Sch
IP9 ....**150** D3
Capell Wlk ◻ IP31 ...**34** E4
Capps La IP19 .....**23** F5
Captain's La IP14 ...**51** A2
Caraway Rd IP24 ....**16** F6
Carbonels ◻ CO10 ..**92** C6
Carders Cl IP7 .....**149** D4
Cardew Drift IP5 ....**141** D8
Cardiff Ave IP2 ....**139** B1
Cardigan St
Ipswich IP1 ....**155** A4
Newmarket CB8 ....**121** A3
Cardinal Cl IP32 ....**123** E6
Cardinal Pk IP1 ....**155** B2
Cardinal St IP1 ....**155** B2
Cardinal Way CB9 ..**132** D7
Cardinalls Rd IP14 ..**124** D7
Carlford Cl ◻ IP5 ...**98** A8
Carlton Cl
Great Yeldham CO9 ...**90** A1
Haverhill CB9 ......**132** D8
Carlton Colville Prim Sch
NR33 ....**114** B2
Carlton Cross NR33 ..**114** C2
Carlton Ct Hospl
NR33 ....**114** C3
Carlton Gn Rd CB8 ..**74** A7
Carlton Marshes Nature
Reserve★ NR33 ....**114** A7
Carlton Pk Ind Est
IP17 ....**128** C5
Carlton Rd Brinkley CB8 ...**59** F1
Carlton IP17 ......**128** C5
Ipswich IP5 ....**141** A7
Lowestoft NR33 ....**115** B6
Carlton Sq NR33 ....**114** C2

Carlton Way IP4 ....**139** E8
Carlton Wlk IP7 ....**149** E4
Carlyle Cl IP1 .....**134** F4
Carmarthen Cl IP2 ..**139** A2
Carnation Way ◻ IP28 ...**46** A8
Carnoustie Dr
◻ Fornham St Martin IP28 ...**48** C6
Carol Ave ◻ IP12 ...**84** A1
Carol Cl IP11 ......**153** C5
Carolbrook Rd IP12 ..**138** E1
Carr Ave IP16 .....**129** D6
Carr Rd Felixstowe IP11 ...**152** E1
Felixstowe IP11 ....**153** H11
Carr St IP4 ....**155** C3
Carriage Cl IP11 ...**152** C8
Carriers Ct CO7 ....**151** D5
Carrops The CB8 ...**46** A7
Carrs Hill IP13 ....**56** B6
Carsons Dr
◻ Sudbury CO10 ...**92** B3
◻ Sudbury CO10 ...**92** B3
Cart Score NR32 ....**113** E3
Carter Rd CB5 .....**44** A6
Carter St CB7 .....**29** B1
Carters Hill CO4 ...**103** A3
Carters La IP14 ....**80** E6
Carters Vineyard★
CO4 ....**102** F3
Casburn La ◻ CB5 ..**44** A6
Case La IP9 ....**104** E8
Castle Ave CB9 ....**132** C6
Castle Cl
Felixstowe IP11 ....**153** D6
Weeting-with-broomhill
IP27 ....**5** E3
Castle Hill
Beccles NR34 ......**111** C4
Dedham CO7 ......**103** F2
Eye IP23 ....**117** D2
Eyke IP12 ....**85** B6
Halesworth IP19 ...**118** C3
Orford IP12 ....**131** C2
Thorndon IP23 ....**37** E1
Castle Hill Jun Sch
IP1 ....**135** A3
Castle La Bungay NR35 ...**110** A4
Hadleigh IP7 ......**149** C7
Haverhill CB9 ......**132** C6
Offton IP8 ....**81** A4
Orford IP12 ....**131** C2
Thetford IP24 .....**16** C5
Castle Manor Upper Sch
CB9 ....**132** C6
Castle Mdw IP8 ....**81** A4
Castle Orch NR35 ...**110** B4
Castle Rd
Bury St Edmunds IP33 ...**154** A1
Hadleigh IP7 ......**149** B7
Ipswich IP1 ....**134** E1
Mettingham NR35 ..**110** F2
Offton IP8 ....**81** A4
Castle Rise
Hadleigh IP7 ......**149** B7
◻ Haughley IP14 ...**51** C1
Castle St Eye IP23 ...**117** D2
Framlingham IP13 ..**126** C4
Framlingham IP13 ..**126** C4
Thetford IP24 .....**16** C5
Woodbridge IP12 ..**147** A5
Castle Terr IP12 ....**131** C2
Castleton Cl ◻ NR32 ...**113** B4
Castleton Way
Eye IP23 ....**117** B3
Yaxley IP23 ....**37** C5
Catchpole Cl ◻ NR33 ...**11** B1
Catchpole Way ◻ IP31 ...**34** E4
Catchpole Wlk IP21 ...**21** C5
Caters Rd IP13 ....**84** C8
Catesbray IP9 .....**150** D3
Cathcart St ◻ NR32 ..**113** D2
Catherine Rd IP12 ..**146** E6
Catkin Cl CB9 .....**132** B7
Cat's La CO10 .....**148** E5
Cattawade St ◻ CO11 ...**104** E4
Catts Cl IP9 ......**105** C5
Cattsfield IP9 .....**105** C5
Caudle Ave IP27 ...**109** E4
Cauldwell Ave IP4 ..**139** F6
Cauldwell Hall Rd IP4 ...**140** A5
Caulfield Cl IP33 ...**122** F3
Causeway
Huntingfield IP19 ...**40** F5
Lowestoft NR33 ....**115** B4
Causeway Cl
Brockdish IP21 .....**21** F2
◻ Glemsford CO10 ..**77** B3
Causeway End CO11 ...**104** D3
Causeway Est IP7 ...**79** F7
Causeway The
Barking IP6 ....**125** B2
Boxford CO10 .....**93** C3
Burwell CB5 ......**44** A5
Burwell CB5 ......**44** A6
Earl Soham IP13 ...**54** F2
Great Horkesley CO6 ...**102** D1
Haverhill CB9 .....**132** C6
Hitcham IP7 ......**79** E6
Isleham CB7 ......**29** C5
Middleton IP17 ....**58** A6
Needham Market IP6 ...**125** D4
◻ Occold IP23 ....**37** F1
Ridgewell CO9 ....**89** C4
Soham CB7 ....**28** D3
Walsham-le-willows IP31 ...**35** B2
Westhall IP19 .....**25** C4
Causton Sch IP11 ....**152** E6

Caustons Cl ◻ CO10 ...**92** B3
Cautley Rd IP18 ....**119** D6
Cavan Rd IP1 .....**134** D2
Cavendish CE Prim Sch
CO10 ....**76** E1
Cavendish Dr ◻ CO11 ...**104** D2
Cavendish La CO10 ..**76** F2
Cavendish Rd
Bury St Edmunds IP33 ...**122** C6
Clare CO10 ....**90** B8
Felixstowe IP11 ....**152** F3
Stowmarket IP14 ..**124** B6
Cavendish St IP3 ...**139** F4
Cavendish Way ◻ CO10 ...**148** D5
Cavenham Rd IP28 ..**31** A1
Caville White CB9 ..**132** A6
Caxton Mews ◻ NR34 ...**111** B5
Caxton Rd NR34 ....**111** B6
Cecil Lodge Cl CB8 ..**120** F3
Cecil Rd IP1 ......**155** A4
Cecilia St IP1 .....**155** B2
Cedar Ave IP5 .....**141** A6
Cedar Cl Bacton IP14 ...**51** F6
◻ Brantham CO11 ..**104** E5
◻ Great Bricett IP7 ..**80** D6
◻ Lakenheath IP27 ...**13** F2
Occold IP23 ......**37** F2
Cedar Cres ◻ CO11 ..**104** D2
Cedar Ct Alderton IP12 ...**99** E5
◻ Beck Row, Holywell
Row & Kenny Hill IP28 ...**13** B1
Cedar Dr
Lowestoft NR33 ....**114** C5
Worlingham NR34 ..**111** F3
Cedar Rd ◻ Barrow IP29 ...**47** A2
◻ Bentwaters Airfield IP12 ...**85** E8
Cedarcroft Rd IP1 ..**134** F2
Cedars La IP9 .....**150** D3
Cedarwood Prim Sch
IP5 ....**141** C6
Celandine Cl NR33 ..**114** C5
Cemetery La
East Bergholt CO7 ..**151** A4
Ipswich IP4 ....**135** F1
Woodbridge IP12 ..**146** E4
Cemetery Rd
Ipswich IP4 ....**155** C3
Lakenheath IP27 ...**109** D6
Wickhambrook CB8 ...**61** E2
Central Ave IP3 ....**144** D8
Central Rd IP3 ....**129** C5
Centre Cl NR34 ....**111** C3
Centre Dr CB8 ....**121** D2
Centre Rd CB7 ....**28** E2
Century Dr IP5 ....**141** E7
Century Rd IP23 ...**117** C4
Chadacre Rd IP29 ..**77** B7
Chaffinch Dr ◻ CO12 ...**106** F1
Chainhouse Rd IP6 ..**125** D3
Chalfont Dr ◻ IP17 ..**72** C8
Chalk Hill La IP6 ...**81** F5
◻ Ixworth IP31 ....**34** B1
Chalk Rd (N) IP33 ..**154** A2
Chalk Rd (S) IP33 ..**154** A2
Chalk Rd IP27 .....**5** D1
Chalkeith Rd IP6 ...**125** E3
Chalkners St ◻ IP7 ..**150** E3
Chalkstone Mid Sch
CB9 ....**132** E6
Chalkstone Way CB9 ...**133** A6
Challice Rd IP33 ...**154** A3
Chalon St IP1 .....**155** A2
Chamberlain Way IP8 ...**138** C2
Chamberlayne Rd
IP32 ....**123** E4
Chamberlin Cl ◻ IP7 ..**79** F4
Champion Rd IP15 ..**130** E3
Chancellery Mews
IP33 ....**154** A4
Chancery La ◻ IP14 ..**53** F2
Chancery Rd IP1 ...**155** A2
Chandlers Ct ◻ CB5 ..**44** A6
Chandlers Way IP16 ..**129** C3
Chandos Ct ◻ IP12 ..**84** A1
Chandos Dr ◻ IP12 ..**84** A1
Channel The IP8 ...**81** C1
Chantry Cl IP13 ...**71** C2
Chantry Gn IP2 ....**138** D3
Chantry High Sch IP2 ...**138** E3
Chantry Jun Sch IP2 ...**138** E3
Chantry Rd IP17 ...**128** C3
Chapel Cl
Capel St. Mary IP9 ...**150** D3
◻ Fressingfield IP21 ..**39** E8
Garboldisham IP22 ..**18** D4
◻ Great Waldingfield CO10 ...**92** C6
Chapel Cut ◻ CO11 ..**105** A2
Chapel End Way CO9 ...**89** A1
Chapel Farm La IP23 ...**37** A4
Chapel Field IP8 ...**134** A2
Chapel Hill
Belchamp Walter CO10 ...**90** E3
Framsden IP14 ....**69** B7
Thorpe Morieux IP30 ...**79** A8
Chapel La Belstead IP8 ...**142** C7
Botesdale IP22 ....**36** A6
◻ Brockley IP29 ...**63** A4
Claydon IP6 ......**134** A1
Copdock & Washbrook
IP8 ....**138** A1
Drinkstone IP30 ...**65** B7
Great Glemham IP17 ...**56** D5
◻ Grundisburgh IP13 ..**83** E5
Horham IP21 .....**38** F2

Chapel La continued
Kirby Row NR35 ....**8** E7
Kirtling CB8 ......**60** E3
Little Cornard CO10 ...**92** B1
◻ Somersham IP8 ...**81** C3
Stoke-by-nayland CO6 ...**103** B7
Wenhaston With Mells Hamlet
IP19 ....**42** C6
Wicken CB7 ......**28** A1
Wickham Market IP13 ...**127** C5
Wortham IP22 ....**36** E8
Chapel Pond Hill IP32 ...**123** C8
Chapel Rd
Beck Row, Holywell Row
& Kenny Hill IP28 ...**29** F6
Bedingham NR35 ..**7** A3
Boxted CO4 ......**103** A2
Bradfield Combust with
Stanninghall IP29 ...**64** A3
Bucklesham IP10 ..**98** B4
Cockfield IP30 ....**64** D2
Grundisburgh IP13 ...**83** E5
Langham CO4 ....**103** B2
Lowestoft NR33 ...**114** B3
Mendlesham IP14 ..**52** E5
Mutford NR34 ....**10** D3
Old Newton with Dagworth
IP14 ....**52** A1
Otley IP6 ....**69** D3
Rendham IP17 ....**56** E3
Ridgewell CO9 ....**89** C7
St Andrew, Ilketshall
NR34 ....**8** C7
Saxmundham IP17 ...**128** C3
Saxtead IP13 .....**55** A4
Scole IP21 ....**21** B5
Stoke Ash IP23 ...**37** B2
Theberton IP16 ...**58** C5
Wattisfield IP22 ...**35** C4
Wrentham NR34 ...**26** C5
Chapel Row ◻ CB8 ..**60** F8
Chapel St ◻ Bildeston IP7 ...**79** E4
Diss IP22 ....**20** C2
Exning CB8 ......**120** B8
Peasenhall IP17 ...**56** F8
Steeple Bumpstead CB9 ...**88** E4
Stoke-by-clare CO9 ...**89** C4
Woodbridge IP12 ..**147** A5
Chaplains Cl CB9 ...**132** D7
Chaplin Rd CO7 ....**151** C5
Chaplin Wlk ◻ CO10 ..**92** B3
Chappel Rd CO6 ....**101** C2
Chapple Dr CB9 ....**132** E7
Chare Rd IP31 .....**34** C5
Charity La IP13 ....**54** D6
Charles Adams Cl
IP16 ....**129** D6
Charles Ave ◻ IP13 ..**83** C4
Charles Burrell High Sch
IP24 ....**16** B5
Charles Cl CB8 ....**120** E3
Charles Melrose Cl
◻ Mildenhall IP28 ..**116** B4
◻ Mildenhall IP28 ..**116** B5
Charles Rd IP11 ...**152** C5
Charles St IP1 ....**155** B3
Charlotte's IP8 ....**95** F5
Charlton Ave IP1 ...**134** F2
Charrington Cl ◻ IP4 ...**133** A4
Charsfield CE Prim Sch
IP13 ....**70** B3
Charter Way ◻ NR33 ..**114** C5
Chartres Piece NR34 ...**25** E7
Chartwell Cl IP4 ...**140** A5
Chase Cl CB9 .....**132** E7
Chase La ◻ CO12 ..**106** F1
Chase Rd IP28 ....**48** C5
Chase The
Beccles NR34 .....**111** E5
Brandon IP27 .....**6** A1
Brantham CO11 ...**104** F5
Dedham CO7 .....**104** A2
Foxearth CO10 ....**91** B7
◻ Manningtree CO11 ...**104** E2
◻ Martlesham Heath IP5 ...**98** A4
◻ Stanton IP31 ...**34** E4
Steeple Bumpstead CB9 ...**88** D4
Chase's La IP17 ...**72** F6
Chatham Rd ◻ IP27 ...**14** A2
Chatsworth Cl ◻ NR32 ...**113** A3
Chatsworth Cres
Felixstowe IP11 ....**152** C7
Ipswich IP1 ....**139** A2
Chatsworth Dr IP4 ..**140** E4
Chattisham Rd IP8 ..**95** E4
Chaucer Rd
Felixstowe IP11 ....**152** F3
Ipswich IP1 ....**134** F3
Sudbury CO10 ....**148** B8
Chaucer St
Bungay NR35 .....**110** A4
Bungay NR35 .....**110** A4
Chaukers Cres NR33 ..**114** C5
Chauntry Rd CB9 ...**132** D5
Chedburgh Rd
Chevington IP29 ...**62** C5
Whepstead IP29 ...**62** F5
Chedgrave Rd NR33 ..**114** F5
Chediston Rd IP19 ..**24** B2
Chediston St
Chediston IP19 ....**41** D8
Halesworth IP19 ...**118** A3
Chelmer Rd CO10 ..**132** F6
Chelmondiston CE Prim Sch
IP9 ....**106** C8
Chelsea Cl
Bury St Edmunds IP33 ...**122** D5
Ipswich IP1 ....**134** F1

Chelsea Ct 4 CO10 ....148 D5
Chelsea Rd 3 CO10 ....148 D5
Chelsworth Ave
Ipswich IP4 ....135 E1
Sudbury CO10 ....148 F4
Chelsworth Rd IP11 ....152 D3
Chelsworth Way IP14 ..124 E3
Cheltenham Ave IP1 ..135 B1
Chepstow Rd
Bury St Edmunds IP33 ...122 D3
Felixstowe IP11 ....152 F5
Ipswich IP1 ....135 B4
Chequer Field IP12 ....85 C2
Chequer Sq IP33 ....154 C2
Chequers La
Bressingham IP22 ....19 E3
Burston & Shimpling IP22 ..20 E8
Glemsford CO10 ....77 B3
Chequers Rd CO11 ....104 E1
Chequers Rise IP6 ....81 F5
Cherry Blossom Cl
IP8 ....138 B2
Cherry Hill IP28 ....30 E3
Cherry Hill Cl 1 NR34 ..111 F4
Cherry La
Belton with Browston NR31 ..2 E8
Lakenheath IP27 ....13 F2
Cherry La Gdns IP4 ...140 B7
Cherry Tree Cl
Mundford IP26 ....6 A8
North Lopham IP22 ....19 A6
Cherry Tree La IP14 ....53 F1
Cherry Tree Rd
Stowmarket IP14 ....124 C8
Woodbridge IP12 ....146 F4
Cherry Tree Row 3 IP31 .35 C2
Cherrytree La
Rickinghall Inferior IP22 ..36 A7
Soham CB7 ....28 D3
Cherrytree Rd CO10 ....148 F5
Cherrywood 10 IP20 ....22 D5
Chesapeake Cl 8 IP9 ..106 C8
Chesapeake Rd 3 IP3 .144 A8
Chesham Rd IP2 ....155 A1
Chessington Gdns IP1 .138 F8
Chester Pl 5 IP31 ....49 A5
Chester Rd
Felixstowe IP11 ....152 F5
6 Southwold IP18 ....119 D5
Chester St 4 IP27 ....14 A3
Chesterfield Dr IP1 ...134 F2
Chesterton Cl IP2 ....138 F1
Chestnut Ave
Great Bricett IP7 ....80 D6
Lowestoft NR32 ....112 E2
Chestnut Cl
4 Beccles NR34 ....111 E3
6 Bentwaters Airfield IP12 85 E8
1 Fornham All Saints IP28 .48 B6
Great Barton IP31 ....49 B6
3 Great Waldingfield CO10 92 C6
Haverhill CB9 ....132 D6
1 Mildenhall IP28 ....116 D4
Rushmere St Andrew
IP5 ....136 E1
4 Stowupland IP14 ....67 A6
Chestnut Cres
Chedburgh IP29 ....62 D4
6 Lowestoft NR33 ....114 C3
Chestnut Dr
Claydon IP6 ....134 C8
6 Soham CB7 ....28 D4
Chestnut Gr 2 IP14 ....124 E5
Chestnut Rd
Dickleburgh IP21 ....21 C5
Glemsford CO10 ....77 A3
Pulham St Mary IP21 ....21 F8
Stradishall CB8 ....75 C6
Chestnut Rise 1 CB5 ....44 A6
Chestnut Way 21 IP27 ...13 F2
Chestnuts The
5 Great Finborough IP14 ..66 B4
11 Ipswich IP2 ....138 C2
Rickinghall Superior IP22 ..36 A6
Wrentham NR34 ....26 E5
Chevalier Rd IP11 ....153 B4
Chevallier St IP1 ....139 A7
Cheveley Rd
Newmarket CB8 ....121 C3
Woodditton CB8 ....60 E6
Chevington Rd
Hargrave IP29 ....62 B6
Horringer IP29 ....63 A7
Cheviot Rd 3 NR32 ...112 D2
Chevy Ct 3 CO12 ....106 E1
Cheyne Ct 10 CO10 ....148 C5
Chichester Cl IP33 ....123 B3
Chichester Dr NR33 ...114 D6
Chichester Rd IP19 ...118 A5
Chickering Rd IP21 ....38 D6
Childer Rd IP14 ....124 D6
Childers Cl 1 IP9 ....107 A5
Childers Field 2 IP11 ..152 D5
Chiltern Cres NR32 ....112 E2
Chilton Ave IP14 ....124 C6
Chilton Ct CO10 ....148 E5
Chilton Hall* CO10 ....92 B5
Chilton Ind Est CO10 ...148 F6
Chilton Lodge Rd
CO10 ....148 E5
Chilton Rd IP3 ....140 C4
Chilton Way IP14 ....124 B7
Chilton Way Sports Club
IP14 ....124 A7
Chimer's La IP13 ....70 A4
Chimney Mills IP28 ....32 C1
Chimswell Way CB9 ...132 A6
Chippenham Rd
Chippenham IP28 ....29 E2
Fordham CB7 ....29 C1
Moulton CB8 ....45 F3
Moulton CB8 ....45 F4
Chipperfield Rd 20 NR33 .11 C1
Chippings The IP15 ...130 C6
Chislehurst Rd 5 NR33 114 C4
Chiswick Ave IP28 ....116 C6
Chivers Rd CB9 ....132 B5
Christ Church Sq
NR32 ....113 E1
Christchurch Dr IP12 ..146 D3
Christchurch Mansion*
IP1 ....155 C3
Christchurch Pk Hospl
(private) IP1 ....155 B4
Christchurch St IP4 ...155 C3
Christmas La
Lowestoft NR32 ....112 C1
Metfield IP20 ....23 D3
Christopher La CO10 ...148 C5
Church Ave NR32 ....112 C2
Church Cl
Aldeburgh IP15 ....130 E4
Bucklesham IP10 ....98 A5
Carlton IP17 ....128 D7
4 Cavendish CO10 ....76 E1
Creeting St Mary IP6 ....125 F8
Dullingham CB8 ....59 F4
Exning CB8 ....120 C8
Fornham St Martin IP28 ...48 D5
Hepworth IP22 ....35 A5
Ipswich IP5 ....141 B8
Pulham St Mary IP21 ....22 A8
Rede IP29 ....62 E3
Risby IP28 ....47 E5
1 Roydon IP22 ....20 A3
15 Stanton IP31 ....34 E4
Wangford NR34 ....26 B2
Wilby IP21 ....39 C3
Wortwell IP20 ....22 F7
Church Cres IP8 ....138 A6
Church Dr IP13 ....71 E5
Church Farm Cl IP21 ...38 F3
Church Farm La 3
IP19 ....118 A3
Church Farm Rd
Aldeburgh IP15 ....130 E5
Bramfield IP19 ....41 F4
Church Field
Monks Eleigh IP7 ....79 C2
Walberswick IP18 ....119 A2
Church Field Rd CO10 .148 F7
Church Gdns
1 Barningham IP31 ....34 E7
6 Beck Row, Holywell
Row & Kenny Hill IP28 ...29 F6
Church Gn IP8 ....134 B1
Church Hill Benhall IP17 .72 C8
Burstall IP8 ....95 D7
Cookley IP19 ....41 C5
Helions Bumpstead CB9 ...88 B4
Hoxne IP21 ....38 C8
Kersey IP7 ....94 A6
Lawford CO11 ....104 C2
Monks Eleigh IP7 ....79 C2
Pakenham IP31 ....49 E6
Ramsey & Parkeston
CO12 ....106 D1
Saxmundham IP17 ....128 D2
Starston IP20 ....22 C7
Westhall IP19 ....25 D3
Whepstead IP29 ....63 B5
Wyverstone IP14 ....51 E6
Church La
Aldeby/Wheatacre/Burgh
St Peter NR34 ....2 B1
Aldham IP7 ....94 D7
Aldringham cum Thorpe
IP16 ....129 E1
Alpheton CO10 ....77 F5
Arwarton IP9 ....106 E5
Barnham IP24 ....16 C2
Barton Mills IP28 ....116 D1
Baylham IP6 ....81 E6
Beck Row, Holywell Row
& Kenny Hill IP28 ....29 F6
Bedfield IP13 ....54 E5
Blo' Norton IP22 ....18 E2
Blythburgh IP19 ....42 E6
Brantham CO11 ....104 F5
Bressingham IP22 ....19 E3
Brockdish IP21 ....21 F2
Bromeswell IP12 ....85 A5
Broome NR35 ....8 B7
Brundish IP13 ....55 C8
Bucklesham IP10 ....98 A5
Burrough Green CB8 ....59 F2
15 Burwell CB5 ....44 A5
Carlton IP17 ....128 D7
1 Cheveley CB8 ....60 E7
Claydon IP6 ....134 E8
Clopton IP13 ....83 E8
Cockfield IP30 ....64 C1
Copdock & Washbrook
IP8 ....142 A7
Corton NR32 ....3 C4
Creeting St Mary IP6 ....125 D7
Dalham CB8 ....46 C1
Ditchingham NR35 ....7 F7
Dullingham CB8 ....59 F4
Earl Soham IP13 ....55 A2
Exning CB8 ....120 B8
Felixstowe IP11 ....152 E6
Finningham IP14 ....52 A8
Fritton & St Olaves NR31 ...2 C7
Frostenden NR34 ....26 C4
Church La *continued*
Harkstead IP9 ....106 B6
3 Harwich CO12 ....107 B3
Hemingstone IP6 ....82 C8
Hemley IP12 ....98 E5
Henley IP6 ....82 E5
Hepworth IP22 ....35 A5
Hitcham IP7 ....79 E6
Hockwold cum Wilton IP26 ..5 A2
Hoo IP13 ....70 B6
Iken IP12 ....72 F3
Kennett CB8 ....45 F6
Kenton IP14 ....54 A4
Kirton IP10 ....98 E2
Levington IP10 ....145 E3
Lowestoft NR32 ....112 C2
Lowestoft NR33 ....114 B2
5 Lowestoft NR33 ....114 C3
Martlesham IP12 ....84 B1
Mistley CO11 ....104 F2
3 Mundford IP26 ....6 B8
Nayland CO6 ....102 D5
Newmarket CB8 ....121 A3
Norton IP31 ....50 C4
2 Occold IP23 ....37 F1
Playford IP6 ....137 B4
Preston St Mary CO10 ....79 A5
Redenhall with Harleston
IP20 ....22 E7
Rendlesham IP12 ....85 C7
Rickinghall Superior IP22 ..36 A5
Ridgewell CO9 ....89 D3
St James, South Elmham
IP19 ....23 F4
St Mary, South Elmham
Otherwise Homersfield
IP20 ....23 B8
Semer IP7 ....79 F1
Shottisham IP12 ....99 C7
Somersham IP8 ....81 D3
Spexhall IP19 ....24 F3
Sproughton IP8 ....138 B6
Stetchworth CB8 ....60 A5
Stoke Ash IP23 ....37 B1
Stonham Earl IP14 ....67 E6
Stuston IP21 ....37 D8
Swilland IP6 ....83 A7
Thelnetham IP22 ....18 E1
Thwaite IP23 ....52 F7
Timworth IP31 ....48 E8
Troston IP31 ....33 E3
9 Ufford IP13 ....84 F7
Walberswick IP18 ....43 C5
Wenhaston With Mells Hamlet
IP19 ....42 C6
Westerfield IP6 ....135 F4
Westley Waterless CB8 ....59 D3
Weston NR34 ....9 E2
Winfarthing IP22 ....20 B8
Worlington IP28 ....30 B4
Yaxley IP23 ....37 C4
Church La Cl IP28 ....116 D2
Church Mdw
Barton Mills IP28 ....116 D2
Rickinghall Inferior IP22 ...35 F6
Church Mdws 1 IP6 ....82 D6
Church Pk CO10 ....89 E6
Church Rd Alburgh IP20 ...7 A2
Ashbocking IP6 ....68 E1
Bacton IP14 ....51 F6
Bardwell IP31 ....34 B4
Barningham IP31 ....34 E7
Barrow IP29 ....47 A3
Battisford IP14 ....66 E1
Bedfield IP13 ....54 E5
Bentley IP9 ....142 A1
Beyton IP30 ....49 F1
6 Bildeston IP7 ....79 F4
Blaxhall IP12 ....71 F4
Blundeston NR32 ....3 A4
Boxted CO4 ....102 F3
Bradfield Combust with
Stanningfield IP29 ....63 F3
Bradfield St George IP30 ..64 D6
Brandon IP27 ....5 E1
Brettenham IP7 ....65 C1
Brockdish IP21 ....21 F2
Bruisyard IP17 ....56 C5
Bulmer CO10 ....91 C2
Butley IP12 ....86 B5
Carlton CB8 ....74 A8
Chevington IP29 ....62 C6
Combs IP14 ....124 E2
Cotton IP14 ....52 B5
Cratfield IP19 ....40 D5
Crowfield IP6 ....68 C4
Dallinghoo IP13 ....70 C1
Denham IP21 ....38 C5
Dickleburgh & Rushall
IP21 ....20 F3
Earsham NR35 ....7 F3
Ellingham NR35 ....8 D7
Ellough NR34 ....111 F1
Elmswell IP30 ....50 E2
Felixstowe IP11 ....153 C6
Felsham IP30 ....65 A4
Flixton NR35 ....7 E1
Friston IP17 ....72 F7
Garboldisham IP22 ....18 D4
Gillingham NR34 ....9 C7
Gisleham NR33 ....11 A3
Great Barton IP31 ....49 A5
1 Great Finborough IP14 ..66 B4
Great Yeldham CO9 ....89 F1
Haskerton IP13 ....146 B7
Hedenham NR35 ....7 E8
Henstead with Hulver Street
NR34 ....26 E8
Church Rd *continued*
Heveningham IP19 ....40 E3
Holbrook IP9 ....105 F6
Honington IP31 ....33 F5
Kessingland NR33 ....11 B1
Kettleburgh IP13 ....70 C7
Kirby Cane NR35 ....8 E8
Knodishall IP17 ....58 A1
Leiston IP16 ....129 B6
Lindsey IP7 ....93 D7
Little Glemham IP13 ....71 E5
Little Thurlow CB9 ....74 D6
Little Waldingfield CO10 ...92 E8
Lowestoft NR32 ....113 C3
Lowestoft NR32 ....113 D2
Market Weston IP22 ....18 C1
Marlesford IP13 ....71 C5
Mendlesham IP14 ....52 E4
Milden IP7 ....79 B1
Monewden IP13 ....69 F5
5 Moulton CB8 ....45 F3
Mutford NR34 ....10 D3
Nacton IP10 ....145 B4
Newton CO10 ....92 D3
North Lopham IP22 ....19 A5
Old Newton with Dagworth
IP14 ....51 F1
Otley IP6 ....69 C1
Pettaugh IP14 ....68 E6
Playford IP6 ....137 B5
Redlingfield IP23 ....38 C1
Rushbrooke with Rougham
IP30 ....49 C1
Shelfanger IP22 ....20 B6
Snape IP17 ....72 D5
Stambourne CO9 ....89 B1
Stowmarket IP14 ....124 D3
Stowupland IP14 ....67 B7
Stutton IP9 ....105 D5
Sudbury CO10 ....148 E3
Sutton IP12 ....85 A1
Tattingstone IP9 ....105 B7
Theberton IP16 ....58 B4
Thistley Green IP28 ....29 F6
6 Thorpeness IP16 ....73 F6
Thurston IP31 ....49 E4
Tostock IP30 ....50 B2
Uggeshall NR34 ....26 A3
Weybread IP21 ....22 D2
Wheatacre NR34 ....2 A1
Wicken CB7 ....28 B1
Wilby IP21 ....39 C3
Wingfield IP21 ....39 A7
Worlingworth IP13 ....54 E7
Wormingford CO6 ....101 F2
Wortham IP22 ....19 F1
Wrabness CO11 ....105 F2
Wyverstone IP14 ....51 E6
Church Row
Bury St Edmunds IP33 ...154 B3
Framsden IP14 ....69 C6
Church Sq 4 CO8 ....101 C4
Church St 2 Ashley CB8 ..60 F8
Belchamp Otten CO10 ....90 D5
1 Boxford CO10 ....93 C3
Boxted CO4 ....103 A4
5 Chelmondiston IP9 ...106 C8
6 Clare CO10 ....90 A8
Diss IP22 ....20 C2
Exning CB8 ....120 C8
Eye IP23 ....117 D2
Fordham CB7 ....29 B1
Framlingham IP13 ....126 D3
2 Fressingfield IP21 ....39 E8
Gestingthorpe CO9 ....90 F1
Groton CO10 ....93 C5
1 Hadleigh IP7 ....149 D5
23 Harleston IP20 ....22 D6
5 Harwich CO12 ....107 C3
Hundon CO10 ....75 D3
10 Isleham CB7 ....29 C5
Kenninghall NR16 ....19 B8
Lavenham CO10 ....78 D3
Orford IP12 ....131 C2
Peasenhall IP17 ....56 F8
Saxmundham IP17 ....128 D3
12 Southwold IP18 ....119 D5
Steeple Bumpstead CB9 ...88 D4
Stoke-by-nayland CO6 ....102 E6
Stoke-by-nayland CO6 ....102 E7
Stradbroke IP21 ....39 B4
Sudbury CO10 ....148 B4
Wangford NR34 ....26 B2
Wetherden IP14 ....51 A1
Wetheringsett-cum-brockford
IP14 ....53 A6
Withersfield CB9 ....74 A2
Woodbridge IP12 ....147 A5
Worlingworth IP13 ....54 F7
Church Terr IP13 ....127 C6
Church View
Halesworth IP19 ....118 E4
Harleston IP20 ....22 E6
1 Haughley IP14 ....51 C1
Stowlangtoft IP31 ....50 B7
Wyverstone IP14 ....51 E6
Church View Cl IP12 ...147 C7
Church Walks IP33 ....154 C1
Church Wlk
Aldeburgh IP15 ....130 E4
3 Laxfield IP13 ....40 B3
Long Melford CO10 ....77 E1
Mildenhall IP28 ....116 B4
Shelfanger IP22 ....20 B6
Stowmarket IP14 ....124 D6
Sturmer CB9 ....133 C2
2 Sudbury CO10 ....148 C5
Church Wood IP19 ....118 E4
Churchfields Dr 1 CB9 ..88 D3
Churchgate CO10 ....77 B3
Churchgate St
Bury St Edmunds IP33 ...154 B2
15 Soham CB7 ....28 D4
Churchill Ave
Hadleigh IP7 ....149 D7
Haverhill CB9 ....132 F7
Ipswich IP4 ....140 B5
Newmarket CB8 ....120 D5
Churchill Cl
3 Lawshall IP29 ....63 D1
Lowestoft NR32 ....113 C4
7 Woodbridge IP12 ....146 E4
Churchill Cres IP13 ...127 C7
Churchill Dr
Mildenhall IP28 ....116 B5
Sudbury CO10 ....148 C8
Churchill Rd
Halesworth IP19 ....118 B5
5 Southwold IP18 ....119 C8
Thetford IP24 ....16 C6
Churchman Cl IP12 ...147 B8
Churchway 3 IP22 ....36 A8
Churchyard The IP28 ..116 B4
Civic Dr IP1 ....155 A2
Clacton Rd CO11 ....104 E1
Clapgate La IP3 ....140 A1
Clapham Rd Central 3
NR32 ....113 D1
Clapham Rd S NR32 ...113 D1
Clare Ave IP12 ....146 E4
Clare Castle (remains of)*
CO10 ....90 A8
Clare Cl
2 Bury St Edmunds IP33 .122 D4
Mildenhall IP28 ....116 D5
Stowmarket IP14 ....124 E3
Clare Cty Prim Sch
CO10 ....90 A8
Clare Mid Sch CO10 ....90 B8
Clare Pl CB8 ....121 B2
Clare Rd Hundon CO10 ...75 E2
Ipswich IP4 ....139 F8
2 Kessingland NR33 ....11 C1
Poslingford CO10 ....76 A2
Claremont Rd 1 NR33 .115 C6
Clarence Rd
7 Clare CO10 ....76 A1
1 Clare CO10 ....90 A8
Ipswich IP3 ....140 B1
1 Lowestoft NR32 ....113 D2
Sudbury CO10 ....148 C6
Clarendale Est CB9 ....74 C7
Clarendon Rd CB9 ....132 D5
Clark Rd NR35 ....110 C7
Clarke Cl IP22 ....20 C1
Clarke's La NR34 ....8 F3
Clarkes La NR33 ....114 C6
Clarke's Rd 3 CO12 ....106 F2
Clark's Dro CB7 ....28 B4
Clarkson Rd NR32 ....112 D1
Clarkson St IP1 ....155 A3
Claude Oliver Cl CO11 .104 D1
Claude St IP1 ....155 B3
Claudian Cl CB9 ....133 B5
Claverton Way IP4 ....140 D5
Clay Hill Dennington IP13 .55 F5
Hintlesham IP8 ....95 B5
Monks Eleigh IP7 ....79 D2
Ubbeston IP19 ....40 E3
Clay La Bacton IP14 ....51 F6
Hadleigh IP7 ....94 F4
Henley IP6 ....82 E7
Hepworth IP22 ....35 B5
Ixworth IP31 ....34 A2
Lavenham CO10 ....78 E4
Stoke Ash IP23 ....37 B1
Clay Rd
20 Bury St Edmunds IP32 ..48 C5
Bury St Edmunds IP32 ...122 E8
Fornham All Saints IP32 ..48 B5
Clay St Soham CB7 ....28 D4
Thornham Magna IP23 ....36 F1
Claydon Dr NR32 ....112 F3
Claydon High Sch IP6 .134 C8
Claydon Prim Sch IP6 ..82 B5
Clayhall La CO10 ....92 C7
Clayhall Pl CO10 ....92 C7
Clayhill La Hitcham IP7 ..79 F6
Wattisham IP7 ....80 A6
Clayhill Rd IP17 ....128 E5
Clayhills 8 IP19 ....118 A3
Clayhive Dr 4 CB9 ....132 D5
Claypits Ave 1 CO8 ....101 D4
Claypits La CO10 ....91 B7
Clayton Ct IP12 ....146 D3
Clayton Rd 2 CO12 ....106 E1
Clematis Cl 4 IP28 ....30 B1
Clemence St NR32 ....113 C1
Clement Rd NR33 ....115 B6
Clement Sq NR33 ....115 B6
Clements Cl
3 Haverhill CB9 ....132 D5
8 Scole IP21 ....20 F1
Clements Dr 2 CB9 ....132 D5
Clements La CB9 ....132 D5
Clements Prim Sch
CB9 ....132 D5
Clements Rd 4 IP12 ...84 E6
Clement's Way 11 IP28 ..30 B8
Clench Cl IP4 ....155 C3
Clench Rd IP9 ....105 E8
Clerk's Piece NR34 ....111 D3

Clermont Ave CO10 ....148 C8
Cleveland Rd NR33 ....115 C7
Cleves Rd CB9 ....132 B4
Clicket Hill CO8 ....101 D4
Cliff La
  Great Yarmouth NR31 ......3 B8
  Ipswich IP2 ....139 E3
Cliff La Prim Sch IP3 .139 E3
Cliff Rd
  Felixstowe IP11 ....153 D6
  Harwich CO12 ....107 B2
  Ipswich IP3 ....139 E3
  Lowestoft NR33 ....115 C6
  Waldringfield IP12 .....98 E7
Clifford Dr NR33 ....114 E5
Clifford Rd IP4 ....139 F5
Clifford Rd Prim Sch
  IP4 ....139 F6
Cliffs The NR33 ....115 B2
Clifton Rd NR33 ......115 C7
Clifton Way IP2 ......138 D2
Clifton Wood **2** IP9 ...105 E7
Cliftonville NR33 .....115 B2
Cliftonville Rd NR33 ..115 B3
Clink The IP19 ....41 C5
Clint Hill IP31 ....33 F6
Clint Rd IP23 ....37 D1
Clive Ave IP1 ....135 B2
Clockhall La CO10 ......75 D3
Clockhouse La IP14 ....67 F7
Cloncurry Gdns IP11 ..152 D3
Clopton Dr **2** CO10 ...91 E7
Clopton Gdns IP7 .....149 E4
Clopton Rd IP6 ....136 C7
Close The Corton NR32 ...3 D4
  9 Harwich CO12 .....107 A4
  Kennett CB8 ....45 F7
  North Lopham IP22 .....19 A6
  Sudbury CO10 ....148 D6
  3 Tattingstone IP9 ..105 B8
Clough Dr **10** IP26 .....4 E5
Clovelly Cl IP4 ....140 F4
Clovelly Rise NR32 ...113 B3
Clover Cl Ipswich IP2 ..138 F4
  Needham Market IP6 ...125 D3
Clover Field CB9 .....132 B6
Clover Way
  Lowestoft NR32 ......113 C5
  1 Red Lodge IP28 .....30 C1
Cloverfield Dr CB7 ....28 C5
Cloverfields **2** IP31 ..49 E4
Clowes's Cnr IP14 .....54 D2
Cluanie Orch CO10 .....76 F1
Clumps The IP12 ....86 A4
Coach La CB8 ....60 E7
Coachman's Paddock **3**
  IP9 ....105 E7
Coakers La IP13 ....70 A1
Coalpit La IP29 ....46 F4
Coast Guards The **8**
  IP16 ....73 F6
Coast Rd NR32 ....3 C5
Coastguard La NR33 ...11 C1
Coastguard La **22** NR33 ..135 C7
Coates Dro **1** CB7 ....29 C5
Cobbler's Cnr IP8 .....95 B5
Cobbold IP14 ....66 C1
Cobbold Mews IP4 ....155 C3
Cobbold Rd
  Felixstowe IP11 ....153 A4
  Woodbridge IP12 .....146 E7
Cobbold St Diss IP22 ...20 B2
  Ipswich IP1 ....155 C3
Cobden Pl IP4 ....155 C3
Cobham Rd IP3 ....140 C2
Coblers Way **3** CO10 ..92 B7
Cock & Bel La CO10 ...91 E8
Cock La CO10 ....78 F2
Cock Rd IP14 ....52 A6
Cockfield Hall La IP6 ..15 E2
Cockfield Rd IP30 .....65 A3
Cockpen Rd IP14 ......28 F1
Cockrell's Rd CO6 ....102 A2
Cocks Gn La IP30 ......64 A5
Cock's Rd IP23 ....117 F1
Coddenham Rd IP6 .....67 E1
Coddington Way **8** IP31 .34 B1
Codling Rd IP32 ......123 E6
Cody Rd IP3 ....140 C1
Coggeshall Rd
  Dedham CO7 ....104 A2
  Foxash Estate CO7 ....103 F1
Colchester Cl **4** IP27 ..13 F2
Colchester Rd
  Bures CO8 ....101 C4
  Dedham CO7 ....103 E2
  Ipswich IP4 ....135 F1
  Ipswich IP4 ....135 F1
  10 Manningtree CO11 ..104 E2
  Wormingford CO6 .....102 A1
Cold Store Rd IP11 ...152 B2
Coldfair Cl IP17 .....129 B3
Coldfair Gn Prim Sch
  IP17 ....129 B2
Coldham La IP23 ....36 D2
Cole Ness Rd IP3 .....144 A8
Cole St IP21 ....39 B2
Coleman Cl IP22 ....20 C1
Coleridge Rd IP1 .....134 F3
Coles Hill IP19 ....42 C7
Coles La CB8 ....59 E1
Coles Oak La CO7 .....103 E3
Colethorpe La IP14 ....46 F3
College Cl **8** IP29 ....63 A8
College Gn IP11 ......153 C5

College Heath Mid Sch
  IP28 ....116 C6
College Heath Rd
  IP28 ....116 C6
College La
  Bury St Edmunds IP33 ..154 B1
  Worlingham NR34 .....111 F2
College Mdws **2** NR32 ..113 A3
College Rd
  Framlingham IP13 .....126 C4
  Hockwold cum Wilton IP26 ...4 F3
  Lowestoft NR33 ......115 C6
  2 Soham CB7 ....28 D3
College St
  Bury St Edmunds IP33 ..154 B1
  Ipswich IP1 ....155 B2
Colletts Chase CO6 ...101 F2
Collett's Wlk IP12 ...146 E5
Collimer Cl **2** IP9 ...106 C8
Collings Pl CB8 ......140 C8
Collingwood Ave **6** IP3 140 B3
Collingwood Fields
  CO7 ....151 B6
Collingwood Rd IP12 ..146 E7
Collin's Hill CB7 .....29 B1
Collinson's IP2 ......138 D5
Colman Rd NR32 ....3 D4
Colne Rd CO8 ....101 C4
Colne Springs CO9 .....89 D4
Colne Valley Rd CB9 ..132 E5
Colneis Jun Sch IP11 .153 B6
Colneis Rd IP11 .....153 B6
Colneis Cl CO10 .....148 B2
Colsterdale NR33 .....114 D3
Coltsfoot IP32 ....123 F5
Coltsfoot Cl
  7 Ixworth IP31 ......34 B1
  8 Lowestoft NR33 ...114 F1
  7 Wickhambrook CB8 ...61 E2
Coltsfoot Rd IP2 .....138 E4
Columbia St IP5 .....141 A7
Columbine Cl **7** NR33 ..114 C5
Columbine Gdns IP2 ..138 E5
Columbine Way **3** IP3 ..36 D2
Columbines The CO10 ..76 F1
Columbyne Cl IP14 ....67 A7
Colville Rd NR33 .....114 E6
Colville Way NR33 ....114 C3
Comber Cl IP21 ....21 A2
Combs Ford Prim Sch
  IP14 ....124 E4
Combs Gn IP14 ....66 D2
Combs La IP14 ....124 D4
Combs Mid Sch IP14 ..124 F3
Combs Wood Dr IP14 ..124 D3
Comet Way IP28 ......116 B5
Commerce Way **3**
  CO11 ....104 E3
Commercial Rd
  Ipswich IP1 ....155 A1
  Lowestoft NR32 ......115 C8
Commister La **14** IP31 ...34 B1
Commodore Rd NR32 ..112 E1
Common Gate Dro CB7 ..29 A5
Common La
  Beccles NR34 ....111 C5
  Bromeswell IP12 .....147 F7
  Syleham IP21 ....22 A2
  Troston IP31 ....33 E3
Common La N NR34 ...111 B6
Common Rd
  Aldeby NR34 ....10 B1
  Botesdale IP22 ....36 B5
  Bressingham IP22 .....19 F4
  Hopton IP22 ....18 C2
  St James, South Elmham
    IP19 ....23 D4
  Scole IP21 ....21 B4
  Shelfanger IP22 ......19 F7
Common St **3** CO10 ...90 A8
Common The **1** IP20 ...22 D5
Compass Cl IP27 .....109 D4
Compass St NR32 .....113 E2
Compiegne Way IP33 ..154 B3
Conach Rd IP32 ......146 E5
Coney Hill NR34 .....111 B6
Coney Weston Rd
  Coney Weston IP31 ....34 D8
  Fakenham Magna IP31 ..33 F6
  Sapiston IP31 ....34 A6
Congreve Rd IP1 .....135 A3
Coniston Cl IP11 ....153 E7
Coniston Rd IP3 .....140 B2
Connaught Rd
  Haverhill CB9 ....132 C5
  Ipswich IP1 ....134 D2
Conrad Cl NR33 ......114 D6
Conrad Rd NR33 .....114 D6
Consent La IP7 ....79 E4
Constable Cl
  Halesworth IP19 .....118 A2
  Lowestoft NR32 ......112 F1
  3 Manningtree CO11 ..104 D2
  Nayland-with-wissington
    CO6 ....102 A5
Constable Ct **15** IP20 ..22 D6
Constable Rd
  Bury St Edmunds IP33 ..122 E4
  Felixstowe IP11 ....153 B4
  Haverhill CB9 ....132 B7
  Ipswich IP4 ....135 E1
  Sudbury CO10 ....148 C4
Constable Way IP14 ..155 A2
Constantine Rd IP1 ..155 A2
Constitution Hill
  Ipswich IP1 ....139 B8
  2 Needham Market IP6 .125 D5
  Southwold IP18 ......119 D4

Constitution Hill continued
  Sudbury CO10 ....148 D6
Convalescent Hill
  IP11 ....153 A3
Conway Cl
  Felixstowe IP11 ....153 C7
  Ipswich IP2 ....139 B2
Conway Rd **2** IP32 ....48 C5
Conyers Way IP31 .....49 A6
Cooke Cl NR33 ......114 F2
Cooke Rd NR33 ......114 F2
Cookley & Walpole CE Prim
  Sch IP19 ....41 C5
Cookley La IP23 ......38 B5
Cookley Rd Cookley IP19 .41 B5
  Eye IP23 ....38 A5
Cooks Cl IP5 ....141 E8
Cook's Dro IP26 ......12 D2
Cooks Hill Boxted CO4 ..103 A4
  Letheringham IP13 ....70 D4
Cook's La
  Hawkedon IP29 ....62 E1
  Wortwell IP20 ....22 F6
Cooks Rd IP30 ....50 E2
Coombers IP9 ....150 D3
Cooper Cl **2** IP17 ...128 C4
Cooper La IP29 ....63 E8
Cooper Rd IP6 ....68 C1
Cooper's Cl CB8 ......60 A5
Coopers Dr **27** NR33 ...11 C1
Cooper's La CO7 .....103 F3
Coopers La NR33 .....11 B1
Cooper's Rd IP6 ......82 C6
Coopers Rd **30** IP5 ....98 A8
Coopers Way **4** IP6 ...82 A5
Coopersfield IP14 .....53 F2
Copdock Prim Sch IP8 .95 F4
Copelis Cl **3** IP29 ...132 E8
Copeman Rd **3** IP22 ...20 A3
Copland Way NR34 ....10 A3
Copleston High Sch
  IP4 ....140 C5
Copleston Rd IP4 ....140 B5
Coplow Dale **12** NR33 ..114 E3
Copper Beech Dr **5**
  NR33 ....114 D4
Copperfield Rd IP2 ..138 E5
Copperfield IP33 .....154 C1
Copperwheat Ave
  IP18 ....119 B8
Coppice Cl IP12 .....147 A6
Coppice The IP31 ......49 A6
Coprolite St IP3 .....139 E5
Copse Cl IP33 ....123 B1
Copswood Cl IP5 .....141 F7
Copy Hill CB9 ....132 C1
Coral Dr IP1 ....134 D1
Coram St IP7 ....149 A6
Cordell Pl CO10 ......91 E8
Cordell Rd CO10 .....91 E8
Corder Rd IP4 ....139 D8
Cordwinders CO7 .....151 F3
Cordy's La IP11 .....152 B6
Coriander Dr IP24 ....16 D6
Corks La IP7 ....149 C6
Corkway Dro IP26 .....4 A4
Corn Craft (Craft Centre) ★
  IP7 ....79 D2
Corn Hatches La IP7 ..80 E1
Cornard Rd CO10 .....148 D5
Cornerth Cres CO10 ..148 F4
Cornfield Ave IP27 ..109 D7
Cornfield Cres **5** NR32 ...3 D4
Cornfield Rd IP33 ....154 A3
Cornfields IP21 ......21 B5
Cornflower Cl IP2 ...138 E4
Cornford Way **13** CO11 ..104 D2
Cornhill IP33 ....154 B2
Cornish Hall End Rd
  CO9 ....89 A1
Cornmill Gn **9** IP30 ...50 D1
Cornmills Rd CB7 .....28 E2
Cornwall Cl IP33 ....154 C1
Cornwall Rd IP11 ....152 F5
Cornwallis Cl IP28 ...32 C1
Cornwallis Ct IP33 ..154 A1
Cornwallis Rd CB9 ..132 D4
Cornwell Cl CB7 .....29 B4
Coronation Ave IP12 ..96 D6
Coronation Dr IP11 ..152 D3
Coronation Rd IP4 ..140 B6
Coronation Rise **1** CO10 .92 C6
Corporation Ave IP2 ..139 B1
Corsbie Cl IP33 .....132 C5
Corsican Pine Cl CB8 ..120 F5
Corton CE VCP Sch
  NR32 ....3 D4
Corton Long La NR32 ..113 B8
Corton Rd Ipswich IP3 ..140 B1
  Lowestoft NR32 ......113 D6
Cosford Rd IP7 ....94 C7
Cotes The CB7 ....28 B6
Cotman Ave **8** CO10 ..104 D2
Cotman Cl **3** NR32 ..113 B6
Cotman Rd IP3 ......140 A1
Cotmer Rd NR33 .....114 D7
Cotswold Ave IP1 ....135 B4
Cotswold Dr **1** CO10 ...91 E7
Cotswold Way IP12 ..112 E2
Cottesford Cl IP7 ...149 E5
Cottingham Rd IP8 ..138 B2
Cotton End Rd CB8 ...120 C6
Cotton La
  Bury St Edmunds IP33 ..154 C3
  Cotton IP14 ....52 A6
Coucy Cl IP13 ......126 C4
Coupals Cl CB9 .....133 A4

Coupals Prim Sch
  CB9 ....133 B5
Coupals Rd CB9 .....133 C4
Courier CB9 ....133 B5
Court Knoll (Earthworks) ★
  CO6 ....102 C7
Court St CO6 ....102 D5
Courtenay Cl CO10 ..148 B8
Courts The
  Felixstowe IP11 ....153 B4
  Playford IP6 ....137 B5
Covell Cl IP33 ......122 C4
Coverdale **6** NR33 ..114 E3
Covert Cl CB9 ......132 E7
Covert Rd IP18 .....119 C8
Covey Dr IP27 ......109 E6
Covey Way IP27 .....109 E6
Cow And Sheep Dro
  IP28 ....29 E7
Cow Fair **7** IP30 ....50 D1
Cowell St IP2 ....139 C3
Cowle's Dro IP26 ......4 D1
Cowley Rd IP11 .....153 A4
Cowper St IP4 ......140 B6
Cowslip Cl IP2 .....138 E4
Cowslip Cres NR33 ..114 C5
Cowslip Way IP6 ....125 D3
Cox Hill CO10 ....93 C3
Cox La Great Barton IP31 .49 B6
  Ipswich IP4 ....155 C2
Coxhall Rd IP9 .....142 E1
Cox's Cl NR34 ......111 C3
Cox's Hill CO11 .....104 D2
Cox's La IP18 ......119 C8
Coytes Gdns IP1 ....155 B2
Crabbe St
  Aldeburgh IP15 ......130 F4
  Ipswich IP4 ....140 A6
Crabbe's Cl **8** IP26 ....4 E5
Crabtree Cl IP19 ......9 F8
Crabtree La Aldeby NR34 ...9 F8
  Little Horkesley CO6 ..102 B1
Crabtree Mdw **5** IP30 ..56 D2
Crabtree Rise IP21 ...21 F2
Cracks La IP12 ....85 C6
Crag Farm Rd IP12 ..131 E2
Crag Path IP15 .....130 F3
Craig Cl **7** IP11 ...107 D8
Craig's La CO8 ......101 B3
Cramswell Cl NR33 ..132 B4
Cranborne Chase **1**
  IP4 ....136 A1
Cranbrook La CO10 ...77 C1
Crancrie Cl IP12 ....146 D3
Crane Hill London Rd
  IP2 ....138 E4
Cranes Mdw **31** IP20 ...22 D6
Cranesbill Dr IP32 ..123 E5
Cranesbill Rd NR33 ..114 F3
Cranfield Cl **4** NR33 ..115 A3
Cranfield Pk IP8 .....95 D7
Cranleigh Rd NR33 ..114 F3
Cranley Gn Rd
  Eye IP23 ....117 D2
  Eye IP23 ....117 E1
Cranley La IP21 .....117 F1
Cranmoregreen La
  CO10 ....77 C1
Cranwell Cres IP3 ...140 C1
Cranwell Gr IP5 ....141 C7
Cranworth Gdns **1**
  NR32 ....112 F4
Cranworth Rd IP7 ...149 E4
Cratfield La IP19 .....40 C4
Cratfield Rd
  Bury St Edmunds IP32 ..123 E4
  Fressingfield IP21 .....39 F8
  Huntingfield IP19 .....40 E7
Craven Way CB8 .....120 E6
Crawford Ave IP14 ....66 D8
Crawford La **2** IP5 ..141 C7
Creeting La IP14 ......67 B7
Creeting Rd IP14 ....124 E6
Creeting St Mary Prim Sch
  IP6 ....125 F8
Crepping Hall Dr IP9 ..105 C5
Crescent Rd
  Aldeburgh IP15 ......130 E4
  Felixstowe IP11 ....153 A4
  Felixstowe IP11 ....153 A4
  Ipswich IP1 ....155 A3
Crescent The
  Dullingham CB8 ......59 D5
  East Harling NR16 .....18 C8
  Great Horkesley CO6 ..102 D1
  6 Soham CB7 ....28 D3
  Stowmarket IP14 .....124 D4
  7 Thurston IP31 ......49 D4
  Wicken CB7 ....28 A1
  Wickham Market IP13 ..127 B6
Crescents The IP18 ..119 B8
Cresmedow Way IP30 ..50 F2
Crespigny Rd IP15 ...130 E3
Cresslands La IP29 ...76 D3
Crestland Bsns Pk
  CO10 ....92 A8
Crestview Dr NR32 ..113 A4
Cricket Field Bd CB8 ..121 B2
Cricket Hill Rd IP11 ..152 D5
Crick's Rd
  Beck Row, Holywell Row
    & Kenny Hill IP28 ...30 A6
  Thistley Green IP28 ...29 F6
Crimbold's La IP30 ....64 D1
Crimp Cramp La NR34 ..16 B8
Crisp Cl **3** NR32 ...113 B4
Crisp Rd NR35 ....8 C7

Crispin Cl CB9 ....132 B5
Crockfords Rd CB8 ...121 A1
Crocus Cl IP2 ....138 F4
Croft Cl Beccles NR34 ..111 C4
  Diss IP22 ....20 C2
  10 Harleston IP20 .....22 D6
  3 Wickhambrook CB8 ...61 E2
Croft La Diss IP22 ....20 C2
  Haverhill CB9 ....132 F4
  Trimley St Martin IP10 ..98 C2
Croft Lea CO10 ....92 E8
Croft Pl IP28 ....116 C4
Croft The **15** Isleham CB7 ..29 C5
  Newmarket CB8 ......120 F5
  Sudbury CO10 ....148 C6
Croft Rise IP33 .....123 B1
Croft St IP2 ....139 C3
Croft The **6** Bures CO8 ..101 C5
  1 Glemsford CO10 .....77 A2
  Great Yeldham CO9 ...90 A1
  1 Lowestoft NR32 .....113 C1
Crofton Rd IP4 .....140 B8
Cromarty Rd IP4 ....140 B8
Cromer Rd IP1 ......134 F1
Crompton Rd
  Ipswich IP2 ....138 F7
  Lowestoft NR33 .....114 E7
Cromwell Ave NR34 ..111 B3
Cromwell Cl NR34 ...111 B3
Cromwell Rd
  Ringsfield NR34 ....9 C2
  Weeting IP27 ....5 E4
  Weston NR34 ....111 B1
Cromwell Sq IP1 ....155 B2
Cropley Cl IP32 .....123 E4
Cross Cl CB9 ....132 E7
Cross Field Way CO4 ..103 A3
Cross La Cl IP27 ....109 D6
Cross Rd IP20 ....22 C6
Cross St Bungay NR35 ..110 B4
  Drinkstone IP30 ......65 C7
  Elmswell IP30 ....50 E4
  Eye IP23 ....117 C2
  Felixstowe IP11 ....152 E6
  Hoxne IP21 ....38 C7
  Leiston IP16 ....129 C5
  Sudbury CO10 ....148 B4
Cross The IP23 .....117 C2
Cross Ways IP30 ......50 E2
Crossfields CO6 .....102 E7
Crossing Rd IP22 ....20 C1
Crossley Gdns IP1 ..134 C2
Crotchets Cl **2** IP9 ..150 E3
Croutel Rd IP11 ....153 B5
Crow St IP31 ....34 B1
Crowbrook Pl IP30 ...78 C8
Crowcroft Glebe IP7 ..80 B5
Crowcroft Rd IP7 ....80 B5
Crowe Hall La IP9 ...105 D5
Crowe St IP14 ......124 D6
Crowfield Rd IP14 ....68 C6
Crowfoot Com Prim Sch
  NR34 ....111 D4
Crowfoot Gdns **7** NR34 ..111 B5
Crowhurst Cl **4** NR33 ..114 D4
Crowland Cl **1** IP27 ..139 A2
Crowland Rd CB9 ....132 E6
Crowley Rd IP6 .....125 D4
Crown Cl **10** IP12 ....84 A1
Crown Corner IP6 ....68 B1
Crown Cres **15** IP31 ..34 B1
Crown Gn IP22 ....20 E6
Crown La
  Coney Weston IP31 ....17 E1
  Ixworth IP31 ....34 B1
  Orford IP12 ....131 C2
  Wickham Market IP13 ..127 C6
Crown Mdw Wlk
  NR32 ....113 C2
Crown Mill **3** IP30 ....50 F2
Crown Pl IP12 ......147 A4
Crown Rd IP26 ....6 B8
Crown St Brandon IP27 ..14 C7
  Bury St Edmunds IP33 ..154 C1
  Dedham CO7 ....103 D4
  Felixstowe IP11 ....152 E5
  Ipswich IP1 ....155 B3
  Leiston IP16 ....129 D6
  Needham Market IP6 ...125 D5
  Stowmarket IP14 .....124 D7
Crown St E **5** NR32 ..113 E2
Crown St W NR32 ....113 D2
Crown Swimming Pool
  IP1 ....155 B3
Crownfield Rd **8** CO10 ..77 A3
Crownfields **2** IP13 ...84 F7
Crownland Rd **1** IP31 ..35 C1
Crowswell Ct **6** IP11 ..107 D8
Croxton Pl IP10 ......98 E2
Croxton Rd IP24 .....16 C7
Crunch Croft CB9 ...133 C3
Cryspen Ct IP33 .....154 B3
Cuckfield Ave IP3 ...140 E3
Cuckoo Hill (Tumulus) ★
  IP28 ....47 C8
Cuckoo Hill CO8 ....101 C6
Cuckoo La IP20 ......22 F6
Cucumber La NR34 ..111 D1
Culford Rd
  Bury St Edmunds IP28 ..48 C6
  Ingham IP31 ....32 F1
Culford Sch IP28 ....32 A6
Cullingham Rd IP1 ..139 A6
Cullum Rd IP33 .....154 B1
Culvers Mdw **4** IP31 ...34 E4
Culzean Gdns **1** NR32 ..113 A4

Cumberland Cl
4 Felixstowe IP11 .....153 D6
5 Southwold IP18 .....119 D5
Cumberland Mews
IP12 .....147 A4
Cumberland Pl 13 NR32 113 E2
Cumberland Rd IP18 ...119 D5
Cumberland St
Ipswich IP1 .....155 A4
Woodbridge IP12 .....147 A4
Cundle Gn La IP17 .....72 C5
Cundys Marsh 5 IP15 .130 E5
Cunningham Way
NR33 .....115 B3
Curlew Cl IP27 .....109 D5
Curlew Gn NR32 .....112 C1
Curlew Rd IP2 .....138 D4
Curlews The IP33 .....123 C1
Curriers' La IP1 .....155 A2
Curtis Cl IP18 .....138 C1
Curtis Dr 1 IP26 .....4 D5
Curwen Rd IP14 .....124 C6
Curzon Rd CO10 .....148 F6
Cutler Rd 5 NR32 .....112 D2
Cutler St IP1 .....155 B2
Cutlers La CO7 .....151 D7
Cutler's La IP14 .....66 A6
Cutter's La IP31 .....49 E8
Cutting's Rd IP21 .....21 E4
Cypress Way 4 NR33 ...114 F7

D

Daffodil Cl IP2 .....138 E3
Dagworth La IP14 .....66 D8
Daimler Rd IP1 .....134 C2
Dains Pl IP11 .....152 C7
Daires La IP7 .....147 C7
Dairy Dr 4 IP28 .....48 B6
Dairy Hill IP19 .....118 B4
Dairy La Ixworth IP31 .....34 A2
Mutford NR34 .....10 C3
Dairy Rd IP7 .....80 A1
Daisy Gn La IP23 .....52 D7
Daisy Hill IP21 .....39 F8
Daking Ave CO10 .....93 B3
Daking's Drift IP19 .118 A2
Dakota Rd 6 IP28 .....30 A8
Dale End NR33 .....114 E2
Dale Hall La IP1 .....135 B1
Dale Hall Prim Sch
IP1 .....135 B2
Dale Hill IP14 .....53 A6
Dale Rd
Fressingfield IP21 .....22 D1
Stanton IP31 .....34 E5
Dale Tree Rd 11 IP29 .....47 F2
Dales Rd IP1 .....135 A1
Dales View IP8 .....95 F4
Dales View Rd IP1 .....135 A1
Dalham Rd Ashley CB8 .....61 B8
Moulton CB8 .....45 F7
Dallinghoo Rd IP13 .127 A6
Dalton Rd IP1 .....155 A3
Dam La Burgate IP22 .....36 E7
Kessingland NR33 .....11 A1
Damask Cl 5 NR33 .....114 E4
Damselfly Rd IP3 .....144 C8
Dandalan Pl IP1 .....138 E8
Dane Cl CB9 .....133 E8
Dane Hill Rd
Kennett CB8 .....45 E7
Kennett CB8 .....45 F7
Danes Cl IP14 .....124 C5
Danes Ct CO10 .....148 F2
Danescourt Ave IP14 ...124 C5
Daneway Gdns IP29 .....129 C4
Danforth Dr IP13 .....126 B4
Daniels Cl 8 CO10 .....92 B7
Daphne Rd IP12 .....131 C2
Darby Cl IP32 .....123 F6
Darby Rd NR34 .....111 B3
Darcy Cl IP32 .....123 E4
Dark La
Dickleburgh & Rushall
IP21 .....20 E2
Easton IP13 .....70 E7
Darkings La IP30 .....64 F2
Darrell Rd 1 IP33 .153 H11
Darrow Gn Rd IP20 .....7 A4
Darrow Wood La IP22 ...20 A5
Darsham Cl 13 IP11 .....152 D5
Darsham Rd IP17 .....58 B8
Darsham Sta IP17 .....57 E8
Darter Cl IP3 .....144 C8
Darwin Cl IP28 .....116 C6
Darwin Pl CB8 .....121 B1
Darwin Rd IP4 .....139 F5
Dash End La CB9 .....133 F8
Dashwood Cl IP8 .....138 C1
Daundy Cl IP2 .....138 D5
Davall Cl 16 CO12 .....106 E1
Davey Cl Bungay NR35 ...110 E4
Ipswich IP3 .....139 F1
Davey La IP13 .....70 B4
Davey's La IP31 .....34 C4
Davidson Cl CO10 .....92 B2
Daw St CO9 .....89 A3
Dawes Cl IP9 .....150 D4
Dawson Dr IP11 .....152 C8
Dawson Drift 3 IP5 .....141 C7
Days Gn IP9 .....150 D3
Day's La IP31 .....34 E8
Days Rd IP9 .....150 D3
Dazeley's La CO7 .....151 F2
De Burgh Pl 6 CO10 .....76 A1
De Greys Cl 8 CO10 .....92 B3

De Havilland Ct 7 IP28 116 B5
De Vere Ct IP13 .....126 C3
Deacon Ct 8 IP11 .....153 D6
Deacon's Cl 2 CO10 .....78 D4
Dead La Ardleigh CO7 .....103 E1
Bures St Mary CO8 .....101 F5
Lawford CO11 .....104 E1
Deadman's La
Benhall IP17 .....128 A2
Combs IP14 .....66 A5
Rendham IP17 .....57 A3
Stoke Ash IP23 .....53 A8
Deane's Cl 1 CO12 .....107 A1
Deans Cl CB9 .....132 E2
Deben Ave Ipswich IP5 .141 F8
Martlesham IP5 .....137 F1
Deben Dr CO10 .....148 E6
Deben High Sch IP11 .152 F4
Deben La
Waldringfield IP12 .....98 A2
6 Woodbridge Airfield
IP12 .....85 B3
Deben Rd Haverhill CB9 .132 F6
Ipswich IP1 .....134 A1
Saxmundham IP17 .....128 C4
Woodbridge IP12 .....147 B5
Deben Rise IP14 .....53 F1
Deben Valley Dr IP5 .141 C7
Deben Way IP11 .....152 E3
Debenham CE High Sch
IP14 .....53 E2
Debenham Rd
Crowfield IP6 .....68 E5
Winston IP14 .....53 F1
Debenside The IP12 .147 C2
Decoy Rd IP27 .....12 F8
Dedham Dr 4 IP28 .....112 F3
Dedham Heavy Horse Ctr★
CO7 .....104 A3
Dedham Meade CO7 .103 F2
Dedham Rd
Ardleigh CO7 .....103 E1
Boxted CO4 .....103 A3
Lawford CO11 .....104 C2
Deepdale NR33 .....114 E2
Deepdale Rd 6 CO12 .107 A2
Deer Row NR35 .....8 D5
Defoe Rd IP1 .....135 A4
Degas Gdns 1 NR32 .113 B6
Delbrig Dro CB7 .....29 A5
Delf Cl IP17 .....149 E7
Delius Cl
Lowestoft NR33 .....115 A6
1 Stowmarket IP14 .124 C7
Dell Cl NR33 .....114 E7
Dell Prim Sch NR33 .114 E7
Dell Rd NR33 .....114 E7
Dell Rd E NR33 .....114 F7
Dellwood Ave IP11 .153 B5
Delph Dro IP28 .....12 D1
Delph Rd IP27 .....109 D7
Demesne Gdns 6 IP5 .98 A8
Dene Rd IP3 .....140 D4
Denes High Sch NR32 .113 D4
Denham Cl IP33 .....122 D5
Denham Cnr IP21 .....38 D3
Denham La IP21 .....47 A2
Denham Low Rd IP21 ...38 C5
Denham Rd Dalham CB8 .61 C8
Denham IP29 .....47 A1
Hoxne IP21 .....38 D6
Denmark Gdns 1 IP9 .105 E7
Denmark Hill IP22 .....20 C2
Denmark La IP22 .....20 B2
Denmark Rd
Beccles NR34 .....111 B6
Lowestoft NR32 .....115 C4
9 Lowestoft NR32 .....115 D8
Denmark St Diss IP22 .....20 C2
Diss IP22 .....20 C2
Denney's La IP17 .....128 D7
Dennington CE Prim Sch
IP13 .....55 E6
Dennington Rd
Dennington IP13 .....55 F8
Framlingham IP13 .....126 B5
Laxfield IP13 .....40 B1
Denny Ave IP14 .....66 D8
Denny's Hill IP20 .....23 A6
Denton Cl IP2 .....138 D2
Denton Dr NR33 .....114 F5
Denton Rd IP20 .....7 C2
Depden La IP29 .....62 C5
Depot Rd CB8 .....120 E6
Derby Cl IP4 .....140 A5
Derby Pl 8 IP31 .....49 A5
Derby Rd Ipswich IP3 .140 A4
Ipswich IP3 .....140 A4
Derby Way CB8 .....120 D5
Dereham Ave IP3 .....139 F3
Dereham Cl 17 IP27 .....13 F2
Derry Brook La 1 IP14 .53 F2
Derwent Gdns 5 NR32 .113 A4
Derwent Rd
15 Bury St Edmunds IP32 .48 C5
Ipswich IP3 .....139 F3
Desmond Cl 9 NR32 .112 D2
Dettingen Way IP33 .122 D5
Devereaux Cl 2 IP4 .....155 C3
Devils Dyke Nature Reserve★
CB5 .....44 A3
Devil's La IP17 .....42 C1
Devlin Rd IP8 .....138 B1
Devon Cl IP32 .....122 E4
Devon Rd
Felixstowe IP11 .....152 F5
7 Stowupland IP14 .....67 A6
Devon Way 10 CO12 .106 E1

Devonshire Rd IP3 .....139 F5
Dewar La IP1 .....141 C7
Dewarrene Dr IP27 .....5 E3
Dial La IP1 .....155 B3
Diamond Cl IP1 .....134 D1
Dickens Ct 6 NR32 .....3 A4
Dickens Rd IP2 .....138 E6
Dickinson Terr 8 IP5 .141 D7
Dickleburgh Rd IP21 ...21 A5
Dicks Mount NR34 .....10 D7
Dicky Hill IP20 .....22 D7
Didsbury Ct IP2 .....138 D2
Digby Cl 5 IP5 .....98 A7
Digby Rd IP4 .....140 C7
Dillwyn St W IP1 .....155 A3
Dinsdale Rd IP6 .....129 C6
Diomed Dr IP31 .....49 A5
Dirty La IP21 .....21 F7
Diss Church Jun Sch
IP22 .....20 C2
Diss Cty High Sch IP22 .20 D3
Diss Mus★ IP22 .....20 C3
Diss Rd
Burston & Shimpling IP22 .20 E5
Garboldisham IP22 .....18 D4
Garboldisham IP22 .....18 D4
3 Scole IP21 .....20 F1
South Lopham IP22 .....19 C4
Wattisfield IP22 .....35 D5
Diss Sta IP22 .....20 D2
Diss Town FC IP22 .....20 B3
Ditchingham Dam
NR35 .....110 B5
Ditchingham Gr IP4 .140 F6
Ditton Cl CB8 .....121 A1
Ditton Gn CB8 .....60 B5
Dixon Cl 11 CO01 .....104 D2
Dixon Dr NR33 .....114 E7
Dobbs Drift IP5 .....141 F7
Dobbs La IP5 .....137 E1
Dock La IP12 .....147 C7
Dock Rd
Felixstowe IP11 .....152 C1
Ramsholt IP12 .....99 B4
Dock St IP2 .....155 B1
Dockfield Ave 6 CO12 .106 F2
Dockings La 11 CB7 .....29 C5
Doctor Watson's La
IP5 .....137 A1
Doctor's La Ashen CO10 .89 C5
Orford IP12 .....131 C3
Pulham St Mary IP21 .....22 A6
Doctors La IP21 .....39 B4
Dodmans IP9 .....150 E3
Dodson Vale IP5 .....141 C7
Does Field IP14 .....68 C6
Dog La Shelfanger IP22 .20 A8
Tannington IP13 .....55 A4
Dogs Head St IP4 .....155 B2
Dogs La IP9 .....9 C7
Dogwood Wlk 31 IP27 .13 F7
Doit La IP22 .....20 A3
Doit The IP22 .....19 F2
Dolphin Cl 3 NR33 .....115 B4
Dombey Rd IP2 .....138 E5
Dome Sports Ctr IP28 .116 E4
Donegal Rd IP1 .....134 D2
Donkey La
Bradfield Combust with
Stanningfield IP29 .....63 F2
Friston IP17 .....72 F7
Dooley Rd IP11 .....152 C3
Dorchester Rd
Bury St Edmunds IP33 .122 D3
Ipswich IP3 .....140 D3
Doric Pl IP12 .....147 A4
Doris St CB8 .....120 F3
Dorking Rd NR32 .....3 A6
Dorley Dale NR33 .....114 E3
Dorothy Hodgkin Ct
NR34 .....111 B2
Dorset Cl IP4 .....135 F1
Double St IP13 .....126 D3
Doug Smith Cl CB8 .120 F6
Doughty Wylie Cres
IP16 .....58 B4
Douglas Cl
Halesworth IP19 .....118 C5
Lowestoft NR33 .....114 D3
Douglas Rd 11 CO12 .107 A2
Doune Way 9 IP20 .....22 D6
Dove Cl Debenham IP14 .53 F2
9 Harleston IP20 .....22 D5
Saxmundham IP17 .....128 C4
Dove Cres 9 CO12 .106 E1
Dove Gdns 2 IP14 .....67 A5
Dove House Rd CB9 .132 E7
Dove La IP23 .....117 D2
Dove Rd IP18 .....119 B7
Dove St Ipswich IP4 .139 E5
Lowestoft NR32 .....113 D2
Dovedale
Felixstowe IP11 .....152 D3
2 Lowestoft NR33 .....114 F3
Dovehouse Hill IP29 ...77 D7
Dover Rd IP3 .....140 B4
Dovercourt Sta CO12 .107 B2
Dovercourt Swimming Pool
CO12 .....107 B1
Dowes Hill Cl NR34 .111 B4
Dowling Rd CO8 .....101 C2
Downham Way IP27 .....6 A1
Downing Dr
Bury St Edmunds IP32 .123 E5
Ipswich IP2 .....138 F2
Mildenhall IP28 .....116 C6
Newmarket CB8 .....121 D2
2 Woodbridge IP12 .....146 E4

Downing Dr 4 IP31 .....49 A6
Downing Prim Sch
IP2 .....138 F2
Downlands 5 IP7 .....80 F1
Downs Cres CB9 .....132 D6
Downs Farm La IP20 .....23 B7
Downs The
Felixstowe IP11 .....152 D5
Rushbrooke with Rougham
IP30 .....49 C2
Downside IP14 .....124 B6
Downside Cl IP2 .....142 F8
Downton Dr CB8 .....132 C6
Dowson Dr 2 NR33 .....11 B1
Drab's La IP13 .....83 E7
Drake Cl IP14 .....124 A6
Drake Rd CO10 .....148 E5
Drake Sq S IP7 .....140 B2
Drake's Heath NR32 .113 B2
Drapers Cl 1 IP7 .....149 E6
Drapers Hill IP21 .....39 D5
Drapers La
Ditchingham NR35 .....8 A7
Helions Bumpstead CB9 ...88 A5
Drapery Comm 3 CO10 .77 A2
Drays The CO10 .....91 D7
Drift Rd IP27 .....109 C8
Drift The
2 East Bergholt CO11 .104 E5
Ipswich IP4 .....140 A6
Ipswich IP4 .....140 C1
24 Martlesham Heath IP5 .98 A8
Middleton IP17 .....58 B6
Polstead CO6 .....93 D2
Sudbury CO10 .....92 B3
Tostock IP30 .....50 B2
Wickham Market IP13 .127 D8
Driftway The
15 Grundisburgh IP13 .....83 E5
Ipswich IP4 .....140 A6
Drinkstone Gn Cl IP30 .65 B7
Drinkstone Rd
Beyton IP30 .....49 F2
Gedding IP30 .....65 B5
Drinkwater Cl CB8 .....120 E4
Drive The
Harwich CO12 .....107 A1
Heveningham IP19 .....41 B3
Hitcham IP7 .....80 A8
Lowestoft NR32 .....112 F2
Rushbrooke with Rougham
IP30 .....64 B8
Southwold IP18 .....119 B7
Dro The IP27 .....14 D8
Drout's La IP31 .....34 E7
Drove La IP14 .....51 A3
Drovers Ave IP32 .....123 F5
Drover's Ct IP11 .....152 B8
Druids La IP22 .....20 B6
Druids' La IP22 .....20 A4
Drum Field CO7 .....103 E5
Drummond Ct IP33 .154 A1
Drury Cl 19 NR33 .....11 C1
Drury Dr CO10 .....148 D8
Drury La Milden IP7 .....79 B1
Ridgewell CO9 .....89 D3
Drury Pk IP17 .....72 D5
Drury Rd IP6 .....134 C8
Drybridge Hill IP12 .146 E4
Dryden Rd IP1 .....135 A3
Dublin Rd IP23 .....53 E8
Duchess Dr
Newmarket CB8 .....121 D2
Woodditton CB8 .....60 C8
Duck Dro CB7 .....12 A6
Duckamere IP8 .....134 A1
Ducks La IP8 .....120 C7
Ducksen Rd IP14 .....52 E4
Duddery Hill CB9 .....132 E5
Duddery Rd 6 CB9 .....132 E5
Dudley St IP27 .....109 F1
Duffs Hill CO10 .....77 A4
Duke St Beccles NR34 .111 C4
4 Bildeston IP7 .....79 F4
Hadleigh IP7 .....149 D5
Haughley IP14 .....51 C1
Hintlesham IP8 .....95 C5
Ipswich IP3 .....139 E4
7 Stanton IP31 .....34 E4
Dukes Cl IP11 .....153 D6
Duke's Dr IP19 .....118 A2
Dukes Head St 6 NR32 .113 E2
Dukes Mdw
1 Beccles NR34 .....111 C4
Cockfield IP30 .....64 D3
Duke's Mdw IP12 .....146 D3
Duke's Pk IP12 .....146 D3
Duke's Rd NR35 .....110 C2
Dukesway 1 NR35 .....7 F4
Dulgate Rd NR35 .....7 B7
Dullingham Rd
Newmarket CB8 .....120 F1
Woodditton CB8 .....59 F7
Dullingham Sta CB8 .....59 D5
Dumbarton Rd
3 Ipswich IP4 .....136 C1
Ipswich IP4 .....140 B8
Dumfries Rd 2 IP4 .....136 C1
Dumplingbridge La
IP27 .....109 C6
Dun Cow Rd NR34 .....10 A8
Dunburgh Rd NR34 .....9 A6
Dunche's La IP6 .....67 E4

Dunhill La IP22 .....35 B5
Dunlin Rd IP2 .....138 E2
Dunlop Rd IP2 .....138 F6
Dunn Cl IP7 .....149 E5
Dunsey Wood Cl CB9 .132 C7
Dunstall Gn Rd CB8 .....61 E6
Dunster Dr CB9 .....132 C6
Dunston Dr NR32 .....112 E4
Dunston's Cnr IP6 .....82 B8
Dunton Gr IP7 .....149 E4
Dunwich Heath Nature
Reserve★ IP17 .....41 A2
Dunwich Mus★ IP17 .....43 B1
Dunwich Pl 2 IP31 .....49 A5
Dunwich Rd
Blythburgh IP19 .....42 F5
4 Southwold IP18 .....119 D5
Westleton IP17 .....58 D8
Dunwich Underwater
Exploration Ex★
IP12 .....131 B2
Durban Cl IP19 .....118 B2
Durban Rd NR33 .....115 B7
Durbar Terr IP33 .....154 A3
Durbidge's Hill IP22 .....20 E5
Durham Cl 22 IP32 .....48 C5
Durham Rd 2 IP27 .....14 A3
Durham Way CB8 .....120 E5
Durrant View IP5 .....141 E7
Durrant's Cl 8 NR33 .....11 C1
Dux St IP7 .....65 B1
Dyer Ct IP7 .....149 F5
Dyers La CO10 .....92 E2
Dyers Rd CO9 .....89 C1
Dyke St IP1 .....155 B3
Dyson's Dro CB5 .....44 A7

E

Eagle Ct NR34 .....26 E5
Eagle Dr IP15 .....130 C6
Eagle La CB8 .....59 E5
Eagle St IP4 .....155 C2
Eagle Way IP5 .....98 A8
Eagles Cl 1 IP11 .....152 F4
Earl Soham Prim Sch
IP13 .....54 F2
Earls Cl IP11 .....153 D6
Earl's Cl IP19 .....118 A4
Earlsbrook IP14 .....51 E6
Earlsfield IP27 .....13 F2
Earlsford Rd Mellis IP23 .36 F5
Thornham Parva IP23 .....37 A4
Earsham CE VA Fst Sch
NR35 .....7 F4
Earsham Dam NR35 .....110 A4
Earsham Rd NR35 .....7 E6
Earsham St
Bungay NR35 .....110 A4
Bungay NR35 .....110 A4
Earth La NR32 .....2 F5
Easlea Rd IP14 .....123 E4
East Anglia Transport Mus★.
NR33 .....114 A3
East Barton Rd IP31 .....49 B5
East Bergholt CE Prim Sch
CO7 .....151 A6
East Bergholt High Sch
CO7 .....151 D6
East Bergholt Pl Gdn★
CO7 .....151 F3
East Cl IP33 .....123 C6
East Dock Rd CO12 .106 F3
East End La CO7 .....104 E6
East End Rd
East Bergholt CO7 .....151 F4
Stonham Aspal IP14 .....68 C6
East Fen Dro CB7 .....28 F4
East Fen Rd CB7 .....29 D5
East Harling Rd NR16 .....18 F8
East La Bawdsey IP12 .....99 F2
Dedham CO7 .....104 A2
Middleton IP17 .....58 B6
Ufford IP13 .....85 A7
East Lawn IP4 .....140 C8
East Mill Gn IP9 .....104 F7
East Point Pavillion Visitor
Ctr★ NR33 .....115 D8
East Rd CB7 .....29 C5
East Side CO4 .....103 A2
East St 6 Harwich CO12 .107 B2
Southwold IP18 .....119 D5
Sudbury CO10 .....148 D5
East View IP28 .....29 E3
Eastcliff IP11 .....153 E7
Eastern Ave
Haverhill CB9 .....132 D6
18 Soham CB7 .....28 D4
Eastern Cl IP4 .....140 E4
Eastern Way
Bury St Edmunds IP32 .123 C6
Elmswell IP30 .....50 F2
Lowestoft NR32 .....113 B1
Eastfen Dro IP26 .....5 B2
Eastfield Gdns 3 NR33 .114 E4
Eastgate St IP33 .....154 C2
Eastland Ct IP11 .....152 D7
Eastlands IP21 .....39 B4
Eastlands La IP23 .....52 B8
Eastlands Rd IP16 .....129 E6
Eastlow Hill (Tumulus)★
IP30 .....64 C8
Eastlowhill Rd IP30 .....64 B8

Easton La
Hacheston IP13 70 F5
Reydon IP18 27 A1
Easton Prim Sch IP13 70 E5
Easton Rd
Hacheston IP13 71 A4
Woodbridge Airfield IP12 85 B3
Eastward Ho IP16 129 D5
Eastward Pl IP14 124 C7
Eastwood Ave NR33 114 F6
Eaton Cl IP11 152 C7
Eaton Gdns IP11 152 E2
Eccles Rd IP2 138 D2
Economy Rd NR33 115 C7
Eddies The NR33 114 E4
Eddowes Rd 6 IP6 82 B5
Edelweiss Cl 1 NR33 114 C4
Eden Rd 5 Haverhill CB9 132 E5
Ipswich IP4 140 B5
Edendale NR32 112 D2
Edes Paddock 9 IP31 49 A6
Edgar Ave IP14 124 D3
Edgar Sewter Prim Sch IP19 118 B5
Edgeborough Cl CB8 46 A5
Edgecomb Rd IP14 124 D3
Edgefield Ave 15 CO11 104 D2
Edgerton Rd NR33 115 A7
Edgworth Rd CO10 148 C4
Edies La CO6 102 B7
Edinburgh Cl
6 Barnham IP24 16 C2
Stowmarket IP14 124 E6
Edinburgh Gdns IP6 82 B5
Edinburgh Rd
Lowestoft NR32 113 D3
Newmarket CB8 120 E4
Edith Cavell Way CB9 88 E3
Edmonton Cl IP5 141 A7
Edmonton Rd IP5 141 A7
Edmund Cl CB9 132 D6
Edmund De Moundeford VC Sch IP26 4 E6
Edmund Moundford Rd 11 IP26 4 E5
Edmund Rd IP27 14 D8
Edmunds Rd IP14 65 F4
Edward Cl IP1 138 F8
Edward St 6 CO12 106 F3
Edwards La IP19 41 F5
Edwin Ave IP12 146 F7
Edwin Panks Rd IP7 149 E6
Egglestone Cl IP2 138 F1
Eggshell La CO9 88 F1
Eglantine Way 2 CO6 102 A7
Egremont St CO10 77 A2
Ehringshausen Way CB9 132 F5
El Alamein Rd NR32 113 A4
Elder Crescen 2 IP7 80 D6
Elders The IP27 109 E5
Elderstub La IP30 49 B1
Eldith Ave CB7 29 C1
Eldo Gdns 8 IP28 29 F6
Eldo Rd IP28 29 F6
Eldon La IP28 30 D8
Eldred Cl IP32 123 E4
Eldred Dr CO10 92 B2
Eleanor Pl 6 IP31 49 A6
Eley's Cnr IP7 94 E8
Elgar Cl NR33 115 A6
Eliot Way 4 IP14 124 B8
Elizabeth Ave CB8 120 E5
Elizabeth Bonhote Cl 3 NR35 110 C2
Elizabeth Cl
Leiston IP16 129 C4
Lowestoft NR32 113 A3
Elizabeth Dr IP29 62 D5
Elizabeth Rd 16 CO12 107 A2
Elizabeth Way
Burrough Green CB8 59 F2
Eye IP23 117 C3
Felixstowe IP11 152 D3
Stowmarket IP14 124 E6
Sudbury CO10 148 A3
Elizabeth Wlk 27 IP20 22 D6
Ellenbrook Rd
Ipswich IP2 138 D1
Pinewood IP9 142 E8
Ellingham Prim Sch NR35 8 D7
Ellington Rd 1 IP24 16 C2
Elliott Ave IP18 119 C8
Elliott Cl CB8 121 A6
Elliott St IP1 139 A6
Ellis Rd CO4 102 F2
Ellis St CO10 93 C3
Elliston Cl 4 IP30 50 F2
Ellough Rd
Beccles NR34 111 D4
Worlingham NR34 111 F2
Ellwoods Cl 2 CB7 29 C5
Elm Cl
10 Bentwaters Airfield IP12 85 E8
6 Brantham CO11 104 E5
Dullingham CB8 59 E5
Haverhill CB9 132 D6
Lakenheath IP27 109 C7
Lowestoft NR33 114 C3
Elm Coppice 6 NR33 114 E4
Elm Ct CB9 133 C3
Elm Dr IP30 49 F1
Elm Gdns IP11 152 C7
Elm Gr
Garboldisham IP22 18 D4
5 Nayland CO6 102 C5
Elm La
Capel St. Mary IP9 150 E3
Copdock & Washbrook IP8 95 F4
Elm Lodge Rd 7 IP13 40 B3
Elm Rd
East Bergholt CO7 151 B5
Ipswich IP5 140 F7
Stowmarket IP14 124 C6
Sudbury CO10 148 E5
Thetford IP24 16 B4
Wickham Market IP13 127 B6
Elm St IP1 155 B3
Elm Tree Cl 1 IP14 51 E1
Elm Tree La 5 CO6 102 A7
Elm Tree Mid Sch NR33 114 E5
Elm Tree Prim Sch NR33 114 E5
Elm Tree Rd NR33 114 E5
Elm Tree Rd W NR33 114 E5
Elm Way IP14 51 F6
Elm Wlk 30 IP27 13 F2
Elmcroft La IP11 153 C7
Elmcroft Rd IP1 135 A2
Elmdale Dr
Lowestoft NR33 114 D4
29 Mistley CO11 104 E2
Elmers La IP5 141 D7
Elmham Dr IP10 145 B8
Elmhurst Ave NR32 112 E1
Elmhurst Cl CB9 132 F5
Elmhurst Dr IP3 139 F3
Elmhurst Rd 17 CO12 107 B2
Elms Cl 6 Earsham NR35 7 F4
Great Barton IP31 49 B6
Elms La NR34 26 B2
Elms Rd Cowlinge CB8 75 B7
Freckenham IP28 29 F2
Elms The 4 IP29 63 A8
Elmsett CE Prim Sch IP7 80 F1
Elmsett Cl IP14 124 F3
Elmsett Rd IP8 81 B3
Elmsley Way IP17 57 C8
Elmswell Rd
Great Ashfield IP31 50 F6
Wetherden IP14 51 A1
Elmswell Sta IP30 50 E3
Elmtree Bsns Pk IP30 50 E3
Elsmere Rd IP1 139 C8
Elton Pk IP2 138 D6
Elveden CE Prim Sch IP24 15 C2
Elveden Rd IP24 15 F2
Elvedon Way CB8 120 E5
Ely Cl IP33 123 B3
Ely Rd 5 Claydon IP6 82 B5
Ipswich IP4 135 F1
Soham CB7 28 B6
Embry Cres 10 IP7 80 D6
Emerald Cl IP5 141 C8
Emily Frost Cl 4 CB8 61 E2
Emlen St IP1 155 A3
Emmanuel Cl
Ipswich IP2 138 F2
Mildenhall IP28 116 D5
Emsworth Cl 2 IP32 123 D6
Endway The CB9 88 E4
Engine Rd CB7 28 B5
Ennerdale Cl 2 IP11 153 D6
Enstone Rd NR33 115 B6
Enterprise Bsns Pk IP33 154 C4
Entry The IP23 52 D8
Epsom Dr IP1 135 A4
Erbury Pl CO10 90 A8
Eriswell Dr IP27 109 D5
Eriswell Rd
Beck Row, Holywell Row & Kenny Hill IP28 13 E1
Haverhill CB9 132 F6
Lakenheath IP27 109 D4
Erinleigh Rd IP4 140 B6
Erratts Hill CB8 61 B1
Errington Way IP30 50 B2
Erskine Rd 14 CO11 104 E2
Erwarton Hall* IP9 106 E6
Erwarton Wlk IP9 106 E6
Eskdale Way NR32 113 A4
Essex Ave CO10 148 D7
Essex Rd NR32 113 B1
Essex Way IP3 140 E1
Estuary Cres 5 IP9 107 A4
Estuary Dr IP11 153 D7
Estuary Rd 7 IP9 107 A4
Ethel Mann Rd 5 NR35 110 C2
Ethel Rd NR32 113 D1
Etna Rd IP33 154 B4
Euro Ret Pk IP3 140 E1
Europa Rd NR32 113 C4
Europa Way
9 Harwich CO12 106 F2
Ipswich IP1 138 D8
Euroscope* NR32 113 E2
Eustace Rd IP1 138 E8
Euston Ave IP4 140 F6
Euston Cl IP33 154 A1
Euston Ct 4 IP11 152 C4
Euston Hall* IP24 16 E1
Evans Cl IP18 119 C7
Evans Dr NR32 113 B2
Evans' Heath CO10 93 F4
Eve Balfour Way IP14 66 D8
Evelyn Cl IP21 38 C7
Everard Cl 5 IP32 122 E8
Evergreen La CB8 74 C8
Evergreen Rd NR32 113 B2
Everitt Rd NR33 114 D8
Everton Cres IP1 134 F1
Eves Ct 12 CO12 106 E1
Evesham Cl 7 IP2 139 A2
Exchange Sq 6 NR34 111 B5
Exchange St 32 IP20 22 D6
Exeter Cres IP27 109 F1
Exeter Rd 9 Claydon IP6 82 B5
Felixstowe IP11 152 F5
Ipswich IP3 140 B4
Newmarket CB8 121 A4
Newmarket CB8 121 A4
Exmoor Rd IP11 152 F6
Exning Prim Sch CB8 120 B8
Exning Rd CB8 120 D6
Eye Airfield Ind Est IP23 117 A6
Eye Castle* IP23 117 D2
Eye Hill Dro CB7 28 B7
Eye Rd IP23 37 C5
Eyke CE Prim Sch IP12 85 B6
Eyke Rd IP12 85 A5
Eyre Cl IP33 154 B1

F

Factory La
Brantham CO11 104 E4
Chevington IP29 62 C5
Diss IP22 20 B3
Factory St NR32 113 D2
Fagbury Rd IP11 152 A4
Fair Cl Beccles NR34 111 B5
14 Feltwell IP26 4 E5
Fair View Rd IP19 118 C5
Fairbairn Ave 1 IP5 141 D7
Fairey Fox Dr 2 IP28 116 B5
Fairfax Ct NR34 111 B3
Fairfax Gdns IP6 125 E4
Fairfield Ave IP11 153 A5
Fairfield Cres IP13 126 D3
Fairfield Dr
Lowestoft NR33 114 D6
Saxmundham IP17 128 C3
Fairfield Hill IP14 124 D6
Fairfield Rd
Aldeburgh IP15 130 D5
Bungay NR35 110 C2
Framlingham IP13 126 D2
Ipswich IP3 140 A2
Lowestoft NR33 114 D6
Saxmundham IP17 128 C3
Saxmundham IP17 128 C3
Fairfield Way 12 IP26 4 E5
Fairfields IP24 16 C7
Fairhaven Way CB8 120 E5
Fairhead Loke NR33 114 B1
Fairlawns Rd CB8 120 F2
Fairlight Cl 2 IP4 136 A1
Fairmead IP30 50 F3
Fairstead Cl 2 NR34 111 F4
Fairstead House Sch CB8 121 B4
Fairstead The IP22 36 A7
Fairway The
Aldeburgh IP15 130 C6
6 Great Yarmouth NR31 3 B8
Lowestoft NR33 114 F5
Fairways The IP4 140 E5
Fakenham Hill IP31 33 F5
Falcon Ave IP22 20 D3
Falcon Cl CB9 133 A6
Falcon Dr IP27 6 A1
Falcon Inn Rd NR34 26 C7
Falcon La NR35 110 B5
Falcon Rd 15 IP26 4 E5
Falcon St
Felixstowe IP11 152 E6
Ipswich IP1 155 B2
Falcon Way IP28 13 B1
Falconer Ave 3 IP14 51 E1
Falconer Rd CB9 133 A3
Falkenham Rd IP10 98 E2
Falklands Dr 21 CO11 104 E2
Falklands Rd CB9 132 E7
Fallowfield 2 IP30 49 F2
Fallowfields NR32 112 F5
Falmouth Ave CB8 120 F3
Falmouth Cl IP5 141 B6
Falmouth Gdns CB8 121 A6
Falmouth St CB8 120 F3
Famona Rd NR33 114 C2
Faraday Rd IP3 139 F5
Farford Field 5 CO10 92 B3
Farina Cl IP1 138 F7
Farlingaye Cty High Sch IP12 146 E6
Farlingayes IP12 146 F7
Farm Cl Bungay NR35 110 D3
Bury St Edmunds IP33 123 B1
5 Lowestoft NR33 114 D5
Wissett IP19 24 E2
Farm Ct St IP20 23 A5
Farmerie Rd CO10 75 D3
Farmland Cl IP18 119 B8
Farnham Cl 5 NR32 112 F4
Farnham Rd
Blaxhall IP12 71 F5
Snape IP17 72 D6
Farriers Cl
15 Martlesham Heath IP5 98 A8
Stradbroke IP21 39 B4
Farrier's Rd IP14 124 C3
Farriers Went IP11 152 D7
Farrow Cl IP16 129 B6
Farthing Dro
Beck Row, Holywell Row & Kenny Hill IP27 12 E6
Lakenheath IP27 13 A6
Farthing Rd IP1 138 C7
Farthings The IP28 31 D3
Farthings Went IP9 150 F4
Fastnet Cl CB9 133 B6
Fastolf Cl 4 NR32 113 A3
Faulkeners Way IP11 152 C7
Fawcett Rd IP15 130 E4
Fawley Cl IP4 140 C7
Fayrefield Rd IP12 147 B7
Feast Cl 7 CB7 29 A1
Featherbroom Gdns IP13 127 C5
Feathers Field 3 IP11 152 D5
Feilden Way CB8 120 E5
Felaw St IP2 155 C1
Felix Cl IP5 141 B7
Felix Rd
Felixstowe IP11 153 B4
Ipswich IP3 140 C2
5 Stowupland IP14 67 A6
Felixstowe General Hospl IP11 153 B4
Felixstowe Mus* IP11 107 E2
Felixstowe Rd
Ipswich IP3 139 F4
8 Martlesham IP5 98 A8
Felixstowe Sta IP11 153 A5
Fell Rd CO9 89 A4
Fellbrigg Ave IP5 140 F6
Felsham Chase CB5 44 B5
Felsham Ct IP14 124 F3
Felsham Rd
Bradfield St Clare IP30 64 D4
Rattlesden IP30 65 C5
Felsham Rise IP17 128 C3
Feltons 6 CB7 29 A1
Feltwell Rd IP26 4 F3
Fen Bank CB7 29 C6
Fen Ct NR33 115 A6
Fen La Ardleigh CO7 103 E1
Beccles NR34 111 B7
Beck Row, Holywell Row & Kenny Hill IP28 13 D1
Braiseworth IP23 37 D3
Creeting St Peter or West Creeting IP6 125 D8
Ditchingham NR35 7 E7
Garboldisham IP22 18 D3
Hitcham IP7 79 E5
Rickinghall Inferior IP22 36 A6
Roydon IP22 19 F3
Stonham Earl IP6 67 D4
Thelnetham IP22 18 E1
Fen Mdw IP11 152 C8
Fen Pk Prim Sch NR33 115 B6
Fen Rd Blo' Norton IP22 18 F2
Pakenham IP31 49 F6
Fen St Boxford CO10 93 C3
Hinderclay IP22 18 F1
Nayland CO6 102 D5
Fen View
Copdock & Washbrook IP8 95 F4
Thorndon IP23 53 B8
Fenbridge La CO7 151 B3
Fengate Dro IP27 5 E2
Fenlands Cres NR33 114 F6
Fenn Cl
Halesworth IP19 118 A5
Stowmarket IP14 124 D3
Fenn La IP12 98 D6
Fenstreet Rd IP17 58 A7
Fenton Rd CB9 132 F6
Fentons Way IP5 141 C7
Ferguson Way IP5 141 B8
Fern Ave NR32 112 D2
Fern Gn Cl 1 NR32 112 E4
Fern Gr CB9 132 C6
Fern Hill CO10 77 A4
Ferndale Ave NR32 113 B3
Ferndale Cl CB8 121 B6
Ferndown Rd 3 IP11 153 C6
Fernhayes Cl IP2 139 A3
Fernhill Cl IP12 147 A7
Fernlea Rd 9 CO12 107 B3
Ferry La
Beck Row, Holywell Row & Kenny Hill IP28 29 F5
Felixstowe IP11 152 C3
Ferry Rd Bawdsey IP12 99 D1
Felixstowe IP11 153 D7
Southwold IP18 119 C3
Sudbourne IP12 131 C6
Walberswick IP18 119 B2
Fersfield Rd IP22 19 D5
Festival Cl 4 IP17 72 C8
Festival Rd 14 CB7 29 C5
Feveryears Yd 4 IP21 39 D8
Fiddlers La CO7 151 C5
Fiddler's La IP23 117 F2
Field Cl 3 IP30 49 F2
Field Fuller's IP6 135 E4
Field House Gdns IP22 20 D2
Field La NR33 11 B1
Field Rd
Mildenhall IP28 116 C5
Mildenhall IP28 116 D5
Field Stile Rd 2 IP18 119 D5
Field Terr Rd CB8 120 F5
Field View
Bucklesham IP10 98 A4
Field View *continued*
8 Thurstow IP31 49 E4
Field View Gdns NR34 111 D3
Field Way
Debenham IP14 53 F1
18 Stanton IP31 34 E4
Field Wlk IP28 116 C5
Fields View CO10 148 D6
Fieldview Cl IP18 119 B8
Fieldview Dr NR32 113 A1
Fife Rd IP4 136 B1
Finbars Wlk IP4 139 F5
Finborough Cl IP4 140 F6
Finborough Rd IP14 124 B6
Finborough Sch IP14 66 B5
Finch Cl 7 IP14 67 A5
Finch Hill CO10 91 D4
Fincham Rd IP28 116 B5
Finchingfield Rd
Stambourne CO9 89 B1
Steeple Bumpstead CB9 88 E3
Finchley Ave IP28 116 B6
Finchley Rd IP4 139 E6
Findley Cl IP9 105 C5
Fingal St IP13 39 A1
Finney's Drift IP10 145 C5
Finningham Rd
Gislingham IP23 36 D1
Old Newton with Dagworth IP14 51 F2
Rickinghall Superior IP22 36 A4
Walsham-le-willows IP31 35 D2
Finsbury Pl IP33 154 B1
Finsbury Sq IP33 154 C1
Fir Cl Barnby NR34 10 C4
Mundford IP26 6 B8
Wickham Market IP13 127 C6
Fir La NR32 113 A2
Fir Rd IP24 16 B4
Fir Tree Cl IP21 22 D2
Fir Tree Hill IP9 105 F7
Fir Tree La IP14 51 C3
Fir Tree Rise IP8 138 C2
Fir Wlk 29 IP27 13 F2
Fircroft Rd IP1 135 A2
Firebrass La IP12 85 C2
Firebronds Rd 7 IP9 105 E7
Firefly Way IP3 144 B8
Firfield Cl NR34 111 B3
Firs The Beccles NR34 111 F4
Lakenheath IP27 109 E6
Lowestoft NR33 114 C3
Southwold IP18 119 B8
First Ave
4 Glemsford CO10 77 B3
Sudbury CO10 148 E7
First Dro Burwell CB5 44 B8
Lakenheath IP27 109 A8
Firtree Cl IP32 122 D7
Fish Pond Hill IP9 106 B6
Fishbane Cl 9 IP3 144 A8
Fisher Cl Haverhill CB9 133 B5
2 Saxmundham IP17 128 C2
Fisher Rd IP22 20 D2
Fisher Row
Carlton Colville NR32 114 B8
Lowestoft NR32 112 B1
Fisherman's Way 13 NR33 11 C1
Fisher's Dro IP28 12 D3
Fisher's La
East Bergholt CO7 104 E6
Hoxne IP21 38 C8
Fishpond Rd IP12 98 D7
Fishponds Hill CO6 102 C3
Fishponds La IP9 105 F7
Fishponds Way IP14 66 C8
Fison Way IP24 16 B7
Fitches The IP17 129 A2
Fitzgerald Cl 4 CO11 104 D2
Fitzgerald Rd
Bramford IP8 134 A1
Woodbridge IP12 147 A6
Fitzmaurice Rd IP3 140 B3
Fitzroy St Ipswich IP1 155 B3
Newmarket CB8 120 F3
Fitzwilliam Cl
Ipswich IP2 138 F2
6 Woodbridge IP12 146 E4
Five Acre La NR35 7 E3
Five Acres 12 IP9 105 E7
Five Cross Ways
Butley IP12 86 B4
Sudbourne IP12 131 B6
Wetheringsett-cum-brockford IP23 53 A7
Flatford Cl IP14 124 E3
Flatford La CO7 151 D1
Flatford Mill (National Trust)* CO7 151 D1
Flatford Rd
East Bergholt CO7 151 D2
Haverhill CB9 132 A6
Flatts La IP30 50 B2
Flavian Cl CB9 133 B5
Flax La CO10 77 B2
Fleet Dyke Dr NR33 114 E5
Fleetwood Ave IP11 153 B5
Fleetwood Rd IP11 153 B5
Fleming Ave IP28 116 C5
Flempton Rd IP28 47 D5
Flemyng Rd IP33 122 C5
Fletcher Cl 3 IP6 82 A5
Fletcher Rd IP3 140 A1
Fletchers La IP5 141 E8
Fletcher's La IP17 58 B6
Flindell Dr IP8 134 A2
Flint Cl IP2 139 B2

Flixton Marsh La NR32 ...112 B6
Flixton Rd
Blundeston NR32 ...112 C8
Bungay NR35 ...110 A1
Flixton NR35 ...7 E2
St Mary, South Elmham Otherwise Homersfield IP20 ...23 B8
Somerleyton, Ashby & Herringfleet NR32 ...2 F4
Flora Rd NR33 ...115 A3
Flordon Rd IP6 ...125 E5
Florence Rd NR33 ...115 B3
Flowerday Cl **4** NR31 ...3 B7
Flowton Rd Elmsett IP7 ...81 A1
Flowton IP8 ...95 B8
Somersham IP8 ...81 C3
Floyd Rd IP32 ...122 D8
Flying Hospl CB8 ...121 A3
Foal's Gn Rd IP21 ...39 D2
Fodderfen Dro
Beck Row, Holywell Row & Kenny Hill IP28 ...12 C1
Feltwell PE38 ...4 A3
Foden Ave IP1 ...134 C2
Folly End IP15 ...130 D5
Folly La
Bressingham IP22 ...19 F4
Copdock & Washbrook IP8 ...95 E2
Lawshall IP29 ...63 C3
Folly Rd
Great Waldingfield CO10 ...92 C6
Hundon CO10 ...75 F3
Mildenhall IP28 ...116 A7
Folly The Harleston IP14 ...66 C8
Haughley IP14 ...51 C1
Fonnereau Rd IP1 ...155 B3
Forbes Dr NR34 ...111 B3
Ford Cl
Beck Row, Holywell Row & Kenny Hill IP28 ...29 F7
Stowmarket IP14 ...124 C4
Ford Hill IP12 ...99 B7
Ford Rd IP13 ...71 C5
Ford View Rd IP14 ...124 E4
Fordham Moor CB7 ...28 A3
Fordham Pl **4** IP4 ...140 F5
Fordham Road
Fordham CB8 ...44 F7
Freckenham IP28 ...29 D2
Fordham Rd CO6 ...101 C1
Fordham Road CB8 ...120 F7
Fordham Rd
Snailwell CB8 ...45 A7
7 Soham CB7 ...28 D3
Fordham Road CB7 ...28 F2
Fordham Rd CO6 ...101 E2
Fordhams Cl **21** IP31 ...34 E4
Fordley Rd IP17 ...57 F6
Fore Hamlet IP3 ...139 E5
Fore St
Framlingham IP13 ...126 D3
Ipswich IP4 ...155 C4
Forest End CB8 ...46 A7
Forest Glade CB9 ...132 D8
Forest La **3** IP5 ...98 A7
Forest Mount NR31 ...2 B7
Forest Prim Sch IP27 ...5 F1
Forest Rd IP14 ...66 B6
Forest Ret Pk IP24 ...16 A5
Forest Way IP28 ...116 E4
Forester Cl IP8 ...142 E8
Foresters Wlk **6** IP6 ...82 A5
Forfar Cl **2** Ipswich IP4 ...136 B1
Ipswich IP4 ...140 B8
Forge Cl **2** Benhall IP17 ...72 C8
Bucklesham IP10 ...98 A4
Palgrave IP22 ...20 C1
Forge End IP28 ...48 B6
Forge Gr NR34 ...9 B6
Forge St CO7 ...104 A3
Fornham La IP33 ...122 C6
Fornham Road
1 Bury St Edmunds IP32 ...123 A8
Bury St Edmunds IP32 ...154 B4
Fornham St Martin IP31 ...48 D5
Fornham Rd IP31 ...49 A5
Forties Cl CB9 ...133 B6
Fortress Rd NR33 ...114 E3
Foster Cl IP18 ...119 D6
Foster Rd **7** CO12 ...106 F3
Foundation St IP4 ...155 B2
Foundry La IP1 ...155 B2
Fountain La CB7 ...28 C4
Fountain Rd **4** IP12 ...85 D8
Fountain's La NR34 ...10 C4
Fountains Rd
Bury St Edmunds IP33 ...122 D2
Ipswich IP2 ...139 A1
Four Ash Hill CO9 ...89 C4
Four Wheel Dr IP30 ...49 B2
Fourth Ave **5** CO10 ...77 A3
Fowe's La CO10 ...90 D4
Fowler's Cres **2** NR32 ...3 D4
Fox & Pin La IP29 ...63 E8
Fox Ct IP14 ...124 D6
Fox Gn CB8 ...74 C8
Fox Hill Hollesley IP12 ...99 F9
St Cross, South Elmham IP20 ...23 C7
Fox La IP17 ...42 B1
Fox Lea IP5 ...141 E8
Fox Wood N **7** CB7 ...28 D5
Fox Wood S **11** CB7 ...28 D5

Foxborough Mid Sch NR32 ...113 A5
Foxborough Rd NR32 ...113 A4
Foxburrow Cl CB9 ...132 D7
Foxburrow Hill NR32 ...113 A6
Foxes La Ashen CO10 ...89 E5
Mendham IP20 ...23 B4
Foxes Rd CO10 ...89 E5
Foxglade NR32 ...112 C2
Foxglove Cl
Lowestoft NR33 ...115 A2
1 Worlingham NR34 ...111 E3
Foxglove Cres IP3 ...140 E1
Foxgrove Gdns IP11 ...153 C5
Foxgrove La IP11 ...153 C5
Foxhall Cl CO7 ...151 C6
Foxhall Fields CO7 ...151 C6
Foxhall Rd Foxhall IP10 ...151 A6
Ipswich IP3 ...139 F5
Foxhall Stadium IP4 ...141 A5
Foxtail Rd IP3 ...144 D8
Foxwood Cl CO11 ...104 B1
Foxwood Cres IP4 ...140 F5
Framfield Rd NR33 ...114 C4
Framlingham Cl **4** IP12 ...85 B3
Framlingham Coll IP13 ...126 C5
Framlingham Rd
Dennington IP13 ...39 F2
Easton IP13 ...70 E5
Laxfield IP13 ...40 A2
Framlingham Castle (remains of)★ IP13 ...126 C4
Framlinham Coll Jun Sch IP13 ...70 A7
Frampton Rd IP3 ...144 A8
Framsden Rd IP14 ...69 E7
Francis Cl
Haverhill CB9 ...132 D6
Ipswich IP5 ...141 E8
Francis Rd
13 Kessingland NR33 ...11 B1
1 Sudbury CO10 ...148 C5
Franciscan Way IP1 ...155 B2
Frank Bridges Cl **4** CB7 ...28 D3
Franklin Cl IP15 ...130 D5
Franklin Rd
Aldeburgh IP15 ...130 C5
Ipswich IP3 ...140 B2
Fraser Rd
Bramford IP8 ...134 A4
Ipswich IP1 ...138 F7
Freckenham Rd IP28 ...30 A3
Fred Archer Way CB8 ...121 A3
Fred Dannatt Rd IP28 ...116 A6
Frederick Talbot Cl **14** CB7 ...28 D4
Frederick's Rd **3** NR34 ...111 D4
Freehold Rd
Ipswich IP4 ...140 A6
Needham Market IP6 ...125 C6
Freelands IP14 ...52 E4
Freeman Ave **4** IP6 ...82 D6
Freeman St IP7 ...149 D7
Freeman Prim Sch IP22 ...67 B7
Freewood St IP30 ...64 D6
Frenze Hall La IP20 ...20 D3
Frenze Rd IP22 ...20 D2
Frere Cnr **7** IP22 ...20 A3
Frere St **30** IP20 ...22 C6
Freshfields **17** Harwich CO12 ...106 F1
Newmarket CB8 ...120 F4
Fressingfield CE Prim Sch IP21 ...39 D8
Fressingfield Rd IP20 ...23 C1
Freston Hill IP9 ...143 E4
Freston St IP9 ...143 D3
Freston Twr★ IP9 ...143 F4
Friar Cl CB9 ...132 D7
Friars IP9 ...150 F1
Friars Bridge Rd IP1 ...155 B2
Friars Cl
Bury St Edmunds IP30 ...154 B1
7 Felixstowe IP11 ...153 D6
Friars Croft IP21 ...22 D3
Friar's La IP33 ...154 B1
Friars Mdw IP21 ...22 D3
Friars Rd IP7 ...149 C6
Friars St Ipswich IP1 ...155 B2
Sudbury CO10 ...148 C5
Friary Mdw IP28 ...48 D5
Friday St
Beck Row, Holywell Row & Kenny Hill IP28 ...29 F6
Rendlesham IP12 ...85 D7
Friday's Orch IP16 ...129 C5
Friends Field **7** CO8 ...101 C5
Friends Wlk IP5 ...141 D8
Friston Rd IP12 ...85 C2
Fristonmoor La
Knodishall IP17 ...57 E1
Sternfield IP17 ...72 E8
Fritillary Cl IP8 ...142 E8
Fritton Cl **2** IP29 ...63 A1
Fritton Lake Ctry World★ NR31 ...2 C6
Frobisher Rd
21 Harwich CO12 ...106 F1
Ipswich IP3 ...139 E1
Frog Hall La IP7 ...149 D6
Frogmore CB8 ...120 B7
Frogs Alley IP9 ...106 F6

Frogs Hall Rd CO10 ...78 D5
Frogs Hole NR32 ...2 C5
Fronk's Ave **3** CO12 ...107 B1
Fronk's Rd CO12 ...107 A1
Front Rd IP3 ...144 D8
Front St
Mendlesham IP14 ...52 E4
Orford IP12 ...131 B3
Ousden CB8 ...61 E6
Frostenden Cres **1** NR32 ...113 B4
Frowd Cl CB7 ...29 B1
Fryatt Ave **7** CO12 ...107 A2
Fryth Cl IP9 ...132 E7
Fuchsia La IP4 ...140 A5
Fulchers Field IP13 ...126 B4
Fulford Cl **8** IP28 ...48 C6
Fuller Rd IP20 ...22 D5
Fullers Cl **2** IP7 ...149 E6
Fulmar Way IP14 ...114 D5
Fulmerston Rd IP24 ...16 B5
Furness Cl IP2 ...142 F8
Further St CO10 ...92 E2
Furthest Dro IP27 ...4 D1
Furze Cl **4** IP31 ...49 D4
Furze Way IP22 ...36 D5
Fyffe Way **12** NR33 ...115 D8
Fynn La IP6 ...136 C5
Fynn Rd IP12 ...146 D3

G

Gaell Cres **5** IP7 ...149 D5
Gage Cl IP32 ...154 A4
Gage's Rd CO10 ...90 C4
Gainsborough Dr
Halesworth IP19 ...118 A2
Lowestoft NR32 ...113 B6
Manningtree CO11 ...104 D2
Gainsborough La IP3 ...143 F8
Gainsborough Rd
Bury St Edmunds IP33 ...122 C6
Felixstowe IP11 ...153 A4
Haverhill CB9 ...132 B7
Ipswich IP4 ...155 C4
Stowmarket IP14 ...124 B6
Sudbury CO10 ...148 C5
Gainsborough St CO10 ...148 C5
Gainsborough's House Mus★ CO10 ...148 C5
Galley Rd CO10 ...75 D3
Gallow La IP30 ...78 C7
Gallows Hill
Hadleigh IP7 ...149 C5
Hadleigh IP7 ...149 C2
Gallows La IP14 ...66 C7
Galway Ave IP1 ...134 E1
Gandish Rd CO7 ...151 E4
Ganges Rd **1** IP9 ...107 A4
Gannet Cl CB9 ...133 A6
Gannet Rd IP2 ...138 E3
Ganwick Cl CB9 ...132 D8
Gaol La Beccles NR34 ...111 B5
Sudbury CO10 ...148 C5
Gap The NR33 ...114 F6
Garboldisham Prim Sch IP22 ...18 D4
Garboldisham Rd
Harling NR16 ...18 C7
Kenninghall NR16 ...18 F7
Garden Cl
Bungay NR35 ...110 C3
Shotley IP9 ...106 F6
Garden Ct **2** CB5 ...44 B6
Garden Field **2** IP11 ...152 E5
Garden Fields IP31 ...33 D3
Garden House La IP30 ...65 C6
Garden La
Beccles NR34 ...111 F4
Westley IP33 ...122 A5
Gardeners La **21** CB7 ...28 C4
Gardeners Rd **4** IP14 ...53 F1
Gardeners Wlk IP30 ...50 E2
Gardens The
4 Beyton IP30 ...49 F2
Lowestoft NR33 ...114 C4
Gardiner Cl IP33 ...122 C4
Gardner Rd IP18 ...119 D5
Garfield Cl IP11 ...152 F3
Garfield Rd IP11 ...152 F3
Garland Rd **5** CO12 ...106 F3
Garland St IP33 ...154 B3
Garlic St IP21 ...22 A6
Garnons Chase **3** CO6 ...101 F2
Garrard Pl **12** IP31 ...34 B1
Garrards Rd **3** IP7 ...80 F1
Garrett Cres IP16 ...129 D5
Garrick Way IP1 ...135 A3
Garrison La
Felixstowe IP11 ...152 F4
5 Great Waldingfield CO10 ...92 C6
Garrod App IP12 ...84 E7
Garrods IP9 ...150 F3
Garrods End IP29 ...62 C5
Gas Works Rd NR32 ...113 E2
Gascoigne Dr **3** IP6 ...82 D6
Gashouse Dro IP27 ...5 F1
Gaston End CO7 ...151 C5
Gaston St CO7 ...151 C4
Gatacre Rd IP1 ...139 A7
Gate Farm Rd **2** IP9 ...107 A5
Gatesbury's La IP29 ...62 C2
Gateway The IP33 ...123 C3
Gavell St IP19 ...24 D5

Gawdy Cl **2** IP20 ...22 D6
Gaye Cres IP23 ...117 B3
Gaye St IP1 ...155 A3
Gayfer Ave IP5 ...141 E8
Gaymers La IP11 ...152 B8
Gazeley Prim Sch CB8 ...46 B3
Gazeley Rd Ashley CB8 ...46 A1
Kentford CB8 ...46 A5
Gedding Hill IP30 ...65 B4
Gedding Rd IP30 ...65 B7
Gedge Cl IP33 ...122 C4
Gedgrave Rd IP12 ...131 A1
Geldeston Hill NR34 ...8 E5
Geldeston Rd
Ellingham NR35 ...8 D6
Geldeston NR34 ...9 B6
General Castle Way IP30 ...49 B2
Generals Mews **12** IP11 152 D5
Genesta Dr IP33 ...49 D4
Geneva Gdns **4** NR31 ...3 C6
Geneva Rd IP1 ...155 A4
Gents La IP29 ...77 F7
George Baldry Way **2** NR35 ...110 C2
George Brown Way NR34 ...111 C3
George Frost Cl IP4 ...155 C4
George Gent Cl **7** CB9 ...88 D3
George Gibson Cl CB8 ...120 C8
George Hill IP31 ...34 E4
George La **3** CO10 ...77 B2
George Lambpton Ave CB8 ...120 F5
George St Hadleigh IP7 ...149 E6
4 Harwich CO12 ...107 B3
2 Harwich CO12 ...107 B3
Hintlesham IP8 ...95 C6
George Westwood Way NR34 ...111 C6
Geralds Ave IP4 ...140 A5
Gestingthorpe Rd CO10 ...90 F2
Gibbon Cl IP32 ...123 E5
Gibraltar Cl IP33 ...122 C6
Gibraltar Rd IP6 ...69 B1
Gifford Cl **9** IP9 ...105 E7
Giffords Pl IP4 ...140 F6
Gifford's Hall★ CO6 ...103 B8
Gilbert Cl IP6 ...125 C5
Gilbert Rd **2** CO10 ...90 A8
Giles Way Risby IP28 ...47 C5
4 Witnesham IP6 ...83 A5
Gillingham Rd NR34 ...9 A6
Gillingham Dam NR34 ...111 A4
Gilpin Rd NR32 ...112 D1
Gilray Rd IP22 ...20 D2
Gilstrap Rd IP31 ...48 D5
Gimbert Rd **7** CB7 ...28 D4
Gin La IP13 ...40 C2
Gippeswyk Ave IP2 ...139 A4
Gippeswyk Rd IP2 ...155 A1
Gipping Cl CB9 ...132 C4
Gipping Pl IP14 ...124 D7
Gipping Rd Claydon IP6 ...82 A5
Stowupland IP14 ...67 A7
Gipping Way
Bramford IP8 ...134 B2
Sproughton IP8 ...138 B4
Stowmarket IP14 ...124 D7
Gippingstone Rd IP8 ...134 A1
Gipsy La
Aldringham cum Thorpe IP16 ...129 D1
Frostenden NR34 ...26 D4
Needham Market IP6 ...125 D4
Girling St CO10 ...148 C6
Girton Cl
Mildenhall IP28 ...116 C6
Woodbridge IP12 ...146 D2
Woodditton CB8 ...121 B1
Girton Rd CB9 ...132 F5
Girton Way IP2 ...138 F1
Gisleham Mid Sch NR33 ...114 C1
Gisleham Rd NR34 ...114 B1
Gislingham CE Prim Sch IP23 ...36 D2
Gislingham Rd IP14 ...36 C1
Gissing Rd IP22 ...20 F6
Glade Prim Sch IP27 ...5 F1
Glade The IP24 ...16 C7
Glades The NR32 ...112 D2
Gladstone Rd
1 Corton NR32 ...3 C4
Ipswich IP3 ...139 F5
6 Woodbridge IP12 ...147 A5
Glamis Ct **26** IP20 ...22 D6
Glamorgan Rd IP2 ...139 B1
Glanville Pl IP5 ...141 B6
Glanville Rd IP7 ...149 E4
Glassfield Rd IP31 ...34 D4
Glastonbury Cl IP2 ...138 F1
Glastonbury Rd IP33 ...122 C3
Glebe Cl Baylham IP6 ...81 E6
Horringer IP29 ...63 A7
Ingham IP31 ...33 C1
Lowestoft NR32 ...113 C5
Sproughton IP8 ...138 B6
1 Tattingstone IP9 ...105 B8
Glebe End IP9 ...150 F4
Glebe La IP9 ...144 B1
Glebe Mdws IP13 ...54 F2
Glebe Rd Bredfield IP13 ...84 C7
Gissing IP21 ...21 A3
Weeting IP27 ...5 E3
Glebe Rd E **15** NR33 ...11 C1

Glebe Rd W **18** NR33 ...11 B1
Glebe The
Haverhill CB9 ...132 E7
Lavenham CO10 ...78 D3
Glebe View NR34 ...111 C3
Glebe Way **1** Claydon IP6 82 B5
Mendlesham IP14 ...52 E4
Glebes The IP17 ...72 D5
Glemham Dr IP4 ...140 F4
Glemham Hall★ IP13 ...71 F1
Glemham Rd IP17 ...56 E2
Glemsford Cl IP11 ...152 D3
Glemsford Com Prim Sch CO10 ...77 A3
Glemsford Rd
Lowestoft NR32 ...112 F4
Stowmarket IP14 ...124 E4
Glenavon Rd IP4 ...140 D7
Glenbourne Wlk **2** NR33 ...114 C3
Glencoe Rd IP4 ...136 C1
Gleneagles Cl
4 Bury St Edmunds IP28 ...48 C6
1 Felixstowe IP11 ...153 C6
Gleneagles Dr IP4 ...140 D5
Glenfield Ave IP11 ...153 A6
Glenhurst Ave IP4 ...140 B8
Glenside CO10 ...148 E4
Glenwood Dr NR34 ...111 E4
Gloster Rd IP5 ...98 A8
Gloucester Ave NR32 ...112 F3
Gloucester Pl **4** CO10 ...76 A1
Gloucester Rd
7 Bury St Edmunds IP32 ...48 C5
4 Bury St Edmunds IP32 ...122 E8
Haverhill CB9 ...132 D5
Ipswich IP3 ...140 A2
Gloucester Way CO10 ...148 B8
Gobbets La IP22 ...35 E7
Gobbett's Rd IP22 ...35 E8
Godbold Rd **3** IP5 ...141 D7
Goddard Pl IP14 ...66 B7
Goddard Rd IP1 ...134 C3
Goddard Rd E IP1 ...134 C3
Godetia Ct **8** NR32 ...113 B4
Godfrey's Hill IP19 ...40 F8
Godfrey's Wood IP12 ...147 A4
Godolphin IP33 ...122 C3
Godyll Rd IP18 ...119 C5
Goldcrest Rd IP2 ...138 C5
Golden La IP29 ...63 C2
Golden Lion La **5** CO12 107 B3
Golden Miller Cl CB8 ...120 D7
Goldenlond CO6 ...102 E7
Golding Way **1** CO10 ...77 A2
Goldings Cl CB9 ...132 E8
Golding's La IP16 ...129 C4
Goldsmith Cl IP32 ...122 D7
Goldsmith Rd IP1 ...134 E3
Goldsmith Way IP21 ...21 F8
Golf Links Rd
Barton Mills IP28 ...30 C3
Worlington IP28 ...116 A1
Golf Rd IP11 ...153 D5
Gondree NR33 ...114 E3
Gonville Rd
Mildenhall IP28 ...116 D6
1 Woodbridge IP12 ...146 E4
Goodall Terr IP5 ...141 E8
Goodchilds Gdns **8** CB7 ...29 C5
Goodlake Ct **9** CO10 ...106 F1
Goodwood Cl IP1 ...135 B4
Goose Gn IP31 ...111 C5
Goose Gn W NR34 ...111 C5
Gorams Mill La IP13 ...40 B3
Gordon Rd
5 Harwich CO12 ...107 A1
Ipswich IP4 ...140 A7
Lowestoft NR32 ...113 D1
Gordon Richards Cl CB8 ...120 F6
Goring Rd IP4 ...140 C6
Gorleston Rd
Blundeston NR32 ...112 F8
Corton NR32 ...3 B4
Gorse Cl
Lakenheath IP27 ...109 E4
6 Red Lodge IP28 ...30 C1
Gorse Ind Est IP24 ...16 A3
Gorse La IP18 ...119 C7
Gorse Rd Ipswich IP3 ...140 B2
Southwold IP17 ...58 C8
Gorse View IP17 ...58 C8
Gorsehayes IP2 ...139 B3
Gorseland Prim Sch IP5 ...141 F8
Gorselands IP12 ...99 F7
Gorst Cl **7** IP32 ...122 E8
Gosford Cl **4** CO10 ...90 A8
Gosford Rd NR34 ...111 C5
Gosford Way IP11 ...153 C6
Gostling Pl IP5 ...141 E8
Gothic Cl **2** IP20 ...22 D5
Gotsfield Cl **1** CO10 ...92 B7
Gough Pl **9** IP31 ...34 B1
Gower St IP2 ...155 B1
Gowers Ct IP5 ...141 E7
Gowers End **6** CO10 ...77 B3
Gowle Rd IP14 ...124 C8
Goyfield Cl IP14 ...53 E2
Gracechurch St IP14 ...53 E2
Grafton Cl IP33 ...122 D5
Grafton Rd **2** CO10 ...107 B2
Grafton Way IP1 ...155 B2

168 Gra - Har

Graham Ave IP1 . . . . . .139 B8
Graham Rd
Felixstowe IP11 . . . . .152 F5
Ipswich IP1 . . . . .155 A4
Grainge Way 3 IP14 . . . .51 C1
Grainger Cl IP32 . . . . . .123 F5
Grammar Sch Pl 11
CO10 . . . . .148 C5
Grampian Way NR32 . . .112 D2
Granaries The IP6 . . . . .136 C6
Granary Crafts Brook Farm*
IP14 . . . . .66 A5
Granary The CO10 . . . . . .90 A7
Granby St CB8 . . . . .121 B3
Grand Ave NR33 . . . . . . .115 B3
Grange Cl
Felixstowe IP11 . . . . .152 E5
Ipswich IP5 . . . . .141 F8
Grange Ct IP12 . . . . . . .147 B6
Grange Farm Ave
IP11 . . . . .152 D5
Grange La
Barton Mills IP28 . . . . . . .116 D2
Ipswich IP5 . . . . .141 E8
Grange Mill 3 IP29 . . . . .62 C6
Grange Prim Sch
IP11 . . . . .152 D4
Grange Rd
Beccles NR34 . . . . .111 A4
Felixstowe IP11 . . . . .152 D3
Flixton NR35 . . . . .23 E8
16 Harwich CO12 . . . . . . .107 A2
Ipswich IP4 . . . . .139 E6
Lawford CO11 . . . . .104 C1
Lowestoft NR32 . . . . .112 D2
Wickham Skeith IP23 . . . . .52 D7
Grange View IP17 . . . . . .58 B7
Grantchester Pl IP5 . . .141 A8
Grantchester Rise CB5 . .44 A7
Grantham Cres IP2 . . . .155 A1
Granville Gdns IP28 . . .116 A4
Granville Rd IP11 . . . . .152 F3
Granville St IP1 . . . . . .155 A3
Granworth Cl IP13 . . . . .83 E6
Grasmere Ave 5 IP11 . .153 D6
Gravel Dam NR32 . . . . .112 B2
Gravel Dro IP28 . . . . . . .29 E6
Gravel Hill CO6 . . . . . . .102 D5
Gravel Hill Way CO12 . .106 F1
Gravel Pit La CO11 . . . .104 F5
Grayling Rd IP8 . . . . . . .142 E8
Graylings The 10 NR33 . .114 E4
Gray's La IP19 . . . . .24 D4
Gray's Orch IP10 . . . . . . .98 E2
Grays Rd NR34 . . . . .10 C7
Grayson Ave NR33 . . . . .115 A3
Grayson Dr NR33 . . . . . .115 A2
Great Back La 4 IP14 . . .53 F2
Great Barton Prim Sch
IP31 . . . . .49 B6
Great Colman St IP4 . .155 C3
Great Comm La NR34 . . . . .8 E1
Great Conard Ctry Pk*
CO10 . . . . .92 B2
Great Cornard Mid Sch
CO10 . . . . .92 B2
Great Cornard Upper Sch
CO10 . . . . .148 F2
Great Dro CB7 . . . . .28 A4
Great Eastern Rd
CO10 . . . . .148 D5
Great Fen Rd CB7 . . . . . .28 D8
Great Field IP11 . . . . . .152 C8
Great Gipping St IP1 . .155 A2
Great Harlings IP9 . . . .107 A5
Great Heath Prim Sch
IP28 . . . . .116 D6
Great Oak Cour CO9 . . . .90 A1
Great Tufts IP9 . . . . . . .150 F3
Great Whelnetham CE Prim
Sch IP30 . . . . .63 F6
Great Whip St IP2 . . . .155 B1
Grebe Cl Ipswich IP2 . . .138 E2
Mildenhall IP28 . . . . .116 D3
Stowmarket IP14 . . . . . . .124 A6
Green Acre 2 CO10 . . . . .92 C6
Green Cres IP10 . . . . . . .98 A4
Green Dr NR33 . . . . .115 A4
Green Farm La 5 IP29 . . .47 A2
Green Fleet Dr NR32 . . .112 E4
Green Hill IP6 . . . . .68 B1
Green King Brewing Mus*
IP33 . . . . .154 C1
Green La Boxted CO4 . . .102 E3
Burgh St Peter NR34 . . . . . .10 C8
Cockfield IP30 . . . . .64 D2
Creeting St Mary IP14 . . . . .67 F5
Ditchingham NR35 . . . . . .110 C7
Earsham NR35 . . . . .7 E6
6 Feltwell IP26 . . . . .4 E5
Frostenden NR34 . . . . .26 C4
Great Barton IP31 . . . . .49 B5
Hundon CO10 . . . . .75 D2
Kessingland NR33 . . . . .11 C1
3 Martlesham IP12 . . . . . .84 A1
Pettistree IP13 . . . . .127 D5
Redenhall with Harleston
IP20 . . . . .22 E6
Reydon IP18 . . . . .26 E1
Shipmeadow NR34 . . . . .8 F5
Somerleyton, Ashby &
Herringfleet NR32 . . . . .2 E4
Southwold IP18 . . . . .119 B8
Starston IP20 . . . . .22 D8
Stratford St Mary CO7 . . .103 E6
Green La *continued*
Syleham IP21 . . . . .38 E8
2 Tattingstone IP9 . . . . .105 B8
Thelnetham IP22 . . . . .35 C6
Thetford IP24 . . . . .16 C6
Thrandeston IP21 . . . . .37 B6
Troston IP31 . . . . .33 C5
Tuddenham St Martin
IP6 . . . . .136 C4
Wetheringsett-cum-brockford
IP14 . . . . .53 A6
Green La Cl IP18 . . . . . .119 B8
Green Man Pl IP12 . . . . . .71 F2
Green Man Way IP12 . .147 B6
Green Oak Glade IP8 . .142 D8
Green Pk Brinkley CB8 . . . .59 E1
42 Harleston IP20 . . . . . . .22 D6
Green Rd Brandon IP27 . . .6 A1
Newmarket CB8 . . . . .121 A2
Thorpe Morieux IP30 . . . . . .64 F1
Woolpit IP30 . . . . .50 D1
Green St IP21 . . . . .38 C8
Green The 4 Ashley CB8 . .60 F8
Beck Row, Holywell Row
& Kenny Hill IP28 . . . . . . .29 E7
Chedburgh IP29 . . . . .62 C4
8 Earsham NR35 . . . . .7 F4
1 Grundisburgh IP13 . . . . .83 E5
Hadleigh IP7 . . . . .149 E6
Hessett IP30 . . . . .64 F8
Kersey IP7 . . . . .94 A7
Kirtling CB8 . . . . .60 E3
Lound NR32 . . . . .2 F6
Lowestoft NR33 . . . . .114 F6
Mendlesham IP14 . . . . .52 D2
2 Mistley CO11 . . . . .104 F2
North Lopham IP22 . . . . . . .19 A6
Snailwell CB8 . . . . .45 A6
Green Willows CO10 . . . .78 C2
Greenacre Cres 1
NR32 . . . . .113 B2
Greenacres IP14 . . . . . . .51 F1
Greenbank IP19 . . . . . .118 C5
Greene Rd IP33 . . . . . . .122 C6
Greenfield Rd NR33 . . .114 F5
Greenfields CB8 . . . . . .121 C3
Greenfields Way CB9 . .132 C5
Greenfinch Ave IP2 . . .138 D3
Greenhills CB7 . . . . .28 E3
Greens The
Aldeburgh IP15 . . . . .130 C6
Ipswich IP4 . . . . .140 F4
Greensmill 2 CO11 . . . .104 E3
Greenspire Gr IP8 . . . .138 B2
Greenview IP29 . . . . .77 B7
Greenway 4 IP31 . . . . . .49 A5
Greenway The NR34 . . .111 B4
Greenways IP12 . . . . .85 C2
Greenways Cl IP1 . . . . .139 B8
Greenways Cres IP32 . .123 D6
Greenwich Bsns Pk
IP3 . . . . .139 E2
Greenwich Cl IP3 . . . . .139 E2
Greenwich Rd IP3 . . . . .139 D2
Greenwood Cl CB9 . . . .132 C5
Greenwood Way 1
NR32 . . . . .113 A6
Greenwoods The IP31 . . .49 E6
Gregory Rd IP28 . . . . . .116 A6
Gregory St CO10 . . . . . .148 C5
Grenadier Rd CB9 . . . . .132 A6
Grenville Rd CO10 . . . .148 D8
Gresham Ave NR32 . . . .112 F2
Gresham Cl NR32 . . . . .112 F2
Gresham Rd NR34 . . . . .111 C6
Gresley Gdns 3 IP2 . . .139 C3
Gretna Gdns 1 IP4 . . . .136 B1
Greville Starkey Ave
CB8 . . . . .121 A5
Grey Friars Rd IP1 . . . .155 B2
Greyfriars IP12 . . . . . . .146 D4
Greyfriars Rd IP32 . . . .123 E4
Greyhound Hill CO4 . . .103 C2
Greyhound La IP22 . . . . .18 B1
Greyhound Rd 7 CO10 . . .77 A2
Greys Cl 5 CO10 . . . . . . .76 E1
Greys La CB9 . . . . .75 A3
Grice Cl 3 NR33 . . . . . . .11 C1
Griffith Cl 4 NR33 . . . . . .11 C1
Grime's Graves (Flint
Mines)* IP27 . . . . .6 C4
Grimsey Rd IP16 . . . . . .129 D5
Grimsey's La IP16 . . . . .129 E5
Grimston La IP11 . . . . .107 C8
Grimwade Cl 9 CO11 . . .104 E4
Grimwade St IP4 . . . . . .155 C2
Grinder's La IP21 . . . . . .22 D4
Grindle Gdns IP33 . . . .123 B3
Grindle The IP8 . . . . .95 F8
Grinstead Gdns IP6 . . .125 E3
Grinstead Hill IP6 . . . . .125 E3
Gromford La IP17 . . . . . .72 C5
Groomes Cl 5 NR31 . . . . . .3 B7
Grosvenor Cl IP4 . . . . .139 E8
Grosvenor Gdns IP33 . .122 F3
Grosvenor House Ct 9
IP28 . . . . .116 B5
Grosvenor Rd
Lowestoft NR33 . . . . .115 C7
Sudbury CO10 . . . . .148 B8
Grosvenor Yd CB8 . . . . .121 A3
Groton St CO10 . . . . .93 B5
Grove Ave CO10 . . . . .92 E8
Grove Cty Prim Sch
NR33 . . . . .114 C4
Grove End IP21 . . . . .39 B5
Grove Gdns
Fordham CB7 . . . . .29 A2
Grove Gdns *continued*
Woodbridge IP12 . . . . . . .146 E6
Grove Hill Belstead IP8 . .142 C7
Dedham CO7 . . . . .103 E2
Langham CO4 . . . . .103 C3
Grove La
Ashfield cum Thorpe IP14 . .54 C2
Elmswell IP30 . . . . .51 A3
Harkstead IP9 . . . . .106 C7
Ipswich IP4 . . . . .139 E5
Mendham IP20 . . . . .23 A2
Stanton IP31 . . . . .34 F4
Thetford IP24 . . . . .16 C6
Grove Mews 4 NR34 . . .111 C4
Grove Pk
Bury St Edmunds IP33 . . .154 A3
Fordham CB7 . . . . .29 A2
5 Walsham Le Willows
IP31 . . . . .35 C2
Grove Rd Beccles NR34 . .111 B5
2 Brantham CO11 . . . . . .104 E4
Brockdish IP21 . . . . .21 F3
Bury St Edmunds IP33 . . .154 A3
Felixstowe IP11 . . . . .153 A6
Gissing IP21 . . . . .21 A8
Knodishall IP17 . . . . .72 F7
Lowestoft NR33 . . . . .114 C4
Pettistree IP13 . . . . .127 A4
Starston IP20 . . . . .22 C6
Walsham-le-willows IP31 . .35 C2
Woodbridge IP13 . . . . . . .146 E6
Grove Rd N NR33 . . . . . .114 D5
Grove The
Great Glemham IP17 . . . . . .56 F1
12 Martlesham Heath IP5 . .98 A8
Mildenhall IP28 . . . . .29 F8
5 Woodbridge IP12 . . . . .147 B6
Grove Wlk IP8 . . . . .142 D8
Grove; Henley Rd The
IP1 . . . . .135 C2
Grub La IP19 . . . . .24 E5
Grundisburgh Cty Prim Sch
IP13 . . . . .83 E5
Grundisburgh Hall*
IP13 . . . . .137 C8
Grundisburgh Rd
Clopton IP13 . . . . .83 D8
Great Bealings IP13 . . . . .137 C6
Tuddenham St Martin
IP6 . . . . .136 D6
Grundle Cl 6 IP31 . . . . . .34 E4
Gt Finborough CE VC Prim
Sch IP14 . . . . .66 B4
Gt Waldingfield CE Prim Sch
CO10 . . . . .92 C6
Guildhall Feoffment Cty Prim
Sch IP33 . . . . .154 C1
Guildhall La NR34 . . . . . .26 D5
Guildhall of Corpus Christi
The* CO10 . . . . .78 D4
Guildhall St IP33 . . . . . .154 B2
Guineas Cl CB8 . . . . . . .120 E6
Gules Gn IP21 . . . . .22 F1
Gull Hill IP19 . . . . .25 C3
Gull La
Grundisburgh IP13 . . . . . . .83 D6
Thornham Magna IP23 . . . .37 A2
Gull The IP13 . . . . .70 C2
Gull's La CO7 . . . . .104 A2
Gulpher Bsns Pk IP11 . .152 F8
Gulpher Rd IP11 . . . . . .152 E6
Gun Hill CO7 . . . . .103 D4
Gun La NR32 . . . . .113 E2
Gunton Ave NR32 . . . . .113 A7
Gunton Church La
NR32 . . . . .113 C5
Gunton Cliff NR32 . . . . .113 D5
Gunton Dr NR32 . . . . . .113 D5
Gunton Prim Sch
NR32 . . . . .113 C6
Gunton St Peter's Ave
NR32 . . . . .113 C5
Guntons Cl 12 CB7 . . . . . .28 D4
Gurdon Rd 5 IP13 . . . . . .83 E5
Gurlings Cl CB9 . . . . . . .132 E8
Guscot Cl NR32 . . . . . . .113 A6
Gusford Prim Sch IP2 .138 D1
Guston Gdns IP10 . . . . . .98 E2
Guthrum Rd IP7 . . . . . .149 D6
Guy Cook Cl CO10 . . . . . .92 B2
Guyatt Ct 6 CB5 . . . . .44 A5
Gwendoline Rd IP4 . . . .140 E4
Gwynne Rd 4 CO12 . . . .107 B2
Gymnasium St IP1 . . . . .155 A3

H

Hacheston Rd IP13 . . . . . .70 F5
Hackney Rd
Peasenhall IP17 . . . . .56 E8
Woodbridge IP12 . . . . . . .147 B6
Hackney's Cnr IP6 . . . . . .81 F5
Haddiscoe Sta NR31 . . . . . .2 A5
Hadenham Rd NR33 . . . .114 F1
Hadleigh Bsns Pk IP7 . . . .94 E4
Hadleigh Dr NR32 . . . . .112 F3
Hadleigh High Sch
IP7 . . . . .149 F5
Hadleigh Prim Sch
IP7 . . . . .149 D5
Hadleigh Rd Aldham IP7 . .94 E8
Bildeston IP7 . . . . .79 F3
Boxford CO6 . . . . .93 D2
East Bergholt CO7 . . . . . .151 B4
Elmsett IP7 . . . . .80 F1
Higham CO7 . . . . .103 D7
Ipswich IP2 . . . . .138 E6
Hadleigh Swimming Pool
IP7 . . . . .149 D6
Hadrian Cl CB9 . . . . . . .133 B5
Haggars Mead IP14 . . . . .67 D7
Haglemere Dr IP4 . . . . .139 E7
Halcyon Cres NR32 . . . .113 C1
Hale Cl IP2 . . . . .138 D2
Halesowen Cl IP2 . . . . .142 F8
Halesworth & District Mus*
IP19 . . . . .118 B4
Halesworth Mid Sch
IP19 . . . . .118 C5
Halesworth Rd
Brampton with Stoven
IP19 . . . . .25 E3
Heveningham IP19 . . . . . . .40 F3
Linstead Parva IP19 . . . . . .40 F8
Reydon IP18 . . . . .119 B7
St Andrew, Ilketshall
NR34 . . . . .25 A6
St Lawrence, Ilketshall
NR34 . . . . .24 E8
Sibton IP17 . . . . .41 B1
Uggeshall NR34 . . . . .25 F3
Walpole IP19 . . . . .41 C5
Wenhaston With Mells Hamlet
IP19 . . . . .41 F6
Halesworth Sta IP19 . .118 B4
Half Moon La
6 Grundisburgh IP13 . . . . .83 E5
Redgrave IP22 . . . . .36 A8
Half Moon St IP30 . . . . . .65 D5
Halfar Rd 2 IP31 . . . . . . .33 D5
Halfmoon La IP27 . . . . .109 C7
Halford Ct 6 IP8 . . . . . .138 C2
Halford La IP22 . . . . .19 D3
Halifax Prim Sch IP2 . .139 B2
Halifax Rd Ipswich IP2 . .139 B2
9 Mildenhall IP28 . . . . . . .30 A8
Halifax St IP27 . . . . . . .109 F1
Halifax Way CB8 . . . . . .120 E5
Hall Barn Rd CB7 . . . . . . .29 B5
Hall Cl IP29 . . . . .62 B4
Hall Cl The IP28 . . . . . . .31 D4
Hall Dr 17 Feltwell IP26 . . . .4 E5
Lakenheath IP27 . . . . . . .109 C7
Lowestoft NR32 . . . . .112 C1
Santon Downham IP27 . . . . .6 C2
Hall Farm Cl IP12 . . . . .147 B8
Hall Farm La NR34 . . . . . .10 E1
Hall Farm Rd IP12 . . . .147 B8
Hall Field 1 IP11 . . . . . .152 E5
Hall La Blundeston NR32 . . .3 A4
Bressingham IP22 . . . . .19 D5
Brinkley CB8 . . . . .59 F1
Burston & Shimpling IP21 . .21 A6
Burwell CB5 . . . . .44 A5
Claydon IP6 . . . . .134 E8
Harwich CO12 . . . . .107 A1
Hawkedon CO10 . . . . .76 C7
Otley IP6 . . . . .69 C2
Oulton NR32 . . . . .112 C4
Redgrave IP22 . . . . .36 A8
Ridgewell CO9 . . . . .89 D3
Risby IP28 . . . . .47 D5
Roydon IP22 . . . . .20 A3
Scole IP21 . . . . .21 C4
Shelfanger IP22 . . . . .20 B6
Somersham IP8 . . . . .81 C3
Spexhall IP19 . . . . .24 E4
Wetheringsett-cum-brockford
IP14 . . . . .53 B4
3 Witnesham IP6 . . . . . . .83 A5
Yaxley IP23 . . . . .37 B4
Hall Pond Way IP11 . . .152 D5
Hall Rd Barnardiston CB8 .75 B5
Barsham NR34 . . . . .8 F3
Bedingfield IP23 . . . . .54 A7
Bedingham NR35 . . . . .7 C7
Belchamp Walter CO10 . . . .91 A3
Blundeston NR32 . . . . . . .112 C8
Borley CO10 . . . . .91 D5
Brent Eleigh CO10 . . . . .79 A3
Brockdish IP21 . . . . .22 A3
Burston & Shimpling IP22 . .20 E7
Carlton Colville NR33 . . . .114 B2
Charsfield IP13 . . . . .69 F3
Chelsworth IP7 . . . . .79 E2
Cowlinge CB8 . . . . .75 A7
Earsham NR35 . . . . .7 E4
Ellingham NR35 . . . . .8 C7
Foxhall IP10 . . . . .141 E4
7 Hopton-on-sea NR31 . . . .3 B7
Hundon CO10 . . . . .75 E4
9 Kessingland NR33 . . . . .11 C1
Lavenham CO10 . . . . .78 D4
Little Bealings IP5 . . . . . .137 E2
Lowestoft NR32 . . . . .112 D1
Marlesford IP13 . . . . .71 C5
Mount Bures CO8 . . . . . . .101 C3
Parham IP13 . . . . .71 B7
Pulham St Mary IP21 . . . . .22 A8
Stowmarket IP14 . . . . . . .124 B8
Thorndon IP23 . . . . .53 C7
Wenhaston With Mells Hamlet
IP19 . . . . .42 D5
Hall Rise CO10 . . . . .148 A3
Hall St
Long Melford CO10 . . . . . . .91 E8
Soham CB7 . . . . .28 D4
Hall Wlk IP8 . . . . .81 F1
Hallfields IP27 . . . . . . .109 C7
Hallifax Pl IP29 . . . . .77 F7
Halliwell Rd IP4 . . . . . .140 B6
Hall's La IP31 . . . . .50 B5
Hallwong La IP20 . . . . . .22 D7
Hallwyck Gdns CB8 . . . .120 F2
Halton Cres IP3 . . . . . .140 C1
Hamblin Rd IP12 . . . . . .147 A5
Hambling's Piece NR16 . .18 C8
Hambrook Cl IP30 . . . . . .63 F7
Hambros The 3 IP31 . . . .49 D4
Hamilton Gdns IP11 . . .153 A3
Hamilton Rd
Felixstowe IP11 . . . . .153 A4
Felixstowe IP11 . . . . .153 A4
Ipswich IP3 . . . . .140 B3
Lowestoft NR32 . . . . .113 E1
Newmarket CB8 . . . . .120 D5
7 Sudbury CO10 . . . . .148 C5
Hamilton St
6 Felixstowe IP11 . . . . . .152 E5
4 Harwich CO12 . . . . . . .106 F3
Hamilton Way
Ditchingham NR35 . . . . . .110 C8
Stowmarket IP14 . . . . . . .124 D7
Hamiltons The CB8 . . . .120 F2
Hamlet Ct 2 CO8 . . . . . .101 C4
Hamlet Rd CB9 . . . . .132 F5
Hammond Cl CB8 . . . . . .120 E6
Hammond's Cnr IP14 . . . .67 C6
Hampstead Ave IP28 . . .116 B6
Hampton Rd IP1 . . . . . .138 F7
Hanchet End CB9 . . . . . . .74 A1
Hancocks Cl 5 IP16 . . . .129 D5
Handford Cut IP1 . . . . .139 A6
Handford Hall Prim Sch
IP1 . . . . .139 A6
Handford Rd IP1 . . . . . .155 A3
Hankin Ave 13 CO12 . . . .106 E1
Hanmer Ave IP28 . . . . . .116 C5
Hanover Cl 5 IP32 . . . . .123 A8
Ha'penny Field 8 IP9 . . .105 E7
Ha'penny Pier Visitor Ctr*
CO12 . . . . .107 B3
Harbour Cres 7 CO12 . .107 C3
Harbour La IP22 . . . . .18 D3
Harbour Rd NR32 . . . . . .112 E1
Harbourage The NR34 . .111 C5
Harcourt Ave 1 CO12 . . .107 A2
Harding's La IP31 . . . . . .50 E4
Hardwick Cl IP4 . . . . . . .140 E5
Hardwick La IP33 . . . . . .122 F2
Hardwick Mid Sch
IP33 . . . . .123 B1
Hardwick Pk Gdns
IP33 . . . . .123 A1
Hardwick Prim Sch
IP33 . . . . .123 B2
Hardwick Rd
Haverhill CB9 . . . . .132 F6
Starston IP20 . . . . .22 C7
Hardy Cl
8 Brantham CO11 . . . . . .104 E4
Lowestoft NR33 . . . . .115 A7
Hardy Cres IP1 . . . . . . .134 F4
Hare & Hounds Cnr
IP6 . . . . .82 F8
Harebell Rd IP2 . . . . . . .138 F4
Harebell Way NR33 . . . .114 C5
Harefield CO10 . . . . .77 E1
Hares La IP19 . . . . .25 B4
Hares Rd IP7 . . . . .65 D1
Hares Wlk 1 CO10 . . . . .148 D6
Hargrave Ave IP6 . . . . . .125 D3
Hargrave Rd IP29 . . . . . . .62 B6
Harkstead La
Freston IP9 . . . . .105 F8
Woolverstone IP9 . . . . . . .144 A1
Harkstead Rd 3 IP9 . . .106 A5
Harleston Dove CE Fst Sch
IP20 . . . . .22 D6
Harleston Hill IP21 . . . . .39 E8
Harleston Mus* IP20 . . . .22 D6
Harleston Rd
Metfield IP20 . . . . .23 B3
Pulham Market IP21 . . . . . .21 E8
Scole IP21 . . . . .21 D5
Weybread IP21 . . . . .22 D4
Harling Dro IP27 . . . . .6 E3
Harling Rd
Garboldisham IP22 . . . . . . .18 C6
North Lopham IP22 . . . . . . .19 A6
Harling Way IP16 . . . . . .129 B6
Harman's La IP20 . . . . . .22 C5
Harold Rd NR33 . . . . . . .115 C6
Harpclose Rd 2 CO10 . .148 D6
Harper's Est 9 CO6 . . . .102 C5
Harper's Hill CO6 . . . . .102 C5
Harpers La IP17 . . . . . .128 D3
Harp's Cl Rd NR32 . . . . .113 B3
Harpur's Rd 2 CO10 . . . . .77 A2
Harrier Cl IP3 . . . . .140 B1
Harriers Wlk IP13 . . . . . .70 E5
Harrington Ave NR32 . . .113 C6
Harrington Cl IP33 . . . .154 C1
Harris Ave NR32 . . . . . .113 C4
Harris Ct 12 IP14 . . . . . . .53 F2
Harris Mid Sch NR32 . . .113 D3
Harrison Gn 3 IP18 . . . .119 C8
Harrison Gr IP5 . . . . . . .141 C8
Harrison Rd NR32 . . . . .112 E1
Harrisons La IP19 . . . . .118 C5
Harrop Dale 10 NR33 . . .114 E3
Harrow Cl IP4 . . . . .140 A5
Harrow Gn 2 IP29 . . . . . .63 D1
Harrow La Benhall IP17 . .72 A7
Theberton IP16 . . . . .129 A8
Harrow Rd
Haverhill CB9 . . . . .132 C5
Troston IP31 . . . . .33 D4
Harrow St CO6 . . . . .102 B8
Harry Palmer Cl 1 CB7 . .29 A1
Hart Cl CB9 . . . . .132 D8
Hartest Hill IP29 . . . . . . .77 C6
Hartest La IP29 . . . . .63 C1

Hartest Prim Sch IP29 ..**77** B7
Hartest Rd IP29 ..**63** A1
Hartest Way
  Stowmarket IP14 ....**124** F3
  Sudbury CO10 ....**92** B3
  Sudbury CO10 ....**148** F4
Hartfield Rd CB8 ....**59** F2
Hartington Rd IP15 ...**130** E3
Hartismere High Sch
  IP23 ....**117** B3
Hartismere Hospl
  IP23 ....**117** C3
Hartley St IP2 ....**155** B1
Hart's La CO7 ....**103** E1
Harvard Rd IP26 ....**4** D5
Harvest Cl IP14 ....**51** D1
Harvest Dr NR33 ....**114** F2
Harvesters Way
  Martlesham IP5 ....**141** F6
  Martlesham Heath IP5 ..**98** A7
Harvey Cl CO11 ....**104** E2
Harvey La IP21 ....**21** C5
Harvey's La IP6 ....**82** C6
Harwich Int Port CO12 .**106** F3
Harwich Rd
  Foxash Estate CO11 ....**104** A1
  Lawford CO11 ....**104** B1
  Mistley CO11 ....**105** A2
  Ramsey & Parkeston
  CO11 ....**106** A1
  Wrabness CO11 ....**105** F1
Harwich Town Sta
  CO12 ....**107** B3
Harwood Ave IP24 ..**16** C7
Hascot Hill Barking IP6 .**125** A1
  Battisford IP14 ....**81** A8
Haselmere Cl IP32 .**123** D6
  Woodbridge IP13 ....**146** E6
Hasketon Rd Burgh IP13 .**83** F6
Haskins Wlk IP5 ....**141** E7
Hasse Rd CB5 ....**28** E8
Hasted Cl IP33 ....**122** C4
Hatchley Cl IP12 ....**85** C3
Hatfield Rd IP3 ....**140** A3
Hatley Dr CB5 ....**44** A6
Hatter St IP33 ....**154** B2
Haugh La
  Great Ashfield IP31 ....**50** F5
  Haughley IP14 ....**51** D1
  Woodbridge IP12 ....**146** F7
Haughate Cl IP12 ....**146** F6
Haughley Crawfords CE Prim
  Sch IP14 ....**51** C1
Haughley Dr IP4 ....**140** F6
Haughley Junc IP14 ....**51** D1
Haughley Rd IP14 ....**66** B7
Hauliers Rd IP11 ....**152** D2
Haven Ave NR32 ....**113** B3
Haven Cl IP11 ....**152** D4
Haven Rd IP16 ....**129** D5
Haven The IP16 ....**73** F6
Havens The IP10 ....**144** E7
Haverhill Rd
  Haverhill CB9 ....**132** F8
  Helions Bumpstead CB9 ..**88** B5
  Kedington CB9 ....**133** E8
  Steeple Bumpstead CB9 ..**88** D5
Haverhill Rovers FC
  CB9 ....**132** F4
Haward St NR32 ....**113** C1
Hawbridge IP9 ....**150** E4
Hawe's La Norton IP30 ..**50** B4
  Wicken CB7 ....**28** A2
Hawes St IP2 ....**155** C1
Hawk End La IP30 ....**50** E2
Hawke Rd IP3 ....**139** E1
Hawker Dr IP5 ....**98** A8
Hawkes La IP11 ....**152** D6
Hawkins Rd CO10 ....**148** E8
Hawk's La IP29 ....**63** E6
Hawks Mill St IP29 ....**125** D5
Hawstead La IP29 ....**63** E6
Hawthorn Ave NR33 ..**115** A7
Hawthorn Cl
  Beccles NR34 ....**111** E4
  Bury St Edmunds IP32 .**122** D8
  Knodishall IP17 ....**129** B2
  Stowupland IP14 ....**67** A6
Hawthorn Dr
  Horringer IP29 ....**63** A8
  Ipswich IP2 ....**138** D2
Hawthorn La IP27 ..**13** F2
Hawthorn Pl IP12 ....**146** E6
Hawthorn Rd
  Haverhill CB9 ....**132** B7
  Middleton IP17 ....**58** A5
  Sudbury CO10 ....**148** F5
  Theberton IP16 ....**57** F4
Hawthorn Way IP2 ..**138** D2
Hawthorn Wlk IP28 ..**30** B8
Hawthorns The IP31 ..**49** D4
Hay Barn Mdw IP30 ..**50** D1
Haycocks Rd CB9 ....**132** A7
Haygate IP23 ....**117** C3
Hayhill Rd IP4 ....**139** E7
Hayland Dro IP26 ....**29** D7
Haylings Gr IP16 ....**129** C4
Haylings Rd IP16 ....**129** C4
Hayman Rd IP3 ....**139** F1
Haynings Mill IP13 ..**126** D4
Haysborder Rd NR29 ..**46** F3
Haythill La IP26 ....**4** D6
Haywards Fields IP5 ..**141** D8
Hazel Cl
  Bentwaters Airfield IP12 **85** E8
  Haverhill CB9 ....**132** C6
  Mildenhall IP28 ....**116** E4

Hazel Dr
  Horringer IP29 ....**63** A8
  Ipswich IP3 ....**140** E1
Hazel Rise IP6 ....**134** C8
Hazelcroft Rd IP1 ....**135** B2
Hazels La IP17 ....**42** C5
Hazelville Cl CO12 ..**106** F1
Hazelwood IP7 ....**80** F1
Hazelwood IP31 ....**49** D4
Hazlitt Rd IP1 ....**135** A3
Head La CO10 ....**148** F2
Headingham Cl IP2 .**139** A2
Headland Ave CB9 ....**132** C5
Headland Dro IP26 ....**4** A1
Heasman Cl CB8 ....**120** F5
Heath Cl
  East Bergholt CO7 ....**151** D5
  Hessett IP30 ....**64** F8
  Polstead CO6 ....**93** F3
Heath Ct IP11 ....**107** D8
Heath Dr IP12 ....**99** C7
Heath Farm Rd IP28 ..**30** A1
Heath La
  Ipswich IP4 ....**140** C5
  Pakenham IP31 ....**49** D8
Heath Prim Sch IP5 ..**141** B8
Heath Rd Burwell CB5 ..**44** C2
  East Bergholt CO7 ....**151** D5
  Exning CB8 ....**120** A4
  Fritton & St Olaves NR31 ..**2** B5
  Geldeston NR34 ....**9** A7
  Hessett IP30 ....**64** F8
  Ipswich IP4 ....**140** C5
  Ixworth IP31 ....**33** E2
  Kenninghall NR16 ....**19** A7
  Lowestoft NR33 ....**114** F8
  Mildenhall IP28 ....**116** C6
  Mistley CO11 ....**105** A2
  Newmarket CB8 ....**121** C3
  Norton IP31 ....**50** B4
  Polstead CO6 ....**93** F2
  Sapiston IP31 ....**34** B7
  Swaffham Prior CB5 ....**44** A1
  Thurston IP31 ....**49** D4
  Troston IP31 ....**33** F4
  Wenhaston With Mells Hamlet
  IP19 ....**42** B7
  Woolpit IP30 ....**50** D1
Heath The
  Dedham CO7 ....**104** A2
  Great Waldingfield CO10 .**92** C6
  Woolpit IP30 ....**65** F8
Heath View
  Ipswich IP5 ....**141** A6
  Leiston IP16 ....**129** E5
Heath Way CO10 ....**92** C6
Heath Wlk IP12 ....**72** A4
Heathbell Rd IP28 ....**121** C3
Heather Ave IP3 ....**140** C2
Heather Cl
  Great Barton IP31 ....**49** D4
  Martlesham Heath IP5 .**141** F6
Heather Rd NR32 ....**113** D4
Heather Way NR34 ..**111** F3
Heathercroft Rd IP1 ..**135** A3
Heatherhayes IP2 ....**139** A3
Heatherset Way IP30 ..**30** C1
Heathfield
  Martlesham Heath IP5 ..**98** A7
  Martlesham Heath IP5 .**141** F6
Heathfield Mews IP5 .**141** F6
Heathfield Rd IP9 ..**105** E7
Heathfields IP11 ....**98** D1
Heathgate Piece IP11 .**152** C8
Heathlands Pk IP4 ....**140** E4
Hedley La IP30 ....**114** A3
Heigham Dr NR33 ....**114** F5
Heights The NR34 ....**111** C4
Heldhaw Rd IP32 ....**123** B5
Helena Rd IP3 ....**139** E4
Helens Cl IP2 ....**36** A8
Helions Bumpstead Rd
  CB9 ....**132** D3
Helions Pk Ave CB9 ..**132** E5
Helions Rd CB9 ....**88** D4
Helions Service Rd
  CB9 ....**132** E5
Helions Wlk CB9 ....**132** E5
Helmingham Hall & Gdns★
  IP14 ....**69** A4
Helmingham Prim Sch
  IP14 ....**69** B5
Helmingham Rd IP6 ..**69** C2
Helston Cl IP5 ....**141** B7
Hemmant Way NR34 ....**9** B7
Hemplands The
  NR32 ....**113** D2
Hempnall Rd NR35 ....**7** A8
Hempstead Rd CB9 ..**132** A7
Hencote La
  Horringer IP29 ....**63** C8
  Nowton IP33 ....**123** C8
Henderson Cl
  Bramford IP8 ....**134** A1
  Haverhill CB9 ....**132** A7
Hengrave Cl IP2 ..**139** A2
Hengrave Hall★ IP28 ..**48** A7
Hengrave Rd IP28 ....**48** B6
Henham Rd NR34 ....**113** A5
Henley Ave IP1 ....**135** B3
Henley Cl IP2 ....**128** C3
Henley Prim Sch IP6 ..**82** E6
Henley Rd Henley IP6 ..**82** E6
  Ipswich IP1 ....**135** B3
  Ipswich IP1 ....**155** B4
Henniker Rd
  Debenham IP14 ....**53** F2
  Ipswich IP1 ....**138** C8

Henny Rd CO8 ....**101** A7
Henry Rd IP3 ....**140** B1
Henry St IP14 ....**53** E2
Henry Ward Rd IP20 .**22** D6
Henslow Rd IP4 ....**140** B5
Henstead Gdns IP3 ..**140** A1
Hepworth Ave IP33 ..**122** D5
Hepworth Rd
  Barningham IP31 ....**34** F7
  Hepworth IP22 ....**35** A7
  Stanton IP31 ....**34** E4
  Thelnetham IP22 ....**35** B7
Herbert Human Cl
  CB7 ....**28** D4
Herbert Rd IP5 ....**141** E8
Hereward Ave IP28 ..**116** C5
Hereward Way
  Feltwell IP26 ....**4** D5
  Littleport CB7 ....**12** B7
  Weeting-with-broomhill
  IP27 ....**5** E3
Heritage Gn NR33 ....**11** B1
Herivan Cl NR32 ....**112** E4
Herivan Gdns NR32 .**112** E4
Hermitage Ct IP13 ..**126** B3
Hermitage Mdws CO10 .**76** B1
Herolf Way IP20 ..**22** D6
Heron Cl
  Mildenhall IP28 ....**13** B1
  Stowmarket IP14 ....**124** A6
Heron Hill IP14 ....**66** C6
Heron Rd
  Bury St Edmunds IP33 .**123** B2
  Ipswich IP2 ....**138** E3
  Saxmundham IP17 ....**128** B3
Herons Cl NR32 ....**112** D2
Herring Fishery Score
  NR32 ....**113** E1
Herringfleet Rd NR31 ..**2** B5
Herringswell Rd
  Herringswell IP28 ....**30** D2
  Kentford CB8 ....**46** A6
Hertford Cl IP32 ....**48** C5
Hertford Pl IP15 ....**130** E3
Hertford Rd CO10 ..**76** A1
Hervey Cl IP9 ....**107** A5
Hervey Rd IP33 ....**122** E3
Hervey St Ipswich IP4 .**155** C4
  Lowestoft NR32 ....**115** C8
Hessett St IP14 ....**124** F3
Hethersett Cl CB8 ....**120** E8
Heveningham Long La
  IP17 ....**41** A1
Heveningham Rd IP19 .**40** C5
Hewitt Rd CO12 ....**106** E1
Hexham Cl IP2 ....**139** A2
Heycroft Way CO6 .**102** C5
Heyford Ct IP28 ....**116** B5
Heyford Rd IP31 ....**33** D5
Heywood Ave IP22 ....**20** C3
Heywood Cl IP2 ....**138** D1
Heywood Rd IP22 ....**20** C4
Hibbard Rd IP8 ....**134** C2
Hickford Hill CO10 ....**90** B7
Hickling Dr IP33 ....**123** B1
Hicks Way CB9 ....**133** C3
High Baxter St IP33 ..**154** B2
High Beach NR32 ....**113** B2
High Beech IP11 ....**153** C4
High Comm Rd IP22 ....**18** F5
High Ct IP20 ....**22** E6
High Hall Cl IP11 ..**107** D8
High House Farm Rd
  IP12 ....**131** D8
High House La IP7 ....**79** B5
High La IP14 ....**53** B6
High Leas NR34 ....**111** C3
High Leas NR34 ....**111** C3
High Lighthouse Wireless
  Mus★ CO12 ....**107** C3
High Lodge Visitor Centre
  Thetford Forest Pk★
  IP27 ....**15** C7
High London La IP22 ..**20** A8
High Rd Badingham IP13 .**56** C6
  Bressingham IP22 ....**19** F4
  Felixstowe IP11 ....**152** B8
  Great Finborough IP14 ..**66** A2
  Kettleburgh IP13 ....**55** B2
  Leavenheath CO6 ....**102** A7
  Needham IP20 ....**22** B3
  Roydon IP22 ....**20** A3
  Swilland IP6 ....**83** A7
  Trimley St Martin IP11 ..**98** C1
  Wortwell IP20 ....**23** A7
High Rd E IP11 ....**153** B5
High Rd W IP11 ....**152** F5
High Row Field IP11 ..**153** C5
High St Acton CO10 ....**92** B7
  Aldeburgh IP15 ....**130** E3
  Ashley IP5 ....**60** F8
  Brandon IP27 ....**5** F2
  Brinkley CB8 ....**59** F1
  Bures CO8 ....**101** C5
  Burwell CB5 ....**44** A5
  Cavendish CO10 ....**76** E1
  Cheveley CB8 ....**60** E8
  Chippenham CB7 ....**45** C8
  Clare CO10 ....**90** A8
  Debenham IP14 ....**53** F2
  Dedham CO7 ....**103** F3
  Dunwich IP17 ....**43** B1
  Felixstowe IP11 ....**152** E6
  Feltwell IP26 ....**4** C5
  Flowton IP8 ....**81** C1
  Gislingham IP23 ....**36** D2
  Great Yeldham CO9 ....**90** A1
  Hadleigh IP7 ....**149** D6

  Harwich CO12 ....**107** B2
  Haverhill CB9 ....**132** E5
  Hemingstone IP6 ....**68** C1
  Hitcham IP7 ....**79** F4
  Hopton IP22 ....**18** C2
  Ipswich IP1 ....**155** B3
  Ipswich IP1 ....**31** B1
  Ixworth IP31 ....**34** B1
  Kessingland NR34 ....**11** B1
  Lakenheath IP27 ....**109** C6
  Langham CO4 ....**103** B2
  Lavenham CO10 ....**78** D4
  Laxfield IP13 ....**40** B3
  Leiston IP16 ....**129** C6
  Long Melford CO10 ....**77** E1
  Lowestoft NR32 ....**113** E2
  Lowestoft NR32 ....**113** E3
  Manningtree CO11 ....**104** E2
  Mildenhall IP28 ....**116** C4
  Nayland CO6 ....**102** D5
  Needham Market IP6 ..**125** D5
  Newmarket CB8 ....**120** F2
  Orford IP12 ....**131** C2
  Pettistree IP13 ....**127** C5
  Rattlesden IP30 ....**65** D6
  St Margaret, Ilketshall
  NR35 ....**24** D7
  Saxmundham IP17 ....**128** D3
  Soham CB7 ....**28** D4
  Southwold IP18 ....**119** D5
  Sproughton IP8 ....**138** A6
  Stansfield CO10 ....**76** C6
  Stetchworth CB8 ....**60** A5
  Thelnetham IP22 ....**18** E1
  Thorndon IP23 ....**53** C8
  Tuddenham IP28 ....**30** F7
  Tuddenham St Martin
  IP6 ....**136** B5
  Wangford with Henham
  NR34 ....**26** B2
  Wicken CB7 ....**28** A1
  Wickham Market IP13 .**127** C7
  Wrentham NR34 ....**26** E5
  Yoxford IP17 ....**57** D8
High St Ex Gall★ IP1 .**155** B3
High View Rd IP1 ....**134** D1
Higham Hill IP7 ....**103** D8
Higham Race Course
  CO7 ....**103** D7
Higham Rd
  Higham CO7 ....**103** D6
  Tuddenham IP28 ....**31** A1
Highbridge Gravel Dro
  IP27 ....**109** B7
Highbury Cres IP33 ..**122** E5
Highbury Rd IP33 ....**122** E5
Highbury Way CO10 ..**148** F4
Highclere Cl CB8 ....**120** D8
Higher Dr NR32 ....**112** F2
Highfield
  Blythburgh IP19 ....**42** F6
  Clare CO10 ....**90** B8
  Eye IP23 ....**117** C3
Highfield App IP11 .**134** F1
Highfield Ave CO12 ..**107** A2
Highfield Cl NR33 ....**114** B1
Highfield Dr IP6 ....**134** D8
Highfield Rd
  Felixstowe IP11 ....**153** A4
  Halesworth IP19 ....**118** B2
  Ipswich IP1 ....**134** F2
  Stowupland IP14 ....**67** A6
  Sudbury CO10 ....**148** E7
Highfields Bentley IP9 .**104** F7
  Great Yeldham CO9 ....**90** A1
  Lakenheath IP27 ....**109** C6
Highfields Dr IP27 ..**109** D6
Highgate La IP13 ....**70** B2
Highgrove Cl NR32 ..**113** A3
Highland Dr NR34 ....**111** E4
Highland Way NR33 .**114** F6
Highlands IP27 ....**109** E6
Highlands Cl IP6 ....**125** C5
Highlands Rd
  Hadleigh IP7 ....**149** E5
  Monks Eleigh IP7 ....**79** C4
Highlands The CB8 ..**120** D8
Highview Cl CO10 ....**148** C8
Highwood Cres CB8 ....**46** B2
Highwood La CO10 ....**92** E5
Highwood Rd CB8 ....**46** B2
Hill Cl
  Long Melford CO10 ..**91** E8
  Newmarket CB8 ....**120** E3
Hill Cres CB9 ....**132** E7
Hill Farm La IP9 ..**106** C8
Hill Farm Rd
  Grundisburgh IP13 ....**83** D6
  Halesworth IP19 ....**118** C3
  Playford IP6 ....**137** B4
  Rendham IP17 ....**56** C4
Hill House Gdns NR33 .**115** C4
Hill House La IP6 ....**125** C6
Hill House Rd IP4 ....**139** E5
Hill La CB9 ....**133** D1
Hill of Health (Tumulus)
  IP28 ....**32** D2
Hill Rd Lowestoft NR32 .**113** C1
  Southwold IP18 ....**119** C6
  Wangford with Henham
  NR34 ....**26** B1
  Westley IP33 ....**122** A5
Hill Rise IP14 ....**124** F3
Hill Rise IP26 ....**4** E5
Hill The North Cove NR34 .**10** C4
  Shipmeadow NR34 ....**8** F4
  Westleton IP17 ....**58** C8
Hill Top IP31 ....**34** E5

Hill View CB8 ....**61** C4
Hill View Bsns Pk IP6 .**134** D6
Hillary Cl IP4 ....**140** A5
Hillcrest IP17 ....**129** A3
Hillcrest App IP8 ....**134** B2
Hillcrest Cl NR34 ..**111** E3
Hillcrest Dr NR32 ....**113** B4
Hillcrest Gdns NR32 ..**113** B3
Hillcrest Rd
  Beccles NR34 ....**111** B3
  Sudbury CO10 ....**148** C8
Hillcroft Prep Sch IP14 .**51** D2
Hillrise Cl NR34 ....**111** E3
Hillside Brandon IP27 ..**14** D8
  Stowmarket IP14 ....**124** D3
Hillside Ave NR34 ....**111** E4
Hillside Com Prim Sch
  IP2 ....**139** C3
Hillside Cres IP3 ..**140** B3
Hillside Cl NR35 ....**110** C2
Hillside Mdw CB7 ....**29** B1
Hillside Rd
  Southwold IP18 ....**119** C7
  Sudbury CO10 ....**148** C8
Hillside Rd East NR35 .**110** D3
Hillside Rd West
  NR35 ....**110** D3
Hillside Way IP19 ....**118** B5
Hilltop Gn NR32 ....**113** A4
Hilltop Rise NR34 ..**111** E3
Hilltop Way IP31 ....**34** E5
Hilly Cl IP31 ....**33** F5
Hilly Fields IP12 ....**146** E4
Hilton Rd CO11 ....**104** E2
Hilton Rd Ipswich IP3 .**140** C1
  Martlesham Heath IP5 ..**98** A8
Hinderclay La IP22 ....**18** E1
Hinderclay Rd
  Redgrave IP22 ....**19** A1
  Rickinghall Inferior IP22 .**35** F6
Hines Rd IP3 ....**140** A4
Hintesham Cl IP2 ..**140** E5
Hintlesham & Chattisham
  Sch IP8 ....**95** D6
Hintlesham Cl IP14 .**124** E3
Hintlesham Dr IP11 ..**152** D4
Histon Cl IP2 ....**139** A2
Hitcham Causeway IP7 .**79** E6
Hitcham Rd
  Debenham IP14 ....**53** F2
  Wattisham IP7 ....**80** B6
Hitcham's La NR34 ....**26** E4
Hitchcock Pl CO10 ..**148** C7
HMS Ganges Mus★
  IP9 ....**107** B4
Hobart Cl NR32 ....**112** E3
Hobart Way NR32 ....**112** E3
Hobbies La IP14 ....**52** D4
Hobbs Dr CO4 ....**103** A3
Hobbs La CO10 ....**77** B2
Hobland Rd
  Belton with Browston NR31 .**2** F8
  Bradwell NR31 ....**3** A8
Hocket Cres IP12 ....**71** F2
Hockey Hill IP14 ....**53** A5
Hockney Gdns IP3 ..**144** A8
Hockwold Prim Sch
  IP26 ....**5** A2
Hodgkinson Rd IP11 .**152** C3
Hodson Cl IP32 ....**122** E8
Hoe La CO10 ....**90** F8
Hog La
  St Lawrence, Ilketshall
  NR34 ....**24** F6
  Wenhaston With Mells Hamlet
  IP19 ....**42** C5
  Westhall NR34 ....**25** A6
Hogarth Rd IP3 ....**139** F1
Hogarth Sq IP3 ....**140** A1
Hogarth Wlk NR32 ..**113** B6
Hogg La NR35 ....**7** C5
Hoggars Rd IP14 ....**52** C4
Hogsty La IP21 ....**22** A5
Holbecks La IP7 ....**149** C4
Holbein Way NR32 .**113** B6
Holborn Ave IP28 ....**116** B6
Holbrook Barn Rd
  CO10 ....**93** C3
Holbrook Cl CO10 ..**92** C6
Holbrook Cres IP11 ..**152** D4
Holbrook Cty High Sch
  IP9 ....**105** E8
Holbrook Prim Sch
  IP9 ....**105** E7
Holbrook Rd
  Haverhill CB9 ....**132** C4
  Holbrook IP9 ....**106** A5
  Ipswich IP3 ....**139** F1
  Lowestoft NR32 ....**112** F4
  Stutton IP9 ....**105** D5
Holcombe Cres IP2 ..**138** D2
Holdans La IP17 ....**56** D2
Holdans Mdw IP17 ....**56** E2
Holden Cl Ipswich IP2 .**139** D3
  Lowestoft NR32 ....**112** C1
Holden Rd IP28 ....**31** F1
Holderness Rd IP32 ..**123** C7
Holeywall La IP31 ....**35** A1
Holiday Village NR31 ..**3** C7
Holkham Cl IP4 ....**140** F5
Holkham Mead CB5 ..**44** B5
Holland Pk CB8 ....**60** E8
Holland Rd
  Felixstowe IP11 ....**152** F3

Holland Rd continued
Ipswich IP4 . . . .**139** F6
Holland Rise IP19 . . . . .**41** A4
Holland's La NR35 . . . . . .**7** C7
Hollands Rd CB9 . . . . . .**132** E4
Hollesley Ave CB9 . . . . .**132** A6
Hollesley Prim Sch
IP12 . . . .**99** F7
Hollesley Rd
Hollesley IP12 . . . .**99** D7
Rendlesham IP12 . . . . . .**85** D7
Hollingsworth Rd
Lowestoft NR32 . . . .**113** C3
 Stowmarket IP14 . . . .**124** E5
Hollow Gr Way NR33 . .**114** C4
Hollow Hill CB9 . . . .**74** A2
Hollow Hill Rd NR35 . . .**110** B7
Hollow La
Badingham IP13 . . . .**56** C6
Barningham IP31 . . . .**34** F8
Bures St Mary CO8 . . . .**101** C6
Carlton Colville NR33 . . .**114** C4
 Chelmondiston IP9 . . .**106** C8
Coney Weston IP31 . . . . .**18** A1
Earl Soham IP13 . . . .**54** F3
Mendham IP20 . . . .**23** A4
Thurston IP31 . . . .**49** F3
Tostock IP30 . . . .**50** A2
Hollow Rd Ashen CO10 . .**89** F6
Bury St Edmunds IP32 . .**123** C6
Copdock & Washbrook
IP8 . . . .**95** E4
Hollow Way Hill NR34 . . .**9** D8
Hollowell Cl NR32 . . . .**112** E4
Hollows The IP6 . . . .**67** F2
Holly Blue Cl IP8 . . . . .**142** E8
Holly Bush Corner
CO7 . . . .**103** E7
Holly Cl Beccles NR34 . .**111** E3
 Horringer IP29 . . . .**63** A8
Little Bealings IP13 . . . .**137** D5
 Red Lodge IP28 . . . .**30** B1
Holly Ct IP20 . . . .**22** D6
Holly End IP5 . . . .**141** F6
Holly Gr NR34 . . . .**111** C4
Holly Hill NR32 . . . . . .**112** C3
Holly La Belstead IP8 . .**142** C7
Great Horkesley CO6 . . .**102** E2
Little Bealings IP13 . . . .**137** D5
Mutford NR34 . . . .**10** E3
Rushmere St Andrew
IP5 . . . .**136** E2
Stutton IP9 . . . .**105** C6
Holly Oaks CO6 . . . . . .**101** F2
Holly Rd
 Great Bricett IP7 . . . . .**80** D6
Ipswich IP1 . . . .**155** A4
Lowestoft NR32 . . . .**112** E1
Willisham IP8 . . . .**81** A5
Holly Wlk IP28 . . . .**30** B8
Hollybush Dr IP11 . . . .**153** D7
Hollybush La IP30 . . . . .**64** D6
Hollycroft Cl IP4 . . . . .**135** A3
Hollydene Cl NR32 . . . .**112** D2
Holm Cl NR34 . . . .**9** F4
Holme Cl IP22 . . . .**18** C2
Holmere Dr IP19 . . . . . .**118** A3
Holme's Hill IP17 . . . . . .**41** A1
Holmes La CB7 . . . .**28** D5
Holmsey Gn
Beck Row, Holywell Row
& Kenny Hill IP28 . . . . .**13** C1
Mildenhall IP28 . . . .**30** B8
Holmsey Gn Gdns
IP28 . . . .**30** B8
Holst Cl NR33 . . . .**115** A6
Holst Mead IP14 . . . . . .**124** C8
Holt Rd CO6 . . . .**93** E2
Holton Ave NR32 . . . . .**112** F4
Holton Rd IP19 . . . .**118** C3
Holton St Peter Prim Sch
IP19 . . . .**118** E4
Holt's La IP6 . . . .**125** F6
Holt's Rd CO6 . . . .**102** A2
Holy Wells Rd IP3 . . . . .**139** E3
Holyhouse Drift IP31 . . .**49** A6
Holyrood CO12 . . . .**106** F1
Holyrood Cl IP2 . . . . . .**138** F1
Holywell Cl IP33 . . . . .**123** A3
Holywell Dro IP28 . . . . .**13** C2
Holywells Cl IP3 . . . . . .**139** E4
Holywells High Sch
IP3 . . . .**140** C2
Home Cl CB9 . . . .**88** E4
Home Farm La IP33 . . . .**123** B1
Home Farm Rd NR35 . . . .**8** C7
Home Mdw IP13 . . . .**40** B3
Home Piece IP22 . . . . . .**35** A8
Homefield Boxford CO10 .**93** C3
Capel St Mary IP9 . . . . .**150** F3
Homefield Ave
 Beccles NR34 . . . .**111** B5
Lowestoft NR33 . . . .**114** F6
Homefield Paddock
NR34 . . . .**111** B5
Homefield Rd CB9 . . . . .**132** C4
Homefield Rd Ind Est
CB9 . . . .**132** D4
Homer Cl IP1 . . . .**134** F4
Homestall Cres CB9 . . . .**93** E1
Homestead Dr IP28 . . . . .**30** B8
Homey Bridge Rd CO6 . .**93** E1
Honey Hill IP33 . . . . . .**154** C1
Honey La CO6 . . . .**102** B6
Honeymeade Cl IP31 . . . .**34** E4

Honeypot La
Kelsale cum Carlton IP17 . .**57** E4
Mendham IP20 . . . .**23** C4
Monewden IP13 . . . .**69** F4
Wattisfield IP22 . . . .**35** D4
Honeypot Mdw NR35 **110** B3
Honeysuckle Cl
Haverhill CB9 . . . .**132** C7
 Lowestoft NR33 . . . . .**115** A3
 Red Lodge IP28 . . . . . .**46** A8
 Soham CB7 . . . .**28** C4
Honeysuckle Gdns
IP2 . . . .**138** E4
Honeysuckle Way
IP32 . . . .**123** E6
Honington Rise IP31 . . . .**33** E5
Honington VC Prim Sch
IP31 . . . .**33** F5
Hoo La IP12 . . . .**71** E4
Hood Dr IP6 . . . .**81** F5
Hood Rd IP3 . . . .**139** E1
Hood's La NR34 . . . .**25** F4
Hook La IP7 . . . .**149** F4
Hooper Sq IP33 . . . . . .**122** C6
Hop Mdw CO7 . . . .**151** B4
Hope Cres IP12 . . . .**147** A6
Hopelyn Cl NR32 . . . . .**113** B4
Hopton CE Prim Sch
IP22 . . . .**18** C1
Hopton Fst Sch NR31 . . . .**3** C6
Hopton Gdns NR31 . . . . .**3** B7
Hopton Rd
Barningham IP31 . . . .**34** F8
Thelnetham IP22 . . . .**18** D1
Hopton Rise CB9 . . . . .**132** A6
Horham Rd IP21 . . . .**38** E1
Horkesley Hill CO6 . . . .**102** D4
Horkesley Rd CO6 . . . .**102** D4
Horn Hill NR33 . . . .**115** C7
Horn La CB8 . . . .**60** D3
Hornbeam NR34 . . . . . .**111** E4
Hornbeam Dr IP29 . . . . .**63** A8
Hornbeam Rd
Mildenhall IP28 . . . .**116** E5
 Stowupland IP14 . . . . .**67** A6
Horringer Ct Mid Sch
IP33 . . . .**122** D3
Horringer Rd IP29 . . . .**122** D2
Horsecroft Rd
Bury St Edmunds IP33 . .**122** F2
Horringer IP29 . . . .**63** C8
Horsefair IP30 . . . .**50** D1
Horsefair Cl IP14 . . . . . .**52** E4
Horseheath Rd CB9 . . . .**74** A2
Horseshoe Dr IP28 . . . . .**30** C1
Horseshoe La CB9 . . . .**132** C5
Horsham Ave IP3 . . . . .**140** D3
Horsham Rd CB9 . . . . . .**132** A4
Hospital Rd
Bury St Edmunds IP33 . .**154** A1
Orford IP12 . . . .**131** B6
Sudbourne IP12 . . . . . .**131** B6
Hossack Rd IP3 . . . . . .**144** A8
Hotson Rd IP18 . . . . . .**119** D6
Houghton Dr NR32 . . . .**112** E4
Houghton Pl IP14 . . . . .**140** F5
Houghtons La CB7 . . . . .**29** D5
Houldsworth Valley Prim Sch
CB8 . . . .**120** F4
How Hill (Tumulus) ★
IP27 . . . .**31** B7
Howard Cl
 Framlingham IP13 . . . .**126** C3
Harleston IP20 . . . .**22** E6
Howard Com Prim Sch
IP32 . . . .**122** F8
Howard De Walden Way
CB8 . . . .**121** A4
Howard Mid Sch IP28 . .**122** D8
Howard Rd NR35 . . . . .**110** D3
Howard St IP4 . . . .**140** B7
Howards Way IP5 . . . . .**141** D8
Howe Ave IP3 . . . .**140** C3
Howe La Cockfield IP30 . .**64** C1
Thornham Parva IP23 . . . .**37** A3
Howe Rd CB9 . . . .**132** D7
Howes Ave IP31 . . . .**49** D4
Howlett Cl IP5 . . . .**141** E7
Howlett Way IP24 . . . . .**16** B7
Howley Gdns NR32 . . . .**113** A6
Hoxne Cl IP14 . . . .**124** E3
Hoxne Rd Eye IP23 . . . .**117** E2
Hoxne IP21 . . . .**38** D3
Syleham IP21 . . . .**21** F1
Hoxter Way CO10 . . . . .**148** C8
Hoylake Cl IP28 . . . . . .**48** C6
Hubbard's Ave IP7 . . . .**113** C6
Hubbard's Hill IP17 . . . .**41** B1
Hubbard's La IP30 . . . . .**64** F8
Hubbard's Loke NR32 . .**113** C6
Hudson Cl
 Harwich CO12 . . . . . .**107** A1
Haverhill CB9 . . . .**133** A4
Hudson Way IP29 . . . . . .**47** A2
Hudsons La CO6 . . . . . .**103** A7
Huggins La IP23 . . . .**37** B1
Hughes Cnr CO7 . . . . . .**151** A6
Hughes Rd CO7 . . . .**151** A6
Hull St IP27 . . . .**109** F1
Hulver La IP17 . . . .**72** C6
Hulver Rd NR34 . . . .**9** F1
Humber Doucy La IP4 . .**136** A2
Humber Doucy Sports Ctr
IP4 . . . .**140** D7
Humphry Rd CO10 . . . .**148** C6
Hundon Rd CB8 . . . .**75** B6
Hundon Prim Sch
CO10 . . . .**75** D3

Hundon Rd
Hundon CO10 . . . .**75** B1
Kedington CB9 . . . .**133** F8
Hundred La
Old Newton with Dagworth
IP14 . . . .**51** F3
Hungate NR34 . . . .**111** B5
Hungate La NR34 . . . . .**111** B5
Hungerdown La CO11 . .**104** B1
Hunston Rd IP31 . . . . . .**50** E7
Hunt Cl
 Redenhall with Harleston
IP20 . . . .**22** D6
Stowmarket IP14 . . . . .**124** D3
Hunter Dr
 Manningtree CO11 . . .**104** D2
 Thurstow IP31 . . . .**49** D4
Hunter Rd
Bury St Edmunds IP32 . .**122** D8
Honington IP31 . . . .**33** D5
Ipswich IP3 . . . .**144** C8
Hunter's Chase CO7 . . .**103** F1
Hunters End IP11 . . . . .**152** C7
Hunter's La IP20 . . . .**23** A3
Hunters La IP20 . . . .**23** B2
Hunters Ride IP5 . . . . . .**98** A8
Huntingdon Cl NR33 . . .**115** A3
Huntingfield Rd
Bury St Edmunds IP33 . .**122** C4
Cratfield IP19 . . . .**40** D5
Leiston IP16 . . . .**129** C5
Huntley Cres IP19 . . . . .**118** C5
Hunts Hill CO10 . . . .**77** A2
Hurdle Dro IP28 . . . .**29** F8
Hurdle Makers Hill IP8 . .**95** F6
Hurn Crag Rd IP18 . . . .**119** C7
Hurricane Pl IP31 . . . . .**140** B1
Hurstlea Rd IP6 . . . . . .**125** C5
Hurth Way IP24 . . . .**16** C6
Hurts Croft CB7 . . . .**29** A1
Hut Hill (Tumulus) ★
IP31 . . . .**17** E3
Hutland Rd IP4 . . . . . .**139** F7
Hyams La IP9 . . . .**105** C7
Hyam's La IP9 . . . .**105** C5
Hyde Rd CO10 . . . .**148** C5
Hydewood Rd CO9 . . . . .**90** A2
Hyem's La IP11 . . . . . .**153** B7
Hyntle Cl IP2 . . . .**138** E5
Hyperion Way CB8 . . . .**120** D8
Hythe Cl CB5 . . . .**44** A6
Hythe La CB5 . . . .**44** A6
Hythe Rd IP26 . . . .**4** E7

Iceni Way CB8 . . . .**120** B8
Icepits Cl IP31 . . . .**49** C6
Icewell Hill CB8 . . . . . .**121** A4
Icklingham Rd IP28 . . . . .**32** B2
Icknield Cl CB8 . . . .**60** E7
Icknield Way IP24 . . . . .**16** B5
Ickworth Cres IP4 . . . . .**140** F5
Ickworth Ct IP11 . . . . . .**152** C3
Ickworth Dr IP33 . . . . .**154** A1
Ickworth House Pk & Gdn ★
IP29 . . . .**62** F8
Ickworth Pk CP Sch
IP29 . . . .**63** A8
Ilex Cl IP33 . . . .**123** A3
Iliffe Way IP7 . . . .**124** D6
Imperial Mews NR31 . . . .**3** B6
Impson Way IP26 . . . .**6** A8
Ingate NR34 . . . .**111** C4
Ingestre St CO12 . . . . .**107** B2
Ingham Rd
Haverhill CB9 . . . .**132** E6
West Stow IP28 . . . .**32** C1
Ingram's La IP21 . . . . . .**21** F3
Ingram's Well Rd
CO10 . . . .**148** D5
Inkerman Cl IP7 . . . . . .**149** D6
Inkerman Terr IP7 . . . .**149** D6
Innes End IP7 . . . .**138** C2
Inverness Rd IP4 . . . . .**136** A2
Inworth La CO6 . . . .**101** B1
Ion Rd IP32 . . . .**122** E8
Ipswich Ave IP32 . . . . . .**85** B3
Ipswich Cl IP12 . . . .**85** B3
Ipswich Ct IP33 . . . . . .**154** B3
Ipswich High Sch IP9 . .**144** C2
Ipswich Hospl The
IP4 . . . .**140** C7
Ipswich Mus ★ IP1 . . . .**155** B3
Ipswich Rd
Brantham CO11 . . . .**104** E5
Charsfield IP13 . . . .**70** B2
Dedham CO4 . . . .**103** D3
East Bergholt CO7 . . . .**151** A6
Elmsett IP7 . . . .**95** A8
Grundisburgh IP13 . . . . .**83** E5
Hadleigh IP7 . . . .**149** F7
Hadleigh IP7 . . . .**149** F8
Harkstead IP9 . . . .**106** A6
Holbrook IP9 . . . .**105** E8
Lowestoft NR32 . . . . . .**113** D3
Nacton IP10 . . . .**145** A5
Nedging-with-naughton
IP7 . . . .**80** C4
Needham Market IP6 . . .**125** E4
Newbourne IP12 . . . .**98** C6
Orford IP12 . . . .**131** B4
Otley IP6 . . . .**69** B2
 Scole IP21 . . . .**20** F1
Scole NR15 . . . .**21** C7
Stowmarket IP14 . . . . .**124** E4

Ipswich Rd continued
Stratford St Mary CO7 . .**103** E4
Waldringfield IP12 . . . . . .**98** D7
Willisham IP8 . . . .**81** B4
Winston IP14 . . . .**53** F1
Woodbridge IP12 . . . . .**146** E3
Yaxley IP23 . . . .**37** B3
Ipswich Rugby Union FC
IP5 . . . .**136** C2
Ipswich Sch IP1 . . . . . .**155** B4
Ipswich St
Bury St Edmunds IP33 . .**154** B3
Lakenheath IP27 . . . . . .**109** F1
Stowmarket IP14 . . . . .**124** D6
Ipswich Sta IP2 . . . . . .**155** A1
Ipswich Transport Mus ★
IP3 . . . .**140** C2
Ipswich Way IP14 . . . . . .**68** E6
Ireland Rd IP3 . . . .**139** F1
Irex Rd NR33 . . . .**115** B3
Iris Cl IP2 . . . .**138** F5
Irlam Rd IP2 . . . .**138** D2
Isaacson Rd CB5 . . . . . .**44** B4
ISCA Maritime Collection ★
NR32 . . . .**112** D1
Isinglass Cl CB8 . . . . . .**121** E2
Isleham Rd CB7 . . . .**29** B2
Ivry St IP1 . . . .**155** A4
Ivy Cl IP13 . . . .**54** E7
Ivy La NR33 . . . .**114** C7
Ivy Lodge Rd IP12 . . . . .**71** D1
Ivytree La IP7 . . . .**94** C7
Ixer La IP30 . . . .**64** B5
Ixworth Abbey IP31 . . . .**34** A1
Ixworth CE Prim Sch
IP31 . . . .**34** B1
Ixworth Mid Sch IP31 . . .**34** B1
Ixworth Rd
Haverhill CB9 . . . .**132** C4
Honington IP31 . . . .**33** F5
Stowlangtoft IP31 . . . . . .**50** B6
Walsham-le-willows IP31 . .**35** A1

Jack Jarvis Cl CB8 . . . .**121** A3
Jack's Gn Rd IP6 . . . . .**125** E6
Jack's La IP14 . . . .**124** C4
Jackson Rd IP12 . . . .**98** C5
Jackson Way IP29 . . . . .**125** D4
Jacob Way IP12 . . . . . .**147** A5
Jacobs Cl IP31 . . . .**34** E4
Jacobs Mdw IP30 . . . . . .**65** D5
Jacobs St NR32 . . . . . .**113** D2
Jacqueline Cl
Bury St Edmunds IP33 . .**154** A1
 Grundisburgh IP13 . . . .**83** E5
James Boden Cl
IP11 . . . .**152** E5
James Carter Rd IP28 . .**116** A4
Janus Cl CB9 . . . .**133** B4
Jaques Cl CO10 . . . .**77** B3
Jarman Cl IP33 . . . .**123** C3
Jarman's La IP28 . . . . . .**29** F7
Jarrold Cl IP31 . . . .**34** F7
Jarvis Way CB8 . . . . . .**120** E5
Jasmine Cl
 Felixstowe IP11 . . . . .**107** D8
Ipswich IP2 . . . .**138** F3
Java Lodge Rd IP13 . . . .**127** B3
Jay Cl CB9 . . . .**133** A5
Jay La NR32 . . . .**3** A6
Jays Croft Rd IP12 . . . . .**85** E8
Jay's Gn IP20 . . . .**22** D6
Jay's Hill Rd
Ellough NR34 . . . .**10** B2
Sotterley NR34 . . . .**10** B1
Willingham St Mary NR34 . .**26** A3
Jaywick Rd CB9 . . . . . .**132** E6
Jeavons La IP5 . . . .**141** E7
Jefferies Rd IP4 . . . . . .**139** E6
Jellicoe Ave NR33 . . . . .**114** D6
Jenkins Gn NR32 . . . . . .**113** A5
Jenkinsons Pightle
NR35 . . . .**7** B8
Jenner Cl NR35 . . . .**110** C2
Jenners Cl IP21 . . . . . .**147** B6
Jennings Way IP22 . . . . .**20** C3
Jermyn Ave IP32 . . . . .**123** F5
Jermyn Way IP19 . . . . .**118** A2
Jermyns Cl IP9 . . . .**150** F4
Jermyns Rd IP18 . . . . . .**119** B8
Jervis Cl IP9 . . . .**105** E7
Jewell View IP5 . . . . . .**141** E8
Jim Mollison Ct IP28 .**116** B5
Jimmy's La CO11 . . . . .**104** F5
Jocelyn Cl IP32 . . . .**48** C5
Jockey's La Combs IP14 . .**66** C2
Framsden IP14 . . . .**69** B7
Joes Rd CO10 . . . .**92** C3
John Childs Way
NR35 . . . .**110** C2
John Lawrence Cl
NR34 . . . .**111** B4
John Russell Gall ★
IP3 . . . .**155** C2
John Shepherd Rd
IP21 . . . .**39** D8
John St Leiston IP16 . . .**129** C5
Lowestoft NR33 . . . . . .**115** C7
John Swain Cl IP6 . . . .**125** C5
John Tibauld Ct CB9 . . . .**88** D3
Johnson Cl IP2 . . . .**139** C3
Johnson Rd IP7 . . . .**47** A2
Johnson Way NR32 . . . .**113** A5
Jolly's Way IP31 . . . .**35** C1
Jones Rd CO10 . . . .**76** C3

Jordan Cl IP6 . . . .**125** E7
Jordayn Cl IP7 . . . .**149** E6
Jordayn Rise IP7 . . . . .**149** E6
Joshua Cl NR31 . . . .**3** B8
Josselyns The IP11 . . . .**152** B8
Joyce Rd NR35 . . . .**110** D3
Jubilee Ave IP14 . . . . . .**124** C4
Jubilee Cl Claydon IP6 . .**82** B5
 Felixstowe IP11 . . . . .**107** D8
 Harwich CO12 . . . . . .**106** F1
 Isleham CB7 . . . .**29** C5
 Laxfield IP13 . . . .**40** B3
Weeting IP27 . . . .**5** E3
Jubilee Cres IP14 . . . . . .**67** A7
Jubilee Ct CB8 . . . .**60** A5
Jubilee End CO11 . . . . .**104** E3
Jubilee Rd
Bungay NR35 . . . .**110** B3
Lowestoft NR33 . . . . . .**115** A2
Sudbury CO10 . . . .**148** D6
Jubilee Terr IP30 . . . . . .**50** F7
Jubilee Way NR32 . . . . .**113** C2
Judas La IP23 . . . .**37** B5
Judith Ave IP17 . . . . . .**129** B2
Julian Cl CB9 . . . .**133** B5
Julian Way NR31 . . . .**3** B7
Julius Martin La CB7 . . .**28** C4
Junction Rd IP28 . . . . .**116** B5
June Ave Ipswich IP1 . . .**135** B2
Lowestoft NR32 . . . . . .**113** B3
Juniper Cl IP28 . . . .**116** E5
Jupes Hill CO7 . . . .**104** B3
Jupiter Cl CB9 . . . .**133** B4
Jupiter Rd IP4 . . . .**140** B7
Justinian Cl CB9 . . . . . .**133** B4

Karen Cl Ipswich IP1 . . .**135** B1
 Scole IP21 . . . .**20** F1
Kate's La IP14 . . . .**51** A1
Katwijk Way NR32 . . . .**115** D8
Keating Cl CO11 . . . . . .**104** D2
Keats Cres IP1 . . . .**134** F3
Kebbles CO10 . . . .**77** A3
Kedington Hill CO10 . . . .**92** A1
Kedington Prim Sch
CB9 . . . .**133** E8
Keel Cl NR33 . . . .**114** B4
Keens La IP18 . . . .**119** B7
Keeper's La
Marlesford IP13 . . . .**71** D5
Stoke-by-nayland CO6 . .**102** C8
Trimley St Mary IP11 . . .**152** A5
Keightley Way IP6 . . . .**136** B5
Kell's Acres NR34 . . . . . .**8** F7
Kell's Way NR34 . . . .**8** F6
Kelly Rd IP2 . . . .**138** E5
Kelsale CE VCP Prim Sch
IP17 . . . .**128** D5
Kelso Rd IP33 . . . .**122** D2
Kelvedon Dr IP4 . . . . . .**140** F5
Kelvin Rd IP1 . . . .**134** F1
Kemball St IP4 . . . .**140** A5
Kembold Ct IP32 . . . . . .**123** E5
Kemps La NR34 . . . .**111** B3
Kempson Dr CO10 . . . . .**92** B3
Kempson Way IP30 . . . .**123** F4
Kempsters The IP11 . . .**152** D7
Kempton Cl IP1 . . . . . .**135** A3
Kempton Cross NR34 . . .**111** E4
Kempton Rd IP1 . . . . . .**135** A3
Kemsley Rd IP11 . . . . .**152** F5
Kendal Rd NR33 . . . . . .**115** B5
Kennedy Ave IP19 . . . . .**118** A1
Kennedy Cl
Halesworth IP19 . . . . . .**118** B1
Ipswich IP4 . . . .**140** A6
Kennedy Rd CB7 . . . . . .**29** C5
Kennel Loke NR31 . . . . . .**3** B8
Kennels La IP13 . . . . . .**146** C8
Kennels Rd
Brightwell IP10 . . . .**98** A6
Foxhall IP10 . . . .**141** F2
Kennetside CB8 . . . .**61** B1
Kennett Rd Or Moulton
CB8 . . . .**45** E3
Kennett Sta CB8 . . . . . .**45** F6
Kenney Cl IP8 . . . .**95** C7
Kenninghall Prim Sch
NR16 . . . .**19** A8
Kenninghall Rd NR16 . . .**19** A7
Kennyhill Dro IP28 . . . . .**13** A3
Kensington Rd
Ipswich IP1 . . . .**139** A8
Lowestoft NR33 . . . . . .**115** C5
Lowestoft NR33 . . . . . .**115** C5
Stowmarket IP14 . . . . .**124** D5
Kent Rd Lackford IP28 . . .**31** F1
Lowestoft NR32 . . . . . .**113** B1
Stowmarket IP14 . . . . .**124** C7
Kentford Rd IP11 . . . . .**152** C4
Kenton Rd IP14 . . . .**53** F2
Kents La Bungay NR35 . .**110** C3
Soham CB7 . . . .**28** D4
Kentwell Cl IP4 . . . . . .**140** F4
Kentwell Hall ★ CO10 . .**77** E2
Kentwell Pl CB5 . . . .**44** B5
Kenyon Dr IP7 . . . .**103** C5
Kenyon Rd IP9 . . . .**92** C6
Kenyon Row NR34 . . . . . .**9** B6
Kenyon St IP2 . . . .**155** B1
Kerridge Way IP20 . . . . .**22** D6
Kerridges NR16 . . . .**18** C8
Kerridge's Cut CO11 . . .**105** A2

Kerrison Con Ctr IP23 ..37 D1
Kerrison Rd NR35 ..110 D2
Kerry Ave IP1 ..134 D1
Kerrys Farm La IP14 ..51 F4
Kersey Ave CO10 ..148 F4
Kersey CE Prim Sch
　IP7 ..94 A6
Kersey Cl IP14 ..124 E3
Kersey Pottery★ IP7 ..94 A7
Kersey Rd IP1 ..152 A6
Kersley Hall La IP11 ..39 A3
Kesgrave Cty High Sch
　IP5 ..141 C8
Kesgrave Dr NR32 ..112 F2
Kesteven Rd IP2 ..155 A1
Kestrel Cl 1 IP28 ..13 B1
Kestrel Dr IP14 ..67 A5
Kestrel Rd
　Bury St Edmunds IP33 ..123 B2
　Haverhill CB9 ..133 A5
　Ipswich IP2 ..138 D3
Keswick Cl IP11 ..153 C6
Kettle La IP6 ..67 E1
Kettlebaston Way 3
　IP1 ..135 D1
Kettleborrow Cl 21 IP31 ..34 B1
Kettleburgh Rd IP13 ..126 E1
Kettlefields CB8 ..59 F5
Kevington Dr NR32 ..112 C2
Key St IP3 ..155 C2
Keynes Way 18 CO12 ..106 F1
Khartoum Rd IP4 ..139 F7
Kilbourn Rd 6 NR33 ..115 A3
Kilbrack NR34 ..111 C5
Kilbrack Gdns NR34 ..111 C5
Kildare Ave IP1 ..134 D2
Kilmaine Rd 22 CO12 ..106 F1
Kiln Dr CO10 ..148 E4
Kiln Farm La IP22 ..35 F5
Kiln Field 1 IP11 ..152 D5
Kiln La Benhall IP17 ..128 C1
　Buxhall IP14 ..65 F3
　Dickleburgh & Rushall
　　IP21 ..21 C2
　Elmswell IP30 ..50 E1
　Friston IP17 ..72 D7
　1 Mistley CO11 ..104 F1
　Needham IP20 ..22 A4
　Rede IP29 ..62 E4
　Stowlangtoft IP31 ..34 E1
Kiln Rd NR34 ..26 C3
Kilverstone Rd IP24 ..17 A6
Kimberley Rd NR33 ..115 A7
Kimms Belt IP24 ..16 B5
King Edward Ave
　IP13 ..127 C7
King Edward Rd
　Ipswich IP3 ..140 B3
　Leiston IP16 ..129 C6
King Edward VI Sch
　IP33 ..154 A3
King Edward VII Dr
　IP9 ..107 A4
King Edward VII Rd
　CB8 ..120 E5
King George Ave CB8 ..120 B8
King George's Ave
　3 Harwich CO12 ..107 A2
　Leiston IP16 ..129 E6
King St Aldeburgh IP15 ..130 E4
　Felixstowe IP11 ..152 E6
　Ipswich IP1 ..155 B3
　Mildenhall IP28 ..116 C4
　1 Mildenhall IP28 ..116 C4
　Sudbury CO10 ..148 C5
　Weybread IP21 ..22 D3
King William St 3 IP6 ..125 D5
Kingfisher Ave IP2 ..138 D3
Kingfisher Cl CB9 ..133 A6
Kingfisher Cres IP18 ..119 A7
Kingfisher Ct NR33 ..114 C6
Kingfisher Dr
　6 Burwell CB5 ..44 A6
　Claydon IP6 ..81 F5
　13 Harwich CO12 ..107 A2
Kingfisher Way 6 IP14 ..67 A5
King's Ave IP13 ..126 B5
Kings Ave IP4 ..139 E5
Kings Cl 7 Acton CO10 ..92 B7
　1 Manningtree CO11 ..104 E2
　Mildenhall IP28 ..116 D5
King's Dam NR34 ..9 B6
Kings Dr CB8 ..121 B1
Kings Fleet Prim Sch
　IP11 ..153 C6
Kings Fleet Rd IP11 ..152 E3
Kings Head La IP22 ..19 A6
King's Head St 2 CO12 ..107 C3
King's Hill CB9 ..133 E7
King's La Blyford IP19 ..42 A4
　Gosbeck IP6 ..68 D3
　Long Melford CO10 ..92 A7
　Sotherton NR34 ..25 D2
　Tannington IP13 ..55 B7
　Walsham-le-willows IP31 ..35 C3
　Weston NR34 ..9 D1
Kings Mdw
　Great Cornard CO10 ..148 E4
　Kedington CB9 ..133 E7
Kings Mead CB8 ..60 E8
Kings Par CB7 ..28 D3
Kings Rd
　Bury St Edmunds IP33 ..154 A2
　Harwich CO12 ..107 A2
　Topcroft NR35 ..7 A8
Kings Rd Bungay NR35 ..110 C2
　Glemsford CO10 ..77 A3

Kings Rd continued
　Leiston IP16 ..129 C5
King's Way IP3 ..140 B2
Kingsbury Rd IP11 ..152 C7
Kingsfield Ave
　6 Ipswich IP1 ..135 D1
　Ipswich IP1 ..139 D8
Kingsgate Dr IP4 ..139 F8
Kingshall St IP30 ..64 B8
Kingsland IP9 ..106 F5
Kingsland La 3 CO6 ..102 A7
Kingsley Cl 8 IP1 ..135 A7
Kingsmead Cl 3 IP14 ..124 C7
Kingsmead Rd IP14 ..124 C7
Kingston Cl NR33 ..115 A3
Kingston Dr NR34 ..111 C5
Kingston Farm Rd
　IP12 ..147 A4
Kingston Pas 3 CB8 ..121 A3
Kingston Rd
　Ipswich IP1 ..138 F8
　Woodbridge IP12 ..147 A4
Kingsway 4 Earsham NR35 ..7 F4
　9 Harwich CO12 ..107 B2
　Mildenhall IP28 ..116 C4
　Newmarket CB8 ..120 F4
　Woodbridge IP12 ..147 B5
Kingswood Ave NR33 ..114 D4
Kingsworth Rd IP32 ..123 D6
Kinross Rd IP4 ..136 B1
Kipling Cl 5 NR33 ..11 C1
Kipling Rd IP1 ..134 F3
Kipling Way IP14 ..124 B8
Kirby Cane Wlk NR32 ..113 A3
Kirby Cl IP4 ..140 A7
Kirby St IP4 ..140 A7
Kirkdale Ct 4 NR33 ..115 B4
Kirkham Cl 2 IP2 ..139 A2
Kirkley Cliff Rd NR33 ..115 C5
Kirkley Gdns NR33 ..115 B6
Kirkley High Sch
　NR33 ..115 A7
Kirkley Mid Sch NR33 ..115 A7
Kirkley Pk Rd NR33 ..115 B6
Kirkley Run NR33 ..115 A7
Kirkley St NR33 ..115 B6
Kirkstead Rd IP33 ..122 D3
Kirkstone Way 4 NR32 ..113 A4
Kirkton Cl IP9 ..107 A5
Kirkwood Dr 1 NR33 ..114 C3
Kirtling Rd CB8 ..60 E5
Kirton Rd IP11 ..107 D8
Kitchen Hill CO10 ..91 D4
Kitchener Rd
　Ipswich IP1 ..138 F8
　Leiston IP16 ..129 C6
Kitchener Way 5 IP7 ..107 A5
Kitson Mdws IP33 ..122 A5
Kittiwake Cl
　Ipswich IP2 ..138 E3
　Lowestoft NR33 ..114 D5
Klondyke IP32 ..122 F8
Knaves Acre Dro CB7 ..29 B6
Knights Cl
　7 Debenham IP14 ..53 F2
　10 Felixstowe IP11 ..153 D6
　6 Manningtree CO11 ..104 E2
　4 Old Newton with Dagworth
　　IP14 ..51 E1
Knights La 5 IP5 ..141 D7
Knightsdale Rd IP1 ..135 A1
Knightswood 3 NR32 ..113 B5
Knoll The IP13 ..126 D3
Knowle The 17 IP31 ..34 E4
Knox La IP31 ..34 C4
Knutsford Cl IP8 ..138 C1
Kreswell Gr 7 CO12 ..107 A1
Kylborne Cl IP33 ..122 C4
Kyson Hill National Trust★
　IP12 ..146 F2
Kyson Prim Sch IP12 ..146 D4

L

Laburnum Ave IP28 ..116 E5
Laburnum Cl
　3 Ipswich IP8 ..138 C2
　Ipswich IP3 ..140 D2
　Red Lodge IP28 ..30 B1
　Worlingworth IP13 ..54 E7
Laburnum Gdns IP5 ..136 E1
Laburnum La 11 CB5 ..44 A6
Laburnum Rd 3 NR35 ..110 B3
Laburnum Way 2 CO6 ..102 C5
Lacey St IP4 ..139 E6
Lacey's La CB8 ..120 B7
Lackford La IP28 ..47 D6
Lackford Wildfowl Nature
　Reserve★ ..31 F1
Lacon Rd 2 IP8 ..134 A2
Lady La Hadleigh IP7 ..149 E7
　Ipswich IP1 ..155 A3
Lady La Ind Est IP7 ..149 E7
Lady Margaret Gdns
　CB7 ..29 C5
Lady St 13 CO10 ..78 D4
Ladyfield IP14 ..66 D8
Lady's La IP22 ..19 F5
Ladywell Rd IP14 ..51 F7
Ladywood Rd IP4 ..140 C7
Lagonda Dr IP1 ..134 C1
Lake Ave IP32 ..48 C5
Lake Side IP14 ..124 C6
Lake View Rd NR33 ..114 E8

Lakeland 3 IP26 ..5 A3
Lakeland Rd NR32 ..112 F1
Lakenheath Airfield
　IP27 ..14 B5
Lakenheath American High
　Sch IP27 ..109 F1
Lakenheath Prim Sch
　IP27 ..109 D6
Lakenheath Sta IP27 ..4 F1
Lakeside Ave IP16 ..73 C6
Lakeside Cl IP18 ..119 B7
Lakeside Pk Dr IP18 ..119 B6
Lakeside Rd IP7 ..138 E2
Lakeside Rise NR32 ..112 C8
Lakforth 4 CO10 ..91 E8
Lamarsh Hill 1 CO8 ..101 C5
Lamarsh Rd CO8 ..101 A4
Lambert Cl IP1 ..118 B3
Lambert Dr CO10 ..92 B7
Lamberts 21 IP26 ..4 E5
Lambert's La
　Mendlesham IP14 ..52 C3
　Sudbourne IP12 ..73 B1
Lamberts La IP5 ..136 C3
Lambert's Way NR35 ..110 C6
Lambeth Cl 1 IP1 ..139 A7
Lambeth Way IP14 ..67 F7
Lamble Cl IP28 ..30 B8
Lambourne Cl 3 IP32 ..123 E6
Lambourne Rd IP1 ..135 B4
Lambs La IP29 ..63 D1
Lambsale Mdw IP17 ..128 D4
Lambseth St IP23 ..117 C3
Lamdin Rd IP32 ..48 C5
Lammas Cl IP31 ..34 C4
Lanark Rd IP4 ..136 B1
Lancaster Ave IP32 ..122 F8
Lancaster Cl IP29 ..62 C4
Lancaster Dr 8 IP5 ..98 A7
Lancaster Rd
　5 Feltwell IP26 ..4 E5
　Ipswich IP4 ..139 E6
　7 Mildenhall IP28 ..30 A8
　Sudbury CO10 ..148 B8
Lancaster Way
　10 Claydon IP6 ..82 B5
　Stradishall CB8 ..75 C7
Lancers Dr IP32 ..146 E3
Lancewood Wlk 27 IP27 ..13 F7
Lancing Ave IP4 ..140 A8
Landguard Fort★
　IP11 ..107 E2
Landguard Nature Reserve★
　IP11 ..107 E2
Landguard Rd IP11 ..153 I11
Landsdown Rd CO10 ..148 E7
Landseer Cl IP3 ..140 A1
Landseer Rd IP3 ..139 E2
Landspring La NR33 ..114 E6
Landwade Rd CB8 ..44 D6
Lane The
　Creeting St Peter or West
　　Creeting IP6 ..67 B5
　3 Mistley CO11 ..104 F2
　Wrentham NR34 ..26 E5
　Yoxford IP17 ..57 C8
Lanercost Way IP2 ..139 A1
Lang Gate Way NR35 ..7 A5
Langdale 2 IP3 ..113 D6
Langdale Pk NR32 ..113 A4
Langer Cty Prim Sch
　IP11 ..152 E2
Langer Rd IP11 ..152 E2
Langford Cl IP14 ..124 B8
Langham La CO4 ..103 B1
Langham Rd
　Blaxhall IP12 ..72 B4
　Boxted CO4 ..102 F1
Langham Way CB9 ..74 A1
Langley Ave IP11 ..152 E4
Langley Gdns NR33 ..114 F5
Langley Hill CO8 ..101 B6
Langmere Rd IP21 ..21 C4
Langridge The IP31 ..34 B2
Langstons IP11 ..152 D7
Langton Rd 4 IP33 ..122 D4
Lanman Mus★ IP13 ..126 D4
Lansbury Rd IP19 ..118 B3
Lansdowne Rd
　Felixstowe IP11 ..153 B6
　Ipswich IP4 ..140 A5
　Lowestoft NR33 ..115 B4
Lanwades Bsns Pk CB8 ..46 A5
Lapwing Cl 17 IP31 ..49 D4
Lapwing Ct 4 IP28 ..116 D4
Lapwing Rd IP2 ..138 D3
Larch Cl IP27 ..109 D7
Larch Gr 6 CO6 ..102 C5
Larch Rd IP3 ..143 B3
Larchcroft Cl IP1 ..135 B2
Larchcroft Rd IP1 ..135 A2
Larches The NR34 ..26 E5
Larchwood Cl IP3 ..138 C5
Largent Gr IP5 ..141 E8
Lark Cl
　4 Stowmarket IP14 ..67 A5
　Worlingham IP28 ..30 A5
Lark Hill CB8 ..45 F3
Lark Rd IP28 ..116 D4
Lark Rise
　23 Martlesham Heath IP5 ..98 A8
　Sudbury CO10 ..148 B3
Lark Valley Dr IP28 ..48 C6
Larkhall Rd CB7 ..28 E5
Larkhill Rise IP4 ..140 E5
Larkhill Way 9 IP11 ..152 D5
Larks Cl CB9 ..133 A5
Larks Rise IP19 ..118 C3

Larksfield Cres 5 CO12 ..107 A2
Larksfield Rd IP9 ..105 D5
Larkspur Cl
　Corton NR32 ..113 B8
　1 Red Lodge IP28 ..30 B1
Larkspur Rd IP2 ..138 F3
Larksway IP11 ..152 E5
Larters La IP14 ..67 D8
Lattens Sq 4 NR32 ..113 C2
Lattice Ave IP4 ..140 C6
Laud's Cl IP11 ..152 B8
Laundry La
　Bury St Edmunds IP33 ..123 D3
　Huntingfield IP19 ..41 A4
Laureate Gdns
　CB8 ..120 E6
Laureate Paddocks
　CB8 ..120 E6
Laureate Prim Sch
　CB8 ..120 E6
Laureate Sch Rd CB8 ..120 E6
Laurel Ave
　1 Harwich CO12 ..106 F1
　Ipswich IP5 ..141 A7
Laurel Cl Haverhill CB9 ..132 B7
　4 Red Lodge IP28 ..30 C1
　19 Thurstow IP31 ..49 D4
Laurel Ct 9 IP30 ..50 F2
Laurel Dr 13 Claydon IP6 ..82 A5
　8 Long Melford CO10 ..91 E8
Laurel Rd NR33 ..115 B6
Laurel Way 5 IP6 ..134 C8
Laurelhayes IP2 ..139 A3
Laurels The
　8 Hopton on Sea NR31 ..3 B7
　Worlingham NR34 ..111 F3
Lavender Cl 3 IP28 ..30 B1
Lavender Hill IP2 ..138 F4
Lavender Rd
　Great Waldingfield CO10 ..78 D1
　Ipswich IP2 ..138 E5
Lavenham Prim Sch
　CO10 ..78 D4
Lavenham Rd
　Great Waldingfield CO10 ..78 D1
　Ipswich IP2 ..138 E5
Lavenham Way
　3 Lowestoft NR32 ..112 F3
　4 Stowmarket IP14 ..124 E3
Lawn Way IP11 ..152 E5
Lawns The IP4 ..140 C8
Lawrence Dr NR32 ..113 B6
Law's Drift IP10 ..98 C2
Lawshall Rd
　Hartest IP29 ..77 B8
　Hawstead IP29 ..63 D4
Lawshall Row IP29 ..63 D2
Lawson Cour NR33 ..115 C7
Lawson Pl IP32 ..123 E5
Lawson Rd NR33 ..115 C7
Laxfield & District Mus★
　IP13 ..40 B3
Laxfield Rd
　Badingham IP13 ..56 B8
　Dennington IP13 ..55 E6
　Fressingfield IP21 ..39 F7
　Laxfield IP13 ..40 C1
　Stradbroke IP21 ..39 E4
Laxfield Way NR33 ..114 F4
Layer Rd CB9 ..132 C5
Layham Dr 23 IP32 ..123 A8
Layham Gdns IP14 ..124 F3
Layham Rd IP7 ..149 D4
Layhill Cl IP32 ..123 D5
Laywood Cl 1 IP32 ..123 D6
Layzell Croft CO10 ..92 B2
Lea Rd Aldeburgh IP15 ..130 E4
　Harwich CO12 ..107 B2
Leabrook Cl IP32 ..123 E6
Leader's Way CB8 ..120 E4
Lea's Drift 1 NR33 ..114 C5
Leas The NR32 ..112 F5
Leather La
　Great Yeldham CO9 ..90 A1
　Haverhill CB9 ..132 C5
Leathes Cl NR32 ..112 F1
Lee Rd Aldeburgh IP15 ..130 E4
　Harwich CO12 ..107 B2
　Ipswich IP3 ..139 F3
Leeks Hill IP12 ..147 A7
Leggatt Dr IP8 ..134 A2
Leicester Cl IP2 ..138 F1
Leighton Rd IP3 ..144 A8
Leighton Sq 8 IP3 ..144 A8
Leiston Abbey★ IP16 ..58 C3
Leiston High Sch IP16 ..129 E5
Leiston Mid Sch IP16 ..129 C6
Leiston Prim Sch
　IP16 ..129 E5
Leiston Rd
　Aldeburgh IP15 ..130 D7
　Coldfair Green IP17 ..129 B3
　Haverhill IP16 ..132 C5
　4 Lowestoft NR32 ..113 D1
　Theberton IP16 ..58 B5
　Theberton IP17 ..58 B5
Leiston Sports Ctr
　IP16 ..129 E6
Leisure Way NR32 ..113 B7
Lely Rd IP3 ..143 F8
Lemons Hill IP9 ..105 B8
Lentins The IP14 ..68 E6
Leona Cres NR33 ..114 C2
Leonard Dr 2 NR32 ..113 A6
Leonard's La IP26 ..4 D5
Leopold Gdns IP4 ..140 B8
Leopold Rd
　Felixstowe IP11 ..153 A3
　Ipswich IP4 ..140 C1
Leslie Rd IP3 ..140 C1
Lester Piggott Way
　..120 F6
Letton Cl IP9 ..150 E3
Leverett's La IP18 ..119 B2

Levington La IP10 ..98 A3
Levington Rd
　Felixstowe IP11 ..152 A1
　Ipswich IP3 ..140 A4
　Nacton IP10 ..145 C4
Lewes Cl IP1 ..140 E3
Lewis Cl
　Ditchingham NR35 ..110 C8
　Hopton IP22 ..18 C3
Lewis La IP9 ..105 B5
Ley Rd Barrow IP29 ..47 A2
　Stetchworth CB8 ..60 A5
Leys La IP23 ..37 B5
Leys Rd IP30 ..50 B2
Leyton Ave IP28 ..116 B6
Lidgate Ct 1 IP11 ..152 C4
Lidgate Rd CB8 ..61 C8
Lifeboat Mus★ IP18 ..119 D4
Lighthouse Score 2
　NR32 ..113 E3
Lilac Cl IP27 ..14 D8
Lilac Dr
　Lakenheath IP27 ..109 D6
　Lowestoft NR32 ..113 B3
Lilac Wlk IP6 ..125 D3
Lilley Cl IP33 ..122 C3
Lily Cl NR34 ..10 A7
Lily Way NR33 ..114 C5
Lime Ave
　Harwich CO12 ..107 A2
　Lowestoft NR32 ..113 B3
Lime Cl 7 Harleston IP20 ..22 D5
　Lakenheath IP27 ..109 D5
　Mildenhall IP28 ..116 E5
　6 Ufford IP13 ..84 F7
　Wickham Market IP13 ..127 B6
Lime Gr CO10 ..148 A3
Lime Kiln Quay Rd
　IP12 ..147 B5
Lime Tree Ave IP16 ..129 C6
Lime Tree Cl 3 IP30 ..64 F8
Lime Tree Pl IP14 ..124 E5
Lime Wlk IP30 ..65 A3
Limecroft Cl 1 IP1 ..135 A3
Limekiln Cl 7 IP6 ..134 C8
Limerick Cl IP1 ..134 E2
Limes Ave IP8 ..134 C5
Limes The
　Halesworth IP19 ..118 A3
　6 Horringer IP29 ..63 A8
　Long Melford CO10 ..91 E8
　Rushmere St Andrew
　　IP5 ..136 D1
Limestone La CB7 ..29 C5
Limetree Cl IP6 ..125 E4
Limetree Dr IP3 ..140 D2
Limmer Ave IP21 ..21 C5
Lincoln Ave IP17 ..128 B2
Lincoln Cl IP1 ..135 B3
Lincoln Ct 11 NR33 ..11 B1
Lincoln Gdns 8 IP6 ..82 B5
Lincoln Gn IP32 ..123 B2
Lincoln La CO6 ..102 E1
Lincoln Rd 10 IP28 ..30 A8
Lincoln Terr 1 IP11 ..152 F3
Linda Cl 11 NR32 ..3 D4
Lindbergh Rd 2 IP3 ..140 C1
Linden Cl
　Aldeburgh IP15 ..130 D6
　20 Manningtree CO10 ..104 D2
Linden Rd IP15 ..130 C5
Linden Wlk 11 IP28 ..13 B1
Lindisfarne Cl 1 IP2 ..139 A1
Lindisfarne Rd IP33 ..122 D2
Lindsey Ave CO10 ..148 F4
Lindsey Rd IP4 ..140 C7
Lindsey Way IP14 ..124 E3
Ling Rd Palgrave IP22 ..20 B2
　Wortham IP22 ..19 F2
Lingfield Rd IP1 ..135 B4
Lingheath Rd IP27 ..6 A1
Lings Field IP13 ..70 C7
Ling's La IP9 ..106 B7
Lingside 1 IP5 ..98 A7
Link La IP9 ..104 E7
Link Rd
　Capel St. Mary IP9 ..150 A3
　7 Shotley Gate IP9 ..107 A5
Link The IP9 ..104 E7
Links Ave IP11 ..153 B6
Links Cl
　Bury St Edmunds IP33 ..123 B1
　Lowestoft NR33 ..114 F5
　Worlingham IP28 ..30 B4
Links Rd
　Great Yarmouth NR31 ..3 B8
　Lowestoft NR32 ..113 D5
Links The Flempton IP28 ..32 B1
　Wooddiitton CB8 ..59 E8
Links View CO10 ..92 D3
Linksfield IP5 ..140 E7
Linksfield Gdns IP5 ..140 E7
Linkwood Rd IP30 ..64 B7
Linnet Pl IP33 ..154 C1
Linnet Rd
　Bury St Edmunds IP33 ..122 E4
　Ipswich IP2 ..138 D4
Linnetts La IP33 ..133 E2
Linstead Rd IP19 ..40 F1
Linton Cl CB8 ..120 F5
Linton Gdns IP33 ..122 E3
Linx The IP13 ..40 B3
Lion La IP6 ..125 C3
Lion Mdw CB9 ..88 D4
Lion Rd Glemsford CO10 ..77 A3

Lion Rd *continued*
Palgrave IP22 ... 20 B1
Wortham IP22 ... 36 F8
Lion St IP1 ... 155 B3
Lionel Hurst Cl 15 CO10 ... 92 B3
Lisburn Rd CB8 ... 121 B3
Lister Rd Hadleigh IP7 ... 149 F5
Ipswich IP1 ... 134 F1
Liston La CO10 ... 91 D7
Lithgo Paddock 8 IP31 ... 49 A6
Little Back La 8 IP14 ... 53 F2
Little Fen Dro CB5 ... 44 A7
Little Gipping St IP1 ... 155 A3
Little Gn CB8 ... 60 E6
Little Gn Cl IP23 ... 36 C3
Little Gr IP9 ... 150 E2
Little Gulls IP9 ... 150 D3
Little Hasse Dro CB7 ... 28 E6
Little Horkesley Rd CO6 ... 102 A2
Little Hyde Cl CO9 ... 90 A1
Little Hyde Rd CO9 ... 90 A1
Little London Hill IP14 ... 53 E3
Little London La CB7 ... 29 B5
Little Mdws Dr IP6 ... 69 C2
Little Mill La IP29 ... 47 A3
Little Oulsham Dro IP26 ... 4 B6
Little St IP17 ... 57 C8
Little St John's St 8 IP12 ... 147 A5
Little St Mary's CO10 ... 91 E7
Little Tufts IP9 ... 150 F3
Little Whip St IP2 ... 155 B1
Little Yeldham Rd CO9 ... 90 B2
Littlemoor Rd IP17 ... 57 E6
Little's Cres IP2 ... 155 B1
Livermere Drift IP31 ... 48 E6
Livermere Rd
Great Barton IP31 ... 49 A6
Troston IP31 ... 33 D2
Lloyd Rd 3 IP9 ... 107 A4
Lloyds Ave Ipswich IP1 ... 155 B3
15 Kessingland NR33 ... 11 B1
Lloyds The IP5 ... 141 C7
Loam Pit La IP19 ... 118 C4
Locarno Rd 1 IP3 ... 140 B3
Lock Cl 14 IP14 ... 53 F2
Lockhart Rd NR35 ... 8 D7
Lockington Cl 4 IP14 ... 124 E5
Lockington Cres IP14 ... 124 D5
Lockington Rd IP14 ... 124 D5
Lock's La
6 Leavenheath CO6 ... 102 A7
Shipmeadow NR34 ... 8 F5
Wrentham NR34 ... 26 F6
Lock's Rd NR34 ... 25 C5
Lockwood Cl 1 IP12 ... 147 A5
Loddon Rd
Ditchingham NR35 ... 110 C7
Gillingham NR34 ... 9 B6
Kirby Cane NR35 ... 8 E8
Lode Cl 1 CB7 ... 28 D3
Lode La CB7 ... 28 A1
Lodge Farm Dr IP11 ... 153 C5
Lodge Farm La
Barsham NR34 ... 9 B4
8 Melton IP12 ... 84 E6
Lodge Farm Rd CO10 ... 77 B1
Lodge La Claydon IP6 ... 134 A8
Riddlesworth IP22 ... 18 A3
Shelfanger IP22 ... 20 B5
Lodge Rd Feltwell IP26 ... 4 F6
Great Bealings IP13 ... 137 E5
Hollesley IP12 ... 99 D7
Holton IP19 ... 118 E5
St John, Ilketshall NR35 ... 110 F2
1 Ufford IP13 ... 84 F7
Walberswick IP18 ... 119 A2
Lodge Way IP24 ... 16 B7
Lofft Cl 11 IP31 ... 34 E4
Loftus Ave IP18 ... 119 C7
Loggers La IP22 ... 18 E1
Loke The
Blundeston NR32 ... 3 A4
Ditchingham NR35 ... 110 B7
Lombardy Rd CO10 ... 148 B8
Lonbarn Hill CO11 ... 105 D1
London City Rd IP21 ... 39 C3
London La
Harleston IP14 ... 66 C7
4 Mundford IP26 ... 6 B8
London Rd
Beccles NR34 ... 111 B2
Blythburgh IP19 ... 42 E5
Brampton with Stoven NR34 ... 25 E6
Brandon IP27 ... 14 E8
Capel St. Mary IP9 ... 150 F2
Copdock & Washbrook IP8 ... 138 A1
Elveden IP24 ... 15 C2
Great Horkesley CO6 ... 102 C1
Halesworth IP19 ... 118 A2
Halesworth IP19 ... 118 B3
Harleston IP20 ... 22 D5
Icklingham IP27 ... 31 E8
Ipswich IP1 ... 155 A3
Kessingland NR33 ... 11 B2
Lowestoft NR33 ... 115 A2
Pinewood IP8 ... 138 B2
Thetford IP24 ... 16 A5
Westley Waterless CB8 ... 59 A4
Weston NR34 ... 9 D2
Wrentham NR34 ... 26 E4
London Rd N NR32 ... 113 D1
London Rd Pakefield NR33 ... 115 A2
London Rd S NR33 ... 115 C5
Lone Barn Ct IP1 ... 138 D8
Lonely Rd IP21 ... 21 C6
Long Acre
Lowestoft NR33 ... 115 B3
Southwold IP18 ... 119 B7
Long Bessels IP7 ... 149 D6
Long Brackland IP33 ... 154 B3
Long Dolver Dro CB7 ... 28 D6
Long Field IP11 ... 152 D6
Long La Bawdsey IP12 ... 99 E3
Burston & Shimpling IP22 ... 20 E8
Feltwell IP26 ... 4 D5
Long Mdw Wlk NR33 ... 114 D5
Long Mdws 2 CO12 ... 106 F1
Long Melford CE Prim Sch CO10 ... 91 E8
Long Pastures 2 CO10 ... 77 B2
Long Perry IP9 ... 150 F3
Long Rd
Lowestoft NR33 ... 114 E3
Lowestoft NR33 ... 114 E3
Manningtree CO11 ... 104 D1
Manningtree CO11 ... 104 D2
Long Rd E CO7 ... 104 A2
Long Rd W CO7 ... 103 F2
Long Row IP16 ... 129 D6
Long Shop Steam Mus* IP16 ... 129 C6
Long St IP3 ... 139 E5
Long Thurlow Rd IP31 ... 51 A7
Longacre Gdns IP33 ... 122 E3
Longbeach Dr NR33 ... 114 D3
Longcroft IP11 ... 152 E6
Longden Ave NR32 ... 112 F2
Longfield Rd IP9 ... 150 E4
Longfield Way 6 NR32 ... 112 D2
Longfulans La NR31 ... 3 B6
Longmeadow IP33 ... 122 E5
Longmere La CB7 ... 28 C5
Longrigg Rd NR35 ... 110 C7
Lonsdale Cl IP4 ... 139 F7
Looe Rd IP11 ... 153 C5
Looms La IP33 ... 154 B2
Lopham Rd NR16 ... 18 D8
Lophams Cl CB9 ... 132 D8
Loraine Way
Bramford IP8 ... 134 A1
Bramford IP8 ... 134 A2
Lord Rd IP22 ... 20 D2
Lord's Croft La CB9 ... 132 E5
Lord's Highway The IP14 ... 67 E5
Lord's La CB8 ... 61 E5
Lord's Wlk IP27 ... 13 F2
Lorne Pk Rd NR33 ... 115 C6
Lorne Rd
Lowestoft NR33 ... 115 C6
Southwold IP18 ... 119 D5
Lothing St NR32 ... 112 F1
Lothingland Mid Sch NR32 ... 3 A5
Lotus Cl IP1 ... 134 C1
Loudham Hall Rd IP13 ... 127 D3
Loudham La IP13 ... 85 A7
Louie's La IP22 ... 20 C3
Lound Dam NR14 ... 2 A3
Lound Rd
Belton with Browston NR31 ... 2 E8
Blundeston NR32 ... 3 A4
Louse La Dedham CO7 ... 103 F2
Rattlesden IP30 ... 65 D3
Louvain Rd 13 CO12 ... 107 A1
Lovat Cl IP20 ... 22 E6
Love La Lowestoft NR33 ... 114 F4
Thorndon IP23 ... 53 B8
Westleton IP17 ... 58 C7
Love Rd NR32 ... 113 C1
Lovers La IP9 ... 106 B6
Lover's La IP16 ... 129 E8
Lovetofts Dr IP1 ... 134 D1
Lovewell Rd NR33 ... 115 C6
Low Comm IP22 ... 19 B3
Low Comm La NR34 ... 2 A1
Low Comm Rd IP22 ... 19 B3
Low Farm Dr NR33 ... 114 C3
Low La Brandeston IP13 ... 70 A7
Creeting St Mary IP6 ... 125 E8
Low Lighthouse Maritime Mus* CO12 ... 107 C3
Low Rd Alburgh IP20 ... 7 A1
Bramfield IP19 ... 42 A5
Brampton with Stoven NR34 ... 25 D5
Burwell CB5 ... 44 A5
Carlton IP17 ... 128 D6
Cransford IP17 ... 56 C4
Darsham IP17 ... 57 F8
Debenham IP14 ... 53 E1
Denham IP21 ... 38 C2
Denton IP20 ... 7 B1
1 Dickleburgh & Rushall IP21 ... 20 F2
Earl Soham IP13 ... 54 E2
Eyke IP12 ... 85 B7
1 Fressingfield IP21 ... 39 E8
Friston IP17 ... 72 F6
Great Glemham IP17 ... 56 C1
Harwich CO12 ... 106 F1
Hasketon IP13 ... 146 B8
Hedenham NR35 ... 7 D8
Marlesford IP13 ... 71 C5
Mettingham NR35 ... 110 F5
Monk Soham IP13 ... 54 D3
Low Rd *continued*
Redenhall with Harleston IP20 ... 22 F5
St John, Ilketshall NR34 ... 8 D3
Starston IP20 ... 22 C7
Stratford St Andrew IP17 ... 71 F7
Swefling IP17 ... 56 E3
Ubbeston IP19 ... 40 D3
Wenhaston With Mells Hamlet IP19 ... 42 C7
Wortham IP22 ... 19 E2
Wortwell IP20 ... 23 A7
Low St Badingham IP13 ... 56 A7
Bardwell IP31 ... 34 C3
Glemsford CO10 ... 77 B3
Hoxne IP21 ... 38 B8
Kettleburgh IP13 ... 70 B7
St Margaret, Ilketshall NR35 ... 24 B8
Low Wr La IP22 ... 20 A1
Lower Barn Rd IP8 ... 95 D5
Lower Baxter St IP33 ... 154 B2
Lower Brook St IP4 ... 155 B2
Lower Broom Rd IP30 ... 50 C1
Lower Byfield IP7 ... 79 C2
Lower Coney Gr IP8 ... 81 A4
Lower Cres IP6 ... 82 A6
Lower Dales View Rd IP1 ... 139 A8
Lower Downs Slade 5 CB9 ... 132 E6
Lower Drag Way IP22 ... 19 A4
Lower Farm Rd
Boxted CO4 ... 103 A4
Ringshall IP7 ... 80 E6
Lower Harlings 4 IP9 ... 107 A4
Lower House La IP12 ... 98 C5
Lower Houses Rd IP9 ... 106 B5
Lower Marine Par CO12 ... 107 B1
Lower N St CO10 ... 75 D3
Lower Oakley IP21 ... 37 F8
Lower Olland St NR35 ... 110 B4
Lower Orwell St IP4 ... 155 C2
Lower Pk Wlk IP19 ... 118 E4
Lower Rd Borley CO10 ... 91 D6
Coddenham IP6 ... 68 B1
Falkenham IP10 ... 98 F1
Glemsford CO10 ... 77 B1
Grundisburgh IP13 ... 83 E5
Hemingstone IP6 ... 68 C1
Hundon CO10 ... 75 D3
Lavenham CO10 ... 78 D4
Little Blakenham IP8 ... 81 D3
Melton IP13 ... 84 F6
Mount Bures CO8 ... 101 D3
Onehouse IP14 ... 66 B5
Westerfield IP6 ... 135 D4
Wicken CB7 ... 28 A2
Lower Rose La IP21 ... 20 D1
Lower St Baylham IP6 ... 81 E7
Cavendish CO10 ... 76 E1
Great Bealings IP13 ... 137 E6
Rattlesden IP30 ... 65 D6
Sproughton IP8 ... 138 A6
Stansfield CO10 ... 76 C6
Stanstead CO10 ... 77 C3
Stratford St Mary CO7 ... 103 E5
Stutton IP9 ... 105 D5
Ufford IP13 ... 85 A6
Wickham Market IP13 ... 127 C7
Lower Ufford La IP13 ... 127 D3
Lower Ufford Rd IP13 ... 127 C1
Lowes Hill IP17 ... 128 E7
Lowestoft & E Suffolk Maritime Mus* NR32 ... 113 E3
Lowestoft & N Suffolk Hospl NR32 ... 113 D1
Lowestoft Coll NR32 ... 113 C2
Lowestoft Mus* NR33 ... 114 D8
Lowestoft Rd
Beccles NR34 ... 111 E4
Blundeston NR32 ... 112 E8
Hopton-on-sea NR31 ... 3 B6
Lowestoft NR33 ... 114 D3
Reydon IP18 ... 119 C8
Worlingham NR34 ... 10 A4
Lowestoft Sta NR32 ... 115 D8
Lowestoft Town FC NR32 ... 113 C2
Lowgate St IP23 ... 117 D2
Lowlands Cl 11 NR33 ... 11 C1
Lowry Cl CB9 ... 132 B7
Lowry Gdns 6 IP3 ... 144 A8
Lowry Way
Lowestoft NR32 ... 113 C5
Stowmarket IP14 ... 124 B7
Low's La IP22 ... 20 C1
Loxley Rd NR33 ... 114 E6
Lucas Rd CO10 ... 148 D5
Lucena Ct IP14 ... 124 C6
Lucerne Cl
Lowestoft NR33 ... 114 C5
5 Red Lodge IP28 ... 30 B1
Ludbrook Cl IP6 ... 125 C5
Ludgate Cswy IP23 ... 117 E2
Ludlow Cl IP1 ... 135 B4
Luff Mdw IP6 ... 125 D5
Lugano Ave IP12 ... 98 B8
Lulworth Ave IP3 ... 140 D3
Lulworth Dr CB9 ... 132 C6
Lulworth Pk 8 NR32 ... 113 A4
Lummis Vale IP5 ... 141 C7
Lundy Cl CB9 ... 133 B5
Lunnish Hill CO12 ... 106 C2
Lupin Cl IP18 ... 119 B6
Lupin Rd IP2 ... 138 E4
Lupin Way IP6 ... 125 D3
Lushington Rd 5 CO11 ... 104 E2
Luther Rd IP2 ... 155 B1
Lutus Cl CO10 ... 90 A7
Lydgate Cl
11 Bury St Edmunds IP32 ... 48 C5
14 Lawford CO11 ... 104 D2
Lydgate Rd IP14 ... 124 C7
Lymingster Cl 6 IP32 ... 123 D6
Lymm Rd NR32 ... 113 B5
Lyncroft Rd NR33 ... 115 B3
Lyndhurst Ave IP4 ... 140 C5
Lyndhurst Rd NR32 ... 113 D4
Lyng La IP22 ... 18 F5
Lyngate Ave NR33 ... 114 F5
Lynn's Hall Cl CO10 ... 92 C6
Lynton Gdns NR32 ... 113 C3
Lynwood Ave IP11 ... 153 B5
Lynx Bsns Pk CB8 ... 44 F7
Lyon Cl IP23 ... 37 C4
Lysander Dr IP3 ... 144 C8

M

Macaulay Rd IP1 ... 134 F3
Mackenzie Dr IP5 ... 141 B8
Mackenzie Pl IP30 ... 78 C8
Mackenzie Rd IP24 ... 16 A5
Macpherson Robertson Way 3 IP28 ... 116 B5
Magdalen Cl 3 NR32 ... 113 A3
Magdalen Dr IP12 ... 146 D3
Magdalen Rd IP7 ... 149 D6
Magdalen St IP23 ... 117 C2
Magdalene Cl IP2 ... 138 F2
Magingley Cres IP4 ... 140 F6
Magnolia Cl
9 Beck Row, Holywell Row & Kenny Hill IP28 ... 13 B1
2 Red Lodge IP28 ... 30 B1
Magnolia Ct 3 NR32 ... 113 B2
Magpie Cl 1 IP8 ... 138 C2
Magpie Ct 33 IP20 ... 22 D6
Magpie Hill IP22 ... 19 E1
Maid Marion Ct IP33 ... 122 F3
Maidenhall App IP2 ... 139 B2
Maidenhall Sports Ctr IP2 ... 139 C2
Maids Cross Hill IP27 ... 109 E6
Maids Cross Way IP27 ... 109 D6
Maidstone Rd
Felixstowe IP11 ... 152 E5
Lowestoft NR32 ... 113 C1
Main Rd Benhall IP17 ... 72 C8
Bucklesham IP10 ... 141 F1
Chelmondiston IP9 ... 106 B8
Darsham IP17 ... 42 A1
Hacheston IP13 ... 127 D8
Harwich CO12 ... 106 F1
Henley IP6 ... 82 D6
Ipswich IP5 ... 141 A8
Kelsale cum Carlton IP17 ... 128 C8
Marlesford IP13 ... 71 D4
Martlesham IP12 ... 146 C1
Parham IP13 ... 70 F8
3 Ramsey & Parkeston CO12 ... 106 D1
Somersham IP8 ... 81 C3
Tuddenham St Martin IP6 ... 136 B4
Woolverstone IP9 ... 143 F2
Wormingford CO6 ... 101 F2
Main St
Hockwold cum Wilton IP26 ... 4 F3
Leiston IP16 ... 129 C6
Maine St 4 IP24 ... 16 A5
Maisie's Mdw IP13 ... 54 D7
Maitland Rd IP6 ... 125 E3
Major La IP23 ... 37 A2
Major's Cl IP29 ... 62 C5
Makins Rd 2 CO12 ... 106 F3
Malcolm Way CB8 ... 121 A5
Maldon Ct CO10 ... 148 F5
Malin Cl CB9 ... 133 B5
Mallard Rd IP18 ... 119 B7
Mallard Way
Hollesley IP12 ... 99 F7
Ipswich IP2 ... 138 F3
Stowmarket IP14 ... 124 A6
Sudbury CO10 ... 92 B3
Mallards The IP27 ... 109 D5
Mallets La IP12 ... 131 C2
Mallow Rd IP24 ... 16 C6
Mallow Way NR33 ... 114 C4
Mallowhayes Cl IP2 ... 139 B3
Malmesbury Cl IP2 ... 139 A2
Malt Cl 5 IP13 ... 40 B3
Malt Office Ave IP19 ... 24 B4
Malt Office La IP19 ... 24 A4
Malthouse Ct 24 IP20 ... 22 D6
Malthouse La
Bury St Edmunds IP32 ... 154 B4
Gissing IP22 ... 20 F8
Malthouse Rd 22 CO11 ... 104 E2
Malting End CB8 ... 60 E2
Malting Farm La CO7 ... 103 E1
Malting La 10 Clare CO10 ... 90 A8
Isleham CB7 ... 29 C5
Malting Row IP31 ... 33 F5
Maltings IP14 ... 52 D3
Maltings Cl
2 Bures Hamlet CO8 ... 101 C5
1 Chevington IP29 ... 62 C6
Halesworth IP19 ... 118 B4
Maltings Cl *continued*
Moulton CB8 ... 45 F3
Maltings Dr 6 IP20 ... 22 D6
Maltings Garth 9 IP31 ... 49 D4
Maltings The NR35 ... 110 C4
Malt's La IP26 ... 4 F3
Maltsters' Way
3 Lowestoft NR32 ... 112 D1
Lowestoft NR32 ... 114 D8
Maltward Ave IP33 ... 122 C5
Malvern Cl Ipswich IP3 ... 140 B3
Newmarket CB8 ... 121 B2
Malvern Rd IP33 ... 122 D3
Malvern Rise NR32 ... 113 B3
Manchester Rd IP2 ... 138 D2
Manderston Rd CB8 ... 120 E3
Manderville Rd IP33 ... 122 C4
Mandeville 14 CB5 ... 44 A5
Mandy Cl IP4 ... 140 A6
Mannall Wlk IP5 ... 141 E8
Manners Rd IP31 ... 48 D5
Manning Rd IP11 ... 152 E2
Manning's La IP22 ... 35 D5
Mannings La IP9 ... 144 A2
Mannington Cl 3 IP4 ... 140 F5
Manningtree High Sch CO11 ... 104 D2
Manningtree Mus* CO11 ... 104 E2
Manningtree Rd
Dedham CO7 ... 104 A3
East Bergholt CO7 ... 151 F3
Stutton IP9 ... 105 C5
Manningtree Sports Ctr CO11 ... 104 D2
Manningtree Sta CO11 ... 104 D3
Manor Ash Dr IP32 ... 123 E6
Manor Cl 9 Beccles NR34 ... 9 F4
3 Cavendish CO10 ... 76 E1
Walberswick IP18 ... 119 A2
Worlingham NR34 ... 9 F4
Manor Farm Cl 11 IP18 ... 119 D5
Manor Farm Rd
St John, Ilketshall NR34 ... 8 D3
1 Thistley Green IP28 ... 29 F6
Manor Garth IP31 ... 49 E6
Manor Gdns
7 Hopton on Sea NR31 ... 3 C6
Saxmundham IP17 ... 128 E2
Manor House Mus* IP33 ... 154 C1
Manor La Gosbeck IP6 ... 68 D2
14 Harwich CO12 ... 107 A2
1 Horringer IP29 ... 63 A8
Horringer IP29 ... 122 B1
Stutton IP9 ... 105 C5
Manor Pk Rd
Corton NR32 ... 3 C4
9 Southwold IP18 ... 119 D5
Manor Rd 10 Bildeston IP7 ... 79 F4
Brandon IP27 ... 5 E1
Bungay NR35 ... 110 B2
Clopton IP13 ... 69 E1
Elmsett IP7 ... 80 F2
Felixstowe IP11 ... 152 B8
Harwich CO12 ... 107 A2
Hasketon IP13 ... 146 D6
Haverhill CB9 ... 132 F5
Hessett IP30 ... 64 F7
Hopton-on-sea NR31 ... 3 B6
Ipswich IP4 ... 139 D8
11 Martlesham Heath IP5 ... 98 A8
Mildenhall IP28 ... 116 B4
Roydon IP22 ... 20 B3
Sudbury CO10 ... 148 C7
Trimley St Martin IP11 ... 153 I11
Manor Terr IP11 ... 107 F3
Manor View IP28 ... 116 D2
Manor Wlk 20 NR33 ... 11 B1
Manorhouse La 8 NR34 ... 111 B6
Manse La IP19 ... 40 C6
Mansfield Ave IP1 ... 134 F2
Manthorp Cl IP12 ... 147 B8
Manwick Rd IP11 ... 152 E2
Maple Cl
6 Great Bricett IP7 ... 80 D6
Ipswich IP2 ... 139 A3
12 Lakenheath IP27 ... 13 F2
Yaxley IP23 ... 37 B5
Maple Gn 3 IP31 ... 49 A6
Maple Gr IP6 ... 82 A6
Maple Hill CO10 ... 75 E1
Maple Rd
5 Lowestoft NR33 ... 114 F7
Stowupland IP14 ... 67 A6
Sudbury CO10 ... 148 F3
Maple Way
Beccles NR34 ... 111 C5
Eye IP23 ... 117 D3
Leavenheath CO6 ... 102 B7
Maples The IP5 ... 140 E8
Marbled White Dr IP9 ... 142 E8
March Pl 2 CO10 ... 76 A1
Marcus Cl CB9 ... 133 B5
Marcus Rd IP11 ... 153 D5
Mardle Rd Reydon NR34 ... 43 B8
Wangford with Henham NR34 ... 26 C1
Mardle The NR33 ... 114 C2
Mare Hill CO10 ... 75 D3
Margaret Rd 2 IP14 ... 124 C7
Margaret St IP11 ... 152 E5
Margate Rd IP3 ... 140 B3
Marham Rd 4 NR32 ... 113 B2
Maria St 7 CO12 ... 107 B3
Marigold Ave IP2 ... 138 E3

Marigold Dr **3** IP28 ....46 A8
Marina **6** NR32 ....113 E1
Marina Gdns IP11 .....152 E2
Marine Cl **3** NR31 ......3 B8
Marine Par
  12 Harwich CO12 ......107 B2
  Harwich CO12 ....107 B2
  Lowestoft NR33 ....115 D7
Mariner's Cl **2** NR31 ....3 B8
Mariner's Compass NR31 ..3 B8
Mariners Pk Cl **11** NR31 ...3 B7
Mariners St NR32 ....113 E2
Mariners Way IP15 ....130 D5
Marion Cl **5** NR34 .....111 C1
Mark Jennings La
  IP33 ....154 C3
Markant Cl IP27 ....6 C2
Market Cross Pl IP15 ..130 F4
Market Gr CO9 ....90 A1
Market Hill **8** Clare CO10 .90 A8
  Clopton IP13 ....83 D8
  Framlingham IP13 ....126 C3
  Haverhill CB9 ....132 E6
  Orford IP12 ....131 C2
  6 Sudbury CO10 .....148 C5
Market La
  Blundeston NR32 ....3 B4
  Burston & Shimpling IP22 .20 E5
  Somerleyton, Ashby &
    Herringfleet NR32 ......2 D6
Market Pl Hadleigh IP7 .149 D5
  2 Halesworth IP19 ...118 A3
  22 Harleston IP20 .....22 D6
  8 Kessingland NR33 ...11 B1
  11 Lavenham CO10 ....78 D4
  Saxmundham IP17 ....128 D3
Market Row NR34 ....111 B5
Market St
  1 Beccles NR34 .....111 B5
  Fordham CB7 ....29 A1
  3 Harwich CO12 ....107 C3
  Laxfield IP13 ....40 B3
  3 Mildenhall IP28 ...116 C4
  2 Newmarket CB8 ...121 A3
  16 Soham CB7 ....28 D4
Market Weston Rd
  IP22 ....35 A7
Markhams Cl CB9 .....132 D7
Marlborough Ct NR32 .112 F1
Marlborough Dr **4**
  CO10 ....148 D6
Marlborough Rd
  Ipswich IP4 ....140 A5
  Lowestoft NR32 ......112 F1
  Saxtead IP13 ....55 A4
  Southwold IP18 ......119 D6
Marlesford Rd IP13 .....71 B5
Marlow Rd IP1 ....140 A5
Marriott's Wlk **5** IP14 .124 D5
Marsden Cl **5** NR33 ...115 A3
Marsh La Aldeby NR34 ....2 A2
  Carlton Colville NR33 ..114 A4
  3 Earsham NR35 ....7 F4
  Felixstowe IP11 ......153 C8
  26 Kessingland NR33 ...11 C1
  Kessingland NR33 ......27 C8
  North Cove NR34 ......10 B5
  Reydon IP18 ....26 D2
  Somerleyton, Ashby &
    Herringfleet NR32 ......2 D6
  Worlingham NR34 ......9 F5
  Wortham IP22 ....20 A1
Marsh Rd Boxford CO10 .93 C3
  Fritton & St Olaves NR31 ..2 B7
  Lowestoft NR33 ......114 D7
  Stoke-by-nayland CO6 .103 C7
Marsh View NR34 ....111 D5
Marshall Cl IP5 ....141 C8
Marshalls Mdw **3** IP14 .67 A6
Marshams Piece **4**
  NR33 ....114 C5
Marshy La CO10 ....90 B4
Martello La IP11 .....153 D5
Martello Rd NR32 ....113 B4
Marten's La CO6 .....102 F8
Martin Cl
  Lowestoft NR33 ......114 D3
  Mildenhall IP28 ......116 D3
  8 Soham CB7 ....28 D3
Martin Rd **16** Burwell CB5 .44 A6
  Harleston IP20 ....22 E6
  Ipswich IP2 ....155 B1
Martinet Gn IP3 ......140 C1
Martin's Ave NR33 ...115 B6
Martins La IP13 ....69 F2
Martins Mdw CO **4** IP23 ..36 D2
Martins Rd CO10 .....148 F7
Martinsyde **9** IP3 ...140 B1
Martlesham Beacon Hill Prim
  Sch IP12 ....84 A1
Martlesham Heath Control
  Twr Mus ★ IP5 .....98 A8
Martlesham Rd IP13 .137 F3
Martyns Rise **5** CO10 .91 E7
Mary La CO10 ....75 C3
Maryon Rd IP3 ....140 B1
Mary's La IP7 ....80 E4
Masefield Rd Diss IP22 .20 D2
  Stowmarket IP14 .....124 B8
Mashay Rd CO9 ....90 B3
Maskell's La IP7 ......80 E4
Mason Ct **1** IP6 .....82 A5
Mason Gdns **2** IP28 ..29 F6
Mason Rd CB5 ....44 A7
Masons Cl IP4 ....139 F6
Mason's La **5** IP30 ....50 D1
Mast Cl NR33 ....114 B4

Masterson Gr IP5 ....141 C6
Mat Dawson Cl CB8 ..120 F6
Mather La IP20 ....22 B5
Mather Way IP2 ......155 C1
Matlock Cl **18** IP8 ...138 C2
Matlock Dale **11** NR33 .114 E3
Matson Rd IP1 ....138 F8
Matthews La CB8 ......74 C7
Maudslay Rd IP1 ....134 C2
Mautby Way NR33 ...114 F5
May Rd Ipswich IP3 ...140 C2
  Lowestoft NR32 ......113 C1
Maybury Rd IP3 .....140 B1
Maybush La IP11 .....153 C5
Maycroft Cl **2** IP1 ...135 A3
Mayes La CO12 ......106 D1
Mayfair Rd NR35 .....110 C3
Mayfield Cl6 ....102 B7
Mayfield Ave **12** NR33 ..11 C1
Mayfield La **7** IP5 ...98 A7
Mayfield Rd
  Bury St Edmunds IP33 .123 B1
  Ipswich IP4 ....140 C7
  Lowestoft NR33 ......114 C4
Mayfield Way IP14 ....52 E5
Mayfields
  Lakenheath IP27 ......109 C7
  6 Martlesham Heath IP5 .98 A7
Mayflower Ave
  8 Harwich CO12 .....107 C3
  Saxmundham IP17 ....128 B2
Mayflower Way
  14 Harleston IP20 .....22 D5
  Sudbury CO10 ....148 D8
Maynewater La IP33 ..154 C1
Maypole La CB8 ....60 C6
May's La CO7 ....103 F2
Mccalmont Way CB8 .121 E2
Mclaren Cl **1** NR33 ..111 C3
Mclean Dr **16** NR33 ....11 B1
Mead The CO10 ......148 F2
Mead Way IP14 ....52 E5
Meadow Barn IP14 ....66 C2
Meadow Cl
  Bury St Edmunds IP33 .122 E3
  8 Felixstowe IP11 ....107 D8
  Felsham IP30 ....65 A4
  Lavenham CO10 ....78 D3
  8 Soham CB7 ....28 D3
  Westhall IP19 ....25 B4
Meadow Ct
  4 Great Yarmouth NR31 ..3 B8
  16 Stanton IP31 ......34 E4
Meadow Dr
  Horringer IP29 ....63 A8
  Lakenheath IP27 .....109 D7
Meadow Gdns NR34 .111 A3
Meadow La
  Newmarket CB8 ......121 D1
  Sudbury CO10 ....148 C5
  Thurston IP31 ....49 E4
Meadow Prim Sch
  NR33 ....115 B6
Meadow Rd
  Bungay NR35 ....110 D2
  Lowestoft NR32 ......112 F4
Meadow Valley IP7 ....80 D5
Meadow View
  Needham Market IP6 ..125 C5
  Woolpit IP30 ....65 E8
Meadow View Rd
  CO10 ....148 B4
Meadow Way
  Assington CO10 ....92 F1
  8 Barrow IP29 ....47 A2
  Lowestoft NR33 ......114 C2
Meadow Wlk **3** IP17 ..72 C7
Meadowlands
  1 Blundeston NR32 ....3 A4
  11 Burwell CB5 ....44 A5
  Kirton IP10 ....98 D2
  4 Woolpit IP30 ....50 D1
Meadowlands Cl IP17 ..57 C8
Meadows The
  Drinkstone IP30 ....65 B7
  Worlingham NR34 .....30 B4
Meadows Way IP7 ...149 D6
Meadowside
  Blo' Norton IP22 ......18 E2
  Wickham Market IP13 .127 C7
Meadowside Gdns
  IP4 ....140 E8
Meadowsweet Cl
  Haverhill CB9 ....132 C7
  3 Lowestoft NR33 ...114 D5
Meadowvale Cl
  Beccles NR34 ....111 B2
  Ipswich IP4 ....139 F8
Meads The NR32 ....113 D5
Meadway **22** CO11 ..104 D2
Mear Cl IP12 ....85 C2
Mechanical Music Mus &
  Bygones ★ IP14 .....52 A6
Medway Rd IP3 ......139 F2
Meekings Rd CO10 ..148 F6
Meeting Field **10** CO10 .91 E8
Meeting La
  Grundisburgh IP13 ....83 E5
  Ridgewell CO9 ....89 D4
Melbourne Dr IP28 ..116 B9
Melbourne Rd
  Ipswich IP4 ....140 D7
  Lowestoft NR33 ......115 D5
Melford Cl **2** Burwell CB5 44 B5
  2 Ipswich IP4 ....140 F5
Melford Hall ★ CO10 ..77 E1
Melford Rd Acton CO10 .92 A8
  Cavendish CO10 ......76 F1

Melford Rd continued
  Lavenham CO10 ....78 C3
  Lawshall IP29 ....63 D1
  Stowmarket IP14 .....124 F4
  Sudbury CO10 ....148 B7
Melford Way IP11 ....152 C3
Mellis Cl CB9 ....74 A1
Mellis St **18** IP11 ...152 D5
Mellis Rd
  Gislingham IP23 ....36 D3
  Thrandeston IP21 .....37 B6
  Wortham IP22 ....36 E7
  Yaxley IP23 ....37 B5
Melplash Cl IP3 .....140 E4
Melplash Rd IP3 ....140 E4
Melrose Cl NR32 ....112 F5
Melrose Gdns
  Ipswich IP4 ....140 B8
  Newmarket CB8 ......120 E4
Melton Cl CB8 ....121 B2
Melton Grange Rd
  IP12 ....147 A6
Melton Hill IP12 ....147 B6
Melton Mdw Rd **4** IP12 .147 B6
Melton Prim Sch IP12 .147 B7
Melton Rd
  Hollesley IP12 ....99 F8
  Woodbridge IP12 ....147 B6
Melton Sta IP12 ....147 D7
Melville Rd IP4 .....139 F5
Mendham Cl **38** IP20 ..22 D6
Mendham La
  38 Harleston IP20 .....22 D6
  St Cross, South Elmham
    IP20 ....23 C6
Mendham Prim Sch
  IP20 ....23 A6
Mendham Rd IP20 ....23 A4
Mendip Dr IP5 ......140 F6
Mendip Rd NR32 ....112 C2
Mendlesham Prim Sch
  IP14 ....52 E4
Mendlesham Rd IP14 ..52 B5
Mercers Rd IP32 ....123 D7
Mere Cl IP31 ....49 C6
Mere Gdns IP4 ......140 F4
Mere La IP28 ....48 A6
Mere Side IP7 ....28 C4
Meredith Rd IP1 ....134 C2
Meriton Rise IP7 ...149 F4
Merivale Rd **17** CO11 .104 C2
Merlewood IP21 ....21 C5
Merlin Rd IP2 ....138 C3
Merriam Cl **5** CO11 .104 E4
Merrifield Rd IP4 ...134 E3
Merrion Cl **12** IP8 ...138 C2
Merrylees NR34 ....111 C4
Mersey Rd IP3 ......139 F2
Merville **9** NR33 ...114 E3
Messenger Cl NR35 .110 B2
Metfield Rd IP20 .....23 D3
Metfield St IP20 ......23 C3
Methersgate Hall Dr
  IP12 ....84 C1
Meynell Gdns CB8 ..121 A5
Micawber Mews **4** NR32 .3 A4
Michaelhouse Way **12**
  IP31 ....34 E4
Michaels Mount IP13 .137 D5
Michaelstowe Cl **1**
  CO12 ....106 E1
Michigan Cl IP5 ....141 B7
Mickfield Mews **16**
  IP11 ....152 D5
Micklegate Rd IP11 .152 E2
Micklesmere Dr **23** IP31 .34 B1
Mid Suffolk Leisure Ctr
  IP14 ....124 B7
Middle Dro CB7 ......28 E1
Middle Gn CO6 .....101 B1
Middle La NR34 ......10 D8
Middle Rd
  Blo' Norton IP22 ......18 F2
  Earsham IP20 ....7 C1
Middle Way CO10 ....91 E8
Middle Wlk NR32 ...113 C5
Middlefield Dr **3** IP14 ..66 B4
Middlefield Rd **10** CO11 .105 A2
Middleton Cl IP2 ...138 D2
Middleton Prim Sch
  IP17 ....58 A6
Middleton Rd
  Sudbury CO10 ....148 B4
  Yoxford IP17 ....57 E7
Midhurst Cl **3** IP32 .123 D6
Midmeadow **4** NR34 ..111 B5
Mid-Suffolk Light Rly Mus
  The ★ IP14 ....53 B4
Mights Rd IP18 .....119 C6
Milano Ave IP12 ......98 B8
Milburn Rd CB8 ......45 F3
Milden Cl **6** IP14 ...124 E3
Milden Rd
  Brent Eleigh CO10 .....79 A2
  Ipswich IP2 ....138 E5
Mildenhall Airfield
  IP28 ....30 B7
Mildenhall Dro IP28 ...12 F3
Mildenhall Mus ★
  IP28 ....116 C4
Mildenhall Rd
  Barton Mills IP28 .....116 C2
  Beck Row, Holywell
    Row & Kenny Hill IP28 .116 C8
  2 Bury St Edmunds IP32 .123 A8
  Fordham CB7 ....29 C1
  Icklingham IP28 ....31 A5
  Littleport CB7 ....12 A8

Mildenhall Stadium
  IP28 ....29 D8
Mildenhall Upper Sch
  IP28 ....116 E4
Mildmay Rd IP3 .....140 B1
Mile End IP27 ....14 E8
Mile End Rd CB7 ......12 A7
Miles Hawk Way IP28 .116 A5
Miles Paddock IP14 ...52 A6
Military Rd CB7 ....28 E2
Military Way **5** CO12 ..116 E1
Mill Bank **1** NR32 ...112 F2
Mill Broadway IP12 .131 C4
Mill Chase CB9 ....88 E3
Mill Cl **6** Burwell CB5 ..44 B5
  Capel St. Mary IP9 ...150 C3
  Exning CB8 ....120 B8
  1 Felixstowe IP11 ...107 D8
  Felixstowe IP11 .....152 D4
  Kirby Row NR35 ....8 E7
  1 Walsham-le-willows
    IP31 ....35 C2
  Woolpit IP30 ....50 D1
Mill Cnr CB7 ....28 C3
Mill Croft **9** CB7 ....28 D3
Mill Drift **9** CB7 .....5 A3
Mill Dro CB7 ....28 C3
Mill End La IP14 ......67 C7
Mill Field
  3 Aldeburgh IP15 ...130 E5
  Bramford IP8 ....134 B2
  Pettaugh IP14 ....68 E6
Mill Fields IP14 ......51 D1
Mill Gdns
  Bedingham NR35 ....7 B8
  Elmswell IP30 ....50 F2
Mill Hill (Tumulus) ★
  NR31 ....2 C8
Mill Hill Burgh IP13 ...83 F6
  Capel St. Mary IP9 ...150 C3
  Cotton IP14 ....52 A6
  Earl Soham IP13 ......54 E1
  Hadleigh IP7 ....94 B7
  Haverhill CB9 ....132 D5
  Lawford CO11 ....104 B2
  Leiston IP16 ....129 C2
  Manningtree CO11 ...104 E2
  Mettingham NR35 ......8 D5
  Newmarket CB8 ......121 A4
  Peasenhall IP17 ......56 F8
  Rattlesden IP30 ......65 D6
  Sudbury CO10 ....148 B5
  Wormingford CO6 ...101 F3
Mill Hill Dr IP19 ....118 A4
Mill Hoo IP12 ....99 E4
Mill La
  All Saints & St Nicholas,
    South Elmham IP20 ...23 E5
  Barnham IP24 ....16 B2
  Barrow IP29 ....47 A2
  Baylham IP6 ....81 F7
  Benhall IP17 ....72 C8
  Boyton IP12 ....86 B2
  Bradfield CO11 ......105 B1
  Bramford IP8 ....134 B1
  Brandeston IP13 ......70 A7
  Bruisyard IP17 ....56 C5
  7 Burwell CB5 ......44 B5
  Butley IP12 ....86 B6
  Campsey Ash IP13 ...127 F6
  Cavendish CO10 ......90 B8
  Chelmondiston IP9 ...106 D8
  Coddenham IP6 ....68 B1
  Combs IP14 ....124 B1
  Copdock & Washbrook
    IP8 ....138 A1
  Corton NR32 ....3 D4
  Cowlinge CB8 ....75 D8
  Creeting St Peter or
    West Creeting IP6 ...125 D8
  Dedham CO7 ....103 F4
  Dennington IP13 ......55 D5
  Ellingham NR35 ....6 F1
  Exning CB8 ....120 B8
  Felixstowe IP11 .....152 F4
  Fordham CB7 ....29 B1
  Garboldisham IP22 ...18 D3
  9 Great Blakenham IP6 ..82 A5
  Great Yeldham CO9 ...90 A2
  Haskston IP13 ....146 A7
  Henley IP6 ....82 D6
  Hockwold cum Wilton IP26 ..5 A3
  Hoo IP13 ....70 C6
  Hopton IP22 ....18 C3
  Hundon CO10 ....75 D3
  Kersey IP7 ....94 A7
  Layham IP7 ....149 E2
  Leiston IP16 ....129 C2
  18 Manningtree CO11 .104 E2
  Marlesford IP13 ......71 C5
  Metfield IP20 ....23 C3
  North Cove NR34 .....10 C4
  Polstead CO6 ....102 E8
  Pulham St Mary IP21 ..21 F8
  4 Redgrave IP22 .....36 A8
  St John, Ilketshall NR34 ...8 E2
  Shadingfield NR34 ....25 D7
  Somersham IP8 ....81 C3
  Southwold IP18 .....119 D5
  Stetchworth CB8 ......59 F5
  Stoke Ash IP23 ....52 F8
  Stonham Earl IP14 ...67 D5
  Stradbroke IP21 ......39 C5
  Sudbury CO10 ....148 B5
  Thetford IP24 ....16 B5
  Thurston IP31 ....49 D5
  Tunstall IP12 ....72 B1
  Weybread IP21 ....22 C3

Mill La continued
  Wickham Market IP13 ..127 C6
  2 Witnesham IP6 ......83 A5
  Woodbridge IP12 ....147 A5
  Woolpit IP30 ....50 D1
  Wrentham NR34 ....26 F5
Mill Piece IP10 .....145 C6
Mill Rd (South) IP33 .154 A1
Mill Rd
  Aldeby/Wheatacre/Burgh
    St Peter NR34 ....10 B8
  Ashley CB8 ....45 F1
  Badingham IP13 ......56 A7
  Barningham IP31 .....34 E7
  Battisford IP14 ....80 B8
  Beccles NR34 ....111 C2
  Birdbrook CO9 ....89 C5
  Botesdale IP22 ....36 B6
  Boxted CO4 ....102 F2
  Brockdish IP21 ....21 E3
  Brockley IP29 ....63 A1
  Burston & Shimpling IP22 ..20 E6
  Bury St Edmunds IP33 .154 A2
  Buxhall IP14 ....65 F4
  Chevington IP29 ......62 C6
  Clare CO10 ....90 B8
  Coldfair Green IP17 .129 A2
  Cotton IP14 ....52 A6
  East Bergholt CO7 ...151 E4
  Ellingham NR35 ....8 D7
  Foxearth CO10 ....91 B7
  Friston IP17 ....72 C6
  Gazeley CB8 ....46 B3
  Great Barton IP31 ....49 A6
  Halesworth IP19 ....118 E3
  Haverhill CB9 ....132 E5
  Hemley IP12 ....98 E5
  Hengrave IP28 ....48 A7
  Honington IP31 ....33 F5
  Hundon CO10 ....75 D4
  Ipswich IP3 ....140 F1
  Kedington CB9 ......133 E8
  Kirtling CB8 ....60 F3
  Lakenheath IP27 ....109 D6
  Laxfield IP13 ....40 B2
  Lowestoft NR33 .....115 C7
  Mendlesham IP14 .....52 D4
  Moulton CB8 ....46 A1
  Mutford NR34 ....10 D3
  Newbourne IP12 ......98 D5
  Occold IP23 ....37 F1
  Peasenhall IP17 ......56 E8
  Redlingfield IP23 .....38 C2
  Ridgewell CO9 ....89 D3
  Rumburgh IP19 ....24 B4
  Saxmundham IP17 ...128 C3
  Stambourne CO9 ......89 B2
  Swefling IP17 ....56 E3
  Thelnetham IP22 ......18 E1
  Westleton IP17 ....58 C7
  Weybread IP21 ....22 C4
  Winfarthing IP22 .....20 B8
  Wissett IP19 ....118 A5
  Worlingworth IP13 ...54 D7
  Wyverstone IP14 .....51 D6
Mill Rd S IP22 ....36 B6
Mill Reef Cl CB8 ....120 D7
Mill Rise **11** Holbrook IP9 105 E7
  Saxmundham IP17 ...128 C2
Mill St Gislingham IP23 ..36 B2
  Isleham CB7 ....29 C5
  Middleton IP17 ....58 A6
  Mildenhall IP28 .....116 B3
  Nayland CO6 ....102 D5
  Stowupland IP14 ......67 A6
  Westleton IP17 ....58 C7
Mill Tye CO10 ....148 E2
Mill View CB8 ....46 B3
Mill View Cl IP14 ...146 E5
Millbank CB8 ....120 F4
Millennium Grandstand
  CB8 ....120 C2
Millennium Way NR32 .113 A4
Miller Cl Elmswell IP30 ..50 F2
  Lowestoft NR33 .....115 B5
Millers Cl IP14 ......124 C3
Millers Ct **5** IP6 ....82 A5
Millers Dr IP21 ....21 B5
Millfield IP23 ....117 B3
Millfield Ave IP14 ..124 C5
Millfield Cl
  Ditchingham NR35 ...110 C8
  1 Saxmundham IP17 .128 C2
Millfield Dr IP14 .....65 F4
Millfield Gdns IP4 ..140 A7
Millfield Rd
  2 Barningham IP31 ...34 A8
  Walberswick IP18 ...119 A2
Millfields
  2 Peasenhall IP17 ....56 F8
  Wangford NR34 ....26 B2
Millfields Way CB9 ..132 E6
Millmarsh Dro IP27 .109 A7
Mills Dr NR32 ....3 D4
Mills La CO10 ....91 E6
Mills Mdw IP13 .....126 D3
Mills Rd CO10 ......148 E6
Mills The
  Framlingham IP13 ...126 C3
  Ipswich IP4 ....140 E8
Millside IP23 ....37 C4
Millway NR34 ....10 C4
Millway La
  Palgrave IP22 ....20 A1
  Wortham IP22 ....19 F1

Millwood Rd CO6 .....94 A3
Milner Rd Chilton CO10 ..92 B4
  Sudbury CO10 ....148 F6
Milner St IP14 ....139 E6
Milnrow 10 IP8 ....138 C2
Milton N Rd 4 IP14 ...124 D6
Milton Rd CO11 ......104 D1
Milton Rd E
  Lowestoft NR32 ......113 D1
  Stowmarket IP14 .....124 C6
Milton Rd S IP14 .....124 E6
Milton St IP4 ....140 B7
Mimosa Wlk NR32 ....113 B2
Minden CI IP33 ......154 C2
Minden Dr
  Bury St Edmunds IP33 ..122 D5
  Leiston IP16 ....129 D5
Minden Rd
  Lowestoft NR32 ......113 C2
  Sudbury CO10 ....148 D5
Minerva CI CB9 ......133 B4
Minos Rd NR32 ......113 C4
Minsmere House Hospl*
  IP4 ....140 C6
Minsmere Nature Reserve*
  IP17 ....58 E6
Minsmere Rd IP17 ....58 F8
Minsmere Rise IP17 ...58 A6
Minsmere Way CO10 ...92 B3
Minster Rd CB9 ......132 D7
Mirbeck's CI 6 NR34 ...9 F4
Misburgh Way NR31 ....3 C6
Mission La CO7 ......104 D6
Mission Rd IP22 ......20 D2
Mistley Secret Bunker*
  CO11 ....105 A2
Mistley Sta CO11 .....104 F2
Mistley Way IP12 .....146 F6
Mitchell Ave IP32 .....48 C5
Mitchery La IP14 .....65 E4
Mitford CI 11 ....135 A4
Mitford Rd IP17 ......72 B8
Mitre CI 6 IP30 ......50 D1
Mitre Way IP3 ....139 E4
Moat Farm CI IP4 ....139 F8
Moat La
  Alphamstone CO8 .....101 A6
  Rushbrooke with Rougham
  IP30 ....49 D1
Moat Rd Birdbrook CO9 ..89 B4
  Theberton IP16 ....57 F4
Mobbs Way NR32 .....112 C3
Mockbeggars Hall*
  IP8 ....134 C6
Moffat Ave IP4 ....136 B1
Moles La NR34 ....8 D1
Moll's La NR34 ....25 D5
Monarch CI IP32 .....132 A6
Monarch Way IP8 ....142 D8
Monastery Hill IP17 ...43 B1
Monckton Ave NR32 ..112 F2
Monckton Cres NR32 ..112 F2
Monet Sq 1 NR32 ....113 B5
Monewden Rd IP13 ...70 A3
Moneyhole Cnr CO10 ..78 E5
Moneypiece CI CB9 ...132 D5
Moneypot La IP22 ....19 B1
Monks CI IP11 ......153 D6
Monks Eleigh CE VC Prim
  Sch IP7 ....79 B2
Monks Gate IP8 .....138 A6
Monk's La CO7 ......103 E2
Monksgate IP24 ......16 B6
Monkshood CI NR33 ..114 F2
Monmouth CI IP2 ....139 B1
Montague Rd IP11 ...153 A4
Montana Rd IP5 .....141 A7
Montgomery Ave
  NR32 ....113 B4
Montgomery Rd IP2 ..139 B1
Monton Rise IP2 .....138 D2
Montpelier Dr 1 IP24 ..16 A5
Monument Farm Rd
  IP10 ....141 B4
Moon Hall La CB9 ...132 E3
Moonhall Bsns Pk
  CB9 ....132 E3
Moor Rd
  Burston & Shimpling IP21 ..21 B6
  Langham CO4 ....103 B2
  Middleton IP17 ......57 F6
Moorbridge La IP14 ...66 B8
Moore Rd Ipswich IP1 ..134 F3
  Rushbrooke with Rougham
  IP30 ....49 B2
Mooreland Dr IP31 ...49 C6
Moore's CI 17 IP14 ...53 F2
Moorfield Rd IP12 ...146 F6
Moorhall Cswy IP23 ..117 C1
Moor's Way IP12 ....146 E6
Moorsfield CO10 ....148 F2
Moot Hall (Museum)*
  IP15 ....130 F4
Moreton Hall Prep Sch
  IP32 ....123 D5
Morgan Ct IP6 ......134 C8
Morgan Dr IP1 ......134 C1
Morgan Mdw IP14 ...124 C2
Morland Prim Sch
  IP3 ....144 A8
Morland Rd 1 IP3 ...144 A8
Morley Ave IP12 ....146 F4
Morley CI 3 IP28 .....30 B8
Morleys La IP23 ......36 D3
Mormor La IP21 ......21 F4

Mornington Ave 2 IP1 .134 F1
Morris Way IP6 ......125 D4
Mors End 2 CO7 .....103 E5
Morston Hall Rd IP11 ..98 B1
Mortimer La IP28 .....29 E3
Mortimer PI 3 CO10 ...76 A1
Morton Peto CI NR32 ...3 D7
Morton Rd NR33 .....115 B4
Moss La IP6 ....135 F4
Mother Quy's IP24 ....15 C5
Mottram CI 14 IP8 ...138 C2
Moulton Ave CB8 ......46 A5
Moulton CE Prim Sch
  CB8 ....45 F3
Moulton Packhorse Bridge*
  CB8 ....45 F3
Moulton Rd
  Cheveley CB8 ....121 D4
  Gazeley CB8 ....46 B3
  Moulton CB8 ....45 F1
Mount CI 5 IP30 ......64 F8
Mount Dr IP3 ....140 F1
Mount Pleasant
  Framlingham IP13 ....126 B4
  Halesworth IP19 .....118 B5
  Lowestoft NR32 ......113 C3
  1 Peasenhall IP17 ...56 F8
  Southwold IP18 ......119 C8
Mount Rd
  Bury St Edmunds IP32 ..123 D6
  Haverhill CB9 ....132 C5
  Rushbrooke with Rougham
  IP30 ....49 A3
Mount St IP22 ....20 C3
Mountbatten CI CO10 .148 D8
Mountbatten Rd
  Bungay NR35 ....110 B2
  Lowestoft NR32 ......113 B4
  Sudbury CO10 ....148 D8
Mounts The IP17 .....56 F8
Mouse La IP30 ....49 C2
Moverley Way 1 IP15 .130 E5
Mow Hill IP6 ....83 A5
Mowbrays Rd IP13 ...126 D3
Mowlands IP9 ....150 F3
Moyes Rd NR32 .....112 D1
Moyn's Pk* CO9 ......88 F3
Moyse Ave 4 IP18 ...119 C8
Moyses Hall Mus*
  IP33 ....154 B2
Mulberry CI
  Beccles NR34 ....111 C5
  18 Feltwell IP26 .....4 E5
  Mildenhall IP28 ......4 F4
Mulberry Gdns 11 IP6 .82 A5
Mumford Rd IP1 ....138 E8
Munday's La IP12 ...131 B3
Mundford Prim Sch
  IP26 ....6 B8
Mundford Rd
  Brandon IP27 ....5 F2
  Thetford IP24 ....16 B7
  Weeting-with-broomhill
  IP27 ....6 A4
Mundy's Rd IP20 ....23 A5
Munnings CI
  Haverhill CB9 ....132 B7
  3 Lowestoft NR33 ...114 C3
Munnings Way CO11 .104 D3
Munson's La IP26 ....4 E6
Munson's PI IP26 ....4 E6
Murfitt's La CB7 ....29 A2
Muriel CI 4 IP7 .....149 E6
Murillo Dr 1 NR32 ...113 C6
Murray Rd IP3 ......140 A3
Murrayfield Prim Sch
  IP3 ....140 A3
Murrills Rd IP3 .....140 E1
Murton CI 10 CB5 ....44 A6
Museum of E Anglian Life*
  IP14 ....124 D5
Museum St IP1 .....155 B3
Musgrave CI 22 CO12 ..106 F1
Mustow St IP33 ....154 C2
Mutford CI NR32 ...112 F1
Mutford Gn IP27 ...27 D1
Mutford Wood NR33 ..10 D4
Mutfordwood La
  NR33 ....114 A2
Mutton La IP13 .....70 A8
Mylford CI IP32 ....123 D4
Mylodon Rd NR32 ..113 C4
Myrtle CI 20 Eriswell IP27 ..13 F2
  Lowestoft NR32 ......113 B2
Myrtle Rd IP3 ......139 E4

N

Nacton CE VC Prim Sch
  IP10 ....145 C5
Nacton CI 5 IP12 ....85 B3
Nacton Cres IP3 ....140 B2
Nacton La IP31 .....49 A6
Nacton Rd
  Felixstowe IP11 .....152 E1
  Ipswich IP10 ....144 D7
Nan Hazle's La IP22 .36 B4
Nansen Rd IP3 .....140 B2
Naples CI 5 NR31 ...3 C6
Narrow Way IP19 ...42 C6
Nash CI CO11 ......104 D3
Nash Gdns 2 IP3 ...144 B8
Nat Flatman St CB8 ..121 B3
National Horseracing Mus*
  CB8 ....121 B3
National Stud* CB8 ..59 B8
Naughton Gdns 8 IP14 124 E3

Naughton Rd IP7 ....80 C1
Naunton Rd IP12 ...146 E5
Navarre St IP1 .....155 B3
Naverne Mdw IP12 ..147 A5
Nayland Prim Sch
  CO6 ....102 D5
Nayland Rd
  Bures St Mary CO8 ..101 D4
  1 Felixstowe IP11 ..152 C3
  Great Horkesley CO6 ..102 D2
  Haverhill CB9 ....132 C4
  Little Horkesley CO6 ..102 C3
Neale CI IP16 ......129 B6
Neale St IP1 ....155 B3
Neath Dr IP2 ......139 A1
Neaves La IP21 .....39 B4
Nedging Rd IP7 .....79 F3
Needham La IP7 .....79 F4
Needham Lake Visitor Ctr*
  IP6 ....125 E4
Needham Mkt Mid Sch
  IP6 ....125 D4
Needham Mkt Sta IP6 .125 E4
Needham Rd
  Coddenham IP6 ......67 F1
  Needham IP20 ....22 C5
  Stowmarket IP14 ....124 E4
Needle Cnr IP9 .....106 B5
Nelson CI IP6 ....83 A8
Nelson Rd
  Bury St Edmunds IP33 ..154 A2
  1 Lowestoft NR33 ...115 A3
  Sudbury CO10 ....148 E7
Nelson Way
  Beccles NR34 ....111 A4
  Woodbridge IP12 ...146 F7
Nelson Wharf NR33 .114 F7
Neptune Sq IP3 ....155 C2
Neptune St IP3 .....115 C8
Ness Rd Arwarton IP9 ..106 D5
  Burwell CB5 ....44 B7
Nether Hill CO9 .....90 E2
Nether Rd 2 CO10 ...76 E1
Nethergate St
  Bungay NR35 ....110 A5
  Clare CO10 ....90 A7
  Hopton IP22 ....18 B2
Netherhall CI IP14 ...52 A1
Netley CI IP7 ....142 F8
Netley Rd IP33 .....122 D3
Nettlestead Rd IP8 ...81 D1
Neve Gdns IP28 .....30 A6
New Cangle Prim Sch
  CB9 ....132 D7
New Cardinal St IP1 ..155 A3
New Cheveley Rd CB8 .121 C3
New Comm Rd IP22 ..35 B8
New Cut 5 Bures CO8 ..101 C4
  8 Glemsford CO10 ....77 A2
  Hadleigh IP7 ....149 E6
  Halesworth IP19 ....118 B4
  Saxmundham IP17 ...128 D3
New Cut W IP2 .....155 C1
New Dro
  Beck Row, Holywell Row
   & Kenny Hill IP28 ...12 E1
  Soham CB7 ....28 A4
New England Way 2
  IP24 ....16 A5
New Gn Ave 13 IP31 ..49 E4
New Hampshire Way 5
  IP24 ....16 A5
New House La CO10 ..76 B3
New La IP9 ....105 F6
New Mkt NR34 .....111 B5
New Path 4 CB8 ....29 A1
New Pleasurewood Hills
  Leisure Pk* NR33 ...113 C8
New Queens Rd CO10 .148 C5
New Rd Ampton IP31 ..33 A1
  Aspall IP14 ....53 E4
  Badingham IP13 .....56 B8
  Barnby NR34 ....10 C4
  Barrow IP29 ....47 B3
  Beccles NR34 ....111 B7
  Brettenham IP24 ....17 B6
  5 Burwell CB5 ......44 A6
  Chevington IP29 .....62 C7
  Dickleburgh & Rushall
   IP21 ....21 A4
  Elmswell IP30 ....50 E2
  Exning CB8 ....120 B8
  Felixstowe IP11 ....152 C7
  Fritton & St Olaves NR31 ..2 B7
  Gissing IP22 ....20 F8
  Great Glemham IP17 ..71 E8
  Helmingham IP14 ....69 A5
  19 Harwich IP31 .....34 B1
  Little Livermere IP31 ..33 A2
  Long Melford CO10 ..91 D8
  Manningtree CO11 ...104 E2
  Marlesford IP13 .....71 C6
  Melton IP12 ....84 D6
  Mettingham NR35 ...110 F2
  Nedging-with-naughton
   IP7 ....80 C3
  Rumburgh IP19 .....24 C4
  Rushbrooke with Rougham
   IP30 ....49 D1
  St Cross, South Elmham
   IP20 ....23 D5
  Sibton IP17 ....41 D1
  Thelnetham IP22 ....35 B7
  Thrandeston IP21 ...37 C8
  Timworth IP31 ......48 E8
  Tivetshall St Mary NR15 ..21 B8

New Rd continued
  Tostock IP30 ....50 B2
  Troston IP31 ....33 D4
  Worlingworth IP13 ...54 F8
New River Gn CB8 ...120 B8
New St Chippenham CB7 ..29 E1
  Framlingham IP13 ...126 A4
  Fressingfield IP21 ...39 D8
  Glemsford CO10 .....77 A3
  4 Mildenhall IP28 ..116 C4
  Stradbroke IP21 .....39 A4
  Sudbury CO10 ....148 C6
  9 Woodbridge IP12 .147 A5
New St CI IP21 ......39 A4
New Way IP2 ....138 E6
New Wolsey Theatre*
  IP1 ....155 A3
Newall Rd 2 IP24 ...16 C7
Newark CI IP7 .....138 F1
Newark Rd
  3 Lakenheath IP27 ..13 F2
  Lowestoft NR33 ....115 B6
Newberry 7 IP7 ....79 F4
Newbourn Rd IP10 ..98 C4
Newbourne Gdns
  IP11 ....152 D3
Newbourne Rd
  Brightwell IP10 ......98 A4
  Martlesham IP12 ....84 B1
  Waldringfield IP12 ..98 C7
Newbury Rd IP14 ...140 C6
Newby Dr IP4 ......140 F5
Newcastle CI 6 IP27 ..13 F2
Newcombe Dr 16 IP26 ..4 E5
Newcombe Rd NR32 .113 C1
Newdelight Rd IP22 ..35 F2
Newell Rise IP6 ....134 C8
Newfen Gravel Dro
  IP27 ....109 A8
Newgate Beccles NR34 .111 B5
  Beccles NR34 ....111 B6
  Kirby Row NR35 ......8 E7
Newgate La NR35 ....8 E7
Newhaven Way IP7 ..149 E7
Newland Ave NR34 ..111 E4
Newlands 2 Elmsett IP7 .80 F1
  Otley IP6 ....69 D2
Newlands CI
  40 Harleston IP20 ...22 D6
  Lowestoft NR33 ....114 F3
Newlands La CO6 ...102 D5
Newman's Rd CO10 .148 C6
Newmarket Com Hospl
  CB8 ....120 F5
Newmarket Lawn Tennis
  Club CB8 ....120 E3
Newmarket Race Course
  CB8 ....120 B1
Newmarket Rd
  1 Ashley CB8 ....60 F8
  Barton Mills IP28 ...116 D1
  Burwell CB5 ....44 B5
  Bury St Edmunds IP33 ..122 D6
  Cowlinge CB8 ....61 B2
  Fordham CB7 ....44 E8
  Moulton CB8 ....45 F3
  Newmarket CB8 ....121 B8
  Red Lodge IP28 ......30 C2
  Risby IP28 ....47 C5
  Snailwell IP28 ......45 A5
Newmarket Sports Ctr
  CB8 ....121 A4
Newmarket Sta CB8 .121 B2
Newmarket Swimming Pool
  CB8 ....120 F3
Newmarket Upper Sch
  CB8 ....120 F4
Newmill La CO11 ...105 C4
Newnham Ave IP12 .146 D4
Newnham CI IP28 ..116 D5
Newnham Ct IP2 ...138 E1
Newnham Dro CB5 ...44 A6
Newnham La 14 CB5 ..44 A6
Newport Ave CB7 ....29 C1
Newport CI 7 IP27 ...13 F2
Newquay CI IP5 ....140 F6
Newry Ave IP11 ....152 F4
Newson Ave NR34 ...10 C3
Newson St IP1 .....155 A4
Newson's Mdw NR32 .113 C2
Newthorpe IP30 ....49 C1
Newton Croft CO10 .148 C5
Newton Rd
  17 Harwich CO12 ...107 A2
  Ipswich IP3 ....140 A4
  Stowupland IP14 ....124 D8
  Sudbury CO10 ......148 D5
Newton St IP1 .....155 C3
Nicholas Dr IP18 ...119 C7
Nicholas Rd IP11 ...152 C4
Nicholls CI 7 IP13 ...84 F7
Nichols CI 24 CO11 .104 D2
Nicholson Dr NR34 ..111 C2
Nicholson Sq 2 NR32 .113 C2
Nicholsons Ct CO10 ..92 D3
Nick's La IP23 .....117 B6
Nidderdale 8 NR33 ..114 C3
Nightall Rd 5 CB7 ...28 C5
Nightingale Ave IP18 .119 B7
Nightingale CI
  Bury St Edmunds IP33 ..154 A1
  19 Harwich CO12 ...106 F1
  5 Mildenhall IP28 ..116 D4
  5 Stowmarket IP14 ...67 A5
Nightingale Hill CO4 .103 C3
Nightingale La
  9 Feltwell IP26 ......4 E5
  3 Feltwell IP26 ......4 E5

Nightingale Piece
  IP12 ....131 C3
Nightingale Rd
  Ipswich IP3 ....144 A8
  Lowestoft NR33 ....115 B6
Nightingale Sq 5 IP3 .144 A8
Nimbus Way IP28 ...120 E8
Nine Acres IP2 .....138 D6
Ninfield CI NR33 ...114 D4
Noahs Dr 5 NR33 ...11 B1
Noakes Rd IP7 ......94 F1
Noel CI NR31 ....3 F6
Noel Murless Dr CB8 .120 F6
Noel Rd NR32 .....112 C1
Noel's Wlk NR34 ...111 B6
Noller's La IP19 ....24 F4
Nonsuch Mdw 2 CO10 .148 C4
Norbury Rd IP4 ....140 B7
Nordalls The 16 NR33 ..11 C1
Norfolk & Suffolk Aviation
  Mus* NR35 ....7 D2
Norfolk Ave CB8 ....120 C5
Norfolk Cres 1 IP13 .126 C3
Norfolk Rd
  Bury St Edmunds IP32 ..123 A8
  9 Honington IP31 ...33 D5
  Ipswich IP4 ....155 C3
  Thetford IP24 ....16 C6
  Wangford NR34 ......26 B2
  Wangford with Henham
   NR34 ....26 B1
Norfolk St NR32 ....113 B1
Norgate La IP21 .....21 B2
Norman CI
  Felixstowe IP11 ....153 D6
  Woodbridge IP12 ...147 A7
Norman Cres IP3 ...140 A2
Norman Rd
  6 Bury St Edmunds IP32 .48 C5
  Bury St Edmunds IP32 ..122 F8
  23 Manningtree CO11 .104 E2
Norman Way 1 CO10 .148 C6
Normandie Way 8 CO8 101 C4
Normandy CI IP4 ...124 D3
Normandy Rd NR32 .113 B4
Normanhurst CI NR32 .113 A2
Normanston Dr 5 NR32 .113 B2
Nornea La CB7 .....28 A8
Norse Ave IP29 .....64 A3
North Acres IP8 ....81 A6
North Ave CB9 .....132 C6
North CI Bacton IP14 ..51 F6
  Ipswich IP4 ....135 E1
  9 Stanton IP31 ......34 E4
North Cres CB9 .....88 D4
North Dr
  Newmarket CB8 ....120 F5
  1 Soham CB7 ....28 C5
North End CB8 .....120 B8
North End Ave IP16 ..73 F6
North End Rd CO9 ...90 C2
North Entrance IP17 .128 C3
North Field CI 3 NR32 .112 F5
North Gn Rd
  Cratfield IP19 ......40 C7
  Pulham St Mary IP21 ..22 A8
North Hill IP12 .....146 F6
North Hill Gdns IP4 .139 E6
North Hill Rd IP4 ...139 E6
North Lawn IP4 ....140 B8
North Lopham Rd
  NR16 ....19 A7
North Par
  Lowestoft NR32 ....113 D4
  Southwold IP18 ....119 E6
North Par Gdns IP18 .119 E6
North PI IP28 ......116 C4
North Rd
  Great Yeldham CO9 ..90 A1
  Lakenheath IP27 ....109 E4
  Southwold IP18 ....119 D6
North Rise IP3 .....148 E4
North St Burwell CB5 ..44 A6
  Freckenham IP28 ....29 E3
  Hundon CO10 ....75 D4
  11 Manningtree CO11 .104 E2
  Steeple Bumpstead CB9 .88 E4
  Sudbury CO10 ......148 C6
  Wicken CB7 ....28 A1
North St Par 5 CO10 .148 C5
North Terr IP28 ....116 C5
North Warren IP15 ..130 C8
Northacre 12 NR33 ..11 B1
Northcroft 1 CO10 ..148 C5
Northern Rd CO10 .148 F7
Northern Way IP32 ..48 C5
Northfield Pk CB7 ..28 C5
Northfield Rd
  Onehouse IP14 ......66 C6
  Soham CB7 ....28 C5
Northfield St Nicholas Sch
  NR32 ....113 C3
Northgate
  Beccles NR34 ....111 B6
  11 Harleston IP20 ...22 D5
  Lowestoft NR32 ....113 B2
Northgate Ave NR32 .154 B4
Northgate Cty High Sch
  IP4 ....136 A1
Northgate Sports Ctr
  IP4 ....136 A2
Northgate St
  Bury St Edmunds IP33 ..154 C3
  Ipswich IP1 ....155 B3
Northumberland Ave
  IP32 ....122 E8
Northwood CI NR33 .114 F6

Norton CE Prim Sch
　IP31 ....50 B5
Norton Rd
　Haverhill CB9 ....132 C4
　Hunston IP31 ....50 C6
　11 Thurstow IP31 ....49 D4
　Tostock IP30 ....50 B2
Norway Cres 2 CO12 ......106 F2
Norwich La
　Bardwell IP31 ....34 C8
　Coney Weston IP31 ....17 E2
Norwich Rd Barham IP6 ..82 A6
　Claydon IP6 ....134 C8
　Denton IP20 ....7 B3
　5 Dickleburgh & Rushall
　　IP21 ....20 F1
　Ditchingham NR35 ....110 A8
　Earsham NR35 ....7 E5
　Gillingham NR34 ....111 A8
　Halesworth IP19 ....118 C5
　Ipswich IP1 ....155 A3
　5 Lakenheath IP27 ....1.3 F2
　Lakenheath IP27 ....109 F1
　Lowestoft NR32 ....113 C1
　Pulham St Mary IP21 ....21 B5
　Scole IP21 ....21 B5
　Stockton NR34 ....9 A8
　Thetford IP24 ....16 C6
　Thetford IP24 ....16 C6
Norwich Rd Sch IP24 ....16 C6
Norwood Rd IP27 ....14 E8
Notcutts CO7 ....151 E3
Notley Dr CB9 ....132 A7
Notley Ent Pk CO7 ....95 A2
Notley Rd NR33 ....115 A7
Nottidge Rd IP4 ....139 E6
Nova Scotia La IP7 ....79 B4
Nowton Rd
　Bury St Edmunds IP33 .....123 C1
　Nowton IP29 ....63 E8
Noyes Ave IP13 ....40 B3
Nuffield Hospl (Private)
　IP33 ....154 C1
Nunn Cl 1 IP12 ....84 A1
Nunnery Gn 2 CB8 ....61 E2
Nunn's Hill IP19 ....24 C3
Nunn's La IP19 ....23 E1
Nuns' Bridges Rd IP24 ...16 B5
Nuns Wlk CO9 ....89 F1
Nursery Cl CB7 ....29 B4
Nursery La IP26 ....5 A2
Nursery Rd CO10 ....148 F2
Nursery Wlk IP11 ....152 F4
Nursey Cl NR35 ....8 D7
Nuttery Vale IP23 ....38 B6

O

Oak Ave NR34 ....111 F5
Oak Cl
　Bury St Edmunds IP28 ....48 C6
　Felixstowe IP11 ....152 E4
　4 Great Finborough IP14 ..66 B4
Oak Cres IP23 ....117 C3
Oak Dr 6 IP28 ....30 B8
Oak Eggar Chase IP8 ....142 D8
Oak Gn IP19 ....118 B2
Oak Gr
　Fornham St Martin IP31 ......48 D5
　Sproughton IP8 ....138 A6
Oak Hill Cl NR34 ....26 E5
Oak Hill La IP32 ....139 B3
Oak La Beccles NR34 ......111 D2
　Cheveley CB8 ....60 E6
　Elmswell IP30 ....50 F3
　Lakenheath IP27 ....13 F2
　Rushbrooke with Rougham
　　IP30 ....64 D8
　Woolpit IP30 ....65 E8
Oak Mdw Cl IP19 ....42 C6
Oak Rd 3 Sudbury CO10 ..92 B3
　Sudbury CO10 ....148 F4
Oak St IP26 ....4 E5
Oak Tree Way 8 IP20 ....22 D5
Oak Way IP19 ....118 A1
Oakdene IP10 ....98 D2
Oakes Cl IP32 ....122 E7
Oakes Rd IP32 ....122 E7
Oakey Field Rd 6 IP31 .....49 E4
Oakey Ley IP30 ....64 D6
Oakfield Rd Bacton IP14 ..52 A6
　Copdock & Washbrook
　　IP8 ....142 A6
Oakfield Wood Nature
　Reserve ★ CO11 ....105 E3
Oakland 15 CO12 ....107 B2
Oaklands CO6 ....102 B8
Oaklands Dr IP27 ....14 D8
Oakley Church La IP21 .....37 F8
Oakley Rd
　11 Harwich CO12 ....106 E1
　Ramsey & Parkeston
　　CO12 ....106 E1
Oaks Bsns Pk CB8 ....120 E7
Oaks Dr CB8 ....120 F7
Oaks La NR34 ....2 B1
Oaks The
　7 Horringer IP29 ....63 A8
　Martlesham Heath IP5 .....141 F6
　Soham CB7 ....28 D3
　Wattisfield IP22 ....35 C5
　Woolpit IP30 ....65 F8
Oaksmere Gdns 8 IP2 ...139 A2
Oakwood Pk IP17 ....57 D7
Oakwood Rd NR33 ....114 F5
Oast Ct IP33 ....154 C1

Oatfields 6 IP21 ....39 D8
Oatlands Cl 4 NR33 ....114 E4
Oban St IP1 ....155 A4
Occold Prim Sch IP23 .....37 F1
Occold Rd IP23 ....38 B2
Offton Rd Elmsett IP7 ......81 A2
　Great Bricett IP7 ....80 F5
Ohio Cl 4 NR33 ....114 E3
Old Barn Rd CO8 ....101 C3
Old Barningham Rd 1
　IP31 ....34 E4
Old Barrack Rd IP12 ......146 E4
Old Brandon Rd IP26 ....4 F5
Old Buckenham Hall Sch
　IP7 ....79 B7
Old Bungay Rd NR35 ....8 D8
Old Bury Rd
　Alpheton CO10 ....78 A6
　Lackford IP28 ....31 F1
　Palgrave IP22 ....37 A8
　Stanton IP31 ....34 E4
　Stuston IP21 ....20 D1
　Wortham IP22 ....36 F8
Old Cattle Mkt IP1 ....155 B2
Old Church La
　Bulmer CO10 ....91 C1
　Westley IP33 ....34 E4
Old Church Rd NR31 ....3 B6
Old Clements La 5
　CB9 ....132 D5
Old Convent Orch
　IP33 ....154 B1
Old Dairy Bsns Pk IP31 ....49 B5
Old Farm Rd
　Beccles NR34 ....111 C5
　4 Lakenheath NR33 ....114 D5
Old Forge Cl IP22 ....36 D8
Old Foundry Pl IP16 ....129 C6
Old Foundry Rd IP4 ....155 C3
Old Gram La NR35 ....110 B3
Old Hall Cl 2 IP30 ....82 D6
Old Hall La Bentley IP9 ....95 F2
　Bury St Edmunds IP28 ....48 D5
　Cockfield IP30 ....64 D5
　Westleton IP17 ....58 B8
Old Hall Mdw IP30 ....65 D6
Old Hall Rd IP13 ....56 E8
Old Harleston Rd NR35 .....7 E3
Old Haverhill Rd CB9 ....74 F2
Old High Rd
　Roydon IP22 ....20 B3
　Yoxford IP17 ....57 D7
Old Homes Rd 7 IP16 .....73 F6
Old House La CO4 ....103 A1
Old House Rd CO6 ....102 D1
Old Ipswich Rd IP6 ....134 C7
Old Kirton Rd IP11 ....107 D4
Old La
　Bradfield Combust with
　　Stanningfield IP29 ....63 F3
　Corton NR32 ....113 B8
　Thelnetham IP22 ....35 C6
Old London Rd IP9 ....150 D1
Old Maids' La IP13 ....70 A7
Old Methwold Rd IP26 ......4 E6
Old Mill Dr IP21 ....21 F8
Old Mill La
　Barton Mills IP28 ....116 F2
　Beccles NR34 ....111 B4
Old Mill Rd CO4 ....103 B3
Old Mill Terr 2 NR34 .....111 B6
Old Mkt NR34 ....111 B6
Old Mkt Pl 21 IP20 ....22 D6
Old Mkt Plain 8 NR32 ....113 E2
Old Mkt St IP14 ....52 E4
Old Nelson St 4 NR32 ....113 E1
Old Newton CE Prim Sch
　IP14 ....52 A1
Old Norwich Rd
　Whitton IP1 ....134 D5
　Yaxley IP23 ....37 C5
Old Orch IP7 ....149 F1
Old Orch Cl IP19 ....118 A2
Old Paper Mill La 8
　IP6 ....134 C8
Old Post Office La
　Blaxhall IP12 ....72 A4
　Kirby Row NR35 ....8 E7
　Sutton IP12 ....99 A8
Old Post Office Rd
　IP29 ....62 C6
Old Priory Gdns NR34 .....26 E4
Old Rd The CO6 ....102 B8
Old Rectory Cl
　2 Claydon IP6 ....82 B5
　6 Roydon IP22 ....20 A3
Old Rectory Gdns 3
　IP23 ....37 F1
Old Rectory La IP29 ....77 E6
Old Rectory Rd IP13 ....56 A6
Old Rly Rd Alburgh IP20 ...7 B2
　Bungay NR35 ....110 A4
Old Rope Wlk CB9 ....132 C5
Old Sch Cl
　Brampton with Stoven
　　NR34 ....25 E5
　5 Burwell CB5 ....44 B6
　4 Soham CB7 ....28 D5
Old Sch La CB8 ....59 F1
Old Sch Rd IP29 ....63 A5
Old Sch The NR34 ....10 E1
Old Schools Ct IP30 ....50 E2
Old St IP14 ....51 C1
Old St The IP9 ....150 F3
Old Sta Rd
　Halesworth IP19 ....118 B5
　Mendlesham IP14 ....52 E3
　Newmarket CB8 ....121 B4

Old Stores Cl IP13 ....54 E7
Old Stowmarket Rd
　IP30 ....50 D1
Old Town La IP33 ....123 C1
Old Vicarage Dr IP31 ....50 E7
Old Vicarage Rd 13
　CO12 ....107 A2
Oldfield Rd IP8 ....138 B1
Oldhall IP9 ....106 F6
Olding Rd IP33 ....122 D6
Olive Cl 2 IP27 ....13 F2
Olive Ct NR32 ....113 B4
Oliver Cl NR33 ....114 D2
Oliver Rd IP33 ....122 C6
Olivers Cl CO10 ....91 E8
Olympus Cl IP1 ....134 C2
One Eyed La IP21 ....22 D3
Onehouse La IP1 ....135 C1
Onehouse Rd IP14 ....124 B6
Onner's La IP16 ....58 C4
Ontario Rd NR33 ....115 C6
Opal Ave Ipswich IP1 .....134 D1
　Ipswich IP1 ....138 D8
Orch Way The 2 IP29 ......63 A8
Orchard Ave NR33 ....114 E6
Orchard Cl
　2 Blundeston NR32 ....3 A4
　Elmswell IP30 ....50 F3
　Great Livermere IP31 ....33 C2
　6 Haverhill CB9 ....132 D5
　Lidgate CB8 ....61 C4
　2 Ramsey & Parkeston
　　CO2 ....106 D1
　Ridgewell CO9 ....89 D3
　Risby IP28 ....47 D5
　Rushbrooke with Rougham
　　IP30 ....64 D8
　Woodbridge IP12 ....147 A7
Orchard Croft 2 NR33 ....114 E4
Orchard Dr IP14 ....65 F4
Orchard End 16 IP13 ....83 E5
Orchard Farm Barns 2
　IP29 ....47 A2
Orchard Farm Bsns Pk
　CB7 ....28 C7
Orchard Gate
　Ipswich IP2 ....138 C5
　1 Needham Market IP6 ...125 D5
Orchard Gn NR34 ....111 C4
Orchard Gr
　Claydon IP6 ....134 C7
　Ipswich IP5 ....141 A7
Orchard La
　3 Blundeston NR32 ....3 A4
　Thurston IP31 ....49 E5
Orchard Pl IP13 ....127 B6
Orchard Rd
　6 Bramford IP8 ....134 A4
　Leiston IP16 ....129 C5
Orchard Rise
　Badingham IP13 ....56 A7
　Beccles NR34 ....111 F4
Orchard Row CB7 ....28 E2
Orchard St
　Bury St Edmunds IP33 .....154 B3
　Ipswich IP4 ....155 C3
Orchard The
　5 Ashley CB8 ....60 F8
　Brandon IP27 ....5 F1
　Felsham IP30 ....65 A4
　Shadingfield NR34 ....25 B7
Orchard Valley IP19 ....118 C4
Orchard Way
　Badwell Ash IP31 ....50 F7
　12 Barrow IP29 ....47 A2
　4 Burwell CB5 ....44 A6
　9 Glemsford CO10 ....77 A2
　Scole IP21 ....21 A2
Orchards The 1 IP13 ....40 B3
Orchid Cl
　Halesworth IP19 ....118 C4
　Ipswich IP2 ....138 E4
Orchid Way IP6 ....125 D3
Orchids Cl NR35 ....110 D3
Oregon Rd IP1 ....134 C8
Orford Castle & Visitor Ctr★
　IP12 ....131 B2
Orford CE VA Prim Sch
　IP12 ....131 B3
Orford Dr NR32 ....113 A2
Orford Ness National Nature
　Reserve★ IP12 ....87 C3
Orford Ness National Trust★
　IP12 ....131 C1
Orford Rd
　Bromeswell IP12 ....147 F7
　Butley IP12 ....86 A6
　Felixstowe IP11 ....152 E1
　Haverhill CB9 ....132 D4
　Tunstall IP12 ....71 F2
Orford St IP1 ....155 A4
Oriel Cl CO10 ....148 F4
Orkney Cl CB9 ....133 B5
Orkney Rd 4 IP4 ....136 A1
Orttewell Rd IP32 ....123 E6
Orvis La CO7 ....151 E3
Orwell Ave IP17 ....128 C4
Orwell Dr 1 NR32 ....112 F3
Orwell High Sch IP11 .....152 E5
Orwell Jun Sch IP3 ....139 F1
Orwell Pk Sch IP10 ....145 B3
Orwell Pl IP4 ....155 C3
Orwell Rd
　Felixstowe IP11 ....152 E4
　10 Harwich CO12 ....107 B2
　Ipswich IP3 ....140 A4
　Stowmarket IP14 ....124 D4
Orwell Ret Pk IP2 ....139 A5

Orwell Rise 10 IP9 ....106 C8
Orwell View Rd IP9 ....106 F6
Osborne Rd IP3 ....140 A4
Osborne St 4 NR32 ....113 E3
Osier Cl IP12 ....147 B6
Osier Rd IP33 ....154 B3
Osprey Rd CB9 ....133 A5
Oswyn Cl IP32 ....123 D4
Otley Coll IP6 ....69 C1
Otley Ct 6 IP11 ....152 D5
Otley Hall★ IP6 ....69 C2
Otley Prim Sch IP6 ....69 C2
Otley Rd IP12 ....85 C2
Otten Rd CO10 ....90 D5
Oulton Broad N Sta
　NR32 ....112 F1
Oulton Broad Prim Sch
　NR32 ....112 C2
Oulton Broad S Sta
　NR33 ....114 D7
Oulton Broad Water Sports
　Ctr NR33 ....114 D7
Oulton Cl 6 CO12 ....106 F2
Oulton Rd Flixton NR32 ..112 F7
　Ipswich IP3 ....139 F2
　Lowestoft NR32 ....112 F5
Oulton St NR32 ....112 F4
Ousden Rd IP29 ....62 A6
Out Northgate IP33 ....154 B4
Out Risbygate IP33 ....122 E6
Out Westgate IP33 ....154 B1
Outney Rd NR35 ....110 A4
Overbury Hall Rd IP7 .....149 D1
Owell The IP31 ....49 E6
Oxer Cl IP30 ....50 F2
Oxford Cl
　Mildenhall IP28 ....116 A4
　Sudbury CO10 ....148 E4
Oxford Rd 2 Feltwell IP26 ..4 E5
　Ipswich IP4 ....139 E5
　Ipswich IP5 ....141 A7
　Lowestoft NR32 ....113 D3
　25 Manningtree CO11 .....104 E2
Oxford St CB8 ....120 B8

P

Packard Ave IP3 ....140 B2
Packard Pl IP8 ....134 B2
Packards La
　Fordham CO6 ....102 A1
　Wormingford CO6 ....101 F1
Packway La IP31 ....50 A5
Packway The IP20 ....23 A7
Paddock Farm IP31 ....34 D8
Paddock Hill NR33 ....114 F2
Paddock Rd 13 IP20 ....22 D6
Paddock St CB7 ....28 D4
Paddock The 16 IP31 ....34 B1
Paddock Way
　Chedburgh IP29 ....62 C4
　Troston IP31 ....33 D3
Paddock Wood Cl 8
　NR33 ....114 C4
Paddocks Dr CB8 ....121 A2
Paddocks Gn NR34 ....111 F4
Paddocks Prim Sch
　CB8 ....120 E4
Paddocks The
　Ashen CO10 ....89 E5
　6 Bures CO8 ....101 C4
　12 Burwell CB5 ....44 A5
　Halesworth IP19 ....118 C4
　3 Martlesham Heath IP5 ..98 A8
　Tuddenham St Martin
　　IP6 ....136 B5
　Worlington IP28 ....30 B4
Padstow Rd IP5 ....141 A6
Pageant Pl IP13 ....126 E3
Page's Cl IP14 ....124 C6
Pages Hill Rd IP29 ....63 B6
Paget Cl IP6 ....125 C5
Paget Pl CB8 ....121 A6
Paget Rd IP1 ....155 A4
Pains Cl 2 NR34 ....9 F4
Pains Hill IP14 ....67 F6
Pakefield Mid Sch
　NR33 ....115 A3
Pakefield Rd NR33 ....115 A3
Pakefield St NR33 ....115 B4
Pakenham Rd IP31 ....49 D6
Palace La CB7 ....45 B8
Palace St 4 IP4 ....121 A3
Palgrave VC Prim Sch
　IP22 ....20 C1
Palmcroft Cl 10 IP1 ....135 A4
Palmcroft Rd IP1 ....135 A4
Palmer Cl NR32 ....113 B6
Palmer Dr IP27 ....109 C2
Palmer St IP31 ....35 C1
Palmer's La IP18 ....119 A2
Palmerston Rd IP4 ....139 E6
Palmerswent Cl CO10 ......91 B7
Pamment's La IP28 ....29 F6
Pannels Cl 5 CO10 ....77 A2
Pantile La 12 CB5 ....44 A4
Papeley Mdw NR29 ....47 B2
Paper Mill La IP8 ....134 B4
Parade Rd N 18 NR33 .....115 D8
Parade Rd S NR33 ....115 D8
Paradise Pl IP16 ....129 C5
Pardoe Pl IP4 ....140 E5
Parish Bush Dro CB7 ....12 A1

Park Ave
　Felixstowe IP11 ....153 B5
　3 Fornham St Martin IP28 ..48 C6
　Newmarket CB8 ....121 B3
　Saxmundham IP17 ....128 C3
Park Cl
　2 Bentwaters Airfield
　　IP12 ....85 D8
　1 Lowestoft NR33 ....114 D4
　5 Martlesham Heath IP5 ..98 A8
　4 Moulton CB8 ....45 F3
　Sudbury CO10 ....148 E6
Park Cotts CB8 ....121 B2
Park Dr NR34 ....111 E4
Park End IP7 ....128 C2
Park Farm Dr
　Barton Mills IP28 ....30 C2
　Stanton IP31 ....34 E3
Park Farm La
　Euston IP24 ....33 E8
　Hoxne IP21 ....38 E6
Park Hill IP16 ....129 C6
Park La Aldeburgh IP15 ...130 E4
　Bulmer CO10 ....91 C2
　Charsfield IP13 ....70 C3
　Eye IP23 ....117 D1
　Glemsford CO10 ....77 B3
　Hawstead IP29 ....63 D7
　Kirton IP10 ....98 E3
　Langham CO4 ....103 C2
　Newmarket CB8 ....121 B3
　Southwold IP18 ....119 D4
　Thornham Parva IP23 ....37 A3
Park Mdws NR32 ....112 F6
Park N IP1 ....139 D8
Park Pl IP17 ....57 D7
Park Rd
　Aldeburgh IP15 ....130 D4
　Benhall IP17 ....72 A7
　Burwell CB5 ....44 A5
　Bury St Edmunds IP33 .....122 D4
　Cheveley CB8 ....60 D7
　Combs IP14 ....124 B2
　Diss IP22 ....20 C2
　Drinkstone IP30 ....50 B1
　East Bergholt CO7 ....104 D5
　Great Horkesley CO6 ....102 D4
　Grundisburgh IP13 ....83 E5
　Halesworth IP19 ....118 A5
　3 Harwich CO12 ....107 B2
　Haverhill CB9 ....132 B7
　Ipswich IP1 ....139 C8
　Lavenham CO10 ....78 D4
　Letheringham IP13 ....70 D4
　Lowestoft NR32 ....113 D3
　Needham Market IP6 ....125 D4
　St Cross, South Elmham
　　IP20 ....23 C7
　Southolt IP23 ....54 A8
　Stoke-by-nayland CO6 ......102 F6
　Sudbury CO10 ....148 E6
　Wetherden IP14 ....51 A1
Park St CO6 ....102 E7
Park The 3 IP31 ....49 E6
Park View
　Botesdale IP22 ....36 B7
　Weeting IP27 ....5 E3
　Wetherden IP14 ....51 A1
Park View Rd IP1 ....135 B1
Park Wlk IP19 ....118 E5
Parker Ave IP11 ....152 B4
Parker's Dro 3 IP28 ....29 F6
Parkers Pl 1 IP5 ....98 A8
Parker's Rd IP14 ....52 E4
Parker's Way CO6 ....102 D5
Parkers Wlk CB8 ....120 E8
Parkeston Rd
　Felixstowe IP11 ....152 D4
　Harwich CO12 ....107 A2
Parkhill NR32 ....112 F5
Parklands Cl 9 CO10 ....77 B3
Parklands Gn 2 IP28 ....48 C6
Parklands The NR33 ....114 D4
Parklands Way 41 IP20 ....22 D6
Parkside
　Chippenham CB7 ....45 C8
　Mildenhall IP28 ....30 C8
　3 Stanton IP31 ....34 E4
Parkside Ave IP4 ....155 C4
Parkside Dr NR32 ....113 A2
Parkway
　Bury St Edmunds IP33 .....154 A2
　Wickham Market IP13 ......127 C7
Parkway Mid Sch CB9 ....132 B6
Parkwood Dr CO10 ....148 C8
Parliament Rd IP4 ....140 B5
Parmenter Dr 13 CO10 .....92 B3
Parnell Cl IP1 ....134 F3
Parnell La IP30 ....50 D3
Parnell Rd IP1 ....134 F3
Parnham Pl 2 IP4 ....140 F5
Parr Rd CB8 ....132 B4
Parrington Way 26
　CO11 ....104 D2
Parsonage Cl
　5 Burwell CB5 ....44 A5
　Felixstowe IP11 ....152 D4
Parsonage Farm La
　CB8 ....60 C5
Parsonage Gr CO8 ....101 C4
Parsonage La
　Burwell CB5 ....44 A5
　Chelsworth IP7 ....79 E3

Parsons Ct IP33 ....122 A6
Parsons Field 4 IP15 ...130 E5
Parson's Field CO7 ...104 A3
Parsons Hill IP12 ....99 F7
Parson's La IP6 ....125 B2
Parsons Yd 24 CO11 ....104 E2
Partridge Cl 15 IP31 .....49 D4
Partridge Rd IP2 ....138 D3
Pashford Cl IP27 ....109 D6
Paske Ave CB9 ....132 D5
Pastures The
  Ipswich IP4 ....140 F5
  Oulton NR32 ....112 F6
Patricia Cl NR32 ....112 D2
Patrick Stead Hospl
  IP19 ....118 C5
Patten La NR15 ....21 B7
Patterdale Gdns 3
  NR32 ....113 A4
Pattern Bush Cl 4
  CO11 ....104 E4
Patteson Rd IP3 ....139 E4
Patticroft 7 CO10 ....77 A3
Pauline St IP2 ....155 B1
Paul's Rd IP2 ....138 F5
Pavilion Ct CB9 ....132 F5
Paxton Chadwick Cl 1
  IP16 ....129 D5
Payne St NR33 ....115 C7
Payne's La IP26 ....4 E5
Peacock Cl
  Hockwold cum Wilton IP26 ..4 F3
  5 Ipswich IP8 ....138 C2
  Lowestoft NR33 ....114 C2
Peacock Rise 18 IP31 ....34 B1
Peacock St IP5 ....141 E7
Peacocks Cl 1 CO10 .....76 E1
Peacock's Pyghtle
  IP12 ....131 C3
Peacocks Rd CO10 ....76 E2
Peak Dale NR33 ....114 E3
Pear Cl 2 IP23 ....36 D2
Pearce Rd IP3 ....140 A4
Pearce's Cl 2 IP26 ....5 A3
Pearcroft Rd IP1 ....135 B3
Pearl Rd IP1 ....138 D8
Pearse Way IP3 ....140 E1
Pearson Rd IP4 ....140 C5
Pearsons Way IP8 ....95 F5
Peartree Cl IP17 ....128 C6
Peartree Hill CO8 ....101 D2
Peasecroft Rd 3 IP31 ....34 B1
Peasenhall Cl 2 IP12 .....85 B3
Peasenhall Prim Sch
  IP17 ....56 F8
Peasenhall Rd IP19 ......41 C3
Pebble Cl NR33 ....113 A3
Pebble View Wlk 8 NR31 ...3 C6
Peckham St IP33 ....154 B3
Pecockes Cl 10 CO10 .....92 B3
Peddars Cl 1 IP31 ....34 B1
Peddars La NR34 ....111 B4
Peddars Way NR32 ......113 B4
Peel St IP1 ....155 B3
Peel Yd 2 IP5 ....98 A8
Pegasus Mews 1 NR32 112 D1
Pegg's Hill IP29 ....22 F2
Pelham 21 CO12 ....106 F1
Pelican Cl IP2 ....138 E3
Pemberton Rd 6 IP20 ....22 D5
Pembroke Ave IP12 .....146 E4
Pembroke Cl
  Ipswich IP2 ....139 B3
  Mildenhall IP28 ....116 C5
  Newmarket CB8 ....121 B2
Pembroke Pl CO10 ......148 B8
Pembroke Rd
  Bury St Edmunds IP32 ...122 D3
  Framlingham IP13 ......126 B4
Pembrooke Way 1
  NR32 ....113 A3
Pendleton Rd IP2 ....138 D1
Penfold Rd IP11 ....153 A4
Penn Cl IP9 ....150 F4
Pennine Way NR32 .....112 E2
Penny La Ipswich IP3 ...140 F1
  Lowestoft NR32 ....112 E3
Penny Mdw 3 IP9 ......150 E3
Pennyfields NR35 ....110 B2
Pennygate Dr NR33 ....114 E6
Pennyroyal Gdns IP2 ...138 E4
Penryn Rd IP5 ....141 A7
Penshurst Rd IP3 ......140 D4
Pentland Wlk 9 NR32 ..113 A4
Pentlow Dr CO10 ....76 F1
Pentlow Hawke Cl
  CB9 ....133 A5
Pentlow Hill CO10 ....91 A8
Penzance Rd IP5 ....141 A6
Pepper La IP31 ....49 E3
Peppercorn Way 2 IP2 138 E3
Peppers Cl IP27 ....5 E3
Pepper's Rd CO4 ....102 F1
Peppers Wash IP13 .....126 B6
Pepys Ave 1 NR34 ....9 F4
Peregrine Way 18 NR33 ..11 C1
Periwinkle Cl 8 NR33 ...114 C5
Perkins Rd IP30 ....49 E2
Perkins Way
  Ipswich IP3 ....139 F1
  Tostock IP30 ....50 B3
Perry La CO4 ....103 D2
Perrydown La IP30 ....64 C1

Persimmon Wlk CB8 ....120 E7
Pesthouse La IP6 ....82 A6
Petch Cl IP33 ....154 B3
Peterhouse Cl IP2 ......138 F2
Peterhouse Cres IP12 ..146 D4
Peterhouse Dr CB8 .....121 A2
Peter's Gr 4 IP9 ....150 E3
Petingo Cl CB8 ....120 D7
Petit Couronne Way
  NR34 ....111 D3
Peto Way NR32 ....113 A1
Pettaugh La IP6 ....68 E2
Petticoat La
  9 Barrow IP29 ....47 A2
  Bury St Edmunds IP33 ..154 A1
Pettitts La IP21 ....20 F3
Pheasant Cl 14 IP31 .....49 D4
Pheasant Rd IP2 ....138 E3
Pheasant Rise IP8 ....95 F4
Pheasants Wlk NR35 ......7 E4
Philip Ave IP11 ....152 E3
Philip Rd
  Bury St Edmunds IP32 ..122 F8
  Ipswich IP2 ....155 B1
Philipps Cl CB8 ....120 D4
Phillipps Rd 3 IP6 ....82 B5
Phillips Cres IP12 ......125 E4
Phillips Field Rd CO10 ..148 E3
Phoenix Day Hospl
  IP33 ....154 A1
Phoenix Rd IP4 ....140 A7
Picketts Rd IP1 ....153 C5
Pickwick Dr 5 NR32 .....3 A4
Pickwick Rd IP2 ....138 E6
Picton Ave 5 IP1 ....135 D1
Pier Ave IP18 ....119 D6
Pier Terr NR33 ....115 D8
Pigeon La IP28 ....48 B6
Pigeon's La IP8 ....138 A3
Pightle Cl IP30 ....50 E2
Pightle The
  Capel St. Mary IP9 .....150 F4
  Haverhill CB9 ....132 E6
  4 Needham Market IP6 125 D3
  North Cove NR34 ....10 B4
Pilgrims Way
  Bungay NR35 ....110 C3
  6 Great Finborough IP14 ..66 B4
Pilgrim's Way 7 IP20 ....22 D5
Pilgrims Way 1 IP16 ....73 F6
Pimpernel Rd IP2 ....138 F3
Pin Mill Cl IP8 ....138 C1
Pin Mill Cliff National Trust★
  IP9 ....106 D8
Pinbush Cl NR33 ....114 F2
Pinbush Rd NR33 ....114 F2
Pine Ave IP1 ....135 B1
Pine Bank IP5 ....141 E6
Pine Cl
  1 Brantham CO11 ......104 E4
  Eye IP23 ....117 D3
  4 Harleston IP20 ....22 D5
  9 Lakenheath IP27 ......13 F2
Pine Gr 14 IP13 ....83 E5
Pine Leys IP32 ....122 F8
Pine Sq IP7 ....80 D6
Pine Tree Cl NR34 .....111 F4
Pine Tree Ct IP22 ....18 C2
Pine Trees Ave IP28 ....116 E4
Pine View IP14 ....52 A6
Pine View Rd IP1 ......139 B8
Pinecroft Rd IP1 ....135 A2
Pinecroft Rise CO10 ....148 B3
Pinecroft Way IP6 .....125 E4
Pines Ind Est The CB8 ...44 F6
Pines The IP11 ....153 E6
Pinetree Cl IP5 ....140 F7
Pinetrees NR31 ....2 B7
Pineview Cl IP14 ....124 D5
Pineway Cl 1 IP29 ......63 A1
Pinewood IP12 ....146 E3
Pinewood Ave NR33 ...114 F6
Pinewood Dr IP7 ....14 F8
Pinewood Gdns NR34 ...10 B4
Pinewood Nature Reserve★
  IP9 ....142 A7
Pinkney's La 19 IP18 ...119 D5
Pinkuah La CO10 ....90 F7
Pinmill Rd IP6 ....106 C8
Pinners La IP13 ....146 B7
Pinners Way IP33 ......122 E4
Pintail Cl IP2 ....138 E3
Pinza Cl CB8 ....120 E8
Piperell Way CB9 ......132 E3
Pipers Cl IP9 ....133 A4
Pipers Mdw IP13 ....54 E7
Pipney Hill IP17 ....56 F4
Pippin Cl 2 IP32 ....123 E6
Pippin Post Cl CO10 ....76 C6
Pippins The
  Blundeston NR32 ....3 A4
  Glemsford CO10 ....77 B2
Pipp's La IP6 ....135 E6
Pirnhow St NR35 ....110 D5
Pit Rd NR34 ....10 B8
Pitcairn Rd IP1 ....138 E8
Pitches Mount★ CO10 ..93 C5
Pitman's Gr IP19 ....42 A4
Pitmire La CO8 ....101 A7
Pits The CB7 ....29 C4
Pitts End CO7 ....151 D5
Place Farm Com Prim Sch
  CB9 ....132 D6
Plampin Cl CO10 ....92 B3
Plantation The IP5 .....130 D5
Plantation Way IP14 ....66 C1
Planters Gr 3 NR33 ....114 F7
Plash Rd IP23 ....53 F7

Plashwood Rd IP14 .....51 B1
Platers Wlk IP16 ....129 C5
Platten Cl IP6 ....125 C5
Platters Cl IP3 ....144 A7
Platters Rd IP11 ....152 E2
Playfield Rd IP4 ....140 A7
Playford Hall★ IP6 ....137 A4
Playford La IP5 ....136 E2
Playford Rd
  Ipswich IP4 ....140 E8
  Playford IP5 ....137 B2
Pleasant Pl NR34 ......111 B3
Pleasant Row IP4 ......155 C2
Pleasurewood Cl 5
  NR32 ....113 B5
Pleasurewood Hill
  NR32 ....113 A7
Plough Cl CO10 ....76 C7
Plough La
  Leavenheath CO6 ......102 B7
  Sudbury CO10 ....148 B5
Plough Rd
  Capel St. Mary IP9 .....150 D3
  Woolpit IP30 ....50 D1
Plough St IP3 ....139 E4
Ploughman's Dro IP26 ...4 B5
Plover Cl 4 IP28 ....13 B1
Plover Rd IP2 ....138 E2
Plovers Way
  Bury St Edmunds IP33 ..123 C1
  Hockwold cum Wilton IP26 ..4 F3
  Lowestoft NR33 ....114 D5
Plum St CO10 ....77 A3
Plum Tree Rise 3 IP7 ...80 D6
Plummer Cl 22 IP31 .....34 B1
Plummers Dell 10 IP6 ..82 A5
Plumpton Ave IP28 ....116 C5
Plumtrees 8 NR32 .....112 D2
Plymouth Rd
  Felixstowe IP11 ....152 F6
  4 Troston IP31 ....33 D5
Pole Hill (Tumulus)★
  IP10 ....141 F5
Police Sta Rd 5 IP33 ...113 D1
Pollards La IP28 ....29 F7
Polls La NR34 ....9 C2
Polstead Cl IP14 ....124 F4
Polstead Hill CO6 ....93 F1
Polstead St CO6 ....102 E7
Pond Cl IP11 ....152 D5
Pond End IP6 ....82 E6
Pond Gn CB7 ....28 A1
Pond Gr Cl IP32 ....123 E6
Pond Hall Rd IP7 ......149 F5
Pond Piece IP13 ....70 A7
Ponds End La IP22 ......35 A8
Poole Cl IP3 ....140 D3
Poole St CO10 ....76 E1
Pooley St IP22 ....19 C3
Popes Ct CB9 ....133 C3
Pope's Gn La IP7 ....94 B2
Poplar Cl 1 Barrow IP29 ..47 A2
  4 Claydon IP6 ....134 C8
  Haverhill CB9 ....132 B7
Poplar Farm Rd IP12 ....73 A2
Poplar Hill IP14 ....124 E4
Poplar La IP8 ....138 B3
Poplar Rd
  Lowestoft NR33 ....114 D3
  Sudbury CO10 ....148 F5
Poplars Cl 1 CB5 ....44 A5
Poplars CP Sch NR32 ..113 B3
Poplars The
  Beck Row, Holywell Row
    & Kenny Hill IP28 ....13 D1
  3 Brantham CO11 .....104 E5
  Spexhall IP19 ....24 F5
Poppy Cl
  Bury St Edmunds IP32 ..123 E5
  Ditchingham NR35 .....110 B7
  Ipswich IP2 ....138 F5
  Worlingham NR34 ......111 F3
Poppy Fields 9 CB7 ....28 D5
Popson St NR33 ....110 A4
Port La IP23 ....37 C3
Port of Felixstowe Rd
  IP11 ....152 C3
Portal Ave IP5 ....84 A1
Portal Cl 4 Barnham IP24 16 C2
  7 Feltwell IP26 ....4 D5
Porter Rd IP3 ....140 F1
Porthole Cl NR34 ......114 B4
Portland Ave 16 CO12 ..107 B4
Portland Cl 18 IP27 .....13 F2
Portland Cres 4 IP24 ..146 E4
Portland Pl 3 IP24 ......16 A5
Portlight Cl 3 CO11 ....105 A2
Portman Rd IP1 ....155 A2
Portman's Wlk IP1 .....139 A5
Portsch Rd IP3 ....114 A3
Portsmouth Cl 19 IP27 ..13 F2
Portsmouth Rd 3 IP31 ..33 D5
Post Mill Cl IP4 ....139 F6
Post Mill Cres 12 IP13 ..83 E4
Post Mill Gdns 10 IP13 ..83 E4
Post Office La
  Glemsford CO10 ....77 A3
  Martlesham IP12 ......146 C1
Post Office Rd IP17 ....129 A3
Posters La IP31 ....35 A2
Pot Kiln Chase CO9 .....90 F1
Pot Kiln Prim Sch
  CO10 ....148 E4
Pot Kiln Rd CO10 ......148 F4
Pot Kilns The CO10 .....92 B3
Potash La Bentley IP9 ..104 F8
Eye IP23 ....117 B5

Potash La continued
  Polstead IP14 ....93 F4
  Wyverstone IP14 ....51 D7
Potkins La IP12 ....131 B3
Potland La 15 CO10 ....78 D4
Pott Hall Rd IP28 ....30 A6
Potters Dr NR31 ....3 B7
Potter's La
  Rickinghall Superior IP22 36 B5
  Stanton IP31 ....34 E4
Potter's St IP16 ....58 C4
Potters Vale IP22 ....35 E7
Pouch Mill IP11 ....152 B8
Poulter's La IP29 ....62 F6
Poultry Rd IP27 ....13 A7
Pound Cl 8 Burwell CB5 ..44 A5
  Halesworth IP19 ......118 B3
  4 Harleston IP20 ....22 D6
  4 Walsham Le Willows
    IP31 ....35 C2
  8 Harwich CO12 ......107 A2
Pound Farm Dr
  NR32 ....112 F4
Pound Farm Par 7
  NR32 ....112 F4
Pound Gn Rd IP13 ......56 C7
Pound Hill Bacton IP14 ..51 F6
  Dallinghoo IP13 ....70 C1
Pound Hill Cl IP14 ......51 F6
Pound La
  Blundeston NR32 ....3 A4
  Bramford IP8 ....81 F3
  Capel St Mary IP9 .....150 D1
  Dallinghoo IP13 ....70 C1
  Ditchingham NR35 ......7 E6
  Hadleigh IP7 ....149 C6
  Isleham CB7 ....29 C5
  Stowmarket IP14 ......124 D7
Pound Mdw 3 IP28 ......48 B6
Pound Pl NR34 ....111 B6
Pound Rd
  3 Beccles NR34 ......111 B6
  Creeting St Peter or West
    Creeting IP6 ....67 B4
  Sotterley NR34 ....26 A7
Pouy St IP17 ....41 B1
Powling Rd IP3 ....140 A2
Powney St IP7 ....93 B8
Pratt St CB7 ....28 D5
Pratt's La IP9 ....144 A2
Prentice Rd IP14 ......124 E6
Prentice St 8 CO10 .....78 D4
Prentices La IP13 ......146 D6
Prescott Dr 11 IP30 ....50 F2
Presmere Rd IP13 .....127 A4
Preston Dr IP1 ....134 F2
Preston Rd CO10 ....78 D4
Prestwick Ave 2 IP11 ..153 C6
Pretty Dr IP21 ....21 A2
Pretty Rd IP16 ....58 A4
Pretyman Ave IP14 ......51 F6
Pretyman Rd
  Felixstowe IP11 ....152 E1
  Ipswich IP3 ....140 B3
Prevetts Way IP15 .....130 E5
Prickwillow Rd CB7 .....12 A2
Priestly Rd IP6 ....125 D4
Primes La Blyford IP19 ..42 B8
  Holton IP19 ....118 F5
Primrose Alley IP18 ...119 D4
Primrose Cl NR33 ......114 D4
Primrose Hill
  Haverhill CB9 ....132 D5
  Ipswich IP4 ....138 F4
Royal Hospital School
  IP9 ....105 E6
Primrose La
  Frostenden NR34 ....26 B4
  Ramsey & Parkeston
    CO11 ....106 A1
  10 Soham CB7 ....28 D5
Primrose Rise NR34 ...111 B3
Primrose Way IP6 .....125 D3
Prince Charles Ave 17
  IP32 ....48 C5
Prince Charles Cl
  CO10 ....148 D6
Prince of Wales Cl
  IP33 ....122 E5
Prince of Wales Dr 9
  IP2 ....139 A2
Prince St CO10 ....148 C6
Princedale Cl IP1 ......135 A6
Princel La CO7 ....103 F4
Princes Gdns IP11 .....152 F4
Princes Gn IP19 ....118 A2
Prince's Rd NR35 ......110 B2
Princes Rd
  Felixstowe IP11 ....152 F4
  13 Harwich CO12 .....107 A2
  Lowestoft NR32 ....113 C2
Princes St
  Bury St Edmunds IP33 ..154 A2
  Ipswich IP2 ....155 A1
Princes Wlk NR32 .....113 A2
Princess Rd 2 IP18 ....119 C8
Princess Way
  5 Earsham NR35 ....7 F4
  Haverhill CB9 ....132 B6
  Newmarket CB8 ....120 E4
Princethorpe Rd IP3 ..140 C4
Printing Mus★ NR34 ..111 B6
Prior's Ave IP33 ......122 E4
Priors Cl
  Lowestoft NR32 ....113 C5
  Rushbrooke with Rougham
    IP30 ....64 D8

Priors' Hill Rd IP15 ...130 D3
Priors Way IP15 ....130 E4
Priory Ave 1 CB9 ......132 D5
Priory Cl 7 Burwell CB5 ..44 A5
  Ingham IP31 ....32 F1
  Palgrave IP22 ....20 C1
  Stradbroke IP21 ....39 B4
Priory Cres IP21 ....39 D8
Priory Ct IP21 ....39 B4
Priory La Bungay NR35 ..110 B4
  Carlton Colville NR33 ..114 A2
  Darsham IP17 ....42 B1
  Debenham IP14 ....53 F2
Priory Rd Beccles NR34 ..111 B4
  Blythburgh IP19 ....42 F6
  Felixstowe IP11 ....153 C5
  Fressingfield IP21 ......39 D7
  Fritton & St Olaves NR31 ..2 A6
  Palgrave IP22 ....20 C1
  Snape IP17 ....72 E5
  Sudbury CO10 ....148 B7
  Wrentham NR34 ....26 E5
Priory Stadium CO10 ..148 C4
Priory Wlk CO10 ......148 C4
Prittlewell Cl IP2 ......113 B8
Private Rd Earsham NR35 ..7 D4
  Mutford NR33 ....10 B2
Privet Gn NR33 ....115 A7
Progress Way IP23 ....117 B5
Promenade
  Harwich CO12 ....107 A1
  Southwold IP18 ....119 D4
Prospect Hill CO10 .....92 B2
Prospect Pl
  Leiston IP16 ....129 D6
  Lowestoft NR33 ....115 B3
Prospect Rd
  Ipswich IP1 ....139 A6
  Lowestoft NR32 ....112 C1
  Norton IP31 ....50 C4
Prospect Row IP33 ....154 B2
Providence La 5 IP1 ..139 A7
Providence Stree IP1 ..155 B3
Provost Rd CO10 ....4 D5
Prussia La IP33 ....154 A1
Puddingmoor NR34 ....111 A5
Puddleduck La NR34 ..111 F3
Pug St IP21 ....21 A6
Pulham Rd IP21 ....21 D5
Pump Cl IP13 ....84 C7
Pump Ct 9 CO10 ....78 D4
Pump House La IP17 ....57 A8
Pump La IP33 ....154 A2
Pump St
  Needham Market IP6 ..125 E4
  Orford IP12 ....131 C2
Punchard Way IP11 ...152 C8
Purcell Rd IP14 ....124 E4
Purdis Ave IP3 ....140 F2
Purdis Farm La
  Foxhall IP10 ....141 C2
  Ipswich IP3 ....140 F2
Purdis Farm IP10 .....141 B2
Purdis Rd IP10 ....141 D2
Purplett St IP2 ....155 C1
Putney Cl IP27 ....14 E8
Putticks La CO7 ....151 E5
Pyes Mdw 1 IP30 ......50 F2
Pykenham Way IP7 ....149 D6
Pytches Cl 2 IP12 ....147 B6
Pytches Rd IP12 ......147 A6

Q

Quadling St IP1 ....155 A3
Quaker La Bardwell IP31 ..34 C4
  Beyton IP30 ....49 F1
Quaker's La 2 CB9 ....132 E6
Quakers' Rd IP28 ......116 F5
Quakers Way
  4 Leiston IP16 ....129 D5
  3 Leiston IP16 ....129 D5
Quantock Cl IP5 ......140 F7
Quarries Cross IP14 ....66 C8
Quaves La NR35 ....110 B4
Quay La Reydon IP18 ...26 D1
  Sudbury CO10 ....148 C4
Quay Side IP12 ....147 A4
Quay St
  Halesworth IP19 ......118 B4
  13 Manningtree CO11 ..104 E2
  Orford IP12 ....131 C2
  Woodbridge IP12 ......147 A4
Quay The 1 CO12 .....107 B3
Quay's Rd IP12 ....47 F5
Quayside Ct IP5 ....109 C7
Quebec Dr IP5 ....141 B8
Queech La IP9 ....105 A4
Queech The IP9 ....150 F4
Queen Edith Dr CB9 ...88 D3
Queen Elizabeth Dr
  NR34 ....111 D3
Queen St Cowlinge CB8 ..61 B1
  Felixstowe IP11 ....152 E5
  6 Hadleigh IP7 ....149 D6
  Haverhill CB9 ....132 E6
  Ipswich IP1 ....155 B3
  Newmarket CB8 ....121 B3
  Southwold IP18 ....119 D5
  Stradbroke IP21 ....39 B5
Queens Ave 5 IP12 ...146 E4
Queen's Cl IP33 ....122 E5
Queens Cl
  Halesworth IP19 ......118 A2
  Sudbury CO10 ....148 C6
Queens Dr IP19 ....118 A2
Queen's Dr IP28 ......116 B4

Queen's Head La IP12 .146 F5
Queen's Head Rd CO4 .102 F1
Queen's Highway
NR32 ...112 C2
Queens La IP29 ...62 D5
Queen's Oak★ IP19 ...41 A5
Queen's Rd
Beccles NR34 ...111 B6
Bungay NR35 ...110 B2
Bury St Edmunds IP33 ...154 A2
Felixstowe IP11 ...153 A3
4 Harwich CO12 ...107 A1
Lowestoft NR32 ...113 D3
Southwold IP18 ...119 D4
Queens Rd Brandon IP27 .14 E8
1 Southwold IP18 ...119 C8
Sudbury CO10 ...148 C6
Queens St CB9 ...74 B2
Queens View CB8 ...120 A8
Queen's Way IP3 ...140 B2
Queensberry Rd
1 Ipswich IP3 ...144 B8
Newmarket CB8 ...121 A3
Queenscliffe Rd IP2 ...139 A3
Queensdale Cl IP1 ...135 B1
Queensdale Rd IP1 ...135 B1
Queensgate Dr IP4 ...139 F8
Queensland IP9 ...106 F5
Queensway 4 Acton CO10 92 B7
7 Earsham NR35 ...7 F4
Exning CB8 ...120 B8
Haverhill CB9 ...132 C6
3 Manningtree CO11 ...104 E2
2 Mildenhall IP28 ...116 B4
8 Soham CB7 ...28 D4
Sudbury CO10 ...148 F3
Thetford IP24 ...16 B5
Queensway Mid Sch
IP24 ...16 B5
Quentin Cl IP1 ...138 E8
Quilter Dr Ipswich IP8 .138 C1
Pinewood IP8 ...142 C8
Quilter Rd IP11 ...153 B4
Quince Cl 9 CO11 ...104 E5
Quinnell Way 5 NR32 .113 A6
Quinton Rd IP6 ...125 C4
Quinton's La IP11 ...153 C5
Quintons Rd CO7 ...151 C5
Quoits Field 2 IP6 ...134 C8
Quoits Mdw IP14 ...68 B6

R

Rackham Cl 1 NR31 ...3 B7
Radcliffe Dr IP2 ...138 D2
Radcliffe Rd 8 IP27 ...14 A2
Radiator Rd CO10 ...148 E3
Radleys La CO6 ...102 B6
Radnor Cl IP32 ...123 E6
Raeburn Rd IP3 ...139 F1
Raeburn Rd S IP3 ...139 E1
Raedwald Dr IP32 ...123 D5
Raglan Rd 2 NR32 ...113 D1
Raglan St NR32 ...113 D1
Rag's La IP30 ...50 D1
Raile Wlk CO10 ...91 E8
Railway App IP11 ...153 A5
Railway Hill IP20 ...22 C6
Railway St 19 CO11 ...104 E2
Raine Ave CB9 ...132 B6
Rainey Ct 37 IP20 ...22 D6
Raingate St IP33 ...154 C1
Raleigh Cl CO10 ...148 E8
Raleigh Rd CO10 ...148 E8
Ram La NR15 ...21 C8
Rampart Way IP24 ...16 C5
Ramsey Cl IP2 ...139 A1
Ramsey Rd
Hadleigh IP7 ...149 F7
Harwich CO12 ...106 D1
Harwich CO12 ...106 E1
Ramsgate Dr IP3 ...140 B3
Randall Cl
2 Hopton on Sea NR31 ...3 B7
Ipswich IP5 ...141 E7
Rands Rd IP7 ...149 B1
Rands Way IP3 ...140 B2
Randwell Cl IP4 ...140 B5
Ranelagh Prim Sch
IP2 ...138 F5
Ranelagh Rd
Felixstowe IP11 ...153 A4
Ipswich IP2 ...155 A1
Ransom Rd IP12 ...146 E6
Ransome Ave IP21 ...21 A2
Ransome Cl IP8 ...138 A6
Ransome Cres IP3 ...140 B2
Ransome Rd IP3 ...140 B2
Ransomes Europark
IP10 ...144 F7
Ransomes Way IP3 ...140 D1
Ranson Rd IP6 ...125 C4
Rant Score NR32 ...113 E2
Ranville NR33 ...114 E3
Ranworth Ave NR33 ...114 E5
Rapier St 6 IP2 ...139 C3
Rare Breeds Farm★
CO7 ...151 A1
Rat Hill IP9 ...106 C5
Rattla Cnr IP16 ...58 C5
Rattlerow Hill IP21 ...39 B6
Rattler's Rd IP27 ...5 F1
Rattlesden CE Prim Sch
IP30 ...65 D6
Rattlesden Cl IP14 ...124 D3
Rattlesden Rd IP30 ...65 C6
Raven Cl IP28 ...116 D3
Raven Rd IP33 ...123 C1
Raven Way IP7 ...149 D4
Raveningham Rd NR34 ...9 C8
Ravens La IP8 ...134 A2
Ravens Way 6 IP12 ...84 A1
Ravensfield Rd IP1 ...134 E1
Ravensmere NR34 ...111 B6
Ravensmere E NR34 ...111 B6
Ravenswood Ave IP3 ...144 B8
Ravenswood Com Prim Sch
IP3 ...144 C8
Ravenwood Mews
NR33 ...115 A5
Ravine The NR32 ...113 E3
Rawlings Way 22 IP26 ...4 E5
Ray Ave CO12 ...107 A2
Ray La 8 CO12 ...106 F3
Raydon Croft IP14 ...124 F3
Raydon La IP12 ...131 D3
Raydon Way CO10 ...92 B3
Rayes La CB8 ...121 A4
Rayleigh Rd IP1 ...134 E1
Rayment Drift 5 IP5 ...141 C7
Rayner's La NR35 ...8 D8
Raynham Rd IP32 ...154 A4
Raynsford Rd IP30 ...63 F7
Reach Rd CB5 ...44 A5
Reade Rd 5 IP9 ...105 E7
Reading Gn IP21 ...38 D4
Reading Rd IP4 ...140 B7
Reading's La IP31 ...35 A2
Rebow Rd 9 CO12 ...107 A1
Reckford Rd IP17 ...58 B6
Recreation La IP11 ...152 F6
Recreation Rd
Haverhill CB9 ...132 D5
Stowmarket IP14 ...124 C6
Recreation Way
Ipswich IP3 ...140 C2
Mildenhall IP28 ...116 C4
Recreation Wlk CO10 ...148 F3
Rectory Cl
Beccles NR34 ...111 F4
3 Glemsford CO10 ...77 A3
Ousden CB8 ...61 E6
Raydon IP7 ...94 F1
Rectory Field 4 IP9 ...106 C8
Rectory Gdns IP30 ...49 F1
Rectory Gr IP29 ...63 B5
Rectory Hill
Botesdale IP22 ...35 F6
East Bergholt CO7 ...151 C3
Polstead CO6 ...102 E8
Rickinghall Superior IP22 ...36 A5
Rectory La Beccles NR34 ...9 F4
Brantham CO11 ...104 F5
Hedenham NR35 ...7 D8
Hintlesham IP8 ...95 C6
Kettlebaston IP7 ...79 B5
Kirton IP10 ...98 D2
Mettingham NR35 ...110 F3
4 Ramsey & Parkeston
CO12 ...106 D1
Scole IP21 ...21 C5
Stuston IP21 ...37 D8
Whatfield IP7 ...80 C1
3 Woolpit IP30 ...50 D1
Rectory Mdw 5 IP28 ...48 B6
Rectory Pk 5 CO10 ...93 C3
Rectory Pl IP29 ...47 A1
Rectory Rd
Aldeby/Wheatacre/Burgh
St Peter NR34 ...10 A8
Bacton IP14 ...51 E5
Blaxhall IP12 ...71 F4
Brome & Oakley IP23 ...117 B7
Broome NR35 ...8 B7
Burston & Shimpling IP22 ...20 E6
Dickleburgh IP21 ...21 B5
Gillingham NR34 ...9 B7
Gissing IP22 ...20 F8
Great Waldingfield CO10 ...92 D6
Harkstead IP9 ...106 B6
Hemingstone IP6 ...68 C1
Hollesley IP12 ...99 F7
Ipswich IP2 ...155 B1
Kedington CB9 ...133 F8
Langham CO4 ...103 C3
7 Lowestoft NR33 ...115 C6
Mellis IP23 ...36 F5
Middleton IP17 ...58 B6
Middleton CO10 ...148 C2
Newton CO10 ...92 D2
Orford IP12 ...131 C3
Shelfanger IP22 ...20 B6
Sotterley NR34 ...26 A7
Tivetshall St Mary NR15 ...21 C8
Whepstead IP29 ...63 B4
Wortham IP22 ...19 F1
Wrabness CO11 ...106 A2
Wyverstone IP14 ...51 D6
Rectory St IP19 ...118 B4
Red Barn Dr 4 CO6 ...102 A7
Red Barn Piece 13 IP13 ...83 E5
Red Dock La CB8 ...61 C1
Red Hill IP7 ...94 D7
Red Hill Rd IP7 ...149 E8
Red House Cl
3 Felixstowe IP11 ...107 D8
Lowestoft NR32 ...112 F5
Red House La
Leiston IP16 ...129 D4
Sudbury CO10 ...148 E2
Red House Wlk IP10 ...145 E4
Red La
Capel St Mary IP9 ...150 E2
Sternfield IP17 ...72 D8
Red Lion Cl IP21 ...38 C7
Red Rose Cl IP12 ...99 E4
Red Sleeve IP9 ...150 D3
Redan St IP1 ...155 A4
Redbarn La IP17 ...72 D7
Redcastle Furze Prim Sch
IP24 ...16 B5
Rede La IP6 ...134 F8
Rede Rd IP29 ...62 F4
Rede Way CO10 ...92 B3
Redenhall Rd IP20 ...22 D6
Redgate IP24 ...16 C6
Redgate La IP9 ...143 D5
Redgrave & Lopham Fen
Nature Reserve★
IP22 ...19 B2
Redgrave & Lopham Fen
Visitor Ctr★ IP22 ...19 C3
Redgrave Rd IP22 ...19 B3
Redhouse Gdns 5 CB7 ...28 D3
Redhouse La
Bawdsey IP12 ...99 E3
Boxted CO4 ...102 E1
9 Sudbury CO10 ...148 C5
Redhouse Rd IP13 ...56 B8
Redisham Cl NR32 ...113 A5
Redisham Rd
Brampton with Stoven
NR34 ...25 B6
Weston NR34 ...9 C1
Redlingfield Rd
Horham IP21 ...38 D2
Occold IP23 ...37 F2
Redshank Cl CB9 ...133 A5
Redwald Rd IP12 ...85 E8
Redwing Cl IP2 ...138 D3
Redwing Rd IP33 ...123 C1
Redwings Visitor Ctr★
NR31 ...2 C8
Redwold Cl IP12 ...146 C1
Redwood Gdns IP33 ...154 C2
Redwood La 23 IP27 ...13 F2
Reedland Way 4 IP11 .152 D5
Reed's Bldgs IP33 ...154 C3
Reeds La CB9 ...132 E6
Reeds Way IP14 ...67 A7
Reet 1 NR32 ...115 D8
Reeve Cl
12 Bury St Edmunds IP32 ...48 C5
Scole IP21 ...21 A2
Reeve Gdns IP5 ...141 C8
Reeve St NR32 ...113 D2
Reeve's Cl NR35 ...110 C3
Reeves La IP26 ...5 A3
Refinery Rd CO12 ...106 F3
Regal Dr CB7 ...28 E3
Regal La CB7 ...28 E3
Regent Pl 3 CB7 ...28 D3
Regent Rd NR32 ...113 D1
Regent St
20 Manningtree CO11 ...104 E2
Stowmarket IP14 ...124 D7
Regent Theatre★ IP4 ...155 C3
Regimental Mus★
IP33 ...122 E6
Regimental Way 6
CO12 ...106 E1
Regina Cl IP4 ...140 B5
Reigate Cl IP3 ...140 B3
Rembrandt Cl 3 NR32 .113 C6
Rembrandt Gdns IP33 .122 F3
Rembrandt Way IP33 ...123 A3
Rembrow Rd IP9 ...150 E3
Rememberance Rd
IP16 ...73 F6
Remercie Rd 7 CO11 ...105 A2
Rendall La IP14 ...67 A8
Rendham Hill IP17 ...56 F7
Rendham Rd
Bruisyard IP17 ...56 D4
Kelsale cum Carlton
IP17 ...128 A6
Peasenhall IP17 ...56 F7
Rendlesham Rd
15 Felixstowe IP11 ...152 D5
9 Ipswich IP1 ...139 A7
Renfrew Rd IP4 ...136 B1
Renoir Pl 2 NR32 ...113 B5
Renson Cl 6 IP30 ...64 F8
Reydon Bsns Pk IP18 ...119 D8
Reydon La IP18 ...26 D1
Reydon Mews NR32 ...113 A6
Reydon Prim Sch
IP18 ...119 C8
Reynolds Ave 2 IP3 ...144 A8
Reynolds Ct 10 IP11 ...152 D5
Reynolds Rd IP3 ...140 A1
Reynolds Way CO10 ...148 E8
Ribblesdale NR33 ...114 E3
Riby Rd IP11 ...152 F3
Richard Burn Way
CO10 ...148 C8
Richard Crampton Rd
NR34 ...111 B3
Richards Dr IP13 ...137 D5
Richardson Rd CO7 ...151 D5
Richardsons La IP9 ...106 B8
Richards's Cl NR33 ...114 E6
Richer Cl IP31 ...50 E7
Richer Rd IP31 ...50 F7
Richmond Cres 8 CO12 107 A1
Richmond Rd
Ipswich IP1 ...138 F7
Lowestoft NR33 ...115 C6
Riddlesworth Hall Sch
IP22 ...17 F4
Rider Haggard La 7
NR33 ...11 C1
Rider Haggard Way
NR35 ...110 C7
Ridgeville 9 NR33 ...114 F3
Ridgeway IP14 ...124 B6
Ridgeway The 10 CO12 .107 A2
Ridgeways The NR33 ...114 D5
Ridgewell Rd
Ashen CO10 ...89 D5
Birdbrook CO9 ...89 C5
Ridings The
3 Beccles NR34 ...111 F4
Leavenheath CO6 ...102 B8
Ridley Rd IP33 ...122 C6
Rigbourne Hill NR34 ...111 C3
Rigbourne Hill La 6
NR34 ...111 C2
Rigby Ave CO11 ...105 A2
Rightup Dro IP27 ...4 E1
Riley Cl IP1 ...134 C1
Ringham Rd IP4 ...140 A6
Ringsfield CE Prim Sch
NR34 ...9 B1
Ringsfield Rd
Beccles NR34 ...111 A4
6 Lowestoft NR32 ...113 A3
Ringsfield NR34 ...9 A1
Ringshall Prim Sch
IP14 ...80 F6
Rio Cl 2 NR33 ...114 C5
Risbridge Dr CB9 ...133 E8
Risby CEVC Prim Sch
IP28 ...47 D5
Risby Cl IP4 ...140 B6
Risbygate St IP33 ...154 B2
Riseway Cl IP33 ...123 B1
Rishton Rd 7 NR32 ...113 D1
Rising Sun Hill IP30 ...65 D5
Rissemere La E IP18 ...119 C8
Ritabrook Rd IP2 ...138 E1
Rivendale 4 NR33 ...114 D3
River La Fordham CB7 ...29 A1
Halesworth IP19 ...118 B3
River View Rd 1 IP9 ...106 A5
Riverbank Cl CO10 ...90 B8
Rivers St IP4 ...139 F7
Riverside
4 Framlingham IP13 ...126 C3
Hasketon IP13 ...146 A7
Palgrave IP22 ...20 B2
Riverside Ave E 6
CO11 ...104 E3
Riverside Ave W 4
CO11 ...104 E3
Riverside Bsns Ctr
NR33 ...115 C8
Riverside Bsns Pk
NR33 ...115 B8
Riverside Cl IP28 ...116 B4
Riverside Ct IP32 ...123 A8
Riverside Ind Est IP13 .127 C7
Riverside Ind Pk IP2 ...139 D3
Riverside Mid Sch
IP28 ...116 B4
Riverside Rd
Ipswich IP1 ...138 F7
Lowestoft NR33 ...115 B8
Riverside View IP13 ...127 C8
Riverview IP12 ...147 C7
Rivish La CO10 ...91 E8
Rixon Cres 3 IP12 ...84 E6
Roamwood Gn La IP14 .53 E3
Robeck Rd IP3 ...139 E1
Robert Boby Way
IP33 ...154 B2
Robert's Hill CO8 ...101 C2
Roberts Rd IP16 ...129 D6
Robertsbridge Wlk 6
NR33 ...114 D4
Robin Cl Haverhill CB9 .133 A5
Mildenhall IP28 ...116 D4
12 Thurstow IP31 ...49 D4
Robin Dr IP2 ...138 D3
Robin Hill NR32 ...113 A2
Robin Rd IP33 ...123 C1
Robin Way CO10 ...148 A3
Robins Cl 16 CB7 ...29 C5
Robinson Cl IP33 ...122 D6
Robinson Rd 7 IP21 ...20 F1
Robletts IP13 ...84 D7
Robletts Way 1 CO6 ...101 F2
Rochdale 3 NR33 ...114 F3
Rochester Rd 1 NR33 .115 B4
Rochester Way CO10 ...148 B8
Rochfort Ave CB8 ...120 E5
Rock Rd NR32 ...112 D1
Rockall CB8 ...61 E6
Rockall Cl CB9 ...133 B5
Rockalls Rd CO6 ...93 F1
Rockingham Rd IP33 ...123 B3
Rockstone La IP19 ...41 C7
Rodber Way NR32 ...113 A6
Rodbridge Hill CO10 ...91 D6
Rodney Ct IP12 ...146 F7
Roebuck Dr IP27 ...109 E4
Rogeron Cl CO10 ...75 D3
Rogers Cl IP11 ...152 F6
Roger's Cl NR31 ...3 B7
Roger's La CO10 ...92 F4
Rogue's La IP13 ...127 C5
Rokewood Pl IP29 ...64 A3
Roman Cl 3 CB5 ...44 A5
Roman Hill Mid Sch
NR32 ...113 C1
Roman Hill Prim Sch
NR32 ...113 C1
Roman Rd NR32 ...113 C1
Roman Way
Felixstowe IP11 ...153 D6
Roman Way *continued*
Halesworth IP19 ...118 A3
Haverhill CB9 ...133 B4
Long Melford CO10 ...91 E7
Romany La NR33 ...11 B3
Romany Rd NR32 ...114 C8
Romany Way IP33 ...123 D3
Romney Pl 6 NR32 ...113 B6
Romney Rd IP3 ...140 A1
Romsey Rd IP33 ...122 D3
Ronald La IP17 ...128 D5
Ronden Cl NR34 ...111 B2
Rookery Chase CO7 ...103 F1
Rookery Cl NR33 ...114 F7
Rookery Dro 2 IP28 ...13 B1
Rookery La IP19 ...23 F4
Rookery Rd Elmsett IP7 ...80 E2
Monewden IP13 ...69 F5
Rookery The
Brandon IP27 ...5 D1
Eye IP23 ...117 D2
4 Manningtree CO11 ...104 E2
Rookery Way IP14 ...51 F1
Rook's La 7 NR34 ...111 B5
Rookwood La CO10 ...78 F6
Rookwood Way CB9 ...132 E4
Roosevelt Wlk 5 NR33 .114 C5
Rope Wlk IP4 ...155 C2
Roper's Ct 3 CO10 ...78 D4
Ropers La CO10 ...91 D7
Ropes Dr IP5 ...141 B8
Rosbrook Cl 1 IP33 ...122 D4
Rose Acre CO7 ...103 F7
Rose Ave IP22 ...20 A3
Rose Ct Lowestoft NR32 .113 B2
Shotley IP9 ...106 F6
Rose Gn CO10 ...101 F8
Rose Gn La 4 IP28 ...30 B8
Rose Hall Gdns NR35 ...110 B3
Rose Hill
Grundisburgh IP13 ...83 E5
Withersfield CB9 ...74 B3
Witnesham IP6 ...135 F7
Rose Hill Prim Sch
IP3 ...140 A4
Rose La Botesdale IP22 ...36 A7
Bungay NR35 ...110 B3
Diss IP22 ...20 D1
Elmswell IP30 ...50 E2
Ipswich IP4 ...155 B2
Wickham Skeith IP23 ...52 D8
Rose La Cl IP22 ...20 C1
Rose Wlk IP6 ...125 D3
Rosebay Gdns 1 CB7 ...28 D4
Rosebery Rd
Felixstowe IP11 ...153 B4
Ipswich IP4 ...139 F5
Rosebery Way CB8 ...120 E5
Rosecroft Rd IP1 ...135 A2
Rosedale Gdns 9 NR33 114 E4
Rosefinch Cl CB9 ...133 A5
Rosehill Cres IP3 ...139 F4
Rosehill Rd IP3 ...139 F4
Rosemary Ave IP11 ...153 B5
Rosemary Cl 4 IP28 ...30 C1
Rosemary Gdns CO10 ...148 D8
Rosemary La
Ipswich IP4 ...155 B2
Kelsale cum Carlton
IP17 ...128 C6
Rosemary Musker Cty High
Sch IP24 ...16 C7
Rosemary Rd 5 IP32 ...48 C5
Rosery La IP13 ...137 F6
Rosewood NR33 ...115 A5
Rosewood Cl 22 IP27 ...13 F2
Ross Cl CB9 ...133 B5
Ross Peers Sports Ctr The
CB7 ...28 D3
Ross Rd IP4 ...136 B1
Rosyth Rd 5 IP31 ...33 D5
Rotheram Rd 9 IP7 ...79 F4
Rotten Row CO10 ...92 D2
Rotterdam Rd NR32 ...113 B1
Rougham CE Prim Sch
IP30 ...49 D1
Rougham Hill IP33 ...123 D3
Rougham Rd
Bradfield St George IP30 ...64 D7
Bury St Edmunds IP33 ...123 C3
Roughlands IP27 ...109 D6
Roundridge Rd IP9 ...150 F4
Roundwood Rd IP4 ...140 A7
Rous Rd CB8 ...121 B3
Rousies Cl 6 IP7 ...149 E6
Routh Ave IP3 ...140 F1
Row The CO7 ...103 E5
Rowan Dr Brandon IP27 ...14 F8
Bury St Edmunds IP32 ...123 F6
Rowan Gn 7 IP30 ...50 F2
Rowan Way
Beccles NR34 ...111 E3
Lowestoft NR33 ...114 D6
5 Thurstow IP31 ...49 D4
Rowanhayes Cl IP2 ...139 B3
Rowans Way 1 CO6 ...102 A7
Rowarth Ave IP5 ...141 C7
Rowell Cl CB9 ...132 E8
Rowell's La IP14 ...51 D4
Rowe's Hill IP13 ...40 C2
Rowley Cl 7 CO11 ...104 E4
Rowley Ct CB9 ...133 C3
Rowley Dr CB8 ...120 F3
Rowley Hill CB9 ...133 B3
Rows The CB8 ...120 E3

Roxburgh Rd IP4 ......136 B1
Roy Ave IP4 ....140 B5
Roy Cl IP5 ....141 B7
Royal Ave NR32 ......113 D3
Royal Hospl Sch IP9 ..105 E6
Royal Naval Patrol Mus★
NR32 ....113 E3
Royal Norfolk & Suffolk
Yacht Club NR33 .....115 D8
Royal Pal Cl CB8 .....120 D7
Royal Terr NR33 ......115 D7
Roydon Fen IP22 ....20 B2
Roydon Prim Sch IP22 ..20 B3
Roydon Rd IP22 ....20 C3
Roylands La CO10 ......93 D3
Royston Dr IP2 ....138 D2
Rozlyne Cl 8 NR33 ....114 E4
Rubens Rd IP3 ....140 A1
Rubens Wlk CO10 .....148 E8
Ruby Cl 9 NR32 ....3 D4
Rudlands IP8 ....138 C1
Rudlands Cl 6 CB7 .....29 C5
Rue's La IP11 ....153 C8
Rugby Rd CO10 ....148 F2
Rumburgh La NR35 .....24 D6
Rumburgh Priory★
IP19 ....24 B4
Rumburgh Rd
Lowestoft NR32 ......113 B5
Rumburgh NR19 ....24 B3
Run Mdw NR33 ....114 C6
Run The NR34 ....26 A7
Runce's La NR33 ......114 C3
Runnacles Way IP11 ..152 D5
Rushall Rd IP20 ....22 B6
Rushbrooke La IP33 ...123 D3
Rushbury Cl IP4 ......140 B8
Rushford Rd
Coney Weston IP31 ....17 E1
Euston IP24 ....16 E2
Rushlake Way 7 NR33 .114 D4
Rushmeadow Way 1
IP11 ....153 F2
Rushmere Hall Prim Sch
IP4 ....136 A1
Rushmere Pl CB9 .....132 F6
Rushmere Rd
Gisleham NR33 ....114 B1
Ipswich IP4 ....140 A7
Rushmere NR33 ....10 F3
Rushmere St IP5 .....136 E1
Ruskin Cl 3 IP14 ....124 B8
Ruskin Rd IP4 ....139 F8
Russell Baron Rd IP31 .48 D5
Russell Rd
Felixstowe IP11 ......152 F2
Ipswich IP1 ....155 A2
Russell's Gn NR34 ......9 C2
Russet Cl
4 Beccles NR34 ......111 C3
Great Barton IP32 ....123 E7
Russett Cl CB9 ....132 A6
Rydal Ave IP11 ......153 D7
Rydal Cl IP14 ....124 B6
Rydal Wlk IP3 ....140 C2
Ryders Way 2 IP22 ....36 A6
Rye Cl Ipswich IP3 ...140 D4
3 Lowestoft NR33 ...114 D4
Ryedale 1 NR33 ......114 F3
Ryeburn Cl 1 NR33 ....11 B1
Ryefields 9 IP31 .....49 E4
Ryes La CO10 ....91 D1
Rylands IP9 ....150 E4
Rylands Cl 1 IP31 ....49 E4

S

Sackville St CB8 .....121 B4
Sackvylle St IP14 .....53 E1
Saddlemakers La
IP12 ....147 C8
Saddlers Mdw IP13 ....83 E5
Saddlers Pl 19 IP5 ...98 A8
Saddlers Yd 17 IP31 ...34 B1
Saffron Sq NR33 .....115 A2
Saffrons IP30 ....50 E1
Sages End Rd CB9 .....88 A4
St Agnes Way IP5 ....140 F6
St Albans CB8 ....121 A6
St Albans Cath High Sch
IP4 ....140 D7
St Andrew Ct 1 NR31 ...3 C7
St Andrews CE VA Prim Sch
IP22 ....19 A5
St Andrew's Church Cl
IP5 ....136 D1
St Andrew's Cl IP12 ..147 D7
St Andrews Cl
2 Barningham IP31 ...34 E7
2 Great Finborough IP14 .66 B4
Ipswich IP4 ....140 D5
3 Isleham CB7 ....29 C5
St Andrew's Ct 4 IP13 .83 E5
St Andrews Dr 3 IP9 .106 C8
St Andrews Dr 7 IP28 ..48 C6
St Andrew's Mead IP14 .68 B8
St Andrew's Pl IP12 ..147 D8
St Andrews Rd
Scole IP21 ....21 A1

St Andrews Rd continued
Sudbury CO10 ....148 E4
St Andrew's St IP28 ..116 C4
St Andrew's St N IP33 .154 B3
St Andrew's St S IP33 .154 B2
St Anne's Cl NR34 ...111 C4
St Annes Cl IP12 ....146 D3
St Anne's Rd NR34 ...111 C4
St Anns Dr IP28 .....116 B4
St Aubyn's Rd 6 NR33 .115 C6
St Aubyns Rd IP4 ....140 A5
St Audrys Pk Rd 5 IP12 .84 E6
St Audrys Rd IP12 ....84 E6
St Augustine Rd IP3 ..140 D4
St Augustine's Gdns
IP3 ....140 C3
St Austell Cl IP5 ....141 A6
St Bartholomews La
CO10 ....148 B7
St Benedicts RC Sch
IP32 ....122 F8
St Benedict's Rd NR34 .111 B6
St Benedicts Rd IP27 ...6 A1
St Benet's Dr NR34 ...111 C3
St Benet's RC Minst
NR34 ....111 A4
St Benets RC Prim Sch
NR34 ....111 A5
St Botolph's La IP33 .154 C1
St Botolphs Prim Sch
IP22 ....36 B7
St Botolph's Way CB9 .132 D6
St Catherine's Cl
NR33 ....114 E4
St Catherines Cl IP16 .116 D6
St Catherine's Ct IP2 .138 E1
St Catherine's Rd 11
CO10 ....91 E8
St Clare Ct 15 NR31 ...3 B7
St Clement Mews 13 NR31 .3 B7
St Clement's Hospl
IP3 ....140 C4
St Cross Rd IP20 ......23 B8
St David's Cl 5 NR34 .111 C2
St Denis Cl 11 CO12 ..107 A1
St Domonic's Dr IP27 ...6 A1
St Edmund Cl 6 IP31 ..34 B1
St Edmund Rd IP27 .....5 E4
St Edmund's Cl IP12 ..85 A5
St Edmunds Cl
2 Beccles NR34 .....111 C2
12 Harwich CO12 .....107 A1
Stowmarket IP14 .....124 C8
3 Woodbridge IP12 ..146 E4
St Edmunds Cres 1
NR33 ....11 C1
St Edmund's Dr IP30 ..50 F3
St Edmunds Gate 11
IP31 ....33 D5
St Edmund's Hill CO10 .101 B7
St Edmunds La CO10 ..101 D5
St Edmund's Pl IP1 ..139 C8
St Edmunds Prim Sch
IP21 ....38 C6
St Edmunds RC Prim Sch
NR35 ....110 B4
St Edmunds RCVA Prim Sch
IP33 ....154 B1
St Edmund's Rd
Felixstowe IP11 ......152 E2
Ipswich IP1 ....139 B8
Southwold IP18 ......119 D6
St Edmunds Rd IP14 ..124 C7
St Edmunds Sq 10 IP31 .33 D5
St Edmundsbury Cath★
IP33 ....154 C2
St Edmundsbury CE Prim Sch
IP33 ....154 A3
St Edmundsbury Ret Pk
IP32 ....123 E4
St Etienne IP14 ....69 B6
St Fabians Ct CB8 ...120 F5
St Felix CEVE Mid Sch
CB8 ....120 F6
St Felix Cl 2 CB7 .....28 D5
St Felix Sch IP18 ....119 A6
St George's Ave 2
CO12 ....107 B1
St George's Rd
Beccles NR34 ....111 B4
Felixstowe IP11 .....153 C6
Lowestoft NR33 ......115 B4
Stowlangtoft IP31 ....50 B7
St George's St 1 IP1 .155 B3
St Gotthards Ave IP12 .98 B8
St Gregorys Cl 1 IP12 .85 E8
St Gregory's Ct CO10 .148 B6
St Gregorys Prim Sch
CO10 ....148 B5
St Helena Wlk IP28 ...116 C6
St Helens Prim Sch
IP4 ....139 E6
St Helen's St IP4 ....155 C3
Saint Helens Way IP24 .16 B7
Saint Isidores IP5 ...141 E7
St Ives IP5 ....141 A4
St James' Gn 7 IP18 .119 D5
St James' La
Chediston IP19 ....24 A3
St James South Elmham
IP19 ....23 F4
St James Mid Sch
IP33 ....123 C5

St James Rd
All Saints & St Nicholas,
South Elmham IP19 ....24 A5
St James, South Elmham
IP19 ....23 F4
St James's St IP17 ....43 B1
St Johns Ave CB8 ....121 A1
St Johns CE Prim Sch
IP4 ....140 A7
St John's Cl IP28 ....116 D6
St John's Hill
Bungay NR35 ....110 C2
4 Woodbridge IP12 ..147 A5
St Johns Mdw IP20 ....23 C3
St John's Pl IP33 ....154 B3
St John's Rd
Bungay NR35 ....110 B3
Ipswich IP4 ....140 A6
Lowestoft NR33 ......115 D7
Saxmundham IP17 ....128 C3
St John's St
Beck Row, Holywell Row
& Kenny Hill IP28 ....30 C8
Bury St Edmunds IP33 .154 B3
Woodbridge IP12 ....147 A5
St John's Terr 5 IP12 .147 A5
St John's Way
13 Feltwell IP26 ......4 E5
Thetford IP24 ....16 A5
St Josephs Coll IP2 .139 A3
St Josephs RC Prim Sch
CO10 ....148 C6
St Lawrence Cl NR34 .111 C2
St Lawrence Prim Sch
NR34 ....24 F6
St Lawrence St IP1 ..155 B3
St Lawrence Way IP5 .141 B8
St Leonards Cl IP21 ...21 A1
St Leonards Hospl
CO10 ....148 D5
St Leonards Rd 2 IP33 .148 A8
St Leonard's Rd NR33 .115 C6
St Leonards St IP26 ...6 B8
St Louis Cath Mid Sch
IP33 ....154 B1
St Louis RC Prim Sch
CB8 ....121 A4
St Margarets CE Prim Sch
IP4 ....155 C3
St Margaret's Cres
IP16 ....129 B6
St Margaret's Pl CB8 ..75 E7
St Margarets Prim Sch
NR32 ....113 C3
St Margaret's Rd
Bungay NR35 ....110 B1
1 Lowestoft NR32 ...113 E3
St Margaret's St IP4 .155 C3
St Margaret's Way 3
NR31 ....3 B7
St Marks RC Prim Sch
IP2 ....138 F3
St Martin's Cl CB8 ..120 C7
St Martins Ct IP5 ...141 E7
St Martins Gn 14 IP11 .107 D8
St Martin's La IP24 ...16 B2
St Martin's St IP33 ..154 B3
St Mary's Ave 5 IP14 ..51 C1
St Marys Cath Prim Sch
IP4 ....139 F6
St Marys CE Prim Sch
Benhall IP17 ....72 C8
Mildenhall IP28 .....116 C5
Woodbridge IP12 ....146 F5
St Mary's Cl Bacton IP14 .51 F6
Bramford IP8 ....134 B1
Felixstowe IP11 .....152 B7
Flixton NR35 ....7 E1
Harleston IP20 ....22 E6
Horham IP21 ....38 F3
Sudbury CO10 ....148 F8
St Marys Cl 1 IP23 ...36 D2
St Mary's Cres
Badwell Ash IP31 .....50 E7
Felixstowe IP11 .....152 F6
St Mary's Gdns IP6 ..125 E6
St Marys Pk IP10 .....98 A4
St Marys Prim Sch
IP7 ....149 E6
St Marys RC Prim Sch
NR33 ....115 C5
St Mary's Rd
Aldeby NR34 ....10 A7
Beccles NR34 ....111 A5
Creeting St Mary IP6 .125 E5
Stowmarket IP14 ....124 B7
St Mary's Sq IP33 ...154 C1
St Mary's St NR35 ...110 B4
St Marys View IP11 ...49 E6
St Marys Way IP6 ....135 F4
St Mary's Wlk 2 CB9 ..88 D3
St Matthew's Ave 3
NR34 ....111 C2
St Matthews CE Prim Sch
IP1 ....155 A3
St Matthew's St 1 IP1 .155 A3
St Michaels CE Prim Sch
NR34 ....9 B6
St Michael's Cl
1 Beccles NR34 .....111 C2
Ipswich IP5 ....141 A6
Lowestoft NR32 .....112 C1
St Michaels Ct 16 CO11 .104 E2
St Michael's Rd 4 CO12 .107 B1
St Michael's Way IP19 .42 C6
St Nicholas Cl
Bury St Edmunds IP32 .123 C6
Rattlesden IP30 ......65 D5

St Nicholas Dr IP26 ....4 E6
St Nicholas St IP1 ...155 B2
St Olaves Rd
Bury St Edmunds IP32 .122 E8
Ipswich IP5 ....141 C8
St Osyth Cl IP2 .....142 F8
St Pancras Cath Prim Sch
IP1 ....134 F2
St Paul's Cl
4 Beccles NR34 ....111 C2
Brockdish IP21 ....21 F2
St Pauls Cl IP15 ....130 E5
St Peter & Paul Ceva Prim
Sch IP23 ....117 D2
St Peter's Ave
13 Claydon IP6 ......82 A5
1 Claydon IP6 .....134 C8
St Peters Cl CB8 ......45 F2
St Peter's Cl
Brockdish IP21 ....21 F2
8 Claydon IP6 ......82 A5
Stowmarket IP14 ....124 B6
Woodbridge IP12 ....146 D4
St Peters Cl
Charsfield IP13 ......70 B3
6 Moulton CB8 ......45 F3
St Peter's Ct IP33 ...154 B1
St Peter's Hall★ NR35 .24 A8
St Peters Pl CB7 .....29 B1
St Peters Rd
Aldeburgh IP15 .....130 E5
Lowestoft NR33 .....114 C3
St Peter's Rd
Lowestoft NR33 .....115 C6
Stowmarket IP14 ....124 B6
St Peter's St
Ipswich IP4 ....155 B2
Lowestoft NR32 .....113 C6
4 Lowestoft NR32 ..113 D2
10 Lowestoft NR32 .113 C6
St Peters Way 11 IP31 ..49 E4
St Peters Wlk IP26 ....4 F3
St Philips Rd CB8 ...120 F5
St Quinton's Ct NR33 .115 B5
St Stephens Cl IP33 .123 C6
St Stephens La IP1 ...155 A2
St Vincent Wlk 14 NR31 ...3 B7
St Wendred's Way
CB8 ....120 B7
Salehurst Rd IP3 ....140 E3
Salisbury Gn IP33 ...123 B3
Salisbury Rd
Ipswich IP3 ....140 A3
Lowestoft NR33 .....115 C7
1 Southwold IP18 ...119 D5
Sallows Cl IP1 ......138 F7
Sally Wood's La IP24 .125 F6
Salmond Dr 5 IP24 ....16 C2
Salter Cl IP32 ......123 E4
Salters Gdns 4 IP13 ..83 E5
Saltgate 5 NR34 ....111 B6
Salthouse La IP4 ....155 C2
Saltwater Way NR33 .114 E8
Samford Cl IP9 ......105 E8
Samford Ct 5 NR34 ..111 C4
Samford Pl IP8 .....138 B6
Sampson Dr 5 CO10 ...91 E8
Samson Cl 14 IP32 ...48 C5
Samson's La IP22 .....19 F4
Samuel Ct IP4 ......155 C3
Samuel Vince Rd 2
IP21 ....39 D8
Samuel Ward Sch
CB9 ....132 F7
San Francisco Wlk 3
NR33 ....114 C5
Sancroft Way
5 Fressingfield IP21 ..39 D8
Wortwell IP20 ....23 A7
Sanctuary Gdns 4
NR32 ....112 F5
Sanctuary The IP16 ...73 F6
Sanctuary Way 9 NR33 .11 B1
Sand Acre Cl IP28 ...116 D5
Sand Hill CO10 ....93 C3
Sand St CB7 ....28 D3
Sandbank Rd 1 NR33 .114 E4
Sanderling Cl 3 IP28 .116 D4
Sanders Cl 2 NR32 ..112 F4
Sandford Rd IP14 ....52 A1
Sandgalls Rd IP27 ...109 D6
Sandholme Cl IP33 ..123 B2
Sandhurst Ave IP3 ..139 F4
Sandling Cres IP4 ...140 E6
Sandlings Prim Sch
IP12 ....85 C3
Sandlings The
Aldeburgh IP15 .....130 E5
Ipswich IP3 ....140 D1
Sandown Cl 3 IP1 ...135 A3
Sandown Rd IP1 .....135 A3
Sandpath 5 IP21 .....39 E8
Sandpiper Cl CB9 ...133 A6
Sandpiper Rd
Bury St Edmunds IP33 .123 C2
Ipswich IP2 ....138 E2
Sandpit Cl IP4 ......140 F5
Sandpit Dr 3 IP31 ....49 E4
Sandpit Hill IP20 .....23 B3
Sandpit La
Thurston IP31 ....49 E4
Worlingham NR34 .....9 F4
Sandringham Cl IP2 .138 F2
Sandringham Rd
NR32 ....113 C1
Sands Cl 9 NR31 ......3 C6
Sands La NR32 ......112 D2
Sandy Cl 5 IP11 .....107 D8

Sandy Dro IP28 ....30 F3
Sandy Hill Barham IP6 .82 B7
Wormingford CO6 ...101 E3
Sandy La Barham IP6 .82 A6
Barningham IP31 .....34 E8
Barsham NR34 ....9 A4
2 Bromeswell IP12 ..85 A5
Bulmer CO10 ....91 D3
Diss IP22 ....20 D2
Gisleham NR33 ....11 A1
Holton IP19 ....118 E4
Hoo IP13 ....70 B4
Iken IP12 ....72 F2
Little Bealings IP13 .137 D2
Marlesford IP13 .....71 C5
Rendham IP17 ....56 F3
Ringshall IP14 ....80 D8
St Mary, South Elmham
Otherwise Homersfield
IP20 ....23 B7
Sternfield IP17 ......72 C8
Stowlangtoft IP31 ....50 A7
Sudbury CO10 ....148 A4
Sutton IP12 ....99 B8
Waldringfield IP12 ...98 E8
Westerfield IP6 .....135 C5
Wickham Market IP13 .127 D5
Witnesham IP6 ......136 B8
Woodbridge IP12 ....146 D2
Sandyhill La IP3 ....139 E1
Sapiston Rd IP31 .....33 F5
Sapling Pl IP4 ......140 E5
Sarsen Cl IP19 .....118 C4
Saturn Cl NR32 .....113 D4
Sawmill La IP10 ....145 B6
Sawmills Rd IP22 ....20 E2
Sawston Cl 10 IP2 ..139 A4
Sawyers IP7 ....80 F1
Sawyers Cl IP9 .....150 E2
Saxham Bsns Pk IP29 ..47 E4
Saxmundham Mid Sch
IP17 ....128 C2
Saxmundham Prim Sch
IP17 ....128 C4
Saxmundham Rd
Aldeburgh IP15 .....130 C5
Framlingham IP13 ...126 E3
Friston IP17 ....72 E7
Knodishall IP17 ......57 F1
Theberton IP16 ......58 A2
Saxmundham Sports Club
IP17 ....128 C4
Saxmundham Sta
IP17 ....128 C3
Saxon Cl Exning CB8 .120 D8
11 Felixstowe IP11 .153 E5
Saxon Cres 7 IP31 ...33 D5
Saxon Dr 9 CB5 ......44 A5
Saxon La IP8 ....95 E4
Saxon Pl IP27 ....5 E3
Saxon Rd
Lowestoft NR33 .....115 B3
Saxmundham IP17 ...128 B3
Saxon Rise IP33 ....122 E3
Saxon Way 2 IP17 ...147 A2
Saxon Wlk IP26 ......6 A8
Saxonfields IP17 .....72 D5
Saxons Way IP19 ...118 B4
Saxstead Rd
Dennington IP13 .....55 D5
Framlingham IP13 ...126 E3
Scales St NR35 .....110 A4
Scalesbrook La IP19 .118 E2
Scaltback Mid Sch
CB8 ....120 E5
Scama La IP22 ....36 C6
Scarlin Rd IP33 .....122 E3
Schneider Rd 3 IP11 .153 H11
Scholars Wlk IP22 ....20 C3
School Ave IP30 ......50 E2
School Cl
1 Capel St. Mary IP9 .150 E4
Cheveley CB8 ....60 E8
Hadleigh IP7 ....149 E5
Kenninghall NR16 ....19 A4
North Cove NR34 .....10 C4
Norton IP31 ....50 B4
20 Stanton IP31 .....34 E4
School Cres CB9 ....133 E8
School Farm La CO10 ..78 C2
School Hill
Boxford CO10 ....93 C3
Copdock & Washbrook
IP8 ....95 B4
Kettleburgh IP13 .....70 C7
School La Bardwell IP31 .34 C4
Bawdsey IP12 ....99 E2
Benhall IP17 ....72 C8
5 Brantham CO11 ...104 E5
16 Burwell CB5 ......44 A5
Dedham CO7 ....103 F4
East Bergholt CO7 ..151 B5
Easton IP13 ....70 E5
Fornham St Martin IP31 .48 D5
Great Barton IP31 ....49 B6
Great Horkesley CO6 .102 C1
Halesworth IP19 ....118 A4
17 Harleston IP20 ...22 D4
Haverhill CB9 ......132 B5
Hollesley IP12 ....99 F7
Little Horkesley CO6 .102 B3
Long Melford CO10 ...77 E1
Manningtree CO11 ..104 D1
Martlesham IP12 ....146 C1
Metfield IP20 ....23 C3
4 Mistley CO11 ....104 F2
Reydon IP18 ....26 E1

School La continued
Stratford St Mary CO7 ....103 E5
Thelnetham IP22 ....18 E1
7 Thurstow IP31 ....49 E4
Ufford IP13 ....84 F7
School Mdw
1 Stowmarket IP14 ....124 E3
4 Wetherden IP14 ......51 A1
School Rd Alburgh IP20 ...7 A1
Bedingham NR35 ....7 B7
Blaxhall IP12 ....72 A3
Bressingham IP22 ....19 E4
Coddenham IP6 ....68 B1
Coldfair Green IP17 ......129 A3
Earsham NR35 ....7 F4
Elmswell IP30 ....50 E2
Great Ashfield IP31 ......50 F6
Great Barton IP31 ....49 B6
Great Wratting CB9 ......74 F3
Hinderclay IP22 ....35 E2
Hollesley IP12 ....99 F7
Kedington IP29 ....133 E8
Kirby Cane NR35 ....8 E8
Knodishall IP17 ....73 A8
Langham CO4 ....103 C2
Little Horkesley CO6 ....102 B2
Little Yeldham CO9 ......90 B2
Lowestoft NR33 ....114 F8
Monk Soham IP13 ....54 D4
Pentlow CO10 ....90 F7
Ringsfield NR34 ....9 E1
Risby IP28 ....47 E5
St Andrew, Ilketshall
NR34 ....8 E2
9 Shotley Gate IP9 ....107 A4
Sudbourne IP12 ....87 A8
Tattingstone IP9 ....142 D1
Thurstow IP31 ....49 E4
Tunstall IP12 ....71 F2
Waldringfield IP12 ......98 D7
Woodditton CB8 ....60 D6
School St Foxearth CO10 ..91 B7
Needham Market IP6 .....125 D4
Stoke-by-Nayland CO6 ...102 E7
Sudbury CO10 ....148 C5
School View NR34 ....24 F5
Schoolhall La IP33 ...154 B3
Schreiber Rd IP4 ....140 B7
Scofield Ct CO10 ....148 E4
Scole Comm IP21 .....20 F3
Scole Comm Rd IP21 ..21 A2
Scole Prim Sch IP21 ..21 A2
Scole Rd IP21 ....21 F2
Sconch Beck Rd IP20 ..23 A6
Scopes Dr IP5 ....141 C8
Scotland End CB7 ......29 E1
Scotland Pl★ CO6 ....102 F7
Scotland St CO6 ......103 A7
Scotred Cl IP28 ....44 A4
Scott Ave IP28 ....116 C5
Scott La 2 IP12 ......84 E6
Scott Rd Ipswich IP3 ..140 B1
13 Ixworth IP31 ....34 B1
Scotts Cl 14 NR33 ....11 B1
Scott's Hill IP14 .....68 B6
Scott's La IP12 ....84 C7
Scrivener Dr IP8 .....138 B2
Scuffin's La IP14 .....52 A6
Sea Lake Rd NR32 ....114 E8
Sea Rd IP11 ....152 F2
Sea View NR33 ....11 C1
Sea View Rise NR31 .....3 C6
Seabreeze Rd IP4 ....124 D5
Seafield Ave 5 CO11 ..105 A2
Seafield Rd 6 CO12 ..107 A1
Seago St NR32 ....113 D1
Sealodes Rd CB7 ....28 A5
Seaman Ave IP17 .....128 B2
Seaton Cl 18 CO11 ...104 D2
Seaton Rd IP11 ......152 E5
Seavert Cl 3 NR33 ...114 E3
Seaview Rd IP18 .....119 C7
Seaward Ave 2 IP16 ..129 D5
Sebert Rd NR32 ......113 B7
Sebert Wood Cty Prim Sch
IP32 ....123 E5
Seckford Cl 1 IP4 ...140 F5
Seckford Hall Rd
IP12 ....146 D3
Seckford St IP12 .....146 F5
Second Ave
Felixstowe IP11 ....152 B7
2 Glemsford CO10 ......77 B3
Sudbury CO10 ....148 E2
Second Dro IP27 ......13 C2
Sedan Wlk IP1 ....155 A2
Sedgefen Rd IP27 .....12 F7
Sedlescombe Rd 8
NR33 ....114 D5
Sefton Way CB8 ......120 D5
Selby St NR32 ....113 C1
Self's La IP22 ....18 F3
Selkirk Rd IP4 ....136 C1
Selvale Way IP11 ....152 E4
Selwyn Cl Ipswich IP2 .155 B1
Mildenhall IP28 ....116 D6
Newmarket CB8 ....121 A1
Semer Cl IP14 ....124 E3
Semere La IP21 ....21 D8
Serpentine Rd IP3 ....140 B2
Seven Cotts La IP5 ..136 C1
Seven Gdns Rd IP3 ....83 F6
Seven Hills (Barrow Cemetery)★
Brettenham IP24 ....16 F4
Little Livermere IP31 ...33 A4
Sevenhills La IP31 ....33 A4
Several Rd IP13 ....55 B3

Severalls La IP13 .....55 D6
Severn Rd
Bury St Edmunds IP32 ...48 C5
Ipswich IP3 ....139 F3
Sewell Wontner Cl
IP5 ....141 C8
Sewell's La CO10 ......90 D5
Sexton NR35 ....7 D6
Sextons Manor Prim Sch
IP33 ....122 C6
Sextons Md IP33 .....154 C1
Sextons Mdw IP33 ....123 B3
Seymore Dr CB9 ......132 B5
Seymour Ave IP27 .....14 D8
Seymour Cl CB8 ......121 C3
Seymour Rd IP2 ......155 B1
Shackleton Cl 20 CO12 106 F1
Shackleton Rd IP3 ...140 B3
Shackleton Sq 3 IP3 .140 B3
Shaddick Rd IP18 ....119 B8
Shade The CB7 ....28 C5
Shadingfield Cl NR32 .113 A5
Shadowbush Cl CB9 ..132 D7
Shadwell Cl IP7 ....5 E3
Shaftesbury Ave 4
CO12 ....107 A2
Shafto Rd IP1 ....134 E1
Shaker's La IP33 .....123 C5
Shaker's Rd IP29 .....47 B4
Shakers' Rd
Brandon IP27 ....15 A5
Wangford IP27 ....14 E4
Shakespeare Rd
Ipswich IP1 ....134 E3
Stowmarket IP14 ....124 B8
Shamrock Ave IP2 ....138 E4
Shannon Cl CB9 ......133 B5
Shannon Rd 4 IP3 ....144 A8
Shardlow Cl CB9 .....132 A7
Sharman's Rd CB7 .....29 A1
Sharon Dr NR32 ......113 B3
Sharon Rd IP33 ......122 D5
Sharp Rd IP3 ....122 F2
Sharper's Cnr IP27 ...109 B8
Sharpes Cnr IP27 ....109 C7
Sharpe's Hill IP29 ...47 E8
Sharpe's La IP29 .....63 A7
Sharpe's Row IP30 ....65 E8
Sharp's Gn 11 IP29 ...63 A8
Shaw Ave NR33 ....114 D3
Shaw Rd CO10 ....91 E8
Shaw Valley Rd IP12 ..84 A1
Shawlands Ave CO10 ..148 F5
Shawsgate Vinery★
IP13 ....126 F6
Shearman Rd IP7 .....149 F5
Sheepdrift Rd IP12 ...85 B5
Sheepgate La
Badwell Ash IP31 ....51 B7
Falkenham IP10 ....98 F1
Sheepshead Hill 2 CO10 92 B3
Sheepwash La IP17 ....58 E6
Sheerwater Cl IP30 ..123 F6
Shelbourne Cl 7 IP5 ..141 D7
Sheldrake Dr IP2 .....138 E1
Sheldrick's Rd CB7 ...29 D5
Shelley Ave CO10 ....148 F4
Shelley Cl IP14 ......124 F3
Shelley Rd
3 Bury St Edmunds IP32 .48 C5
Layham IP7 ....149 E1
Shelley St IP2 ....155 B1
Shelley Way
Bacton IP14 ....51 E5
Thetford IP24 ....16 C7
Shelterhouse Cnr IP24 .32 C8
Shelton Hill IP21 ....39 B5
Shelton Rd 4 NR33 ..114 F3
Shenley Rd IP3 ......140 B1
Shenstone Dr IP1 ....135 A3
Shepherd Dr IP8 .....138 C2
Shepherds Dr 1 IP29 ..63 D1
Shepherds Gr Ind Est
IP22 ....35 B4
Shepherds La
Burgate IP22 ....36 D7
Glemsford CO10 ....77 A3
Onehouse IP14 ....124 A8
Sheppards Way 6 IP5 .147 D7
Sherborne Ave IP4 ...136 A2
Sherborne Rd IP33 ..122 D3
Sherbourne St CO10 ...93 B4
Sheridan Wlk NR34 ..111 E4
Sheriffs Ct CB8 ......59 F2
Sherrington Rd IP1 ..139 A8
Sherwood Fields 4 IP5 141 C7
Shetland Cl
5 Ipswich IP4 ....136 A1
Ipswich IP4 ....140 A8
Shetland Rd CB9 .....133 B5
Shetlands 13 IP31 ....34 E4
Shickle Pl IP22 ....18 C2
Shilling St CO10 ......78 D4
Shillitoe Cl IP33 ....154 A2
Shimpling Cl 7 IP14 .124 E3
Shimpling Rd IP21 ....21 B5
Shingle Hill IP21 ....38 C4
Ship Gdns IP28 ....59 E8
Ship La Bradfield CO11 105 C2
Bramford IP8 ....134 B1
Ship Launch Rd IP3 ..139 E3
Ship Rd NR33 ....114 E6
Shippea Hill Sta CB7 .12 C7
Shire Hall Yd IP4 ...155 C2
Shires The NR32 .....113 B8
Shirley Cl 9 IP1 .....135 A3
Shi-tennoji Sch IP28 ..30 D1
Shoals Wlk NR33 .....114 E6

Shoe Devil La NR35 ...24 C8
Shoebridge's Hill CO7 .103 F3
Shop Hill CB8 ....61 E1
Shop La IP13 ....71 E5
Shop Rd IP13 ....69 E1
Shop St IP13 ....54 D7
Shore La
Bradfield CO11 ....105 C2
Harkstead IP9 ....106 A5
Nacton IP10 ....145 B3
Shores Cl IP28 ....29 C6
Short Beck 19 IP26 ....4 E5
Short Brackland IP33 .154 B2
Short La Feltwell IP26 ..4 D5
Lowestoft NR33 ....114 C2
Walberswick IP18 ....43 C5
Short Rd
Belton with Browston NR31 .2 D8
Blundeston NR32 ....3 A4
Snailwell CB8 ....45 A5
Short St 2 NR33 ......115 B4
Shortlands IP22 ......138 D1
Shotford Rd IP20 .....22 D5
Shotley Cl
Felixstowe IP11 ....152 D4
Ipswich IP8 ....138 C2
Shotley Mews 8 IP12 ..85 B3
Shotley Prim Sch IP9 .106 F5
Shotley Wlk IP9 .....106 E7
Shrub House Cl 1 IP28 .30 B8
Shrubberies The CB8 .121 D1
Shrubbery Rd IP13 ...146 B3
Shrubland Ave IP1 ...134 E1
Shrubland Dr IP4 ....140 F5
Shrubland Rd 11 CO11 105 A2
Shrublands 2 IP28 ...116 C4
Siam Pl 4 CO10 ......148 C5
Siamhall La CO10 ....92 F3
Sicklesmere Rd
Bury St Edmunds IP33 ..123 D2
Nowton IP30 ....63 D8
Sidegate Ave IP4 ....140 A8
Sidegate La IP4 ......136 A1
Sidegate La W IP4 ...135 F1
Sidegate Prim Sch
IP4 ....140 A8
Sidegate Rd NR31 ......3 A8
Siding Rd NR34 ....10 C5
Silent St IP4 ....155 B2
Silhalls Cl 7 CB8 .....60 F8
Silk Mill Cl 2 IP7 ...149 D5
Silver Dr IP15 ....130 C6
Silver Hill IP8 ....95 D6
Silver Leys IP9 ......104 F7
Silver St Burwell CB5 ..44 A6
Kedington CB9 ....133 F7
Old Newton with Dagworth
IP14 ....51 E2
South Lopham IP22 ......19 C3
Withersfield CB9 ....74 A2
Silverdale Ave IP14 ..124 C7
Silverdale Cl IP1 ....135 A1
Silverley Way 6 CB8 ..60 F8
Silverwood NR33 .....115 A4
Simon's Cross IP13 ..127 B7
Simons Rd IP12 ......147 A7
Simpers Drift IP17 ...56 D1
Simpson Cl IP3 ......139 F1
Sim's La CB9 ....133 F7
Sinclair Dr IP2 ......139 C3
Singleton Ct CO10 ...148 E3
Sir John Leman High Sch
NR34 ....111 A4
Sir John Leman Rd
NR34 ....111 D2
Sir Robert Hitchams CE Prim
Sch IP13 ....126 C4
Sir Robert Hitchams Sch
IP14 ....53 F2
Sirdar Rd IP1 ....139 A6
Siskin Gn 1 NR33 ...114 D5
Sitwell Cl 12 CO11 ..104 D2
Sitwell Gdns 7 IP13 .126 C3
Sizewell Gap IP16 ....58 F1
Sizewell Power Sta
IP16 ....58 F2
Sizewell Rd IP16 ....129 D5
Skamacre Cres NR32 .113 B2
Skate's Hill CO10 ....77 A2
Skelton Cl 9 CO11 ...104 E2
Skelton Rd IP22 ......20 D2
Skelton's Dro IP28 ...13 A2
Skinner St IP33 .....154 B2
Skinner's La
Metfield IP20 ....23 C3
Starston IP20 ....22 B8
Skipper Cl IP8 ......142 E8
Skipper Rd IP2 ......138 D1
Skipper's La IP20 ....74 A3
Skoulding Cl 1 NR33 .114 F7
Sky Hall Hill CO4 ...103 B4
Skylark La IP8 ......138 C2
Slade La IP22 ....19 E2
Slade St IP4 ....155 C2
Slade The IP6 ....134 D8
Slades Cl 7 CO10 .....77 B3
Slaughden Rd IP15 ..130 C3
Sleaford Cl IP2 ......139 A3
Sloe La IP17 ....129 A2
Slough Hill IP29 ......77 E7
Slough La Acton CO10 .78 C1
Horringer IP29 ....122 A2
Slough Rd
Botesdale IP22 ....36 C5
Brantham CO11 ....104 E5

Sir Alf Ramsey Way
IP1 ....155 A2
Slugs La NR32 ....2 C4
Sluice Dro IP26 ....4 E3
Slushy La IP9 ....106 A6
Smaley La 1 CO10 ....91 E8
Smallbridge Entry
CO8 ....101 E4
Smallbridge Hall★
CO8 ....101 E4
Smallgate 6 NR34 ...111 B6
Smallworth La IP22 ..18 E3
Smart St IP4 ....155 C2
Smear La IP18 ....26 D2
Smear La E IP18 .....26 F1
Smeetham Hall La
CO10 ....91 C3
Smith Cres 17 NR33 ..11 B1
Smithbrook La IP29 ..77 A8
Smithers Cl 9 IP9 ...150 E3
Smithfield IP12 .....147 B6
Smiths Dr IP21 ....21 B5
Smiths Pl 9 IP5 .....141 D7
Smith's Wlk NR33 ...114 C6
Smithy Cl
Bradfield Combust with
Stanningfield IP29 .....64 A3
Rushbrooke with Rougham
IP29 ....64 D8
Smock Mdw 8 IP7 ....79 F4
Snab Hill NR33 ....11 A1
Snailwell Rd
Fordham CB8 ....44 F7
Newmarket CB8 ....121 B7
Snailwell Short Rd CB8 .44 F5
Snake's La Lound NR32 .2 F6
Topcroft NR35 ....7 A8
Snape Com Prim Sch
IP17 ....72 D5
Snape Dr NR32 ......113 A4
Snape Hill 2 IP29 ...35 F6
Snape Rd Friston IP17 .129 A2
Sudbourne IP12 ....131 A2
Tunstall IP12 ....72 A2
Snare Dro IP28 ....12 E3
Snipe Farm Rd IP13 ..69 E1
Snow Hill CO10 ....76 A1
Snow Hill La CO6 ...103 B7
Snowberry Way 6 CB7 .28 D5
Snowcroft IP9 ....150 E3
Snowdens Yd 14 IP18 119 D5
Snowdon Hill IP13 ..127 C7
Snowdon Rd IP2 ......138 B2
Snowdrop Cl IP32 ...123 F5
Soames Cl IP14 .....124 C7
Soane St IP4 ....155 C3
Soft Rd CO10 ....90 F3
Soham Rd Ely CB7 ....28 A8
Fordham CB8 ....28 F2
Soham Town Cnr IP13 .54 F3
Solomon Rd 10 NR33 ..11 B1
Somerleyton Hall & Gdns★
NR32 ....2 E4
Somerleyton Prim Sch
NR32 ....2 D4
Somerleyton Rd NR32 .112 F4
Somerleyton Sta NR32 ..2 C3
Somerset Rd IP4 ....139 F8
Somersham Prim Sch
IP8 ....81 C3
Somersham Rd IP8 ...81 F2
Somerton Ave NR32 ..113 C3
Somerton Rd IP29 ....77 A7
Somerville Lea 2 IP15 .130 E5
Sorrel Cl IP2 ....138 F3
Sotterley Rd
6 Lowestoft NR32 .....112 F4
Sotterley NR34 ....10 C1
Willingham St Mary NR34 .25 F7
Sound The NR33 .....114 E6
South Cl Beccles NR34 .111 A3
Bury St Edmunds IP33 ..154 A1
Ipswich IP4 ....139 E8
Leiston IP16 ....129 D5
9 Melton IP12 ....84 E6
South Dr CB8 ....120 F4
South Elmham Terr
NR33 ....114 E8
South Entrance IP17 .128 D2
South Hill IP11 ......152 F3
South Lee Sch IP33 ..123 C2
South Leet Cl 4 NR32 .112 E4
South Lodge Dr 1 IP28 .48 C6
South Lowestoft Ind Est
NR33 ....114 E2
South Pk IP27 ....5 E3
South Rd Beccles NR34 .111 A3
Lakenheath IP27 ....109 E3
South St
Hockwold cum Wilton IP26 ..4 F2
Ipswich IP1 ....155 A4
12 Manningtree CO11 ...104 C2
Risby IP28 ....47 D4
South Strand 1 CO11 .104 E3
South View Cl 8 NR32 .113 B2
South View Gn IP9 ..104 F7
Southend Rd 4 NR35 ..110 B3
Southern La IP21 .....19 A1
Southery Rd IP26 ......4 B6
Southfield Dr IP16 ..129 C5
Southfield Gdns NR33 .114 F6
Southfields CO7 .....103 F3
Southfields Cl CB8 ...120 E4
Southgate IP20 ....22 C6
Southgate Ave IP28 ..116 C4
Southgate Gdns
Bury St Edmunds IP33 ..123 C3
3 Long Melford CO10 ..91 E7

Southgate Rd IP8 ....138 B1
Southgate St
Bury St Edmunds IP33 ..154 C1
4 Long Melford CO10 ..91 E7
Southolt Rd
Athelington IP21 ....38 F1
Bedfield IP13 ....54 D6
Southwald & District Hospl
IP18 ....119 C6
Southwell La NR34 ...26 A6
Southwell Rd NR33 ..115 B7
Southwold Mus★
IP18 ....119 D5
Southwold Prim Sch
IP18 ....119 D5
Southwold Rd
Blyford IP19 ....42 B8
Brampton with Stoven
NR34 ....25 E5
Holton IP19 ....118 F3
Wrentham NR34 ....26 E5
Southwood Cl IP17 ..128 D2
Spalding's Chair Hill
IP24 ....17 B3
Spanbies Rd 3 CO7 ..103 E5
Sparhawk St IP33 ...154 C1
Sparkes Cl 5 CB7 ....29 C5
Sparks La CO9 ....89 D3
Sparrow Ct 11 IP14 ..53 F2
Sparrow Rd CO10 ...148 F4
Sparrowhawk Rd
IP18 ....118 C7
Sparrows Croft Rd 5
IP12 ....85 E8
Spashett Rd 2 NR32 .113 B4
Speed La CB7 ....28 D4
Speedwell Cl 7 NR33 .115 A3
Speedwell Rd IP2 ...138 F4
Speedwell Way 13 IP20 .22 D5
Spencer Dr NR32 ....113 B6
Spencer Dro CB7 .....28 C4
Spencer Rd 4 IP12 ...85 E8
Spencer Way IP14 ...124 B7
Spenser Rd IP1 ......134 E3
Spexhall Way NR32 ..113 B5
Spicers La 2 CO10 ....91 E8
Spiers Way IP22 .....20 B2
Spike's La IP14 ......66 E7
Spindle Rd CB9 .....132 B7
Spinks' La NR35 ....7 D6
Spinnel's Hill CO11 ..105 D1
Spinnel's La CO11 ...105 E1
Spinner Cl IP1 ......138 D8
Spinner's La 3 IP18 .119 D5
Spinney Cl NR34 ......10 B4
Spinney Hill IP7 ......81 A1
Spinney Rd IP31 ......33 B3
Spinney The
Beccles NR34 ....111 D4
Ipswich IP4 ....140 F4
Spire Chase CO10 ...148 E8
Spirkett's La IP20 ...22 D5
Spitfire Cl IP3 ......140 B1
Spong La IP30 ....50 E2
Spong The IP20 ......23 C3
Spooners Cl CB8 ......59 F4
Spooner's La NR34 ...26 E2
Spooners La 5 IP7 ...149 D6
Spout La CO10 ......101 B8
Spring Cl
3 Bentwaters Airfield
IP12 ....85 D8
Burwell CB5 ....44 A5
Spring La
Bury St Edmunds IP33 ..154 A3
Crowfield IP6 ....68 B3
Dennington IP13 ....55 B5
5 Lavenham CO10 ......78 D4
Polstead CO6 ....93 D2
Ufford IP13 ....127 B1
Wickham Market IP13 ..127 D7
Spring Mdw
10 Glemsford CO10 .....77 A3
Playford IP6 ....137 B4
Spring Pk IP6 ....69 C2
Spring Rd Bardwell IP31 .34 C5
Copdock & Washbrook
IP8 ....95 E5
Ipswich IP4 ....139 F6
Spring Row IP14 .....124 D7
Spring St 6 CO10 .....78 D4
Springbank Ave 16
CO11 ....104 D2
Springett's Hill CO8 .101 B5
Springfield IP18 .....119 A7
Springfield Ave
Bury St Edmunds IP33 ..154 A3
Felixstowe IP11 ....153 A5
Springfield Dr IP27 ..109 D6
Springfield Gdns
NR33 ....114 F5
Springfield Jun Sch
IP1 ....138 F8
Springfield La IP1 ...138 F8
Springfield Rd
Aldeburgh IP15 ....130 C5
Bury St Edmunds IP33 ..154 A3
4 Somersham IP8 ......81 C3
Sudbury CO10 ....148 C2
Springhurst Cl IP4 ..139 F6
Springland Cl IP4 ...140 A6
Springlands Way
CO10 ....148 D8
Sprites End IP11 ....152 D7
Sprites Jun Sch IP2 .138 C2

Sprites La IP8 ....138 C1
Spriteshall La IP11 ...152 D7
Sproughton Bsns Pk
 IP1 ....138 D7
Sproughton CE Prim Sch
 IP8 ....138 B6
Sproughton Rd IP1 ...138 C7
Spruce Cl 14 IP27 .....13 F2
Spur End IP12 ....147 C7
Spurgeon Score 12
 NR32 ....113 E2
Spurling Cl 2 CB8 .....60 E7
Square The IP14 ......124 E4
Squires La 4 IP5 ......98 A8
Squires Wlk NR32 ....113 C5
Squirrells Mill Rd 3 IP7 .79 F4
Squirrels The IP9 ....150 E4
Stackwood Rd CO6 ....93 F3
Stafford Ct NR32 .....112 E4
Stafford St CB8 ....121 B2
Staithe Cl NR35 ......110 B4
Staithe Rd
 Bungay NR35 ....110 B4
 Bungay NR35 ....110 C4
 Burgh St Peter NR34 ..10 C7
Staithe The NR35 ....114 C6
Stambourne Rd CO9 ...89 E2
Stamford Cl IP2 ......142 F8
Stamford St CB8 .....121 B2
Stammers Pl IP5 .....141 E8
Stanford St 3 NR32 ..113 C1
Stanhope Cl IP17 .....72 D5
Stanley Ave IP3 ......140 A4
Stanley Rd Diss IP22 ..20 B2
 Felixstowe IP11 ......153 A3
 Lowestoft NR33 ......114 E7
 Newmarket CB8 ......121 C3
 Sudbury CO10 ....148 C6
Stanley St NR32 ......113 D1
Stanley Wood Ave
 CO10 ....148 D7
Stannard Way CO10 ..148 E4
Stanningfield Rd IP30 ..63 F5
Stansfield Cl NR33 ...114 E6
Stanton Cl
 Beccles NR34 ....111 C3
 Lowestoft NR32 ......113 C5
Stanton Hughes Way 10
 CO11 ....104 D2
Stanton Prim Sch IP31 .34 E4
Stanton Rd IP31 ....34 C4
Stanway Cl CO10 ....77 B3
Staple Cl IP31 ....35 C1
Staplehurst Rd 7 NR33 .114 C4
Staples La CB7 ....28 D3
Star La IP4 ....155 C2
Starfield Cl IP4 ......140 B6
Starhouse La IP14 .....66 C5
Starre Rd IP33 ....122 C5
Starston La IP20 ......22 C5
Station App
 Newmarket CB8 ......121 A2
 Saxmundham IP17 ....128 D3
Station Hill
 1 Bures CO8 ....101 C4
 Bury St Edmunds IP33 .154 B4
 Harleston IP20 ....22 D6
 Little Whelnetham IP30 .64 B6
 Thurstow IP31 ....49 D4
Station La 13 CO12 ...107 B2
Station Rd Alburgh IP20 .7 A1
 Bacton IP14 ....52 A6
 Barnham IP24 ....16 B2
 Beccles NR34 ....111 B5
 Bentley IP9 ....104 E7
 Birdbrook CO9 ....89 B4
 Blaxhall IP12 ....71 E3
 Bradfield CO11 ....105 B2
 Brampton with Stoven
  NR34 ....25 C5
 Burston & Shimpling IP21 .20 F6
 Clare CO10 ....90 B8
 Claydon IP6 ....134 B8
 8 Corton NR32 ....3 C4
 Corton NR32 ....113 C8
 Diss IP22 ....20 D2
 Ditchingham NR35 ...110 C6
 Dullingham CB8 ......59 E5
 2 Earsham NR35 ......7 F4
 Ellingham NR35 ....8 D7
 Elmswell IP30 ....50 F2
 Felixstowe IP11 ......152 C7
 Fordham CB7 ....29 A1
 Framlingham IP13 ....126 C2
 Geldeston NR34 ....8 F6
 Haddiscoe NR31 ......2 A5
 Hadleigh IP7 ....149 E5
 Halesworth IP19 .....118 B4
 Harleston IP20 ....22 D6
 1 Harwich CO12 ......106 F3
 8 Harwich CO12 .....107 B2
 Haughley IP14 ....51 D1
 4 Haverhill IP9 ......132 E6
 Hopton on Sea NR31 ..3 B6
 Isleham CB7 ....29 C4
 Kennett CB8 ....45 F7
 Lakenheath IP27 .....109 C7
 Laxfield IP13 ....39 F4
 Leiston IP16 ....129 C6
 Long Melford CO10 ...91 E7
 Lowestoft NR32 ......113 D4
 Manningtree CO11 ...104 E3
 Mildenhall IP28 ......116 B3
 Pulham Market IP21 ..21 E8
 Pulham St Mary IP21 ..22 A8
 Soham CB7 ....28 C4

Station Rd continued
 Somerleyton, Ashby &
  Herringfleet NR32 ....2 C3
 Southwold IP18 ......119 C6
 Sudbury CO10 ....148 C5
 Tattingstone IP9 .....105 A7
 Thetford IP24 ....16 B6
 Wetheringsett-cum-brockford
  IP14 ....53 B4
 Woodbridge IP12 ....147 A4
 Wrabness CO11 ......105 F2
Station Rd E IP14 ....124 E6
Station Rd W IP14 ...124 D6
Station Rd CO12 ......106 F3
Station Sq
 Lowestoft NR32 ......115 D8
 11 Lowestoft NR32 ...115 D8
Station Str IP2 ....139 C3
Station Terr IP13 .....126 C2
Station Yd
 Mildenhall IP28 ......116 B3
 Needham Market IP6 ..125 E4
Staverton Cl IP12 .....85 B6
Staygate Wlk 17 NR32 .112 E4
Stearn Dr IP14 ....66 C6
Stearn's La 7 IP14 ....67 D6
Stebbings La IP12 ....99 E7
Steeds Mdw 7 CO10 ..91 E8
Steeles Rd IP30 ....50 D1
Steeple Bumpstead Pottery ★
 CB9 ....88 D3
Steeple Bumpstead Rd
 CB9 ....88 B4
Steeple End IP19 .....118 B3
Steeplechase CO10 ...75 C4
Steggall Cl IP6 ....125 C6
Stella Maris IP2 .....138 D5
Stennetts Cl IP11 ....152 B8
Stephen Cl
 Haverhill CB9 ....132 D6
 Long Melford CO10 ...91 D7
Stephen Rd IP5 ......141 E8
Stephen's Ct IP14 ....140 B6
Stepping Hill 3 NR34 .111 B5
Stetchworth Rd
 Dullingham CB8 ......59 F4
 Stetchworth CB8 ......60 B4
Stevens St NR32 .....113 C1
Stevenson Rd IP1 ....155 A3
Steward Rd IP33 .....123 C2
Stewart Young Gr
 IP5 ....141 D7
Stimpson Cl 3 NR32 ..113 A6
Stirling Cl
 Lowestoft NR32 ......112 F4
 7 Thistley Green IP28 .29 F6
Stirling Dr CB9 ......132 C6
Stirling Gdns CB8 ...120 E4
Stirrups La NR32 ......3 C5
Stobart Cl NR34 .....111 D3
Stockley Cl CB9 ......133 A5
Stockmers End 8 IP9 .150 E3
Stockton Cl IP7 .....149 F4
Stockton Rd NR34 .....9 A7
Stoke Ash Prim Sch
 IP23 ....52 F8
Stoke Coll CO10 ......89 C6
Stoke Cty High Sch
 IP2 ....139 C3
Stoke Hall Rd IP2 ....155 B1
Stoke Pk Dr IP2 .....139 A1
Stoke Quay IP2 ......155 C1
Stoke Rd Clare CO10 ..90 A7
 Layham IP7 ....149 D1
 Leavenheath CO6 ....102 B8
 Nayland-with-wissington
  CO6 ....102 D5
 Stoke Ash IP23 ......37 D1
 Stoke-by-clare CO10 ..89 F7
Stoke St IP2 ....155 B1
Stoke-by-Nayland CEVC
 Prim Sch CO6 ....102 E7
Stoke-by-Nayland Mid Sch
 CO6 ....102 E7
Stollery Cl IP5 ......141 B7
Stonalls IP30 ....50 C1
Stone Hall Rd IP23 ...36 A2
Stone La
 Bressingham IP22 ....19 F6
 Wrabness CO11 ......105 F2
Stone Lodge La IP2 ..139 A3
Stone Lodge La W
 IP2 ....138 F3
Stone Lodge Wlk IP2 .139 B3
Stone St Boxford CO6 .93 C3
 Crowfield IP6 ....68 C3
 Hadleigh IP7 ....149 B8
 Spexhall IP19 ....118 C8
Stone St Rd 2 CO10 ..93 C3
Stonebridge Ave IP33 .122 F3
Stonebridge La IP14 ..67 A8
Stonechat Rd IP2 ....138 C3
Stonegrove Rd IP11 ..152 D1
Stonehouse Rd IP7 ..149 D6
Stonewell Hill IP6 ....68 D1
Stoney La Barrow IP29 .47 B2
 Thurston IP31 ....49 F4
Stoney Rd IP13 ....83 D6
Stonham Aspal CE Prim Sch
 IP14 ....68 B6
Stonham Rd IP14 .....52 B4
Stony La
 2 Aldringham cum Thorpe
  IP16 ....73 F6
 Debenham IP14 ....53 D2
 Wortwell IP20 ....22 F8
Stopford Ct 8 IP1 ...139 A7
Stour Ave IP11 ......152 E3

Stour Cl Glemsford CO10 .77 B1
 4 Harwich CO12 .....106 E1
 Saxmundham IP17 ....128 C4
Stour Gdns CO10 ....148 E2
Stour Rd CO12 ....107 B3
Stour St Cavendish CO10 .90 D8
 17 Manningtree CO11 .104 E2
 Sudbury CO10 ....148 B5
Stour Vale CO9 ......89 B5
Stour Valley Rd CB9 .132 F5
Stourdale Cl 27 CO11 .104 D2
Stourmead Cl CB9 ...133 E8
Stourside IP9 ....107 A4
Stourview Ave 4 CO11 .105 A2
Stourview Cl 6 CO11 .105 A2
Stoven Cl NR32 ......113 B5
Stoven Rd NR34 ......25 F3
Stow La IP31 ....50 A8
Stow Rd IP31 ....34 B1
Stowmarket High Sch
 IP14 ....124 B7
Stowmarket Mid Sch
 IP14 ....124 C6
Stowmarket Rd
 Badley IP6 ....125 A8
 Great Blakenham IP6 ..81 F6
 Old Newton with Dagworth
  IP14 ....51 E1
 Rattlesden IP30 ......65 E6
 Stonham Aspal IP14 ..68 A6
 Wetherden IP14 ......51 A1
Stowmarket Sta IP14 .124 E6
Stowmarket Town FC
 IP14 ....124 D8
Stowupland Rd IP14 ..124 F7
Stowupland St IP14 ..124 D6
Stradbroke CE Prim Sch
 IP21 ....39 A5
Stradbroke High Sch
 IP21 ....39 B4
Stradbroke Rd
 Fressingfield IP21 ....39 D7
 Ipswich IP4 ....140 F1
 Lowestoft NR33 ......115 A4
 Southwold IP18 ......119 D5
Stradishall Rd CO10 ..75 E5
Straight La 19 IP20 ...22 D6
Straight Rd
 Battisford IP14 ......66 D1
 Boxted CO4 ....102 F1
 Bradfield CO11 ......105 B1
 Capel IP10 ....141 C1
 Lidgate CB8 ....61 B4
 Polstead CO6 ....93 F3
 Whepstead IP29 ......63 C4
Strand The IP2 ......143 C8
Stratford Rd
 Dedham CO11 ....103 E4
 Ipswich IP1 ....134 F2
Stratford St Mary Prim Sch
 CO7 ....103 E5
Strattonhall Drift
 IP10 ....145 F2
Straw La CO10 ....148 B5
Strawberry Fields
 CB9 ....132 B5
Strawberry La IP19 ...25 D3
Street Farm La 4 IP31 .34 B1
Street Farm Rd IP17 .128 D3
Street The Aldeby NR34 ..9 F8
 Alderton IP12 ....99 E3
 Aldham IP7 ....94 E8
 Ashen CO10 ....89 E5
 Ashfield cum Thorpe IP14 .54 C1
 Bacton IP14 ....51 E5
 Badwell Ash IP31 ....50 E7
 Barnham IP24 ....16 B2
 Barrow IP29 ....47 A2
 Barton Mills IP28 ....116 A2
 Bawdsey IP12 ....99 E3
 Beck Row, Holywell Row
  & Kenny Hill IP28 ..30 C8
 Belchamp Otten CO10 .90 A4
 Belstead IP8 ....142 C6
 Benacre NR34 ....27 A7
 Birdbrook CO9 ....89 A3
 Blo' Norton IP22 .....18 E2
 Blundeston NR32 ......3 A4
 Botesdale IP22 ....36 A6
 Boxted IP29 ....77 A6
 Bradfield CO11 ......105 C1
 Bradfield Combust with
  Stanningfield IP30 ..64 B4
 Bramfield IP19 ....41 F5
 Bramford IP8 ....134 A2
 Brampton with Stoven
  NR34 ....25 E4
 Brandon IP27 ....5 E1
 Brantham CO11 ......105 A5
 Bredfield IP13 ....84 C8
 Bressingham IP22 ....19 D6
 Brettenham IP7 .....65 C1
 Bridgham NR16 ....17 E8
 Brockdish IP21 ....21 E2
 Brome & Oakley IP23 .117 D8
 Bruisyard IP17 ....56 D4
 Brundish IP13 ....39 D1
 Bulmer CO10 ....91 C3
 Burrough Green CB8 ..59 E3
 12 Bury St Edmunds IP28 .48 C6
 Butley IP12 ....86 A6
 Capel St. Mary IP9 ...150 D3
 Cavenham IP28 ......47 A8
 Charsfield IP13 ......70 B3
 Charsfield IP13 ......70 C3
 Chattisham IP8 ......95 C4
 Chedburgh IP29 ......62 C4
 Chelsworth IP7 ......79 D3
 Coney Weston IP31 ...17 E1

Street The continued
 Copdock & Washbrook
  IP8 ....95 F5
 Corton NR32 ....3 D4
 Cratfield IP19 ....40 D5
 Cretingham IP13 .....69 E7
 Culford IP28 ....48 B8
 Dalham CB8 ....61 B8
 Dalham CB8 ....61 C8
 Darsham IP17 ....42 B1
 Dennington IP13 .....55 E6
 Dickleburgh IP21 ....21 B5
 Drinkstone IP30 .....65 B8
 Earl Soham IP13 .....54 F2
 Earsham NR35 ....7 F4
 East Bergholt CO7 ...151 B4
 Easton IP13 ....70 E5
 Elmsett IP7 ....80 F1
 Eriswell IP27 ....13 F1
 Eye IP21 ....38 B4
 Eyke IP12 ....85 B6
 Farnham IP17 ....72 A7
 Flixton NR35 ....7 E2
 Foxearth CO10 ......91 B7
 Framsden IP14 ......69 B6
 Freckenham IP28 ....29 E3
 Gazeley CB8 ....46 B3
 Geldeston NR34 ....8 F6
 Great Barton IP31 ...49 B5
 Great Bricett IP7 ....80 D5
 Great Livermere IP31 .33 C2
 Great Waldingfield CO10 .92 D6
 Great Wratting CB9 ..74 F3
 Grundisburgh IP13 ..83 E5
 Hacheston IP13 ......71 A6
 Halesworth IP19 .....118 E3
 Harkstead IP9 ......106 A5
 Hessett IP30 ....64 F8
 Hinderclay IP22 .....35 E7
 Holbrook IP9 ....105 E7
 Hollesley IP12 ....99 F7
 Horham IP21 ....38 E3
 Horringer IP29 ......122 B1
 Huntingfield IP19 ....41 A4
 Icklingham IP28 .....31 D4
 Kersey IP7 ....93 F7
 Kettleburgh IP13 ....70 C7
 Kirtling CB8 ....60 E3
 Lawshall IP29 ....63 E1
 Layham IP7 ....149 E2
 Letheringham IP13 ...70 D4
 Lidgate CB8 ....61 B4
 Little Bealings IP13 ..137 D4
 Little Thurlow CB9 ...74 D5
 Little Waldingfield CO10 .92 E8
 Lound NR32 ....2 F6
 Lowestoft NR32 ......113 D8
 Lowestoft NR33 ......114 C2
 Market Weston IP22 ..35 A8
 Martlesham IP12 ....146 C1
 Middleton CO10 .....148 C1
 Mildenhall IP28 ......30 B8
 Monks Eleigh IP7 ....79 C2
 Moulton CB8 ....45 F3
 Nacton IP10 ....145 C5
 Newbourne IP12 .....98 D6
 North Cove NR34 .....10 B4
 North Lopham IP22 ..19 A6
 Norton IP31 ....50 B4
 Occold IP23 ....37 F1
 Pakenham IP31 ......49 E6
 Parham IP13 ....71 A7
 Peasenhall IP17 .....56 F8
 Pettistree IP13 ......127 C4
 Poslingford CO10 ....76 A3
 Preston St Mary CO10 .79 A5
 Pulham St Mary IP21 .22 A7
 Ramsey & Parkeston
  CO12 ....106 D1
 Raydon IP7 ....94 E1
 Redenhall with Harleston
  IP20 ....22 F5
 1 Redgrave IP22 .....36 A8
 Riddlesworth IP22 ...18 A3
 Rumburgh IP19 ......24 C4
 Rushmere NR33 .....10 B1
 St James South Elmham
  IP19 ....23 F4
 Shotley IP9 ....106 F6
 Shottisham IP12 .....99 B7
 Snailwell CB8 ....45 A4
 Somerleyton, Ashby &
  Herringfleet NR32 ...2 D4
 Somerleyton, Ashby &
  Herringfleet NR32 ...2 D4
 South Lopham IP22 ..19 B4
 Southolt IP23 ....54 B7
 Stanton IP31 ....34 E4
 Starston IP20 ....22 C7
 Sternfield IP17 .....72 D8
 Stoke Ash IP23 ......52 F8
 Stonham Aspal IP14 ..68 B6
 Stowlangtoft IP31 ...50 B6
 Stradishall CB8 ......75 E6
 Stratford St Mary CO7 .103 E4
 Thorndon IP23 ....53 B8
 Thornham Magna IP23 .37 A2
 Troston IP31 ....33 D3
 Tuddenham St Martin
  IP6 ....136 C5
 Ubbeston IP19 ....40 F3
 Walberswick IP18 ...119 A2
 Wattisfield IP22 .....35 C4
 Wenhaston IP19 .....42 C6
 Westleton IP17 ......58 C7
 Westleton IP17 ......58 C5

Street The continued
 Wetheringsett-cum-brockford
  IP14 ....52 F6
 Weybread IP21 ....22 D2
 Whatfield IP7 ....80 C1
 Wherstead IP9 ......143 A6
 Winfarthing IP22 ....20 B8
 Wissett IP19 ....24 D2
 Witnesham IP6 ......136 A8
 Woodbridge IP12 ....147 C7
 Wooddalton CB8 ....60 D5
 Wooddalton CB8 ....60 D6
 Woolpit IP30 ....50 D1
 Worlington IP28 .....30 B4
Streetfield Cl IP29 ...77 F7
Stretham Rd CB7 .....28 A2
Stretton Ave CB8 ....121 B2
Strickland Manor Hill
 IP17 ....57 C8
Strickland Pl 18 IP18 .119 D5
Stricklands Rd 1 IP14 .124 E5
Strickmere CO7 ......103 E5
Strollers Way CB8 ....60 A5
Strowger's Way 6 NR33 .11 C7
Struggler's La IP6 ...136 A8
Stuart Ct
 5 Felixstowe IP11 ...153 D7
 Ipswich IP4 ....139 F7
Stuart Dr NR34 ......111 C4
Stubbing's La IP21 ...22 E3
Stubbin's La CB8 .....46 B3
Stubbs Cl Ipswich IP3 .140 A1
 9 Manningtree CO11 .104 D2
Stubbs Wood NR32 ..113 B6
Studio Cl IP17 ....58 C8
Studlands Pk Ave
 CB8 ....120 D6
Stump St IP13 ....127 A3
Stump's Cross CO9 ..89 D1
Sturdee Ave IP3 .....140 B3
Sturgeon Way 22 IP31 .34 E4
Sturmer End Ind Est
 CB9 ....133 A3
Sturmer Rd CB9 .....133 D5
Stuston La IP21 .....117 B8
Stuston Rd IP21 ......20 E1
Stutton CE Prim Sch
 IP9 ....105 D5
Stutton Cl IP9 ....105 D5
Stutton Gn IP9 ......105 C4
Stutton Hall ★ IP9 ...105 B7
Stutton La IP9 ......105 D5
Stutton Rd CO11 ....105 A5
Sub-station Rd IP11 .152 D2
Sudbourne Rd
 14 Felixstowe IP11 ..152 D5
 Orford IP12 ....131 B5
Sudbury Rd Acton CO10 .92 D2
 Bulmer CO10 ....91 C3
 Bures St Mary CO8 ..101 C5
 3 Felixstowe IP11 ...152 C4
 Gestingthorpe CO9 ..90 F1
 Great Whelnetham IP30 .64 A6
 Lavenham CO10 ......78 D3
 Long Melford CO10 ..91 D6
 Newton CO10 ....92 C4
 Stoke-by-nayland CO6 .102 D7
Sudbury Rugby Union FC
 CO10 ....148 A2
Sudbury Sta CO10 ...148 D5
Sudbury Upper Sch
 CO10 ....148 B3
Sue Ryder Foundation Mus ★
 CO10 ....76 A1
Suffolk Ave IP31 .....33 D5
Suffolk Bsns Pk IP30 .123 F4
Suffolk Dr IP12 ......85 D8
Suffolk Horse Mus ★
 IP12 ....147 A5
Suffolk Nuffield Hospl
 IP10 ....141 B4
Suffolk Owl Sanctuary ★
 IP14 ....68 C3
Suffolk Rd
 18 Bury St Edmunds IP32 .48 C8
 2 Bury St Edmunds IP32 .122 E8
 Ipswich IP4 ....155 C4
 Lowestoft NR32 ......115 D8
 Sudbury CO10 ....148 C6
Suffolk Ret Pk IP1 ...139 A6
Suffolk Ski Ctr ★ IP2 .143 B7
Suffolk Way CB8 .....120 C5
Suffolk Wildlife Pk ★
 NR33 ....11 B3
Suffolk Wr Pk ★ IP8 .134 A5
Sulleys Hill IP7 ......103 D8
Sullivan Pl IP12 ......98 D7
Summer La IP12 .....85 A6
Summer Rd 8 NR32 ..113 D1
Summerfield Cl IP4 ..140 D8
Summerfield Gdns
 NR33 ....115 A6
Summerhill Sch IP16 .129 C7
Summers Rd IP32 ...122 E8
Sumner Rd IP22 .....35 B4
Sun La IP12 ....147 A5
Sun Rd NR35 ....110 D8
Sun St 4 CB7 ....29 C5
Sunderland Rd 2
 IP11 ....153 H11
Sunfield Cl IP4 ......140 E6
Sunley Cl IP3 ....155 D8
Sunningdale Ave
 Ipswich IP4 ....140 D5
 Lowestoft NR33 .....115 A4
 Mildenhall IP28 .....116 B4
Sunningdale Dr IP11 .153 B6
Sunnyfields NR33 ...115 A7

Sunnyhill IP12 . . . . .98 D7
Sunnyside
  Bedingham NR35 . . . . .7 C8
  Diss IP22 . . . . .20 C3
Sunray Ave IP11 . . . . . .153 B6
Surbiton Rd IP1 . . . . . .138 F7
Surrey Cl 8 IP13 . . . . .126 C3
Surrey Rd
  Felixstowe IP11 . . . . . .152 F4
  Ipswich IP1 . . . . .139 A6
Surrey St
  6 Lowestoft NR32 . . . . .113 D1
  4 Lowestoft NR32 . . . . .115 D8
Sussex Crof 9 IP12 . . . .85 B3
Sussex Rd NR32 . . . . . .113 B5
Sutherland Dr NR32 . . . .113 B5
Sutton Cl
  Bury St Edmunds IP32 . . .123 E5
  Woodbridge IP12 . . . . . .147 B5
Sutton Hoo National Trust ★
  IP12 . . . . .147 D5
Swaffham Heath Rd
  CB8 . . . . .59 A7
Swaffham Rd
  Burwell CB5 . . . . .44 A3
  Mundford IP26 . . . . .6 B8
Swainston Way IP13 . . . .55 D5
Swallow Cl
  Felixstowe IP11 . . . . . .153 C7
  12 Harwich CO12 . . . . . .106 F1
Swallow Dr Brandon IP27 . .6 A1
  3 Stowmarket IP14 . . . . .67 A5
Swallow Rd IP2 . . . . . .138 C3
Swallowfields NR33 . . . .114 D3
Swallowtail Cl IP8 . . . . .142 E8
Swamp La IP22 . . . . . . .20 A3
Swan Cl
  Halesworth IP19 . . . . . .118 B3
  29 Martlesham Heath IP5 . .98 A8
  Stowmarket IP14 . . . . . .124 A6
Swan Ct 12 CO11 . . . . . .105 A2
Swan Gn La IP19 . . . . . .40 C5
Swan Gr CB8 . . . . .120 B8
Swan Hill IP8 . . . . .138 A2
Swan La
  Bury St Edmunds IP33 . . .154 C1
  Coney Weston IP31 . . . . .34 D8
  Cretingham IP13 . . . . . .69 E8
  Exning CB8 . . . . .120 B8
  Haverhill CB9 . . . . . . .132 E6
  9 Long Melford CO10 . . . .91 E8
  North Cove NR34 . . . . . .10 C4
  Redenhall with Harleston
    IP20 . . . . .22 D6
  Westerfield IP6 . . . . . .135 A4
Swan Mdw CO7 . . . . . . .103 E5
Swan Rd IP13 . . . . .54 E7
Swan St CO10 . . . . .93 B3
Swanfield CO10 . . . . . . .91 E8
Swansea Ave IP2 . . . . . .139 B1
Swatchway Cl 3 IP3 . . . .144 B8
Swaynes 1 CO7 . . . . . . .103 E5
Sweden Cl 3 CO12 . . . . .106 F2
Swift Cl NR33 . . . . . . .114 D3
Swilltub La IP14 . . . . . .52 A4
Swinburne Rd IP1 . . . . .134 E3
Swine's Gn NR34 . . . . . .111 C4
Swingleton Hill IP7 . . . . .79 C2
Swinton Cl IP2 . . . . . . .138 D1
Swonnell's Wlk
  2 Lowestoft NR32 . . . . .112 D1
  Lowestoft NR32 . . . . . . .114 D8
Sycamore Ave NR33 . . . .114 D7
Sycamore Cl
  Beccles NR34 . . . . . . .111 E3
  7 Great Bricett IP7 . . . . .80 D6
  Ipswich IP8 . . . . .138 C1
  Leiston IP16 . . . . .129 C5
Sycamore Dr
  8 Beck Row, Holywell
    Row & Kenny Hill IP28 . . .13 B1
  5 Mildenhall IP28 . . . . . .30 A8
Sycamore Rd
  Stowupland IP14 . . . . . .67 A6
  Sudbury CO10 . . . . . . .148 F4
Sycamore Way
  Brantham CO11 . . . . . . .104 E5
  Diss IP22 . . . . .20 D3
Sycamore Wlk 20 IP2 . . .138 C1
Syleham Hall La IP21 . . . .22 C1
Syleham Rd
  Brockdish IP21 . . . . . . .22 A2
  Syleham IP21 . . . . .38 D8
Sylvester Rd IP16 . . . . .129 D5
Symonds Rd IP33 . . . . . .123 C4

T

Tacket St IP4 . . . . .155 C2
Tacon Cl IP23 . . . . .117 C2
Tacon Rd IP11 . . . . . . .152 E1
Takers La IP14 . . . . . . .124 E4
Talbot Rd CO10 . . . . . . .148 D7
Tallboys CI IP5 . . . . . . .141 C8
Tallyho Cnr 8 CO7 . . . . .103 E5
Talmash Gdns IP2 . . . . .139 A4
Tamage Rd CO10 . . . . . .92 B7
Tan House La CB5 . . . . . .44 A4
Tan Office La
  Chevington IP29 . . . . . . .62 C5
  Mendlesham IP14 . . . . . .52 E1
Tanners La CB7 . . . . . . .28 D3
Tannersfield Way CB8 . . .120 E8
Tannery Dr IP33 . . . . . .123 B3
Tannery Rd IP14 . . . . . .124 C1
Tannington Long Rd
  IP13 . . . . .39 D1

Tanns La IP22 . . . . .19 A6
Tansy Cl 5 NR33 . . . . . .114 F3
Tansy Mdw 3 IP21 . . . . .39 D8
Target Hill IP20 . . . . . . .23 B6
Tarn Hows Cl 1 IP11 . . . .153 D6
Tasman Cl CB9 . . . . . . .133 A5
Tasmania Rd IP4 . . . . . .140 D6
Tassel Rd IP32 . . . . . . .123 F6
Tattingstone CE Prim Sch
  IP9 . . . . .105 B8
Taunton Cl IP1 . . . . . . .135 B4
Taunton Rd IP11 . . . . . .152 F5
Tavern St Ipswich IP1 . . .155 B3
  Stowmarket IP14 . . . . . .124 D6
Tawneys Ride 2 CO8 . . . .101 D4
Tayfen Rd IP33 . . . . . . .154 B3
Tayfen Terr IP33 . . . . . .154 B4
Tayler Cl 4 IP7 . . . . . . .149 D5
Tayler Rd IP7 . . . . .149 E5
Taylor Dr 8 CO11 . . . . .104 E2
Taylor Rd IP22 . . . . . . .20 B2
Taylors Farm IP14 . . . . .66 C1
Taylors Field CB8 . . . . . .59 F4
Tea Kettle La CB8 . . . . . .59 F5
Teal Cl IP2 . . . . .138 D3
Tedder Cl 3 IP24 . . . . . .16 C2
Tedder Rd NR32 . . . . . .113 B4
Teesdale NR32 . . . . . . .114 D3
Telesia Ct NR32 . . . . . .113 B4
Temperance Pl 8 NR34 . .111 B5
Temple Cl 7 IP28 . . . . . .31 C4
Temple End CB9 . . . . . . .74 C5
Temple Pattle 11 CO11 . .104 F2
Temple Rd Ipswich IP3 . . .140 C4
  Isleham CB7 . . . . .29 B4
  Stowmarket IP14 . . . . . .124 D5
Ten Bell La 10 CB7 . . . . .28 C4
Tenby Rd IP2 . . . . .139 B1
Tennyson Cl IP12 . . . . .146 E6
Tennyson Rd
  18 Bury St Edmunds IP32 . .48 C5
  Lowestoft NR32 . . . . . . .113 D2
Tennyson Way IP24 . . . . .16 C7
Tenter Field 4 CO7 . . . . .103 E5
Tenter Piece 16 CO10 . . . .78 D4
Tenterden Cl 6 NR33 . . . .114 D5
Tenth Rd IP10 . . . . .98 A3
Tentree Rd CO10 . . . . . .92 C7
Terence Airey Ct 25 IP20 .22 D6
Tern Cl IP9 . . . . .133 A5
Tern Rd IP2 . . . . .138 E2
Terr The
  Aldeburgh IP15 . . . . . . .130 E4
  Snape IP17 . . . . .72 D5
Terrace The CB8 . . . . . .121 A3
Tewkesbury Pl 7 IP31 . . .49 A5
Thackeray Gr IP14 . . . . .124 B7
Thackeray Rd IP1 . . . . . .134 E3
Thanet Rd IP4 . . . . .140 B6
Tharp Way CB7 . . . . . . .29 E1
Theatre Royal ★ IP33 . . .154 C1
Theatre St IP12 . . . . . . .146 F5
Theberton Rd IP16 . . . . .73 D2
Thedwastre Cl 8 IP30 . . .50 F2
Thedwastre Rd IP31 . . . .49 E3
Thellusson Rd 3 IP12 . . . .85 B8
Thelnetham Rd IP22 . . . . .18 E2
Thelnetham Windmill ★
  IP22 . . . . .18 E1
Theobald Cl 5 IP6 . . . . .125 D4
Thetford Cl 16 IP27 . . . . .13 F2
Thetford Cottage Hospl
  IP24 . . . . .16 C6
Thetford Gram Sch
  IP24 . . . . .16 B6
Thetford Mus ★ IP24 . . . .16 C6
Thetford Rd Brandon IP27 . .5 F1
  Coney Weston IP31 . . . . .34 D8
  Euston IP24 . . . . .16 C2
  Fakenham Magna IP24 . . . .33 E8
  Fornham St Martin IP31 . . .48 D5
  Garboldisham IP22 . . . . .18 C4
  2 Ipswich IP1 . . . . .139 A7
  Ixworth IP31 . . . . .34 A2
  Ixworth Thorpe IP31 . . . . .33 F3
  Mildenhall IP28 . . . . . . .116 E4
  Santon Downham IP27 . . . .6 B1
  South Lopham IP22 . . . . .19 A4
Thetford Sta IP24 . . . . . .16 B6
Thieves La IP31 . . . . . . .49 F8
Thingoe Hill IP32 . . . . . .154 B4
Third Ave CO10 . . . . . . .77 B3
Thirlmere Dr IP14 . . . . . .124 B6
Thirlmere Wlk NR32 . . . .113 A4
Thirlwall Dr IP1 . . . . . . .29 C1
Thistle Cl IP2 . . . . .138 F4
Thistledown NR33 . . . . .114 D4
Thistledown Dr IP1 . . . . .34 B2
Thomas Arne Cl IP14 . . .124 C8
Thomas Ave IP11 . . . . . .152 C8
Thomas Bardwell Dr 4
  NR35 . . . . .110 C2
Thomas Bole Cl 7 IP2 . . .18 D4
Thomas Cl 20 IP31 . . . . .34 B1
Thomas La IP33 . . . . . . .154 B1
Thomas Mills High Sch
  IP13 . . . . .126 A5
Thomas Walls Cl 3 IP13 . .83 E5
Thomas Young Cl
  IP14 . . . . .124 D3
Thompson Cl IP14 . . . . . .51 D1
Thompson Rd IP1 . . . . . .138 F8
Thomsons La IP6 . . . . . . .69 A2
Thong Hall Rd IP13 . . . . .127 A5
Thorington Rd IP19 . . . . .42 A5
Thorn Cl CB7 . . . . .28 C5
Thorn Way IP11 . . . . . . .152 E4
Thorn Wlk IP2 . . . . .85 D2

Thornbush La IP8 . . . . . .138 A8
Thorndon CE Prim Sch
  IP23 . . . . .53 C8
Thorney Gn Rd IP14 . . . .67 A6
Thorney Rd IP9 . . . . . . .150 E4
Thornham Cl 5 NR33 . . . .114 F4
Thornham Rd IP23 . . . . . .36 D2
Thornhayes Cl IP2 . . . . .139 A3
Thornhill Rd IP6 . . . . . . .82 B5
Thornley Dr IP4 . . . . . . .140 C8
Thornley Rd IP11 . . . . . .153 C4
Thorns Cl CB8 . . . . .61 E2
Thornton Cl 15 IP27 . . . .13 F2
Thornton Rd IP33 . . . . . .122 E2
Thoroughfare IP19 . . . . .118 B3
Thoroughfare The
  Brundish IP13 . . . . .55 C8
  Harleston IP20 . . . . . . .22 D6
  Wilby IP21 . . . . .39 D1
  10 Woodbridge IP12 . . . .147 A5
Thorpe Abbots Rd
  IP21 . . . . .21 D4
Thorpe Hall Rd IP21 . . . .38 F4
Thorpe La
  Ashfield cum Thorpe IP14 . .69 C8
  Debenham IP14 . . . . .53 F1
  Trimley St Martin IP11 . . .107 C8
Thorpe Rd IP16 . . . . . . .130 F6
Thorpe's Hill IP8 . . . . . .95 E6
Threadneedle St
  Dedham CO7 . . . . .103 F4
  1 Hadleigh IP7 . . . . . . .149 C5
Three Marsh La IP18 . . . .119 B6
Throckmorton Rd
  NR35 . . . . .110 D3
Through Duncans
  IP12 . . . . .146 E3
Through Jollys IP5 . . . . .141 D8
Thurleston Cty High Sch
  IP1 . . . . .135 A4
Thurleston La IP1 . . . . . .134 F5
Thurlow CE Prim Sch
  CB9 . . . . .74 B4
Thurlow Ct 2 IP14 . . . . .124 D6
Thurlow Rd CB9 . . . . . . .74 D7
Thurmans La IP11 . . . . . .152 B8
Thurne Rd NR32 . . . . . .114 F5
Thurston CE Prim Sch
  IP31 . . . . .49 E4
Thurston Com Coll
  IP31 . . . . .49 D4
Thurston Ct 6 IP11 . . . . .152 C4
Thurston La CO10 . . . . . .76 C7
Thurston Rd
  1 Beyton IP30 . . . . .49 F2
  Lowestoft NR32 . . . . . . .113 D2
  Thurston IP31 . . . . .49 E3
Thurston Sta IP31 . . . . . .49 D3
Thwaite Rd
  Ditchingham NR35 . . . . .110 C7
  Thorndon IP23 . . . . .53 B8
  Wickham Skeith IP23 . . . .52 D7
Tibbenham's Score 6
  NR32 . . . . .3 D4
Tiberius Cl CB9 . . . . . . .133 B5
Tide Mill ★ IP12 . . . . . .147 B4
Tide Mill Way IP12 . . . . .147 A4
Tideway NR32 . . . . .114 E8
Tidys Ct IP33 . . . . .154 B3
Tiggins La IP17 . . . . . . .128 D8
Tilbury Rd
  Great Yeldham CO9 . . . . . .90 A2
  Ridgewell CO9 . . . . .89 E4
Tile Barn La CO11 . . . . .104 B1
Tillbrooks Hill CB8 . . . . .61 B1
Timperley Cl IP7 . . . . . .149 D7
Timperley Rd IP7 . . . . . .149 E7
Timperleys IP8 . . . . .95 C5
Tinabrook Cl IP2 . . . . . .138 E1
Tinker Rd IP13 . . . . .71 F5
Tinker St CO12 . . . . . . .106 C1
Tinker's La IP7 . . . . . . .149 D5
Tinkers La NR34 . . . . . . .10 D1
Tinker's La NR15 . . . . . .21 C8
Tintern Cl 5 IP12 . . . . . .139 A2
Tippet Ave IP14 . . . . . . .124 C8
Tithe Ave IP28 . . . . .30 B8
Title Rd IP17 . . . . .58 A6
Titlow Rd 28 IP20 . . . . . .22 D6
Toad Row NR34 . . . . . . .10 F1
Todhunter Ave NR34 . . . . .9 B6
Tog La CO6 . . . . .102 D2
Tokio Rd IP4 . . . . .140 A6
Toll Gate Rd 6 IP9 . . . . .150 E3
Tollemache Bsns Pk
  IP7 . . . . .80 E4
Toller Cl IP12 . . . . .131 C4
Toller Rd IP3 . . . . .139 E3
Tolley Cobbold St 3
  IP28 . . . . .30 A8
Tollgate Prim Sch
  IP32 . . . . .122 F8
Tolsey La 3 IP32 . . . . . .123 A8
Tolworth Rd IP4 . . . . . . .140 A6
Tom Jennings Cl CB8 . . .120 F5
Tomline Rd
  Felixstowe IP11 . . . . . .153 A4
  Ipswich IP3 . . . . .140 A5
Tomo Bsns Pk IP14 . . . .124 F6
Tomtit's La IP12 . . . . . . .51 B2
Tonning St NR32 . . . . . .113 C1
Tooks Comm La IP19 . . . .34 B1
Top Rd Hasketon IP13 . . .146 B8
  Rattlesden IP30 . . . . . . .65 D5
  St Andrew, Ilketshall
    NR34 . . . . .8 E1
  Wingfield IP21 . . . . .39 A7
Top St IP12 . . . . .146 C2

Toper La IP33 . . . . .154 C1
Toppesfield Cl 3 IP7 . . . .149 D5
Tortoiseshell Cl IP7 . . . . .142 E8
Tostock Rd IP30 . . . . . . .49 F2
Tot Hill IP14 . . . . .66 C8
Tottington La IP22 . . . . . .20 B2
Tovells 4 IP13 . . . . .84 F7
Tovell's Rd IP4 . . . . . . .139 F6
Tower Field Rd IP12 . . . . .85 D7
Tower Hill NR34 . . . . . . .111 C3
Tower Mill La IP7 . . . . . .149 E6
Tower Mill Rd
  Bungay NR35 . . . . .110 B3
  Ipswich IP1 . . . . .138 F7
Tower Ramparts IP1 . . . .155 B3
Tower Rd
  Felixstowe IP11 . . . . . .152 F4
  Lowestoft NR33 . . . . . . .115 A2
Tower St IP1 . . . . .155 B3
Town Farm Cl IP20 . . . . .23 C3
Town Farm Est IP12 . . . .131 B3
Town Gn IP14 . . . . .134 C7
Town House Cnr IP14 . . . .68 F7
Town House La IP22 . . . . .35 D6
Town La IP14 . . . . .53 A3
Townhouse Rd IP31 . . . . .35 C1
Townlands Dr NR34 . . . .111 B3
Townsend IP33 . . . . .123 B1
Townsend CB7 . . . . .28 C5
Toyse Cl 1 CB5 . . . . . . .44 B6
Toyse La CB5 . . . . .44 A6
Trafalgar Cl IP4 . . . . . . .139 F6
Trafalgar Rd CO10 . . . . .148 E2
Trafalgar St
  4 Lowestoft NR32 . . . . .113 C1
  Lowestoft NR32 . . . . . . .115 C8
Trafford Cl 2 IP14 . . . . .51 E1
Tranmere Gr IP1 . . . . . .134 F2
Traveller's Hill (Tumuli) ★
  IP28 . . . . .32 E5
Travellers Rd IP13 . . . . . .69 C5
Traverse The IP33 . . . . .154 B2
Treetops IP11 . . . . .152 E7
Treeview IP14 . . . . .124 B6
Trefoil Cl IP2 . . . . .138 F4
Trenchard Sq 8 IP26 . . . . .4 D5
Trent Rd
  1 Bury St Edmunds IP32 . .48 C5
  Ipswich IP3 . . . . .139 F2
Trevethan Cl IP32 . . . . .122 E7
Triangle Yd 9 NR32 . . . .113 E2
Trimley Rd IP10 . . . . . . .98 D1
Trimley St Martin Prim Sch
  IP11 . . . . .152 C8
Trimley St Mary Prim Sch
  IP11 . . . . .152 C7
Trimley Sta IP11 . . . . . .152 C7
Trinity Ave
  Felixstowe IP11 . . . . . .152 B3
  Felixstowe IP11 . . . . . .152 B3
  Mildenhall IP28 . . . . . . .116 C5
Trinity Cl Fordham CB7 . . .29 B1
  Ipswich IP5 . . . . .140 F7
  28 Manningtree CO11 . . .104 E2
  16 Southwold IP18 . . . . .119 D5
  Woodbridge IP12 . . . . . .146 D3
Trinity Dr CB8 . . . . .121 B2
Trinity Gdns NR35 . . . . .110 B4
Trinity Gild 7 CO10 . . . . .78 D4
Trinity Link CB9 . . . . . . .132 E7
Trinity Mews IP33 . . . . . .154 A3
Trinity Rd
  Lowestoft NR32 . . . . . . .113 E1
  Manningtree CO11 . . . . .104 E2
Trinity St Bungay NR35 . .110 B4
  15 Southwold IP18 . . . . .119 D5
Trinity Wlk IP4 . . . . .67 A7
Triple Plea La NR35 . . . . .7 B8
Triple Plea Rd NR35 . . . . .7 B8
Troon Cl 5 IP28 . . . . . . .48 C6
Troon Gdns 3 IP4 . . . . .136 B1
Trossachs The 1 NR32 . .112 D2
Troston Mount (Tumulus) ★
  IP31 . . . . .33 D5
Troston Rd IP31 . . . . . . .33 E5
Trotting Horse La CB8 . . .75 A8
Trott's La CO10 . . . . . . .92 F3
Trunch Hill IP20 . . . . . . .7 A3
Trunch Rd IP20 . . . . .7 B2
Tuddenham Ave IP4 . . . .139 E7
Tuddenham CE Prim Sch
  IP28 . . . . .30 F2
Tuddenham Cnr IP28 . . . .46 E6
Tuddenham La IP5 . . . . .136 B2
Tuddenham Rd
  Barton Mills IP28 . . . . . .116 F2
  Ipswich IP4 . . . . .155 C4
  Westerfield IP4 . . . . . . .136 A3
Tudor Ave IP22 . . . . .20 B3
Tudor CE Prim Sch
  CO10 . . . . .148 D7
Tudor Cl
  Chedburgh IP29 . . . . . . .62 D5
  9 Framlingham IP13 . . . .126 C3
  3 Shotley Gate IP9 . . . . .107 A5
  Sudbury CO10 . . . . . . .148 C7
Tudor Ct 1 IP23 . . . . . . .37 F1
Tudor Gn CO10 . . . . . . .148 C8
Tudor Rd CO10 . . . . . . .148 C7
Tudor Wlk
  8 Honington IP31 . . . . . .33 D5
  11 Lowestoft NR33 . . . . .114 E4
Tuffen La IP22 . . . . .35 D8
Tuffields Rd IP29 . . . . . .63 B3
Tumbril La IP29 . . . . . . .63 A3
Tunbeck Cl IP20 . . . . . . .23 A7
Tunbeck Rd IP20 . . . . . . .23 A8
Tunbridge 4 CB5 . . . . . .44 A5

Tunneys La NR35 . . . . . .110 C8
Tuns La IP33 . . . . .154 C1
Tunstall Dr NR32 . . . . . .112 F4
Tunstall Gn IP12 . . . . . . .71 F2
Turin St IP2 . . . . .155 B1
Turin Way 2 NR31 . . . . . .3 C6
Turino Ave IP12 . . . . . . .98 B8
Turkentine Cl 12 CO10 . . .92 B3
Turkeyhall La IP14 . . . . . .51 F6
Turnberry Cl 3 NR33 . . .114 F4
Turnberry Dr 11 IP28 . . . .48 C6
Turner Ave 1 CO11 . . . .104 D2
Turner Cl
  Ditchingham NR35 . . . . .110 C7
  Haverhill CB9 . . . . .132 B7
  4 Lowestoft NR32 . . . . .113 C6
  Sudbury CO10 . . . . . . .148 E8
Turner Gdns IP12 . . . . . .146 D3
Turner Gr IP5 . . . . .141 D8
Turner La 4 IP14 . . . . . .51 C1
Turner Rd Ipswich IP3 . . .144 A8
  Stowmarket IP14 . . . . . .124 B7
Turnpike Hill CB9 . . . . . .74 B2
Turnpike Rd
  Chippenham CB8 . . . . . .45 F8
  Red Lodge IP28 . . . . . . .30 B1
  Woodbridge IP12 . . . . . .147 B6
Turnstone Cl 2 IP28 . . . .116 D4
Turret La IP4 . . . . .155 B2
Tut Hill IP28 . . . . .48 B5
Tutelina Rd IP30 . . . . . . .64 A6
Tutt Hill (Tumulus) ★
  IP24 . . . . .16 D4
Tuyar Wlk CB8 . . . . . . .120 E8
Tweed Cl CB8 . . . . .45 F3
Twelve Acre App IP5 . . . .141 B7
Twin Oak Dr IP13 . . . . . .56 B7
Twinnings The IP14 . . . . .124 C3
Twiss Cl 5 IP22 . . . . . . .20 A3
Two Acres IP9 . . . . .150 F4
Two House Cl IP13 . . . . .127 C7
Two Pole Dro CB7 . . . . . .28 A7
Tydemans Ct 1 IP14 . . . .124 D6
Tye Green CO10 . . . . . . .77 A3
Tye La IP8 . . . . .81 D2
Tyler St 3 Harwich CO12 106 F3
  Ipswich IP1 . . . . .155 B1
Tylers Gn IP11 . . . . . . .152 C7
Tylers Way IP14 . . . . . . .124 D3
Tymmes Pl IP13 . . . . . . .146 C8
Tyrone Cl IP1 . . . . .134 D2

U

Ubbeston Way NR33 . . .114 F4
Ufford Pl 8 IP13 . . . . . . .84 F7
Ufford Rd Bredfield IP13 . .84 D7
  Eyke IP12 . . . . .85 B6
Uggeshall Cl NR32 . . . . .113 A5
Ullswater Ave 4 IP11 . . .153 D7
Ullswater Rd IP12 . . . . . .71 C2
Ulster Ave IP1 . . . . .134 D1
Una Rd CO12 . . . . .106 F2
Uncle's La IP19 . . . . .24 B6
Undercliff Rd E IP11 . . . .153 C4
Undercliff Rd W IP11 . . . .153 A3
Underhill IP14 . . . . .124 C5
Undley Rd IP27 . . . . . . .109 B4
Unicorn Pl IP33 . . . . . . .123 C6
Union Hill IP7 . . . . .94 A8
Union La
  Lowestoft NR32 . . . . . . .112 F5
  Wortham IP22 . . . . .20 A1
Union Pl NR33 . . . . .115 C7
Union Rd
  Lowestoft NR32 . . . . . . .113 C1
  Onehouse IP14 . . . . .66 C6
  Stowmarket IP14 . . . . . .124 A7
Union St IP4 . . . . .155 C3
Union St E IP4 . . . . .124 D6
Union St W IP14 . . . . . .124 D6
Unitarian Meeting House ★
  IP1 . . . . .155 B2
Unity Rd IP14 . . . . .124 D5
Unity St IP3 . . . . .139 E4
Univ Coll Suffolk IP4 . . .139 E5
Up St IP31 . . . . .34 C4
Upland Rd IP4 . . . . .140 A6
Uplands Cl NR33 . . . . . .114 D4
Uplands Cres CO10 . . . .148 C7
Uplands Mid Sch
  CO10 . . . . .148 D7
Uplands Rd
  3 Aldringham cum Thorpe
    IP16 . . . . .73 F6
  Sudbury CO10 . . . . . . .148 C7
Uplands Rd N NR33 . . . .114 D5
Uplands Rd S NR33 . . . .114 C3
Uplands The
  Aldringham cum Thorpe
    IP16 . . . . .73 F6
  Beccles NR34 . . . . . . .111 D4
Uplands Way Diss IP22 . . .20 C3
  Halesworth IP19 . . . . . .118 B5
Upper Ave IP19 . . . . . . .118 B5
Upper Barclay St 4 IP4 . .155 C2
Upper Brook La IP20 . . . .22 B4
Upper Brook St IP4 . . . .155 B3
Upper Burnthouse La
  IP20 . . . . .22 A5
Upper Cavendish St
  IP3 . . . . .140 A5
Upper E St CO10 . . . . . .148 D6
Upper Farm Rd CO10 . . . .89 E4

Upper Grange Rd
NR34 ....111 A4
Upper Harmans La
IP20 ....22 B5
Upper High St IP1 ..155 B4
Upper Melton Terr 10
IP12 ....84 E6
Upper Moorfield Rd
IP12 ....146 F6
Upper Oakley IP23 ...117 F8
Upper Olland St NR35 .110 B3
Upper Orwell St IP4 ..155 C2
Upper Rd CO10 ....101 C8
Upper Rose La IP22 ...20 C1
Upper St Gissing IP22 ..20 F8
  Layham IP7 ....149 F1
  Stansfield CO10 ......76 C6
  Stanstead CO10 ......77 C4
  Stratford St Mary CO7 .103 E5
Upper Tumbril La IP20 ..22 A4
Upperfield Dr IP13 ...153 C6
Upsons Way IP5 .....141 E8
Upthorpe Rd IP31 ....34 F4
Upton Cl IP4 ....139 E6
Urban Rd IP16 ......129 D6
US 100th Bomb Group Meml
  Mus★ IP21 ....21 D4
Uvedale Gdns IP6 ...125 E4
Uxbridge Cres IP3 ...140 C1

V

Vale La
  Bury St Edmunds IP33 ..123 C3
  Kersey IP7 ....94 A6
  Stutton IP9 ....105 A6
Valentine Way IP30 ...64 F7
Valiant Dr IP31 ......33 D4
Valiant St 6 IP28 ....13 B1
Valley Cl
  4 Brantham CO11 ...104 E5
  Halesworth IP19 .....118 E4
  Ipswich IP1 ....135 C1
Valley Farm★ CO7 ...151 D1
Valley Farm Camargue
  Horses★ IP13 ......127 A8
Valley Farm La IP7 ...94 E5
Valley Farm Rd IP7 ...94 E5
Valley La Battisford IP14 ..80 F8
  Buxhall IP14 ....65 F3
  Wherstead IP9 ......143 A3
Valley Rd Battisford IP14 ..66 E1
  Chilton CO10 ....92 C5
  Great Bricett IP7 ....80 D6
  Harwich CO12 ......106 E1
  Ipswich IP1 ....135 B1
  Leiston IP16 ....129 E6
  Little Blakenham IP8 ..81 E4
Valley View CO10 ....77 C4
Valley Wash CO10 ....75 D4
Valley Way CB8 ......120 E3
Valley Wlk IP17 ......152 F5
Vallibus Cl 5 NR32 ...112 E4
Valleyview Dr IP4 ....140 F4
Van Dyck Cl 9 NR32 ..113 B6
Vandyck Rd IP3 .....144 A8
Vanners Rd CB9 .....132 E5
Vaughan St IP21 .....155 B1
Vaunces La IP21 ......21 E4
Vaunce's La IP21 ......21 E4
Vaux Ave 15 CO12 ...106 F1
Velda Cl NR33 ......114 F4
Ventris Cl IP2 ....138 D5
Verdons La IP21 ......39 E4
Verdure Cl 2 NR32 ...112 F5
Vere Gdns IP1 ......135 C2
Vermeer Cl 5 NR32 ...113 B6
Vermont Cres IP4 ....155 C4
Vermont Rd IP4 .....155 C4
Verneuil Ave IP14 ...124 D3
Vernon St IP2 ......155 B1
Veyses End 6 CO7 ...103 E5
Vicarage Cl CB8 .....59 E5
Vicarage Field CO10 ..148 F3
Vicarage Gdns 16 IP14 ..53 B7
Vicarage Hill 7 IP12 ..147 A5
Vicarage La Acton CO10 ..92 A6
  Bramford IP8 ....134 B1
  Bungay NR35 ......110 E3
  Wherstead IP9 ......143 B5
  Woodditton CB8 ......60 B6
Vicarage Rd
  Belchamp St Paul CO10 ..90 D5
  Felixstowe IP11 .....152 D4
  Laxfield IP13 ....40 B3
  Newmarket CB8 ......121 B3
  Thetford IP24 ....16 C6
  Wingfield IP21 ....39 A8
  Winston IP14 ....54 A1
Victor Rd IP31 ......33 D4
Victoria Cl 5 IP31 ...49 E4
Victoria Cres 2 CO11 ..104 E2
Victoria Hill IP23 ...117 C4
Victoria Mill Rd IP13 ..126 B2
Victoria Rd
  Aldeburgh IP15 .....130 E4
  Diss IP22 ....20 D2
  Felixstowe IP11 .....152 F3
  Haverhill CB9 ....132 B5
  Lowestoft NR33 .....114 E2
  Stowmarket IP14 ....124 E7
  Woodbridge IP12 ....147 A5
Victoria St
  Bury St Edmunds IP33 ..154 A2

Victoria St continued
  Felixstowe IP11 .....153 A4
  7 Harwich CO12 ....107 B2
  Ipswich IP1 ....139 A6
  13 Southwold IP18 ..119 D5
Victoria Terr
  3 Fressingfield IP21 ..39 E8
  Lowestoft NR33 .....115 D7
Victoria Way CB8 ...120 E7
Victory Cl IP33 .....123 C2
Victory Rd Ipswich IP4 ..140 A7
  Leiston IP16 ....129 E6
View Point Rd IP11 ..153 H10
Viking Cl IP12 ......84 B1
Viking Hts IP12 ......84 B1
Viking Rd IP14 ......124 C5
Villa Hill IP12 ....99 B7
Village Way
  Lowestoft NR33 .....113 B5
  Waldringfield IP12 ...98 D7
Vincent Cl 7 Feltwell IP26 ..4 E5
  Ipswich IP1 ....138 E8
Vince's Rd IP22 ......20 D2
Vine Cl IP31 ....17 E1
Vine Rd IP6 ....69 C2
Vinefields The IP33 ..154 C2
Vinery Cl IP13 ....127 C6
Vinery Rd IP33 ......122 F3
Vines The IP17 ......128 D7
Vinesse Rd CO6 .....102 B2
Vineway The
  6 Harwich CO12 ...107 A2
  2 Harwich CO12 ...107 A2
Violet Cl
  Bury St Edmunds IP32 ..123 F5
  Ipswich IP22 ....138 F4
Violet Hill Rd IP14 ..124 C7
Virginia Rd 11 IP28 ..30 A8
Vyces Rd IP13 ......126 B3

W

W Suffolk Hospl The
  IP33 ....123 A2
Wacker Field Rd 8 IP12 ..85 B8
Wadd La IP17 ....72 C6
Waddesdon Rd 5 CO12 ..107 B2
Waddlegoose La IP14 ..54 D2
Waddling La NR32 ...112 A7
Wades Gr IP5 ......141 E7
Wade's La Raydon IP7 ..94 E1
  Shotley IP9 ....106 E7
Wades Wood 1 IP30 ...50 D1
Wadgate Rd IP11 ....152 E4
Wadhurst Rd IP3 ....140 D3
Wainford Cl 5 NR34 ..9 F4
Wainford Rd NR35 ...110 E5
Wainwright Cl 4 NR32 ..113 A6
Wainwright Gdns IP6 ..81 F5
Wainwright Way IP5 ..141 E8
Wake Ave IP28 ......116 C5
Wakehall La CO10 ...90 E4
Walberswick Nature
  Reserve★ IP17 ......43 B4
Walberswick Way 8
  NR32 ....113 A3
Walcot Rd IP22 ......20 D3
Walcot Rise IP22 ....20 D3
Walcott Wlk NR33 ...115 B5
Waldegrave Cl 23 CO11 ..104 D2
Waldegrave Rd CO11 ..104 D2
Waldingfield Rd
  10 Acton CO10 .....92 B7
  Chilton CO10 ....148 F8
Waldringfield Prim Sch
  IP12 ....98 D7
Waldringfield Rd IP12 ..84 C1
Walker Cl IP4 ....140 C5
Walker Gdns NR34 ...26 E5
Walks The NR34 .....10 A8
Wall La CO11 ....105 E2
Wallace Rd IP1 ......138 E8
Waller's Gr IP2 ......138 F4
Wallow La IP7 ....80 D4
Walls The CO11 .....104 E2
Walmer Cl NR33 ....115 A5
Walmer Rd NR33 ....115 A5
Walnut Cl Acton CO10 ..92 B8
  Felixstowe IP11 .....153 D7
  Hopton IP22 ....18 C1
  13 Lakenheath IP27 ..13 F2
Walnut Gr IP28 ......30 A4
Walnut Tree La
  2 Harkstead IP9 ...106 A5
  Sudbury CO10 ......148 B5
Walnut Tree Mdw IP14 ..68 B6
Walnuts La IP13 ....127 B5
Walnuts The
  Beccles NR34 ....111 E4
  3 Ufford IP13 ......84 F7
Walnuttree Hospl
  CO10 ....148 B5
Walpole Cl NR35 ....110 D7
Walpole La IP19 .....41 D5
Walpole Rd
  Bramfield IP19 ......41 E4
  Halesworth IP19 .....118 E4
Walsham Le Willows Sch
  IP31 ....35 C2
Walsham Rd
  Finningham IP14 .....36 A1
  Finningham IP14 .....36 B1
  6 Ixworth IP31 .....34 B1
  Wattisfield IP22 .....35 C3
Walsingham Cl 11 CO10 ..92 B3

Walsingham Rd IP33 ..122 D3
Walters Cl 9 NR31 ....3 B7
Waltham Cl IP2 .....139 A2
Walton Ave IP11 ....152 C3
Walton Cl 5 Fordham CB7 ..29 A1
  1 Stowmarket IP14 ..124 B8
Walton Rd NR32 ....113 D1
Wamil Rd IP28 ......30 B5
Wamil Way IP28 ....116 B4
Wangford Rd
  Lakenheath IP27 .....13 F7
  Reydon IP18 ....26 D1
  Southwold IP18 .....119 B8
  Uggeshall NR34 .....26 A3
  Westhall IP19 ....25 B4
Wannock Cl NR33 ...114 D4
Wantisden Cnr IP12 ...86 A6
Ward Rd IP8 ....138 B2
Wardlaw Ct 10 IP14 ...53 F2
Wardley Cl IP2 ......138 D1
Wardley Hill Rd NR35 ...8 D8
Ware Rd IP7 ....80 B6
Wareham Ave IP3 ...140 D3
Warene Cl 3 IP13 ...126 C3
Warham Rd CO12 ...106 F1
Warner Way CO10 ...148 E6
Warren Chase IP5 ...141 E7
Warren Cl Elmswell IP30 ..50 E2
  Lakenheath IP27 ....109 D5
Warren Heath Ave
  IP3 ....140 D2
Warren Heath Rd IP3 ..140 D2
Warren Hill Rd IP12 ..146 E4
Warren La
  Arwarton IP9 ....106 D6
  Elmswell IP30 ....50 E2
  27 Martlesham Heath IP5 ..98 A8
  Woolpit IP30 ....50 F1
Warren Loke NR31 ....2 B7
Warren Rd
  Great Yarmouth NR31 ..3 B8
  Herringswell CB8 .....46 A8
  Hopton on Sea NR31 ..3 C7
  Lowestoft NR32 ....113 D4
  Red Lodge IP28 .....30 C1
Warren's La NR34 ...10 A2
Warrington Rd IP1 ...155 A4
Warrington St CB8 ..121 A2
Warwick Ave
  Halesworth IP19 ....118 C5
  Woodbridge IP12 ...146 F6
Warwick Rd IP4 .....135 B6
Wash La Beccles NR34 ..111 B2
  Boxford CO6 ....93 D2
  Burgh St Peter NR34 ..10 C8
  Dennington IP13 ....55 E6
  Frostenden NR34 ....26 C3
  Great Finborough IP14 ..124 A5
  Hinderclay IP22 .....35 E8
  Kessingland NR33 ...11 C1
  Mendlesham IP14 ...52 E3
  Redgrave IP22 ....19 D1
  Reydon IP18 ....26 D2
  St Peter, South Elmham
    NR35 ....23 F7
  Shelfanger IP22 ....20 B6
  Spexhall IP19 ....118 A7
  Stanton IP31 ....34 F3
  Topcroft NR35 ....7 A8
  Wenhaston With Mells Hamlet
    IP19 ....118 E1
  Westleton IP17 .....58 B8
  Witnesham IP6 ......83 A6
Washington St
  7 Mildenhall IP28 ...13 B1
  4 Mildenhall IP28 ...30 A1
Wassicks La IP14 ....51 E3
Watch House Hill
  NR35 ....110 E4
Water La
  Athelington IP21 .....38 F1
  Barnardiston CB9 ....75 B4
  Barnham IP24 ....16 C2
  Botesdale IP22 ......35 F5
  3 Bures CO8 ....101 C5
  Cavendish CO10 ....76 E1
  Debenham IP14 .....53 F2
  Denston CB8 ....75 F7
  Garboldisham IP22 ..18 A4
  Great Bradley CB8 ...74 C8
  Great Horkesley CO6 ..102 F8
  Great Whelnetham IP30 ..64 A6
  Helions Bumpstead CB9 ..88 B4
  Kersey IP7 ....94 A6
  Layham IP7 ....149 E1
  Lowestoft NR32 ....113 C2
  Polstead CO6 ....102 F8
  Steeple Bumpstead CB9 ..88 D3
  Sturmer CB9 ....133 D3
  Thelnetham IP22 ....18 E1
  Thornham Magna IP23 ..37 A1
  Weybread IP21 ......22 D4
  Worlingworth IP13 ...54 D8
Water Mill La IP21 ...38 C8
Water Run The IP7 ...79 F7
Water St CO10 ......78 D4
Watercourse The CB8 ..121 A4
Waterford Rd IP1 ....134 D2
Waterhead La IP12 ..147 D8
Watering Cl 1 IP8 ....81 C3
Watering La IP17 ....72 C7
Watering Rd IP21 ....38 D5
Waterloo Ave
  Leiston IP16 ....129 B6
  2 Roydon IP22 .....20 A3
Waterloo Cl CB8 ....120 D8
Waterloo Rd
  4 Ipswich IP1 ......139 A7

Waterloo Rd continued
  Lowestoft NR33 ....115 D7
  Sotterley NR34 ......26 A4
Watermill Cl IP7 ....149 E2
Watermill Rd IP12 ...98 C5
Waters Ave NR33 ...114 C3
Waterside CB7 ......29 C5
Waterworks Rd IP28 12 IP28 ..30 A8
Waterworks St IP4 ..155 C2
Watery La IP13 .....146 A8
Watson Way IP12 ...99 E4
Watsons Cl 3 NR31 ..3 C7
Watson's Hill IP7 ....79 F1
Watt Cl IP12 ....99 E4
Wattisfield Rd IP31 ...35 C2
Wattisham Airfield IP7 ..80 C6
Wattisham Airfield Mus★
  IP7 ....80 C6
Wattisham Rd IP7 ....79 F4
Waveney Cl 3 IP17 ..128 C4
Waveney Cres NR33 ..115 B7
Waveney Dr NR33 ...115 A7
Waveney Hill
  Carlton Colville NR32 ..114 B8
  Lowestoft NR32 .....112 B1
Waveney Hts
  Beccles NR34 ....111 B4
  Bungay NR35 ....110 D3
  10 Bury St Edmunds IP32 ..48 C5
  Ditchingham NR35 ...110 C8
  Felixstowe IP11 .....152 E3
  Ipswich IP1 ....138 E8
  10 Lowestoft NR32 ..115 D8
Waveney Sports & Leisure
  Ctr NR32 ....113 C3
Waveney Terr 4 CB9 ..132 E5
Waveney Valley Swimming
  Pool NR35 ....110 D2
Way Bank La CO9 ...89 C7
Wayne Cl NR32 .....113 B6
Wayside Cl IP14 ....124 D3
Weald The NR32 ....112 E2
Weatheralls Cl 9 CB7 ..28 D4
Weaver Cl IP1 ......138 D3
Weavers Cl
  2 Raleigh IP17 .....149 D6
  4 Lavenham CO10 ...78 D4
  Stowmarket IP14 ...124 C3
Weavers Croft 8 IP20 ..22 D6
Weavers Dr 6 CO10 ...77 D2
Weavers La CO10 ...148 C5
Weavers Marsh La
  IP17 ....41 E2
Weavers Way 2 IP6 ..82 A5
Webb Rd IP14 ......124 D3
Webb St 1 IP2 .....139 C3
Webb's Cl IP14 .....124 C1
Webbs Ct IP5 ......141 C7
Webster St NR35 ...110 A4
Weddell Rd CB9 ....133 A4
Weeting Heath Nature
  Reserve★ NR35 .....5 C3
Weeting Heath Visitor Ctr★
  IP27 ....6 C4
Weeting Prim Sch IP27 ..5 E3
Weir Pl IP22 ....98 D2
Weirs Dro CB5 ......44 A6
Welbeck Cl IP11 ....152 C7
Welbourne Way NR34 ..10 D2
Welburn Cl 6 IP12 ...85 D8
Welch Cl NR34 ......10 D3
Welham La IP28 .....47 D5
Well Bottom CB8 ....45 D4
Well La 9 CO10 .....90 A8
Well St IP33 ....154 B2
Wellesley Rd
  Ipswich IP3 ....139 F5
  Troston IP31 ....33 D4
Wellington Cl IP28 ...30 A6
Wellington Esplanade
  NR33 ....115 C6
Wellington Rd
  Eye IP23 ....117 D3
  4 Feltwell IP26 ......4 E5
  6 Harwich CO12 ...107 C3
  2 Lowestoft NR33 ..115 A3
  8 Mildenhall IP28 ...30 A8
  13 Troston IP31 .....33 D2
Wellington St
  7 Harwich CO12 ...139 A7
  1 Newmarket CB8 ...121 A3
Wells Cl IP4 ....139 E6
Wells Cnr IP13 .....39 F2
Wells Ct IP28 ......116 B5
Wells Hall Com Prim Sch
  CO10 ....148 F2
Wells Hall Rd CO10 ..148 F3
Wells' La IP20 ....22 C5
Wells Rd IP20 ......22 C5
Wembley Ave NR34 ..111 B4
Wendy Cl 7 IP9 ....106 C8
Wenham La
  East Bergholt CO7 ...151 D8
  Wenham Magna CO7 ..150 A2
Wenham Rd IP8 .....150 B8
Wenhaston La IP19 ...42 C6
Wenhaston Prim Sch
  IP19 ....42 C6
Wenhaston Rd IP19 ...42 B5
Wenhaston Way 2
  NR32 ....112 F3
Wensleydale 5 NR33 ..114 E3
Wentford View 1 CO10 ..76 A1
Wentworth
  14 Fornham All Saints IP28 ..48 C6
  Hadleigh IP7 ....149 F5

Wentworth Dr
  Felixstowe IP11 .....153 C6
  7 Ipswich IP8 ......138 C2
  10 Mildenhall IP28 ..116 B5
Wentworth Rd IP15 ..130 F4
Wentworth Way 2
  NR33 ....114 F4
Wesel Ave NR33 ....152 D3
Wesley Cl NR34 ....111 B2
Wesley End Rd CO9 ...89 B2
Wesley Way IP1 ....138 F8
West Dock Rd CO12 ..106 F3
West Dr
  Mildenhall IP28 .....116 B4
  Soham CB7 ....28 C4
West Dr Cres CB7 ...28 C4
West Dr Gdns CB7 ...28 C4
West End CB8 ......60 B5
West End La
  Great Thurlow CB9 ...74 B4
  16 Harwich CO12 ...107 A1
West End Rd IP1 ....155 A2
West Gr NR33 ......115 A3
West Hall Rd
  1 Mundford IP26 ....6 B8
  Walsham-le-willows IP22 ..35 F3
West Harling Rd NR16 ..18 B8
West Herne La IP22 ...19 A1
West Lawn IP4 ......140 C8
West Mdws IP1 .....134 C4
West Mill Gn IP9 ....104 F7
West Rd
  Bury St Edmunds IP33 ..122 E4
  Ipswich IP3 ....140 F4
West Row Prim Sch
  IP28 ....29 F7
West Row Rd IP28 ...116 A5
West Side NR32 .....113 C5
West St Harwich CO12 ..107 B3
  Icklingham IP28 .....31 C4
  Isleham CB7 ....29 B5
  Rickinghall Inferior IP22 ..35 A1
West Stow Anglo-Saxon
  Village★ IP28 ......31 F2
West Stow Ctry Pk★
  IP28 ....31 F2
West Stow Rd IP28 ...32 B1
West Suffolk Coll
  IP33 ....122 F6
West Tofts Rd IP26 ...6 D7
West View IP14 .....124 B6
West View Gdns 4 IP23 ..36 D2
West Wood 9 IP31 ...49 A5
Westbourne High Sch
  IP1 ....134 E1
Westbourne Rd IP1 ..134 F1
Westbury Ave IP33 ...122 D5
Westbury Rd IP4 ....140 F4
Westend La IP33 ....133 F8
Westerfield Hall★
  IP6 ....135 E6
Westerfield La IP6 ...136 A5
Westerfield Rd
  Ipswich IP1 ....155 C4
  Westerfield IP6 .....135 E4
  Westerfield Sta IP6 ..135 E3
Westerings The 1 CO6 ..102 C5
Western Ave
  Felixstowe IP11 .....153 D6
  Haverhill CB9 ....132 D6
Western Cl 4 Feltwell IP26 ..4 D5
  Ipswich IP4 ....140 F4
Western Way IP33 ...122 D6
Western's End 6 CO11 ..104 C4
Westfield CO10 ......90 A7
Westfield Com Prim Sch
  CB9 ....132 F5
Westgarth Gdns IP33 ..122 E4
Westgate 5 IP16 ....73 F6
Westgate Cty Prim Sch
  IP33 ....154 A1
Westgate St
  Bury St Edmunds IP33 ..154 C1
  Ipswich IP1 ....155 B3
  Long Melford CO10 ..77 C3
Westhall IP21 ......39 B5
Westhall Rd NR32 ...113 B5
Westholme Cl IP12 ..146 F4
Westholme Rd IP1 ...135 A1
Westhorpe 3 CB5 ...44 A6
Westhorpe Rd IP14 ...52 A8
Westland 26 IP5 .....98 A8
Westland Rd NR33 ...114 E6
Westleton Rd IP17 ...57 E8
Westleton Way 17 IP11 ..152 C6
Westley Bottom Rd
  CB8 ....59 A4
Westley La IP29 .....122 B3
Westley Mid Sch IP33 ..122 C5
Westley Rd IP28 ....122 B8
Westley Way IP31 ...50 F2
Westminster Cl IP4 ..140 C4
Westminster Dr IP33 ..122 D3
Westmorland Cl 8
  CO11 ....105 A2
Westmorland Rd IP11 ..153 D7
Weston Colville Rd
  CB8 ....59 E4
Weston Rd NR32 ....113 B5
Weston Way CB8 ....120 F6
Westropps 6 CO10 ...91 E7
Westward Deals CB9 ..133 F6
Westward House
  IP16 ....129 C6
Westwood Ave
  Ipswich IP1 ....139 A8
  Lowestoft NR33 ....114 E6
Wet La CO4 ....102 F3

Wetherby Cl IP1 .....135 B3
Wetherden Rd
  Elmswell IP30 ....50 F2
  Great Ashfield IP31 .....51 B6
Wetheringsett CE Prim Sch
  IP14 ....53 A5
Wexford Rd IP1 ....134 D2
Weyland Rd IP6 ....83 A6
Weylands Cl IP14 ....67 D7
Whalebone Cnr CO4 ...103 C4
Whapload Rd NR32 ....113 E1
Wharf La 3 CO8 ....101 C4
Wharfedale 114 F3
Wharfedale Rd IP1 ...135 A1
Wharton St 5 NR33 ....110 B4
Whatfield CE Prim Sch
  IP7 ....80 C1
Whatfield Rd
  Aldham IP7 ....94 C7
  Elmsett IP7 ....80 F1
Whatfield Way IP14 ...124 E3
Wheatacre Dr 3 NR32 ...3 C4
Wheatfield Rd NR33 ..114 D4
Wheatfields
  3 Botesdale IP22 ......36 A6
  4 Thurston IP31 ....49 E4
  Whatfield IP7 ....80 C1
Wheatsheaf Cl CO11 ..105 E2
Wheatsheaf La CO11 ..105 E2
Wheelbarrow La IP20 ...23 F5
Wheeler's La IP31 ......51 A5
Wheelwrights The
  IP11 ....152 C8
Whepstead Rd
  Hawstead IP29 ....63 B7
  Horringer IP29 ....122 D1
Wherry Rd 3 NR35 ....110 D3
Wherstead Rd IP2 .....155 B1
Whin Marsh 6 IP15 ...130 C5
Whinchat Cl IP2 ......138 D3
Whinfield 13 IP5 ......98 A8
Whinfield Ave 23 CO12 .106 F1
Whinfield Ct 16 IP5 ....98 A8
Whinneys The IP5 .....141 D8
Whinyard Way 3 IP11 .153 D7
Whiskin 7 NR32 ......112 C2
Whitby Rd
  Bury St Edmunds IP33 .122 D3
  Ipswich IP4 ....139 F8
White Elm Rd IP30 .....50 C1
White Elm St IP3 .....139 E4
White Foot La IP13 .....83 E6
White Hall Cl CO10 .....92 C5
White Hart La 20 CB7 ...28 D4
White Horse Cl 4 IP11 .153 C6
White Horse Hill IP9 ..142 D1
White Horse La IP30 ...64 D7
White Horse Rd
  Capel St Mary IP9 .....150 F3
  East Bergholt CO7 .....151 D3
  Kedington IP29 ....133 E8
White Horse St 4 NR32 113 C4
White House Farm La
  IP21 ....22 B6
White House Gdns
  NR34 ....111 A4
White House Rd IP1 ..134 D2
White Lion Rd NR34 ....10 B8
White Mdw 3 IP14 .....51 A4
White Womans La IP12 ..85 B7
Whitedike Dro IP26 ......4 B4
Whitegates CB8 ....121 B3
Whitehall Rd IP14 ......51 F1
Whitehouse Ind Est
  IP1 ....134 C3
Whitehouse Jun Sch
  IP1 ....134 E1
Whitehouse La
  Belchamp Otten CO10 ...90 D5
  Earsham NR35 ....7 C5
  Stowupland IP14 ....67 D8
Whitepost Cnr IP14 .....54 C1
Whites IP21 ....39 B4
Whites Field CO7 .....151 B5
White's La NR33 ....11 B1
Whitethorn Rd IP3 ....140 F1
Whitewood Wlk 8 IP17 .13 F2
Whiting Rd NR32 .....112 C2
Whiting St IP33 ......154 B1
Whitland Cl IP2 ......143 A8
Whitlands 6 CO10 .....77 A3
Whitlock Dr CO9 ....89 F1
Whittle Rd IP2 ....138 F6
Whitton Church La
  IP1 ....134 F4
Whitton Cl IP1 ....114 E6
Whitton Com Prim Sch
  IP1 ....134 E3
Whitton Gn Prim Sch
  NR33 ....114 F5
Whitton Leyer IP8 ....134 C2
Whitwell House Day Hospl
  IP17 ....128 B3
Whitworth Cl IP2 .....138 D2
Whyteway IP19 ....24 B4
Wick La CO12 ....107 A1
Wick Rd Langham CO4 .103 C4
  Stoke-by-nayland CO6 .103 A6
Wicken CB7 ....28 D1
Wickham Com Prim Sch
  IP13 ....127 B6
Wickham la IP14 ....52 A6
Wickham Mkt FC
  IP13 ....127 C6
Wickham Mkt Sta IP13 .71 C2
Wickham Rd IP23 ......52 F7
Wickhambrook Ct 2
  IP11 ....152 C4

Wickhambrook Prim Sch
  CB8 ....61 E2
Wickhambrook Rd
  IP29 ....62 A5
Wicklow Rd IP1 ......134 D2
Wicks La IP14 ....67 D7
Widgeon Cl IP2 ......138 F3
Wiggin Cl IP28 ....116 D2
Wiggs Acre NR34 ......10 C4
Wigg's Way 3 NR32 .....3 D4
Wigmore Cl IP2 ......138 F1
Wignall St CO11 ......104 C2
Wigston Rd IP33 .....122 C3
Wigwam Hill IP22 ......19 F1
Wilberforce St IP1 ...139 A6
Wilby CE Prim Sch
  IP21 ....39 B2
Wilby La IP13 ....39 C3
Wilby Rd IP21 ....39 A4
Wilbye Cl IP32 ....123 E4
Wild Acres 13 CB5 .....44 A5
Wild Tracks Offroad Activity
  Pk★ CB7 ....45 E7
Wilde St NR32 ....113 E2
Wilde St Est IP28 .....13 D1
Wilderness Cl 3 IP20 ..22 D5
Wilderness Hill IP8 ....95 B6
Wilderness La
  Harleston IP20 ....22 D6
  Woodbridge IP12 .....147 A6
Wildflower Way NR35 .110 B7
Wilding Dr IP5 ......141 D7
Wilding Rd IP8 ......138 C1
Wildmere La IP28 ......13 D1
Wilford Bridge Rd
  IP12 ....147 D7
Wilford Bridge Spur
  IP12 ....147 C7
Wilkinson Dr IP5 ....141 C6
Wilkinson Way IP12 ..147 A6
Wilks Rd IP33 ....123 B2
Willbye Ave IP33 ......20 D3
Willcox Ave IP33 .....122 C6
William Armstrong Cl 6
  IP30 ....50 F2
William Booth Way 11
  IP11 ....152 D5
William Groom Ave 2
  CO12 ....107 A1
William St IP1 ....155 B3
William's Way 4 IP28 ..29 F6
Williamsport Way IP6 .125 F3
Willie Snaith Rd CB8 .120 F6
Willoughby Cl IP3 .....71 A7
Willoughby Rd IP2 ...155 A1
Willow Cl
  Badwell Ash IP31 ......50 F8
  6 Claydon IP6 ....134 C8
  Haverhill CB9 ....132 B7
  Stradbroke IP21 ....39 B5
  1 Sudbury CO10 ......148 C4
  Worlingham NR34 .....111 F3
  Wortwell IP20 ....23 A8
Willow Cres CB8 .....121 B2
Willow Gn IP13 ....54 E7
Willow Gr 3 CO6 .....102 C5
Willow La
  Bedingham NR35 ....7 B7
  Broome NR35 ....8 C7
  Cotton IP14 ....52 B6
Willow Marsh La
  Darsham IP17 ....42 A1
  Yoxford IP17 ....41 F2
Willow Rd NR33 ......115 A2
Willow Tree Cl IP13 ..127 B6
Willow Way
  9 Great Bricett IP7 ...80 D6
  3 Harwich CO12 .....106 F1
Willow Wlk 5 IP20 .....22 D5
Willowcroft Rd IP1 ...135 A2
Willrede Rd NR34 ....111 B3
Wilmslow Ave IP12 ..146 E5
Wilmslow Dr IP8 .....138 C2
Wilson Rd Hadleigh IP7 149 E5
  Ipswich IP8 ....138 B1
  Lowestoft NR33 ......115 C5
Wilton Rd IP26 ....4 E5
Wimbledon Ave IP27 ..14 E8
Wimborne Ave IP3 ...140 D4
Wimpole Cl IP5 ......140 F6
Wincanton Cl IP14 ...136 A1
Winchester Cl IP14 ..124 B6
Winchester Gdns 4 IP6 82 B5
Winchester Rd IP33 ..122 D4
Winchester Way IP2 .142 F8
Windermere Cl IP3 ...144 B8
Windermere Pk NR32 .113 A4
Windermere Rd
  6 Felixstowe IP11 ...153 D7
  Stowmarket IP14 .....124 C6
  Sudbury CO10 ....148 B5
Windgap La IP14 ....51 D1
Windham Rd CO10 ...148 E6
Winding Piece 5 IP9 .150 D3
Windings Rd 4 IP7 .....80 F1
Windmill Ave IP30 .....50 C1
Windmill Cl
  Boxted CO4 ....102 F2
  Ramsey & Parkeston
    CO12 ....106 C1
  Soham CB7 ....28 C1
  3 Somersham IP8 .....81 C3
Windmill Gn 19 IP31 ...34 C8
Windmill Hill
  Capel St Mary IP9 ....150 F3
  Exning CB8 ....120 A4
  Long Melford CO10 ....77 D1

Windmill Rd IP20 ......23 A7
Windmill Rise
  Bury St Edmunds IP33 .154 A1
  Hundon CO10 ....75 D4
  1 Wetherden IP14 .....51 A1
Windmill Row 5 CO10 ..77 B3
Windrush Rd IP5 .....141 C8
Windsor Circ
  1 Lakenheath IP27 ....14 A3
  Lakenheath IP27 .....109 F1
Windsor Cl
  7 Barnham IP24 ....16 C2
  Lawshall IP29 ....63 D2
Windsor Rd
  Felixstowe IP11 ......152 E5
  Ipswich IP1 ....138 F7
  Lowestoft NR33 ......115 C7
  Newmarket CB8 ......120 E4
  Southwold IP18 ....119 B8
Windward Way NR33 ..114 E5
Windyridge Rd IP30 ....65 D5
Winfarthing Rd IP22 ...20 B6
Winfrith Rd IP3 ......140 D4
Wingfield Ave NR33 ..114 E7
Wingfield Mdws IP14 ..68 B6
Wingfield Rd
  Lakenheath IP27 .....109 D7
  Syleham IP21 ....21 F1
  Weybread IP21 ....22 C2
Wingfield St
  Bungay NR35 ....110 B3
  Ipswich IP4 ....155 C3
Wings Rd IP27 ....109 D6
Winnipeg Rd NR32 ...113 D2
Winsford Rd IP32 ....123 E6
Winston Ave
  Ipswich IP4 ....140 C8
  Lowestoft NR33 ....114 E7
Winston Cl
  5 Felixstowe IP11 ...152 D5
  11 Kessingland NR33 ..11 C1
Winston Rd
  Southwold IP18 ......119 C7
  Winston IP14 ....53 F1
Winthrop Rd IP33 ....122 D4
Winthrops The CO10 ...93 B4
Wissett Cl IP19 ......118 B4
Wissett Rd
  Chediston IP19 ....41 B8
  Halesworth IP19 .....118 A5
  Wissett IP19 ....24 D1
Wissett Way NR32 ...113 B4
Wissey View 2 IP26 .....6 B8
Wissington Uplands
  CO6 ....102 A5
Wiston Hall★ CO6 ....102 B4
Wiston Rd CO6 ....102 B4
Withers 2 CB7 ....29 A1
Withersdale Rd
  Mendham IP20 ....23 A5
  Weybread IP21 ....22 D4
Withersfield Rd
  Haverhill CB9 ....132 C7
  Withersfield CB9 ......74 C4
Withipoll St IP4 .....155 C3
Witnesham Church La
  IP6 ....82 F5
Witnesham Prim Sch
  IP6 ....83 A4
Witney Gn NR33 .....115 A3
Witney Rd 3 NR33 ...115 A3
Wittons La IP21 ....38 C7
Wix Rd CO12 ....106 C1
Wlk The Bacton IP14 ...51 D5
  Beccles NR34 ....111 B6
  Ipswich IP5 ....141 B8
Wollaston Cl IP32 ....122 D8
Wollaston Rd NR33 ...114 C3
Wolsey Art Gall★ IP1 .155 C4
Wolsey Gdns IP11 ....153 A3
Wolsey Rd 4 IP14 ....124 C7
Wolsey St IP1 ....155 B2
Wolton Rd IP5 ....141 C7
Wolves Farm La IP7 ...94 E6
Wood Cl
  1 Bentwaters Airfield
    IP12 ....85 D4
  Kenninghall NR16 .....19 A8
  Tostock IP30 ....50 B3
Wood Farm La IP14 ....26 C2
Wood Farm Rd IP13 ....83 C5
Wood La Bedingham NR35 .7 A6
  Bressingham IP22 .....19 E6
  Dallinghoo IP13 ....70 B1
  Dickleburgh & Rushall
    IP21 ....21 C2
  Fressingfield IP21 .....40 A8
  Henstead with Hulver Street
    NR34 ....26 E7
  Hepworth IP22 ....35 A6
  Oulton NR32 ....112 C3
  Reydon IP18 ....26 C1
  Scole IP21 ....21 C4
  Thelnetham IP22 ......35 C6
Wood Rd
  Badingham IP13 ....56 B6
  Woolpit IP30 ....65 F8
Wood Side
  Wood Side NR34 .....124 B5
Wood View 4 IP17 .....56 F8
Woodbridge Mus The★
  IP12 ....147 A5
Woodbridge Prim Sch
  IP12 ....147 B6
Woodbridge Rd
  Alderton IP12 ....99 D5
  Bredfield IP13 ....84 C7
  Butley IP12 ....86 A5

Woodbridge Rd continued
  Framlingham IP13 ....126 C1
  Grundisburgh IP13 ....83 E6
  Ipswich IP4 ....155 C3
  Sutton IP12 ....85 A1
  Tunstall IP12 ....71 E1
  Waldringfield IP12 .....98 D6
  Wantisden IP12 ....85 E5
Woodbridge Rd E
  Ipswich IP4 ....140 C7
  Rushmere St Andrew
    IP4 ....140 D7
Woodbridge Sch IP12 .146 F5
Woodbridge Sta 147 B4
Woodchurch Ave 6
  NR33 ....114 C4
Woodcock Cl CB9 ....133 A5
Woodcock Rd IP2 ....138 E2
Woodcrofts IP29 ......63 A1
Woodcutters Way
  IP27 ....109 D7
Wooddition Rd
  Kirtling CB8 ....60 D3
  Newmarket CB8 ......121 A1
  Woodditton CB8 ....60 B6
Woodfield Cl NR34 .....25 E7
Woodfield Dr IP14 ...124 E5
Woodfield La
  Stowmarket IP14 .....124 D4
  Stutton IP9 ....105 C5
Woodfields IP21 ....39 A4
Woodgates Rd CO7 ..151 D7
Woodhall Bsns Pk
  CO10 ....148 D8
Woodhall Cl CO10 ...148 C7
Woodhall CP Sch
  CO10 ....148 D8
Woodhall Rd CO10 ...148 D8
Woodhouse La IP10 ..141 C2
Woodland Ave NR34 ..111 F4
Woodland Cl
  Onehouse IP14 ....66 C6
  Risby IP28 ....47 D5
  Thurston IP31 ....49 E3
Woodland Dr
  Bungay NR35 ....110 B1
  Ellingham NR35 ....8 E7
Woodland Pl 7 IP31 ...49 A6
Woodlands
  1 Chelmondiston IP9 .106 C8
  Hadleigh IP7 ....149 B7
  35 Harleston IP20 .....22 D6
  Lakenheath IP27 .....109 D8
Woodlands Ave 4
  NR33 ....114 C3
Woodlands Bsns Pk
  IP30 ....49 B3
Woodlands Dr IP24 ....16 C7
Woodlands Rd
  Holbrook IP9 ....105 E8
  Raydon IP7 ....94 F2
  Rushbrooke with Rougham
    IP30 ....49 B3
Woodlands Rise IP27 ..14 D8
Woodlands The NR32 .113 B8
Woodlands Way
  Bramford IP8 ....134 C4
  Mildenhall IP28 ......116 F5
Woodlane Rd IP23 .....38 C1
Woodlark Cl IP14 ....138 E1
Woodley Com Sch
  IP14 ....124 B7
Woodpecker Ave 2
  NR33 ....114 C4
Woodpecker Rd IP2 ..138 E2
Woodrush Rd IP3 ....140 C1
Woods Cl
  Ditchingham NR35 ...110 B7
  Sturmer CB9 ....133 C3
Woods La IP12 ....147 B7
Woods Loke E NR32 .113 A3
Woods Loke Prim Sch
  NR32 ....112 F3
Woods Loke W NR32 .112 F3
Woodside
  Beccles NR34 ....111 D3
  Brampton with Stoven
    NR34 ....25 E5
Woodside Cl
  Bury St Edmunds IP33 .123 B1
  Lowestoft NR33 ......114 C3
Woodspring Cl IP12 ..139 A2
Woodstone Ave IP14 .135 C1
Woodthorpe Cl IP7 ..149 F5
Woodthorpe Rd IP7 ..149 E6
Woodville Rd IP4 ....139 F5
Woodward Ave IP14 ...51 F6
Woolhall St 2 IP33 ..154 B2
Woollards Cl IP14 ....25 E4
Woollards Gdns 3 CO10 .91 E8
Woolmers Cl IP14 ....124 D4
Woolner Cl 7 IP6 ......82 A5
Woolnough Cl 6 CB9 ..88 D3
Woolnough Rd IP12 ..146 F6
Woolnoughs The 2
  IP5 ....141 D7
Woolpit Prim Sch IP30 .50 D1
Woolpit Rd IP30 ......34 C2
Woolverstone Cl IP2 .138 D1
Worcester Cl 5 IP32 .123 E6
Worcester Rd CO10 ..144 A8
Wordsworth Cres IP1 .134 E3
Wordsworth Rd
  4 Bury St Edmunds IP32 .48 C5
  2 Stowmarket IP14 ..124 D4
Worell Dr NR34 ......111 E4

Workhouse Hill
  Boxted CO4 ....102 F3
  Hartest IP29 ....77 B8
Workhouse La IP17 ....57 E2
Workhouse Rd
  Little Horkesley CO6 ..102 B2
  Thornham Magna IP23 .37 A1
Workshop La IP10 ....145 C5
World's End La IP14 ...65 F2
World's End Rd IP13 ..55 B4
Worlingham Hall★
  NR34 ....111 F5
Worlingham Mid Sch
  NR34 ....111 F4
Worlingham Prim Sch
  NR34 ....9 F4
Worlingham Way
  NR32 ....113 A4
Worlington Rd
  Barton Mills IP28 ......30 E3
  Worlington IP28 ......116 A3
Worlingworth CE Prim Sch
  IP13 ....54 E7
Worlingworth Rd IP21 .38 F3
Wortham Ling Nature
  Reserve★ IP22 ....19 F2
Wortham Pl 1 CB8 ...132 E6
Wortham Prim Sch
  IP22 ....36 E7
Worthing Rd NR32 ...113 D3
Wrabness Local Nature
  Reserve★ IP9 ....105 E2
Wrabness Rd 1 CO12 .106 D1
Wrabness Sta CO11 ..106 A2
Wragg Dr CB8 ....121 A6
Wratting Rd
  Great Thurlow CB9 ....74 D5
  Haverhill CB9 ....132 E7
Wren Ave IP2 ....138 D3
Wren Cl
  Mildenhall IP28 ......116 D4
  1 Stowmarket IP14 ...67 A5
  13 Thurstow IP31 .....49 D4
Wrens Pk 2 IP11 ....153 D7
Wriggle St IP13 ....70 A7
Wright Cl IP14 ....124 D3
Wright La IP5 ....141 D8
Wright Rd IP3 ....140 C2
Wrights Way
  Leavenheath CO6 .....102 A7
  Woolpit IP30 ....50 C1
Wroxham Rd IP3 .....139 F3
Wyatt Cl IP30 ....50 F3
Wyatt Way IP24 ....16 B7
Wyatts La CO10 .....101 B8
Wye Rd IP3 ....140 A2
Wyken Rd IP31 ....34 D3
Wykes Bishop St IP3 .139 E4
Wymering Rd 10 IP18 .119 D5
Wyncoll's La IP7 ......94 B2
Wyndham Way CB8 ..121 A6
Wynterton Cl 3 IP3 ..140 B1
Wynton Rise IP14 ....124 E4
Wytchwoods The IP14 .68 C5
Wyvern Rd IP3 ......140 C1
Wyverstone Rd IP31 ..51 B7

Y
Yale Bsns Pk IP3 ....144 F8
Yarmouth Pl 3 CB9 ..132 E6
Yarmouth Rd
  Corton NR32 ....113 A8
  Ditchingham NR35 ...110 D7
  Geldeston NR34 ....9 A7
  Ipswich IP1 ....139 A6
  Kirby Cane NR35 ....8 E7
  Lound NR32 ....2 F7
  Lowestoft NR32 ......113 B5
  Melton IP12 ....84 C6
  Ufford IP13 ....127 B1
  Woodbridge IP12 ....147 C8
Yarrow Dr NR33 .....114 C4
Yaxley Hall La IP23 ...37 C4
Yaxley Rd IP23 ....37 C3
Yeldham Pl IP7 ......132 E6
Yeoman Cres IP7 ....149 E5
Yeoman Rd IP11 .....152 D3
Yeoman Way IP7 ....149 E5
Yeoman's Cl NR35 ...110 C3
Yeovil Rd NR32 ......113 C2
Yerril Gdn CB9 ....132 C5
Yew Cl 1 IP27 ....13 F2
Yew Ct IP2 ....139 A3
Yew Tree Rise IP13 ..127 C7
Yewlands Gr IP30 .....65 A4
Yewtree Gr IP5 ......140 F5
Yewtree Rise IP8 ....138 C1
York Cl
  Bury St Edmunds IP33 .122 E5
  1 Mildenhall IP28 .....30 A4
  Sudbury CO10 ....148 C1
York Cres 12 Claydon IP6 .82 B5
  Claydon IP6 ....134 C8
York Rd
  Bury St Edmunds IP33 .154 A2
  Felixstowe IP11 .....153 A4
  Foxhall IP5 ....98 A4
  Haverhill CB9 ....132 C5
  Ipswich IP3 ....140 A4
  Lowestoft NR32 ......113 C1
  Southwold IP18 ......119 B5
  Sudbury CO10 ....148 C6
York Terr IP33 ......154 A2

Using the Ordnance Survey National Grid

NG	NH	NJ	NK		
NM	NN	NO	NP		
NR	NS	NT	NU		
	NX	NY	NZ		
	SC	SD	SE	TA	
	SH	SJ	SK	TF	TG
SM	SN	SO	SP	TL	TM
SR	SS	ST	SU	TQ	TR
SW	SX	SY	SZ	TV	

Any feature in this atlas can be given a unique reference to help you find the same feature on other Ordnance Survey maps of the area, or to help someone else locate you if they do not have a Street Atlas.

The grid squares in this atlas match the Ordnance Survey National Grid and are at 500 metre intervals. The small figures at the bottom and sides of every other grid line are the National Grid kilometre values (**00** to **99** km) and are repeated across the country every 100 km (see left).

To give a unique National Grid reference you need to locate where in the country you are. The country is divided into 100 km squares with each square given a unique two-letter reference. Use the administrative map to determine in which 100 km square a particular page of this atlas falls.

The bold letters and numbers between each grid line (**A** to **F**, **1** to **8**) are for use within a specific Street Atlas only, and when used with the page number, are a convenient way of referencing these grid squares.

Example   The railway bridge over DARLEY GREEN RD in grid square B1

Step 1: Identify the two-letter reference, in this example the page is in **SP**

Step 2: Identify the 1 km square in which the railway bridge falls. Use the figures in the southwest corner of this square: Eastings **17**, Northings **74**. This gives a unique reference: **SP 17 74**, accurate to 1 km.

Step 3: To give a more precise reference accurate to 100 m you need to estimate how many tenths along and how many tenths up this 1 km square the feature is (to help with this the 1 km square is divided into four 500 m squares). This makes the bridge about **8** tenths along and about **1** tenth up from the southwest corner.

This gives a unique reference: **SP 178 741**, accurate to 100 m.

Eastings (read from left to right along the bottom) come before Northings (read from bottom to top). If you have trouble remembering say to yourself "Along the hall, THEN up the stairs"!

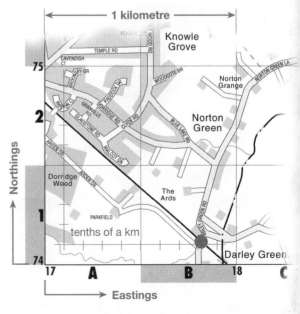

PHILIP'S MAPS

the Gold Standard for serious driving

◆ Philip's street atlases cover every county in England and Wales, plus much of Scotland

◆ All our atlases use the same style of mapping, with the same colours and symbols, so you can move with confidence from one atlas to the next

◆ Widely used by the emergency services, transport companies and local authorities

◆ Created from the most up-to-date and detailed information available from Ordnance Survey

◆ Based on the National Grid

BEST BUY • BEST BUY
Auto EXPRESS
BEST BUY • BEST BUY

STREET ATLAS London
The definitive Lon...
from Britain's national ma...
PHILIP'S

STREET ATLAS Devon
Unique comprehensive coverage
BEST BUY
with time-saving through-routes
Includes Lyme Regis, Saltash and Wellington, plus Exeter and Plymouth city centres at extra-large scale

STREET ATLAS Norfolk
Unique comprehensive coverage
BEST BUY
with time-saving through-routes
Includes Norwich city centre at extra-large scale, plus town maps of Bury St Edmunds and Lowestoft

STREET ATLAS Cumbria
Unique comprehensive coverage
BEST BUY
Every named street, road and lane
Plus town maps of Dumfries and Morecambe, with Carlisle city centre at extra-large scale

BRITAIN'S MOST DETAILED ROAD ATLAS
PHILIP'S
NAVIGATOR Britain
Ultra-large scale mapping 1¾ miles to 1 inch
50 fully indexed town plans
'Extremely clear maps with the most detail by far' Auto Express
Recommended by the Institute of Advanced Motorists

For national mapping, choose **Philip's Navigator Britain** – the most detailed road atlas available of England, Wales and Scotland. Hailed by Auto Express as 'the ultimate road atlas', this is the only one-volume atlas to show every road and lane in Britain.

Street atlases currently available

England
Bedfordshire
Berkshire
Birmingham and West Midlands
Bristol and Bath
Buckinghamshire
Cambridgeshire
Cheshire
Cornwall
Cumbria
Derbyshire
Devon
Dorset
County Durham and Teesside
Essex
North Essex
South Essex
Gloucestershire
North Hampshire
South Hampshire
Herefordshire Monmouthshire
Hertfordshire
Isle of Wight
Kent
East Kent
West Kent
Lancashire
Leicestershire and Rutland
Lincolnshire
London
Greater Manchester
Merseyside
Norfolk
Northamptonshire
Northumberland
Nottinghamshire
Oxfordshire
Shropshire
Somerset
Staffordshire

All England and Wales coverage

Suffolk
Surrey
East Sussex
West Sussex
Tyne and Wear
Warwickshire
Birmingham and West Midlands
Wiltshire and Swindon
Worcestershire
East Yorkshire Northern Lincolnshire
North Yorkshire
South Yorkshire
West Yorkshire
Wales
Anglesey, Conwy and Gwynedd
Cardiff, Swansea and The Valleys
Carmarthenshire, Pembrokeshire and Swansea
Ceredigion and South Gwynedd
Denbighshire, Flintshire, Wrexham
Herefordshire Monmouthshire
Powys
Scotland
Aberdeenshire
Ayrshire
Edinburgh and East Central Scotland
Fife and Tayside
Glasgow and West Central Scotland
Inverness and Moray
Lanarkshire

How to order

Philip's maps and atlases are available from bookshops, motorway services and petrol stations. You can order direct from the publisher by phoning **01903 828503** or online at **www.philips-maps.co.uk**
For bulk orders only, phone 020 7644 6940